MORALITY

MORALITY

Its Nature and Justification

BERNARD GERT

New York   Oxford
Oxford University Press
1998

Oxford University Press

Oxford   New York
Athens   Auckland   Bangkok   Bogota   Bombay
Buenos Aires   Calcutta   Cape Town   Dar es Salaam
Delhi   Florence   Hong Kong   Istanbul   Karachi
Kuala Lumpur   Madras   Madrid   Melbourne
Mexico City   Nairobi   Paris   Singapore
Taipei   Tokyo   Toronto   Warsaw

and associated companies in
Berlin   Ibadan

Copyright © 1998 by Bernard Gert

Published by Oxford University Press, Inc.
198 Madison Avenue, New York, New York 10016

Oxford is a registered trademark of Oxford University Press

Library of Congress Cataloging-in-Publication Data
Gert, Bernard, 1934–
      Morality : its nature and justification / Bernard Gert.
          p.   cm.
      Includes bibliographical references and index.
      ISBN 0-19-512255-0; ISBN 0-19-512256-9 (pbk.)
      1. Ethics.   I. Title.
   BJ1012.G45   1998
   171'.2— dc21   97-31586

9 8 7 6 5 4 3 2 1

Printed in the United States of America
on acid-free paper

To the memory of my mother and my father,
in continuing gratitude for having provided
me with the understanding of morality
that this book makes explicit

Contents

Preface

Common morality is a complex and subtle system. It is far more complex and subtle than the systems of conduct that most philosophers generate from their moral theories, and that they offer as improvements upon common morality. The moral theory presented in this book is not used to generate an improved system of conduct; rather, it is an attempt to describe, explain, and justify the common moral system. I try to provide a description of common morality that does justice to its complexity and subtlety; I explain its nature by relating it to universal features of human nature such as fallibility and vulnerability; and I try to justify it by relating it to impartiality and rationality.

This is most likely the last major revision of the moral theory that was first published in 1970 under the title, *The Moral Rules: A New Rational Foundation for Morality* (New York: Harper and Row, 1970). At that time, I was so taken by being able to show that all of the commonly accepted moral rules had a rational foundation, that I did not make sufficiently clear that the moral rules were only one part of the moral system. Indeed, the title was even mistakenly interpreted as claiming that the moral rules were the rational foundation of morality. In the 1988 revision, I tried to correct this impression by using the title, *Morality: A New Justification of the Moral Rules* (New York: Oxford University Press, 1988).[1] However, this title was open to the misinterpretation that justifying morality simply was justifying the moral rules. I hope that the present title, *Morality: Its Nature and Justification*, makes clear that I am concerned with describing and justifying all of morality, not just the moral rules.

It is not merely the subtitle that has been changed. At the suggestion of my colleague, Walter Sinnott-Armstrong, I have distinguished more clearly between justifying the moral rules and justifying violations of those rules by devoting a separate chapter to justifying violations. I have also tried to make even clearer my view that the moral rules can only be understood by understanding how they fit within morality or the moral system. Morality consists, not merely of rules, but also of ideals, morally relevant features, and a two-step procedure for determining which violations of a rule are strongly justified, which are weakly justified, and which are unjustified.

Only by considering morality as a unified system can the overwhelming majority of the moral decisions and judgments common to most people be described, explained, and justified.

However, emphasis on the systematic character of morality may mistakenly lead to the view that morality always provides unique answers to every moral question. Therefore I have now explicitly incorporated into the definition of morality that it is an informal system that often does not provide unique answers to moral questions. This made me realize that the correctness of a moral decision can never be determined by voting. Rather a moral question, such as abortion, remains unresolved, but the practical problem of whether to allow abortions is resolved by political means.

I have also clarified the hybrid character of rationality, noting explicitly that irrationality is essentially egocentric, whereas reasons need not be egocentric at all. The hybrid character of rationality explains why both rational egoism and the view that rationality requires one to be moral are mistaken. I also try to explain why the correct view that reasons always can serve as motives for rational persons is often confused with the mistaken internalist view that reasons always do serve as such motives. I now devote a separate chapter to reasons and have provided a new account of what makes one reason better than another. This account helps explain both the plausibility of the claim it is irrational to act immorally and why that claim is false.

I recognize more fully now that the fallibility and vulnerability of moral agents are essential presuppositions of morality. Consequently, I have come to a greater appreciation of the importance of humility and provide a fuller account of it. I have also made explicit some additional morally relevant features. The chapter on virtue and vice shows a greater appreciation of their practical importance in teaching what morality is and in living a moral life.

I provide a more detailed account of moral impartiality and show why the standard philosophical accounts employing reversibility (Baier, the Golden Rule), universalizability (Hare, Kant, and the categorical imperative), and the veil of ignorance (Rawls), are inadequate accounts of both general impartiality and the impartiality required by morality. I also show why failure to realize that impartiality, even moral impartiality, is always related to a specific group in a specific respect has created pointless disputes between partialists and impartialists.

I have made clearer the full significance of recognizing that morality is a public system, and so applies only to those to whom it is known. Those who hold that morality is universal must hold that all rational persons know what morality requires, prohibits, encourages, and allows. Thus, unless they deny either that morality is a public system or is universal, they cannot hold that morality is based on any religion, for no religion is known to all rational persons.

I admit that the moral rules (e.g., Do not deceive) can be interpreted somewhat differently in different societies, but I show the limits on interpretation. Although some of the specific claims of ethical relativism are plausible, I show that the plausibility of its central claim — that some societies have totally different moralities — comes from the failure to appreciate that morality is a public system. This failure makes ethical relativism seem plausible because it leads one to overlook how different morality is from law and religion. Thus ethical relativism is not distinguished from defensible forms of value relativism, such as legal or religious relativism.

I have removed former chapters 13 and 14. Chapter 13 was a critique of Kurt Baier's *The Moral Point of View* and John Rawls's *A Theory of Justice*. Although both have acknowledged the force of my criticisms, they have both written new books that do not deal with my objections. I thought it pointless to simply include this chapter unchanged and did not think it worthwhile to make the same objections to their new books. This does not, however, diminish my great admiration and respect for these two philosophers, and their influence is apparent throughout this book.

Chapter 14 was an application of the account of morality to several problems in biomedical ethics. This chapter has been removed because there are two recent books that apply the account of morality presented in this book to problems in biomedical ethics. The first is *Morality and the New Genetics: A Guide for Students and Health Care Providers* (Sudbury, Mass.: Jones and Bartlett Publishers, now distributed by Wadsworth Publishing, 1996) by Bernard Gert, Edward M. Berger, George F. Cahill, Jr., K. Danner Clouser, Charles M. Culver, John B. Moeschler, and George H. S. Singer. It is the result of a three-year grant from the National Institutes of Health to apply my account of morality to the problems that may arise from the Human Genome Project. The second is *Bioethics: A Return to Fundamentals* (New York: Oxford University Press, 1997) by Bernard Gert, Charles M. Culver, and K. Danner Clouser. This book, which we worked on for almost a decade, attempts to show how the account of morality presented in this book is far more useful in dealing with real moral problems in medicine than any of the alternative accounts of morality or of moral reasoning.

Although the descriptions of impartiality, morality, and rationality that I provide differ from most of the standard philosophical accounts, the primary difference between my descriptions and most previous accounts is that I recognize more fully the complexity of these concepts. I claim no originality for my views, for I have appropriated something from all of the standard moral views. Indeed, my view has been characterized as Kant with consequences, as Mill with publicity, and as Ross with a theory. My alternative to Kant's categorical imperative avoids the counterexamples that undermine it. My accounts of rationality and impartiality are more complex and less open to objections than those normally provided by consequentialists. My distinction between moral rules and moral ideals clarifies what is misleading about Ross's list of prima facie duties. There is a surprising similarity between my account of morality and what is known as "discourse ethics," but my specification of the characteristics of those competent to participate in the discourse allows me to make explicit much of what is only implicit in discourse ethics.

From Hobbes, I have come to appreciate Aristotle's recognition of the importance of the virtues and of bringing up children in the right way. Through Hobbes I have also borrowed from both contractarianism and natural law theory, although I allow for moral disagreement in ways that these theories do not. Indeed, I think that my view is best characterized as a natural law theory. However this phrase has taken on connotations that are likely to be misleading. Indeed, I think that my view is best characterized as a natural law theory in the tradition of Hobbes. However, unless one has the correct interpretation of Hobbes, this characterization may be misleading.[2]

Asking, "Why should I favor morality being regarded as the supreme guide to conduct?" is very different from asking, "Why should I be moral?" Recognition of this led me to appreciate the force of the feminist answer to the second question. That both rationality and morality often allow more than one acceptable solution to a problem showed me not only that different people might solve a problem in different ways but also that none of these ways need be superior to the others. I cite these points and affinities so that no one will be surprised when they find so little to disagree with in my moral theory.

The moral theory presented in this book differs from most other moral theories in that it attempts to do far less than any of them. It does not provide unique answers to every moral question, nor does it try to show that it is irrational to act immorally. It only provides a universally acceptable framework for dealing with moral problems. It does this by making explicit and justifying the moral system that people normally use when they make moral decisions and judgments. Attempting to do less enables me to avoid the errors of those who attempt to do more.

I have tried to answer all of the criticisms that have been made of my views, but I have still not spent much time explicitly criticizing the views of others. I often criticize views that I think are held by others, but without mentioning them by name, for I am not sure that I have interpreted their views correctly. Those I do criticize by name are those whose views are sufficiently clear that I have no doubt about my interpretation. To be clear enough to criticize is a virtue, for "Truth arises more easily from error than from confusion." I have tried make my own views as clear as I can. I realize the benefits of explicitly criticizing the views of others, but I prefer to make my book more readable for those not interested in these kinds of philosophical disputes; however, philosophers should have no problem in seeing how my arguments and positions relate to these disputes, not only in normative theory, but also in metaethics.

I have benefited from discussion of the revised versions of the first four (now five) chapters of this book by members of a National Endowment for the Humanities Seminar on Moral Knowledge at Dartmouth College in the fall term of 1994, organized by Walter Sinnott-Armstrong and Kevin Reinhart. I was a senior fellow in the seminar and distributed these revised chapters to those members of the seminar that were interested in discussing them. Among those that were most helpful in reading and commenting on these chapters were Robert Audi, Walter Sinnott-Armstrong, Kevin Reinhart, Dennis Charles Washburn, Amy Hollywood, James B. Murphy, Jean H. Burfoot, Stefen S. Sencerz, Polly Ashton Smith, and William M. Throop.

I also benefited from teaching *Morality* in a graduate seminar at the Nacional Universidad de La Plata during the fall term of 1995. Maria Julia Bertomeu, who invited me to apply for a Fulbright to teach that seminar at La Plata, was a leading participant in the class. She and I had many fruitful discussions about *Morality* both in the class and outside of it. She also persuaded her student Maria Victoria Costa to serve as my translator in this seminar and in a course on medical ethics that I taught at the Universidad de Buenos Aires, as well as at all of my public lectures in Buenos Aires. Victoria was not only an excellent translator she is also an excellent philosopher, and I had many useful conversations about *Morality* with her throughout my stay in Argentina. Florencia Luna and Oswaldo Guariglia were also helpful to me, and I had many productive discussions about *Morality* with them.

I continue to benefit from my discussions with Dartmouth students; this time with the students in my course on rationality and the emotions during the fall term of 1996, when I was leading a foreign study program at the University of Edinburgh. I lead such a program once every five years and have always benefited from discussion with members of the philosophy department there. Most valuable in this regard have been discussions with Vinit Haksar and Michael Menlowe. I have also benefited from discussions I have had at various other universities in England, Scotland, and the United States. Since these discussions have occurred over so many years and since my memory is so poor, I have thought it best not to mention particular places. I also had many friends who are not philosophers but who read early drafts of this book and made important suggestions; especially valuable were the comments of my good friend of over thirty years, Bob Forster.

This book is much improved because of discussions that I have had with those who collaborated with me on the two books applying my theory to problems in genetics and medicine. I have continued to benefit from discussions with George H. S. Singer, who is trying to apply my account of morality to several issues related to the treatment of emotionally disturbed children. Discussions with Edward M. Berger on many issues, including the ethics of scientific research, have been very helpful. Judy Stern, with whom I worked on this latter issue, and who studied the previous version of *Morality* with me, provided many useful suggestions that are incorporated in this edition. I have discussed this book so much and for so long with Charles M. Culver and K. Danner Clouser (both of whom were coauthors with me on both applied books) that I cannot always remember who first had the idea that led to the revision. Of course, I have continued to have fruitful discussions with my colleagues in philosophy at Dartmouth, especially Jim Moor and Walter Sinnott-Armstrong. Indeed, Walter used an abridged version of a draft of this edition in his course in the spring of 1997, and I benefited from many of his and his students' suggestions. I have also had continuing fruitful discussions with Robert Audi, and I have incorporated many of his suggestions, including the division of the book into parts.

Although I enjoy teaching and have benefited from teaching *Morality* to students at Dartmouth, I have been able to devote so much time to the revising of this book and to the writing of the two applied ethics books mentioned above because of the released time provided by the Eunice and Julian Cohen Professorship for the Study of Ethics and Human Values. I have also enjoyed the personal encouragement and support of Eunice and Julian and wish to use this opportunity to tell them how much I appreciate what they have done. I must also acknowledge the benefits of working at Dartmouth College, for it provides the most hassle-free environment for doing research that I can imagine.

Finally, I have enjoyed the benefits of clarification and criticism from discussions with my children, Heather and Joshua. Heather, who is an associate professor of philosophy at Texas A & M University, used a draft of this version of *Morality* in a graduate seminar in the fall of 1997, and in my session with them I received some criticisms that led me to make some significant changes. I have previously explicitly acknowledged my debt to her in my understanding of the concept of rights. Joshua is finishing his Ph.D. dissertation, *Different Sorts of Reasons: A Denial of the Force of the Better Reason* (University of Illinois at Chicago Circle, 1998), and his continuing criticism of my account of reasons and rationality have saved me from some significant errors. Esther, my wife and their mother, has not only had to endure the normal discomfort of listening to the ramblings of a husband who is a philosopher, she also had to endure his long telephone conversations with her children about philosophy. In addition, Esther, Heather, and Joshua helped me in proofreading and correcting the copyedited manuscript. If this book were not already dedicated to the memory of my parents, it would be dedicated to the three of them.

Hanover, New Hampshire   B. G.
January 1998

Notes

1. The prefaces to all of the previous editions to these books can be found in this book. They provide a record of the changes that have occured with each new edition.

2. For the correct interpretation of Hobbes, see my introduction to *Man and Citizen* by Thomas Hobbes (Indianapolis: Hackett Publishing, 1991), and the articles "Hobbes, Thomas," in *The Oxford Companion to Philosophy*, edited by Ted Honderich (Oxford: Oxford University Press 1995), 367–370, and "Hobbes," in *The Cambridge Dictionary of Philosophy*, edited by Robert Audi (Cambridge: Cambridge University Press, 1995), 331–335.

PART I

CONCEPTUAL FOUNDATIONS

The utility of moral and civil philosophy is to be estimated, not so much by the commodities we have by knowing these sciences, as by the calamities we receive by not knowing them.

THOMAS HOBBES, De Corpore, chap. 1, sec. 7

Chapter 1

Morality

What is morality? This question seems as if it could be answered by any intelligent person until one actually tries to answer it. Then a funny thing happens. If one starts by saying "Morality is . . . " nothing one says afterward seems to be quite right. Of course one can say clever things like "Morality is simply the expression of the demands of the superego." But this kind of clever remark does not explain what morality is. The superego makes many demands that are not moral demands. Which of its demands are the moral ones? Simply asking this question makes clear that morality cannot be equated with the demands of the superego. And so it goes with any answer that one initially proposes.

Part of the difficulty is that "morality" is an unusual word. It is not used very much, at least not without some qualification. People do sometimes talk of "Christian morality," "Nazi morality," or of "the morality of the Greeks," but they seldom talk simply of morality all by itself.[1] The widespread belief that there is no common or universal morality, that there is only the morality of this group or the morality of that society, is false. In this book I shall present an account of morality, not of the morality of this group or the morality of that society, but of morality. Further, I shall show that this common or universal morality is justified, that, with the appropriate qualifications, all rational persons would favor adopting it to govern the behavior of all those who are able to understand it and to govern their behavior by it.

Morality versus a Moral Theory

It is important right at the beginning to distinguish between morality and a moral theory that makes explicit, explains, and, if possible, justifies morality. I use the phrase "moral system" to mean the same as "morality" and regard morality or the moral system as the system people use, often unconsciously, when they are trying to make a morally acceptable choice among several alternative actions or when they make moral judgments about their own actions or those of others. I do not claim that

3

everyone uses exactly the same moral system, but I prefer to consider the differences, some of which are quite significant, as variations of a single system.[2] It is, however, an essential feature of morality in all of its variations that everyone who is judged by it knows what morality prohibits, requires, encourages, and allows.[3] Since moral judgments can be made about all rational persons, it follows that morality is universal and that what seem to be different moral systems are simply specifications or variations of a universal morality or moral system. However, if people hold that the differences between particular moralities or moral systems are significant enough that they prefer to talk of different moralities or moral systems that share a common framework, nothing of significance will turn on this.[4]

When readers of this book decide how to act when confronted with a moral problem or when they make a serious moral judgment, I think they all use the moral system that this book describes and justifies. However, I am not suggesting that they consciously and explicitly apply this moral system in order to arrive at these moral decisions and judgments. I do claim, however, that explicit application of this moral system to any moral problem will not classify as immoral any action that a reader considers as morally acceptable. Since morality allows for more than one morally acceptable answer to some moral problems, I do not claim that explicit application of this moral system will rule out as incorrect all moral judgments with which one disagrees. I do claim that this moral system rules out as incorrect all judgments that no one whose moral judgments are taken seriously regards as correct. I have tried to make this account of morality clear and precise enough that all readers can test it for counterexamples by applying it to their own actions, decisions, and judgments.

I realize that there are many controversial moral issues, such as abortion, (discussed in more detail in chapter 6) where each side claims that the position held by those on the other side is morally unacceptable. One of the most important, and perhaps unique, features of the account of morality presented in this book is that it does not decide genuinely controversial moral issues, but rather admits that both sides to the dispute have morally acceptable positions. Even though in almost all normal situations there is complete agreement, morality allows for some unresolvable disagreement among completely informed impartial rational persons. The normal situations are usually not talked about, for they present no interesting moral problems. "Should one lie in order to cause problems for a person one does not like?" is not a question that is discussed in moral philosophy courses, for everyone agrees on the answer. A moral theory should explain not only why agreement in moral judgments is so common in most situations but also why some unresolvable moral disagreements are an unavoidable feature of morality. (This will be discussed in chapters 7, 8, and 9.)

A useful analogy for knowledge of morality is knowledge of the grammar that all competent speakers of a language have. Even though almost no competent speaker can explicitly describe the grammatical system, they all know it in the sense that they use it when speaking themselves and in interpreting the speech of others. If presented with an explicit account of the grammar, competent speakers have the final word on its accuracy. The competency of the speakers is determined by their ability to communicate successfully with most of the other speakers of the language. Although there are some variations in the grammar, the appropriate test for an account of a grammar is to determine if it allows speaking in a way that all competent speakers regard as acceptable and rules out speaking in a way that is recognized as unacceptable by all who are competent speakers of the language. An explicit account of a grammar must accurately describe the way competent speakers actually use the language. Without an adequate reason for doing so, it would be absurd to suffer the inconvenience of changing the way one speaks in order to conform to some proposed explicit account of a grammatical system.

Morality, however, is correctly regarded as rational in a sense that grammar is not. It is perfectly acceptable to explain what looks like a pointless grammatical rule by citing its historical development. That is not true for morality; every feature of morality must serve a purpose. If some feature of morality comes to be regarded as not serving a rational purpose, it ceases to be regarded as a genuine feature of morality. Thus it is logically possible, though extremely unlikely, for everyone to be mistaken about a particular feature of morality and consequently for a universally accepted moral judgment to be incorrect.[5] On the other hand, it is not possible for all competent speakers of the language to speak ungrammatically because they are mistaken about the grammar of the language.[6] What counts as grammatical use is completely determined by the use of competent speakers of the language. Morality's relation to rationality makes it possible for everyone to make mistaken moral judgments and so gives it a kind of universality that a grammar does not have.

Nonetheless, like a description of grammar, a proposed description of morality that conflicts with one's own considered moral decisions and judgments generally should not be accepted. However, recognition of the rationality of morality and of its systematic character may make apparent some inconsistencies in one's moral decisions or judgments. Making the moral system explicit, including making clear which facts are morally relevant and why, may reveal that some of one's moral judgments are inconsistent with the vast majority of one's other moral judgments. Thus one may come to see that what was accepted by oneself as a correct moral decision or judgment is in fact mistaken.

Even though wholesale repudiation of commonly accepted moral judgments amounts to the claim that morality is not justifiable, particular widely accepted moral judgments, even of competent people, may sometimes be mistaken without denying that morality can be justified. Especially when long accepted ways of thinking are being challenged, people may be misled by superficial similarities and differences into making judgments that are inconsistent with the vast majority of their other moral judgments. For example, many people in the United States in the 1950s found that their moral judgments about what were morally acceptable ways of treating African Americans were inconsistent with the vast majority of their other moral judgments. Today, in the 1990s, many people in the United States are finding that their moral judgments about what are morally acceptable ways of treating those with a different sexual orientation are inconsistent with the vast majority of their other moral judgments. That discrimination against both African Americans and homosexuals were sometimes supported by religious scriptures shows the dangers of not distinguishing clearly between morality and religion.

One of the major points of difference between morality and religion is that every feature of morality must be known to and rationally acceptable to all who are judged by it. Every feature of the moral system must be one that is known to and could be chosen by any rational person. No religion is known to all rational persons, and all religions have some features that could not be chosen by all rational persons. Some mistaken moral judgments arise from incorrectly identifying morality and religion. *There are many religions, but only one morality.* It is now universally recognized that morality must be known to everyone who is judged by it. Showing that a proposed account of morality contains some part that is justifiably unknown to any people about whom moral judgments are made shows that the proposed account of morality is inadequate. This was the great insight of those who put forward the doctrine of natural law, which states that all rational persons know what morality requires, prohibits, encourages, and allows. However, some religions make judgments about those who could not know what that religion requires them to do or believe.

Moral Theories

A moral theory should make explicit, explain, and, if possible, justify morality or the moral system. It must provide an explicit account of morality, including its variations. None of the standard moral theories provide anything close to an adequate account of common morality. Even the best of these theories, including those of Hobbes, Kant, and Mill, provide only an outline of the moral system that is commonly used. Unfortunately even they are not completely clear about the distinction between their account of this common morality and their attempt to justify it. Although morality is known to all those about whom moral judgments are correctly made (moral agents), it is more complex than I and other philosophers have recognized. This complexity does not conflict with its being understood by all, but it does make it less vulnerable to the kinds of criticisms that are often brought against it by philosophers. I hope to provide such a clear, coherent, and precise account of this complex common moral system that philosophers and others will no longer dismiss it as obviously inadequate.[7]

Many so-called moral theories do not even attempt to explain or justify common morality but are used to generate guides to conduct intended to replace common morality. These proposed moral guides, those generated by all of the standard consequentialist, contractarian, and deontological theories, are far simpler than the common moral system and sometimes yield totally unacceptable answers to moral problems. Since those philosophers who put forward these theories have usually dismissed common morality as confused, they are completely unaware of the complexity involved in making moral decisions and judgments. It is not surprising that many who take morality seriously and try to apply it to real problems faced by actual people are so critical of moral theory.

Any moral theory that adequately explains and justifies morality must contain explicit accounts of the concepts of rationality and impartiality and that of morality itself. It must also explicitly recognize those features of human nature that explain why morality has the features it has. It must show what features are morally relevant in describing a situation, and it must describe the procedures involved in moral reasoning.[8] I have already started providing an account of morality by pointing out that it has as an essential feature that only those who are not justifiably ignorant of what morality requires, prohibits, encourages, and allows, can be judged morally. It follows that everyone about whom a moral judgment can be correctly made must know what morality requires, and so on. A complete account of the concept of morality must identify and explain all of the other features that are essential to it, such as the relation between morality and impartiality. The failure of all previous moral theories to provide adequate descriptions of rationality, impartiality, and morality explains why none of them provides an adequate explanation and justification of morality.

Although I provide a preliminary account of morality before I begin to explain and justify it, I suspect that I was not always completely clear that an adequate description of morality is essential to any attempt to justify it. I now realize that I continue to provide a clearer, more precise account of morality at the same time that I attempt to justify it. As previously noted, I regard knowing what morality is as knowing how to act morally and how to make appropriate moral judgments. As I justify the moral rules, I provide more precise statements of them and of the two-step procedure used to justify violations of them. I do not regard myself as generating a new moral system from the moral theory, but rather as providing a more precise statement of the common moral system made possible by the understanding provided by the moral theory.

It is true that once one has discovered the nature of morality and seen how it is so intimately related to human nature, it becomes clear that all rational persons would favor adopting the moral system as a universal guide. Thus it is very tempting to think that one can simply start with an account of human nature, including an account of human rationality, fallibility, and vulnerability, and simply generate a code of conduct that all rational persons would favor adopting to guide everyone's behavior. And perhaps one can. However, it would not count as *justifying morality* unless the code of conduct being justified was virtually identical to the moral system that is now implicitly used in deciding how to act morally and in making moral judgments. Further, one test of any such generated system must be examining whether it diverges in any significant way from the common moral system. Any divergence counts against the adequacy of the generated system and ultimately against the moral theory that generated it. This is precisely what happened to utilitarianism.

The starting point has to be common morality. I am not now claiming that it is justifiable, only that it must be believed to be so. Clearly, what some claim to be morality is not justifiable. However, I have been amazed that a careful examination of common morality shows it to be far more sophisticated than almost anyone has taken it to be. Further, although many different moral mistakes have been widespread, each of these mistaken views can be shown to be inconsistent with the moral system as a whole. The moral theory I shall present shows common morality to be justified, that is, to be a kind of system that all rational persons, given appropriate limitations on their beliefs, would favor adopting.[9] Describing and justifying common morality is sufficient to show that morality is universal and provides a conclusive refutation of any serious forms of moral nihilism, relativism, or skepticism.

It is morality or the moral system, not the moral theory, that is applied to the moral problems that arise in business, law, medicine, science, and all other areas of ordinary life. Moral theory is useful because it supplies an explicit account of morality, so that the moral system can be applied to new and difficult situations. It is extremely important for a moral theory to explain why morality does not provide unique solutions to most controversial cases. Recognition that most controversial issues have no unique right answer might prevent people from regarding their opponents as morally corrupt. This could make it easier for both sides to compromise without fearing that they are giving up their moral integrity. Finally, by showing that common morality is justified, a moral theory can justify using morality to decide what policies to adopt, what actions to take, and what judgments to make. Thus moral theory is not merely a theoretical enterprise; it has some practical consequences. These consequences are, however, primarily indirect; it is morality itself that explains moral decisions about what to do and moral judgments on the actions, intentions, motives, and character of others.

An Incorrect View of Morality

The dominant philosophical view of morality now, and perhaps as far back as Socrates, seems to be that morality functions primarily as a guide for the individual person who adopts it.[10] But hardly anyone denies that morality must be such that a person who adopts it must also propose its adoption by everyone. Thus many philosophers have tried to show that the guide to conduct that they were adopting for themselves they would propose to be adopted by all rational persons. This view of morality is sometimes put forward by saying that any guide about how everyone *ought* to act is a moral guide, as if the precept that everyone ought to brush his teeth twice a day is part of a moral guide.

The extreme oddity of the view of morality as a guide that everyone would adopt for themselves is shown by the discussion of what is known as "ethical egoism." Ethical egoism is the position that every person ought to maximize their own self-interest. When morality is regarded primarily as a guide for the individual person who adopts it, ethical egoism, if sufficiently enlightened, becomes a plausible moral guide. This extremely odd view is reinforced by noting that it is a view about what every person "ought" to do, thus clearly confirming that it is a moral guide.[11]

The discussions of ethical egoism show that even those philosophers who hold the view that morality is primarily intended as a guide for the individual person who adopts it have some sense that it is absurd to view ethical egoism as a moral guide. They recognize that a moral view must not merely be one that would be adopted by everyone; it must also be a view that one would put forward to be adopted by everyone. Thus they argue that since no one would put forward ethical egoism to be adopted by everyone, it cannot really be a moral guide. Some even argue that an ethical egoist would be involved in an inconsistency if she told others to act in their own self-interest, because it would not be in her own self-interest for them to act in that way. I shall not consider the arguments for and against ethical egoism, for they seem to me to be beside the point. Ethical egoism is considered a moral guide only because of the mistaken view of morality as primarily intended as a guide for the individual person who adopts it.[12]

A Correct View of Morality

Hobbes is one of the few philosophers who realized that the moral virtues are praised because of the calamities everyone avoids if people act morally.[13] Hobbes's point is that morality is primarily concerned with the behavior of people insofar as that behavior affects others; it prohibits the kind of conduct that harms others and encourages the kind of conduct that helps them. Nietzsche was certainly right when he maintained that morality is what the vulnerable use to protect themselves from those who might prey upon them. Unlike Hobbes, he did not seem to realize that everyone is vulnerable. This vulnerability explains why even those who are not always prepared to act morally favor having morality taught to others.

Anyone who takes the trouble to look at what is normally considered to be morality realizes that morality is best conceived as a guide to behavior that rational persons put forward to govern the behavior of others, whether or not they plan to follow that guide themselves. That is why hypocrisy is so intimately related to morality. Once this feature of morality is recognized, it is quite clear that no rational person would put forward ethical egoism as a moral guide. The statement that morality is about how one ought to act should not be taken as a definition of morality, but rather as a claim that morality is primarily about actions. The mistaken interpretation of the statement as a definition may explain why anyone could possibly view ethical egoism as a moral guide.

It is troubling to have to criticize the statement that morality is about how one ought to act, for interpreted properly that statement is not only correct but important. It corrects another widespread but mistaken philosophical view that morality is primarily about what is the best state of affairs. (See especially *Principia Ethica* by G. E. Moore.) From the moral point of view, the only reason for wanting to know what is the best state of affairs is that it may have some bearing on how one ought to behave. Sometimes, of course, it will not have any bearing on this, as one cannot bring about that state of affairs. Further, it is often dangerous to view morality as being concerned with the best state of affairs because often one cannot bring about that state of affairs in a morally acceptable way.[14] The widely used but poorly worded slogan "The end does not justify the means" is correct if interpreted as claiming that bringing about a better state of affairs does not justify using morally unacceptable means. It is incorrect if interpreted as meaning that the end to be achieved is never a significant factor in determining whether some particular means count as morally unacceptable.

Any definition of morality must include as two of its necessary features that (1) everyone about whom a moral judgment is correctly made knows what morality is and (2) it is not irrational for any of them to use morality as a guide for their own conduct. If one agrees that moral judgments can be correctly made about all rational persons, then one holds that morality is universal. Only those who hold that a person cannot make any moral judgments about people in other societies can hold ethical relativism, for example, that only Germans living at the time can condemn Hitler. However, I doubt that any reader of this book actually holds such a view, for I have never met anyone who was willing to make moral judgments at all who was not willing to make them on some people in other societies. The realization that morality is not primarily a guide for one's own behavior but rather is a guide to behavior that rational persons put forward to govern the behavior of others makes ethical relativism much less plausible. (See the discussion of cheating in chapter 8 for another explanation of how a mistaken model of morality leads to ethical relativism.)

It is the mistaken view that morality is a guide to conduct that people adopt to govern their own behavior that has led people to talk about Nazi morality and Christian morality. In this view, Nazi morality is the code of conduct adopted by all true Nazis and Christian morality is the code of conduct adopted by all true Christians. On this use of "morality," morality is simply any code of conduct adopted by a group. But it isn't. It is only a careless use of language that has allowed "code of conduct adopted by a group" to be taken as equivalent to "morality" and has allowed such monstrous phrases as "Nazi morality." The Nazi code of conduct was not a moral code; on the contrary, it was grossly immoral. Unless one enjoys talking paradoxically, as far too many people do, one should avoid the use of "morality" that forces one to talk of an immoral morality.[15]

Many philosophers realize that viewing morality as a guide to conduct that people adopt to govern their own behavior does not distinguish morality from nonmoral codes of conduct, such as prudential guides. These philosophers then define morality as that code of conduct which a person takes to be overriding. It is significant that such philosophers almost never discuss religion, for religion is just as plausibly regarded as providing a code of conduct that a person takes to be overriding or most important. If they do discuss religion, then philosophers who hold the "overriding" view are likely to classify a religious code of conduct as a moral code. They may not realize that this has the consequence that morality does not have one of its necessary features, namely, that all who are judged by it know what it requires, prohibits, encourages, and allows.

Morality Is an Informal Public System That Applies to All Rational Persons

I use the phrase "public system" to refer to a guide to conduct that has the following two features. (1) All persons to whom it applies, all those whose behavior is to be guided and judged by that system, understand it, and know what behavior the system prohibits, requires, encourages, and allows. (2) It is not irrational for any of these persons to accept being guided and judged by that system. Since morality is public system, any adequate definition of morality must include these two features — that is, (1) everyone who is subject to moral judgment must know what morality requires, prohibits, encourages, and allows, and (2) it is not irrational for any of them to use morality as a guide for their own conduct.

The clearest example of a public system is a game such as baseball or bridge. A game has an inherent goal and a set of rules that form a system that is understood by all of the players. They all know what kind of behavior is required, prohibited, encouraged, and allowed by the game, and it is not irrational for all players to use the goal and the rules of the game to guide their own behavior and to judge the behavior of other players by them. Although a game is a public system, it applies only to those playing the game. If a person does not want the goal sufficiently to abide by the rules, she can usually quit. Morality is the one public system that a person cannot quit. This is the point that Kant, without completely realizing it, captured by saying that morality is categorical. All people are subject to morality, simply by virtue of being rational persons who can control their actions. Morality is a public system that applies to all rational persons.

Public systems can be either formal or informal. Formal public systems are those in which there is a decision procedure, usually involving authorities such as judges, umpires, or referees, that resolves all questions of interpretation of the rules of the system as well as all other disagreements between those to whom the system applies. Informal public systems presuppose overwhelming agreement about their interpretation and cannot function unless disagreements are relatively rare. When it becomes important that all disagreements be settled, public systems tend to become formal. Some games such as professional sports have become formal public systems employing elaborate decision procedures with a hierarchy of referees. Many games however, remain informal public systems, for example, casual card games or neighborhood games of various sports, and disagreements are settled on an ad hoc basis or not settled at all.

Morality is an informal public system that has no authoritative judges and no decision procedure that provides unique answers to all moral questions. When it is important that disagreements be settled, societies use political and legal systems to supplement morality. These systems do not provide a moral answer to the question; rather, the question, being regarded as morally unresolvable, is transferred to the political or legal system. There are, however, limits to legitimate moral disagreement, just as there are limits to disagreements in all informal public systems. In the vast majority of situations there is no disagreement at all, but for this very reason these situations are never discussed.

The claim that some person — for example, the pope — is a moral authority, is the result of failing to distinguish between morality and religion. There can be religious authorities, but there are no moral authorities. It is generally recognized that as long as people are within vague but generally recognized limits no one has the authority to settle moral disputes in the way that the United States Supreme Court has the authority to settle legal disputes in the United States or the pope religious disputes among Roman Catholics. Further, no one has some special knowledge of morality not available to others, for everyone who is subject to moral judgment must know what it requires, prohibits, encourages, and allows.

Of course, some people are better at dealing with moral problems than others, partly due to their training and experience, and partly due to their intelligence and good judgment. But skill in making moral decisions is not an academic specialty, and no one can legitimately claim to be a moral expert. Unfortunately, some people, including some philosophers, have taken the title of "ethicist" as if they were experts concerning moral decisions in fields such as business or medicine in the same way that chemists are experts in chemistry. The primary task of all philosophers, including moral philosophers, is to clarify. They can also sometimes show whether a commonly held view is justified. Moral philosophers clarify the nature of morality and try to show that it is justified, but those who have a better knowledge of the relevant facts and more experience in the relevant field are more likely to make better moral decisions in that field. Clarifying morality cannot settle all moral disputes, because common morality allows for some disagreement. Even in the unlikely event that everyone was in complete agreement on the facts, including their predictions about the consequences of a decision or policy, there would still be some unresolvable moral disagreement.

Regarding morality as an informal public system that applies to all rational persons explains many of the features of morality that almost everyone agrees that it has. That all normal adults are regarded as knowing what morality requires, prohibits, encourages, and allows explains why ignorance of morality is not normally allowed as an excuse. It also explains why it is thought not to be irrational for any person to adopt morality as a guide, even as the overriding guide, for her own conduct.[16] The account of morality as a public system that applies to all rational persons also explains why morality is regarded as categorical or inescapable. No one can simply opt out of it; others will continue to judge a person morally regardless of her claim that she is above it or outside of it.

Even if they do not necessarily want to follow it themselves, rational persons not only want others to adopt morality as their guide to conduct, they know that all rational persons want them to act morally. That is why the question "Why should I be moral?" is a genuine question and why it is recognized by almost all that it is rationally allowed not to adopt morality as the overriding guide, not even as an important guide, for one's own conduct. Those philosophers who claim that the question "Why should I be moral?" is not a genuine question usually also ignore the close relationship between hypocrisy and morality. These errors stem, at least in part, from continuing to regard morality primarily as a guide that each person adopts for her own conduct.

Defining morality as an informal public system that applies to all rational persons has a very tempting simplicity. Defined in this way, morality includes everything that Plato, Aristotle, and Kant discuss under that heading. On this definition, morality includes not only behavior that affects others but also behavior that affects only oneself. The promotion of good for oneself is as much a moral matter as the prevention of evil for others. My view, like that of Hobbes and Mill, is that morality applies primarily to behavior that affects the amount of harm suffered by others. Even though morality does not apply to behavior that affects only oneself, I shall discuss such behavior as well as behavior that affects others. I shall also discuss promoting benefits as well as preventing harms, even though the former is morally relevant only in limited circumstances. The definition of morality has practical as well as theoretical consequences. Too wide a definition of morality may tempt people to improperly interfere with the behavior of people when their behavior affects no one but themselves, or to feel morally required to benefit those who are not deprived.

The Definition of Morality

Although morality has the formal features discussed above, these features do not provide a complete definition of what most people think of when they think of morality.

For most people, morality has a definite content. Morality is not merely an informal public system that applies to all rational persons, nor is it merely such a public system that primarily concerns behavior that affects others. Morality has the goal of lessening the amount of evil or harm suffered. If a public system applying to all rational persons does not have this content, then even if it is justified it does not count as a justification of morality. Further, to be sure that it is common morality rather than some philosophical substitute that is being justified, the commonly accepted moral rules, ideals, and virtues must be included in the definition of morality. It is only the justifying of a public system that includes these moral rules, ideals, and virtues that counts as a justification of morality. Although there is not complete agreement concerning what counts as a moral rule, no one denies that killing, cheating, and lying are prohibited by moral rules. Nor does anyone deny that relieving and preventing pain are moral ideals or that kindness and honesty are moral virtues.

One function of a moral theory is to examine common morality, including the commonly accepted moral rules, ideals, and virtues to see if it is an informal public system that applies to all rational persons. Then it should determine whether common morality is justified by determining if it is a public system that all rational persons could, perhaps would, favor adopting. Further, all of the parts of morality, including the rules, ideals, and virtues, must be justified. If they are not such that all rational persons could favor adopting them as parts of a public system which applies to all rational persons, then morality as commonly conceived cannot be justified and ethical relativism, nihilism, or skepticism is the correct philosophical position. However, showing that common morality is a public system applying to all rational persons and that all rational persons *could* favor adopting it, counts as showing that morality as commonly conceived is at least weakly justified. Showing that all rational persons *would* favor adopting this common morality counts as strongly justifying it. This stronger justification requires the qualification that these rational persons use no controversial factual beliefs, that is, no beliefs not shared by all those who are subject to moral judgments.

In order to guarantee that I am providing a justification of common morality, I shall attempt to justify a moral system that meets the following definition. *Morality is an informal public system applying to all rational persons, governing behavior that affects others, and includes what are commonly known as the moral rules, ideals, and virtues and has the lessening of evil or harm as its goal.* Those preferring a smaller and more formal definition can simply take the first eleven words, *Morality is an informal public system applying to all rational persons,* as the definition. However, as noted earlier, this simpler definition is misleading, as it includes much that is not included in the proper understanding of morality, such as personal virtues like temperance and courage.[17]

Mill's View of Moral Philosophy

The failure to distinguish morality from other general guides to conduct has distorted the work of most moral philosophers. Even Sidgwick, whom I rank as one of the best moral philosophers of all time, equated true moral laws with rational rules of conduct without realizing that the true *moral* laws must be intimately related to the commonly accepted moral rules and moral ideals. This, together with his view that morality is a guide to conduct that people adopt for themselves, is what led him to regard ethical egoism as one of the methods of ethics.[18] The view of morality as primarily intended to provide a guide for the individual person who adopts it makes it very difficult for most philosophers to adequately distinguish morality from other guides to conduct. Even when they realize that morality is intended to be a guide for everyone, they do not adequately distinguish morality from alternative guides to conduct.

In order to show how easy it is for philosophers to provide an inadequate account of morality, I shall examine the views of John Stuart Mill. This choice is prompted by several considerations. First, all of the relevant remarks made by Mill are in his popular work *Utilitarianism*. Since this work is short and easily obtainable, it will be easy for anyone to check whether I am distorting what Mill says. Second, Mill is one of the best known and most respected moral philosophers, so that any confusions found in his writings are likely to be widespread. Third, Mill himself is somewhat concerned with this same problem, the nature and justification of morality, so that I am not attacking someone on an issue which is not his concern. Fourth, Mill writes in English and clearly enough, so that there is no great problem for readers of the present book (in its original language) in interpreting his remarks; when he is unclear, this is due to a confusion of his thought, not of his language. Fifth, utilitarianism is, and promises to remain, one of the most popular of ethical theories, and Mill is one of its principal spokesmen. Thus simply showing where Mill goes wrong at the very beginning of his account of morality is itself of considerable value.

In the very first paragraph of chapter 1 of *Utilitarianism*, Mill maintains: "From the dawn of philosophy, the question concerning the *summum bonum*, or, what is the same thing, concerning the foundation of morality, has been accounted the main problem in speculative thought." In this seemingly innocent sentence, the seeds of a crucial confusion are already apparent. In a paradigm case of a philosophical mistake, Mill has made a significant philosophical claim without realizing it. Without any argument, Mill claims that the question concerning the *summum bonum*, or greatest good, is the same as the question concerning the foundation of morality. This claim, though it is commonly made, is quite doubtful. The same kind of mistake is sometimes made using the phrases "in other words," "that is to say," or simply "i.e."; I call it the fallacy of *assumed equivalence*. It is probably the most common fallacy in philosophy, and it is quite remarkable that it does not already have a name.

In addition to equating the foundation of morality with the *summum bonum*, the following passage, also in chapter 1 (paragraph 3), strongly suggests that Mill also regards the question concerning the foundation of morality as a question of how to provide support for the moral rules.

> The intuitive, no less than what may be termed the inductive school of ethics, insists on the necessity of general laws. They both accept that the morality of an individual action is not a question of direct perception, but of the application of a law to an individual case. They recognize also, to a great extent, the same moral laws; but differ as to their evidence, and the source from which they derive their authority.

It is far from obvious, however, that the *summum bonum* provides a foundation for moral rules, that it provides either evidence or a source of authority for the moral rules. It is more plausible that a foundation for morality is provided by discovering what helps one avoid the *summum malum*, or greatest evil, as Hobbes maintains. Hobbes denies that there is a *summum bonum*, and most contemporary philosophers agree with him. Yet Hobbes, and even philosophers who acknowledge neither a *summum bonum* nor a *summum malum*, are not thereby forced to abandon all efforts to provide a justification for the moral rules. Thus right at the start Mill equates one of the proper tasks of a moral theory, providing a justification for the moral rules, with a different task, determining the *summum bonum*, whose relevance to morality is not at all clear.

Although not completely aware of it, Mill is not always concerned with justifying common morality, rather, he sometimes seems to be attempting to provide an alternative general guide to conduct. It is important to note that Mill has been criticized precisely because his guide to conduct can conflict with the guide provided by common morality. For example, it is sometimes claimed that Mill's guide allows inflicting a significant amount of unwanted pain on one person to provide a great deal of pleasure for very many others. Yet these critics do not fully realize the significance of their criticism. They do not see that Mill's utilitarianism is inadequate because Mill is not clear whether his utilitarianism is primarily concerned with providing a justification for common morality, or with offering an alternative guide to conduct.

Mill himself criticizes all previous moral philosophers for their failure to provide a foundation for the moral rules. He says: "They either assume the ordinary precepts of morals as of *a priori* authority, or they lay down as the common groundwork of those maxims, some generality much less obviously authoritative than the maxims themselves, and which has never succeeded in gaining popular acceptance" (paragraph 3). Ironically, this latter alternative seems a perfect criticism of utilitarianism. However, Mill is so unclear that he is attempting to provide evidence and a source of authority for the moral rules that he has even been interpreted as claiming that the moral rules are merely rules of thumb to be used because there is not enough time to apply the principle of utility directly.

Mill criticizes Kant for offering the categorical imperative, "So act, that the rule on which thou actest would admit of being adopted as a law by all rational beings," as "the origin and ground of moral obligation." For he holds that Kant "fails, almost grotesquely, to show that there would be any contradiction, any logical (not to say physical) impossibility, in the adoption by all rational beings of the most outrageously immoral rules of conduct" (paragraph 4). Whether or not Mill's criticism of Kant is warranted, it shows that Mill criticizes previous philosophers on the same grounds that later philosophers criticize him: namely, the principle he uses to support morality does not always do so, but, in fact, sometimes supports conduct contrary to that required by morality.

In chapter 5 of *Utilitarianism*, Mill provides a much more careful account of the nature of morality.

> We do not call anything wrong unless we mean to imply that a person ought to be punished in some way or other for doing it — if not by law, by the opinion of his fellow creatures; if not by opinion, by the reproaches of his own conscience. This

seems to be the real turning point between morality and simple expediency. It is part of the notion of duty in every one of its forms that a person may rightfully be compelled to fulfill it. Duty is a thing that may be exacted from a person, as one exacts a debt. Unless we think it can be exacted from him, we do not call it his duty. . . . There are other things, on the contrary, which we wish that people should do, which we like or admire them for doing, but yet admit that they are not bound to do; it is not a case of moral obligation; we do not blame them, that is, we do not think that they are proper objects of punishment. (chapter 5, paragraph 14)

In this quote Mill claims to distinguish between morality and other conduct governed by the principle of utility. But actually he is only distinguishing between what is morally wrong and other kinds of wrong actions, such as taking the wrong turn when driving to Cincinnati or using the wrong club to hit a golf ball one hundred yards. By simply equating morality with moral obligations and duties he falsely claims that morality concerns only that conduct that one can be forced to do and can be punished for not doing. Mill uses "punishment" in such a wide sense, including "reproaches of his own conscience" as a punishment, that he does not see that he has excluded many morally good actions from the sphere of morality.

Morality is not limited to conduct that one can be forced to do, as Mill and everyone else would realize, once they think about people who act in morally good ways that go far beyond what anyone would regard as appropriate to force them to do. Those who sacrifice their lives to save others, and even those who spend far more of their time and effort helping others than anyone would expect of them, are acting in morally good ways. They are following moral ideals and no one should be punished simply for not following a moral ideal. Mill's confusion about this may have been aided by the misleading terminology that both he and Kant use, talking about moral ideals as "duties of imperfect obligation." But duties of imperfect obligation are not duties any more than false friends are friends. They share almost none of the features of real duties.[19] The importance of terminology cannot be overestimated. If Mill had used the phrases "moral ideals" and "moral rules" instead of duties of imperfect and perfect obligation, he might have been less likely to come up with an account of morality he should have known to be false. Had he not used this misleading terminology, Mill might have realized that morality is distinguished from other guides by being primarily concerned with the lessening of evil or harm suffered by those protected by it.

That morality is concerned with the lessening of evil explains why many people believe that choosing medicine as a profession is a morally good choice, as is deciding on any career whose primary aim is helping those in need. Unless one's action is morally unacceptable, all behavior that is primarily intended to prevent or to relieve pain and suffering is properly regarded as an object of moral praise. No one has any doubts about this. In fact, it is usually only when one has no obligation or duty to prevent or relieve harm that one's action is regarded as morally good. The false account of morality proposed by many consequentialists, that morality requires doing that action that has the best consequences has led even some nonconsequentialists into claiming that morality is always a matter of obligations.[20] Even though the goal of morality is the lessening of harm, morality does not oblige one to do all those possible actions which lessen harm.

Having distinguished morality from expediency by using the notion of punishment, Mill must then distinguish in some other way between justice, which he takes to be the most important part of morality, and the rest of morality. His distinction between justice and the rest of morality is that justice involves violating someone's rights. If he had realized that morality is distinguished from other general guides to behavior by its aim of lessening the amount of harm, he might have seen that liability to punishment is what marks off justice from the rest of morality, not that which marks off morality from expediency. Rights are an incorrect way of distinguishing the rules of justice, by which he means the moral rules, from the rest of morality which are the moral ideals. Rights are not even involved in all violations of moral rules. Cheating is violating a moral rule, yet need not involve violating anyone's rights. Further, cheating is certainly unfair and fairness is closely related to justice. These errors in Mill's account of morality have had the continuing unfortunate effect not only of leading philosophers to regard all morality as concerned with obligations, they have made it seem as if "rights" were necessary in order to distinguish justice from the rest of morality. Perhaps it is because Mill's account of morality in chapter 5 come so close to getting so many points right that it has had such a profound effect on succeeding accounts of morality.

Moral Theories as Providing Guides to Conduct

Like Mill, most moral philosophers begin by trying to see what support, if any, can be given to common morality. However, also like Mill, they soon lose sight of their original task. Once they find a principle, or set of principles, they forget that the point of the principle is to provide support for common morality. Since their original search was initiated for a principle that would do this, it is not surprising that the application of the principle results in a guide to conduct which resembles to a greater or lesser degree the guide provided by common morality. Although it is barely evident in the works of some philosophers, why their works are regarded as moral theories is the connection their principles have, or seem to have, with common morality. All of the major moral philosophers who offered guides to conduct thought that they were also providing a justification for at least a large part of common morality. Success in this endeavor was the criterion by which they judged the theories of other moral philosophers.

Although this criterion is used by most philosophers, its significance is not appreciated. Philosophers continue to generate guides to conduct in the vain hope that they will coincide with the guide provided by common morality. Philosophers should not, however, offer their own guides to conduct, especially as these cannot differ in any significant way from that offered by the common moral system. They should explain and justify, if possible, the common moral system. The mistaken view that moral philosophers should offer new general guides to conduct arises from the fact that, like Mill, most philosophers are not sufficiently aware of the distinction between offering a general guide of their own and justifying the common moral system. But if a philosopher strays sufficiently far from common morality, as Nietzsche does, almost everyone begins to question whether he is even attempting to provide a *moral* guide. Lack of sufficient overlap with common morality is why hedonism, egoism, and stoicism are correctly regarded as general guides to conduct or philosophies of life rather than as moral theories.

A moral theory should make explicit all the significant features of the common moral system. It is especially important to provide an explicit and precise statement of the moral rules, for everyone is morally required to obey them. It should also clarify the moral ideals which people are morally encouraged to follow. It should make the morally relevant features explicit and explain how they are involved in the two-step procedure for determining morally acceptable violations of the moral rules. It should also clarify the nature of the moral virtues and vices. This explicit account of common morality should be clear, coherent, comprehensive, and yet easy to use when one tries to apply it to a new or complex moral problem.

Making explicit that morality is an *informal* public system is valuable in itself, for it makes clear that not all moral disagreements can be resolved and this promotes moral tolerance. A moral theory should also try to justify the moral system, which requires showing how morality is related to rationality. Showing that the moral system is a public system that applies to all rational persons is the first step in the attempt to justify it. As stated earlier, showing that common morality is a public system that *could* be supported by all rational persons is what I call weakly justifying it; showing that common morality is a public system that *would* be supported by all rational persons is what I call strongly justifying it. I shall attempt to provide a strong justification, but only with regard to rational persons who use no beliefs not shared by all moral agents.

Moral Theory as the Study of Moral Judgments

Although most philosophers did not realize that moral theories should not be used to generate new moral systems, some moral philosophers stopped offering moral guides to conduct and started analyzing moral judgments.[21] In part this was due to the sense of futility that came from looking at such a long succession of proposed moral guides to conduct, all of them inadequate in varying degrees. Since these moral philosophers did not realize that this inadequacy was due, in large part, to the failure to distinguish between common morality and general guides to conduct that were being proposed as replacements for it, their analyses of moral judgments were also doomed to inadequacy. In fact, since common morality is more closely related to general guides to conduct than it is to the making of judgments, most analyses of moral judgments were less related to the proper function of moral theory than providing general guides to conduct. It is impossible to distinguish moral judgments from other kinds of judgments without an adequate account of common morality and the likelihood of even coming close is exceedingly remote. Much of the discussion of the nature of moral judgments is almost completely irrelevant to moral theory, although it has its own intrinsic interest.

The person who did the most to start contemporary moral philosophers on the investigation of the nature of moral judgments was G. E. Moore. His apparent clarity, at least about the task of moral philosophy, resulted in making it almost impossible to distinguish moral judgments from nonmoral ones. Accepting Mill's identification of the study of the foundations of morality with the study of the nature of goodness, Moore stated his initial task to be an investigation of the meaning of the word "good." As a consequence of cogent criticisms of previous accounts of the meaning of "good" and a theory of meaning that he carried to fantastic lengths, he concluded that the adjective "good," in its basic sense, referred to a nonnatural property. For Moore, a statement of the form "X is good," when it does not mean "X is a means to something good," means that X has a certain nonnatural property.

Those statements, which Moore says are his concern as a moral philosopher, are statements attributing this nonnatural property of goodness to an object. Why Moore called goodness a nonnatural property is a complex issue that is not relevant to this discussion, for Moore's primary concern was to show that all persons agree on what things have this property and thus are intrinsically good. The point that was seized on by later philosophers, however, was Moore's assertion that moral judgments are statements of fact, though admittedly of a queer sort of fact. Although most disputed Moore's claim that moral judgments are statements of fact, almost no one seemed to question Moore's claim, which he never argued for, that all statements of the form "X is good" are moral judgments. Thus, right at the beginning, the examination of the nature of moral judgments was presented with an insuperable obstacle by the very person who started the examination. This obstacle has not yet been completely overcome.

As an indication of how remote from moral philosophy these discussions of moral judgments became, one need only cite the supposedly important distinction between the emotive theory of ethics and the subjectivist theory. According to the emotive theory, moral judgments, such as "That is wrong," are expressions of one's feelings, just as "ugh" is an expression of one's feelings. It supposedly makes no more sense to ask if a moral judgment is true than if "ugh" is true. This theory was presented as a great advance over the naive subjectivist theory (which it is not clear that anyone ever explicitly held), namely, that moral judgments are statements about one's feelings. On the subjectivist view, moral judgments are thought to be a disguised form of autobiographical statement, that is, a report about one's feelings toward something or somebody. The difference between these two theories is that emotivism views moral judgments as *expressions of* one's feelings, subjectivism as *statements about* them.

It shows something about the state of moral philosophy that this difference was thought to be crucial. The two theories do indeed differ; according to subjectivism moral judgments can be true or false, while according to emotivism they can be neither. It was rarely noted, however, that according to emotivism moral judgments can be either sincere or insincere. The difference between the two views is as great as the difference between holding your stomach and groaning, and saying "My stomach hurts." The latter can be true or false, the former only genuine or fake.

I do not deny that the emotive theory was important, if only in leading to the rediscovery that not all uses of language can be classified as true or false. The emotive theory paved the way for many more sophisticated attempts to describe the nature of moral judgments. The names indicate fairly clearly what the view was, for example, "the imperative theory" and "the commending theory." There were also the obvious modifications, such as the "emotive-imperative theory." No doubt a more satisfactory understanding of language has generally emerged from all this. I deny none of this. I maintain only that the connection between these theories and a moral theory is extremely remote. Although some made serious efforts, no emotivist or imperativist provided a plausible way of distinguishing moral judgments from other kinds of judgments. In fact, most seemed to believe that there was no significant distinction to be made. These metaethical theories make it puzzling that anyone should have ever distinguished moral judgments from all other kinds of judgments and given them a special name.

This puzzle is primarily due to the unexamined premise that moral judgments can be distinguished from other judgments by examining the words that appear in the judgment. Judgments that include the words "good," "bad," "right," "wrong," "should," or "ought" were examined, as if all judgments containing these words were moral judgments. It is too obvious to be completely neglected (though many tried hard) that the overwhelming majority of judgments including these words have nothing to do with morality.[22] So there were attempts by some philosophers to distinguish moral judgments from other judgments using the same words. They hoped that a proper analysis of the moral use of these words would clarify the nature of moral judgments. Many claimed that using these words in moral judgments gave the judgment some quality of universalizability. It was never completely clear what this amounted to, but insofar as one could find out what was meant, it turned out that all value judgments using these words, such as aesthetic and prudential judgments, had this same quality. Then it was claimed that moral judgments were overriding.[23]

All who attempted to illuminate the nature of moral judgments by comparing them with other uses of language failed to do so, and for the same reason. They were unable to distinguish moral judgments from nonmoral judgments. This was not due to the crudity of the theories that they proposed. The most sophisticated theory, to wit, that moral judgments are in some respects like statements of fact, in some respects like expressions of emotion, and in some respects like commands, is no better than its cruder predecessors in distinguishing moral judgments from nonmoral ones. All linguistic analyses of moral judgments fail because moral judgments are not distinguished from other judgments by their form, or by their function, but by their content.

The Scope of Moral Judgments

The importance of content in distinguishing moral judgments from nonmoral judgments also points to the inadequacy of theories that seek to explain moral judgments by appealing to moral emotions or moral feelings. This is especially evident if one attempts to characterize moral emotions simply by means of introspection, without reference to the subject matter toward which one feels these emotions. Based solely on introspection, the possibility arises that one could have a moral feeling toward anything, or perhaps toward nothing at all. When walking down the street, a person could all of a sudden have a moral feeling, and if he expressed that feeling he has made a moral judgment. How absurd! Nor has someone made a moral judgment about the mosquito that has just stung her child when she expresses her negative feeling toward it. Even though it is quite possible that introspectively one sometimes has the same feeling toward a person who does an immoral action as one has toward an animal who does something harmful, the expression of feeling toward the animal is not a moral judgment.

Substituting attitude for feeling does not help distinguish between the two cases because the word "attitude" is so vague that one cannot be sure whether it is possible to have the same attitude toward the two cases. If having an attitude toward something does not involve having certain beliefs about it, then one could have the same attitude toward a vicious dog as toward an immoral person. If having an attitude involves having certain beliefs, then distinguishing a moral attitude from a nonmoral one will require a specification of the beliefs required for the attitude to count as moral. Further, only if the beliefs have a certain content, will the attitude count as a moral one.

Moral attitudes, judgments, feelings, and so on must be about beings who know what morality is and can guide their actions by it. All and only such beings count as moral agents. Some philosophers talk as if moral judgments can be made about states of affairs independent of their relationship to moral agents. It is sometimes said that a world in which there was less suffering by nonhuman animals would be a morally better world, and that this need have nothing to do with moral agents. I do not deny that such a world would be better, but to say that it would be *morally* better has to mean something like that it would be better for moral agents to act so as to bring about such a world. If there are two possible worlds, completely and permanently inaccessible to moral agents, and one of them has more suffering than the other, it is in no sense *morally* worse than the other. This is perfectly compatible with all moral agents preferring that the world with less suffering be the one that actually exists.

Part of the unfortunate legacy that any judgments using the words "good," "right," "ought," and so on are moral judgments is that most philosophers seem to hold that the phrases "morally good," "morally right," "morally ought," and so on are redundant. Since it is plausible to maintain that what counts as the right decision is the decision that has the best results, some philosophers have put forward the totally implausible view that what counts as the morally right decision is the decision that has the best results. But sometimes a person makes a decision that, by a fluke and completely unforeseeably, has the best results. No one would claim that the person made the morally right decision. To do so would be similar to claiming that a dog who does something that has the best results did the morally right action.

I am not claiming that moral judgments, such as a judgment that a decision is morally right, can be made only about states of affairs in which the suffering of moral agents is affected. I am claiming that they are limited to judgments in which moral agents are involved as actual or possible agents. This does not seem to me to be controversial, even though there is considerable controversy about who has to be affected by the actions of moral agents in order for a moral judgment to be appropriate. Everyone agrees that a moral judgment is appropriate if another moral agent is affected. Some think that only if moral agents are affected are moral judgments appropriate, that nothing that is done to any other being is a matter for moral judgment. Others hold that any actions of moral agents that affect the suffering of any sentient being are a proper subject of moral judgment.

Several positions are possible. Among them are the following: (1) only what is done to presently existing actual moral agents, for example, adult human beings living now, is morally relevant; (2) only what is done to actual moral agents, present or future, thus including future generations, is morally relevant; (3) only what is done to presently existing actual or potential moral agents, including most living human neonates and fetuses, is morally relevant; (4) only what is done to presently existing sentient beings, thus including many animals, but excluding early fetuses, is morally relevant; and (5) whatever is done to actual or potential sentient beings, present or future, is morally relevant (this includes every being in all of the previous categories plus future generations of animals including animal fetuses). There is considerable controversy about the scope of moral judgments, from the narrowest view, (1), to the widest view, (5). However, even on the widest view, the actions of moral agents that are the appropriate subject matter of moral judgments is limited in scope.

Clarity about the nature of moral judgments requires clarity about their scope. What is subject to moral judgment? This is a question that seems not to have been given sufficient weight by any of the philosophers who discuss the nature of moral judgments. Any account of moral judgments that would allow moral judgments to be made about actions or beings that are not subject to moral judgment is clearly inadequate. So that almost all, if not all, of the various accounts of moral judgments that have commonly been offered, namely, that moral judgments are expressions of emotion, statements of emotion, commands, commendations, mistaken projections of internal feelings onto external objects, and so forth, are inadequate. None of these accounts ensures that moral judgments can be made only about actions and beings that are subject to moral judgments. It is true that when one makes a moral judgment one may be expressing one's feelings, giving a command, commending, or condemning, or mistakenly objectifying one's feelings, but when this has been said, nothing has been done to distinguish moral judgments from other kinds of judgments.

It should now be clear that no attempt to distinguish moral from nonmoral judgments can be made without taking into account the subject matter of the judgment. This seems so obvious as to be hardly worth saying. Yet it is surprising how many accounts of moral judgments have been given without mentioning anything at all about the content of the judgment. It has already been pointed out that moral judgments are limited to judgments involving beings who are moral agents. Not all beings, however, are moral agents, only those having certain characteristics. Of a being having all of the necessary characteristics, moral judgments can be made about her actions, intentions, motives, character traits, or simply about the person in general. Of course, not all a person's actions, intentions, motives, and character traits are subject to moral judgments; some of them fall outside the limits of morality.

The two relatively distinct kinds of limitations on moral judgments are (1), they are limited to the actions, intentions, motives, and character of people who have certain characteristics, and (2), they are limited to a subclass of these actions, intentions, and so on, that is, those that have a certain content. The second kind of limitation is related to the kinds of actions that are covered by the moral system. A discussion of the first of these limitations largely overlaps with a discussion of what are commonly known as excuses. Excuses generally consist of showing that a person either does not have, or did not have, one or more of the characteristics that are necessary to be an appropriate subject of moral judgments.

Excuses

What are the characteristics persons must have before their actions, intentions, and so on, are subject to moral judgment? Since nonhuman animals are not subject to moral judgment, at least some of the characteristics that persons must have in order to be subject to moral judgments will be characteristics that these animals do not have. One of the distinguishing features of persons is their knowledge of very general facts. It is not surprising that one of the characteristics that a person must have to be subject to moral judgment is knowledge of a very general sort. Among the things that must be known are the following: persons can be killed by other persons and they do not normally want to be killed; one person can inflict pain on or disable another person and persons do not normally want to be inflicted with pain or disabled; one person can deprive another person of freedom or pleasure and persons do not normally want to be deprived of these things. Failing to know some of these things but not others, would excuse one from some moral judgments but not others. Children are therefore not subject to some moral judgments, even though they are subject to others. A certain minimal intelligence and knowledge is required for one to be subject to moral judgment. Someone lacking this minimal intelligence and knowledge lies outside the scope of moral judgment.

The appropriateness of moral judgments is also affected by the knowledge that the person has or should have had of the particular situation. There is no dispute among philosophers, or even among nonphilosophers, that in some cases lack of knowledge renders a person totally exempt from moral judgment, but not always. For example, sometimes a person does not know the driving regulations in a foreign country but should have made an effort to find out. In these cases it may be felt that a tourist is responsible to some degree for an accident, though perhaps not as much as a native driver would be. The degree of responsibility will depend, in part, on such seemingly unrelated factors as how close to the border it was, how many warnings or reminders there were, how many foreigners (the percentage) fail to find out the regulations, and so on. Although it may be felt that an effort should have been made to find out, the degree of responsibility will depend in part on how actual persons behave. It is unreasonable to expect a person to come to know something if no one with similar knowledge and intelligence given that same opportunity comes to know it. Whether a person can be expected to know the likely or possible consequences of his action will sometimes be an undecidable question. Hence, it will also sometimes be undecidable whether or how much he should be subject to moral judgment.

One also needs some volitional ability or ability to will.[24] Persons who do not understand that there are incentives for acting and for refraining from acting, or who do not respond to any of these incentives no matter how powerful they are, are not subject to moral judgment. Such persons do not really have a will. For to have a will is to have the volitional ability to respond to the incentives for doing or refraining from doing many kinds of actions. It is not clear to what degree nonhuman animals and very young children do have the ability to will. It is clear that it is inappropriate for moral judgments to be made of the behavior of those beings who do not have any ability to will. It is a more complex matter to determine whether a person is subject to moral judgment for an action if she simply lacks the ability to will that kind of action. (See chapter 12.)

Although persons must have some volitional ability or ability to will before they are subject to moral judgment, not only actions that are willed, intentional actions, are subject to moral judgment. If people have volitional abilities, then their unintentional actions, especially if reckless, may also be subject to moral judgments. Even their unintentional failure to act, if the result of negligence, may be the proper subject of moral judgment. Some philosophers have held that it is only intentions and intentional actions that are the proper subject of moral judgments. This mistake is plausible only if one fails to make a distinction between saying that moral judgments can only be made about those who can act intentionally and saying that moral judgments can only be made about the intentional actions of such persons.

Sometimes when one says "José ought not to have done X" one intends to be making a moral judgment. If in response to this remark someone points out that, through no fault of his own, José lacked the relevant volitional ability, that response is not a moral judgment. But since that response is incompatible with the original remark, it may seem odd that the original remark is a moral judgment and the response is not. The response that José did not have the relevant volitional ability does not contradict the moral judgment that José ought not to have done X, but is a denial of one of its presuppositions. Statements about excuses concern matters presupposed by moral judgments. The moral judgment presupposes that José had the relevant volitional ability. When shown that this presupposition is false, the judgment has to be withdrawn. Statements about excuses have a close relation to moral judgments, but they are not themselves moral judgments.

Excuses are generally offered when one is trying to claim exemption from moral judgment. Obviously this occurs almost invariably when the moral judgment would be unfavorable. If one claims exemption from a favorable moral judgment, this is not ordinarily called an excuse. Yet in both cases, the same kind of facts may be cited, namely that when doing the action in question, one lacked at least one of the characteristics necessary before one's actions are subject to moral judgment. Failure to know the consequences of one's action because one lacks either sufficient intelligence or knowledge that one could not have been expected to have, exempts one from both favorable and unfavorable moral judgments. For example, someone shouts, unaware that shouting will distract a child and cause an accident. If one could not have been expected to know this, that action is not subject to moral judgment. Nor, of course, is it appropriate for one to be subject to moral judgment if, in the same circumstances, shouting helps to avert a tragedy. Normally, an unvoluntary action, that is, one done intentionally but without the relevant volitional ability, is also not subject to moral judgment, unfavorable or otherwise. Someone with severe claustrophobia generally is not subject to moral judgment when his phobia prevents him from doing what would otherwise be morally required. But if, like many drug addicts, one is responsible for lacking the relevant volitional ability, then one may be appropriately held responsible for all actions that result from that lack of ability.

The Subject Matter of Moral Judgments

The previous section showed that for an action to be subject to moral judgment, it must have been done by a person who has certain characteristics. If moral judgments were made only about intentional actions, showing which intentional actions were subject to moral judgments would complete the discussion of their scope. As has already been pointed out, however, moral judgments are also made about some unintentional actions, even about some unintentional failures to act. Moral judgments are also made about intentions, motives, character traits, even about the person as a whole. But moral judgments about actions are basic.

Separate moral judgments about intentions are not usually made unless the intentions have not been carried out. If people do what they intended to do, a moral judgment is normally made only about their actions; no separate moral judgment is made about their intentions. Sometimes, however, intentions are not carried out. Where there is no action to make a moral judgment about, or the action is not the one intended, moral judgments are made about intentions. Obviously, the judgment about the intention is closely related to the judgment that would have been made if the action had been carried out. If the intention is not carried out because of circumstances not in the control of the agent, the intention may be judged just as the action would have been judged. If the failure to carry out the intention was due to the agent, not only is the intention judged but also the failure to carry it out. Moral judgments of intentions are so similar to those of actions that there is no need for a separate discussion of them.

Moral judgments about motives are slightly more complex. Sometimes they are indistinguishable from judgments about intentions; sometimes they are more like judgments about character traits. Favorable or unfavorable moral judgments about motives are made insofar as one thinks that this kind of motive normally leads to certain kinds of actions about which one would make favorable or unfavorable moral judgments. Sometimes an unfavorable moral judgment about a particular action may be appropriate, even though a favorable moral judgment is made about the motive for the action. For the motive may be one that is thought more likely to lead to actions about which favorable moral judgments are appropriate. Similarly, moral judgments about a character trait also depend on the moral judgments about the actions that are likely to issue from it. General moral judgments about a person are very similar, though obviously more complex, as people have many different character traits, some may be moral virtues and some may be moral vices.

The Content of Moral Judgments

In discussing the further limitations on moral judgments, only moral judgments about actions, not moral judgments about intentions, motives, and so on shall be considered. Everything said of moral judgments about an action applies, with fairly obvious modifications, to the moral judgments that are made about the failure to act, intentions, motives, character traits, and people as a whole. That there are further limits to moral judgments than that they be about the actions of a person with certain characteristics should be clear. Even if someone had all of the required characteristics, she would not be subject to a moral judgment for putting on her right shoe before her left, at least not in anything like normal circumstances. Not only is the scope of moral judgments limited to actions performed by persons with certain characteristics, it is also limited to a very small proportion of the actions done by people of this sort.

Which actions are subject to moral judgment? The simple answer is, those that are covered by the moral system, that is, by some moral rule or moral ideal. However, this answer, which is largely correct, is of limited use until the content of the moral system, including the moral rules and moral ideals, is precisely known. But, of course, some moral rules, such as "Do not kill," "Do not lie," "Do not steal," are known. And so are some moral ideals, such as "Relieve suffering," "Help the needy." Thus the simple answer is not completely useless. But in order to be completely clear about the scope of moral judgments, a complete and precise account of the moral system must be provided; all of the basic moral rules and moral ideals must be made explicit. It is, however, already clear that not all actions are covered by moral rules or moral ideals. Thus a moral judgment cannot be adequately described as an expression of emotion, a statement about a property, a command, a statement about feelings or attitudes, or as a piece of advice. For all of these can be made about actions that are related in no way to either moral rules or moral ideals. Simply the realization of the limited scope of moral judgments is sufficient to make clear the inadequacy of almost all previous accounts of moral judgments.[25]

Summary

In this chapter I have distinguished between morality or a moral system and a moral theory. I have challenged the prevailing view that morality is best conceived as a guide to conduct that a person or group adopts for itself. I have claimed that there is a common morality that applies to all rational persons and have provided a definition of it. *Morality is an informal public system applying to all rational persons, governing behavior that affects others, and includes what are commonly known as the moral rules, ideals, and virtues and has the lessening of evil or harm as its goal.* I have provided an account of a public system and shown the advantages of recognizing that morality is an informal public system.

I have emphasized a feature of morality that everyone acknowledges it to have; that moral judgments can only be made about those who know what morality requires, prohibits, encourages, and allows. I have shown that recognition of this feature not only allows one to distinguish clearly between religion and morality but also limits the content of morality. I have shown that recognizing that morality has a definite content reveals the inadequacy of normative ethical theories that are used to generate new moral systems and of metaethical theories that simply examine the language used in moral judgments. And I have explained excuses by relating them to this limitation on the subject matter of moral judgments.

Notes

1. This way of talking arises from falsely equating morality with the mores or customs of a society, and it results in equating morality with any code of conduct adopted by a group or with the legal system of a society. See note 15.

2. I prefer to talk of a universal morality with variations, because it not only explains those unresolvable moral disagreements that occur when there are no disagreements about the facts but also explains why these disagreements are always limited and shows that there is always agreement on the morally acceptable ways of settling the disagreement.

3. This may explain why some hold that moral judgments can be made only about those in the same society, and who thus accept ethical relativism. But since people in all societies share those features that are responsible for their having any morality, namely, they are vulnerable, fallible, and rational, morality will have a universal and common content.

4. Kurt Baier takes this view in *The Moral Point of View* (Ithaca, N.Y.: Cornell University Press, 1958). Although I hold that morality is universal, anyone who holds that moralities are limited to societies can take the account presented in this book as an account of the morality of their society.

5. It is not only extremely unlikely; there is no reason to believe that it has ever happened. However, if one accepts any of the standard philosophical accounts of morality, it would follow that everyone is mistaken fairly often.

6. A description of a grammar can be mistaken but still persuade competent speakers to change the way they speak. However, once competent speakers adopt a way of speaking, it becomes grammatical.

7. In *The Outlines of the History of Ethics* (London: Macmillan, 1902) Henry Sidgwick, says, "The truth is that a moral system could not be satisfactorily constructed until attention had been strongly directed to the vagueness and inconsistency of the common moral opinions of mankind: until this was done, the moral counsels of the philosopher, however supreme his contempt for the common herd, inevitably shared these defects" (p. 16). Although Sidgwick is talking about pre-Socratic moral philosophers, it seems clear that he thinks "the common moral opinions of mankind" have continued to be vague and inconsistent.

8. Some of these features are neither consequences nor even reasons; nonetheless, they affect the moral acceptability of a moral decision or action. A moral theory cannot possibly explain or justify these morally relevant features if it does not even acknowledge their existence. See chapter 9 for a fuller discussion.

9. This limitation on beliefs requires that rational persons use no controversial beliefs, that is, no beliefs that are not shared by all those who are subject to moral judgment. I will discusss this limitation on beliefs in more detail in chapter 2.

10. There is a use of the term "ethics" that refers to this kind of guide; however, as I use "ethics" it refers to the same subject matter as "morality." I use the phrase "philosophy of life" to refer to this all encompassing guide for the individual.

11. In *The Methods of Ethics* (7th edition, London: Macmillan, 1907), Henry Sidgwick, presents ethical egoism as one of the three methods of ethics, the other two being utilitarianism and intuitionism.

12. For a further discussion of ethical egoism and how it derives from rational egoism, see chapter 2 and my article "Egoísmo," *Revista Latinoamericana de Filosofía* 22, no. 1 (fall 1996): 5–20.

13. Hobbes was neither an ethical egoist nor a psychological egoist but was considered to be so in part because he held the correct account of morality. See my introduction to *Man and Citizen* by Thomas Hobbes (Indianapolis: Hackett Publishing, 1991); or my articles "Hobbes, Thomas," *The Oxford Companion to Philosophy*, edited by Ted Honderich (Oxford: Oxford University Press, 1995), 367–370; "Hobbes," *The Cambridge Dictionary of Phi-*

losophy, edited by Robert Audi (Cambridge: Cambridge University Press, 1995), 331–335; or "Hobbes's Psychology," *The Cambridge Companion to Hobbes*, edited by Tom Sorell (Cambridge: Cambridge University Press, 1996), 157–174.

14. This is why utilitarianism and many other forms of consequentialism are dangerous views.

15. As this paragraph makes clear, I realize that "morality" is sometimes used as equivalent to "code of conduct adopted by a society"; however, this is most likely due to failing to distinguish between a morality and a legal system. This topic will be discussed in more detail in chapter 14. I also realize that "morality" is used in some other ways with which I am unconcerned. However, I think that insofar as philosophers have attempted to justify morality, they attempted to justify morality in my sense. Further, I think that my account of morality fits a very common, perhaps the most common, use of the concept.

16. I interpret the claim that morality is the overriding guide to mean that no nonmoral considerations should make one act immorally. Rational persons need not regard morality as overriding and many people do act immorally for personal reasons. Almost no one thinks that moral considerations always outweigh nonmoral considerations, that they should always give their extra money to charity rather than indulging themselves with minor luxuries.

17. There may be disputes about whether those virtues like temperance and courage, which primarily benefit oneself, are part of morality, but I regard these disputes as primarily terminological. See chapter 11.

18. See note 10.

19. Duties will be discussed in more detail in chapter 8.

20. This view has continued into the present with such clever philosophers as Bernard Williams making the same mistake as Mill.

21. Moral theories are now standardly regarded as falling into two distinct categories, normative ethics and metaethics. Originally, normative ethical theories were those that generated a moral system and a metaethical theory was an account of the language used in making moral judgments. Justifying the common moral system does not fit neatly into either category and is sometimes regarded as part of normative ethical theory, sometimes as part of metaethical theory. It should be clear from the previous section that I regard what is usually regarded as normative ethics to be the result of a confusion, and it will be clear from this section that I regard what is usually regarded as metaethics to be irrelevant to the central task of moral theory. Thus any attempt to use these categories to classify what I am doing is very likely to be extremely misleading.

22. In fact, a computer search of these words reveals that less than 10 percent of their uses have anything to do with morality.

23. As discussed earlier in this chapter, this creates problems distinguishing morality from religion.

24. For further clarification of this concept, see Timothy Duggan and Bernard Gert, "Voluntary Abilities," *American Philosophical Quarterly* 4, no. 2 (April 1967): 127–135, reprinted in *The Nature of Human Action*, edited by Myles Brand (Glenview, Ill.: Scott, Foresman, 1970); and Bernard Gert and Timothy Duggan, "Free Will as the Ability to Will," *Nous* 13 (1979): 197–217, reprinted in *Moral Responsibility*, edited by John Fisher (Ithaca, N.Y.: Cornell University Press, 1986). See also Charles M. Culver and Bernard Gert, "Volitional Disabilities," *Philosophy in Medicine* (Oxford: Oxford University Press, 1982), chap. 6.

25. The moral virtues and vices cannot replace the moral rules and ideals in determining the scope of moral judgments, for the moral virtues and vices must be explained by using the moral rules and ideals. See chapter 11.

Chapter 2

RATIONALITY AND IRRATIONALITY

Why Be Rational?

I am concerned with the concept of rationality such that the question "Why be rational?" makes no sense. This is the evaluative or normative sense of "rational" that applies to the actions, beliefs, and decisions of moral agents. It is not the sense of "rational" where rationality is taken to be a capacity for reasoning, which is often regarded as distinguishing human beings from other animals. However, the two senses sometimes get confused, or some fairly obvious naturalistic fallacy is being committed. Some philosophers (from the present time to even farther back than Plato and Aristotle) seem to claim that human beings are essentially rational (reasoning) beings; therefore reasoning is the highest goal or best activity of human beings and they should reason as much as possible. But even if rationality (reasoning) is a unique characteristic of human beings, it does not follow that people should be rational if that means that reasoning is the best activity or that people should reason as much as possible. In some circumstances, a person can understand what it is to engage in reasoning and prefer some other activity. In the sense of "rational" with which I am concerned, no person who understands what "rational" means would *ever* ask why be rational.

This is the sense of rationality that plays the most basic role in justifying claims, not only in moral philosophy, but in all of philosophy as well as in everyday life. It is only this evaluative or normative sense of rationality with which I shall be concerned, and for which I will attempt to provide an analysis or definition. I believe that this is the sense of rationality with which most philosophers have been concerned and for which all the standard philosophical analyses, descriptions, or definitions must be wrong. As commonly described by philosophers, rationality could not do what it in fact does, namely, provide the basis for many of the evaluative and normative claims both in ordinary life and in philosophy, medicine, and all of the social sciences. The low esteem into which rationality has fallen in many circles is due primarily to its being almost universally misdescribed by philosophers, economists, and others. Although a clear account of the concepts of rationality and irrationality has a value far beyond that of understanding and justifying morality, I shall generally limit my discussion to those features of rationality and irrationality that are relevant to these tasks.

Irrationality More Basic Than Rationality

Rationality and irrationality are primarily concerned with actions. Irrationality is the more basic normative concept of the pair. To regard an action as irrational is always to want that it not be done by anyone for whom one is concerned.[1] However, there may be two or more rational alternatives, so that to regard an action as rational is not necessarily to want it to be done by everyone for whom one is concerned. "Everyone always ought to act rationally" is true because it means that no one should ever act irrationally. It is not true if it is taken as meaning that if an act is rational, it should be done. This is because rational actions include not only rationally required actions, but also those that are merely rationally allowed, that is, neither rationally prohibited nor rationally required. Most of the actions of most people, for example, going to a movie, belong in this category; they are neither rationally required nor rationally prohibited. However, rationally allowed actions are clearly rational actions, and any attempt to classify them as nonrational involves a distortion of the concept of rationality.

A Test of Irrational Actions

An essential feature of the actions that are irrational in the basic sense is that no fully informed rational person would ever advocate doing them to any person for whom he is concerned.[2] When I talk of "rational persons" in this context, I mean "persons insofar as they have neither irrational beliefs, desires, nor motives, and are not acting irrationally." Thus, in talking about rational persons, I am not making any empirical claims about actual rational persons, but am simply making explicit what is involved in being rational. To be fully informed about something, a rational person must have all of the relevant information about it that is possessed by all other rational persons at that time. This does not involve the unattainable ideal of omniscience; on the contrary, it seems likely that most people are fully informed about most of their actions.[3]

All fully informed rational persons would advocate to everyone for whom they are concerned that they not perform an irrational action. In the basic sense of an irrational action, the test of an irrational action is whether any fully informed rational person could advocate that someone for whom he is concerned perform this action. Because some people are not fully informed or perhaps not even rational, it is clear that people may be mistaken in regarding an action as irrational. This shows that there is an objective sense of irrationality which is more basic that that which simply regards the action as one that a person never wants either himself or those he cares about to do.

Any descriptive account of this basic sense of rationality that would ever result in a fully informed rational person advocating to any persons for whom she is concerned, including herself, that they act irrationally is an inadequate account of rationality. An adequate descriptive account of rationality must have the result that every fully informed rational person would advocate to her friends that they never perform an irrational act. Whether it has this result can be used as a test of the adequacy of that account. If it does not, then it fails the test and is an inadequate account. It is tempting to regard this test of the adequacy of all descriptive definitions as itself being a descriptive definition. It can be formulated as follows: *An act is irrational if and only if every fully informed rational person would advocate that all persons for whom they are concerned, including themselves, never do that act.*[4]

There are two problems with this definition of an irrational act. The first problem is that it does not distinguish between irrational actions and those that are simply based on false beliefs or the absence of relevant true beliefs. No fully informed rational person would advocate that any persons for whom she is concerned act in a way that would count as irrational if the person acting were himself fully informed. No fully informed rational person would advocate that a child for whom she is concerned take a pill that will cause the child great pain and provide no benefit to anyone. However, the child may not have sufficient knowledge and intelligence to have the belief that the pill will have this affect. Thus, it would not be irrational for the child to take the pill even though no fully informed rational person concerned with him would advocate that he do so.

The second problem with accepting this definition of an irrational act is that using "rational person" as part of the definition makes it circular, for a rational person is partly defined in terms of rational actions. This problem could be avoided if one could make explicit who is being referred by the phrase "rational person," so that the word "rational" could be eliminated from the definition. The same problem arises if "rational person" is taken as referring to all those whom we hold responsible for their actions — that is, moral agents — because a necessary feature of moral agents is that they be rational persons. Further, talking about those whom "we" hold responsible, brings in the same problem again: Who is referred to by "we"? It is both surprising and disappointing how many philosophical definitions of rational action depend upon limiting their "we" to rational persons, without explicitly noting that they are doing so and without explaining what they mean by "rational persons."

I have already pointed out that I use "rational persons" to refer to people insofar as they are rational, but this does not eliminate the circularity or explain what is meant by "rational persons." For present purposes "rational persons" must also have sufficient knowledge and intelligence to be subject to moral judgment, but not merely this. These people must also advocate to those for whom they were concerned, necessarily including themselves, that they not act in any ways that would cause them, or increase their chances of, death, pain, loss of ability, freedom, or pleasure, unless they believe that someone, either themselves or someone else, would avoid an equal or greater harm or gain some compensating benefit.[5] I am not saying that I use "rational persons" to refer only to those who accept a particular account of rationality. I am saying that I use it to refer only to those people who know enough to be morally responsible for their actions and who want to avoid death, pain, or loss of ability, freedom, or pleasure for themselves and their friends unless they believe there will be compensating benefits for someone. I expect that all readers of this book belong in this category. My goal is the Socratic one of convincing these readers.

Any acceptable definition of an irrational action must meet the test described above, of never allowing any fully informed rational person to advise her friends to act irrationally. If it does not meet this test, then rationality and irrationality cannot serve the purpose that they do in almost all philosophical theories. Philosophers who hold as diverse views of reason as Plato, Hobbes, and Kant, nonetheless agree that reason should always be obeyed. Those who deny that reason always ought to be followed, like Hume, are properly regarded as skeptics. If it is ever acceptable to advocate that any person for whom one is concerned perform an irrational act, what purpose would be served by showing that an act is irrational? But any definition of an irrational action that passes this test results in a concept of an irrational action that is not only normative but also objective. A descriptive definition of an irrational action that passes this test yields a concept of irrationality that is both descriptive and normative, thus allowing one to move from descriptions to prescriptions. If no definition passes this test then there is no rationality in the basic sense with which I am concerned, and skepticism is correct.

In the first published version of my theory, I described an irrational action as being "prohibited by reason," a rationally required action as being "required by reason," and a rationally allowed action as being "allowed by reason."[6] I stopped using these phrases because they create such a strong temptation to think of "reason" as a faculty that issues commands and prohibitions. Plato, Hobbes, and Kant all succumb to this temptation, and, except for Hobbes, there seems no way to eliminate the faculty way of talking without wholesale modification of the theories involved. *Talk of rationality and irrationality is not talk about some faculty of human nature, it is a way of talking about the fundamental normative judgments concerning human actions.* Irrational actions are not usually called "irrational"; more often, terms like "crazy," "idiotic," "stupid," or "silly" are used. Which of these terms is used and the tone of voice in which it is said depend on how irrational the action is regarded, that is, how much it is taken to count against the person being rational.

Whenever there is any significant disagreement as to whether an action is rational or irrational, I shall regard it as rational. Thus if any significant group of rational persons, as characterized previously, regard an action as rational, I shall regard it as rational.[7] This makes it quite likely that I shall call some actions rational that others would prefer to call irrational. This disagreement will have no significant consequences unless one mistakenly regards all immoral actions as irrational or regards any sacrifice of one's own interests in order to benefit others as irrational. I am primarily concerned with avoiding calling any action irrational that any significant group of people would normally regard as rational. I want to use "irrational action" to refer only to actions that everyone would advocate that they or their friends never do.

Irrationality applies primarily to actions, and the concept of an irrational action is necessary for explaining why some beliefs, desires, and motives are called irrational as well as for explaining the concept of an irrational person. I shall discuss irrational beliefs, desires, and motives, but I shall have very little to say about distinguishing rational persons from irrational persons.[8] At least since Freud it has been commonly held that the rationality of persons is a matter of degree. All people act irrationally some of the time. It is extremely common to use the term "irrational" simply as a term of great disapproval, but I do not use the term in that way. I am concerned with a comprehensive account of the concept of rationality, so that to regard an action as irrational is to count it in favor of the person being irrational. A person who continually performs serious irrational actions is an irrational person. Rational persons can be held responsible for doing irrational actions, but irrational persons are not held responsible for these actions. This shows that I do not simply use "irrational" as a term of disapproval, but regard it as having significant content. How serious a person's irrational actions have to be before he is considered irrational is a matter of responsibility standards (see chapter 12).

Who Can Act Rationally and Irrationally?

The term "rational" applies to the actions of a being only if the term "irrational" can also be applied to the actions of the same being. Since "rational" and "irrational" are opposing normative terms, if one of these terms can apply to the actions of a being the other should also apply. This does not rule out applying rationality and irrationality to the intentional actions of some nonhuman animals as well as of human beings, for it seems that nonhuman animals can act in irrational ways. It seems possible that an animal can become so angry that it acts in a way that it knows will be harmful to itself and have no good results. However, newborn babies do not act either rationally or irrationally, nor do most nonhuman animals, because when they act in ways that are harmful to themselves, they do not know any better.

Applying the term "rational" to the actions of any being, including nonhuman animals, whose actions can also be called irrational, would have the positive consequence that it would avoid the view that human beings are fundamentally different from all other animals with regard to rationality and irrationality. What distinguishes human beings from all other animals is not rationality, but morality. Only the actions of human beings are subject to moral judgment. No actions of any nonhuman animals are considered as being moral or immoral, only the actions of some as yet unspecified class of human beings are judged as moral or immoral.[9] It is tempting to describe this class simply as the class of all adult human beings, but this is obviously inadequate. It excludes older children, whose actions are subject to moral judgment and it includes adults who are so severely mentally retarded that they are not regarded as subject to moral judgment.

"Rational" and "irrational" can apply to the actions of a wider group of beings than do the terms "moral and "immoral," but I shall limit my use of "rational" and "irrational" to the actions, beliefs, desires, and motives of those who have sufficient knowledge and intelligence to be subject to moral judgment. A person has sufficient knowledge and intelligence to be subject to moral judgment only if he knows some very general facts about people, such as that they are fallible and vulnerable. Having sufficient knowledge and intelligence to be subject to moral judgment is not sufficient for a person to be subject to moral judgment, but it is important to recognize that some general knowledge is necessary in order to be subject to moral judgment.

I realize that this leads to the somewhat paradoxical-sounding conclusion that it is necessary for a person to have at least a certain minimal knowledge and intelligence in order for his actions, beliefs, desires, and motives to be called irrational, but this is merely a verbal problem.

Irrational (Rationally Prohibited) Beliefs

In order for a person's actions to be subject to moral judgment, she must have sufficient knowledge and intelligence to hold an irrational belief.[10] A belief is irrational if and only if (1) it conflicts, either logically or empirically, with a great number of beliefs which that person knows to be true; and (2) almost all people with similar relevant knowledge and intelligence would not only hold the belief to be false, but would regard the conflict between it and the other beliefs of the person to be obvious.[11] Briefly, a belief is irrational if and only if it is held in the face of overwhelming evidence or logical truths that are, or should be, known to the person holding it.

A person does not have to know that she knows things that contradict her belief or that the overwhelming evidence would lead almost everyone with similar relevant knowledge and intelligence to hold that it is false. All that is necessary for a belief to be irrational is that almost everyone with similar relevant knowledge and intelligence would hold the belief to be false. An irrational belief is not merely a false belief, not even simply an obviously false belief; it is an obviously false belief held by a person who has sufficient relevant knowledge and intelligence to know that it is false. I call these kinds of beliefs irrational because holding them significantly increases the chances of a person acting irrationally.

To say of a belief that it is irrational is to say something very strong about it, much stronger than saying that the belief is mistaken. Many beliefs are mistaken and yet not irrational. For example, the belief that Oswald did not participate in the assassination of President Kennedy is mistaken but it is not an irrational belief. It would be irrational to believe that Kennedy was not assassinated. It is hard to formulate precisely the difference between the two cases. It is not sufficient to say that there is overwhelming or conclusive evidence that Kennedy was assassinated. It can be claimed, with some justification, that there is overwhelming or conclusive evidence that Oswald participated in the assassination. Nor is it sufficient to talk of the former being known and the latter only being believed. For it could be claimed that it is known that Oswald participated in the assassination; that it had been proved beyond the shadow of a doubt. Nonetheless there does seem to be an important difference between the two beliefs. There can be rational disagreement about whether Oswald participated in the assassination, but it would be irrational for anyone to deny that Kennedy was assassinated.

Of course, the above discussion has an implicit limitation; generally speaking, it is limited to normal adults living in America in the sixties. It would not be irrational for someone in China to believe that Kennedy was not assassinated but that the whole thing was faked. Talk of irrational beliefs presupposes a group of people with similar relevant knowledge and intelligence for whom it would be irrational to accept those beliefs. It is irrational for normal adults to believe in Santa Claus; it is not irrational for children to believe in him. Providing a list of irrational beliefs requires making clear what group of people one has in mind. Here there is a choice. Specifying some intelligent and highly educated class, such as readers of this book, would make it possible to list a great number of irrational beliefs. By specifying this class I could list as irrational beliefs the belief that the earth is flat, that the book of Genesis is literally true, that walking under a ladder brings bad luck, and so on. This is a tempting choice for I am primarily interested in persuading readers of this book that a certain attitude toward morality is rationally required.

However, I want to be able to speak of irrational beliefs without excluding anyone who is subject to moral judgment. It is of little value to say that certain beliefs about morality are rationally required, if this does not mean rationally required of all those who are subject to moral judgment. Thus, from now on when I talk about irrational beliefs or rationally prohibited beliefs, I shall mean beliefs which would be irrational to anyone with enough knowledge and intelligence to be a moral agent, that is, to be subject to the moral judgment.

Prominent among the kinds of beliefs that would be considered irrational by all moral agents are those that are put forward by philosophical skeptics. The philosophical skeptic puts forward these beliefs in order to force people to examine more carefully the opposing or commonsense views. But genuinely holding the beliefs that are put forward by the skeptic, that is, basing any of one's actions on these beliefs, would be irrational. These irrational skeptical beliefs include the following: no one can ever know, or even be reasonably sure, what will happen in the future; no one can ever know what any of the effects of an action will be; no one can ever know anything about the world outside of his immediate sensations; no one can even know if there is such a world; in particular, no one can ever know if there are any other people in the world. Barring extraordinary conditions, any person with sufficient knowledge and intelligence to be a moral agent would be irrational to accept any of the beliefs listed above. None of the beliefs in this list of rationally prohibited beliefs, is in the slightest degree plausible as a genuine belief, that is, as a belief that should affect one's everyday actions.

It is, however, not only skeptical beliefs that are rationally prohibited; it is also irrational to believe that anyone knows everything that is going to happen. Even if one believes in determinism, whatever that comes to, it is irrational to believe that any person knows all of the consequences of any action. Any action, especially if it is at all significant, has so many consequences that it is impossible for any person to know them all. It is irrational to believe that anyone knows completely how he will be affected by breaking a moral rule, not merely whether he will feel guilt, shame, or remorse, but also how his character will be affected. It is also irrational to believe that anyone knows completely how breaking a moral rule will affect others, or even whether they will come to know about it.

It is irrational to believe that any person is infallible. However, the infallibility of people is often assumed by philosophers when they present moral problems for discussion. They present an action, usually a violation of a moral rule, together with all of its consequences as if everyone involved knew all of the consequences of that action. This is one reason why they often arrive at such counterintuitive results. Just as it is irrational to believe that no moral agent can know anything, it is also irrational to believe that any moral agent can know everything. It is also irrational to believe that any moral agent never makes any mistakes. The fallibility of persons, that is, that persons sometimes mistakenly believe that they know more than they actually do, is one of the features of human nature that is presupposed by morality.

Rationally Required Beliefs

Only a small number of the rational beliefs that people hold are rationally required beliefs, for these must be beliefs that any moral agent would be irrational not to hold. One kind of rationally required belief is a general belief, that is, a belief that makes no reference to any particular person, group, place, or time that is not known to all rational persons. One group of these general rationally required beliefs consists of the beliefs that the previously listed irrational skeptical beliefs are false. There is a simple logical relation between those beliefs that it would be irrational for anyone to hold, that is, rationally prohibited beliefs, and rationally required beliefs. If a belief is rationally required, then to hold that this belief is false is rationally prohibited. If a belief is rationally prohibited, then to hold that this belief is false is rationally required.[12]

Another important group of rationally required beliefs are personal beliefs, that is, beliefs about oneself. However, even most of one's beliefs about oneself which a person would be irrational to doubt are only rationally allowed beliefs, for other rational persons would not be irrational to deny them about themselves. I count only those personal beliefs which all rational persons must have about themselves as rationally required beliefs. Thus, no beliefs about one's race or gender count as rationally required beliefs. The personal beliefs that are rationally required include the following: I am mortal, I can suffer pain, I can be disabled, I can be deprived of freedom, and I can be deprived of pleasure. These beliefs can be summarized by the belief, I am vulnerable. Other rationally required beliefs are, I know something but not everything, and I am fallible. Since rationally required personal beliefs are beliefs that all rational persons hold about themselves, it should be clear that only a very small proportion of rational personal beliefs are rationally required; the overwhelming majority are only rationally allowed.

Closely related to the rationally required personal beliefs are some rationally required positive general beliefs. If extraordinary circumstances are ruled out, some general beliefs can be listed that any moral agent would be irrational not to believe. The following list of general beliefs is not complete; it contains only those beliefs that are immediately relevant to the present task. People are mortal, they can be killed by other persons, and they do not generally want to be killed. One person can inflict pain on or disable another; people do not generally want to have pain inflicted on them or to be disabled. It is possible for some persons to deprive others of their freedom, and people generally do not want to be so deprived. People do not want to be deprived of pleasure, but they can be so deprived by the actions of other persons. And finally, people are fallible and have limited knowledge, they know some things, but not everything.[13]

A strong justification of a universal morality must be based on beliefs that every moral agent accepts. Accepting these beliefs cannot involve any special knowledge nor require that a person live at a particular time or place. They must be accepted by all moral agents, for morality does not allow people to be judged if they are justifiably ignorant of the beliefs on the basis of which they are judged. There are strange circumstances in which a person might come to believe that some person or group of persons were not mortal, nor subject to pain or disability, nonetheless, in normal circumstances, it would be irrational for anyone to doubt or deny any of the beliefs listed above. Rationally required beliefs are completely uncontroversial; no rational person doubts them. Indeed, only rationally required beliefs are completely uncontroversial, for they are the only beliefs that no rational person doubts.[14] Morality can be strongly justified, that is, it can be shown that all rational persons would favor adopting morality as the guide to conduct to be followed by everyone, only when rational persons use no controversial beliefs.

Rationally Allowed Beliefs

As noted earlier, very few rational beliefs are rationally required, almost all are merely rationally allowed. The beliefs that are classified as rationally allowed include all those beliefs which it would not be irrational for some moral agent to believe to be true and another to believe to be false. Thus it is rationally allowed to believe that the holy writings of any of the major religions are true, and to believe that they are false. Of course, it will be irrational for some people, such as readers of this book, to hold some rationally allowed beliefs, for example, that the earth is flat. Nonetheless this belief is rationally allowed rather than irrational (rationally prohibited) because it would not be irrational for some moral agents to believe the earth is flat. Beliefs that have been proven true by modern science are still only rationally allowed, for it is not irrational for some moral agents not to accept them.

It may seem surprising that both scientific beliefs and religious beliefs are in the class of rationally allowed beliefs. I agree that some scientific claims are so well supported, for example, that the sun is much farther away from the earth than the moon is, that it might be irrational for someone who knew all of the evidence for them not to believe them. However, rationally required beliefs are limited to those that it would be irrational for any moral agent not to accept, and some moral agents do not know the facts that would make it irrational for them not to accept most scientific beliefs. Similarly, someone who had an extremely powerful religious experience might be irrational not to believe certain religious claims, yet it is still only rationally allowed to believe those claims, for most who are subject to moral judgment have not had such an experience.

Although rationally allowed beliefs cannot be part of the moral system or used in justifying it, they not only can but must be used in supporting particular moral judgments. All particular moral judgments, such as judgments that some particular person did something morally wrong, must involve rationally allowed beliefs. In no way do I want to minimize the importance of rationally allowed beliefs in the making of moral judgments. I do, however, want to distinguish between those beliefs that are part of the moral system or are used to justify it, which must be rationally required, and those beliefs that are used in applying the moral system to particular actions, people, institutions, and practices. Few moral disagreements result from disagreements about morality; most are disagreements about the way the moral system applies to particular actions, people, institutions, and practices. Indeed, one aim of this book is to make clear how much agreement there is concerning morality itself, so that more attention is paid to the particular context in which a moral decision or judgment is made. The view that a universal morality must result in ignoring the particular context is completely confused. It is like claiming that since mathematics is universal the particular context must be ignored when it is applied.

My categorizing of beliefs as rationally required, rationally prohibited, and rationally allowed allows me to list the beliefs in each category without being concerned about the knowledge and intelligence of the particular person holding the belief. I realize that this may create odd-sounding consequences; sometimes it will be irrational for a person not to hold a rationally allowed belief and sometimes it will be irrational for a person to hold a rationally allowed belief. For example, some people, such as readers of this book, are rationally required to hold a rationally allowed personal belief, such as that they can understand English. These same people are rationally prohibited from holding many rationally allowed general beliefs, for example, that the earth is flat. However, having made clear that the irrationality of a belief is dependent on the knowledge and intelligence of the person holding it, I see no problem in classifying beliefs by relating them to persons who have sufficient intelligence and knowledge to be moral agents. It is very useful to be able to classify and talk about beliefs as either rationally required, rationally prohibited, or rationally allowed without being concerned about the particular person who holds the belief.

The Centrality of Action

Action is central to the analysis of rationality and irrationality. It is primarily and basically actions that are judged rational and irrational. This does not mean that rationality and irrationality are incorrectly applied to beliefs. In the previous sections I provided a detailed account of what it is to hold an irrational belief, and a rational belief is any belief that is not irrational. But this account supports the view that what I call irrational beliefs are appropriately called irrational because of their connection with irrational actions. Irrational beliefs, or delusions, not only are intimately associated with mental disorders, which often cause irrational actions, but they often cause irrational actions directly. Once again, the concept of irrationality is more basic than that of rationality, for rational beliefs do not directly lead to rational actions. Although only rational beliefs can count as reasons, there is a much closer connection between irrational beliefs and irrational actions than there is between rational beliefs and rational actions.

First Definition of Irrational Action

I had intended to provide criticisms of other definitions of rationality before presenting my own. However, my criticisms are based on the test of definitions of rationality that I provided earlier and addressed to readers who have the characteristics that a "rational person" (see earlier in this chapter) has, so I suspect that the definition has already been implicitly provided. It therefore seems preferable to provide an explicit first definition. I do not think that this definition is completely adequate as it stands, nor do I believe that it will be entirely understandable yet. However, it is close enough to adequate and should be understandable enough that it will aid in understanding my criticisms of the other definitions.

An action is irrational in the basic sense if and only if it is an intentional action of a person with sufficient knowledge and intelligence to be fully informed about that action, and who, if fully informed, (1) would believe that the action involves significantly increased risk of his suffering death, pain, loss of ability, loss of freedom, or loss of pleasure, and (2) would not have an adequate reason for the action.[15] *All other intentional actions are rational.*[16] It is not necessary that the actions be voluntary actions, that is, that the person have the volitional ability to do that kind of action. Many irrational actions are intentional but not voluntary; they are either due to a person's irrational beliefs (delusions) or to a volitional disability, such as an addiction, compulsion, or phobia.[17]

According to Aristotle, health is primarily and basically a property of persons, and all other things that are called healthy are called healthy because of their relationship to a healthy person; for example, a healthy complexion is a sign of a healthy person. A complete enough description of a healthy complexion could be given to enable such a complexion to be recognized without ever mentioning a healthy person. But a person who did not know the connection between a healthy complexion and a healthy person would not understand why such a complexion was called healthy. Those who knew of the connection but thought healthy complexion more fundamental than healthy person would be even more confused. For they would not understand why some foods were called healthy when they had no connection with one's complexion.

In a similar manner a person who did not know the connection between irrational beliefs and irrational actions would not understand why some beliefs are called irrational. Taking irrational belief to be more fundamental than irrational action would make it impossible to understand how there can be irrational desires, which have no connection to irrational beliefs. Only the account of irrationality as not avoiding harms for oneself without an adequate reason, and the recognition that "rational" means "not irrational," explain the coherent use of the concepts of rationality and irrationality as the basic normative terms.

Scientists may claim that the basic sense of rationality involves reasoning correctly and irrationality, reasoning incorrectly. Scientific rationality consists of using those scientific methods best suited for discovering truth. This account of rationality, if taken as fundamental, makes two mistakes: it takes rationality as more fundamental than irrationality, and it regards rationality as being primarily involved with belief rather than with action. Although I do not deny that it is correct to talk of scientific rationality, it cannot be taken as the fundamental sense of rationality. Scientific rationality cannot explain why it is irrational not to avoid suffering avoidable harms when no one benefits in any way, and rational to avoid such harm. The avoiding-harm account of rationality does explain why it is rational to reason correctly and to discover new truth; doing so helps people to avoid harms.

Hume's View of Reason

Hume is the philosopher who is most responsible for the current misunderstanding of rationality. He regarded rationality to be primarily and fundamentally concerned with beliefs. He held that, considered apart from beliefs, actions were neither rational nor irrational. He thought that only if actions were related to beliefs in some way could they be regarded as rational or irrational. He held that all actions based on mistaken beliefs were irrational actions and that all actions based on true beliefs were rational actions. He said: "It is not contrary to reason for me to choose my total ruin to prevent the least uneasiness of an Indian, or person wholly unknown to me. It is as little contrary to reason to prefer even my own acknowledged lesser good to my greater, and have a more ardent affection for the former than the latter" (*A Treatise of Human Nature*, book 2, part 3, section 3). According to Hume, no matter what one does, one is acting rationally if the action is not based on a mistaken belief. It should be clear that this account of rationality is not merely inadequate, it is totally false and misleading.

It is impossible to defend Hume's account of rationality as it stands, but some philosophers have attempted to defend what they consider a slightly modified Humean view. If one asks them "Why is it rational to act on true beliefs?" they do not answer as a strict following of Hume would require, "That is just what is meant by acting rationally." What they generally say is "Acting on true beliefs generally results in maximizing satisfaction of one's desires." If one now asks, "Why is it rational to do that which generally results in maximizing satisfaction of one's desires?" one is likely to get the answer "Everyone just does want to do that which they believe will result in maximizing satisfaction of their desires." This answer is false. Some people do not want to do that which they believe will result in maximizing satisfaction of their desires, at least if these words are used in their normal sense. "Well," they might reply, "Anyone who does not want this is crazy." This is just the point. Defining rational action as action based on true beliefs is plausible only because those holding this definition include only rational people in their "everyone," that is, one would have to mean by "rational people" people insofar as they are acting rationally. Once one recognizes that some people with mental disorders have irrational desires not based on false beliefs, and that even persons with no mental disorders sometimes act irrationally even though they have no relevant false beliefs, then defining rational action in terms of true beliefs loses its plausibility.

The Maximum Satisfaction of Desires View

The most popular way in which Hume's account has been modified is to maintain that rational action is action compatible with the maximum satisfaction of one's desires. Note, however, that this modification completely changes Hume's view of reason. For Hume, rationality has no goal, it is rational to act in any way one desires; all that rationality requires is that one act on true beliefs. It may seem only a slight revision to require that one not act in any way one desires, but limit oneself to acting in ways compatible with the maximum satisfaction of one's desires. But the change is indeed drastic, for now rationality has a goal, maximum satisfaction of one's desires.

Moreover, one can act contrary to this goal even though one has no false beliefs, but rather because of a strong passion or emotion.[18] Thus rationality is no longer tied to beliefs, and rational action can no longer be defined in terms of true beliefs. Indeed, it is now rational to have true beliefs primarily because of their connection with attaining the goal of rationality, the maximum satisfaction of one's desires.

This account of the goal of rationality leads to the view that rationality is concerned only with means; desire sets the ends. However, this is also very misleading; it is rationality that requires maximum satisfaction of desires. Hume said, "Reason is, and ought only to be, the slave of the passions, and can never pretend to any other office than to serve and obey them" (*A Treatise of Human Nature*, book 2, part 3, section 3). On the modified view, rationality is not the slave of each and every passion; rationality is the slave of the passions only when they are considered as forming a system. Hume meant rationality to be a slave to the passions in the first sense; most followers of Hume, in the second. There is, as I have shown, an extraordinary difference between the two views. Hume's view has no plausibility; the view of his followers is extremely persuasive.

On their account, as well as on Hume's, there is no kind of passion or desire that rationality prohibits a person from acting on simply because she feels like doing so. But unlike Hume, they maintain that rationality does prohibit people from acting on a particular desire when so acting conflicts with maximum satisfaction of their desires considered as a whole. If a person acts on one desire when she knows that this conflicts with satisfying a desire which she regards as greater or more important, then acting on the first desire is irrational. Considered by itself, no coherent desire is irrational. If there is no conflict with some more important desire, it is never irrational to act solely in order to satisfy any desire. Further, each individual decides for herself which desires she considers most important. Rationality serves only as a means for harmonizing one's desires. On this view all desires, considered apart from their effect on the satisfaction of other desires, are rationally allowed; none is either prohibited or required.

This view is extremely persuasive, primarily because the vast majority of one's desires are neither rationally required nor prohibited. It is rationally allowed to desire to eat an orange or to desire not to. It is rational to desire to go to a concert, and it is also rational to desire to stay home. Especially when considering such a wide class of people as all those subject to moral judgment, it may seem to be impossible to find any desire that is not rationally allowed. Diversity of desires is so widespread that to classify any desire as rationally prohibited seems completely arbitrary. Generally, a desire is regarded as irrational to act on only when the person acting believes, or should believe, that so acting will result in the failure to satisfy some more important desire or set of desires. Whether a person who likes to drink but dislikes the hangover he always gets is acting irrationally or not depends on whether he considers the desire to avoid the hangover significantly more important than the desire to drink. If he does, then he is acting irrationally when he acts on his desire to drink; if he does not, he is not acting irrationally. But the desire to drink is, in either case, not a rationally prohibited desire. If it is irrational to act on it, it is because it conflicts with the satisfaction of some more important desire. A person need not be irrational if he acts simply in order to satisfy his desire to drink.

The "Cool Moment" Modification

A serious problem in this account of the rationality of desires is how to decide which of a set of desires is most important. Of course, sometimes a person may act on a desire, knowing full well at the time that it is irrational; that he is sacrificing or risking the satisfaction of much more important desires. But what of the more common case, where at the moment of acting the lesser desire seems the greater. The pleasure of drinking seems to be worth the misery of the hangover. Of course, the next day one does not think so. When confronted with the same situation again, is it rational to drink? Here one can see that simply saying that the person who acts decides which is the more important desire is not enough. Is it what the person feels at the moment of acting, when in the grip of one desire? Or is it later, when there is a realization of the cost of satisfaction of that desire? A promising solution to this problem has been to talk of a considered judgment in a "cool moment." The relative weight of one's desires must be judged in a moment of reflection when one is not in the grip of either. Only when one neither has a strong desire to drink nor is suffering from the aftereffects of drinking can one decide if drinking is worth the hangover it causes. It is what one decides then that determines whether or not it is rational to drink. If on careful reflection one decides that it is worth it, it is not irrational to drink.

Of course, one may decide that there is not enough difference between the two desires to make either choice irrational. Just as with beliefs, it does not follow that in a conflict between two incompatible desires one must be irrational. There must be a significant difference between the two desires before satisfying one rather than the other is irrational. On this account, people decide for themselves which desire is the rational one for them to satisfy. This account still leaves open the possibility that persons may often act irrationally, for they can sacrifice one desire to another when in a cool moment they consider the former significantly more important than the latter. But the final court of appeal for the rationality of acting on any desire is what that particular person would decide in a cool moment. It is not per se irrational to act so as to satisfy any desire.

For those who hold the view I have been describing, an irrational desire would be defined as follows: A *desire is irrational if and only if one believes (or should believe) that acting on that desire will result in one's failing to satisfy some desire or set of desires that in a cool moment one would decide is significantly more important.*[19] The following example should show the inadequacy of the "cool moment" definition of an irrational desire.

José begins to have a slight desire to kill himself. At first it is not an important desire. From time to time he considers various ways in which he might kill himself. But he has other desires that in a cool moment he considers more important than this desire, so, being rational, he does not act on this desire. As time passes, however, the desire to kill himself becomes more and more important. Finally there comes a time when even in a cool moment he decides that the desire to kill himself is more important than any of his other desires, more important even than all of them put together. At this moment, according to the "cool moment" definition, it becomes rational for him to kill himself. Since this is obviously mistaken, the objection immediately comes to mind: he cannot have decided this in a cool moment. The very fact that he takes the desire to kill himself as more important than all the rest of his desires put together shows that the decision was not made in a cool moment. This objection is self-defeating. The fact that he regards certain desires as more important than others cannot be used as conclusive evidence that he cannot have done so in a cool moment. To do so is to regard certain desires taken by themselves to be irrational, not to limit irrational desires to those which conflict with desires considered more important in a cool moment.

The absurdity of taking what is decided in a cool moment as decisive for the rationality of acting on a certain desire comes out even more clearly in the following example. Maria decides in a cool moment that her desire to kill herself in the most painful possible way is her most important desire. It is not her only desire, but she thinks it more important than all of her other desires put together. Among her other desires is a desire to go to a psychiatrist and see if she can be cured (notice how natural this word is) of this desire. She talks to her friend the philosopher, describes her situation, and asks for advice. The philosopher who believes what she says and who accepts the "cool moment" definition of an irrational desire should tell her that it would be irrational for her to go to a psychiatrist. For if she goes to a psychiatrist, this will result in her failing to satisfy a desire which in a cool moment she considers more important. The plausibility of the "cool moment" definition of irrational desire depends on overlooking people who suffer from mental disorders.[20] The "cool moment" account has no way to deal with what I shall call basic irrational desires.

Some philosophers have attempted to answer this objection by talking not merely of actual desires but of possible future desires. They claim that killing oneself results in the frustration of many possible future desires and so conflicts with a maximum satisfaction of desires. This view, however, either begs the question by assuming that the possible future desires will be rational, or it runs into the same problems as the original "cool moment" view. A person with a mental disorder may continue to desire to kill herself in the most painful possible way. Or, someone may continually desire to cause herself pain or to disable herself. Frustration of possible future desires do not rule out desires to harm oneself, for there will always be clear cases of irrational actions, such as actions caused by mental disorders, that are not ruled out by this version of the "cool moment" view.[21]

Richard Brandt provides another account of the "cool moment" view that does try to rule out the irrational desires of mental disorders.[22] This account defines "a cool moment" in terms of the correctness of one's beliefs. On this account it is rational to act so as to maximize the satisfaction of those desires that one would have if one were completely aware of what it would be like for all of those desires to be satisfied. This awareness must not merely be an intellectual awareness, but an awareness that has the force to change one's desires if one realizes that satisfaction of a desire will not be like what one formerly believed it to be. This is probably the best attempt to provide a formal account of "a cool moment." By counting as relevant only the satisfaction of those desires one would continue to have even after full knowledge of what was involved in their satisfaction, it no longer requires satisfying those desires due to the influence of drugs that have distorted one's beliefs about what is involved in their satisfaction. It also rules out all those desires due to false beliefs that are the result of being overcome by some emotion or because of a mental disorder.

On this account, rationality requires maximizing only the overall satisfaction of those desires that one has with full knowledge and appreciation of what it would be like to have them satisfied. Further, it even condemns as irrational satisfying a desire that, with full knowledge, one would recognize as being incompatible with maximizing the overall satisfaction of those desires that one would continue to have with full knowledge. However, Brandt's view presupposes what is false, namely, that all irrational desires are based on false beliefs and would be extinguished by full appreciation of the facts. It assumes that once a person fully realizes what it would be like to satisfy a desire for pain or disability, he would no longer have such a desire. However, it is now known that no amount of "cognitive psychotherapy" will remove some irrational desires, but that only the taking of some medicine will do so. Would anyone favor people for whom one is concerned not taking medicine that, with no side effects, will result in their no longer having desires to seriously harm themselves? If not, then everyone thinks that there are some basic irrational desires.

Basic Desires versus Derived Desires

The basic criterian of desires is intentional action; desires are distinguished from wishes, which one can have without doing anything to make them come true.[23] What a person desires is generally determined by seeing what she tries to get. For the purpose of being able classify desires as irrational, rationally allowed, and rationally required, I shall distinguish between basic desires and derived desires. When a person has no motive for desiring X, that is, when she simply feels like doing or having X, I shall say that she has a basic desire for X. When a person has a motive, which may also be a reason, for desiring X, such as desiring X because she believes it will help her satisfy her desire for Y, or because she believes it will help her avoid death, pain, or disability, I shall say that she has a derived desire for X. Using this distinction, it is probably true that though most people have a desire for money, it is a derived desire, not a basic one, for they want money because they believe it will help them satisfy other desires. However, the desire to avoid pain, which all rational people have, is a basic desire, not a derived one. Some people have a derived desire to take a walk because they believe it is good for their health, and others have a basic desire to do so, that is, they simply feel like taking a walk. People can have both a basic and a derived desire to take a walk: Although they have a motive for walking, (e.g., because they believe that it is healthy), they may also simply desire to do so, that is, they may simply feel like walking.

Contrary to the popular view, the natural result of satisfying a desire is not pleasure, though, of course, pleasure does sometime result from satisfying a desire. What satisfying a desire usually does is to prevent displeasure. When someone tries to satisfy a desire and fails, he is generally displeased. But sometimes desires simply go away, and this normally does not result in displeasure. Watching people attempting to satisfy their desires reveals that often they display none of the criterian of pleasure when they have been successful. However, if they fail to satisfy their desires, they will generally display the criterian of displeasure. Sometimes a person is displeased even after satisfying his desire. This phenomenon leads some people to talk of false or mistaken desires and makes clear that it is a mistake to equate pleasure and the satisfaction of desire. Complete clarification of the relations between pain, pleasure, displeasure, and desire is an important and difficult philosophical project. Although I do discuss this topic briefly in this book, I plan to treat these issues more extensively in a later book on human nature.

Irrational Desires

I define an irrational desire as follows: A *desire is irrational if it is always irrational to act on it without an adequate reason.* This definition covers both basic and derived desires. Since basic desires are not derived from motives, it is most unlikely that one will have any reason, let alone an adequate reason, to act on them.[24] However, there are also derived desires, and whether it is irrational to act on one of these desires often depends upon whether one has an adequate reasons for acting on it. If not, then the desire is irrational; for example, acting on a desire to commit suicide, because of some motive that is not a reason, such as believing that someone else will suffer because of that action, is irrational. It is not arbitrary to regard some desires as irrational in the sense defined. There are limits to what desires it is considered rational to act on without reasons. This does not mean that one can simply list a number of desires and say that it is always irrational to act on them. There are reasons for acting on almost any desire that would make that action rational. Although it would be irrational for John to want to have an arm cut off just to see what he looked like with one arm, it would not be irrational for him to want to have his arm amputated if he thought that by so doing he would save his life.

Classifying certain desires as irrational desires only means that it is always irrational to act on them without an adequate reason. I do not claim that it is always irrational to act on these desires, nor even that it is usually irrational to do so, for people usually not only have reasons, they have adequate reasons for acting on these desires. Indeed, if people are acting rationally they must have adequate reasons for acting on these desires. Given this understanding, I shall, as with beliefs, provide a list of desires that it would be irrational for anyone to act on without an adequate reason.

The Desire to Die

The desire to die is irrational. Unless one has some reason, acting on this desire is irrational. Even if, in a cool moment, Maria decides that her desire to die is stronger than all of her other desires put together, she would still be acting irrationally if she acted on this desire. This does not mean it is always irrational to kill oneself; one may have an adequate reason for doing this. Dying may be the only way to escape constant severe pain, but to kill oneself for no reason, simply because one desires to die, is irrational. There may be some dispute as to what constitutes an adequate reason for killing oneself, that is, a reason sufficient to make the action rational, but there is no dispute that one needs some reason. It is not enough simply to desire to do so. The desire to die is quite different from most of one's desires. A person needs no reason to act on his desire to wear pink shirts, acting on this desire simply in order to satisfy it, is not irrational. Even though it may not be possible to determine precisely what counts as an adequate reason for killing oneself, the desire to die can still be distinguished from most other desires.

Although I talk about the desire to die, it would be more accurate to characterize this irrational desire as the desire for a permanent loss of consciousness.[25] Death in the normal sense is important to people because of its relationship with the permanent loss of consciousness. Until recently there was little point in distinguishing between death and permanent loss of consciousness. Not only did the former entail the latter, but the latter almost never occurred without the former. However, due to the wonders of modern medicine it is now possible for someone who has permanently lost all consciousness to be kept alive. Thousands of human beings in permanent vegetative states live many years after they are no longer persons, that is, after they have permanently lost all consciousness and thus all of their psychological features. I do not claim that it would be irrational for anyone to prefer to die rather than to live in a permanent vegetative state. I claim only that without an adequate reason, it is irrational to desire to lose permanently all consciousness.[26]

Understood as a desire for a permanent loss of consciousness, it should be clear that the claim that the desire to die is irrational is not at all controversial. If one believes that when one dies, in the normal sense of that term, one's conscious life continues but without one's body, then it is not irrational to want to die. I am not claiming that believers in Christianity and Islam have irrational desires when they look forward to dying. They are not looking forward to the permanent loss of consciousness, rather they are looking forward to a much more pleasant conscious life. On the other hand, Buddhists who do look forward to a permanent loss of conscious life are not considered irrational on this account either, for they believe that life contains much more pain and suffering than pleasure and happiness, and so they have a reason for wanting to end it. I do not know how many members of these religions really hold the beliefs I have listed. Even though only a few act as if they prefer death, one cannot say that only a few do hold these beliefs, for each of these religions contains provisions that lead their adherents to seek to avoid death. My own view is that if they did not have these provisions they would have far fewer living adherents. This discussion of religious beliefs is meant to show only how uncontroversial is my claim that the desire to die is an irrational desire. I shall continue to talk of the desire for death rather than the desire for a permanent loss of consciousness, for death and a permanent loss of consciousness almost always go together, and I think that the latter phrase is more likely to create misunderstanding.

The Desire for Pain and Other Unpleasant Feelings

The claim that the desire for pain is irrational is equally uncontroversial. Of course, there are many reasons that can make acting on this desire rational, for example, the belief that it is necessary to suffer pain in order to cure a disease that threatens one's life. Although I am primarily concerned with nontrivial pains, it is irrational to cause oneself even a trivial pain for no reason, although one is likely to use the term "silly" rather than "irrational" or any of the other more serious terms to describe such an action. Nonetheless, the desire for pain, like the desire for death, is an irrational desire.

Saying that seeking pain is irrational brings up the troublesome case of a masochist. Is a masochist acting irrationally in seeking pain? In keeping with the policy of not calling any action irrational unless there is no doubt about the matter, I shall call masochistic behavior rational if the masochist, as described by Freud, seeks pain in order to increase his sexual pleasure. This does not conflict with the view that the desire for pain is irrational. For, as has already been noted, it is not irrational to act on an irrational desire if one has an adequate reason. A masochist may have an adequate reason for seeking pain, namely, it increases his sexual pleasure. However, if the pain suffered is out of all proportion to the increase in pleasure, a masochist does not have an adequate reason and his behavior is irrational. A person who seeks pain but does not believe it will increase his pleasure, and has no other reason, is acting irrationally. But many masochists are no more irrational than those who stay hungry during the day in order to enhance the pleasure of a special meal in the evening.

Although "pain" often refers only to physical pain, I intend more. It is equally irrational to desire to suffer any of the various kinds of unpleasant feelings that are sometimes referred to as mental suffering. Desires to feel sad, anxious, or displeased are irrational. It is also irrational to desire to feel the various emotions, such as guilt, shame, and remorse that involve these unpleasant feelings. Often one has reasons for wanting to have these feelings and emotions, but this is a very complex subject that I shall not discuss now but shall postpone until the chapter concerning reasons for being moral. Many problems in the philosophy of human nature and in aesthetics, particularly the popularity of tragedies, horror films, and works of art that cause people to feel outrage, depend for their solution on being clear about the different feelings and emotions and the reasons that one might have for wanting to feel them. I hope to discuss them more fully later in a book on human nature.

Facial expressions, such as those associated with wincing, together with involuntary avoidance reactions, serve as part of the criterian of pain. Other unpleasant feelings, such as sadness, anxiety, and feeling displeased, also have facial expressions and involuntary bodily reactions as part of their criterian.[27] People generally act so as to avoid that which causes them pain, sadness, anxiety, or displeasure, and act so as to continue feeling pleasure. Normally, this intentional behavior is perfectly correlated with the appropriate facial expressions and involuntary reactions, and there is no doubt about what the person is feeling. However, if there is a discrepancy between the facial expressions and involuntary bodily reactions on the one side and the intentional behavior, including verbal behavior, on the other, then it is often not clear what to think. However, in most cases I think that one should go with the facial expressions and bodily reactions. This discrepancy that sometimes arises between what one intentionally does and says and one's facial expressions and bodily reactions gives sense to the talk of people being alienated from their feelings.

The Desire to Be Disabled

The desire to be disabled, or to lose any ability, is also an irrational desire. It is irrational to desire to be blind or deaf, or to be unable to walk or talk. It is irrational to desire to be less intelligent or talented in any way. It is also irrational to desire to have a phobia, compulsion, addiction, or any other volitional disability. As with the previous irrational desires, there are reasons, such as increasing the probability of being cured of a life-threatening disease, that would make it rational to want to be disabled, for example, by having one's leg amputated. I am merely making the uncontroversial claim that the desire to be disabled for no reason is irrational. It is also irrational to desire to lose or lessen any ability that one has, physical, mental, or volitional, unless one has an adequate reason. To desire to lose even a trivial ability, for example, to wiggle one's ears, without any reason, is irrational, but in this case the term "silly" would probably be used rather than any of the more serious terms. The desire to lose some ability, the exercise of which may cause one to suffer harm, need not be irrational, because one may have an adequate reason. It is rational to want to lose an ability if one has a rational belief that having that ability makes it likely that one will use it, thereby significantly increasing the probability of suffering a greater harm.

As with the previous irrational desires, there often are adequate reasons for wanting to be disabled or to lose some ability, but "I feel like it" is not enough to make it rational to act on this desire. This desire, like the other irrational desires, is significantly different from most desires, such as the desire to go for a walk, for which no reason is needed for it to be rational to act on it. To desire to be disabled in a cool moment is even worse. To say "I've thought it over for a long time and I simply want to have my arm cut off," is not sufficient to make it rational. On the contrary, in the absence of any reason, acting on this desire in a cool moment is more irrational than acting on it in a fit of anger at being so clumsy.

The Desire for Loss of Freedom to Act
or from Being Acted Upon

Very similar remarks can be made about the desire to have less freedom. By "freedom" I do not mean merely, or even primarily, political freedom, that is, the absence of constraints against voting and engaging in other activities that are intended to affect the way one's society is governed. Freedom to act is taken away by all external restrictions on one's behavior, such as being imprisoned or in chains. Serious threats of harm like those involved in coercion also count as external constraints on one's behavior. The serious punishments attached to some violations of the criminal law count as coercion. Total freedom to act would be the absence of all external constraints on one's behavior. I do not claim that people want total freedom of this kind, for they may correctly believe that they could not handle such freedom, that it would turn out to be disastrous for them. I am only claiming that it would be irrational for people to want to have less freedom than they already have, unless they have an adequate reason for wanting to have more constraints on their behavior.

It is sometimes difficult to know whether a person cannot do something because she lacks the ability to do so, or because she lacks the freedom to do so. For example, can she not enter the park because the fence around it has taken away her freedom to enter, or because she lacks the ability to climb the fence? However, when considering a loss of ability or loss of freedom it is usually clear which is involved, because the status quo is the place to start. If a person cannot do something because of a change in herself, it is a loss of ability; if it is because of a change in circumstances, it is a loss of freedom. Freedom and ability are closely related, indeed the definition of each may involve the other. It is also clear that a desire to have less freedom, like a desire to have less ability, is irrational.

Sometimes one cannot engage in some behavior, not because one lacks the appropriate ability, or because there are physical constraints or threats, but because one lacks the resources, often money, to engage in that activity (e.g., doing philosophical research for a year). On these occasions it is more customary to talk of a lack of opportunity rather than a lack of freedom. I do not regard this as an important philosophical distinction, and I use the term "freedom" to include what might more commonly be called "opportunities." It is irrational for a person to desire to have either more constraints on his behavior or fewer resources for engaging in some behavior, unless he has an adequate reason. Although it is understandable that a person angered by his failure to make anything of his opportunities might desire to restrict them, that does not make it rational. And, again, absent a reason, were one to desire a loss of freedom after reflection, this would make it more irrational, not less.

There are, of course, many reasons for wanting to have less freedom or opportunity. It might be necessary to accept more constraints on one's behavior in order to have others accept more constraints on theirs. A person also may justifiably believe that he will make such bad use of his freedom, for example, he will kill himself, that it will be rational for him to have his freedom severely restricted by having himself voluntarily committed to a mental institution. Someone with insight into his character might conclude that he will never get his book written if he does not put himself in a situation that severely limits his freedom or opportunity to do anything else. But, as with the other irrational desires, a person needs an adequate reason to want to restrict his freedom or opportunity or acting on it is irrational.

The concept of freedom includes not only being free to act, but also being free from being acted on. It is not only irrational to desire more constraints on, or fewer resources for, acting, it is also irrational to desire less control over what is done to oneself, including one's body. By "less control" I mean less freedom to determine what one sees, hears, smells, tastes, or what touches one's body or goes into it. Unless one has an adequate reason, it is irrational to want to lose the freedom to determine what one will see, hear, and so on. Similarly, it is irrational to want to lose the freedom to decide whether one will be touched, even if that touching is not painful. The same is true for what enters one's body. To be given medicine when one is sleeping, especially when one has clearly stated that one did not want to be given that medicine, is to be deprived of the freedom to control what enters one's body. As with every other irrational desire, it is irrational to desire to lose this freedom unless one has an adequate reason; for example, a person may want to be touched independently of her consent if she has a severe phobia of needles, but an injection is necessary to save her life.

As I use the concept of freedom, its loss involves either (1) an increase in external limitations on; (2) a decrease in resources for acting as one wants; or (3) a loss of control over what others do to one. I do not include freedom from fear, hunger, and other unpleasant experiences, as part of the concept of freedom. Having listed desires for pain and other unpleasant feelings as irrational desires, it is redundant to include in the irrational desire for the loss of freedom, a loss of freedom from pain and other unpleasant feelings. It is not redundant to include a loss of freedom to control what is done to oneself, including one's body, as part of what is meant by a loss of freedom. This loss of control is not part of any other irrational desire and is often referred to as a loss of freedom. Thus, the irrational desire to suffer a loss of freedom should be understood to include both a loss of freedom to act and a loss of freedom from being acted upon.[28]

The Desire for Loss of Pleasure

The final irrational desire is a desire for loss of pleasure. Those who equate pleasure with satisfaction of desire may regard it as not merely irrational to desire a loss of pleasure for oneself, but impossible. However, although it is irrational to desire not to experience pleasure, it is clearly possible to do so. As with the other irrational desires, it is usually only those who are mentally ill or who are overcome by some strong negative emotion that have this desire without an adequate reason. However, people who have been brought up in some religious traditions may continue to desire not to experience pleasure even after they have given up any religious belief that could count as an adequate reason for having such a desire. Pleasure is not the same as satisfaction of desire, and there are those who, when they find themselves experiencing pleasure, act so as to stop themselves from feeling it. Someone suffering from neurotic guilt or a sense of worthlessness may stop listening to music when she realizes that she is enjoying it. If one has no reason for not experiencing pleasure, then it is irrational to act so as to lose that pleasure. Of course, there are reasons that make it rational to deprive oneself of a particular pleasure. Continued enjoyment may be harmful to one's health, as smoking cigarettes or taking other drugs may be. Nonetheless, like other irrational desires, without an adequate reason, acting on the desire to deprive oneself of pleasure is acting irrationally.

Pleasure does have an important conceptual relationship to desires, but the relationship is not as simple as is often maintained. The criterian for pleasure is different from and more complex than that for desire. The defining criterian for desire is intentional action, but intentional action is only part of the criterian for pleasure. Indeed it is more accurate to say that what gives one pleasure is what makes one smile rather than that what gives one pleasure is what satisfies one's desires. For human beings, facial expressions, primarily some kinds of smiles, together with associated bodily reactions, serve as the most important part of the criterian of pleasure. It is true that intentional behavior is also part of the criterian, but it is not as central as those contemporary utilitarians who have substituted the satisfaction of desires for pleasure have claimed.

Infants, at first, do not have any intentional behavior, but they do have facial expressions and other involuntary bodily reactions that are used by all as showing how they are feeling, especially whether they are pleased or displeased. The criterian contains all those observable features, including both behavior and circumstances, that are used to teach and test the use of psychological terms, such as "pleasure," "pain," "sadness," and "jealousy." The criterian determines what these psychological terms refer to, and the defining criterian is actually used to define the term. Crying, being the salient part of the criterian for the term "sad," serves as the defining criterian, and sadness can be defined as feeling like crying. However the criterian, even the defining criterian, does not guarantee the presence of the psychological phenomena for which it is the criterian; it provides neither necessary nor sufficient conditions for the presence or absence of that to which the psychological terms refer.[29] People need not show what they are feeling, and they can exhibit behavior for feelings they do not have.

The List of Irrational Desires Is Fundamental

I regard this list of five basic irrational desires (the desires for death, pain, disability, loss of freedom, and loss of pleasure) as complete. I cannot prove that it is complete, indeed I cannot prove that any of the desires that I have included in this list are basic irrational desires. I have not derived this list of irrational desires from any more basic account of irrationality. My position that the items on this list are fundamental is extremely hard for most philosophers to accept as a philosophical view, even though there is no disagreement with any of the items on the list. I have never met anyone, including any philosopher, who does not avoid the items on the list, or acts in any way differently than those who do accept the list. I sometimes get a kind of pseudo-tolerance, to wit, a claim that they would never attempt to keep others from acting simply to satisfy their desires for any item included on this list. Even this fades when the person acting so as to satisfy one of these desires is imagined to be a close friend or family member.

I cannot and would not try to provide arguments for any item on the list, but if someone claimed that it was not irrational to desire any nontrivial instance of one of the items on the list, I would simply try to make clear what was involved in such a claim. If I were persuaded that he understood me completely, that he thought that there was nothing irrational about simply flipping a coin and deciding to suffer any of the items on the list, for example, cutting off his arm if the coin came up heads, I would urge him to seek psychiatric help. To provide arguments for accepting the list would be to deny that the list is basic. I am not denying that the general acceptance of the list can be explained. Evolution provides an obvious explanation why most human beings not only do not have desires for any of the items on the list of evils, but treat those who do have such desires as having a mental disorder.[30] But accepting the list in no way depends upon accepting any theory of evolution.

Other Irrational Desires

Acting on a basic irrational desire without an adequate reason is only one way of acting irrationally. It is also irrational to act on any desire simply because one feels like it when one believes that acting in this way will significantly increase one's chances of dying, suffering pain, or losing some ability, freedom, or pleasure. If one believes (or should believe) that satisfying a desire will result in any of the consequences listed above, with no compensating benefit for anyone, then such a desire must be regarded as irrational. Someone who desires to wash his hands every hour and acts on this desire without a reason, even when he knows that doing so will significantly increase his chances of suffering pain or disability, is acting irrationally.

Someone who acts like the handwasher described above is also regarded as suffering from a compulsion, a kind of mental disorder. That someone who suffers from a compulsion or other mental disorder often acts irrationally has resulted in some blurring of the distinction between acting irrationally and suffering from a mental disorder or malady. Even though acting irrationally is often a symptom that one is suffering a mental malady, the two do not always go together. Indeed, it is probably true that most irrational actions are not the result of mental disorders and that most mental disorders do not result in irrational actions.

Suppose that the compulsive handwasher described above, because of the sores caused by so much washing, had tried to stop washing his hands in order to avoid increasing his pain and disability. However, when he refrained from washing his hands, he suffered such acute anxiety that he felt compelled to continue washing his hands. If he now washes his hands in order to avoid the unbearable anxiety that comes when he refrains from washing them, then even though he knows that he is causing himself pain and disability he may no longer be acting irrationally. If psychiatric help is not presently available, then it may be rational for him to continue washing his hands. However, even if it is rational for him to continue to wash his hands, he is still suffering from a compulsion, a mental malady. A person who suffers acute anxiety when he does not wash his hands every hour is suffering from a mental disorder, but it does not follow that he is acting irrationally. He is acting irrationally not to seek psychiatric help if he knows that it is available and has a high probability of curing the compulsion. Without an adequate reason, not seeking such psychiatric help is failing to avoid continuing suffering of anxiety, pain and disability, and is irrational.

Rationally Required and Rationally Allowed Desires

So far only those desires that are rationally prohibited have been discussed, but there are also desires that are rationally required and rationally allowed. Irrational desires are those that it is irrational to act on without an adequate reason. Like rationally prohibited beliefs, I talk about rationally prohibited desires only with regard to those who have sufficient knowledge and intelligence to be subject to moral judgment. It is irrational for any moral agent to act on an irrational desire simply because she feels like doing so. Similarly, it is irrational for anyone not to act on a rationally required desire simply because she does not feel like doing so. It is not only irrational to desire death, pain, disability, loss of freedom, and loss of pleasure, it is irrational not to desire to avoid them. Unless, of course, one has an adequate reason for not desiring to avoid them. Desires that are neither rationally prohibited nor rationally required are rationally allowed.

Acting on a desire to avoid death, pain, and so on, requires some positive action, whereas not acting on a desire for pain, and so on, does not require one to do anything except refrain from acting. If someone acts on a desire for pain, and so on, simply because he feels like doing so, no matter how trivial the pain, he is acting irrationally, although if the harm is trivial his action would probably be described as stupid or silly. However, if without an adequate reason, someone fails to have, or to act on, a desire to avoid a trivial harm, many would not regard his lack of behavior as even silly. Partly this may be due to the ubiquity of trivial pains and losses. If the anticipated pain or loss is trivial enough, it is usually regarded as rationally allowed to simply ignore it or to take no action to prevent it from occurring.

It would be neater if there were complete symmetry between rationally prohibited desires and rationally required ones. However, like most concepts, the concept of rationality is not quite so neat. Whereas it is irrational to act on any desire for pain, loss of ability, and so on, no matter how trivial, it is rationally required to avoid only nontrivial pains and losses. Similarly, it is irrational to desire to increase even by a small amount the risk that one will suffer some harm. But it is not rationally required that one desire to avoid an insignificant increase in risk of pain, loss of ability, and so on. It is only rationally required to desire to avoid an increase in risk if that increase is significant and the pain or loss is nontrivial. Of course, there will be some disagreement about whether a risk counts as significant or whether a pain or loss counts as trivial. Although it is misleading to pretend to a precision that the concept of rationality does not have, the area of vagueness is quite small and is unlikely to have any important consequences, since it involves only whether an increase in risk counts as significant or a pain or loss counts as trivial.

Notes

1. When I use the phrase "for whom one is concerned," I mean either that I am as concerned with that person as with anyone else, including myself, or that there is no conflict of interests between that person and anyone for whom I am more concerned, including myself. Otherwise there would be counterexamples.

2. There are unusual cases where an action may count against the rationality of the person performing it because he does not have any conscious belief that anyone will benefit from the harm he is causing himself to suffer. However, others may know that someone, perhaps even he himself, will have some significant benefit. In this kind of case someone may advocate that a person for whom he is concerned act in a way that the person would regard as acting irrationally. But although acting in that way counts against the rationality of the person, the act itself is rational, for *some fully informed rational persons* may advocate that someone for whom they are concerned act in that way.

3. See chapter 3, the section on reasons as beliefs versus reasons as facts.

4. The earlier statements of this test were not clear in specifying that the person doing the advocating must be both fully informed and rational. See my articles "Rationality, Human Nature, and Lists," *Ethics* 100, no. 2 (January 1990): 279–300, and "Defending Irrationality and Lists," *Ethics* 103, no. 2 (January 1993): 329–336.

5. Nothing will increase or decrease one's chances of dying for it is 100 percent certain that one will die. When I talk about an action "increasing one's chances of dying" or "decreasing one's chances of dying," I mean increasing or decreasing one's chances of dying earlier than one would die without that action.

6. *The Moral Rules: A New Rational Foundation for Morality* (New York: Harper and Row, 1970).

7. Usually this will involve their regarding a reason as adequate for an action that would otherwise be irrational, though other significant groups of persons do not regard that reason as adequate for that action.

8. In this paragraph, I do not use "rational persons" in the way I normally use this phrase in this book, that is, as a person insofar as she is rational. In this more ordinary context, ratio-

nal persons sometimes act irrationally. Further, as I normally use the phrase "rational persons," such a person would never make errors in reasoning. Although this is certainly false, it allows me to avoid continually adding the qualifying phrase "if they are reasoning correctly" when I talk of what all rational persons would hold or advocate. I mention this explicitly because otherwise one might misinterpret my remarks about what all rational persons would hold or advocate, as claiming that some philosophers are acting irrationally, rather than just making a mistake, if they do not hold or advocate what I claim all rational persons hold or advocate.

9. Although no beings other than human beings are now considered to be moral agents, the characteristics that are needed to be a moral agent do not include any biological facts. Thus, it is an open question whether beings from other planets will have these characteristics and so be moral agents.

10. I use the term "belief" to refer to both factual beliefs and quasi-factual beliefs such as that $7 + 5 = 12$ and Jesus is God. These are beliefs to which the terms "true" and "false" are normally applied.

11. Holding an irrational belief is identical to what the *Diagnostic and Statistical Manual of Mental Disorders* of the American Psychiatric Association calls having a delusion. The differences in the definitions are primarily stylistic and reflect the difference between philosophical and psychiatric terminology. See my article "Irrationality and the DSM-III-R Definition of Mental Disorder," *Analyse und Kritik* 12, no. 1 (July 1990): 34–46.

12. A parallel relationship holds with regard to irrational actions and actions that it is rationally required not to do. This was pointed out to me by Logi Gunnarsson.

13. It might be simpler to regard the positive general beliefs as applying to all moral agents, and then have only one rationally required personal belief, namely, that I am a moral agent. However, there are rhetorical considerations that favor providing parallel accounts of the personal and general beliefs.

14. It is a rationally required belief that some moral agents care about some sentient beings when the sentient beings are potential moral agents, such as infants. That this belief is rationally required explains why all regard morality as providing some protection to infants and many would want infants to have the full protection of morality even though infants are not moral agents. Another less obvious morally relevant rationally required belief is the belief that some moral agents care about some sentient beings even when they are not potential moral agents. This belief explains why causing pain to nonhuman sentient beings for no reason might be prohibited by all impartial rational persons. However, it does not require that one regard the prohibition against causing pain to nonhuman sentient beings to be as strict as the prohibition against causing pain to moral agents, and many people will regard almost any reason as providing an adequate justification for causing pain to such nonhuman animals. Thus acknowledging this belief as rationally required does not settle any significant issue about when it is morally justified to cause pain to sentient beings who are not potential moral agents or, more generally, about the scope of morality.

15. Irrational actions in this basic sense will be irrational either because the agent should know better or because, despite being fully informed, he acts in a way he knows will result in his suffering harm without an adequate reason for so acting.

16. "Intentional actions" include intentional failures to act or inactions as well as positive actions.

17. For further discussion of volitional disabilities, see Bernard Gert and Timothy Duggan, "Free Will as the Ability to Will," *Nous* 13, no. 2 (May 1979): 197–217, reprinted in *Moral Responsibility*, edited by John Martin Fisher, (Ithaca, N.Y. Cornell University Press, 1986), and Richard B. Farrell, Trevor P. Price, Bernard Gert, and Bernard J. Bergen, "Volitional Disability and Physician Attitudes toward Noncompliance," *The Journal of Medicine and Philosophy* 9, no. 4 (November 1984): 333–351.

18. Hume recognizes this but must make his point using different terminology like "calm passions."

19. This account of rationality is held by the overwhelming majority of contemporary moral philosophers.

20. For an account of mental disorders, see the *Diagnostic and Statistical Manual of Mental Disorders*, fourth edition (*DSM IV*) (Washington, D.C.: American Psychiatric Association, 1994), and "Malady," chapter 5 of *Bioethics: A Return to Fundamentals*, by Bernard Gert, Charles M. Culver, and K. Danner Clouser (New York: Oxford University Press, 1997).

21. For more detail on the relation between irrationality and mental disorders, see my article "Irrationality and the DSM-III-R Definition of Mental Disorder."

22. See Brandt, "The Concept of Rationality in Ethical and Political Theory," in *Nomos*, vol. 17, *Human Nature in Politics*, edited by J. Roland Pennock and John W. Chapman (New York: New York University Press, 1977): 265–279, and his book, *A Theory of the Good and the Right* (Oxford: Oxford University Press, 1979).

23. This spelling of "criterian" is intended to highlight that I am using this term in a technical sense derived from Wittgenstein. See the sources cited in note 29.

24. There are unusual cases where one can have an adequate reasons for a basic irrational desire. For example, one may have a basic desire to die and believe that doing so will result in saving the lives of many other people. However, that one's action will save the lives of many other people may not be a motive at all for one's desire to die, yet having the belief that one's action will do this is still a reason, and an adequate reason, for acting on the desire to die.

25. Discussions with Matthew Weiss, whose senior honors thesis I directed, made this point clear to me. Unless the context makes it clear otherwise, "permanent loss of consciousness" can always be substituted for "death."

26. See Bernard Gert, Charles M. Culver, and K. Danner Clouser, *Bioethics: A Return to Fundamentals* (New York: Oxford University Press, 1997), chap. 11.

27. See Charles Darwin, *The Expression of the Emotions in Man and Animals*, (Chicago: The University of Chicago Press, 1965).

28. Note to translators: Teaching a course on an earlier version of my theory in Argentina showed me that there may be no word in some other language that corresponds closely enough to the English word "freedom" to encompass all that I mean by that word. I think it important that my use of "freedom" be close enough to its normal meaning in English that what I say is easily understood. I do not regard myself as inventing a technical sense of the term and would prefer that any translation enlarge the list of things it would be irrational to desire rather than invent some technical term that does not include all that I include. It is not crucial that there be only five items on this list. Since every item on the list must be one that everyone knows refers to something that it is irrational to desire, I am not concerned that the list will grow to unmanageable proportions. This problem arose in discussing "freedom," but the same point may also apply to "death," "pain," "ability," and "pleasure."

29. See my articles "Psychological Terms and Criteria," *Synthese* 80 (1989): 201–222, and "Criterian and Human Nature," *Wittgenstein: Eine Neubewertung, Toward a Re-Evaluation*, vol. 2, edited by Rudolf Haller and Johannes Brandl (Wien: Verlag Hölder-Pichler-Tempsky): 106–114.

30. See my article "Rationality and Sociobiology," *Monist* 67, no. 2 (April 1984): 216–228.

Chapter 3

Reasons

A Formal Definition of Reasons

It is always irrational to act so as to achieve the object of an irrational desire: death (permanent loss of consciousness), pain, loss of ability, loss of freedom or loss of pleasure, without a reason. If one acts so as to achieve the object of an irrational desire, one needs a reason for acting in that way in order for one's actions to count as rational. However, people usually have reasons for acting in these ways, and if the reason is adequate the action is no longer irrational. *Reasons for acting are conscious rational beliefs that can make some otherwise irrational actions, rational.*[1] The belief that having one's right arm cut off will save one's life is a reason for having one's arm cut off. In the discussion of irrational desires, several of these kinds of beliefs were mentioned. Beliefs that one's action will decrease one's own or anyone else's chances of dying, of suffering pain, or of losing some ability, freedom, or pleasure count as reasons. These beliefs are reasons because they can sometimes make acting to achieve the object of an irrational desire rational. Other reasons are beliefs that one's action will maintain or increase one's own or anyone else's consciousness, abilities, freedom, or pleasure. These beliefs can also make some otherwise irrational actions rational.

As with the list of irrational desires, I have no argument that the beliefs on this list count as reasons. If someone denies that beliefs about decreasing one's own or anyone else's chances of dying (permanently losing consciousness), suffering pain, losing some ability, freedom and pleasure, and increasing their chances of maintaining or gaining consciousness, abilities, freedom, and pleasure, count as reasons, I have no arguments to support my claim. In fact, I do not know anyone who denies that these beliefs are reasons. If someone says that he would never count some of these beliefs as reasons for acting, I would take him to be using reasons to mean motives, and claiming that these beliefs would never move him to act. I do not claim that all reasons are motives to all persons, I claim only that having these beliefs can make otherwise irrational actions rational. That these beliefs count as reasons is as fundamental as that the previously listed desires are irrational. No argument can be provided for these lists that is as worthy of being accepted as the lists themselves.

Basic irrational desires are limited to desires that oneself and those one cares about suffer any of the harms. Basic reasons are not limited to beliefs that oneself and those one cares about will avoid some harm. Beliefs about anyone, whether one cares about them or not, avoiding harms, or gaining benefits are also basic reasons. It is not irrational to give to a charity that aids people about whom one does not care and perhaps does not even know. However, it is also not irrational not to give to such a charity. Irrational actions and desires involve an egocentric reference, while reasons need have no egocentric element.

A Formal Definition of Adequate Reasons

The beliefs that count as reasons for acting can simply be listed, but what counts as an adequate reason depends on the context. A reason adequate to make one otherwise irrational action rational may not be adequate to make some other irrational action rational. That one will avoid some significant pain, such as that involved in having a tooth pulled, is an adequate reason for accepting a temporary loss of ability, that involved in taking anesthesia; it is not an adequate reason for committing suicide. A stronger reason is needed for wanting to die than for wanting to lose some pleasure. This can be seen from the fact that it would be rational to deprive oneself of any pleasure in order to avoid dying, but it would be irrational even to risk death in order to avoid losing most pleasures. Thus although acting because one believes that it will result in pleasure is acting on a reason, if the consequences are serious enough it is not an adequate reason.

An adequate reason for acting is a conscious rational belief that makes *the otherwise irrational action for which it is a reason, rational.* Although there is far more agreement on what counts as a reason than on what counts as an adequate reason, in general there will be complete agreement in most situations on what reasons count as adequate for doing some otherwise irrational action. It is clear that the belief that a temporarily painful injection would prevent total permanent paralysis is an adequate reason to take it. However, in some situations, a significant group of people will regard a reason as adequate, and a different significant group of people will not regard that reason as adequate. In these situations, obviously, people will disagree about the rationality of the action. Those who regard the action as irrational will never advocate that anyone for whom they are concerned act in that way, whereas those who regard the action as rational may advocate either that it be done or that it not be done.

In keeping with the policy of not classifying any action as irrational if any significant group of otherwise rational people would regard it as rational, I count any reason as adequate if any significant group of otherwise rational people regard that reason as adequate, that is, if they regard the harm avoided or benefit gained to compensate for the harm suffered. People count as otherwise rational if they do not normally act on irrational desires without an adequate reason. Whether a belief is a reason is a completely objective matter, but whether a belief is an adequate reason depends upon whether there is any significant group of people who regard it as adequate. Although this vagueness presents some practical problems in determining what counts as an adequate reason, one should not demand more precision in a subject matter than that subject matter permits.[2]

Death, pain, loss of ability, loss of freedom, and loss of pleasure cannot be ranked in the abstract. Indeed, one cannot even rank different kinds of pain, different kinds of disabilities, or the loss of different kinds of freedom in the abstract. Some pain is so severe that it would not be irrational to want to die in order to escape from it. However, there are also lesser degrees of pain from which everyone would consider avoidance by death to be irrational. Death has no degrees. It seems never to be irrational to want not to die, even when it is rational to want to. Although it is sometimes rationally allowed to want to die, it never seems rationally required. Many people prefer to remain alive and conscious even though almost all of what they will be conscious of is pain and suffering. This means that it is never irrational to desire to continue living even though there may be circumstances, such as painful terminal cancer, when it would not be irrational to want to die. In general, most actual decisions are those in which it would be rational to act in either way.

People almost always have adequate reasons for acting in ways that would be irrational if they did not have such reasons. However, people can differ on whether a particular reason is adequate to make an otherwise particular irrational action rational. There is significant disagreement concerning whether a belief about preventing harm to a nonhuman animal is an adequate reason for suffering a similar amount of harm oneself. This question arises only when one does not have any concern for that animal, otherwise there are likely to be additional reasons for preventing that harm.[3] People also rationally rank harms and benefits differently, and these different rational rankings may affect how they regard the adequacy of some reasons and hence whether they regard some actions as rational or irrational.[4]

That, within limits, rational people rank the goods and evils differently accounts for some of the plausibility of the "cool moment" account of rationality. However, the "cool moment" account has no objective limits. Indeed, in the "cool moment" account, the rational way to act is simply that way that maximizes the satisfaction of those desires that a person would have after calm reflection. But though a person's rankings of harms and benefits may determine what reasons he takes as adequate, everyone agrees that some reasons are adequate and some are not. A person who cuts off her hand in order to get rid of an irritating wart does not have an adequate reason for doing so, no matter how she ranks the goods and evils; one who cuts if off in order to prevent a fatal infection from spreading does have an adequate reason. That people are often allowed to overrule the irrational decisions of others provides a reason for classifying as rational any action or decision that any significant group of otherwise rational persons regard as rational.[5] This is why when there is legitimate disagreement about whether a reason counts as an adequate reason for a particular act, I always count that reason as adequate.

The Egocentricity of Irrationality

The account of irrational actions and desires in the previous chapter is egocentric, almost egoistic. No action (or inaction) counts as irrational unless the agent knows or should know that the action (or inaction) will result in some harm for herself or those she cares about. And why it is irrational to act in a way that those one cares about will be harmed is that their suffering harm will result in suffering for oneself. It follows from this account of irrational actions that the only actions that are rationally required are those that increase the chances of the agent avoiding some harm. It is never rationally required to help others unless helping others is necessary for avoiding some harm to oneself. If the concept of rationality only included actions that were rationally prohibited and rationally required, then the account of rationality that I am putting forward would be appropriately described as rational egoism.

The Nonegocentricity of Reasons

However, rationality does include a third category, namely, those actions that are rationally allowed. Neglect of this third category has resulted in the inadequacy of all previous accounts of rationality. It is rationally allowed to do anything, including helping or hurting others, as long as acting in that way does not result in harm to oneself. However, helping others need not count as irrational even when helping them does result in harm to oneself, whereas hurting others will be irrational if it results in harm to oneself. If the concept of a reason were as egocentric as the concept of an irrational action, then it would never be rational to help others if doing so resulted in harm to oneself. But as indicated above, reasons need not be egocentric. Whether or not a belief is a reason for acting is unaffected by who is believed to benefit from one's action.

The Complex Hybrid Concept of Rationality

The complexity of the concept of rationality and the difficulty of presenting an adequate account of it stem from the following combination of features. Reasons can make it rational to act in ways that would be irrational if one did not have those reasons; yet reasons need not be egocentric in any way, and irrational actions are determined egocentrically. The importance of this discrepancy between actions that count as irrational being determined in an egocentric way and the reasons that can make an irrational act rational *not* being determined in an egocentric way has not been appreciated. There is a tremendous temptation to regard both irrational actions and reasons to be determined egocentrically or to claim that neither irrational actions nor reasons are determined egocentrically.

One example of giving in to this temptation to make the concept of a rational action simpler than it actually is, is the attempt to define a rational action in terms of reasons. The seemingly trivial definition "A rational action is one that is based on reasons" also shows how misleading a positive definition of a rational action is.[6] Even though this definition of a rational action is of little use without an account of what reasons are, it is still misleading; for on any plausible account of "based on reasons," these definitions exclude from the category of rational actions all those rationally allowed actions that are done without a reason, or simply because one feels like acting in that way. Although all rationally required actions can be described as based on reasons, rationally allowed actions are also rational, and many of them cannot be correctly described as based on reasons.

Awareness of the category of rationally allowed actions enables one to avoid oversimplified accounts of the relationship between reasons and rationality. When an action involves no risk of harm to oneself, then it is rationally allowed to act for no reason at all, but simply on a whim or because one feels like doing so. For example, no reason is needed for it to be rationally allowed to go for a walk. That one always needs a reason for acting in a way that involves a risk of harm to oneself, does not mean that one always needs a reason for acting in a way that does not involve a risk of harm to oneself. Further, the belief that one's action will benefit another, even someone whom one does not know, may be an adequate reason to make it rationally allowed to act in a way that does risk harm to oneself. Reasons need not be egocentric at all, and rationality is only partially egocentric.

The failure to realize that reasons are related to irrational actions in a complex way gives rise to the plausible but false claim that it is irrational to chose to do B when A is supported by reasons and B is not. However, irrationality is completely egocentric, so that although reasons can make an irrational action rational, it need not be irrational to chose to do B when A is supported by reasons and B is not. For example, it is not irrational to refuse to give to some very worthy charity simply because one does not feel like doing so. Even when one has no reason for doing so, it is rationally allowed to act contrary to what is supported by reasons when those reasons involve only the interests of others. Requiring rational actions to be those that are supported by reasons in any way whatsoever excludes this kind of rational action.[7] Although all rationally required actions are supported by reasons, many rationally allowed actions are not. Not counting such actions as rational seriously distorts the concept of rationality. Defining rational actions as those that are not irrational allows for the category of rationally allowed actions.

Reasons concerning the interests of others can make otherwise irrational actions rational, but failure to act on these kinds of reasons never makes otherwise rational actions irrational. This complex relationship between reasons and irrationality is necessary to account for the coherent use of irrationality as the basic normative concept while still including as reasons all the beliefs that are normally counted as reasons. Defining reasons as beliefs that can make an irrational act rational makes clear what it means to say that one needs a reason for acting, namely, that it would be irrational to act in that way without a reason. It also explains why a person sometimes needs a reason for acting and sometimes not. Finally, it enables one to distinguish between beliefs that are not adequate reasons for a particular act and beliefs that are not reasons at all.

The failure to recognize the importance of the category of rationally allowed actions is partially explained by the standard practice of defining an irrational action in terms of a rational action rather than the reverse. Recognition that rationally allowed actions are rational actions makes it clear that a rational action is simply one that is not irrational. All attempts to provide a positive definition of a rational action are inadequate because rational actions share no positive feature or even any significant similarity other than simply being not irrational. Defining a rational action simply as an action that is not irrational does not impose a fictitious and misleading uniformity on all rational actions. It also allows for the complex relationship between irrational actions and reasons.

Seeking for those positive characteristics that all rational actions share and that distinguishes them from other actions, inevitably leads to a distortion of the concept of rationality. Positive definitions of rationality tend to lead people to equate rational actions with actions based on calculations about costs and benefits and to regard spontaneous actions as irrational. Since almost everyone would sometimes advocate to those for whom they are concerned that they act spontaneously, this account of an irrational action fails the test for an irrational action. Indeed, all positive definitions of rational actions result in irrational actions that fail the test for an irrational action. The absurdity of regarding all actions not satisfying the definition of a rational action as irrational — for example, regarding spontaneous actions as irrational — has led to the introduction of a category of nonrational actions. It is not clear what is meant by calling ordinary actions, for example, cheering for one's team, nonrational, but even so, it is better than calling them irrational. Recognition of the complex hybrid character of rationality, with irrationality being egocentric and reasons not, avoids the counterintuitive results of all other accounts of rationality.

Basic Reasons

Since reasons for acting in a certain way are not limited to beliefs that acting in this way will benefit oneself, but also include beliefs that acting in this way will benefit someone else, rationality cannot be equated with rational self-interest. A person is not irrational when he acts in a way that he believes is contrary to his self-interest if he believes that acting in this way will benefit someone else. There should be little disagreement that beliefs to the effect that acting in a certain way will benefit anyone, either oneself or someone else, are reasons. However, I expect that the claim that no other beliefs count as reasons unless they are related to these reasons will be more controversial. Beliefs that acting in a certain way will benefit anyone, either oneself or someone else, are what I call basic reasons, and I claim that these beliefs are the only basic reasons. I do not claim that no other beliefs count as reasons, only that there are no other basic reasons, and that any other belief that counts as a reason must involve these basic reasons.

On this account of basic reasons, all basic reasons are beliefs about the present or the future; a belief about the past can never be a basic reason. This means that acting in order to gain revenge, for example, having as one's only motive for wanting to harm another the belief that she harmed a member of one's family, is not acting on a basic reason. It also means that the fact that someone intentionally, voluntarily, and freely, broke a justified law, by itself, provides no basic reason for punishing that person. Nor does the fact that someone did a person a favor provide a basic reason for that person to show gratitude. This account of basic reasons has the consequence that, if a person believes that a particular act of taking revenge or showing gratitude will result in her suffering some harm and that no one will benefit from that act, that act is irrational. Unless one's belief that the person "hurt someone close to one" or "did one a favor" is appropriately related to a basic reason, it is not a reason for acting at all. I realize that this may sound somewhat paradoxical, but upon reflection, especially on the fact that often one needs no reason in order to be acting rationally, the air of paradox should disappear.

I do not deny that people talk about beliefs concerning the past as reasons, but often that simply means that they are motives, not that they are reasons. They are cited to explain one's actions, not to justify them. Sometimes, however, people do take beliefs about the past to be genuine reasons, and I do not claim that this way of talking is incorrect. But these beliefs about the past count as reasons only when they are related to basic reasons in an appropriate way. Often a belief about the past is closely related to a belief about the future, for example, that someone broke a law does provide a reason for believing that if not punished she or others will be more likely to break the law in the future. Thus one way that a fact about the past can provide a reason without providing a basic reason is that it provides a reason for holding a belief about the future, which is a basic reason for acting. When I talk about reasons in the rest of this book, I usually mean basic reasons.

Desires Are Not Reasons

In denying that desires are reasons I am not merely making the verbal point that since reasons are beliefs, desires are not reasons; I am making the more significant point that desires never make beliefs into reasons. This means that a belief that an action will satisfy one's desire is never a reason for doing that action. An irrational desire is a desire that it is irrational to act on without a reason. This not only implies that irrational desires are never reasons for doing what one desires to do, it also implies that the belief that one's action will satisfy one's desire is not a reason for acting. Indeed, it should be clear that an irrational desire cannot make any otherwise irrational act rational. The desire to become blind cannot make it rational to stare at the sun. Not even philosophers explicitly claim that irrational desires are reasons, but some philosophers explicitly claim that rational desires are.[8]

It might be claimed that rationally required desires are reasons or at least make beliefs into reasons. Doesn't the rationally required desire to cure my otherwise fatal disease make the belief that this medicine will cure my otherwise fatal disease into a reason? It does not. This belief is a reason whether or not I have the desire to cure my disease. It is extremely misleading to regard rationally required desires as having any influence on what beliefs count as reasons. Any belief that a rationally required desire could turn into a reason is already a reason independent of whether the agent has that desire or not.

I have shown that the claim that desires are reasons, or that they can make beliefs into reasons, does not work with regard to either rationally prohibited or rationally required desires. If the claim is to have any plausibility, it must be a claim about rationally allowed desires. It does seem plausible to say that my desire to buy a paper is a reason for buying it. Although there is a sense of "a reason" in which a desire does provide a reason, this sense of "a reason" has nothing to do with rationality; it simply explains one's actions. A reason must be able to make some otherwise irrational action rational, so citing an action for which one needs no reason cannot show that a desire is a reason.

The question under consideration is whether a rationally allowed desire, by itself, can make acting in a way that one knows will result in oneself suffering some harm rational. I claim that it cannot, and that any plausibility that it can stems from the fact that frustration of desires generally results in displeasure and satisfaction of desires sometimes results in pleasure.[9] If one knows that failing to satisfy a desire will result in displeasure or that satisfaction of a desire will result in pleasure, then one has a reason for acting on that desire, even though the desire is an irrational one. I have already discussed this kind of case when I concluded that masochism could be rational if the pain suffered was not out of proportion to the pleasure anticipated. It is the anticipated pleasure, not the desire, that makes that otherwise irrational action rational.

However, persons suffering what is sometimes inappropriately called "moral masochism" do not anticipate experiencing any pleasure. These persons intentionally act so as to "punish" themselves for being bad persons. They do not expect to receive any pleasure from so doing. Their desire to suffer harms does not make it rational for them to inflict harms on themselves. They are just like the compulsive handwasher whose desire to wash his hands does not make it rational for him to do so when he knows that pain and disability result from such frequent washings. However, just as it may become rational for the compulsive handwasher to wash his hands when he becomes aware of the horrible anxiety he suffers if he does not do so, so moral masochists may be acting rationally in inflicting pain on themselves if they become aware of the great anxiety or displeasure they will suffer if they do not do so.

It is a belief about the pleasure that will result from satisfying a desire, or a belief about the mental suffering that will result if one does not satisfy a desire, that makes it seem as if desires themselves are reasons. However, if it is clear that one will receive no pleasure from satisfying a desire and will not be bothered by not satisfying it, then the desire provides no reason for acting in any way that one knows will result in harm to oneself. This state of affairs is, in fact, quite common, and many people have desires that they forget about completely in a few moments. It is important not to confuse frustration of a desire that one is unsuccessfully trying to satisfy, and which almost invariably results in displeasure, with simply failing to satisfy a desire one happens to have. Indeed, as many ancient philosophers have pointed out, it is often rational to seek to rid oneself of some of one's desires.

Distinguishing between satisfying a desire and pleasure, and between failing to satisfy a desire and displeasure, removes most of the plausibility of thinking that desires are reasons. Whatever other plausibility remains should be removed when one compares the relationship between reasons and irrational actions to the relationship between reasons and irrational desires. What is true about irrational actions and the reasons that can make them rational is also true about irrational desires to do an action and the reasons that can make these desires rational. For purposes of assessing their rationality, desires can be treated just like actions. Unless having the desire is itself pleasurable, or relieves one of pain, if it is irrational to do something, it is also irrational to desire to do it.

Every belief that counts as a reason for acting also counts as a reason for wanting to act in that way. The belief that I will enjoy seeing a certain movie is a reason for going to see that movie, and it is also a reason for wanting to see that movie. Satisfying a desire to see a certain movie may sound like a reason for going to see that movie, but it does not even sound like a reason for wanting to see that movie. The belief that I will gain greater abilities is a reason for undergoing an unpleasant training regime, and it is also a reason for wanting to undergo an unpleasant training regime. Satisfying a desire to undergo an unpleasant training regime does not even sound like a reason for undergoing an unpleasant training regime, and it is clearly not a reason for wanting to undergo an unpleasant training regime. If the action I desire to do is irrational, the desire to act in that way will not make it rational. Indeed, the desire to act in that way will be an irrational desire.

However, it might be claimed that strong and persistent desires to act irrationally can make it rational to act in that way.[10] I have already discussed the cases of masochism and compulsive handwashing, and what was said there also applies to other irrational desires. It is not the desire itself that makes it rational to act in an otherwise irrational way; it is the belief about the pleasure to be gained from satisfying that desire, or the belief about the harm to be suffered from not satisfying it. A strong, persistent, and incurable desire to die may make it rational to commit suicide, but that is because such a strong, persistent, and incurable desire is invariably related to extreme suffering, either physical or mental. It is universally recognized that if one is suffering from an incurable and painful physical illness, such as extreme arthritis, it is not irrational to want to die. In the same way, if one is suffering from an incurable and painful mental illness, such as severe depression, it is equally rational to want to die. Of course most depressions are not incurable, and if they are curable, then it is irrational to act on the accompanying desire to die. Indeed, it is rationally required that one seek to cure the depression. But if a depression is incurable, and it is accompanied by a strong and persistent desire to die, it is not irrational to act on that desire.

Reasons as Beliefs versus Reasons as Facts

When talking about actions, I use "a reason" to mean a conscious rational belief that can make an otherwise irrational action rational. My use of "conscious" does not require having a belief introspectively present in one's mind prior to, or at the time of, acting. I count beliefs about the consequences of an action as conscious if, when asked whether one believes that the action has those consequences, one would immediately assent. A belief that an agent sincerely denies having cannot count as a reason, but whether one actually acts on, plans to act on, or would act on the belief is irrelevant to its being a reason. Simply having an appropriate conscious belief is not only necessary for its being a reason, it is also sufficient. Its being a reason is an objective matter, not something that is determined by the person who has the belief.

It might be thought that for reasons to be objective, they should be facts rather than conscious beliefs. Some might prefer to say that it is the fact that taking an aspirin will relieve one's headache that is the reason for taking the aspirin, whereas I claim that it is a person's conscious belief that taking an aspirin will relieve his headache that is the reason for taking it. The latter way of talking allows for a unified concept of rationality by maintaining the close connection between reasons, the rationality of actions, and the rationality of persons. If facts were reasons, it would weaken the conceptual connection between reasons, the rationality of actions, and the rationality of persons. Many facts are such that not only is the agent unaware of them, no one could be expected to be aware of them. These facts do not affect the rationality of an action when the rationality of an action counts in determining a person's rationality. The only facts that determine the rationality of an action are those that the person should know, that is, that the person has sufficient knowledge and intelligence to know.

Suppose a person acts in a way that she believes will kill herself, for example, takes an overdose of some pills. If she has no conscious belief that serves as an adequate reason for committing suicide, then on the view of reasons as beliefs, her action is irrational. But if reasons are facts, then if the pills were, in fact, an antidote to some poison she had unknowingly taken earlier, she would have acted rationally. This is an extremely misleading way of describing her action. Conversely, if she takes some unpleasant medicine because she — due to her lack of sufficient knowledge or intelligence — has a rational belief that it will cure her illness, on the view of reasons as beliefs, her action is rational, even though her belief is mistaken and the medicine will not cure her. However, if reasons are facts then her action is irrational, rather than merely mistaken. Irrational actions count against the rationality of the person; they cannot simply be due to lack of information.

Of course, one might distinguish between external and internal reasons. External reasons are facts and are the kind of reason normally referred to when one says, "There is a reason." Internal reasons are beliefs and are normally referred to by saying, "One has a reason."[11] If there are external reasons to do something, then if one knows of these facts, one has internal reasons to do it. If one has internal reasons to do something, then one believes that there are external reasons to do it. External reasons determine the external rationality, sometimes misleadingly called "the objective rationality" of an action. Internal reasons determine the internal rationality, sometimes misleadingly called "the subjective rationality" of an action. In the ideal case, which I hope is also the standard or normal case, external and internal reasons coincide, so that the external and internal rationality of an action are the same. However, sometimes the external and internal reasons do not coincide. For the rationality of actions to have the appropriate relationship to the rationality of persons, internal rationality must be taken as the basic sense of rationality.

Accepting internal rationality as the basic sense of rationality is regarding basic reasons as beliefs rather than facts. However, for a conscious belief with the appropriate content to count as a reason, it must be a rational belief. This limitation is necessary to maintain the close conceptual connection between reasons, rational actions, and rational persons. Ruling out irrational beliefs as reasons eliminates all of the standard counterexamples used as objections to regarding beliefs as reasons, such that it allows the belief that avoiding stepping on the cracks in the sidewalk will prevent one's mother from suffering a broken back to count as a reason for not stepping on the cracks. I shall always use "a reason" to mean "an internal reason," or more precisely, a conscious rational belief. But, when it is obvious that the facts are known, I shall sometimes talk of the facts as providing reasons.

Reasons for Believing

There are reasons for believing as well as reasons for acting. A reason for believing is a belief that can make holding an otherwise irrational belief rational. I am now not talking about beliefs that are irrational for any moral agent to hold, but about those beliefs that are irrational for a person with some specified level of knowledge and intelligence. For readers of this book, the belief that the earth is flat, or that the sun is smaller than the earth and about the same size as the moon, is an irrational belief. The distinction between reasons for believing and reasons for acting is as important as the distinction between irrational desires and irrational beliefs. Failing to distinguish clearly between them can lead to the caricatures of William James's pragmatism, where reasons for acting are given as reasons for believing. Although the relationship between irrational beliefs and reasons for believing is completely parallel to the relationship between irrational desires and reasons for acting, the beliefs that count as basic reasons for believing are completely different from the beliefs that count as basic reasons for acting.

The belief that one sees a bird is a basic reason for believing that there is a bird where one sees it to be. The belief that one remembers taking an aspirin is a basic reason for believing that one took an aspirin. The belief that a proposition is entailed by something one knows is a basic reason for believing the proposition. Philosophers sometimes give basic reasons for holding irrational beliefs such as skeptical beliefs. In more normal cases, reasons are beliefs that are offered in order to persuade a rational person to accept some rationally allowed belief.

It would be irrational for readers of this book to doubt any of their basic ordinary beliefs about the world unless they had an adequate reason to do so. It would also be irrational for them to doubt any of their basic ordinary beliefs about themselves without an adequate reason. Arguments that do not make use of any new information, such as philosophical arguments, provide reasons, but never adequate reasons for doubting any basic ordinary belief about the world. It is important to keep in mind that I am talking about real doubts, those that if relevant would affect everyday actions. Philosophers who accept skeptical arguments concerning the existence of the external world, or of other minds, do not act any differently when they move around or talk to others than do those who reject those arguments.

Neither induction nor deduction has to be justified, for no rational person claims that it is irrational to use them as methods of reasoning. Normal moral views, such as that killing, causing pain, deceiving, and so on, are immoral unless justified, are even in less need of justification. No rational person has any doubts about the immorality of pointless infliction of pain or disability. When I claim to be justifying the common moral system, I am not responding to real doubts about morality, but rather am providing explicit arguments that show that all rational persons *could* favor adopting morality as a public system that applies to all rational persons, and that they *would* do so if they were limited to uncontroversial or rationally required beliefs. I am also attempting to provide such a clear, precise, and comprehensive account of morality that it will help resolve some real doubts that some people have about particular aspects of morality. I hope to show that unresolvable disagreements about some very important moral questions, such as abortion, do not cast any doubt on the complete agreement on most other moral matters.

Distinguishing between Reasons and Motives

It is the failure to distinguish reasons from motives, or perhaps the attempt to regard it as a necessary feature of a reason that it motivates, that explains some of the formal definitions of reasons and rationality that are commonly offered. Many philosophers are not satisfied with an account of reasons such that most reasons serve as motives for most rational people most of the time; they seem to demand that all reasons be motives for all rational people all of the time.[12] But since complete egoists or limited altruists can be rational persons, it is quite clear that some rational persons can have reasons for acting, that is, conscious beliefs that someone will benefit, but if those who benefit are people for whom they do not care, these reasons will not be motives for them. In addition, some motives, those beliefs involved in revenge, are not reasons. Finally, people sometimes act irrationally: beliefs that they will avoid some harm do not motivate them at all; on the contrary, they are motivated by beliefs that they will suffer harms. Thus, for some rational people some reasons are not motives, and for some irrational people most reasons may not be motives and most motives may not be reasons. An account of rationality and reasons is part of an account of how people should behave, whether or not they actually do behave in those ways.

By "a motive" I mean *a conscious belief that at the time of deliberating or acting the agent regards as, and which is part of, an acceptable explanation for her doing the action.*[13] Everything I call a reason can serve as a motive for a rational person; however, not all reasons serve as motives for all persons. Further, someone may be motivated to act by a belief that someone will be harmed by his action, for example, he may commit suicide in order to make someone else feel guilty. Such motives are not reasons. The belief that someone will be harmed by his action, may be a person's motive for doing it, that is, it may be sincerely offered and provide an acceptable explanation for his doing it, but it is not a reason. Such a belief cannot, by itself, make any otherwise irrational act rational.[14]

This definition of a motive makes clear that "unconscious motives" are not motives, for at the time of acting or deliberating, the agent does not regard them as part of an acceptable explanation of her action.[15] However, they may, in fact, be part of an acceptable explanation for the action. I do not deny the reality of unconscious motivation, however, I do not regard "unconscious motives" as motives.[16] Partly this is because it is not even clear that unconscious motives are beliefs, for when unconscious motives become conscious beliefs, they normally cease to motivate. This account of motives also rules out "rationalizations" as motives. A rationalization is a conscious belief that the agent puts forward, sincerely or not, as part of an acceptable explanation of her action, but which is not part of such an explanation. A motive must actually be part of the explanation of the action.

Conscious beliefs often become motives, that is, come to be regarded by the agent as, and are part of, an acceptable explanation of his action, because they are related to desires. A desire often makes a belief into a motive; for example, it is a person's desire for a drink that makes his belief that drinks are in the refrigerator a motive for opening the refrigerator. When asked why he did something, a person often cites a desire rather than a belief. It is also quite common to cite an emotion, which contains beliefs, desires, and feelings, when explaining some action. However, although it is common to call jealousy a motive, I prefer to say that the belief involved in jealousy, such as, that one's spouse loves another, is the motive. There is no substantive disagreement between those who say that jealousy is a motive and my view that it is the belief that is part of jealousy that is the motive. To say that a belief that one's spouse loves another is a motive for harming one's spouse is to say that the person is jealous. It adds nothing to say that jealousy is the motive for wanting to harm. Motives do not always provide complete explanations of intentional actions. In order to reserve the term "motive" for the belief, I distinguish between a belief and the desire that makes it into a motive, or the emotion that contains that belief. I believe that this results in greater clarity and precision in describing the relation among motives, reasons, desires, and emotions.

Philosophers have not usually distinguished clearly enough between beliefs that *can* make otherwise irrational actions rational (reasons) and beliefs that *do* explain them (motives). Further, they have not clearly distinguished desires from either of these. That a person desires to do something is neither a reason for doing it nor his motive for doing it. Of course, a person seldom needs a reason for doing what he desires to do, and if he desires to do something he does not normally need a motive to explain his doing it. His desire to do something may explain why he does it, but it can never make his doing it rational. But of course, acting as one desires to act is not usually irrational and so seldom needs to be made rational. Failure to distinguish desires from pleasure or enjoyment may explain why some mistakenly regard desires as reasons. A belief that one would enjoy doing something is always a reason, and often a motive, for doing it.

A person usually needs no reason for doing those things she desires to do. If she desires to see the place where Kennedy was assassinated, she does not need a reason. If someone asks her why she desires to see it, her reply "I simply want to" may be taken in several ways. It may explain her action by ruling out any motives for it, that is, she may deny that she has any conscious beliefs that she regards as explaining why she desires to see it. It may also be taken as denying that she needs a reason for her desire to see it. It does not provide a reason for her desire to see the place, so it cannot make it rational to do so. But since it is not irrational to desire to see this place, there is no need to make it rational; it already is rational. This account of reasons explains ordinary expressions like "I don't have a reason, I just want to do it" and "But you need a reason for doing something so dangerous."

Egoisms — Psychological, Rational, and Ethical

The confusion between motives and reasons is one of the explanations for the plausibility of psychological egoism. According to psychological egoism no belief to the effect that an action will benefit someone else is ever part of an adequate explanation of that action. If an agent regards this belief as even partially explaining her action, she is mistaken, and the belief is merely a rationalization. Sometimes psychological egoism is taken as making the claim that no one even regards her own actions as explained by a belief that it will help someone else. But this claim is so obviously false that there is no point in discussing it. Psychological egoism is plausible only if one accepts the claim that beliefs about helping others, unless related to one's own self-interest, are never part of an adequate explanation of any action. Accepting this claim may be the result of failing to distinguish motives from reasons and so failing to recognize the difference between psychological egoism and rational egoism.

Rational egoism starts with the correct view that it is irrational to act contrary to one's self-interest without a reason. Rational egoism's distinctive claim is that only beliefs to the effect that something is in one's self-interest count as reasons for doing that action and so it is always irrational to act contrary to one's self-interest. This view is so plausible that it seems to have been put forward by Bishop Butler in his famous remark at the end of Sermon 11, "Let it be allowed that though virtue or moral rectitude does indeed consist in affection to and pursuit of what is right and good, as such: yet that, when we sit down in a cool hour, we can neither justify to ourselves this or any other pursuit, till we are convinced that it will be for our happiness, or at least not contrary to it."[17] That Butler is often regarded as having conclusively refuted psychological egoism shows the plausibility of rational egoism.

It is very easy to go from rational egoism to psychological egoism. According to rational egoism the only rational way to act is in order to benefit oneself. This is a view about reasons and rationality, not about motives and psychology. However, when combined with what seems like merely a definition, rational egoism turns into psychological egoism. Interpreting Aristotle's definition of human beings as rational animals to mean that human beings always act rationally, psychological egoism seems to follow from rational egoism. If it is always irrational to act contrary to one's self-interest and human beings always act rationally, then human beings never act contrary to their own self-interest. To the obvious objection that human beings do sometimes act contrary to their own self-interest, the obvious reply is that they do this only because they are mistaken about what is in their own self-interest. They always act in what they believe is their own self-interest, that is, their motive is always one of self-interest.

The close connection between rational egoism and psychological egoism explains many of the peculiarities of psychological egoism. Rational egoism is correctly stated in a positive form. "All reasons for human action are beliefs that the action is in one's self-interest." Substituting the term "motive" for "reason" results in a positive statement of psychological egoism: "All motives for human action are beliefs that the action is in one's self-interest." But stated in this way, psychological egoism denies the possibility of irrational action, for example, harming oneself because of a belief that others will be harmed. Strictly speaking, psychological egoism should deny that revenge ever serves as a motive. However, psychological egoism does not wish to deny irrational action, only altruistic action. Psychological egoism takes rational egoism's claim that acting contrary to one's self-interest in order to aid someone else is irrational, and simply substitutes "impossible" or "unintelligible" for "irrational." This turns it into the claim that any action that is not explained by a motive of self-interest is impossible or unintelligible. But acting contrary to one's self-interest is clearly neither impossible nor unintelligible. Indeed, it is fairly common for some people to sacrifice their own self-interest for the greater interest of others. The confusion between reasons and motives has led some of those who hold rational egoism to put forward their view as if they held psychological egoism.

Ethical egoism is also very easy to derive from rational egoism. Start by accepting a standard definition of morality discussed in chapter 1, that morality provides a guide everyone *ought* to follow. Then add the following generally accepted and correct statement: "Everyone always ought to act rationally." Now add a statement of rational egoism, "Acting rationally is acting in one's own self-interest." The conclusion is "Everyone always ought to act in her own self-interest." Taking this conclusion to be a statement of a moral view yields ethical egoism. However, this conclusion is not a statement of a moral view, so that even if rational egoism were correct, ethical egoism would still be mistaken. As pointed out in chapter 1, not every guide that tells everyone how they ought to act is a moral guide. Everyone is clear that a guide that tells everyone how they ought to exercise is not a moral guide. Unfortunately, everyone is not as clear that a guide that tells everyone how to achieve peace of mind is also not a moral guide. The discussion of the definition of morality in chapter 1 should have made clear that not all "oughts" are moral oughts. To say what one ought to do, even what everyone ought to do, is not necessarily to say what they morally ought to do.

Even when, after realizing that the "ought" of rational egoism is not a moral "ought," rational egoism provides powerful support for ethical egoism. It is universally acknowledged that acting morally cannot be irrational. The correct answer to "Is it always at least rationally allowed to act morally?" must be "Certainly!" Rational egoism claims that it is always rationally required to act in one's own self-interest. It follows that acting morally cannot conflict with acting in one's self-interest. The best way to guarantee that acting morally is always in one's self-interest is to make self-interest the goal of all moral action. This is another way that rational egoism seems to lead to ethical egoism.

Most people recognize that it is never irrational to act morally. But most people also recognize that it is never irrational to act in your own self-interest. Since both of these views are correct, there should be no problem in holding both of them. However, these views have not always been distinguished from two views that are not compatible. The first of these views, whose most famous champion is Kant, is that it is always irrational to act immorally. The second is rational egoism, that it is always irrational to act contrary to your own self-interest. Both of these views are false, but if one holds either of them, reconciling self-interest and morality becomes a serious problem.[18]

If one holds that morality and self-interest sometimes conflict, and that it is always irrational to act immorally, one must hold that it is sometimes irrational to act in one's own self-interest. If one accepts rational egoism and that morality and self-interest sometimes conflict, one must hold that it is sometimes irrational to act morally. If one accepts rational egoism and does not want to hold that it is ever irrational to act morally, one must hold that self-interest and morality cannot conflict, which is very close to ethical egoism. That both ethical egoism and psychological egoism are derived from rational egoism explains why people accused of holding either one of the former views are also likely to be accused of holding the other, even though it is generally recognized that they are incompatible views.[19]

Although rational egoism is more plausible than either of the other forms of egoism, it is also an incorrect view. Rational egoism does start with the correct view that it is irrational to act contrary to one's self-interest without a reason. However, it makes the common mistake of thinking that since irrational actions are defined egocentrically, reasons also should be defined in that way. Thus rational egoism falsely claims that all reasons for acting are reasons of self-interest. Some forms of rational egoism allow for an action to be rational even though one has no reason for it, such as helping others when this has no effect on one's self-interest. Butler probably held this form of rational egoism, but like all other rational egoists he regards any sacrifice of self-interest to help others as irrational. However, even the slightest reflection makes it clear that helping others, even when doing so is contrary to one's own self-interest, is not irrational. Urging people to sacrifice their own lesser interests to the greater interests of others is not regarded by anyone as advocating irrational action.

Rationality and Self-Interest

In the previous chapter I listed five irrational desires: the desire to die, to suffer pain, to be disabled, to lose freedom, and to lose pleasure. To the question "Why do you call these desires irrational?" I replied that everyone would advocate to everyone for whom they are concerned not to act on any of these desires without an adequate reason. Anyone who acts on any of these desires simply because he feels like doing so is regarded as acting irrationally. This answer may seem unsatisfying. Many would like an answer with a more self-evident ring to it. Some might prefer to say that these desires are irrational because acting on them simply because one feels like it is acting contrary to one's self-interest for no reason.[20] They might argue as follows: to act contrary to one's self-interest for no reason is to act irrationally. To act on certain desires simply because one feels like doing so is to act contrary to one's self-interest for no reason. Therefore to act on these desires simply because one feels like doing so is irrational. These kinds of desires are called irrational desires.

As the discussion of rational egoism shows, the desire for a simple theory of rationality leads some to go from the correct view that all irrational desires are contrary to one's self-interest to the incorrect view that all reasons are beliefs that something is in one's self-interest. Rationality is often equated with rational self-interest. This false equation is furthered by the fact that it is always rational to act in one's self-interest. But that it is always rationally allowed to act in one's self-interest does not mean that it is always rationally required to act in one's self-interest and hence prohibited to act contrary to one's self-interest. However, if no reasons other than one's self-interest are involved, then it is rationally prohibited to act contrary to one's self-interest. When self-interest is interpreted in terms of the lists that account for irrational desires and the reasons related to them, it is irrational for a person in isolation to act on any desire when she knows that acting on that desire will have the overall result of sacrificing her self-interest.

Reasons and the Interests of Others

However, persons do not live in isolation. They almost always live in a society with others, and, as noted before, reasons are not limited to beliefs that one's action is in one's own self-interest. If a person believes that she will save someone else's life, relieve someone else's pain, prevent someone else being disabled, prevent someone else from losing his freedom, prevent someone else's loss of pleasure, or increase the chances of someone else's gaining consciousness, or obtaining more ability, freedom, or pleasure, then she has a reason for acting. Sometimes these reasons will be adequate to make it rational to do what she knows will result in a sacrifice of her own self-interest, such as depriving herself of some pleasure or suffering pain, even giving up her own life.

Unlike irrational desires, which are limited to desires to cause harm to oneself and those for whom one is concerned, beliefs about avoiding harms or gaining benefits for oneself or those for whom one is concerned are not the only beliefs that count as reasons. Reasons need not be egocentric. Beliefs that one's actions will prevent harms to unknown others can make it rational to deprive oneself of pleasure or to suffer pain. However, it is also rational not to act on these reasons, no matter how strong they are. It is rationally allowed both to deprive oneself of pleasure or to suffer pain for the sake of greater benefit to unknown others, and to cause much greater harm to these unknown others in order to avoid much less harm to oneself.

The hybrid nature of rationality, which has been almost completely unrecognized, explains why the category of rationally allowed actions is so important. Reasons are not limited to beliefs that one's action is in the interest of those for whom one is concerned, and so it is not irrational to act contrary to one's self-interest in order to benefit others. However, it is also never irrational to act contrary to reasons involving the interests of unknown others, even if one has no reason for acting in that way. It is rationally allowed to act in the greater interests of unknown others even if the action is contrary to the interests of those for whom one is concerned (necessarily including oneself). And in the same circumstances it is rationally allowed to act in the interests of those for whom one is concerned. Although irrational actions are egocentric, reasons need not be.

Without the category of rationally allowed actions it would be impossible for it to be rational both to act in one's own interests at a greater cost to someone else and to act to benefit others at some cost to oneself. The hybrid nature of rationality explains why rationality does not require benefiting others, even if doing so involves no cost for oneself. The hybrid account claims only that it is rationally allowed to sacrifice one's self-interest for the greater interests of others, but this is an uncontroversial claim. A person is not considered to be acting irrationally if she gives her time or money for the benefit of others. Indeed, even giving up one's life in an attempt to save others is not considered irrational. Although irrationality necessarily involves acting contrary to one's self-interest, because rationality also includes reasons which need not be egocentric, it is also rationally allowed to act contrary to one's self-interest.

Beliefs about preventing anyone's pain or disability, not merely one's own or those for whom one is concerned, are reasons. Like all reasons, they can make acting on an otherwise irrational desire rational. But reasons involving self-interest have a closer relationship to irrationality than reasons involving the interests of others. Both the belief that an action will enable oneself to avoid suffering pain and the belief that an action will enable someone else to avoid suffering pain are reasons for doing that action. But unless one has another reason not to act in this way, it is irrational not to avoid suffering pain oneself, but not irrational not to avoid suffering for others, even though one has no other reason not to act in this way.[21] On this account of reasons for acting, both beliefs about oneself avoiding suffering some harm and beliefs about others avoiding suffering some harm are reasons. And they are reasons for all persons, whether or not these persons are motivated to act on these reasons. But it is only failure to act on reasons concerned with one's own self-interest that is ever irrational; failure to act on reasons concerned with the interests of others is never irrational.

Recognizing the hybrid nature of rationality, that irrationality is egocentric whereas reasons need not be explains why it is compatible to hold both (1) that it is not irrational to harm others for whom one is not concerned even when one has no reason to harm them and (2) that it is always a reason for acting that one will avoid causing harm to others, even for those for whom one is not concerned. Only by recognizing the hybrid nature of rationality can one hold that avoiding causing harm to others, even those for whom one is not concerned, is a reason, even though it is not irrational to cause harm to those for whom one is not concerned, for no reason. One can hold both of these views when one realizes that it is only irrational to act contrary to one's self-interest, and therefore it is never irrational to act contrary to reasons involving others, even when one has no reason for doing so. Although this may sound paradoxical stated in the abstract, it results in explaining the coherent use of the concept of rationality better than any alternative. It explains why it is not irrational to refuse to give to a worthy charity simply because one does not feel like doing so and also not irrational to risk one's life to save the lives of those one does not even know.

Insofar as a person is rational, her belief that her action will help her or her friends to avoid death, pain, and so on, will be a motive for her to do that act. However, reasons include beliefs that anyone, not merely those for whom one cares, will avoid death and pain, or gain additional abilities. But these beliefs about avoiding or preventing harm for those for whom one does not care may not be motives for some people. Indeed, some may be motivated to act on a belief that someone for whom they do not care, whom they actually dislike, will suffer a harm. But such a belief is not a reason, for it cannot make rational an otherwise irrational action. If it is irrational to act in a given way, the belief that someone else will also suffer some harm cannot, by itself, make that action rational.

No Beliefs Unrelated to Avoiding Harms or
Gaining Benefits Are Basic Reasons

Gratitude

It may seem odd that no beliefs solely about the past are basic reasons for acting, for the fact that someone unjustifiably harmed another is often taken as a basic reason for punishing him. I shall talk about revenge and punishment in the next chapter, so that here I shall use gratitude to explain why a belief about the past, such as a belief about past favors, is not a basic reason for acting. Suppose that showing gratitude requires suffering some significant harm. If past favors provide a basic reason, then it might be rational to suffer that harm, even if no one, neither oneself nor the person to whom one is showing gratitude, were to benefit either directly or indirectly from one's action. It might be objected that one cannot show gratitude if the person to whom you are showing gratitude does not benefit either directly or indirectly from one's action. But this objection does not count against my point that beliefs about the past not being basic reasons. If showing gratitude to someone requires that she benefit either directly or indirectly from one's action, then one always has a reason for showing gratitude. But that reason is not the past favor that was done to one, but the benefit to be gained by the person who did the favor.

Hobbes's account of gratitude as acting so that the giver will "have no reasonable cause to repent him of his good will" strongly suggests that showing gratitude is intended to benefit the giver. It is because one believes one is benefiting that person, or at least, attempting to prevent him from feeling regret, that showing gratitude can make an otherwise irrational action, such as causing a loss for oneself, rational. Thus, the reason for showing gratitude is the belief that one will benefit that person, not the belief that this person did you a favor. Since this reason involves the future, not the past, gratitude does not count against the view that beliefs about the past do not count as reasons. However, I do not deny that beliefs about the past can serve as motives or that people are motivated by past favors. Nor do I deny that showing gratitude for past favors is rational. Generally, showing gratitude does not involve one's suffering any harms; quite the contrary, it is often enjoyable to show one's gratitude. Even when showing gratitude does involve suffering some harm, it need not be irrational, for the person to whom one is showing gratitude benefits.

I have so far been talking about "showing gratitude," not "feeling gratitude." Showing gratitude is an action, and so if it involves suffering some harm it needs a reason to make it rational. However, there is always a reason for showing gratitude; it benefits the person who did one a favor. Many people feel gratitude, that is, feel like showing gratitude, toward those who did them favors, and there is nothing irrational about this feeling. On the contrary, insofar as it is possible, I think children should be brought up to feel gratitude toward those who have benefited them. The more widespread such feelings, the more likely it is that people will benefit one another. Thus my claim that past favors do not provide a basic reason for showing gratitude should not be taken as denying that past favors are a reason for showing gratitude, they are simply not a basic reason. I do not regard feeling gratitude as irrational in any way. Impartial rational people would even favor children being brought up to be motivated to show gratitude for past favors and would count it a virtue that one is so motivated.

Obeying Rules

Another consequence of limiting reasons to beliefs that someone will benefit is that the belief that one's action is in accordance with a rule or custom is not a basic reason for acting in that way. Of course, generally no reason is needed for acting in conformity with a rule or custom, but if a reason is needed, the mere belief that one's action is in accord with a rule or custom does not provide that reason. Such a belief cannot make it rational to act in conformity with that rule or custom. However, if one believes the rule to be a good one, that is, that the closer to universal the following of the rule the better the results, then one does have a reason for acting in accordance with it. Knowledge that the rule is a good rule provides a reason for believing that less harm or more benefit will result from following the rule than from violating it. The rationally required belief in the fallibility of all people, including oneself, should give one pause before violating a good rule, for one knows that violations often have bad consequences. The belief that one's action is in accordance with a good rule is thus a reason for following the rule without being a basic reason.

The fact that everyone is fallible, that no one knows all of the consequences of his actions including all of the consequences of his action on his own future behavior, makes clear the importance of following good rules. Violating a rule may erode support for it and increase the probability that greater harm will result. Especially when a person violates the rule in circumstances when she would not want everyone to know that they are allowed to violate the rule, this violation may have a bad effect on her future behavior. Thus the belief that one's action is in accordance with a good rule is a reason for following it; so acting in accordance with that rule may make an action rational, even when this involves some cost or loss for oneself. However, when all rational people would favor everyone knowing that they are allowed to break the rule in these circumstances, there may not be a reason to act according to a good rule. In these cases, when breaking the rule is justified, it may not even be rational to follow a good rule, for the circumstances may be such that obeying the rule will result in harm to oneself and perhaps others as well, and there are no compensating benefits for anyone.

Moral rules are good rules. People have a reason to obey moral rules, especially when they are considering violating a rule in circumstances in which they would not want everyone to know that they are allowed to violate the rule. Of course, violating moral rules like those prohibiting killing always results directly in someone suffering some harm. With regard to these kinds of rules, it is clear that there is always a reason for obeying the rule, for doing so avoids causing harm to someone. The problematic situations arise when violating a rule does not directly cause harm to anyone and acting in accordance with the rule does result in harm to oneself, as is sometimes the case with moral rules like those that prohibit cheating. These kinds of cases make it important to recognize there is a reason for acting in accordance with a good rule. Although the belief that one's action is in accordance with a good rule, even a moral rule, does not provide a basic reason for acting in that way, recognition of one's fallibility, provides a reason for believing that there is a basic reason for obeying the rule.

The question of whether the reason for acting in accordance with the rule is adequate does not arise unless one would be harmed by acting in accordance with the rule. When one would be harmed, then one does need a reason, and it is not obvious that the reasons I have mentioned would always be adequate. I have already admitted that it is possible that sometimes it may be irrational for someone to act in accordance with a good rule, even a moral rule. But in these cases, it will always be morally justified for one to break the rule. All of the moral rules have exceptions, and even though it is never irrational to act morally, that does not mean it is never irrational to act in accordance with a moral rule. I claim only that it is never irrational to avoid unjustifiable violations of moral rules. In the chapter on why one should be moral (chapter 13), I shall try to show that when one is not morally justified in violating a moral rule, one always has an adequate reason for acting in accordance with it.

Even if one does not know whether a rule or custom is a good one, one may have a reason for acting in accordance with it; other people may be very upset if one violates a commonly observed rule or custom. Also, one often feels very uncomfortable acting contrary to a custom or rule when previously one had always acted in accordance with it. One may believe that avoiding the unpleasant feeling that would result from violating the rule is an adequate reason for undergoing the harm that results from following it. This is very similar to the self-conscious compulsive handwasher, for whom avoiding the anxiety that results from refraining from washing them is an adequate reason for washing them. Denying that the mere fact that there is a rule or custom provides a basic reason for acting is perfectly compatible with admitting that there are many reasons for acting in accordance with commonly accepted rules or customs.

In all examples where some belief about the past, by itself, seems to provide a basic reason for acting, it does not really do so; rather, it provides a reason for believing that there is a basic reason for acting, a reason that concerns someone benefiting in the present or future. Although the belief that an act is in accordance with a rule or custom never by itself provides a basic reason for acting, there are almost always reasons for acting in accordance with good rules and customs, including moral rules. All reasons for acting that are not basic reasons are reasons for believing that there are basic reasons for acting. The only beliefs that count as basic reasons are beliefs that one is decreasing someone's chances of dying, of suffering pain, or of losing abilities, freedom, or pleasure, and beliefs that one is increasing someone's chances of gaining consciousness, or of obtaining more ability, freedom, or pleasure. Anything else that counts as a reason for acting does so only because it involves the basic reasons listed above. If anyone shows that there is some reason for acting that does not involve these basic reasons, I shall have been proved wrong.

Stronger or Better Reasons

Since some reasons are not motives and some motives are not reasons, it should not be surprising that the better or stronger reasons will often not be the stronger motives or vice versa. The strength of a motive is determined by how it fares in competition with other motives. If a person has a belief that acting one way will have certain consequences while acting another way will have significantly different consequences, which belief is the stronger of the two motives will be determined by which way he acts or tries to act. Strength of motive is completely person relative; that one motive is stronger than another for one person does not imply that it will be stronger for a different person. Indeed, the strength of a motive not only differs for different people, it also differs for the same person at different times. Of course, one belief may always provide a stronger motive than another belief for a given person, but motives also may change in strength over time. The strength of a motive may even fluctuate, depending on one's health, mood, recent past history, and other personal factors. In general, some motives are stronger than others for most people, but which motives are stronger for most people is an empirical matter, not a philosophical one.

Although not all people agree on what reasons are better or stronger than others, there are limits to this disagreement. In the absence of other considerations, beliefs about avoiding greater harms are stronger or better reasons than beliefs about avoiding lesser harms. A person has a better or stronger reason to avoid being sent to prison for five years than for two years. Insofar as the harms that a person will avoid are all for himself, there is no question that the better or stronger reasons are those that involve avoiding the greater harms or gaining the greater benefits. Insofar as there is disagreement on which of two harms is greater or which of two benefits is larger, there will be disagreement as to which belief is the better reason.[22] All of this is fairly straightforward.

Problems arise when the competing reasons concern different kinds of harms or both benefits and harms. However, although there is no precise way to compare different kinds of harms, all rational people would regard a harm of one kind, if sufficiently large, to be greater than a fairly small harm of another kind (e.g., suffering some pain for a short time to prevent a significant permanent disability). Similarly, there is no precise way to compare benefits with harms, but everyone would regard some benefits as compensating for some harms and lesser benefits as not doing so. For example, many people would regard significantly increased abilities as compensating for the unpleasant work necessary to achieve them but would not regard only minimally increased abilities as compensating for the same amount of unpleasant work. Indeed, knowing how minimal the results would be beforehand, some would regard undergoing so much unpleasant work for so little benefit as irrational. Since rational persons rank harms and benefits differently, they can disagree about whether or not some belief about benefits is an adequate reason for suffering some harm. When rational persons disagree, I do not count either reason as stronger than the other. However, all rational persons agree that some reasons involving harms are stronger than some reasons involving benefits, and may even agree that some reasons involving benefits, if they are great enough, are stronger than some reasons involving harms, if the harms are small enough.

The above discussion should make it clear that reasons can be ranked by determining which irrational acts the reason can make rational. If everyone agrees that reason A would be an adequate reason for every otherwise irrational act that reason

B would be an adequate reason for, and for some otherwise irrational acts as well, then reason A is a stronger or better reason than reason B. A stronger reason will be adequate for more serious irrational acts than a weaker reason. Since the seriousness of the irrationality of an act depends on the amount of harm that one will suffer by doing that act, a stronger reason will compensate for greater harm than a weaker reason. The difficulty in ranking reasons about gaining benefits with those about avoiding harms is due to the wide variation in views about whether any given good adequately compensates for suffering some nontrivial harm. Nonetheless, everyone admits that it would not be irrational to suffer some nontrivial harms in order to gain some benefits, even if they personally would not suffer that harm to gain that benefit.

What makes an action irrational is the harm that the agent will suffer, not the harm caused to anyone else, unless the agent suffers because of that person suffering. However, reasons are beliefs that anyone will avoid a harm or gain a benefit, even if the agent does not care about that person. The question whether reasons of self-interest are stronger than reasons involving the interests of others arises only if one confuses reasons with motives. If the amount of harm to be avoided and the benefit to be gained is the same, then reasons involving self-interest cannot make rational any acts that reasons involving the interests of others cannot make rational. Any irrational act that would be made rational by a reason of self-interest would also be made rational by a reason of the same strength involving the interests of others. A mere change of person affected does not affect the strength of a reason.[23]

If it would be rational to spend all of one's money to prevent a painful death for oneself, then, if there are no other reasons involved, it would also be rational to spend all of one's money to prevent a painful death for someone else. If it would be irrational to spend all of one's money to gain a momentary pleasure for oneself, then, if there are no other reasons involved, it would also be irrational to spend all of one's money to gain a momentary pleasure for someone else. A reason has the same strength regardless of the agent who will benefit. The strength of a reason is determined by the amount of harm avoided or benefit gained. It is not dependent on which reason provides the strongest motive to the agent. Of course, beliefs about benefits to oneself are almost always going to provide stronger motives than beliefs about benefits to those for whom one is not concerned, but the strength of a reason is not correlated with the strength of a motive. The same belief retains the same strength as a reason, independent of who has the belief; the same belief usually has different strengths as a motive, depending on who has the belief.

On the above account of the strength of reasons, avoiding a greater amount of harm for others is a stronger reason than avoiding a lesser amount of harm for oneself. Avoiding a temporary discomfort is not an adequate reason for losing one's arm, and may not even be an adequate reason for risking losing one's arm. Thus it might be irrational for a machine operator to avoid the discomfort of taking the safety precautions if he thereby puts his arm at serious risk for being amputated. But given the same probabilities, it would not be irrational for him to put his arm at risk to save someone else's life. This account of the strength of reasons provides the kind of non-question-begging objectivity that has been one of the goals of those who have tried to show that rationality requires acting morally. That one has a stronger reason to prevent greater harm to others rather than lesser harm to oneself seems to support those who claim that rationality requires being moral. However, given the hybrid nature of rationality, this is not true, for rationality does not require acting on stronger or better reasons.

This objective account of the strength of reasons does not show that rationality requires regarding the interests of others as important as one's own. It is not irrational to be motivated more by one's own interests than by the interests of others, even if the interests of others provide objectively stronger reasons than one's own interests. It is not irrational not to act to save the life of someone else, even though saving that life is a stronger reason than any reason one has for not saving it.[24] The relationship between reasons, even stronger or better reasons, and morality is far more complex than most philosophers have realized. Given that one reason is better than another only if all rational persons agree that it is better, there may not always be better reasons for acting morally rather than in one's self-interest. In fact, acting morally sometimes seems to require acting in a way that results in more harm for oneself than the harm that is avoided for anyone else. Refraining from cheating on a test may result in many of the harms that accompany failing, and no one else may avoid any comparable harm or gain any compensating benefit.[25] However, it is true that someone who always acts on better reasons will never act to benefit himself at greater cost to others.

The Desire to Harm Others

Basic reasons include not only beliefs that one's action is in one's own self-interest but also beliefs that it is in the interest of someone else. The strength of reasons is an objective matter that does not change merely on the basis of whose interests are involved. Recognition that reasons need not be egocentric may tempt one to claim that irrational desires should also not be limited to those that are egocentric. It is plausible to claim that irrational desires should not be limited to desires to act contrary to one's own self-interest, that it is irrational to desire to kill, inflict pain on, disable, deprive of freedom, or deprive of pleasure anyone, and not merely oneself, for no reason. This claim need not imply that it is irrational to be immoral, but it does suggest that it is irrational not to act on better reasons.

It is compatible with this claim that it is not irrational to cause harm to others if a person believes that he will benefit himself sufficiently, or even derive sufficient pleasure from doing so. It does not even require considering sadism, getting pleasure from inflicting pain on others, irrational. Like masochism (in which one gets pleasure from being inflicted with pain), sadism may be a mental disorder, but acting sadistically need not be irrational. Indeed, getting pleasure from seeing the pain of others may not even be unusual, considering how many people enjoy boxing, how many laugh at accidents, and so on. That it is irrational to harm others for no reason, or to cause greater harm to them than the harm one avoids for oneself, is a plausible claim. If one accepts this claim, it will make my justification of morality even easier. However, I do not accept it, and not merely because of my principle of not regarding any action as irrational unless there is no significant disagreement concerning it.

Is it irrational to act on a desire to harm others simply because one feels like doing so? In other words, is the desire to harm others an irrational desire? It is very tempting to say this, for people do talk of senseless killing. People who simply act on their desire to kill others do seem to be irrational. The student who, several decades ago, shot and killed all the people he saw from a tower on the University of Texas campus, was certainly acting irrationally. Since he seems to have done this without any reason, it is tempting to conclude that anyone who acts on a desire to kill others simply because he feels like doing so is acting irrationally. But it is not clear that the student acted irrationally simply because he acted on his desire to harm others. He had sufficient knowledge and intelligence to know that his action was one that significantly increased his own chances of being harmed. He may be considered irrational on the same grounds that a compulsive hand washer is considered irrational, namely, acting without a reason on a desire that he knows or should know would significantly increase his own chances of being harmed. Thus the example of the Texas student does not show that the desire to harm people is, in itself, any more irrational than the desire to wash one's hands. However, it is far more likely that harming others will result in harm to oneself than it is that washing one's hands will harm oneself. This may explain why many think it is irrational to act on the desire to harm others simply because one feels like doing so.

However, if a person takes care that he will not suffer harm himself, it does not seem irrational to act on a desire to harm someone, for example, for revenge, without any reason. But if the desire for revenge is so strong that it leads one to act in such a way that one seriously harms oneself in order to carry out the revenge, then such action is irrational. So revenge that harms oneself is irrational, whereas revenge which does not is rationally allowed. If this is the case, then acting on the desire to harm another simply because one feels like doing so is not an irrational desire. To harm someone because he has made you angry is usually irrational, not because one needs a reason for harming others, but because one knows one is increasing one's own chances of being harmed. Envy, at least in some mild form, is almost universal. Although the person who seeks to harm those he envies is not admired, if he does it without harming himself, he is not regarded as acting irrationally.

Regarding desires to harm others as irrational as desires to harm oneself creates a problem in relating irrational actions to irrational persons. As noted earlier, a person is regarded as irrational and hence not responsible for his irrational acts if he continually acts in seriously irrational ways. To regard a person who continually seriously harms others for no reason to be as irrational as someone who continually seriously harms himself for no reason means that neither is responsible for their behavior. But if someone knew he was in a situation where he would suffer no harm by harming others, he would not be irrational even if he continually did cause them harm. Of course, it would be monstrous of him to do that, but he would not be irrational. Those who worked in the Nazi concentration camps and knew that they could indulge their desires to kill and torture others without suffering any harm themselves were not acting irrationally. Rather, they were acting in a morally monstrous way. They should be held responsible for their actions.

It may seldom be the case that anyone who is not suffering from a mental malady ever simply desires to harm another. But people have other desires, for example, the desire to feel superior to someone else, and this desire may lead them to act

so as to harm others for no reason. Envy is exceedingly common, and it often involves a desire to harm another, even though one will not thereby avoid a harm or
gain a benefit.[26] The desire for status seems to be one of the most prevalent desires
and often leads one to harm another with no motive other than to satisfy that desire.
As long as one takes care not to harm oneself, such a person is not usually regarded
as acting irrationally. If this desire for status, however, becomes so strong that he
harms himself, then he is regarded as acting irrationally, unless he believes that he
will get sufficient pleasure from having that status that it compensates for the harm
he suffers.

I can understand why many would like to classify pointless violence as irrational.[27] Although someone who is completely indifferent to the suffering of other
people is probably suffering from a mental disorder, it does not seem that he is acting irrationally if he harms another simply on a whim. I have given my objection to
classifying acting on such desires as irrational, namely, it seems to absolve the Nazi
concentration camp guards and other similar moral monsters of responsibility. It
does the same for much vandalism. Thus, in addition to following my principle of
classifying all controversial cases as rational, I prefer to regard the harming of others
when one does not increase one's own chances of suffering harm as rationally allowed. Regarding those who harm others for no reason as generally responsible for
their actions makes clear that to classify an act as rationally allowed is in no way
whatsoever to praise it.

Rationality, Interests, and Lists

Limiting irrational desires to desires to harm oneself does not support those who
want to make rationality essentially a matter of self-interest. Although acting contrary
to self-interest is central to the concept of irrationality, reasons are beliefs about anyone benefiting anyone. It is often rational to sacrifice oneself to benefit others, but it
is always irrational to sacrifice oneself to harm others. The sadist may be acting rationally to make some sacrifice to harm others if he gets pleasure from so doing, for
this pleasure may outweigh the sacrifice he makes. The person who gets no pleasure
from harming others is irrational to make any sacrifice to do so unless he has some
reason for doing so.

Causing harm to others never, by itself, makes rational an action that would otherwise be irrational; whereas helping others, by itself, can make an action that would
otherwise be irrational, rational. If by depriving herself of some pleasure a person
enables others to gain greater pleasure, what was an otherwise irrational action becomes rational. Moreover, though it may not be irrational simply to harm others, it is
irrational to do so if one thereby harms oneself, and gets no pleasure or benefit. It is,
however, rationally allowed for a person to harm others simply because he feels like
doing so when he will not harm himself. Only actions that harm oneself are irrational, therefore one needs no reason to act on any desires except those that are
contrary to one's self-interest, such as suffering death, pain, and the other harms.
However, reasons are beliefs about anyone benefiting, so that it need not be irrational to help others even if one thereby harms oneself. As a hybrid concept, ration-

ality includes both an egocentric element, and a nonegocentric element. Thus self-sacrifice often counts as rational.

Although I have summarized my account of rationality, irrationality, and reasons, using the phrases "self-interest" and "contrary to self-interest," it is important to remember that these phrases are not essential to my account. It is death, pain in all of its manifestations, loss of abilities, loss of freedom, and loss of pleasure that determine what counts as contrary to one's self-interest. What is in one's self-interest is to avoid suffering these harms and to maintain and obtain goods, namely, consciousness, abilities, freedom, and pleasure. To harm others or to act contrary to their interests is to cause them to suffer death, pain, loss of ability, loss of freedom, or loss of pleasure, or to prevent them from maintaining or increasing their consciousness, abilities, freedom, or pleasure. To help others, to benefit them, or to act in their interests, is to prevent their suffering death, pain, loss of ability, loss of freedom, or loss of pleasure, or to enable them to maintain or increase their consciousness, abilities, freedom, or pleasure.

That rationality is ultimately defined by a list rather than a formula will be, for many, a sufficient motive for rejecting this account. This preference for a formula over a list goes back at least as far as Plato. Like most such long-standing preferences there is no argument in its favor. The supposed arguments against a list consist primarily of epithets like "arbitrary." A list is supposedly arbitrary in the way that a formula is not, but the only sense in which my list is arbitrary is that it is a list rather than a formula. I have talked to no one who disputes any of the items on my list, and who does not use this list, or something very like it, to test any formula that is put forward. If rationality and irrationality are in fact the fundamental concepts that most philosophers take them to be, then they have to be defined in terms of a list, for all fundamental definitions must be ostensive rather than verbal. This point has been consistently overlooked.

Rationality does not require concern for the welfare of others, especially when this conflicts with one's own welfare; it does not even seem to exclude what is generally called "senseless killing." Nonetheless, it is important to see that when one's own interest conflicts with the interests of others, it is rationally allowed to act either according to one's own interests or to sacrifice one's interests to others. Indeed, the greater interests of others provide stronger reasons than one's own lesser interests. However, rationality does not offer the guide to conduct that either those who equate it with rational self-interest or those who equate it with morality assign it. Rationality does not provide the support to morality that it is sometimes claimed to do; yet, despite appearances, it is not the enemy of morality that it has also sometimes been claimed to be. Unfortunately, the fact that in a conflict between morality and self-interest, it is rational to act either way has led some philosophers to claim that rationality is in conflict with itself. I do not understand what this claim means, except if it is taken as a lament that rationality does not prescribe a unique course of action in important cases of conflict.[28]

Final Definition of a Rational Action

The concept of a rational action can now be seen to be quite complex: it is a hybrid concept. A rational action is one that is not irrational, and this requires that it participate in the egocentric character of an irrational action. Any action that is not irrational counts as rational; that is, any action that does not have foreseeable harmful consequences for oneself or those for whom one cares is rational. However, the concept of a rational action also incorporates the concept of a reason, and reasons need not be egocentric. A conscious rational belief that anyone will benefit from one's actions is a reason. Reasons are not limited to beliefs about benefits to oneself or those for whom one cares. Thus an action that has foreseeable harmful consequences for oneself can be rational if there are compensating benefits for others, even if one does not care about them.

A clear consequence of this hybrid character is that it need not be irrational to act contrary to what one has a reason for doing, even if one has no reason at all for acting contrary to this reason. If the reason for doing something is that someone for whom one does not care will benefit, then it is not irrational not to act on that reason, for no reason. As previously stated, it is not irrational to refuse to give to a worthy charity simply because one does not feel like doing so. But also it is not irrational to act contrary to self-interest for the very same reason, that is, it is not irrational to give to the same worthy charity even though this will result in one not being able to take the vacation that one was looking forward to.

It is the failure to recognize the hybrid character of rationality that is responsible for the inadequacy of all of the previous accounts of that concept. Those who focused on irrational actions recognized only the egocentric feature of rationality. Rational egoism is the clearest example, but all of the desire-based accounts, including all of the versions of the "cool moment" theories are examples. Internalism — the view that for rational persons, all reasons must be motives — is also partly the result of focusing on the egocentric part of rationality. Those who focus on the concept of reasons make a different error. They take rationality to be entirely objective. Kant and others who regard it as irrational to be immoral provide the clearest examples. Other examples are those who recognize that reasons are objective and then try to define a rational action as one that is based on reasons. Of course, defining a rational action as one based on reasons can also result in making reasons egocentric, if reasons are regarded as dependent on one's desires.

It is only by recognizing the hybrid character of rationality, acknowledging that it has both an egocentric component (irrational actions) and a nonegocentric component (reasons), that an adequate definition can be formulated. Such a definition must start by defining irrational actions and define rational actions as those action that are not irrational. Only such a definition allows for the category of rationally allowed actions and adequately accounts for all of the relevant uses of the related concepts. An adequate definition must also pass the test that all fully informed rational persons would advocate that anyone for whom they care never act irrationally. Only the definition formulated below, or one that is equivalent to it, passes this test.

An action is irrational in the basic sense if and only if it is an intentional action of a person with sufficient knowledge and intelligence to be fully informed about that action and who, if fully informed, (1) would believe that the action involves signifi-cantly increased risk of his suffering death, nontrivial pain, loss of ability, loss of free-dom, or loss of pleasure and (2) would not have an adequate reason for the action.[29] *A reason for acting is a conscious rational belief that one's action will increase the prob-ability of someone's avoiding any of the harms listed above or gaining greater con-sciousness, ability, freedom, or pleasure. A reason is adequate if any significant group of moral agents regard the harm avoided or benefit gained as compensating for the harm suffered. Any intentional action that is not irrational is rational.*

This definition is intended to classify an action as irrational if someone would believe that an alternative action would result in his suffering less harm with no in-crease in harm suffered (or decrease in benefits gained) by anyone else, even if, in the absence of that alternative action, the action would count as rational. The exam-ple of the compulsive handwasher presented in chapter 2 is an example of this kind of irrational action. It is irrational for him to continue to wash his hands rather than seek psychiatric help, even though if no such help is available, it is rational for him to continue washing his hands in order to avoid the overwhelming anxiety.

There is no mention of desires in this definition, because, as noted before, de-sires are not reasons, nor can they make beliefs into reasons. On the "cool moment" account of rationality, it is irrational to act on a desire only when one believes that this will significantly decrease one's chances of satisfying some other desires, which in a cool moment, one considers significantly more important. This view does not even require that the more important desires be rational ones.[30] Part of the plausibil-ity of this view stems from the fact that the frustration of desires generally causes dis-pleasure. Unless other benefits and harms are involved, one desire counts as more important than another if in a cool moment its frustration results in more displea-sure (duration included) than the frustration of a less important desire. These con-siderations explain why, unless one has an adequate reason, it is irrational to cause the frustration of more important rational desires. But it is the greater displeasure caused by the frustration of one's more important desires that makes it irrational to frustrate them without a reason. Failing to satisfy a desire is not the same as frustrat-ing it. Similarly, it is the belief about the pleasure that will come from satisfying a desire that is a reason for acting to satisfy the desire; having a desire provides no rea-son for acting to satisfy it.

Although not irrational in the basic sense, there are two parasitic kinds of irra-tional action; the first resembles the Humean account of an irrational action as one based on a false belief. This kind of irrational action is one that is based on an irra-tional belief, independent of the consequences of acting on that belief. These ac-tions are often regarded as irrational because so many of them meet the definition of an irrational action in the basic sense defined above. Many actions based on irra-tional beliefs result in a person with sufficient knowledge and intelligence to know better, suffering an increased risk of death, pain, and the other evils, without an ade-quate reason. Further, even when acting on an irrational belief does not directly in-crease one's risk, it seems that this is merely accidental, that is, if the situation were to change, the person would not react to it in a rational way and so would increase his risk of suffering some harm. But this is a parasitic sense of an irrational action, the basic sense is the one previously defined.

The second kind of parasitic irrational action is far less common. Suppose a person acts in a way that he knows will harm himself, but believes that some others will avoid greater harms or will gain compensating benefits from his action. However, this reason is not a motive for his acting in that way — and may even be a motive for his not acting in that way. An example of such a case is José who is extremely angry and depressed, and so desires to kill himself. However, his belief that the proceeds from his life insurance policy will enable his wife and children to get medical treatments that will cure their crippling and painful diseases does not serve as a motive for his killing himself. Rather this belief, which is a reason for his killing himself, is — for him — a motive for his not killing himself. The belief that does serve as a motive for his killing himself is his belief that his wife and children will feel guilty and thus suffer even more. Although José may have an adequate reason for killing himself, that reason is not his motive for doing so. José seems to be acting irrationally whether or not the belief that his family will benefit from his death is a strong enough motive to prevent him from killing himself. But just as one must distinguish between a moral judgment about an action and a moral judgment about the motives of a person who acts in that way, one must also distinguish between the rationality of an action and the rationality of the motives of the person who is acting in that way.[31]

A person who does not kill or otherwise harm himself, no matter what his motive for not doing so, is not acting irrationally in the basic sense. Of course, if it is known that he wants to kill himself and that his motive for not killing himself is that his death will prevent greater harms for others, then we would regard it as simply an accident that he does not act irrationally. That he is motivated in this way counts in favor of judging him to be irrational, and that is why his decision to kill himself is regarded as a parasitic kind of irrational action. Also, if a person does kill himself, but has an adequate reason for doing so, his action is not irrational in the basic sense, regardless of whether that reason is a motive for his killing himself. Indeed, it makes no difference if that reason is a motive for his not killing himself, but is simply not strong enough to make him refrain from killing himself. His action is not irrational in the basic sense even though it is irrational in the sense that its motivation is irrational and so counts against the person being regarded as rational. In the basic sense, the rationality of an action is completely determined by the rational beliefs that a fully informed person should have. If he should not have a belief that his action will result in any harm to himself, his action is never irrational, regardless of his motive for acting or not acting. The same is true if he believes that his action will result in his being harmed, but also has an adequate reason for his action. His action is not irrational even if his reason is a motive against doing the action. Rationality is parallel to morality in that motives do not count at all in judging the rationality or the morality of the act, they count only in judging the rationality or the morality of the person.[32]

Summary

I have attempted to provide an account of rationality such that every action that is classified as irrational is one that no one wants to do. In this basic sense, an action is irrational only if every fully informed rational person would advocate that any person for whom they are concerned, including themselves, not act in that way.[33] All intentional actions that are not irrational are rational. Since some rational persons would sometimes advocate that a fully informed person for whom they are concerned act in a way that is motivated by a false belief or even do an act which is irrationally motivated, actions motivated by false beliefs or based on irrational motivation may still be rational actions in this basic sense. I realize that many people would prefer that these and other actions that I classify as rationally allowed be classified as irrational. I also do not deny that a plausible case can also be made for calling sadism, masochism, and the desire to harm others irrational. (Although once irrationality is distinguished from having a mental malady, the case seems less compelling.) However, I do not want to classify as irrational any action that anyone can plausibly want to classify as rational. When I show an action to be irrational, I expect complete agreement that it should not be done.

To call an action, desire, or belief rationally allowed does not even suggest that one favors it. Although actions, desires, or beliefs that are rationally allowed are rational and "rational" is often used as a word of praise, I use it only to rule out one kind of condemnation. Only when I say that an action, desire, or belief is rationally required do I mean to commend it, for then not doing that action, or having that desire or belief is irrational. It is "irrational" that has the primary normative force; to call an action, belief, or desire "irrational" is to condemn it. This account of rationality shows that those who claim that the gulf between facts and values or between the descriptive and the prescriptive cannot be bridged are mistaken.[34]

Notes

1. Irrational beliefs do not count as reasons, for they can never make it rational to do an otherwise irrational action. Nor can unconscious beliefs make it rational to do an otherwise irrational action. I discuss unconscious beliefs further in this chapter when I distinguish between reasons and motives.

2. This vagueness is similar to the vagueness involved in determining when a belief is a delusion or an irrational belief.

3. The disagreement about the adequacy of beliefs about preventing harm to animals is easier to discuss when talking about the strength of reasons. See note 23.

4. Since I classify as rational any action that any significant group of people would regard as rational, these different rankings of the harms and benefits do not affect how I classify the rationality of these actions and decisions. I use the terms "reasonable" and "unreasonable," respectively, for decisions and actions that are in accord with and counter to the rankings of the agent. When all of the harms and benefits involved are those of agent, as when discussing with patients their decisions about which treatment to accept, these terms are clear and have no misleading connotations. When the harms and benefits involve different people, as when considering harming others in order to benefit oneself, there may be some misleading connotations. For its use in considering the decisions of patients, see Bernard Gert, Charles M. Culver, and K. Danner Clouser, *Bioethics: A Return to Fundamentals* (New York: Oxford University Press, 1997), chap. 7.

5. The reason is that it prevents a loss of freedom.

6. Variations of this definition modify it by replacing "reasons" with "the best reasons" or "adequate reasons." The additional difficulties with the view that a rational action is one that

is based on the best reasons will be discussed in the section of this chapter on the stronger or better reasons.

7. See Bruce W. Price, "Comment on Bernard Gert's Analysis of Rational Action," *Ethics* 102 (October 1991): 110–116, and B. C. Postow, "Gert's Definition of Irrationality," *Ethics* 102 (October 1991): 103–109, for examples of this view.

8. See B. C. Postow, "Gert's Definition of Irrationality."

9. This may not be a completely contingent matter, for it may be part of the criterian for desires that their frustration results in that behavior which is part of the criterian for displeasure. It does not, however, seem to be part of the criterian for desires that their satisfaction results in that behavior which is part of the criterian for pleasure.

10. See Stephen Nathanson, *The Ideal of Rationality: A Defense within Reason*, revised ed. (Chicago: Open Court Publishing, 1994).

11. Since the rationality of an action in the basic sense may depend upon one having a reason, even if reasons were facts, they would not be related to the rationality of an action unless the person knows those facts.

12. That all reasons are motives for all rational people all of the time is called an internalist view. It is due to an inadequate account of the nature of reasons, including a failure to distinguish clearly enough between reasons and motives. The derivation of psychological egoism from rational egoism is based on a similar failure. (See the next section, "Egoisms — Psychological, Rational, and Ethical.")

13. This is the basic sense of "motive," but in an extended sense, a motive for an action is a conscious belief that would be a motive in the basic sense if the person were to do the action. In a more extended sense, a motive can be a conscious belief that would be a motive in the extended sense if there were not opposing motives. Finally, a motive can be a fact that if believed would be a motive in either of the previous senses.

14. Baier marks this distinction by using "justifying reasons" and "explanatory reasons." See *The Moral Point of View*, abridged ed. (New York: Random House, 1965), 40 ff.

15. See my article "Hobbes, Mechanism, and Egoism," *Philosophical Quarterly* 15, no. 61 (October 1965): 341–349.

16. Regarding "unconscious motives" as motives is an example of what I call the fallacy of "ignoring the modifier." This fallacy is fairly common; other examples are regarding a dead person as a person and an immaterial object as an object. More prosaic examples would include regarding a rubber duck as a duck and a false friend as a friend.

17. Bishop Butler, *Fifteen Sermons upon Human Nature* (London, 1726; 2nd ed., 1729).

18. Both of these views are the result of failing to recognize the hybrid complexity of rationality, that is, that irrationality is egocentric and that reasons need not be.

19. For a fuller account of how rational egoism leads to both ethical and psychological egoism, see my article "Egoismo," *Revista Latinoamericana de Filosofia* 22, no. 1 (Fall 1996): 5–20.

20. See Nathanson, *The Ideal of Rationality.*

21. See my review of Thomas Nagel, *The Possibility of Altruism*, in *Journal of Philosophy* 64, no. 12 (June 15, 1972): 340–344.

22. This disagreement, like disagreements about the adequacy of a reason, are what Charles Stevenson called "disagreements in attitude." These differ from disagreements about the facts in that they always involve the way one acts or wants to act. Since neither person need be incorrect, the disagreements may never be resolved. However, there may sometimes be a correct answer, and if the persons are rational they may come to agreement.

23. Of course, it is very unlikely for there to be "a mere change of person affected," especially when one of those persons is oneself and the other someone for whom one has no concern. Moreover, there are sentient beings who are not persons, and people can disagree

over whether a belief that one will avoid a certain amount of pain for a sentient being who is not a person — for example, a dog — is as strong a reason as a belief that one will avoid the same amount of pain for a person. Most people would not regard avoiding pain for a dog as providing as strong a reason as avoiding pain for a person, but some might. This disagreement is closely related to the disagreement about the scope of morality, that is, about who is protected by it.

24. See Nicholas Rescher, *Rationality* (Oxford: Oxford University Press, 1988), who seems to represent the majority philosophical view when he claims, "A rational person is someone . . . who endeavors to let all his proceedings be governed by . . . the strongest reasons" (10).

25. This point will be discussed in more detail in chapter 8, especially the section on cheating, and in chapter 13, "Why Should I Be Moral?"

26. But what Rawls meant by ruling out envy as a source of rational desires — that acting on envy never makes an otherwise irrational action rational — is correct.

27. It would have very little effect on my attempt to provide a justification of morality, that is, to show that all rational persons advocate adopting morality as a public system that applies to all rational persons, if the desire to harm others were listed as an irrational desire. If anything, it would make it easier to provide that justification. However, it would still allow it to be rational to be immoral, for most immoral acts are done for adequate reasons, either to benefit oneself or to benefit those for whom one cares. I do not list one's desires to harm others for no reason as irrational, because to do so would destroy the close connection between the rationality of actions and the rationality of persons. I do not see what is gained by listing them as irrational.

28. Sidgwick seems to have meant this in the seventh edition of *Methods of Ethics* (London: Macmillan, 1907) when he lamented the fact that there was no way to prove that one should follow morality rather than self-interest. Unfortunately, Sidgwick held the view that ethics was simply a matter of rational rules of conduct, so that he said that self-interest and morality were different methods of ethics, when what he actually held was that in cases of conflict it was equally rational to act morally or to act in one's self-interest.

29. "Nontrivial" applies not only to pain, but also to loss of ability, freedom, and pleasure.

30. For an excellent account of rationality as acting for the best, which presents a version of the "cool moment" account of rationality that rules out what I call irrational desires, see Nathanson, *The Ideal of Rationality*. Although an extremely plausible view, it still suffers from the mistake of regarding desires as reasons.

31. See chapter 11's discussion of motives and the morality of an action.

32. The explicit recognition that rationality and morality are parallel in this way is the result of several long conversations with my son Joshua. He is also responsible for several other changes in the account of rationality, including improvements in the definition of a rational action. For further discussion of the problems that arise when beliefs are considered to be reasons only when they are also motives, see his dissertation, *Different Sorts of Reasons: A Denial of the Force of Better Reason* (Chicago: University of Illinois at Chicago Circle, 1998).

33. Not "if and only if," for every fully informed rational person would advocate that any person for whom they are concerned not act in a mistaken way, that is, a way that would be irrational if they had sufficient knowledge and intelligence to be fully informed about the consequences of their action.

34. That certain representations are both prescriptive and descriptive is argued for by Ruth Garrett Millikan in her article "Pushmi-pullyu Representations," in *Philosophical Perspectives*, edited by James Tomberlin (Reseda, Calif.: Ridgeview Publishing, 1995), and *Mind and Morals*, edited by Larry May, Marilyn Friedman, and Andy Clark (Cambridge, Mass.: MIT Press, 1996).

Chapter 4

Goods and Evils
(Benefits and Harms)

Evils or Harms More Important Than Goods or Benefits

In most discussions of goods and evils, goods receive most of the attention. Indeed, sometimes evils are completely ignored, almost as if they did not exist. Theologians through the centuries have recognized that there is at least a seeming inconsistency between the view that there is an all-knowing, all-powerful, and completely benevolent God and the existence of so much pain and suffering. I use the term "evil" as it is used in stating this "problem of evil," that is, the problem of reconciling believing in such a God with the fact that there is so much evil in the world. Some theologians have even explicitly claimed that evils do not really exist. This view is, I believe, a central tenet of one branch of Christianity. There is no disagreement among theologians about what counts as an evil. Even those who deny the existence of evils agree about the sorts of things whose existence they are denying. They are agreed that if there really is pain, then there really is evil. Some of them are prepared to assert that there really is no pain; or that pain is not really something positive, but is a kind of privation. I shall not go into these theological subtleties. Pain is an evil. No rational person has any doubts on this matter.

To say that pain is an evil is not to deny that pain often serves a useful purpose. Pain provides a warning that a part of the body may need attention. Lack of the ability to feel pain in certain parts of the body is in fact a symptom of some diseases, such as leprosy. If a person does not feel pain, then he is likely not to take appropriate care and as a result might suffer serious injuries and even die. This fact about the function of pain is sometimes used in an attempt to solve the problem of evil. It is sometimes claimed that this is the best of all possible worlds and all the evils in it are necessary evils. Even if that is so, a necessary evil is an evil. I am not now concerned with showing the futility of all solutions to the problem of evil. I am only providing an account of evils. Pain is an evil. To use the fact that pain helps one to avoid death as a point in favor of pain only shows that death is generally considered an even greater evil than pain.

89

The claim that there are evils in the world needs no defense. Unfortunately, there is so much evil suffered in this world that many people look forward to the next world, which, at least for the deserving, has far less. Not all of these evils are caused by people, although they seem to be increasing their share consistently. But in this chapter I am only concerned with providing a general list of things that are evils and things that are goods and also in providing a definition of a good and an evil. It should be apparent that by an evil, I mean a harm, such as a pain, not an immoral action; similarly, by a good, I mean a benefit, such as pleasure. My discussion will differ from most philosophical discussions in that evils or harms rather than goods or benefits will receive the most attention. As Hobbes realized, evils or harms play a much more important role in morality than goods or benefits. The moral rules prohibit causing evils, and the moral ideals encourage preventing evils. Normally, promoting goods is not a moral matter at all. However, promoting goods for those who are deprived, that is, those who have too little pleasure or freedom, counts as relieving (preventing) evils and so counts as following a moral ideal. Causing loss of a good is causing an evil, so that a complete account of evils must also include an account of goods.

Definition of an Evil

Everyone agrees that death and pain are evils or harms.[1] In the previous chapter I pointed out that desires for pain or death are irrational desires. Since desires for death and pain are irrational desires and since death and pain are evils, it seems likely that there is a close relationship between the objects of irrational desires and evils. In fact, an evil or a harm can be initially defined as the object of an irrational desire. Defining an evil or a harm in this way provides a list of evils: death, pain, disability, loss of freedom, and loss of pleasure.[2] Everything on this list is regarded as an evil or harm. No rational person insofar as she is rational (this phrase is always to be understood when I talk of rational persons) desires any evil for herself without an adequate reason. But rational persons not only do not desire evils for themselves, they avoid evils for themselves, unless they have an adequate reason not to. That there are circumstances in which rational people do not avoid death, pain, or disability, and may even seek them, does not count at all against the view that these things are undesirable or evils. It only shows that people sometimes have an adequate reason for seeking to be harmed. An evil or harm is best defined as that which all rational persons avoid unless they have an adequate reason not to.

Some people are color-blind, and there are conditions in which even normal observers will not see yellow objects as yellow. This does not count against the view that some objects really are yellow. Whether a given object is really yellow is determined by making sure that it is in normal conditions and that those who are going to decide have normal vision. Normal conditions are generally those in which people usually see most things, but sometimes it is the conditions in which they normally see that object. Normal vision is determined by relatively simple tests in which, in normal conditions, people demonstrate their ability to discriminate between yellow objects and those of another color. With appropriate provisions for those who speak a different language there is nothing wrong with defining "yellow" as the color that people with normal vision in normal conditions call "yellow."

The objectivity of yellow is maintained by the proviso "people with normal vision in normal conditions." When all of these people in these conditions call a color "yellow," it is yellow. If normal people in normal conditions do not agree whether a color is yellow or not yellow, the concept of yellow is to that extent vague. In most cases, all people with normal vision in normal conditions agree on whether or not a color is yellow. This makes the concept of yellow a useful concept. It is also an objective concept; it does not contain, even implicitly, any egocentric terms, and a person can apply it sincerely but mistakenly.

The concept of an evil or a harm is as objective as the concept of yellow. Further, the concept of an evil is more precise than the concept of yellow. This should not be surprising. It is much more important to be precise about what is an evil than about what is yellow. All rational persons desire to avoid evils; they need have no particular attitude toward yellow. Defining an evil as that which all rational people avoid provides an objective account of evils, and yet not one that is independent of rational people. The definition makes it clear that all rational persons avoid evils for themselves, but it does not require that they avoid evils for others. No rational person inflicts an evil on himself unless he has an adequate reason, but some rational persons inflict evils on others without any reason, let alone an adequate reason. Indeed, an increasing amount of harm in the world is caused by some persons inflicting harm on others. Even so, not all harm in the world is caused by the actions of persons. Floods, earthquakes, disease, and so on still cause a significant amount.

Definition of a Good

Using the initial definition of an evil as the object of an irrational desire, it is tempting to define a good as the object of a rational desire. But unlike irrational desires there are two kinds of rational desires: those that are rationally required and those that are rationally allowed. Since rationally required desires are limited to desires to avoid harms, defining a good as the object of rationally required desires would limit goods to the absence of evils. This conclusion, although it is at least as worthwhile as defining evils as the absence of goods, is inadequate. More things are good than the absence of evil. To allow for positive goods, a good would have to be defined as the object of a rationally allowed desire. However, since rationally allowed desires are not shared by all rational persons, defining a good as the object of a rationally allowed desire does not provide an objective list of goods. Nonetheless, defining a good as the object of a rationally allowed desire does explain a common use of the word "good." On this definition what is good to one person need not be good to another, and indeed what is good to a person at one time need not be good to her at some later time. People commonly do call the object of their rationally allowed desires "good," and there is nothing wrong in doing so. I am concerned, however, with a concept of a good such that all rational persons agree on what is a good.

Since agreement on what is an evil stems from the fact that all rational persons avoid them, it might be thought that agreement on the goods might be reached by defining a good as what is desired by all rational persons. Since beliefs that one will gain greater ability, freedom, and pleasure are reasons, it is plausible that all rational persons must desire them. However, if one is not deprived, it is not irrational not to make any effort to gain a significant amount of additional ability, freedom, or pleasure. As pointed out above, all that is rationally required is to avoid the evils. People are not regarded as irrational if they do not take advantage of all opportunities to benefit themselves by increasing their abilities, freedom, or pleasure. There seems to be an asymmetry in rationality between seeking additional goods and losing the goods one already has.[3] It seems to be irrational to be indifferent to any nontrivial loss of ability, freedom, or pleasure, for this is the same as being indifferent to suffering a nontrivial harm. It is unclear how much effort must be made in order to avoid some evils, but if one is rational some effort must be made to avoid suffering any nontrivial evil, unless one has an adequate reason for not making such an effort.

Realizing that evils are avoided by all rational persons suggests defining a good as that which no rational person would avoid without a reason. In the absence of an adequate reason to do so, no rational person would give up or avoid any good. This suggests the following definition: *A good is that which no rational person will give up or avoid without an adequate reason.*[4] This definition yields a list of all of those things which are normally regarded as goods. Consciousness, abilities, freedom, and pleasure are the basic goods on this definition, for no rational person gives up or avoids these things without an adequate reason. To do so would be equivalent to causing a loss of ability for oneself or depriving oneself of freedom or pleasure without an adequate reason, actions which are clearly irrational. This results in parallel definitions of goods and evils. *In the absence of reasons, evils or harms are what all rational persons avoid, and goods or benefits are what no rational person gives up or avoids.*

This definition of a good, together with the list of basic goods, explains all of those things that are universally regarded as goods. Health is a good, for no rational person would give up or avoid health without an adequate reason. To do so would be to increase one's chances of an earlier death, pain, or disability, which is irrational. Wealth is a good, for to give it up or avoid it without an adequate reason would be to deprive oneself of the freedom to do or get the things money can buy. To give up or avoid knowledge is to give up or avoid an ability, clearly an irrational act unless one has an adequate reason. Although most rational persons desire health, wealth, and knowledge, whether one desires them or not, they are goods because no rational person will give up or avoid them without an adequate reason. (The phrase "without an adequate reason" should be understood from now on.) Many other goods such as love and friendship could be listed if my primary purpose were to compile a complete list of all goods. However, my primary purpose is to provide a correct understanding of the concepts of a good or benefit and of an evil or harm.

Everything that is a good or benefit seems to be related to the basic goods of consciousness, abilities, freedom, and pleasure, or to the avoidance of the evils or harms of death, pain, disability, loss of freedom, and loss of pleasure. Although it might seem that life itself is a good, all rational persons would give up life if they were in a persistent vegetative state, that is, if they permanently lacked consciousness. This suggests, correctly, I now think, that consciousness should be included in the list of basic goods.[5] Like the other goods, when people have a normal amount of consciousness, they do not usually seek additional consciousness, but they do not give up or avoid consciousness without an adequate reason. Moreover, some people do take drugs to attain what they regard as heightened states of consciousness, and this does not seem to be irrational even if they take some risk of suffering harms in taking the drugs.

Although temporary loss of consciousness, as in sleep, is not regarded by most as a harm, this may be due to the need for sleep to avoid other harms. Most people do regard sleep as good only because of its benefits, and sometimes even regard sleep as a necessary evil, especially if they need too much of it. This suggests that even temporary loss of consciousness, were it not for its capacity to prevent or relieve other evils, would be regarded as a harm, and hence that consciousness is a good. Further, it is usually not considered irrational for a person to want to stay conscious during a minor operation or dental procedure, even though what they are primarily conscious of is painful or unpleasant. It is even clearer that it is not irrational for terminally ill patients to seek to remain conscious, even if what they are primarily conscious of is also painful or unpleasant. For these behaviors to count as rational, temporary as well as permanent loss of consciousness must count as an evil. Thus, it seems to follow that consciousness is a good.

Personal Goods and Evils

In addition to providing objective accounts of an evil or harm and a good or benefit, another advantage of these definitions is that they allow for many things to be neither a good nor an evil. Everything that is not irrational not to avoid, but which it is also not irrational to give up or avoid, is neither a good nor an evil. Sticks and stones are neither good nor evil; neither is taking a walk, nor believing in God. Collecting stones is not the object of an irrational desire; nor is it irrational to avoid going stone collecting. Some rational people desire to believe in God; others desire not to. I call inherently evil only those things that it is irrational to desire; I call inherently good only those things that are irrational to avoid. I shall call those things that are inherently good, "personal goods," and those that are inherently evil, "personal evils."

I use the phrases "personal good" and "personal evil" to emphasize that a good is what it is irrational to avoid for oneself personally; an evil is what it is irrational not to avoid for oneself personally. Although there is a close connection between what I call personal goods and what philosophers have traditionally called intrinsic goods, the terms are not synonymous. Only pleasure has uniformly been considered an intrinsic good, though ability (especially knowledge), freedom, health, and friendship have also been considered intrinsic goods. However, wealth has always been considered an instrumental rather than an intrinsic good. Philosophers have rarely discussed intrinsic evils, although it is generally acknowledged that pain is an intrinsic evil. Further, the concept of intrinsic goods and intrinsic evils suggests that goods and evils can be characterized completely independently of the desires of rational persons. This makes it a mystery why rational people have such a uniform aversion to the evils and never avoid any of the goods.[6]

Although everyone admits that there is an extraordinarily close connection between goods and evils and the aversions and desires of rational people, some might object to defining a personal evil as that which it is irrational not to avoid and a personal good as that which no rational person would give up or avoid. Some might prefer to define rationality in terms of goods and evils rather than defining goods and evils in terms of rationality.[7] Others might prefer to define them independently. It is not crucial to my view which of these alternatives are chosen, as long as the relationship between rationality (irrationality and reasons) and goods and evils is recognized to be conceptual rather than contingent or empirical. If something is an evil, it is necessarily true that, unless they have an adequate reason, all rational persons avoid it. If something is a good, it is necessarily true that, unless they have an adequate reason, no rational person avoids it. Similarly, if all rational persons avoid something, it is necessarily an evil; if no rational person avoids something, it is necessarily a good.

As long as it is agreed that death, pain, disability, loss of freedom, and loss of pleasure are personal evils, and that consciousness, ability, freedom, and pleasure are personal goods, it is not important for my purposes whether one claims that it is a synthetic a priori truth that all rational persons avoid the evils and no rational person avoids the goods, or whether rationality (irrationality and reasons) is defined in terms of goods and evils or vice versa. What is important is that the items included in the lists are used to define either goods and evils or rationality (irrationality and reasons), and that there be a very close conceptual relationship between these concepts. I prefer to use the lists to define irrationality and reasons and to use these concepts to define the goods and evils, for this does not raise misleading ontological questions about the goods and evils. I do not see how these problems can be avoided by starting with goods and evils, unless irrationality and reasons are at least implicitly used to define them. However, if these ontological problems can be avoided, I do not think it is of philosophical significance which set of concepts is taken as basic.

Values

If, as seems plausible, what is good has positive value and what is evil has negative value, then some values are objective; that is, all rational persons will hold some things to have positive value and other things to have negative value. I find it difficult to find a philosophical use for the noun "value" that is not more clearly served by the terms "good," "bad," "harm," and "benefit" and related terms like "better" and "worse." I know that the term "values" is extremely popular now; people talk of "family values," "religious values," and "spiritual values." I find much of this talk confusing, and do not know what is meant by it. I think that I do know what is meant by "moral values"; they are those virtues that result in people acting in morally good and morally right ways. Moral values, like goods and evils, are objective values. Honesty, dependability, and kindness are traits of character that all impartial rational persons want everyone to have. Other traits of character, like courage and prudence, are virtues that everyone wants for themselves, whether or not they want others to have them.[8]

Perhaps "family values," "religious values," and "spiritual values" have to do with those traits of character that all impartial rational persons who favor a certain kind of family or religion want everyone to have. There may be good reason to believe that this kind of family or religion does result in significantly less evil being suffered. Members of that kind of family or religion may not only cause less evil for others, they may also suffer less evil themselves. If that is true, and if there are traits of character, in addition to the moral and personal virtues, that support that kind of family or religion, then those traits of character would be objective values. However, it may be that there is no agreement on any traits of character, other than the moral and personal virtues, that are favored by everyone favoring a certain kind of family or religion. Or it may be that there are no good reasons for favoring a certain kind of family or religion, so that it has no philosophical significance that all impartial rational persons who favor that kind of family or religion would favor certain values.

Social Goods and Social Evils

Philosophers have called that which causes a personal good, such as pleasure, an instrumental good, and that which causes a personal evil, such as pain, an instrumental evil. However, depending on circumstances, the very same kind of thing, such as a piece of pie (or an act, such as eating a piece of pie), may be both an instrumental good and an instrumental evil, because it gives one person pleasure and causes another person to feel uncomfortable. Thus, it seems that the categories of instrumental goods and instrumental evils are misleading, for having a category suggests that certain things (or acts) belong to that category and other things (or acts) do not. It is useful to have a category that includes all those things that by their very nature increase personal goods, even though they may contingently increase personal evils. And another category that includes all those things that by their very nature increase personal evils, even though they may contingently increase personal goods. I call those things that belong to these categories social goods and social evils. I use the phrases "social good" and "social evil" to emphasize that almost all of the things that belong in these categories are social in character.

The categories of social goods and social evils are best understood by providing a list of social goods and social evils. One of the greatest social goods is peace, for peace necessarily prevents personal evils. Education and medicine are social goods: the former increases knowledge, which is an ability; the latter decreases disabilities, as well as preventing and relieving pain. Everyone approves of those who seek peace and those who seek to improve education and medicine. Clearly, one of the greatest social evils is war, especially nuclear war, for war necessarily increases personal evils. Poverty and slums are great social evils. Thus, unless there are adequate reasons to act differently, everyone favors eliminating war, poverty, and slums.

The social goods and evils listed in the previous paragraph are uncontroversial: no one disputes that war and slums are bad and that peace and medicine are good. However, some other social goods and evils are more controversial. Science is a social good because, like education, it necessarily increases abilities. I am aware, however, that science has many bad consequences, such as more destructive weapons of

war. My claim that science is a social good is simply the claim that science necessarily leads to an increase in the personal good of knowledge, whereas its bad effects
are only contingent. This does not mean that the contingent bad effects are less important than the essential good effects, but since the bad effects are only contingent,
it should be possible to lessen, if not eliminate, those bad effects while still favoring
the scientific enterprise. One needs no reasons for favoring science but must provide reasons for being against it. However, social goods like science, education, and
medicine, may have sufficiently harmful contingent consequences that one can have
adequate reasons for limiting them.

Punishment is a social evil, for it necessarily involves the infliction of personal
evils. Since I favor punishment for serious violations of the moral rules, it should be
clear that in calling punishment a social evil, I am not recommending its elimination. However, it does mean that I realize that punishment needs to be justified, so
that if one cannot show that punishment has sufficiently beneficial consequences to
compensate for the evils that are necessarily caused, punishment is not justifiable. It
also means that insofar as alternatives to punishment that are not social evils can
provide equally beneficial consequences, they should be employed.

Earthquakes, floods, and hurricanes often cause great personal evil, but these
things do not necessarily affect people. Some floods, hurricanes, and earthquakes affect no one. This is not true of war and slums. When floods, earthquakes, or hurricanes cause great personal evil, they are called disasters or tragedies. War and slums
always cause personal evil, so that they are evils by their very nature. Nonetheless,
earthquakes, floods, and hurricanes often do cause considerable suffering, so that
scientific attempts to predict and control them in order to minimize the suffering
they cause are themselves social goods.

I use the phrases "social good" and "social evil" only for those things that have
only good consequences by their very nature and those things that have only bad
consequences by their very nature. I do not use these phrases to refer to anything
that has both good and bad consequences by its very nature, for I do not know of
anything that by its very nature has a greater balance of good consequences over bad
or vice versa. Thus I do not regard a government as either a social good or a social
evil, for it both provides security and deprives of freedom. I do not classify something either as a social good or as a social evil on the basis of the consequences that
it has only contingently. As I use these phrases, they are primarily of theoretical
significance in that they enable one to talk about some kinds of social institutions
without depending on a particular context. For practical purposes, the contingent
consequences of any social institution are often more important than its essential
consequences.

Personal and social goods and evils are things that by their very nature are good
and evil. It may be true that nothing is pleasant or unpleasant but thinking makes it
so, but it is not true that nothing is good or evil but thinking makes it so. What a
good is, or an evil, does not depend on the opinion of any person or particular group
of persons, but is an objective matter. I do not claim that every use of the words
"good" (benefit) and "evil" (harm) is objective. As noted earlier, there is a common
and correct use of "good" and "evil" by people to express their rationally allowed desires and aversions. However, even this use can best be understood as parasitic on the

objective use, as I shall attempt to show shortly. The objective sense of "good" and "evil" is the important one in morality, and most major philosophers have been concerned with this sense.

Better and Worse

The definitions of a good and an evil are such that though neither is defined in terms of the other, they are logically related to each other in the appropriate way. An evil is what it is irrational not to avoid without an adequate reason; a good is what it is irrational to avoid without an adequate reason. Nothing, therefore, can be both a good and an evil. All rational persons prefer goods to evils. This account of a good and an evil is easily extended to provide an account of better and worse. One alternative is better than another if all rational persons would choose it over the other, unless they had an adequate reason for not doing so. It is better to have a thousand dollars than to have only a hundred; better to have an opportunity to choose between five alternatives than to have the opportunity to choose between only two of them. One alternative is worse than another if no rational person would choose it over the other unless she had an adequate reason. It is worse to be disabled for two months than for only two weeks; worse to be deprived of freedom for ten years than for only five.

This account explains how one can be confronted with a choice of two evils, one of them worse than the other, or two goods, one of them better than the other, and why a rational person always chooses the lesser of two evils and the better of two goods. It also follows from these definitions that when confronted with two alternatives, one good, the other evil, the former is always better than the latter; the latter is always worse than the former. Rational persons do not always agree which of two evils is worse, or which of two goods is better. When confronted with choosing between increasing wealth and increasing knowledge, rational persons may make different choices. Especially since both wealth and knowledge have degrees, it is pointless to talk of knowledge being better than wealth, or vice versa. Similarly there will not be complete agreement among rational persons about which is worse, pain or loss of freedom. There are degrees of pain, to escape from which all rational persons would choose some loss of freedom, but complete agreement cannot be expected when different kinds of evils are involved. Death is usually considered the worst evil, for almost all rational persons are prepared to suffer extremely high degrees of the other evils in order to avoid death. But now, especially among those suffering from serious maladies, the other evils have become so great that death has come to be regarded by many as the lesser evil.

No Unique Ranking of the Goods and Evils

In a memorable phrase, John Stuart Mill maintained that "it is better to be Socrates dissatisfied than a fool satisfied."[9] Mill tried to support this by claiming that the pleasure of Socrates was of a higher quality than the pleasure of a fool. He made this claim because he was committed to the view that pleasure was the only good. If he were not committed to this mistaken view, Mill might have claimed that the goods of knowledge and other mental abilities were better than pleasure. Although my personal preference is the same as Mill's, I have to admit that it is merely a personal preference. All rational persons need not prefer increasing knowledge to gaining pleasure. Indeed, very few actually do. Since those who do are generally those who read philosophy, it is not surprising that Mill's view, although mistaken, has met with what seems like general approval.

One must be very careful in doing philosophy not to mistake agreement among philosophers for agreement among all rational persons. That the life of the mind has been considered by philosophers as the best life shows only that philosophers prefer the life of the mind. This is not surprising; one would not expect them to be philosophers if they did not. Persons who do not prefer the life of the mind seldom write philosophy books extolling their way of life as the best. But books have been written extolling a life of pleasure over that of knowledge. Rationality does not require emphasizing any one of the goods over the others, but, within wide limits, allows each person to have her own ranking.

Given this account of goods and evils, it should not be surprising that there may be nothing that all rational persons will agree is the worst of all possible evils, or the best of all possible goods. That there are several different kinds of goods and evils, not just pleasure and pain as the classical utilitarians maintained, has important consequences. It means that two persons, both rational and both agreeing on all the facts, even when they are concerned with the same people, may favor different courses of action. This can happen because they may rank differently the goods and evils involved. One may regard a certain amount of loss of freedom as worse than a certain amount of pain, while another person may regard the pain as worse. Within limits, it is rationally allowed to rank in either way. That there is not always a unique best decision, however, does not mean that there are not usually better and worse decisions.

The fact that when confronted with two evils or two goods it is often rationally allowed to choose either has had an extraordinary effect on some philosophers. They have concluded that when presented with any two alternatives, even if one is a good and the other an evil, rationality never requires choosing one of them. This is obviously absurd. When confronted with a choice between a good and an evil it is rationally required to choose the good and prohibited to choose the evil. Even in many of the cases where one is confronted with two goods or two evils, one choice is rationally required, the other rationally prohibited. It is clearly a mistake to hold that if rationality does not provide a complete guide, then it does not provide any guide at all.

However, all rational persons do not always agree on which consequences are better and which worse. Further, even if they agree on which are better and worse, they can still disagree on how to act. Disagreement on how to act can stem from differences about who will be harmed or benefited by one's action. One person may prefer to cause a greater evil to those she does not care about rather than cause a lesser evil to those she does care about while another person may choose to cause the lesser evil regardless of who is harmed. Although the latter is acting on the stronger reasons, it is not irrational to act on weaker reasons. Accepting rationality as one's guide does not require giving up any real freedom of choice. Rationality prohibits doing only those things that no rational person would choose to do. There are no real decisions to be made in which rationality requires one alternative over the other. No rational person even feels that a decision is called for when one alternative results in evils for everyone including himself and the other results in goods for everyone including himself.

Acting rationally and acting on the best reasons are not the same. Although someone acting on the best reasons is always acting rationally, the reverse is not always true. A person who has to choose between avoiding a lesser harm for himself and a much greater harm for others is acting rationally, no matter which choice he makes. In those cases where rational persons genuinely feel that a decision is called for, either alternative is always rationally allowed. A person dying of terminal cancer must decide if he wants to be kept alive or not. Both choices are rationally allowed. A talented young person must choose between medical research and a well-paying private practice. Again, both choices are rationally allowed. The lack of complete agreement among all rational persons on the relative rankings of the various goods and evils, and how these goods and evils should be distributed, does not show that there is not complete agreement on what is a good and what is an evil.

Good of Its Kind

This analysis of good and evil can be extended to particular things, like tools, by specifying the interests and qualifications of rational persons. A good tool is one that all qualified rational persons would select when choosing the tool for its normal use, unless they had an adequate reason not to. ("Qualified," "normal use," and the "unless" clause should be understood from now on.) A bad tool is one that all rational persons would avoid. One tool is better than another if all rational persons would prefer it. Thus two tools can be good, but one better; two tools can be bad, but one better; and naturally if one tool is good and the other bad, the former is better than the latter. This analysis works not only for tools, but also for anything that has a standard function or purpose, even athletes. Good athletes are those who are more likely to win or to help their team to win.

A tool may have several characteristics that are relevant to its performance, so it may not always be possible to decide which tool is best. Each tool might be better in one characteristic with no agreement on which combination is best. All rational persons may agree that A, B, and C are good tools, that D, E, and F are bad ones, and that A and B are better than C, without agreeing on whether A or B is better. Even when judging purely functional items, there will not always be agreement among all qualified rational persons. However, lack of complete agreement does not mean that there will not be substantial agreement. Reading through any issue of *Consumer Reports* illustrates this point very clearly.

Also, that there is no right answer to the question "Who was the best hitter in baseball?" does not mean there are no wrong answers. That there is no agreement on whether Babe Ruth, Ty Cobb, or Hank Aaron was the best hitter does not mean that there is no agreement that all three of them are better than 99 percent of all hitters, past or present.[10] The lack of complete agreement affects the objectivity of these judgments as little as the fact that normal people sometimes disagree about whether an object is yellow affects the objectivity of judgments about color. It is surprising how often people forget how limited are their disagreements in ranking players and teams as better or worse. From the fact that disagreements are more interesting to talk about than agreements and so are discussed more often, it is sometimes mistakenly concluded that the former are more common than the latter.

Aesthetic Judgments

Aesthetic judgments differ radically from judgments of functional items. This does not mean that no aesthetic judgments are objective. In judging such things as paintings, music, novels, or poems, all qualified rational persons who accept the same standards will undoubtedly reach substantial agreement. However, since works of art have no "normal function," qualified rational persons need not accept the same standards. The view that each work of art should be judged by the standards appropriate to it does not result in anarchy, for the appropriate standards will be determined by the "purpose" of the work of art. Those who believe that the only purpose of a work of art is to express the creativity of the artist will hold that there is a single standard for all works of art. However, if one accepts that a work of art can be designed merely to entertain, then, with some qualifications, it should be judged by how well it does that. It is also relevant for whom the work of art is intended. A children's book should not be written like a novel for intellectuals. As long as a work of art is judged on its own terms, generally determined by the intentions of the artist, I see no reason why aesthetic judgments should not be as objective as any other kind of value judgment.

However, when one says that certain kinds of paintings or music are better than others, then one reaches an area where judgment rapidly deteriorates into expression of preference. It is common for sophisticated composers to scorn popular music as inferior. Popular music can be composed with much less knowledge of music than is required to compose serious contemporary music. It does not follow that one who can compose good serious contemporary music can also compose good popular music. Nor does it follow that because something is more difficult to do, the result should be judged superior to something less difficult to do. Even the designation "great" is applied to performers who seek merely to entertain. Thus I see no point in ranking works of art that have different purposes, nor do I see how one can expect to reach agreement on who counts as a qualified rational person, nor on what counts as the appropriate standard by which they are to judge.

Judgments versus Expressions of Likes and Dislikes

All judgments using the terms "good," "bad," "better," and "worse" must be made on the basis of standards. These standards will always be related to the purposes of the things being judged. Sometimes this relationship will be indirect, as in the case of judging dogs. Dogs used to have certain functions and certain forms were characteristically associated with good performance of those functions. Standards for judging dogs developed using these forms as a basis. It must, however, be admitted that many standards are now almost completely conventional, the function that originally generated the standards having been forgotten long ago.

Although all judgments using "good" must be made on the basis of standards, this is more a comment on the concept of judgment than on the use of the term "good." For "good" is often used not in making judgments but in expressing one's likes, just as "bad" is often used to express one's dislikes. In calling a movie bad, someone may not be making a judgment of the movie at all, but simply expressing her dislike of it. Similarly when someone says that a meal was good, she may simply mean she liked it and be using no standard at all. However, even this use of "good" and "bad" is best understood when related to the objective sense of these terms. Since pleasure is a good, it is most natural to call that which gives one pleasure "good." Similarly, "bad" applies to what one dislikes, for the displeasure one feels is an objective harm.

It may be that it was concentration on the use of "good" and "bad" as expressing one's likes and dislikes that led those who put forward the emotive theory to deny the objectivity of goods and evils. They correctly pointed out that people differed in what they called "good." What gives one person pleasure may not give pleasure to another, indeed what gives pleasure to a person at one time may not give her pleasure at some future time. This is supposed to explain why good is not used in an objective way. But recognizing that even in these cases it is because a thing pleases her that a person calls it good, shows that the objectivity of goods and evils underlies even the seemingly subjective use of these terms. It is surprising how many people, including philosophers, have denied the objectivity of goods and evils without realizing that these concepts play a central role in defining other concepts, such as punishment, reward, and malady or disease, which are usually regarded as objective.

Punishment

Examination of punishment provides further support for defining an evil in terms of the list that I have provided. Punishment necessarily involves the infliction of an evil, though, of course, not all infliction of evil is punishment. A full account of punishment must include an account of the relationship between the person inflicting the evil and the person who suffers it. It must also include an account of why the evil is inflicted, such as that the person violated a law. I am not now attempting to provide a complete account of punishment; I am concerned only with the showing how the relationship between punishment and the inflicting of evils supports the present account of an evil.[11]

All of the evils on the list have been used as punishments. The death penalty is usually regarded as the most severe punishment, reinforcing the view that death is usually considered the worst evil. The infliction of pain used to be a much more common punishment than it now is, although some countries still retain flogging, and spanking is still used by parents. Since it admits of degrees, one cannot say that infliction of pain is more or less severe than other types of punishment. There are degrees of pain that may make death seem the lesser punishment, but some pain may be so light that one prefers it to any other punishment. Disabling has also been used as a punishment; for example, pickpockets used to have their hands cut off, and this punishment may still be used in some countries. The most common punishment is deprivation of freedom. It has many advantages: the longer one is deprived of freedom the greater the punishment, and there can be very precise gradations in the amount of punishment. It is fairly easy to administer, and, since it can be combined with other evils or even goods, it allows for great flexibility. The mildest form of punishment is generally deprivation of pleasure. This punishment is usually restricted to children.

All punishments involve one or more of the evils mentioned above. If one of these evils has not been inflicted on a person, then the person has not been punished. The suffering of these evils is so closely connected with punishment that some psychologists now talk of punishment whenever a person suffers an evil contingent upon performance of an action, even though the person may have done nothing wrong at all. The close connection between suffering an evil and being punished is also shown by the fact that even when a guilty person suffers an evil through natural causes, he is sometimes said to have been punished.

Since being punished involves being inflicted with an evil and no rational person wants to suffer an evil, it seems I must hold that it is irrational for a person to voluntarily confess his crime and willingly submit to punishment. But I do not claim that all people who confess are acting irrationally, so I seem faced with an inconsistency. But this inconsistency is only apparent. Those people who want to be punished for their actions, if they are not acting irrationally, have an adequate reason for wanting to be punished. These reasons fall into two broad categories. One is psychological: some people feel extraordinarily uncomfortable when they know they are guilty of some crime and are not punished. They submit to punishment in order to relieve themselves of these unpleasant feelings. The other reason I shall call moral: some people seek to be punished because they believe that by confessing they are making it more likely that less evil will be suffered by others. Generally, but not necessarily, one who has the moral reason will also have the psychological reason.

The fact that some people seek punishment for psychological reasons shows that punishment may benefit the one being punished; it does not show that this is why they are punished. That people sometimes benefit from being punished may have led Plato to claim that punishment is for the benefit of the person being punished. Even granting his theory that the health of the soul is more important than the health of the body, his view does not seem very plausible. It is hard to see how killing someone benefits him. Being made to suffer pain or disability benefits a person only insofar as it convinces him to act in ways that will not lead to further punishment. Being deprived of freedom or pleasure also usually benefits the person being punished only in this very limited fashion.

Examination of the actual administration of punishment shows quite clearly that it is almost never intended for the benefit of the punished. Although punishment itself is not for the benefit of the person punished, it is sometimes possible to benefit someone while he is being punished. This is not possible with punishments such as killing, and it is very unlikely with inflicting pain, disabling, and deprivation of pleasure. Depriving a person of freedom, however, may be combined with benefiting him. Rehabilitation of criminals is not a replacement for punishment, but it can go on during punishment. Even though rehabilitation should be a goal of punishment, it is clearly not the primary goal and in most instances it does not occur.

The strongest *motive* of most people for inflicting punishment may not be to make it less likely that people, including the person being punished, will perform the punishable action, but this is the best *reason* for punishment. Regardless of why most evils are actually inflicted as punishments, the only reason justifying that infliction of evils is the belief that the person being punished or others will be deterred from committing a punishable action. But punishment will not deter unless there is a significant probability that a person will be punished if he does a punishable action. This is why an efficient police force and judicial system is so important. As shown by sayings such as "This will put the fear of God in him [and others like him]" or "This will teach him [and others like him] to respect the law," talking about deterrence may lead one to think that this must be done by means of threats.

Although the justification of punishment is deterrence, rational persons have no interest in scaring people. They are primarily concerned with lessening the number of immoral actions. Fear may deter, but it need not be the best way to prevent future punishable action. Deprivation of freedom, since it can be graduated in both duration and intensity, allows great flexibility in preventing future punishable action. Deprivation of freedom by itself serves as a deterrent, but it can be combined with rehabilitation so as to decrease further the chances of one's committing a future punishable action. Unfortunately, the two rarely seem to be combined; on the contrary, imprisonment often seems to increase the chances of the prisoner committing further crimes upon being released from prison. Nonetheless, were a government to have a rational policy concerning punishment, rehabilitation would universally accompany imprisonment.

Rewards

Rewards, like punishments, are used to influence future behavior. Whereas punishment is generally used to discourage people from performing actions, rewards are generally used to encourage people to perform them. To give people rewards is to give them goods, thus providing them with reasons for doing the kind of action being rewarded.[12] The most common social reward is money, for reasons similar to deprivation of freedom being the most common punishment: flexibility, ease of administration, and ability to make very precise gradations. Rewards, like punishments, are often not primarily concerned with influencing the behavior of the person rewarded; they are often used to influence others who may be in a position to earn such a reward later. Like punishments, rewards require some prior behavior on the part of the person rewarded, but all that I am concerned with now is the relationship between rewards and goods. A reward must be the giving of a good or the removal or lessening of an evil, but in this context, I regard the removal or lessening of an evil as the giving of a good. Of course, the goods of consciousness and abilities are not normally used as rewards, but this is because one person cannot normally offer these to someone else.

That rewards are the giving of goods, and punishments always the infliction of evils, affects the ways in which they can be used to influence future behavior. If one wants to prohibit some kind of action from ever being performed, for example, stealing, it will be very difficult to discourage this kind of behavior by means of rewards. Suppose that one tries to do this by offering a reward every week to everyone who does not steal. If no one steals then, of course, there will be no further problem. But what if someone does steal, then what does one do, deprive him of his reward for that week? Suppose that the thief wants what he steals more than he wants the reward and so continues to steal. What is to be done now? Can one raise the general reward for not stealing so high that the thief will finally prefer to get the reward rather than steal? When dealing with any large group of people in anything like normal circumstances, this is impossible. One certainly cannot increase the reward only for the thief, for this would have the effect of encouraging everyone to steal at least once.

Clearly rewards are not suited for enforcing universal prohibitions. On the other hand, punishment is perfectly suited for this. Evil is inflicted only on the thief and can be increased if more discouragement is needed. Punishment also seems well suited when one wants to require everyone to perform some kind of behavior. One can inflict an evil on anyone who does not act in the specified way; for example, make a public declaration of loyalty. However, rewards might be equally suitable for encouraging this kind of behavior. Partly, it would depend on how important it was for everyone to act in this way. If it were not critical that everyone declare his loyalty, then rewards might be as good as punishment. However, if it were important that everyone perform the specified act, then punishment seems more suitable.

Rewards are best suited for encouraging behavior that one does not expect, let alone require, everyone to perform, for example, an act of heroism. It might be possible to encourage acts of heroism by punishing everyone who did not perform one when they had the opportunity, but this is far less suitable than rewarding those who do. There are a number of reasons why punishment is not suitable for encouraging heroic acts. First, it would lead people to avoid occasions for heroic acts. Second, it would force unnecessary action on occasions where there were several people who could perform the act. Third, given the character of most heroic acts, the punishment would have to be extremely harsh in order to encourage such action on the part of people not naturally inclined to do so. For those kinds of actions one wants to encourage, but not to require of everyone, rewards seem more suitable. For actions required of everyone, punishments generally are more suitable than rewards. For universal prohibitions, punishments are far more suitable than rewards.

That punishments are more suitable than rewards for those cases in which universal obedience is desirable is also related to the following difference between goods and evils. An evil is that which all rational persons seek to avoid, so that punishment will affect, at least to some degree, all rational persons. This is what is required for universal obedience. A good is only that which no rational person will give up or avoid, not that which all persons seek; hence there need be no good that will affect every rational person in the desired way. Some rational persons may be completely unmoved by the reward. Hence rewards are most suitably used only in those cases where universal obedience is not required.

This examination of punishment and reward serves to support the analysis of goods and evils in several ways. It supports the objectivity of goods and evils and provides empirical evidence that what I have listed as goods and evils is in accord with the normal view of the matter. It makes use of the fact that the definitions show that all rational persons seek to avoid evils, but that they do not all seek to gain goods. That punishments, rather than rewards, are always used when universal obedience is required, supports the view that all rational persons are motivated by threats of evils, but that not all of them are motivated by promises of goods. Since the moral rules are universal prohibitions of certain kinds of behavior such as killing and lying, it is not surprising that punishment is more suitable for preventing violations of moral rules than rewards. This is further evidence that evils are more relevant than goods to discussions of these rules.

Evils and Maladies

Further support for the account of an evil presented in this chapter is provided by an examination of the concepts of disease, injury, and other conditions of persons that lead them to seek medical attention. To suffer any of these conditions is to suffer a malady, which is a condition of an individual who is suffering or at increased risk of suffering an evil in the absence of a distinct sustaining cause.[13] For present purposes it is sufficient to note that an examination of maladies, including diseases, both infectious and genetic, injuries, birth defects, and headaches, in order to see what they all have in common reveals that they all involve suffering, or a significantly increased risk of suffering a nontrivial evil or harm. It is a necessary feature for a condition being classified as a malady that it involves at least a significantly increased risk of suffering an evil. This is not sufficient, for the condition must also be independent of the environment in certain ways, but here I am only concerned with the relationship between maladies and evils.

Death, pain, and disability are the three evils that are most clearly related to maladies. Any condition of a person that has the other necessary features of a malady, and that results in death, pain, or disability, or an increased probability of suffering them, is a malady. Cancer, malaria, a broken bone, and schizophrenia are all maladies because all of them result either in death, pain, or disability or a significantly increased risk of suffering one or more of these evils. The loss of freedom and loss of pleasure are also involved in maladies, but are less commonly involved than the first three evils. However, some maladies involve only these latter two evils, and if they were not included in the list of evils, one could not explain why the conditions that result in these evils are counted as maladies.

Someone who has an allergy has a malady. However, if he knows what he is allergic to, he may not suffer any of the first three evils, or even be at significantly increased risk of suffering them. Someone may move to Arizona to escape his severe allergic reactions to various kinds of pollen and be perfectly happy to stay there. Nonetheless he still has his allergy and so still has a malady. What evil does he suffer? He suffers from a loss of freedom. He is not free to leave Arizona. Someone who has a severe allergy to chocolate is not free to eat chocolate. This is true, even if he no longer has any desire to do so. A prisoner does not become free simply because he longer wants to get out of jail.

Loss of pleasure is a common symptom of many maladies, especially mental maladies such as depression, but usually it is not the only evil suffered. However, someone who suffers from a sexual dysfunction that prevents her only from experiencing pleasure also has a malady. Her loss of pleasure, if combined with the other necessary features of maladies, is sufficient to make her condition a malady. Someone who could not experience any pleasure, anhedonia, would certainly be suffering from a malady, even if she suffered none of the other evils. It is true that most maladies involve suffering or a significantly increased risk of suffering one of the first three evils, but some maladies do not. Allergies and some sexual dysfunctions show that loss of freedom and loss of pleasure, together with the other features, are sufficient to classify a condition as a malady. Thus all of the evils are involved in the definition of a malady, just as all of them are involved in the definition of a punishment.

Summary

In this chapter I have provided both a definition of a good and an evil and a list of the personal goods and evils. The definition of an evil as that which all rational persons will avoid clearly depends on the account of irrationality provided in the previous chapter. The definition of a good as that which it is irrational to give up or avoid also depends on that account of irrationality. In that chapter, I made it clear that the list that I used in defining an irrational desire, and which is now used to define an evil, might be formulated somewhat differently. One can have distinct categories for different kinds of pain and other kinds of suffering, such as anxiety. Loss of opportunity and loss of wealth can be listed separately from loss of freedom. Loss of freedom to act can be distinguished from loss of freedom to be acted on. However, all of these changes in the lists are stylistic; there is no significant disagreement about what belongs on the list, even if there are some disagreements on the best way to formulate it. Similarly, the list of what counts as a personal good can be formulated differently. Opportunity and wealth can be included as distinct goods, and health could be listed as a good all by itself. In this chapter I showed that death is an evil because it entails a permanent loss of consciousness. This led to the realization that consciousness should be included in the list of basic goods. I admit that my motives for formulating the lists in the way that I do are primarily aesthetic, cultural, and historical.[14]

The lists of social goods and evils can also be formulated differently. Nonetheless, there is no disagreement that war, slums, and poverty are social evils, and that peace, education, medicine, and science are social goods. That punishment is listed as a social evil is meant to show that, given the way the world is, some social evils may be necessary. Defining social goods and evils so as to include contingent consequences might be a more useful way of defining these categories if one's purpose were to provide a practical guide to political action; however, that would not yield a universal list of social goods and evils. Since I am trying to avoid any controversial empirical claims, I thought it best to define social goods and evils solely in terms of their inherent characteristics. Nonetheless, unlike the list of personal goods and evils, the list of social goods and evils I have provided is not complete.

It is primarily the list of personal evils (death, pain, disability, loss of freedom, and loss of pleasure), and also the list of personal goods (consciousness, ability, freedom, and pleasure), that I will make use of in the following chapters. These lists, which derive from the definitions of an evil in terms of what it is irrational not to avoid without an adequate reason, and of a good in terms of what it is irrational to give up or avoid without an adequate reason, coincides with almost everyone's view of what counts as an evil or harm and as a good or benefit. Examination of punishment and maladies shows that the list of evils does, in fact, explain the unity of these concepts; punishments and maladies must involve one or more of these evils. Examination of rewards confirms that all rewards involve the giving of goods or the lessening of evils. That the goods of consciousness and abilities are not normally used as rewards does not count against their being goods, for they are normally not the kinds of things that one person gives to another. But complete agreement on what is good and evil does not preclude disagreement on what is better and worse; rational people differ in their rankings of the goods and evils.

That morality is concerned with the lessening of evil explains why it is a mistake to focus on goods rather than evils when discussing morality. The close relationship between punishment and the moral rules also supports the view that evils are much more important than goods in discussing morality. It was, in part, the neglect of evils and the concentration on goods that made it impossible for previous moral philosophers to give an adequate account of morality, and in particular of the moral rules.

Notes

1. I realize "evils" does not mean exactly the same as "harms" and that "goods" does not mean exactly the same as "benefits." However, the primary function of both sets of terms is to refer to the items on the lists of goods and evils, and using both sets of terms eliminates any misleading connotation that might come from using only one of them. Further, using both sets allows me to contrast my view with the standard views more clearly.

2 For purely stylistic or aesthetic considerations, I shall now generally use "disability" in place of "loss of ability." Disability is the most common result of loss of ability, and loss of ability that does not result in disability is usually less serious. Nonetheless, unless the context indicates otherwise, whatever I say about disabilities applies to loss of ability.

3. The asymmetry between seeking goods and avoiding evils, plus the greater importance of avoiding evils, helps explain the fact that many people will make different decisions based on the same information presented in different ways. The greater salience of avoiding evils, though rationally based, may sometimes lead to confused decision making. For example, many people will refuse an operation if told the probability of dying is 5 percent, but will consent to it if told that the probability of surviving is 95 percent, and all of the other information is the same.

4. This means "knowingly" give up or avoid. Similarly, people only avoid an evil if they are aware that it is an evil.

5. It may have been the substitution of death for permanent loss of consciousness, that obscured the fact that loss of consciousness is an evil, and hence that consciousness is a good.

6. It should be clear that I do not regard the naturalistic fallacy as a fallacy. It is not an open question whether what all rational persons avoid is an evil and whether what no rational person avoids is a good. But, of course, "rational" is a normative term, so this may not count as a naturalistic fallacy. However, defining rationality by means of the lists would be regarded as committing the naturalistic fallacy and my view is that rationality must be defined by means of these lists. For the classic statement of the naturalistic fallacy, see G. E. Moore, *Principia Ethica* (Cambridge: Cambridge University Press, 1903).

7. See E. J. Bond, *Reason and Value* (Cambridge: Cambridge University Press, 1983), who holds this view and criticizes my definitions of good and evil in terms of rationality.

8. I call these traits of character, "personal virtues." I shall discuss the moral and personal virtues in more detail in chapter 11 on virtues and vices.

9. *Utilitarianism*, chap. 2, par. 6.

10. For those unfamiliar with baseball, the same point can be made by considering soccer, cricket, rugby, or any other sport in which evaluation is complex.

11. For a more detailed account of punishment, see my article "Moral Theory and Applied Ethics," *Monist* 67, no. 4 (October 1984): 532–548.

12. The removal or lessening of harms can also be rewards. Indeed, providing some goods to deprived persons is just lessening the harms they are suffering.

13. See K. Danner Clouser, C. M. Culver, and Bernard Gert, "Malady: A New Treatment of Disease," *Hastings Center Report* 11, no. 3 (June 1981): 29–37. See also Bernard Gert, Charles M. Culver, and K. Danner Clouser, *Bioethics: A Return to Fundamentals* (New York: Oxford University Press, 1997), chap. 5.

14. In another language, aesthetic and historical reasons may lead to a different formulation of the lists, including the fact that there may be more than five general categories. Nothing of philosophical significance turns on this.

Chapter 5

Moral Rules

Moral Rules Are Concerned with Kinds of Actions

Talking about moral rules is a convenient way of talking about those general kinds of actions that are morally required and prohibited, for example, keeping promises and killing. These rules can be stated in many different ways, such as "Killing is wrong" or "Do not kill." I have chosen the formulation "Do not kill," for it has the advantage that this is a common formulation for precepts that are taken to be moral rules, such as the Ten Commandments. Nothing of philosophical significance turns on the choice of this formulation; the same points can be made using other formulations, or even in talking about the general kinds of actions that are required and prohibited. However, the formulation I have chosen allows the points to be made in a simple and understandable way, without creating philosophical problems.

As pointed out in the first chapter, knowledge of morality is knowledge of what it requires, prohibits, encourages, and allows. Knowledge of the moral rules involves knowing what general kinds of actions are morally required and prohibited. Knowledge of these rules also includes knowledge that a particular action of this general kind might not be required or prohibited, that is, that these rules have exceptions. In order to save a life, it is not only morally allowed to do a kind of action that is generally prohibited, such as telling a lie, but it is morally encouraged to do so. However, common knowledge of the moral rules does not include explicit knowledge of those characteristics that all moral rules have and which distinguishes them from all other rules. In this chapter I shall attempt to make this knowledge explicit.

Defining Conditions of Moral Rules

Showing that moral rules, or at least the most important general moral rules, share a set of characteristics that distinguishes them from all other rules is providing the defining conditions for moral rules. This set of characteristics must be such that the rules can be part of a public system that applies to all rational persons, for the moral rules are part of morality and morality is such a system. (This point is discussed in more detail in chapters 8 and 9.) Whether these characteristics provide defining conditions will be tested by seeing if they distinguish between general moral rules and all other rules. They must include all clear examples of moral rules and must exclude all rules that are clearly not moral rules. Thus whether these characteristics provide defining conditions is tested by seeing if they provide the desired results. It would be futile to offer as defining conditions of general moral rules ones that either exclude "Do not kill" or include "The bishop may only move diagonally." What rules are ordinarily regarded as general moral rules (and what rules are not) must be used in order to arrive at the set of characteristics that are their defining conditions.

I am primarily concerned with general moral rules, those that mention only such a general kind of behavior that all rational persons might perform them or fail to do so. Unless I explicitly say otherwise, when I talk about moral rules, I mean general moral rules such as "Do not kill" and "Do not lie." Testing the adequacy of the definition of these general moral rules is similar to the test given to axioms in mathematics or logic. Just as the axioms are tested by seeing if they yield theorems known to be true, and do not yield theorems known to be false, so the definition is tested by seeing if it includes all the rules that are clearly moral rules and excludes all the rules that are clearly not moral rules. This still leaves open the possibility that, once a definition of moral rules has been provided, it will be of some help in deciding cases about which we were previously unsure. If the definition works well enough, it may enable a clearer and more precise formulation of the moral rules and show that a rule that was considered by many to be a moral rule is not a general moral rule and may not be a moral rule at all.

Providing defining conditions of moral rules that distinguish them from all other rules requires providing those characteristics a rule must have in order to be a moral rule (its necessary conditions) and a set of characteristics, such that if a rule has them, it is a moral rule (its sufficient conditions). These characteristics must also be distinguished from those characteristics which, though often associated with moral rules, are not essential characteristics. In other words, it must be made clear what characteristics a rule must have if it is a moral rule, and what characteristics one can deny a rule has, without being forced to deny that the rule is a moral rule. I am concerned solely with the logically necessary and sufficient conditions for a rule to be a moral rule. Denying that a rule has one of these logically necessary conditions while claiming it is a moral rule or claiming that a rule has the set of logically sufficient conditions while denying that it is a moral rule shows a lack of understanding of the concepts involved.

Of course, there may be no defining conditions of moral rules; that is, there may be no set of necessary and sufficient characteristics that distinguish moral rules from all others. Moral rules might simply have a family resemblance to one another; that is, there might be a number of different characteristics, none of them necessary, which, together with the common necessary characteristics, are sufficient to make a rule a moral rule. That there are some necessary characteristics cannot be doubted. Moral rules must be rules that rational persons can both obey and disobey. In this chapter I try to make explicit all of the necessary characteristics of moral rules, and to see if there is a set of characteristics that is both necessary and sufficient to make a rule a moral rule. To make explicit such a set of characteristics is to provide the defining conditions or definition of a moral rule.

Preliminary List of General Moral Rules

Some general kinds of actions are commonly regarded as immoral unless one has a justification for doing them; among them are killing, lying, stealing, committing adultery, breaking a promise, cheating, and causing pain. Someone who kills people, lies to them, and so on, and does so without an adequate justification, is commonly regarded as acting immorally. That a general kind of action is immoral unless one has an adequate justification for doing it is all that I mean by saying that there is a moral rule prohibiting that kind of action. Most people realize that moral rules have exceptions. They know that there is often a justification for doing the general kinds of actions prohibited by the moral rules. Philosophers seem to want to formulate moral rules so that they have no exceptions; unlike philosophers, most people correctly regard moral rules as those rules which it is immoral to violate unless one has an adequate justification for doing so.

Given this common understanding of moral rules, the following moral rules would be accepted by most people: "Do not kill," "Do not lie," "Do not steal," "Do not commit adultery," "Keep your promises," "Do not cheat," and "Do not cause pain." These seven rules will be discussed in great detail in chapters 8 and 9; now I am only maintaining that they are generally considered to be paradigm examples of general moral rules. Undoubtedly other rules could be added, but simply showing that these seven rules share a common set of characteristics that distinguishes them from all other rules would be interesting and significant. If, in addition, these defining characteristics show that these moral rules or some closely related rules are part of a public system that applies to all rational persons, then that would be extremely significant. Showing that, with appropriate qualifications, all rational persons would favor adopting such a system would be sufficient to count as a justification of these moral rules.

Formal Characteristics

First, I shall be concerned with what I call formal characteristics, those that do not specify the content of the rules. All seven of these rules apply to all persons who know them and can both obey and disobey them. For the general moral rules, with which I am most concerned, this includes all those who are morally responsible for any of their actions. To say that the moral rules apply to all moral agents means essentially the same as to say that they apply to all rational persons.[1] A moral rule applies to a person when it is appropriate to use a person's obeying or violating the rule as a basis for making a moral judgment on that act of the person. Thus the universality of the general moral rules requires that the rules must be such that rational persons in every society at any time in history might have acted upon them or broken them.

They must not concern the kinds of actions that rational persons in some society at some time could not have done. All who accept the seven rules that I have listed as moral rules believe that the kinds of actions prohibited by them were real possibilities to all rational persons in all societies at all times. With the possible exception of adultery and stealing there is no human society in which rational persons did not have a chance to commit the kinds of actions prohibited by these moral rules. Killing and causing pain are always possible, and given that every society demands some group activities and cooperation, it is obvious that opportunities to lie, cheat, and break one's word are ubiquitous.

This universal applicability distinguishes general moral rules from the rules of a legal system, which apply only to those within the jurisdiction of that legal system. Someone who completely understands a law and is capable of obeying it may still correctly say that the law does not apply to her. Someone who completely understands a general moral rule and is capable of obeying it cannot correctly say that the rule does not apply to her. An "amoral" person is not one to whom the moral rules do not apply, but only one who claims that they do not apply to her and acts accordingly. When considering general moral rules, no one does or should take that claim seriously.

It is an essential feature of moral rules that they apply to all persons who know them and can obey them. For the general moral rules this means all rational persons. Thus, knowledge of these rules cannot depend on some specialized knowledge known only to some cultures. Any rational person who is subject to moral judgment must know what the general moral rules require and forbid. Ignorance of these rules does not count as an excuse for not obeying them unless it counts against regarding the person as a moral agent. Although these rules are taught to children, this teaching consists in training them to follow the rules, clarifying how they are to be interpreted, and explaining how violations are to be justified. It is not providing them with knowledge of new rules in the way that we provide beginning players with the rules of a game. Thus, the commandment to remember the Sabbath day and to keep it holy is not a general moral rule, for it does not have this necessary feature of general moral rules. Many rational persons know nothing about a Sabbath day and keeping it holy. Indeed, they may not even have the concept of a week with seven days.

Particular Moral Rules

The claim that a rule is not a general moral rule unless the actions prohibited by it are open to all rational persons in every society may be inconsistent with including the prohibitions against adultery and stealing in the list of general moral rules. Even if there is some question whether the institutions of marriage and private property, upon which these actions depend, are present in every human society, this question casts no doubt on the wrongness of adultery and stealing. So it may seem that a general moral rule need not concern actions that are open to all rational persons in every society. It seems clearly false to say that if one society has no private property, then it would not be morally wrong to steal in any society. Similarly, it seems obviously false to say that if one society does not have the institution of marriage, adultery is not immoral in any society.

But I do not claim that no action is immoral if that kind of action could not have been performed by any person in any society. My claim is only that a *general* moral rule is one that concerns actions open to all rational persons in all societies at all times. It is not necessary for the rules against adultery and stealing to be general moral rules for adultery and stealing to be morally wrong. In addition to the general moral rules there are particular moral rules that apply to all rational persons in a given society. However, a particular moral rule is also a particular instance of a general moral rule, that is, it is a general moral rule applied to an institution or practice in a particular society.[2]

Particular moral rules share the essential formal features of general moral rules, they apply to all persons who know them and can both obey and disobey them, but unlike the general moral rules, this does not mean that they apply to all rational persons. If a society has the appropriate institutions or practices of marriage and private property, then members of that society know the prohibitions against adultery and stealing and can both obey and disobey them. So the prohibitions against adultery and stealing can be particular moral rules in those societies. That it is not possible to steal without the ownership of property, or commit adultery in societies without the appropriate practice of marriage, only shows that these moral rules are not general moral rules; it does not show that such rules are not particular moral rules. Similarly, the rule concerning the Sabbath might be a particular moral rule. It must, however, be possible to show that all violations of particular moral rules are also violations of general moral rules. Otherwise, the particular moral rules of a society might be completely unrelated to the general moral rules and morality would not be universal.

Driving while drunk is immoral, but obviously this kind of action would not be understood and could not be done in societies with no automobiles. Thus, the rule "Do not drive when drunk" is not a general moral rule in the sense with which I am concerned. It would, however, be appropriate to regard it as a particular moral rule. It is obvious that violations of this particular moral rule involve violations of one or more general moral rules. The general moral rules against killing and causing pain together with some facts known to everyone in that society, such as that driving while drunk significantly increases one's chances of killing and causing pain, explain why it is morally wrong to drive while drunk. Similarly, even if one decides that stealing and adultery are not general moral rules, analyses of the concepts of stealing and adultery may show that stealing and adultery involve violations of one or more general moral rules.

Other Formal Characteristics of General Moral Rules

From the formal characteristics of general moral rules listed above, together with the feature that they apply to all rational persons, it is possible to infer some other formal characteristics. A general moral rule is unchanging and unchangeable; discovered rather than invented. It is not dependent on the will or decision of any person or group of persons. These characteristics are obviously closely connected, for to say that these rules are unchangeable is to say that they cannot be subject to the will or decision of any person or group of persons. Since general moral rules apply to all rational persons at all times, obviously they cannot be invented, or changed, or subject to the will of anyone. Unless one holds the extremely implausible view that there is some particular individual or group that every rational person knows about, it follows that the general moral rules cannot depend in any way on knowing about any individual or group, including those mentioned in any scripture or religious writings. No adherent of any major religion holds that, prior to the moment that the teachings or scriptures of that religion were revealed, killing, causing pain, or lying needed no justification.

Although a general moral rule may have been first made explicit, articulated and promulgated by some one person or group at some period in history, they are regarded as having discovered the moral rule rather than having invented it. This is particularly true of all of the religions that put forward what they take to be moral rules. A plausible interpretation of the claim that these rules come from God is as a denial that the rules were invented or created by human beings. No religion claims that God created these rules at the moment they were revealed to the founders of that religion. Rather, it is universally acknowledged that these rules have existed as long as rational people have existed. The doctrine of natural law that was adopted by Christianity was clearly an acknowledgment of the universality of the moral rules. The attempt to show that these rules were also revealed by God in the Scriptures in no way conflicts with the view that these rules apply to people who have never heard of the Scriptures.

People knew that killing, causing pain, and lying had to be justified before anyone explicitly stated the rules prohibiting these activities. The analogy with grammar is fairly close; people knew how to speak grammatically before anyone explicitly stated the rules of grammar. To hold that someone invented a general moral rule requires holding that the kind of behavior that this rule prohibits did not need to be justified prior to the time the moral rule was invented. No one thinks that general moral rules came into existence at some definite moment in time. General moral rules have a status similar to the laws of logic. No one invents the laws of logic, though articulation of them, or perhaps discovery of them, may have taken place at some definite time or times. The general moral rules are not like the laws of logic in all respects; however, any account of general moral rules that makes them subject to human decision must be mistaken.[3]

Universality, Generality, and Absoluteness

Even though the general moral rules are completely universal in the sense described, it would be misleading to leave it at this. To say that these rules are universal means that they apply to all moral agents. In discussing the scope of morality in chapter 1, I emphasized that the application of the moral rules were limited to this class; now I am pointing out that a general moral rule cannot be limited to any group smaller than this class. If a rule applies to any group smaller than the class of all rational persons, it is not a general moral rule. But even particular moral rules share the most important sense of universality of the general moral rules in that they apply to all those who know the rules and can guide their actions by them. Both general and particular moral rules, unlike almost all other rules, apply to all those who know them and can guide their actions accordingly. For the general moral rules, that includes all rational persons.

In addition to applying to all moral agents, the general moral rules simply state what kind of action is to be avoided or done, where all rational persons know about that kind of action. In none of these rules is there any reference to any particular person, group, place, or time; they are completely general. These rules are to be obeyed impartially with regard to (at least) all those to whom they apply, that is, all moral agents. Within this class no person or group has any special status; all must obey the rules with regard to all. There is, however, some disagreement on who else in addition to moral agents are protected by the moral rules. This will be discussed in more detail in the following chapter on impartiality.

The compete generality of these rules explains why rational persons do not want them to be obeyed with no exceptions; everyone recognizes that circumstances must be taken into consideration. The rules prohibit doing those kinds of actions that cause harm or increase the probability of someone suffering some harm; however, in some circumstances performing one of these kinds of actions may prevent far more harm than it causes. The claim that the moral rules are absolute is a claim that one ought never to break any moral rule. Although some moral fanatics claim this, it has little support even from those who have some relevant religious views. Almost everyone is aware that there are circumstances when any rule can be broken without the person thereby doing anything immoral. Even killing that is done in self-defense is usually regarded as morally justified. Breaking a promise to save a life is regarded by all rational persons as more than morally justified; it is morally encouraged.

Hence one further characteristic of the moral rules must be mentioned that is often overlooked, namely, moral rules have exceptions. A person to whom a moral rule applies may in some circumstances intentionally, voluntarily, and freely break it and not be acting immorally. Physicians and dentists regularly cause pain to their patients, but since they do so with the patients' consent and for their benefit, no one thinks that they are acting immorally in the slightest. In these cases, as in many others, it is morally encouraged to violate a moral rule. Further, the moral rules may sometime conflict, so that it would be impossible not to violate at least one of them. In talking about the general moral rules, neither universality, applying to all those who know them and can guide their conduct by them, nor generality, simply stating the kind of action to be done or avoided, should be confused with absoluteness. All general moral rules have exceptions.

These formal features of the general moral rules are all compatible with the moral rules being included in a public system that applies to all rational persons. Their universality guarantees that the rules are understood by all rational persons; their generality guarantees that the rules concern behavior that is open to all rational persons. All that is necessary to show that these moral rules are part of a public system that applies to all rational persons is to show that it would not be irrational for any rational person to adopt a system containing these rules as a guide for his own conduct and to judge the conduct of others. To show this requires making explicit not only the formal features of moral rules, but also their content.

The Content of General Moral Rules

In the account of general moral rules given so far, nothing of significance has been said about the content of the rules. From what has been said so far, "Break your promises" could be a general moral rule. It is universal in the necessary sense, and it also has the necessary generality. An adequate account of the defining characteristics of general moral rules must provide some limit to the content of the rules. Almost all moral philosophers have tried to deal with this problem. Among the different answers, the most common seem to focus on the consequences of following the rules, such as, that moral rules lead to self-realization or to the greatest overall happiness. However, even the most casual look at the seven moral rules listed earlier in this chapter shows that these positive consequentialist accounts are inadequate descriptions. Moral rules do not require promoting good for oneself or for others. They do not even require preventing harm to others. Rather they require avoiding causing evils or harms.[4] It is not an accident that all moral rules can be stated as prohibitions.

The fact that moral rules prohibit causing evils or harms rather than requiring the promotion of goods or the prevention of harms has some unexpected consequences. For example, it makes plausible the Platonic view of a moral person as one who minds his own business. Of course, what will count as minding one's own business will depend upon the circumstances. A person who cheats is not minding his own business, nor is a person who fails to keep his promises. Although it is sometimes contrary to one's interests or desires to obey the general moral rules, obedience will usually not require doing some action which it is not one's business to do. Moral rules are therefore not quite so demanding as they are sometimes made out to be. It is ordinarily not a burden to obey them; they can generally be obeyed by doing hardly anything at all.

That it is not ordinarily a burden to obey the moral rules does not mean that it never is. Quips such as "Everything I like is either illegal, immoral, or fattening," make clear that moral rules may and often do conflict with one's desires and interests. Some philosophers have tried to minimize the significance of this characteristic by talking of true desires and real interests, but in any ordinary sense of desires and interests moral rules sometimes require action contrary to persons' interests and their desires. Although it is generally more conducive to satisfying one's desires and advancing one's interests to act morally, almost everyone would benefit from unjustifiably breaking a moral rule on some occasion. Speaking literally, most of the time, that is, most moments in a day, no one wants to break or would benefit by breaking, a moral rule. However, it is also correctly and commonly held that almost everyone at some time either wants to break, or would benefit from breaking, a moral rule unjustifiably.

Tests of Definitions of Moral Rules

All of the rules in the preliminary list of moral rules seem to have all of the characteristics, mostly formal, that have been discussed in the previous sections. Even the rules prohibiting adultery and stealing have them with only slight qualifications, namely, though these two rules apply to all who can know them and guide their conduct by them, this may not include all rational persons. It is not yet clear whether this set of characteristics is sufficient to define a moral rule, but it is useful in examining the adequacy of some proposed definitions. Before I set out my own definition, it will be worthwhile to examine these other definitions of moral rules. This examination will show that there is no simple definition that is compatible with the set of characteristics distinguishing moral rules from all other rules. The inadequacy of all of the commonly offered definitions is usually the result of overlooking the formal characteristics that almost everyone agrees that moral rules have.

The Religious Definition

One of the more popular definitions offered to distinguish moral rules from others is religious: moral rules are the rules given by God. This definition suffers from the obvious difficulty that different religions offer different rules that are supposedly given by God. Hence even if it were an adequate definition, it can never be known if it is satisfied. No one can ever know if the rules that are said to come from God really do so. It is also a consequence of this view that atheists cannot consider anything to be a moral rule. Further, not only atheists, but deists, or anyone who does not believe that God gave persons any rules to live by, would also be logically excluded from holding that anything is a moral rule.[5] Also, anyone who doubted that the rule against killing came from God would necessarily have to doubt that it was a moral rule. None of these consequences is true. Hence it cannot be a necessary condition for a rule to be a moral rule that it be a command of God.

The above argument says nothing about the actual origin of moral rules, only that being God-given is not a logically necessary condition for being a moral rule. The following considerations also show that it is not a logically sufficient condition. According to all religions, God gave rules that are not moral rules. Even the Ten Commandments, often called moral laws and which provide some paradigm cases of moral rules, contain rules that are not moral rules. As noted above, the commandment to remember the Sabbath day and to keep it holy is not a moral rule. Nor is it so regarded in Jewish law. Rather, it is addressed solely to those who accept Judaism as their religion. Serious consideration of this rule shows that it lacks a necessary feature of general moral rules, namely, that all rational persons know what a moral rule requires or prohibits. Unless they are aware of some particular scripture, many moral agents could not know that one day of the week should be distinguished from all the others and given a special status.

Accepting the claim that all the moral rules are, in fact, God-given does not require accepting that being God-given is either a necessary or a sufficient condition for a rule being a moral rule. According to all religions, God gave rules other than moral rules, so that further characteristics are still needed to distinguish moral rules from other rules. Thus being God-given is not a sufficient condition. That atheists can accept some rules as moral rules shows that it is not a necessary condition. Being God-given provides neither a necessary nor a sufficient condition for moral rules, so it is clear that a religious definition is inadequate. It is important to emphasize again that denying that being God-given is an essential feature of moral rules is compatible with accepting the claim made by many religions that God does explicitly require obedience to all moral rules.[6] The common insight of all religious thinkers who put forward various religious natural law theories, that is, who held that God engraved knowledge of the moral law in the hearts of all people, is that such knowledge is independent of knowledge of any particular revelation or scripture.

The Societal Definition

Another popular definition of moral rules commonly offered is social or cultural. It has been maintained that moral rules are those rules to which a society or culture demands obedience of all of its members.[7] However, this definition suggests that the original question, "What are the characteristics of general moral rules?" should be replaced by the question "What are the characteristics of the particular moral rules of such and such society?" This question seems to presuppose some form of ethical relativism. However, if all particular moral rules must have the formal characteristics of the general moral rules and their content as well, it would be an ethical relativism in name only. The particular moral rules of all societies would all be particular interpretations of general moral rules. I have no objection to this form of ethical relativism.

As the societal definition is normally put forward, moral rules need have none of the previously listed formal characteristics, and certainly need not have a content compatible with the general moral rules. According to this kind of definition, the only characteristic that is both necessary and sufficient for a rule to be a moral rule is that the rule be one to which a society requires obedience from all of its members. The plausibility of regarding it as a necessary condition of a moral rule that obedience by all is required by a society stems from the fact that all civilized societies require obedience to all the rules in the preliminary list of moral rules. Indeed, except for the rule concerning adultery, it is hard to imagine any society continuing for any significant period of time without prohibitions on killing, lying, cheating, and so on, at least with regard to other members of the society. However, no one thinks that a rule ceases to be a moral rule if a society ceases to require obedience by all. Indeed, it is generally taken as a serious moral criticism of a society that it does not require all of its members to obey all the moral rules. Thus, being enforced by society is not regarded as a necessary condition for a rule being a moral rule.

It is almost superfluous to show that obedience by all being required by society is not a sufficient condition for a moral rule. Everyone is aware that all civilized societies require everyone to obey rules that are not moral rules. No one maintains that all laws, including traffic laws, are moral rules, and yet obedience to laws is required of all. Moreover, obedience to laws is required even for laws that are regarded as immoral, for example, the old apartheid laws of South Africa. That the law is immoral is used as grounds for holding that the government should no longer enforce it. Hence, even if it were a necessary condition for being a moral rule that obedience by all is required by the society, it would not be a sufficient one. Those rules to which society requires impartial obedience by all and that are moral rules would still have to be distinguished from those that are not.

The claim that all and only those rules to which their society demands obedience by all members count as moral rules is as inadequate as the claim that all and only those rules that have been commanded by God count as moral rules. Just as it is compatible with the claim that God, in fact, requires obedience to all of the moral rules, that being God-given is neither a necessary or sufficient condition of a rule being a moral rule, so even if every society enforced all of the moral rules, that would not make being enforced by a society either a necessary or a sufficient condition for a rule to be a moral rule. In fact, it is very likely that most societies do enforce obedience to all of the moral rules, at least with regard to members of their own society.

The Universal Obedience Definition

The two popular definitions discussed in the previous sections were inadequate because they did not necessarily include those features, both formal and of content, that all moral rules have. Similarly, in showing the inadequacy of some philosophical definitions, I do not take them as necessarily including these features. I present them, perhaps misleadingly, as simple definitions in which the characteristic used in the definition is taken, by itself, as sufficient to make a rule a moral rule. However, those proposing the definition may hold that the characteristic is sufficient, because having this characteristic entails that moral rules have all of the required formal and content features.

One common philosophical definition is that a moral rule is any rule that any individual wants universally obeyed. Stated in this way, this definition does not even require that the individual be rational. On this account "Do not walk on the cracks in sidewalks" might be one's only moral rule. Or even worse, "Kill yourself in the most painful fashion possible" might be one's only moral rule. These consequences are so absurd that the fact that this account allows each person to have her own set of continually changing moral rules seems almost a minor objection. Even if this account is modified by requiring that the individual be rational, it does not help much. "Do not study philosophy" is a rule that a rational individual could want universally obeyed. This proposed definition, even as modified, has the effect of denying that there is any distinction between moral rules and all other rules, hence it is obvious that it cannot be an adequate definition.

However, slightly modifying the condition so that a moral rule must be a rule that a rational individual puts forward as a rule to be universally obeyed, yields a very plausible necessary condition. Although some philosophers have put forward this characteristic as both a necessary and a sufficient condition, it is not plausible as either if it requires a rational person to put the rule forward as a rule that he, himself, must obey. Holding this view would result in hypocrites not being able to put forward any rule as a genuine moral rule. Further, to be plausible, putting forward a rule to be universally obeyed must mean putting it forward to be obeyed by everyone unless a person has an adequate justification to violate it. It is not a necessary condition for a rule to be a moral rule that a rational person puts it forward to be obeyed absolutely, that is, without exceptions. On the contrary, no rational person wants any of the preliminary list of moral rules put forward to be obeyed without exception. Indeed, given the complexity of the world, no rational person wants any simple general rule put forward to be obeyed without exception. Unfortunately, many philosophers have claimed that no person can consider any rule to be a moral rule unless she is committed to obeying it. Further, they have regarded "genuine moral rules" to have no exceptions.[8] This results in a moral rule being so complex as to be unstatable. However, when properly modified and interpreted, the claim that a moral rule must be one that a rational person wants universally obeyed does something that neither of the popular accounts does: it provides a necessary condition for a rule being a moral rule.

The Utilitarian Definition

Probably the most well-known philosophical definition of moral rules is that suggested by those who put forward rule utilitarianism.[9] This definition may be stated as follows: A rule is a moral rule if and only if universal obedience to it would promote the greatest happiness.[10] Taken literally, universal obedience to the rule "Improve your sexual technique" would give greater pleasure to one's sexual partner and so would undoubtedly increase the pleasure in the world by vast amounts.[11] I do not think, however, that anyone regards such a rule as a moral rule. Thus it is clear that the utilitarian definition is not a sufficient condition of moral rules and hence cannot be an adequate definition of moral rules.

More significant, the utilitarian formulation of the definition requires that moral rules be exceptionless. However, none of the rules on the preliminary list of moral rules is exceptionless, so that none of these rules would count as moral rules. If each exception is built into the rule, it becomes unknowable, and knowledge of the rule must continually change as new exceptions are discovered. However, it is a formal feature of moral rules that everyone knows them. General moral rules must have exceptions; however, I do not know of any rule utilitarians who have provided an adequate procedure for determining justified exceptions to the moral rules. If an exception is justified if and only if it results in better overall consequences, rule utilitarianism collapses into act utilitarianism, and act utilitarianism does not even regard violating moral rules as needing any special justification. Rule utilitarians claim that these indefinitely long moral rules are justified if universal obedience to them would result in the greatest balance of pleasure over pain, but no one has ever provided an actual example of such a rule. No one has done so because it is impossible to provide an example of a rule such that it is even plausible that no change in it would result in better consequences if universally obeyed. It is ironic that utilitarianism, which is usually taken as the most straightforward and precise account of morality, actually has an account of moral rules that makes them ineffable.

A Negative Utilitarian Definition

A more promising definition of moral rules is the following: A rule is a moral rule if widespread violation of the rule would lead to bad consequences. Certainly the consequences of widespread violation of the rules against killing, stealing, or lying would have bad consequences, so that this definition includes what are normally considered to be moral rules. It also excludes some rules that are not considered to be moral rules. Widespread violation of the rule "Do not step on the cracks in side-walks" would not have bad consequences. However, although this definition in-cludes all of the moral rules and excludes many nonmoral rules, it does not exclude some rules that are clearly not moral rules. "Do not stand on your head all day" is a rule that, if widely disobeyed, would have bad consequences, yet it is not a moral rule. Thus the proposed definition does not adequately distinguish moral rules from all other rules.

This definition does, however, suggest another necessary condition. But in order for this characteristic to actually provide a necessary condition, it must be modified. A rule can be a moral rule if no bad consequences would result from widespread vi-olation of it, if all of these violations are justified. The formulation of the necessary condition must take into account that it is unjustified violations of moral rules that generally cause harm, and so the formulation must claim that a necessary condition of a rule being a moral rule is that bad consequences would result from widespread unjustified violations of it. Thus it is similar to the necessary condition that devel-oped from the universal obedience definition, namely, that a moral rule must be a rule that a rational individual wants put forward as a rule to be universally obeyed unless a person has an adequate justification to violate it. In fact, these two condi-tions fit very nicely together. That bad consequences would follow from widespread unjustified violations of a moral rule explains why a moral rule is one that a rational person puts forward to be universally obeyed unless a person has an adequate justifi-cation to violate it. Thus two of the philosophical definitions, when properly modi-fied, do provide necessary conditions for rules to be moral rules.

Definition Must Contain Features
Shared by All Moral Rules

The inadequacy of all of the simple definitions discussed above does not prove that there can be no simple adequate definition, but it does make it seem a reasonable hypothesis. Rather than offering another simple definition, I shall use the features shared by all of the commonly accepted moral rules to provide the defining condi-tions of moral rules. Since moral rules may be distinguished from all other rules by the attitude that rational persons take toward them, I shall also examine the attitude that rational persons take toward these rules. It is an essential feature of a moral rule that a certain attitude is taken toward it, so it is not out of place to include this atti-tude in the defining conditions of a moral rule.

Acting in Accordance with a Rule
versus Following a Rule

Distinguishing between acting in accordance with a rule and following it makes it easier to express an important difference between moral rules and most other guides to conduct. Acting in accordance with a rule simply means not violating it and does not require that the rule influence one's acting in accordance with it. Following a rule is not merely acting in accordance with the rule, it involves guiding one's action by the rule. Everyone is required to act in accordance with the moral rules at all times unless they have a justification for violating them. Acting in accordance with moral rules is usually done with no thought of them at all. Most of the time one never even considers whether one should break a moral rule. In fact, it would normally be worse than pointless to violate moral rules more than a small fraction of the time.

Everyone is required to act in accordance with moral rules whenever they have no justification for not acting in accordance with them. All violations of a moral rule need to be justified. There is no similar requirement to act in accordance with those general precepts encouraging people to prevent or relieve the suffering of evil or harm, the moral ideals. Nor is there a requirement to act in accordance with those precepts that encourage the promotion of good, the utilitarian ideals. Failing to act in accordance with moral or utilitarian ideals does not usually require any justification. Further, people do not usually merely act in accordance with these ideals; rather, they follow them.

It is not surprising that rules that are prohibitions of general kinds of actions are the kind of rule that people are most likely simply to act in accordance with rather than to follow. For most people it is very rare that they are tempted to kill someone, so that it is very rare that they consciously follow the rule against killing and decide to refrain from killing. Rather, they almost always simply act in accordance with the rule against killing; they simply do not kill. Although people may be tempted to lie, cheat, or steal somewhat more often than they are tempted to kill, it is still relatively rare that not lying, cheating, or stealing is the result of consciously refraining from doing so. Most often, one simply does not lie, cheat, or steal. This may partly explain why Kant says that one does not deserve any moral praise for simply acting in accordance with the moral rules. When a moral rule imposes a positive requirement, such as the requirement to keep one's promises, it is far more likely that people follow the rule rather than simply act in accordance with it.

"Promote Pleasure" Is Not a General Moral Rule

That everyone is required to act in accordance with general moral rules all of the time supports the view about the content of general moral rules, that they demand only that one avoid causing harm, not that one promote good. Neither "Promote pleasure" nor "Increase the balance of pleasure over pain" have this formal characteristic of general moral rules. For example, with regard to the rule "Do not cause pain" and all other general moral rules, the question "When should one obey these rules?" should not be taken as a question about time. The answer "Always," followed perhaps by a statement about justified exceptions, is not an answer about time. It would be a joke to answer this question by listing a certain time of day, or year, or even by giving a certain proportion of time, for example, 10 percent of your waking hours. Time per se has no relevance to general moral rules. There is no proportion of time when one need not obey the moral rules, nor is there any particular time of day or night at which they do not apply.

However, when the precept "Promote pleasure" is being considered, questions about time are relevant. The question "When should one obey the precept 'Promote pleasure'?" cannot be answered correctly by "Always," nor can one make it correct by adding a statement about exceptions. When this question is asked of the precept "Promote pleasure," time per se is relevant. This question could be answered quite plausibly by citing a certain proportion of one's time that should be devoted to following it. People have, in fact, said things strikingly like this: for example, "Spend an hour every day trying to make life more pleasant for those around one." It also would be understandable if one listed certain particular times of the day or year — such as every Sunday morning — when one should obey the precept.

Another question that shows an important difference between general moral rules and the precept "Promote pleasure" is the question "Toward whom should one obey the rule?" With regard to general moral rules, insofar as this question makes sense, it is a question about the scope of the moral rules, about what group of beings is protected by the moral rules. Within this group, one is required to obey the rules impartially with regard to everyone. This is possible because moral rules do not generally require positive action, but only the avoidance of certain kinds of actions. If one is not killing, one is not killing anyone, and so on for all other general moral rules, including the rule prohibiting breaking promises. Even keeping a promise with regard to one individual is normally compatible with not breaking a promise with regard to anyone else. When one acts in accordance with these rules, one can act in that way with regard to everyone impartially.

With the precept "Promote pleasure," the question "With regard to whom should one obey the rule?" is not so easily answered, even when talking only about those protected by the moral rules. There can be genuine disagreement with regard to whom one should obey this rule. As noted above, one is sometimes advised to promote the pleasure of those around one. Some may claim that the precept should be primarily followed with regard to those in one's local community. Others might say that it should be followed with regard to everyone in one's country. Still others might say that it should be treated like a moral rule and followed with regard to everyone protected by the moral rules. However, since promoting pleasure requires positive action, one must be doing something that actually promotes the pleasure of everyone. Even if "everyone" is taken to mean everyone in one's local community, let alone everyone in one's country, it is humanly impossible to be following the precept with regard to everyone. However, with regard to all of the moral rules, doing nothing is often compatible with acting in accordance with the rule with regard to everyone, not only in one's country but in the whole world.

Another point, closely related to the previous one, can be raised to distinguish "Promote pleasure" from general moral rules. Moral rules protect all persons equally. The question "Should the rule be obeyed impartially?" must be answered positively. However, when the question is asked of the precept "Promote pleasure," the answer is not obvious. As already noted, it could be held that this rule should be followed primarily with regard to those in one's local community. This answer suggests that the precept should be followed more with regard to those in one's local community, even if some regard should be given to those outside. This precept, unlike moral rules, does not require that everyone be treated equally, nor does anyone actually follow it impartially.

These considerations show that the precept "Promote pleasure" differs from general moral rules in significant ways. Whereas, ignoring the question of justified exceptions, moral rules are to be impartially obeyed with regard to everyone protected by the rules, the precept "Promote pleasure" is not and should not be followed impartially with regard to everyone protected by the moral rules. It is not only possible but relatively easy to obey all moral rules all of the time, but it is humanly impossible to follow the precept "Promote pleasure" all of the time. These considerations are all very closely connected to the fact that all general moral rules are or can, with no change in content, be stated as prohibitions on actions. Obeying these rules at all times impartially with regard to everyone is accomplished simply by not breaking them at any time with regard to anyone. The precept "Promote pleasure" demands positive action, hence the impossibility of following it at all times with regard to everyone equally or impartially. A precept that can never be obeyed impartially with regard to all those protected by morality is not a moral rule.

General moral rules require people not to cause harm to anyone protected by morality; they do not require people to promote the general good. Any account of moral rules that characterizes them as leading to the greatest good, or even as being for the good of everyone alike, is seriously misleading. It is not the promoting of good but the avoidance of causing evil or harm that characterizes the moral rules. Of course, if a rule is for the good of everyone alike, it cannot allow causing evil or harm to anyone; hence the plausibility of regarding moral rules as rules that are for the good of everyone alike. But a rule that would simply promote the good of everyone alike, even one that had the formal characteristics of a moral rule, would not be a moral rule. It is not easy to think up such a rule, but the following seems to fit the description: "Greet people with a smile." This rule seems to meet all of the formal requirements of a moral rule. It is both universal and general. It applies to all rational persons. It mentions no person, group, time, or place. However, it would not be regarded as a general moral rule because of the fact that it requires the promotion of good, not merely the avoidance of causing evil or harm. That the moral rules do not require promoting of goods, only avoiding causing evils, has significant consequences for what counts as a general moral rule.

Preventing Evils versus Promoting Goods

It is a universally accepted criticism of some forms of utilitarianism that it would allow the infliction of significant pain on one person in order to promote a great amount of pleasure for many others if a sufficiently large number will receive the pleasure. This criticism of utilitarianism depends on there being a morally significant difference between a good like pleasure and an evil like pain, for the argument does not have the same force when preventing evil is substituted for promoting good. It is not obviously wrong to allow the infliction of significant pain on one person in order to prevent a greater amount of pain for many others if a sufficiently large number will avoid the pain.

Suppose if a plague is not stopped, it will result in countless painful deaths. Suppose, further, that the circumstances are such that only by causing a painful death to an innocent person can the plague be stopped. Although one might cringe at taking such a step oneself, it may be morally justifiable to cause such a painful death in order to prevent a harm of the same kind to a sufficiently large number of others, say, in the millions. Alyosha's answer to Ivan in *The Brothers Karamazov*, that he would not kill one innocent baby in order to produce a perfect world, is not obviously the morally right answer. If one considers the countless number of innocent babies who die in the world today, let alone the other evils suffered by almost all of humankind, it seems as if one would be a moral coward if one failed to take the opportunity presented to Alyosha. Strict deontologists who hold that no amount of harm prevented justifies causing significant harm to one unconsenting innocent person can plausibly claim that the situation presented to Alyosha is not a real one.

However, during terrible times such as a war or plague there seem to be situations where enough evil will be prevented to innocent others to make it justifiable to cause a significant evil to an unconsenting innocent person. But in order for it to be justifiable to cause significant harm to an innocent person, the difference between the harm caused and the harm prevented must be far greater than that proposed by act utilitarians. Although these situations are not merely science fiction situations, they are rarer than is usually claimed. The proposed position of the strict deontologists has much to recommend it, and if forced to choose between it and that of act utilitarians, it should be chosen. However, neither of these positions need be accepted; there is a middle position, that put forward by common morality, which is superior to both of them.

As noted above, some consequentialists even seem to hold that gaining significant benefits for sufficiently many people may justify causing some significant harm to an unconsenting innocent person. No strict deontologist accepts this. While strict deontologists are correct when talking about individuals in their relationship to each other, they do not seem correct when governments are involved. Taking money by taxation is often regarded as a significant harm, and some tax money is spent on promoting culture and the arts. The classical utilitarians, Bentham and Mill, were primarily concerned with the actions of governments, and their view is far more plausible than that of contemporary utilitarians who make similar claims about individual persons. Why the situation is different for governments and how great the benefits need to be in order for a government to justify causing harm to an unconsenting innocent person will be discussed in chapters 9 and 14.

Strict deontologists are correct that it is not justifiable for an individual to cause significant harm to one person in order to promote goods, no matter how many are benefited. No consequentialist has provided a plausible way of comparing goods and evils such that if it is justifiable to cause some harm in order to prevent greater harm, there is some equivalent amount of good that also justifies causing that harm. It is only because consequentialists, like most moral theorists, have never gone beyond a schematic account of morality that they think it unimportant to distinguish between promoting good and preventing evil. However, any attention to the actual details of common morality shows that the distinction between promoting good and preventing evil is a significant moral distinction.

Avoiding Causing Harm versus Preventing Harm

In addition to distinguishing between promoting goods and preventing evils, it is also necessary to distinguish between avoiding causing evil and preventing evil. Since the precept "Prevent evil" demands positive action, it can not be a general moral rule for the same reasons advanced against regarding the precept "Promote pleasure" as a general moral rule; namely, no one can, so no one can be required to, follow the precept all of the time with regard to everyone equally. Preventing harms, however, often provides a justification for an individual person to break a moral rule, even without the consent of the person toward whom one is violating the rule. In this respect preventing harms has a moral relevance that promoting goods does not. Because moral rules only require that one avoid causing harm, precepts that encourage preventing harm cannot be classified as moral rules, but that preventing evil or harm is obviously a moral matter explains why I call those precepts that encourage preventing harms *moral ideals*. The precepts that encourage promoting good, I call *utilitarian ideals*. Both kinds of ideals will be discussed in more detail in chapter 10.

Specifying the content of moral rules as prohibiting doing those kinds of actions that cause, or increase the probability of causing, people to suffer harm, makes clear that there is always a reason for following these rules. That following moral rules involves avoiding causing others some harm makes it plausible that it would not be irrational for anyone to follow the moral rules. Further, the universality of the general moral rules makes it plausible that they could be known by all rational persons. Examining the preliminary list of general moral rules reveals a set of characteristics that enables these moral rules to be included in a public system that applies to all rational persons. These same characteristics also make it plausible that all rational persons who use only rationally required beliefs would favor adopting a system containing these rules as a public system that applies to all rational persons. The details of how the rules fit into such a public system will be examined in chapters 7 and 8. In the remainder of this chapter I shall show how the characteristics of the preliminary list of moral rules results in all rational persons taking a certain attitude toward these rules. This attitude is another feature that allows general moral rules to be distinguished from all other precepts.

The Attitude of Rational Persons toward Moral Rules

One defining characteristic of moral rules is that they prohibit those kinds of actions that harm people or increase their probability of being harmed. A second defining characteristic of general moral rules is that all rational persons who use only rationally required beliefs favor all people always acting in accordance with them and are prepared to enforce obedience by punishing unjustified violations.[12] These two characteristics, by themselves, result in all of the preliminary list of moral rules being counted as general moral rules. They also exclude all of those rules, such as rules of games, that are obviously not general moral rules. Only those rules that have all of the content and formal features presented earlier are rules that all rational persons would favor everyone always acting in accordance with. And only with regard to these rules would all rational persons be prepared to punish unjustified violations.

In order for all rational persons to take the attitude toward a rule that all unjustified violations may be punished, the rule must be universal, general, and have all of the other features that follow from these two. Further, rational persons would only take this attitude toward rules with a certain content. They would not take this attitude toward rules that require committing harmful actions, such as "Kill all unbelievers." Regarding this attitude of all rational people as a defining condition also excludes trivial or insignificant rules, such as "Do not cut your hair" as general moral rules. Nonetheless, accepting these defining characteristics does allow for the discovery of a general moral rule that had not been previously formulated. Further, a general moral rule, as normally formulated, may not have the all of the required features, so that some reformulation of the moral rules is possible. However, talking about a general moral rule is talking about those general kinds of actions that are required or prohibited. Everyone agrees that not doing one of these required actions, or doing one of these prohibited actions, is immoral if one does not have a justification. Thus there will be no surprising new moral rules.

Most of the defining characteristics I have listed are purely formal. They simply make clear what is meant by the universality and generality of moral rules. The universality of moral rules means that they apply to all and only those who know them and can guide their actions by them. Given that all moral agents know them and can guide their actions by them, this means that they apply to all those who are held morally responsible for any of their actions. Thus moral rules satisfy a necessary condition for a rule to be a part of a public system that applies to all moral agents. This universality also makes clear the independence of moral rules from the will or decision of any person or group of persons, and entails that moral rules are unchanging. However, that the moral rules apply only to moral agents, and that only moral agents can be judged by them, does not mean that they protect only moral agents. Whether the protection of the moral rules extends beyond those who are required to obey them is a controversial issue on which rational persons disagree.

The generality of moral rules, that they simply prohibit or require general kinds of actions, means that considerations of person, place, group, or time are irrelevant. It also explains why moral rules have justified exceptions. That there are justified exceptions to moral rules makes clear that it is impossible to apply them mechanically in deciding how to act or in making moral judgments. Moral rules require acting in accordance with them all of the time with regard to everyone equally. Since positive actions cannot be done all of the time with regard to everyone equally, the moral rules cannot require positive actions like preventing evils or promoting goods. The only rules that are moral rules are those that prohibit causing or increasing the risk of evils being suffered by others. Preventing evils, although normally not required by moral rules, is encouraged by moral ideals, and these ideals often justify breaking a moral rule, even by individuals. However, governments may sometimes be justified in violating moral rules in order to promote benefits.

Rational persons sometimes may not want to act in accordance with a moral rule, even when they would not be justified in violating that rule. Sometimes an unjustified violation of a moral rule will not be contrary to a person's self-interest. Thus it is often not irrational to unjustifiably violate a moral rule. However, whenever it is unjustifiable to violate a moral rule, it will never be irrational for a person to act in accordance with it. Were it ever irrational to refrain from unjustifiably violating a moral rule, there would be a conflict between rationality and morality that no supporter of the rationality of morality could accept. And if morality is not rational, then clearly it cannot be a public system at all, let alone one that applies to all rational persons.

Regardless of whether or not they want to obey the rules themselves, rational persons never want others to unjustifiably violate a moral rule with regard to themselves. In order to be a moral rule, all rational persons who use only rationally required beliefs must take a certain attitude toward the rule. This attitude must include the view that everyone act in accordance with that rule with regard to themselves, although this is not meant to exclude exceptions. However, the attitude that others should obey the moral rules with regard to oneself is not the appropriate moral attitude toward the moral rules. Everyone believes that the appropriate moral attitude toward the moral rules is that they should be followed impartially by everyone with regard to all those protected by the rules. Everyone also agrees that all moral agents are protected, even though there is some disagreement on who else is protected by them. The final characteristic that all moral rules have is that they are believed to be justified, that is, it is believed that all properly qualified rational persons would favor impartial obedience to them by all moral agents with regard to all who are protected by the moral rules.

The moral rules prohibit causing harm to others, require no one ever to violate them without justification, and are part of a public system that applies to all rational persons. These three characteristics together with the fact that all rational persons would favor adopting a public system that contains the moral rules, distinguishes these rules from all other guides to conduct. Making all of these characteristics precise requires precise accounts of morality as a public system, rationality and impartiality. In chapter 1 I tried to provide a precise account of morality as a public system. In chapters 2 and 3 I tried to present a precise account of rationality. In the following chapter I shall try to provide a precise account of impartiality.

Notes

1. I shall generally use "rational person" and "moral agent" interchangeably. Although I recognize that rational persons with locked-in syndrome could have such extensive voluntary disabilities that they might not be subject to moral judgments, this possibility is so remote, that I will ignore it. Voluntary disabilities are disabilities to perform voluntary actions. They may be due to physical disabilities, mental disabilities, or volitional disabilities. For a more detailed account of these concepts see Bernard Gert and Timothy Duggan, "Free Will as the Ability to Will," *Nous* 13, no. 2, (May 1979): 197–217, reprinted in *Moral Responsibility*, edited by John Martin Fisher (Ithaca, N.Y.: Cornell University Press, 1986).

2. For a more detailed analysis of the relationship between general moral rules and particular moral rules, see chapter 3 of Bernard Gert, Charles M. Culver, and K. Danner Clouser, *Bioethics: A Return to Fundamentals* (New York: Oxford University Press, 1997).

3. This is a misleading characteristic of all contractarian accounts of morality.

4. As stated in chapter 4, I use the terms "evil" and "harm" as synonyms. I use the phrase "evil or harm" to minimize the misleading connotation of either term used by itself. When I

think that there will be no misleading implication, I use whichever term seems most natural in the context.

5. This point is explicitly made by Hobbes when discussing the laws of nature, or the moral law, in the first chapter of *De Cive*.

6. This is the same point that is made by Plato in the *Euthyphro* and by Kant in the *Groundwork for the Metaphysics of Morals*.

7. Although this is a completely inadequate definition of moral rules, it is much closer to adequate if taken as a definition of legal rules. A more detailed definition of law is provided in chapter 9 and a more detailed discussion of the confusion between ethical relativity and legal relativity is in chapter 14.

8. Kant claimed that a necessary condition for a maxim to be a moral rule is that it fit the categorical imperative, "Act only on that maxim that you would will to be a universal law." Kant also claimed that these maxims had no exceptions.

9. Rule utilitarianism is intended to repair the obvious flaws of act utilitarianism, which claims that one determines the moral goodness or rightness of an action by comparing its consequences with the consequences of all possible alternative actions. If the relevant consequences are taken as actual consequences, act utilitarianism leads naturally to skepticism. No one can possibly know all the actual future consequences of his proposed action, let alone all of the actual future consequences of all of the possible alternative actions, so there is no way that anyone can ever know that any given act is morally good or right. Using foreseeable consequences eliminates this flaw, but act utilitarianism is still implausible as an account of morality, or as a plausible alternative public guide.

10. If taken literally, the view that it is the consequences of universal obedience that is important indicates a striking similarity to the views of Kant, where the possibility of universal obedience plays a crucial role.

11. It is, however, a very plausible precept, and many books have been written to help people follow this precept.

12. That moral rules involve punishment for violations is often overlooked, but is crucial in distinguishing moral rules from moral ideals, as well as from other precepts. Punishment and the moral attitude are discussed in detail in chapter 7.

Chapter 6

Impartiality

Impartiality Is a Complex Concept

Impartiality has been almost universally misdescribed by philosophers. Like simultaneity, impartiality is usually taken to be a simpler concept than it really is. Einstein made the conceptual discovery that it was inadequate to characterize the simultaneity of two events by simply considering those two events. The point of view of the observer must also be considered. Einstein showed that it is incomplete to say merely "A and B occurred simultaneously." A complete characterization requires saying "A and B occurred simultaneously to an observer at C." This point had not been previously recognized because all of the known observers were at C. Thus it seemed sufficient to use the simpler characterization of simultaneity. Once it is clear that observers need not be at C, but can be at D or E, it becomes apparent that A and B can occur simultaneously with regard to one observer, but not occur simultaneously with regard to another. There is no answer to the question "But did A and B really occur simultaneously?" because this question presupposes an account of simultaneity that Einstein has shown to be inadequate.

A person is sometimes described as impartial as if that characterization were a complete one. But it is not. Understanding what is meant by saying that a person is impartial requires knowing both toward which group the person is impartial and also in what respect the person is impartial with regard to this group. A teacher may be impartial toward all of the students in her class with respect to grading their papers, that is, she is not influenced in her grading of a paper by whose paper it is; however, she may not be impartial toward her students in providing time and effort in helping them to write better papers. She may spend more time and effort with the boys or with those who are members of other disadvantaged groups, even though once the papers are handed in she grades them impartially. Usually, the group and respect are presupposed when talking about impartiality, but failure to make these presuppositions explicit has led to a misunderstanding of the concept. Also, people are sometimes mistaken about either the group with regard to which a person is supposed to be impartial or the respect in which she is supposed to be impartial with regard to this group.

When a baseball umpire is described as impartial, it is usually clear that this means that in making such decisions as calling balls and strikes, he is not influenced by which team benefits or is harmed. An explicit characterization of the impartiality of an umpire involves stating that the umpire is impartial with regard to the competing teams in making his decisions about balls and strikes. Having an explicit characterization of impartiality allows a number of problems concerning impartiality to be stated more clearly. Suppose that an umpire has a friend playing on one of the teams, can he be impartial? This is now clearly seen to be an empirical question. Stated more fully, the question becomes "Can a person who has a friend on one team make his decisions between the competing teams without being influenced by which team benefits?" This is certainly difficult to do. It is not merely that he must avoid consciously favoring one team over the other, he must be able to detect and compensate for any unconscious tendency to favor one team. And not only this, he must be careful not to overcompensate, not to make decisions favoring the team without his friend in order to avoid being partial toward his friend's team.

The difficulty of being an impartial umpire if one has some personal interest in a team explains why umpires are usually required to avoid having a personal interest in any team. In more important matters, judges are supposed to disqualify themselves if they have any personal interest in the outcome of a case. In the administration of justice it is not merely impartiality, it is also the appearance of impartiality that is important. Thus an attempt is made to avoid anything that would lead either side to suspect the judge of not being impartial. The difficulty of directly checking the impartiality of the judge or umpire makes it important to avoid any situation that increases the likelihood of partiality.

Moral Impartiality

It is surprising how few detailed analyses of impartiality have been proposed.[1] Perhaps the apparent simplicity of the concept makes it seem that no detailed analysis is necessary. It has not been realized that stating that someone is impartial is always elliptical, that a complete statement must always include the group with regard to which the person is impartial and the respect in which he is impartial with regard to that group. Perhaps this failure to provide an analysis is due to a lack of interest in the general concept of impartiality. Most philosophers have been primarily interested in the kind of impartiality that is required by morality, what I shall call *moral impartiality*. They may have believed that it was obvious toward which group morality requires impartiality and also in what respect morality requires a person to be impartial with regard to this group. If they did believe this, they were clearly mistaken.

Impartiality has been so neglected that it is not surprising that the brief characterizations of it by philosophers have been so inadequate. This inadequacy is significant because, before an adequate account of moral impartiality can be given, it is necessary to provide an account of the general concept of impartiality. Philosophers have not realized that it is important to make explicit the group toward which and the respect in which impartiality is required by morality. Instead of detailed analyses of moral impartiality, or of impartiality in general, philosophers have simply substituted technical concepts like reversibility, universalizability, and the veil of ignorance for the kind of impartiality required by morality.[2] There has also been talk about moral impartiality as involving a God's eye view, or the point of view of the universe, or some other profound-sounding but useless and misleading characterization.

The realization that impartiality requires reference to a group with regard to which one is impartial, and a respect in which one is impartial with regard to that group, suggests the following definition: *A is impartial in respect R with regard to group G if and only if A's actions in respect R are not influenced by which member(s) of G benefit or are harmed by these actions.* Briefly, one is impartial with regard to a group in a given respect if one does not favor any member of the group over any other member in that respect.

Common Mischaracterizations of Impartiality

Unfortunately, most characterizations of impartiality fail to take into account the elliptical nature of statements of impartiality and therefore are seriously mistaken. A common characterization of impartiality is "to be unbiased by one's personal preferences or interests in one's judgments." Although this characterization sounds like a truism, explaining impartiality by use of the term "unbiased," it is in fact quite misleading. Suppose that a baseball umpire prefers a high-scoring game to a low-scoring one. This may lead him to have a very narrow strike zone, thus making it more likely that batters will have better pitches at which to swing. Such an umpire can be completely impartial with regard to the two teams when he calls balls and strikes, yet he is not unbiased by his personal preferences and interests. He also may not be impartial with regard to batters and pitchers, but that does not affect his impartiality with regard to the two teams.

The most common characterization of impartiality is that it requires that like cases be treated alike. This latter characterization is taken as trivially true by almost all philosophers, but unfortunately it is also mistaken. Consider the umpire again. It is clear that his preference for a high-scoring game need not interfere with his calling balls and strikes impartially with regard to the two teams. But now suppose that he becomes upset because he comes to believe that umpires are not properly appreciated. He decides that he will change the strike zone every three innings, starting with a narrow zone, going to a wide one, and then returning to a narrow one. This certainly makes him a bad umpire, and may even lead many to suspect him of not being impartial with regard to the two teams. But if he simply decides to change the strike zone every three innings without being influenced by which team benefits or is harmed by this change, then he does not cease to be impartial with regard to the two teams in calling balls and strikes. This is true even though he does not treat like cases alike; for the same pitch that he calls a ball in the first inning, he calls a strike in the fifth inning.

Impartiality and Consistency

Defenders of the view of impartiality as treating like cases alike might claim that the inning in which the ball is pitched has to be included in determining what counts as a like case. This rather desperate maneuver leads to bizarre results, for the umpire can maintain his impartiality and decide to change the strike zone at five-minute intervals, or whenever he hears a certain sound. Indeed, he can change it whenever he feels like it, and if he is not influenced by which team is benefited or harmed by this erratic change in the strike zone, he remains impartial with regard to the two teams. He will not be consistent, but impartiality should not be confused with consistency. A good umpire is supposed to be consistent as well as impartial. An inconsistent umpire will certainly be a bad umpire and will probably even be suspected of not being impartial, but if he is not influenced by which team is benefited or harmed, he remains impartial with respect to calling balls and strikes with regard to the two teams. He does not favor either team with respect to calling balls and strikes.

This example of the umpire who changes strike zones at random intervals shows that the common characterization of impartiality as requiring that like cases be treated alike, that is, consistently, is not correct. But one might think that although impartiality does not require consistency, if one is consistent, then one must be impartial. Although consistency is not a necessary condition of impartiality, it may seem as if it is a sufficient condition. But this is also not true. Consistency, which in this context involves making the same decision whenever the circumstances are the same, does not require impartiality, because one can count as part of the *same* circumstances that certain members of the group toward which one is supposed to be impartial will benefit. One can consistently favor men over women for an executive position, although one is supposed to be impartial with regard to all job applicants. A person can consistently make decisions favoring some members of a group over others, even though she is supposed to be impartial with regard to that group. So consistency does not entail impartiality any more than impartiality entails consistency.

The common assumptions that a person who makes consistent decisions must make impartial decisions and that a person who makes impartial decisions must make consistent decisions have both been shown to be incorrect. Consistency is neither necessary nor sufficient for impartiality, indeed, the two concepts are completely distinct. Normally, impartiality and consistency do go together, but either can occur without the other. Inconsistency, however, is quite likely to cause suspicion of partiality. But although consistency does not have the close connection with impartiality that it is normally taken to have, it is a valuable trait in itself. The example of the umpire shows that inconsistent decisions make it more difficult for people dependent on those decisions to plan for the future as successfully as they could have if the decisions had been consistent. For example, pitchers will have a harder time deciding how to pitch and batters will have a harder time deciding what pitches to swing at.

Rationality and Impartiality

It should also be clear that, contrary to the claims of many philosophers, there is no conceptual relationship between rationality and impartiality. With regard to almost any group and in almost any respect that one is supposed to be impartial, it is rationally allowed either to be impartial or not to be impartial. Although a rational person need not be concerned with anyone other than himself, it is also rational to be concerned with every sentient being. That a rational person need not be impartial with regard to any group, including the group of all other rational persons goes contrary to the views of many philosophers. Kant regarded impartiality, or rather his substitute for it, to be intimately related to rationality, and many philosophers have followed him in this. But Kant had an extremely unusual concept of rationality. On the concept of rationality where it is the basic normative concept and it makes no sense to ask "Why be rational?" no one ever wants to act irrationally. When this basic normative concept of rationality is the one being used, it is clear that rationality can never require impartially, not even the kind of impartiality required by morality.

Of course, it is not irrational for a person to act impartially in the way required by morality, but it is also not irrational for a person not to do so. Impartiality and rationality are completely distinct concepts; that one is rational implies neither that one is impartial in the way required by morality, nor that one is not. Perhaps surprisingly, even that one is impartial with regard to all moral agents with respect to the moral rules does not imply either that one is rational or that one is irrational. If one is irrational, one may simply unjustifiably violate the moral rules without being influenced by who is hurt by one's violations and allow others to violate them in the same way. It is only if one is both rational and impartial with respect to the moral rules with regard to the appropriate group that one will act in a morally acceptable way. Indeed, what counts as a morally acceptable way to act with respect to the moral rules is determined by the way that a person who is rational and impartial in the way required by morality can advocate that one act. Rationality is part of moral impartiality because the impartiality required by morality is an impartiality that can be part of a public system, and it is never irrational to act as a public system requires.

Impartiality Is Not a Moral Virtue

Impartiality is not like honesty and kindness. Unless the group and respect are specified in certain ways, it is not a moral virtue, that is, a character trait, that all rational persons want everyone else to have. Unless the group and respect are of a certain kind, impartial decisions are not guaranteed to be morally acceptable decisions. All that impartiality guarantees is that actions or decisions in the specified respect will not be influenced by whether they benefit or harm one person rather than another in the specified group. Impartiality only involves not differentiating between the members of a group toward which one is supposed to be impartial; it does not require that one be impartial in any particular respect. How one treats the members of that group is not a relevant consideration in determining one's impartiality with regard to its members. It was said of a famous football coach that he treated all of his players impartially, like dogs.

The proposed definition of impartiality explains how there can be impartial enforcement of bad or unjust laws. Those enforcing the rules can be impartial with regard to all violators of the law. If they enforce the laws in the same way, regardless of who the violator is, they are enforcing the law impartially. Even if it would be morally better for them not to enforce the law at all, this has no bearing on whether or not they are enforcing the law impartially. It is a common mistake to equate impartiality with justice or fairness. Both justice and fairness are moral terms, whereas impartiality is not. Someone who is impartial with regard to all high-income persons in planning his burglaries of their homes is not regarded as acting justly or fairly. Justice and fairness require acting in morally acceptable ways, impartiality does not.

The performance of many jobs, not merely umpires and judges, requires both impartiality and consistency. This is true even when the group toward which one is expected to be impartial in important respects is small and does not include oneself, such as teachers with regard to their students. I am not in any way claiming that impartiality is not relevant to morality; in fact, I regard impartiality as one of the key concepts in defining morality. That is why I think it is important to provide a definition of impartiality that is independent of morality. My effort in this chapter is not only to provide an account of impartiality that adequately describes all kinds of impartiality but also to provide an account of the kind of impartiality required by morality. That one is impartial, as the definition that I have provided shows, does not in any way guarantee that one is acting morally. This account of impartiality distinguishes general impartiality from those other characteristics, both moral and nonmoral, with which it is so commonly but mistakenly associated, such as fairness and consistency.

General impartiality requires neither consistency nor any effort to avoid inflicting undeserved harm. However, the kind of impartiality that is required by morality does involve both consistency and avoiding causing undeserved harm. General impartiality is mistakenly regarded as a moral virtue because it is not distinguished from moral impartiality, which is a moral virtue. But moral impartiality is not merely acting impartially with regard to all moral agents. It is possible to be impartial with regard to a group including oneself and all other moral agents and not be rational. One can easily imagine someone, perhaps due to some perverted religious or evolutionary belief, who impartially does nothing to relieve the pain of anyone, including himself. Such a person is neither rationally nor morally preferable to a person who relieves the pain only of those who are suffering from AIDS. In fact, the person who aided only victims of AIDS would be morally preferable to the person who impartially refused to help anyone. Being impartial with regard to everyone, including oneself, with regard to refusing to relieve pain is certainly not a moral virtue. A person can act impartially with regard to all moral agents and not be rational. It is the false assumption that impartiality with regard to all moral agents also involves being impartial in the appropriate respect that leads some to regard impartiality toward an appropriate group as sufficient to make it a moral virtue.

The Respect In Which Morality Requires Impartiality

I claim that all rational persons who are impartial with regard to a group including at least all moral agents, in the respect of choosing a public system to apply to their behavior with regard to each other, would choose morality as the public system. In order for this claim to have any significance it is essential that the concepts of a public system, rationality, and impartiality be characterized in nonmoral terms. It would be worse than trivial to explain morality in terms of a public system, rationality, and impartiality if one could not provide accounts of a public system, rationality, and impartiality that were independent of morality. Further, on the accounts I have provided, rationality does not require impartiality with regard to all moral agents, nor does impartiality with regard to all moral agents require rationality. It is only the two concepts together with a public system that yield moral impartiality.[3] In the remainder of this chapter I shall try to specify the kind of impartiality required by morality.

All those who hold an objective account of morality, that is, that the correctness of a moral judgment does not depend on who makes the judgment, agree that morality requires impartiality with regard to a group that includes, at least, all moral agents. Before discussing the specification of this group in more detail, it would be useful to specify the respect in which morality requires one's actions to be impartial. Most philosophers have paid little explicit attention to specifying the respect in which morality requires impartiality. John Stuart Mill says in chapter 2 of *Utilitarianism*, "As between his own happiness and that of others, utilitarianism requires him to be as strictly impartial as a disinterested and benevolent spectator."[4] Many philosophers, accepting what Mill says, claim that morality requires impartiality in all of one's actions that might affect the pleasure, pain, or happiness of any moral agent. However, it is humanly impossible for anyone to act impartially with respect to preventing or relieving the pain and suffering of all moral agents, much less to promoting their pleasure or happiness. It is absurd to claim that morality requires one to act impartially toward all moral agents with respect to the consequences of one's actions on their happiness when it is humanly impossible to do so.

The respect in which morality requires impartiality must be a respect in which it is humanly possible to be impartial toward a group as large as all moral agents. This is possible only with regard to prohibitions such as "Do not kill" and "Do not lie" and the other moral rules listed in the previous chapter. Morality does indeed require impartiality whenever one is considering violating a moral rule. However, when neither saving a person nor not saving him involves violating a moral rule, morality does not require impartiality when one is considering risking one's life to save someone. If two children fall off of a boat and one of them is one's child, morality does not require flipping a coin in order to decide which one to rescue first. However, if one's child needs a heart transplant, morality does not allow one to kill some other child in order to obtain a suitable heart.[5] Morality does not require impartiality when acting on a moral ideal.

It is clear that morality requires impartiality with respect to obeying the moral rules, but it is less clear how to characterize this kind of impartiality. The problem arises because the impartiality required by morality does not always require one to act in accordance with a moral rule. Two moral rules can sometimes conflict, so that it is sometimes impossible to act in accordance with both. How does one determine what counts as acting impartially with respect to the moral rules in this kind of case? Further, there are some situations where a moral ideal, such as saving a life, conflicts with a moral rule, like keeping a promise, such that morality encourages breaking the promise. Thus it is not sufficient to characterize moral impartiality as impartiality with respect to the moral rules. It is necessary to provide a more detailed account of what counts as acting impartially with respect to the moral rules. Later in this chapter, I will consider three of the most popular ways of characterizing, or rather replacing, moral impartiality.

The Scope of Moral Impartiality

The scope of moral impartiality concerns who is included in the group toward which one must act impartially with respect to following the moral rules. In the previous chapter, the question of who is required to act in accordance with the moral rules was answered. In the discussion of the universality of the moral rules, it was pointed out that the moral rules apply to all moral agents, those who can understand them and guide their conduct by them, that is, to all rational persons with the relevant voluntary abilities. Here, I am concerned with the group toward which all of these persons are required to act impartially with respect to the moral rules. To act impartially with respect to the moral rules with regard to a given group requires that one not violate the rule toward some members of that group in the same circumstances where one would not allow the rule to be violated with regard to other members of the group. It also requires that one not allow the rule to be violated because certain members of that group will benefit when one would not allow the rule to be violated in order to benefit other members of the group.

It is the latter requirement of moral impartiality that makes it important to realize that the agent himself must be a member of the group toward which morality requires impartiality. To be appropriately impartial with respect to the moral rules requires that one not make special exceptions that benefit oneself or one's friends and relatives. Nor can one limit the group toward which one is impartial with regard to the moral rules to oneself and one's friends and relatives, nor even to members of one's own society. Limiting the group to these people is clearly incompatible with the kind of impartiality required by morality. Someone who obeyed the moral rules impartially, but only with regard to a small circle of friends or only his fellow citizens would be correctly regarded as acting impartially toward the group smaller than the one toward which moral rules require impartiality.

That oneself is a part of the group toward whom one must be impartial distinguishes moral impartiality from the impartiality required of a judge or umpire. An umpire must be impartial with regard to his decisions regarding the two teams; it does not even make any sense to say he must also include himself in the group toward which he must be impartial, for he makes no decisions regarding himself. Of course, an impartial umpire cannot take a bribe that would influence his decisions. But this is because taking a bribe may lead him to favor one team over the other, not because he must be impartial with regard to himself. It is the likelihood of being influenced by a bribe to make decisions favoring one team that makes taking a bribe from one team seem incompatible with impartiality.

Moral impartiality also does not allow one to make special exceptions to the moral rules to benefit members of one's race, religion, gender, or country. Nor can one limit the group toward which one must be impartial with regard to the moral rules to members of one's race, religion, gender, or country. It is quite clear that being impartial only with regard to members of one's race, religion, gender, or country is not the kind of impartiality required by morality. Those who obey the moral rules impartially, but only with regard to members of their own race are properly regarded as racist, not moral. Those who would kill or deceive those who are not members of their religion in circumstances when they would never kill or deceive members of their religion are religious fanatics, not moral persons. Similarly, those who would deprive females of freedom in circumstances when they would never deprive males of freedom are sexist, not moral. Those who obey the moral rules impartially only with regard to members of their own society also are not being impartial with regard to a large enough group. For those people who do not interact with people of a different race, religion, or country, it may never be clear if the scope of their impartiality is with regard to a large enough group. Confusion about the scope of moral impartiality is an essential feature of those who hold various forms of ethical relativism.

Moral impartiality requires that one include in the group toward which one is impartial all those to whom the moral rules apply, that is, all moral agents. Some, for quasi-aesthetic reasons, limit the group toward which morality requires one to be impartial to moral agents. There is a satisfying symmetry to the view that morality requires acting impartially with respect to the moral rules only with regard to the same group that morality requires to act impartially with respect to these rules. However, given that one uses only rationally required beliefs, this limitation is not only an irrational limitation, it is also an incorrect account of the group toward which common morality requires impartiality. Common morality requires impartiality to all former moral agents such as those who, no matter what the cause, have regressed to the state where they are no longer held morally responsible for their actions. Moral impartiality does not allow such people to be killed, caused pain, or disabled for the benefit of those who are still moral agents when it would not allow moral agents to be killed, caused pain, or disabled for their benefit. Common morality also requires impartiality toward children, at least those who have the capacity to become moral agents.

Rational Attitudes toward the Scope of Moral Impartiality

All rational persons, if limited to rationally required beliefs, would endorse including former moral agents in the group toward which morality requires impartiality. Of course, they would require that these former moral agents be conscious, but insofar as former moral agents can suffer the harms that the moral rules prohibit causing, rational persons agree that former moral agents are protected by the moral rules. But they need not require that former moral agents be treated exactly as moral agents. They can differ about whether institutions like hospitals need to have the same duties toward moral agents and former moral agents. So, although rational persons would agree that morality does not allow killing former moral agents, they might disagree about whether there is a duty to spend the same resources in order to help former moral agents to stay alive as there is to spend on actual moral agents.

It is not clear that all rational persons would agree that children be included in the group that is impartially protected by morality, but many would. Certainly all would agree that children whose parents want them to be impartially protected should be so protected, for any of them might be a parent of such a child, and it is a rationally required belief that some parents view the well-being of their children as more important than their own. Further, some rational persons would want the group toward which morality requires impartiality to include additions beyond former moral agents and those who can become moral agents. However, every addition to the group impartially protected by morality restricts the freedom of moral agents. This is why, unless there is an overwhelming consideration in favor of adding to the group of beings impartially protected by morality, not all rational persons will agree that they should be added to this group.

Moral Agents Include Future Actual Moral Agents

Although everyone agrees that the group toward which one must impartially obey the moral rules includes all moral agents, it is important to be more precise in stating what is meant by "all moral agents." To interpret "all moral agents" as "all presently existing moral agents" is to claim that one needs to include in the group toward which one must impartially obey the moral rules only all presently existing actual moral agents. However, common morality interprets "all moral agents" to mean "all present and future actual moral agents," and this is the most plausible interpretation. It is not morally allowable to break moral rules toward other moral agents simply because they are spatially distant, even though psychologically it may be easier to do so. Since there does not seem to be any morally relevant difference between time and space, what holds for spatial distance should also hold for temporal distance. It is not morally allowable to break moral rules toward other moral agents simply because they are temporally distant, even though psychologically it may be easier to do so.

That future actual moral agents are included in the group toward which morality requires impartiality does seem to have some practical consequences. That morality requires impartiality toward future actual moral agents means that morality requires some concern about the effect of present actions on future generations. Spatial distance is not morally relevant. When the numbers of people affected at both sites would be the same, morality does not allow causing significant risks of harm, such as might arise from building a dangerous nuclear or other toxic waste facility, in a far-off place if it does not allow causing the same risks by building a similar facility nearby. Similarly, if morality does not allow causing significant risks of harm to people now living, it does not allow causing the same risks to people who are temporally distant.

Imagining the following action in which only future actual moral agents, but no presently existing actual moral agent, will be harmed, makes it absolutely clear that such an action would be morally unacceptable. Even though it is outlandish, consider someone who, simply for the fun of it, builds and plants a big bomb, capable of destroying thousands of people, arranging for it to go off in two hundred years. Anyone who accepts the plausibility of this example, would regard the action as morally unacceptable. This would be true even if the bomb builder could prove that his bomb posed no risk at all for anyone prior to that time. However, as a practical matter, it is not clear that future actual moral agents being included in the group toward which one must be impartial has a significant impact on the moral acceptability of different policies.

Given that some presently existing actual moral agents may be living one hundred years from now, detrimental effects within one hundred years increases the risk to these presently existing actual moral agents. Thus that future actual moral agents are included in the morally protected group does not seem to have an important impact on the moral acceptability of any present economic or environmental policies. The reason for this is not that these policies will not have important implications for future generations, but rather that these economic or environmental policies will also affect presently existing actual moral agents. Only actions that have their significant effects so far in the future that no presently existing actual moral agents will still be alive would have their moral status determined primarily by the consequences on future actual moral agents. Since effects so far in the future are usually unforseeable and so have little moral relevance, very little freedom of action is lost by including future actual moral agents in the group protected by the moral rules. Since rational persons know that they may have descendants, they would accept common morality's interpretation of "all moral agents" as all presently existing and future actual moral agents.

One theoretical effect of including future actual moral agents in the group protected by morality is that it becomes even more implausible that the actual consequences rather than the foreseeable consequences of an act and its alternatives determine the moral rightness or wrongness of an act. Indeed, that actual consequences to distant generations determines the moral rightness and wrongness of all actions has the consequence that no one can ever know whether any act is morally right or wrong. Only moral skeptics should welcome this consequence. For nonskeptics, explicitly including future actual moral agents in the group impartially protected by the moral rules removes any doubt that morality is concerned with foreseeable rather than actual consequences.

Another theoretical effect of including future actual moral agents in the group impartially protected by morality is that it highlights the misleading nature of contractarian theories of morality. It is extremely implausible to talk about contracts, even hypothetical ones, between people separated by many generations. Morality is not the result of any contract, actual or hypothetical. Natural law is a better metaphor for morality than the contractarian metaphor. Morality is an informal public system that develops out of human nature with its features of rationality, fallibility, and vulnerability, and the human situation. Although morality does serve a purpose, it is not consciously created for a purpose. A moral theory is an attempt to justify the moral system that is already an existing feature of human life, not an attempt to create a new code of conduct.

No one disagrees that all presently existing and future actual moral agents are protected by the moral rules. Common morality also includes all those who have been actual moral agents and are still conscious. This addition is supported by noting that all rational persons who are moral agents would want to retain the protection of the moral rules if they were to lose their capacity to act as moral agents but could still suffer harms. All moral agents know that they can become former moral agents who remain conscious, so it is clear why they agree with common morality in including these former moral agents in the group protected by morality. These actual and former moral agents comprise the smallest group toward which all rational persons agree that morality requires impartiality. I therefore call it *the Minimal Group*.

Presently Existing Potential Moral Agents — Infants and Children

Rational persons can disagree about all other additions to the minimal group. The addition that seems least controversial is adding children who will become moral agents and whose parents want them to be included in the impartially protected group. Every reader of this book probably also would want to include all human infants, even neonates, in the group toward which the moral rules should be impartially followed.[6] However, even in Western society there are those who regard it as morally acceptable to kill neonates whose life prospects are very poor when they would not allow the killing of moral agents or former moral agents with similar prospects. It is primarily those human infants who do not have the prospect of ever becoming actual moral agents, such as severely brain-damaged infants, who are most likely not to be included in the group toward which the moral rules require impartial obedience. Everyone in American society wants to include in the group toward which the moral rules require impartial obedience infants who with proper care would become moral agents, and almost everyone wants to include all children.

It is not clear that an argument can be given to prove that children, including infants, should be included in the group toward which the moral rules must be impartially obeyed, nor is it clear that any argument is needed. It is simply a fact that almost everyone in a technologically advanced society (or a society in which lack of enough food to sustain life is not a problem), wants to include human infants who will become moral agents in the group toward which the moral rules must be impartially obeyed. In the past, human infants were not always included in this group, but presently there seems to be no genuine controversy about including them. Sociobiological considerations may explain why human moral agents include human infants and children in the morally protected group, but they do not show that it is rationally required for them to be accorded the impartial protection of morality.

Presently Existing Potential Moral Agents — Embryos and Fetuses

That there is substantial agreement for including human infants and children in the group toward which the moral rules should be impartially obeyed may lead one to think that all presently existing potential moral agents should also be included. But embryos and fetuses are also presently existing potential moral agents, and even those who are concerned about protecting fetuses may not regard them as belonging to that group toward which the moral rules require impartial obedience. Those who allow abortion for rape or incest, or even to protect the life of the mother, may not regard the fetus as having the same level of protection from the moral rules as do actual moral agents, or potential moral agents that are already born.[7] Some have claimed that there is no relevant difference between a fetus and a neonate, since neither are actual moral agents and both are potential moral agents.[8] Yet most people feel that a distinction should be made between a neonate and an embryo or a fetus, especially in its early stages of development.

This difference might be captured by drawing a parallel with former moral agents who are still conscious, but who are no longer moral agents. They are impartially protected, but beings in a persistent vegetative state, those that have permanently lost all consciousness, are not included. All normal neonates are presently existing *sentient* beings, that is, are capable of feeling, and are also potential moral agents. This does not distinguish neonates from late fetuses, but it does distinguish neonates and fetuses in the latter stages from embryos and fetuses in the earliest stages. Many would like a distinction that allows including fetuses in the later stages in the group toward which the moral rules should be impartially obeyed. Others do not want to include fetuses at any stage in the group toward which the moral rules must be impartially obeyed. I know of no argument that would persuade all rational persons either to include or not to include all presently existing sentient beings who are potential moral agents in the group toward which one should impartially obey the moral rules. Common morality is undecided on this matter, and arguments do not seem to determine most people's attitude on this issue.

The Role of Emotional Involvement

Many claim that there is a continuum between moral agents and potential moral agents. They claim that it is impossible to draw a nonarbitrary line between those who are already moral agents and those who have not quite acquired the intellectual and volitional abilities to be held morally responsible for their actions. Although this claim is true, it is not helpful in deciding who should be included in the group toward which the moral rules require impartial obedience. There is no doubt that babies, even as old as a year, are not moral agents, yet every reader of this book would want to include babies of this age in the group toward which the moral rules require impartiality. This is undoubtedly due to the fact that the interaction between moral agents and these babies is as deep and intimate as any among moral agents. Moral agents are not distinguished from those who are not moral agents by the degree of emotional involvement it is possible to have with them. Most moral agents care for babies as much as they care for other moral agents and so want them accorded the full protection of morality.

When people are choosing who they want added to the group that has the full and impartial protection of the moral rules, the considerations that incline them one way or the other are often related to emotional factors. It is adult interaction with babies that makes adults want to include them in the group that must be treated impartially. Some would claim that this interaction begins at birth and that this is why the infant or neonate is accorded the full protection of the moral rules whereas the fetus is not. These considerations have considerable psychological force. Related considerations may explain why killing a fetus in the very early stages of pregnancy is regarded as much less serious than killing a fetus in the very late stages. Even if the interaction is somewhat one-sided, people are more emotionally involved with the fetus in the later stages.

Emotional involvement with children is one factor that leads to including them in the group accorded the impartial protection of the moral rules. The power of emotional attachment to other beings is not affected by whether or not they are moral agents. Since all moral agents must be accorded the full protection of the moral rules, if there is any group of beings with whom moral agents are as emotionally involved as with other moral agents, then they will be accorded as much protection as moral agents. Human babies are in this group for most human moral agents. People do not have this same emotional involvement with fetuses, especially in the early stages of pregnancy.

Emotional involvement with those who are moral agents or potential moral agents is usually stronger than emotional involvement with those who are not. However, some people are emotionally involved with animals, especially pets, in a way that equals or exceeds their emotional involvement with other moral agents. These people may want animals to be included in the group toward which the moral rules should be impartially obeyed.[9] Some may even be inclined to include all sentient beings in the group to be treated impartially, but not include potential moral agents who are not yet sentient beings, that is, fetuses in the earlier stages of pregnancy. Emotional involvement usually requires a being with whom interaction is possible, or at least one with whom empathy is possible. This explains why those who are anti-abortion try to portray the fetus as if it were just like a human infant, differing only in size and location.

The Role of Metaphysical, Religious, and Scientific Beliefs

Direct emotional involvement is not the only factor that influences how people determine who they want in the group toward which morality affords impartial protection. Many are influenced by religious or metaphysical beliefs. If a person believes that what is most significant about moral agents is that they have a soul, then she will probably want to include in the group toward which one should be impartial all beings that she believes have a soul. If she believes that the soul enters the body at the moment of conception, then she will want fetuses from the moment of conception included in the group. If she believes that the soul enters the body at birth then she may not include any fetuses in the protected group. And if she believes that the soul enters the body at some time during pregnancy, for example, when the fetus becomes sentient, then she will want to include all fetuses after that time in the protected group and may not include fetuses before that time. If she has some belief about transmigration of souls, such that the souls of moral agents sometimes come back in the bodies of animals, then she may want animals to be included in the group.

Metaphysical beliefs about the nature of actuality and potentiality may lead one to include all potential moral agents in the group. I shall not list all of the religious and metaphysical beliefs that may lead one to accept or reject an increase in the size of the group toward which morality requires impartial obedience, because these beliefs, even if true, are not beliefs that are shared by all rational persons. The same is true of scientific beliefs, that fetuses are members of the same biological species as all moral agents, or that there is a continuous development of a fetus from conception to birth. Since morality applies to all rational persons, all of the essential features of morality must be understood and acceptable to all rational persons, and hence no religious, metaphysical, or even scientific belief that is not shared by all rational persons can be used to determine the essential features of morality.

The religious, metaphysical, and scientific beliefs that incline one to accept or reject a proposed increase in the size of the group, like one's emotional involvement, only explain why one wants to increase the size of the group in a certain way; they do not provide arguments that are persuasive to all rational persons. Presenting these arguments is like showing people a picture of a fetus in order to get them emotionally involved. Its success will depend in part on the skill of the presenter. However, even if people become emotionally involved or are persuaded of the correctness of the argument, they may still not want to enlarge the group in the way that is being argued for.

Concern for those beings that are not moral agents, regardless of the cause of that concern, is what leads people to want to include them in the group that is impartially protected by the moral rules. However, a person can have some concern with these beings and yet not want to include them in the minimal group, because every enlargement of this group restricts the freedom of those already in the group. However, denying that nonhuman mammals should be included in the impartially protected group does not mean that one denies that nonhuman mammals should be treated humanely. People can favor some protection even for animals that they do not want afforded impartial protection. People can favor laws protecting animals from mistreatment, even though they do not believe that animals belong in the group that is impartially protected.

Some Possible Additions to the Minimal Group

The categories that can be used in enlarging the group toward which one must impartially obey the moral rules must be categories that are understood by all rational persons. The group cannot be increased by adding cats and dogs, because some rational persons have never heard of cats and dogs. The group can be increased by adding sentient beings, which would include cats and dogs, but the more general category would also include many other animals, and so remove the bias in favor of those animals that have become pets. A more direct approach would be to add that group of sentient beings that are pets of moral agents, but this clearly biased attempt is also unacceptable, because some rational persons have no concept of pet. The following categories all satisfy the condition that all rational persons know about that category, even if they do not understand my particular way of formulating it. Since these categories are known to all rational persons they can be part of a public system applying to all rational persons and so are possible additions to the group toward which morality requires impartial obedience to the moral rules.

The first three categories are related to the concept of a potential moral agent. Almost all would enlarge the minimal group by including human infants and children. This is Addition 1. Many want to enlarge the minimal group by adding sentient beings who are potential moral agents. This would enlarge the group by adding both human infants and fetuses after they had become sentient beings. This is Addition 1a. Others want to enlarge the group by adding all potential moral agents, regardless of whether or not they are already sentient beings. This enlarges the group by adding fetuses at conception or shortly thereafter. I call this Addition 1b.

There may be other combinations or distinctions with regard to what potential moral agents should be included in the group, but I have already listed enough to make it clear how one might propose to add potential moral agents to the minimal group. However, others may want to make additions to the minimal group that do not use the concept of potential moral agent at all, but rather that use the concept of a sentient being or a potential sentient being. Some may hold that all actual sentient beings should be included in the group toward which one should impartially obey the moral rules. This is Addition 2. Others may hold that all potential sentient beings should be included. This is Addition 2a, and it creates the largest group toward which any rational person would claim that morality requires impartial obedience to the moral rules. No one claims that flowers, trees, or species, belong to the group toward which the moral rules must be impartially obeyed. Rational persons can accept any of this additions, but they need accept no addition to the minimal group at all. Apart from including children, common morality takes no position.

It is tempting to claim that morality requires impartiality in determining who belongs in the group toward which the moral rules require impartial obedience. Since impartiality must include reference to some group, it must be determined which group is the one toward which morality requires this impartiality. But there is no group from which those who belong in the protected group should be impartially picked. Common morality includes all moral agents and former moral agents who are still conscious in the impartially protected group. These moral agents may choose to include potential moral agents or sentient beings, but there is no argument that will convince all rational persons that any particular addition should or should not be made to this minimal group. As long as the addition has the required generality, one may expand the group on any basis whatsoever, as long as one is prepared to have all moral agents act impartially with regard to this group whenever considering a violation of the moral rules.

Although no argument will be persuasive to everyone, readers might find it a valuable exercise to consider situations in which members of the minimal group and members of a proposed addition are paired. They can then decide if they are prepared to require obeying the moral rules impartially with regard to those in the minimal group and in the addition. For example, they can decide if they think that since a nonhuman mammal can be killed to save the lives of several human beings a human being can be killed to save an equal number of lives of several nonhuman mammals. If they do think this, then they believe nonhuman mammals should be included in the fully protected group. If they do not think this, then they believe nonhuman mammals should not be included. No rational person would accept any enlargement of the fully protected group beyond all actual and potential sentient beings, and few would accept a group this large.

Holding that some group is a group toward which the moral rules must be impartially followed means that no one, including oneself, is allowed to violate a moral rule with regard to anyone in this group unless everyone is allowed to violate that same rule with regard to anyone else in that group in the same circumstances. Moral impartiality involves impartiality in respect to obeying the moral rules with regard to at least all those in the minimal group, including oneself and one's friends, and many would hold that morality requires impartiality with regard to a larger group. Unlike general impartiality, moral impartiality includes rationality and consistency; a person is not acting as moral impartiality requires unless his actions are both rational and consistent. It may be that confusing moral impartiality with general impartiality has led philosophers to mistakenly hold that rationality and consistency are essential features of general impartiality.

Tests or Characterizations of Moral Impartiality

Previous attempts to characterize the impartiality required by morality have not realized that morality requires impartiality only with respect to obeying the moral rules. This has resulted in all previous accounts of moral impartiality being inadequate. Three of the most popular accounts of the impartiality required by morality have philosophical counterparts. These accounts are sometimes put forward as tests of moral impartiality and sometimes as characterizations of it. It is worth examining all three of them to see why they are inadequate.[10]

The first and most popular of the tests or characterizations of moral impartiality is the Golden Rule, "Do unto others as you would have them do unto you." The Golden Rule is best regarded as a recommendation on how to achieve moral impartiality. It recommends that a person act in a certain way toward someone else if and only if he would want that other person to behave in that way toward himself. This is sometimes called the test of reversibility.[11] It is regarded by some as both necessary and sufficient for achieving moral impartiality.

The second most popular test of moral impartiality is universalizability. Kant's categorical imperative, "Act only on that maxim that you would will to be a universal law," is used by many who do not accept any other aspect of Kant's moral philosophy. Many followers of Kant hold that only if one is willing to make the maxim of one's action a universal law of nature, is one being impartial in the way required by morality. Many who do not follow Kant also regard the willingness to universalize one's actions to be the test of one's moral impartiality. If and only if one would want everyone to act in the way one is acting, is one acting in the way that moral impartiality requires. If and only if one would universalize the maxim of one's action, is one acting impartially in the way required by morality.[12]

The third method of achieving moral impartiality is best exemplified by attempting to formulate in words what is symbolized by the blindfold on the statue of Justice. Rawls's "veil of ignorance" is the best-known philosophical method of this kind.[13] On Rawls's method, all characteristics of a person that would distinguish her from anyone else are removed. She does not know whether she is a man or a woman or any other fact about herself that would differentiate her from anyone else. She also has no personality or character traits that are not universal. On this view, moral impartiality is achieved only by the total elimination of individuality. It is a consequence of this view that all persons who are morally impartial must agree, for any features that could lead to disagreement have been eliminated.[14]

The reversibility and universalizability tests for moral impartiality do not have this consequence. On these tests, two rational persons might contemplate the same action, apply the test, and come out with different results. José may want Maria to do to him what he is considering doing to her, whereas Maria does not want José to do to her what she is contemplating doing to him, even though both are contemplating doing the same kind of action: deceiving in order to prevent the person deceived from suffering some minor anxiety. Similarly, José may want everyone perform such an action, whereas Maria may not want anyone perform it. Thus José and Maria, although both are impartial according to the tests of reversibility and universalizability, would come to different decisions about whether or not to perform a certain kind of action. Indeed, on the first two tests, even with no change in the circumstances, José and Maria can change their minds about what they want to have done to themselves, or by all, and still remain impartial.

The Golden Rule cannot be a test of general impartiality, for it deals only with those instances of impartiality in which the person acting is included in the group with regard to which he should be impartial. But since the Golden Rule is only being put forward as a test of moral impartiality, where the person acting is included in the group with regard toward which he should be impartial, it may still be an adequate test of moral impartiality. The categorical imperative can be a test of general impartiality as well as of moral impartiality. The veil of ignorance also seems as if it could be a test of general impartiality as well as a test of moral impartiality. If one does not know who is going to be benefited or harmed by one's decisions, it is impossible not to be impartial. The veil of ignorance even eliminates the problem of unintentional partiality. Someone cannot be affected by how his decisions may affect different people in the group toward whom he should be impartial if he does not know who his decisions will affect.

Taking away all information about which person from the group toward which one is supposed to be impartial benefits or is harmed by the decision guarantees that the decision will be impartial. Any decision that is made in ignorance of who will benefit or be harmed by that decision is necessarily an impartial decision. This is why Justice, who treats all who come before her impartially, is often portrayed with a blindfold over her eyes. This symbolic representation that Justice is not aware of who it is that comes before her shows that justice is impartial, that she does not favor any one member of the group over another. On the veil of ignorance test of impartiality, decisions must be impartial with regard to members of a given group, for these decisions are made without being influenced in any way by which members of the group will benefit or be harmed. Neither reversibility nor universalizability can guarantee that one is not influenced by which members of the group are benefited or harmed by one's actions. Of the three tests, the only test that guarantees moral impartiality as well as general impartiality is the veil of ignorance test.

Impartial Rational Persons Can Disagree

But the veil of ignorance guarantees impartiality by eliminating all disagreement, and I have already pointed out that people who are impartial with regard to the same group can disagree. Some umpires call pitches that are at the knee strikes, while others call a pitch a strike only if it is above the knee. Yet there is no doubt that both can be completely impartial. Indeed, as mentioned earlier, a single umpire, while retaining his impartiality, can be inconsistent in what he calls a strike. He would not be a good umpire, for a good umpire must be consistent as well as impartial, but his failure would not be due to lack of impartiality. Impartial persons can disagree with each other, even when both are rational persons and equally well informed. This strongly suggests that there can be disagreement among impartial rational persons even when they are being impartial in the way required by morality.

Even if impartial persons make their decisions according to the rules, that does not eliminate all disagreement. Almost all rules are vague to some degree and so require some interpretation. Two different people can make rational, impartial, informed decisions that are in accord with some acceptable interpretation of the rules, and still make different decisions. But often the situation will be such that all impartial, rational persons who are acting in accordance with the rules will make the same decision. For example, if the pitch is over the batter's head no impartial rational person acting according to the rules will call it a strike. Nonetheless, there are situations where impartial rational persons acting in accord with an acceptable interpretation of the rules will disagree.

The United States Supreme Court sometimes comes down with a unanimous decision, but most often the decisions are split. There is no reason to believe that all of these split decisions require an explanation in terms of the defects in one or more of the judges, either as (1) not acting rationally, (2) not acting impartially, (3) not knowing all the relevant facts or laws, or (4) not acting in accordance with the Constitution. The fact that most decisions of the Supreme Court are split decisions should not lead one to the view that impartial rational persons who know all the relevant facts, laws, and the Constitution, will usually fail to agree. The Supreme Court does not hear the overwhelming number of cases on which they would all agree, precisely because it is known that they would all agree. It only makes sense to take to the Court those issues on which it is not clear what fully knowledgeable, impartial rational persons will decide.

Fully knowledgeable, impartial rational persons applying the same rules sometimes disagree even though they usually agree. The ratio of agreement to disagreement will depend on the degree to which the facts allow for differing interpretations of the rules. In most situations where impartial decisions are required, the facts do not often allow differing interpretations to result in different decisions. When supposedly impartial decisions are not in agreement, those adversely affected by the decisions sometimes claim that the decisions were really not impartial. The fact that disagreement sometimes calls impartiality into question may account for the attempt to characterize impartiality in such a way as to rule out any disagreement.

John Rawls's veil of ignorance is the most prominent attempt to rule out any disagreement. What I call the "blindfold of justice" does not rule out all disagreement. It merely removes all knowledge of who will benefit or be harmed by one's decisions. This is sufficient to ensure impartiality but does not guarantee complete agreement. The veil of ignorance eliminates more than the blindfold of justice for it not only removes all knowledge of who will benefit or be harmed by one's decisions, it also removes all individuating characteristics (e.g., no one has a different ranking of the goods and evils than another). This makes it impossible for anyone to actually make decisions under the veil of ignorance. This extra uniformity is not required for impartiality, but it allows the veil of ignorance to guarantee not only impartiality, but also unanimity. However, by requiring unanimity, the veil of ignorance ignores the different rankings of men and women, and results in minorities being taken as having the same rankings as the majority. Although the blindfold of justice is not as large as the veil of ignorance, it is sufficient to guarantee impartiality. Unfortunately, the blindfold of justice has not been previously put forward as a test of impartiality, so the veil of ignorance has been taken as the best test of impartiality.

Universalizability and reversibility do not work as well as the veil of ignorance in guaranteeing impartiality, but they are superior to it in that they both allow for disagreement among impartial rational persons whereas the veil of ignorance does not. However, universalizability and reversibility, by themselves, do not completely rule out favoring one member of the group toward which one is supposed to be impartial over others in that group. Some additional procedure is needed to prevent these tests from being manipulated by using special categories or characterizations. Although no one has as yet come up with any procedure that can do this, requiring that the concepts involved be those that can be part of a public system that applies to all those in the group toward which one is required to be impartial might be sufficient. An adequate test of both general and moral impartiality must guarantee that no member of the group can be favored over any other, and yet allow for some disagreement among impartial rational persons.

Impartial rational persons can differ in their decisions because they may interpret the rule or standard governing their decisions differently. Some basketball referees call a foul for bodily contact between players that other referees do not call. The referees may call fouls the way they do because of their conception of how the game should be played. One may think calling a foul to discourage bodily contact results in a better game because it is a better test of the skill of the players. Another may hold that calling a foul to discourage bodily contact results in a worse game because the flow of the game is disrupted too often. Referees who call fouls or who refrain from calling them from motives like the above do not cease to be impartial. It may be that some teams do in fact benefit from fouls being called one way rather than the other and that other teams are hurt by this policy, but it does not follow from this that adopting one policy or the other is not impartial. Especially if one does not know who will be benefited or harmed by a given policy, it cannot be that one is not acting impartially in adopting that policy.

A referee does not cease to be impartial if he prefers a game with less physical contact. The same is true of the referee who prefers a game with minimal interference. An analog to Rawls's veil of ignorance is not needed in order to guarantee impartiality. On the contrary, it does not even make any sense to talk of the referee having no view whatsoever on how fouls are to be called. If he had no view on this matter it would be impossible for him to interpret the rule concerning fouls in order to make any calls. One may think that he should call fouls in the way the rule intended with no interpretation, but there is no such way. It is the mistaken view that there is one and only one correct way to apply the rules that leads to the view that to be impartial one must not have any views on the way the game should be played. Of course, there are limits on the legitimate interpretations of the rules, and most of the time these limits will determine whether or not a foul should be called. It goes against all human experience, however, to maintain that all qualified impartial rational persons will always interpret or apply a rule in exactly the same way.

Impartiality does not require that one have no views on how to interpret the rules one is applying, only that one not be influenced in one's interpretation by how any particular person or persons within the group toward which one is supposed to be impartial will be affected by that interpretation. This point holds for impartiality with respect to the moral rules as well as with regard to any other rules. The moral rules require impartiality with regard to a group containing oneself, one's friends and family, and at least all those in the minimal group. This means that when considering the violation of a moral rule with regard to a member of this group one cannot allow it to be violated for anyone in this group unless in the same circumstances one would allow it to be violated for everyone in this group. It also means that one cannot allow it to be violated with regard to anyone unless in the same circumstances one would allow it to be violated with regard to everyone. Impartiality with regard to moral rules requires impartiality with regard both to those for whom the rule may be violated and to those toward whom it is to be violated.

Justified Violations Must Be Publicly Allowed

Guaranteeing impartial following of the moral rules requires a way of specifying the same circumstances so that they cannot be intentionally or unintentionally manipulated in order to benefit or hurt particular members of the protected group, such as friends and enemies. Since the moral system is a public system that applies to all rational persons, every feature of the system must be known to and understood by all rational persons. This entails that what counts as the same circumstances be known to and understood by all rational persons. A public system also requires that it not be irrational for any person to whom the system applies to guide his behavior by it. This entails that those to whom the moral rules apply count as the same circumstances only those circumstances that would not be irrational for them to use to determine when people may violate a moral rule. To allow circumstances that discriminate against any subclass of those protected by the moral rules to determine when a moral rule may be violated would be irrational for anyone in that subclass. It would weaken the protection of the moral rules that all rational persons want.

Everyone admits that violations of moral rules are justified only if they are impartial. Since morality is a public system, it is not enough for a violation to be justified that a rational person would allow everyone to violate the rule in the same circumstances. Every rational person must know, understand, and be able to accept the procedure by which this kind of violation is allowed. This is necessary because the procedure cannot be part of a public system unless violations of moral rules are allowed only when they are determined by a procedure that is known by and acceptable to all moral agents. When violations are determined by such a procedure I call them *publicly allowed*. Only publicly allowed violations are justified, but they can be weakly or strongly justified. Strongly justified violations are those all impartial rational persons would publicly allow; weakly justified violations are those on which impartial rational persons can disagree. But when all of a person's violations of moral rules are publicly allowed, he is acting impartially in the way required by morality.

Since the impartiality required by morality is an impartiality that can be part of a public system, violations must be publicly allowed in order to be justified. That justified violations of moral rules must be publicly allowed is not a new condition. It simply makes explicit what is involved in saying that morality as a public system requires an impartiality with respect to acting in accordance with the moral rules impartially. It is because impartiality is part of the public system that justified violations of moral rules must have the same characteristics that moral rules have, namely, to be known to, understood by, and not irrational to follow, by all whose conduct is to be governed by them. This rules out the possibility of a moral system part of which, the moral rules, is known and acceptable to all, and part of which, the procedure for determining justified exceptions, is known and acceptable only to some. The moral rules and the procedure for determining justified exceptions are both part of the same public system, and both must have all of the essential features of that system.

In making moral judgments on particular actions, one must, of course, know the facts of the particular case, and these are not known to all rational persons. But the system of morality itself, which one uses to make judgments about these particular facts, cannot make use of any beliefs that are not held by all rational persons. This limitation to rationally required beliefs derives from the fact that morality is a public system that applies to all rational persons. It derives from the very nature of morality and is not an arbitrary limitation set up simply to rule out the possibility of one group of rational persons using facts known only to them in order to gain some advantage over other rational persons.

The limitation on the beliefs that can be used as part of or in justifying morality to rationally required beliefs resembles the limitations imposed by Rawls's veil of ignorance, but there are two major differences. First, the limitation to rationally required beliefs does not rule out rationally allowed desires and preferences. It allows different desires and preferences as long as one can have them using only rationally required beliefs. Thus it allows impartial rational persons to rank the goods and evils differently and to disagree about whether or not to publicly allow the same violation. Under Rawls's veil of ignorance, rational persons always agree. The limitation to rationally required beliefs allows for some disagreement. Second, the limitation to rationally required beliefs rules out many beliefs that the veil of ignorance allows; for example, it rules out general scientific truths if these are not known to all rational persons. Thus it rules out the claim of more technologically advanced societies that their superior scientific knowledge provides them with greater knowledge of morality than that achieved by less technologically advanced societies.

Moral impartiality not only requires universal knowledge and understanding but also universal acceptability. Advocating that a violation be publicly allowed requires not only that all rational persons know and understand the procedure used in publicly allowing the violation, but also that they can accept it. Using whether a violation can be publicly allowed as a test of moral impartiality resembles the use of universalizability and reversibility as methods for determining moral impartiality in that it does not require that all rational persons agree on what violations they would favor. However, it differs from them in that it guarantees that one cannot unacceptably manipulate the way one formulates the violation. Being publicly allowed eliminates unacceptable eccentricity, because it requires that every rational person know, understand, and accept what counts as the same violation in order for that violation to be allowed. Thus, if the circumstances remain the same, it must be rational for everyone to be willing to be a victim of this kind of violation and rational for everyone to be willing for everyone to commit this kind of violation.

Morality requires impartiality only with respect to obeying moral rules or when one has a duty to be impartial with regard to some smaller group. No matter what test of impartiality one accepts, the claim that all of one's actions be reversible, universalizable, be made under the veil of ignorance, be made using only rationally required beliefs, or even be made under the blindfold of justice, is clearly too strong a requirement. If one is not considering violating any moral rule, there is no need to be impartial, hence no need to satisfy any requirement of impartiality. The failure to realize that it is only when violating a moral rule that morality requires impartiality may have led some to think that impartiality was too stringent a requirement for morality. It is the mistaken acceptance of the standard consequentialist view that morality requires impartiality with regard to all of one's actions that leads to the view that morality must include some special kind of agent-centered prerogative to allow for a normal life.

Summary

In this chapter I have provided a general definition of impartiality, A *is impartial in respect R with regard to group G if and only if A's actions in respect R are not influ-*

enced by which member(s) of G benefit or are harmed by these actions. I have shown that the kind of impartiality morality requires is impartiality with respect to acting in accordance with the moral rules with regard to a group containing oneself, one's friends and family, and at least a minimal group containing all moral agents and former moral agents who are still conscious. Moral impartiality must also be part of a public system that applies to all moral agents. Since a justified violation must be a violation that is consistent with impartially obeying the moral rules, all justified violations of moral rules must be such that a rational person can advocate that they be publicly allowed. The procedure by which the violation is justified must be known, understood, and acceptable to all rational persons. As part of a public system, it must also be rational to act impartially. It cannot be irrational to be impartial in the way required by morality.

In chapter 1 the concept of a public system was introduced and although it is logically dependent on the concept of rationality, it is completely independent of the concept of morality. In chapters 2 and 3 I provided an analysis of the concept of rationality. In this chapter I provided an analysis of the concept of impartiality. These latter two concepts are not only independent of each other, they are also independent of the concept of morality, although the concept of moral impartiality does make use of the concept of morality. In chapter 5 I discussed several rules that are taken to be paradigm examples of moral rules. In the following two chapters I shall show how these three concepts — a public system, rationality, and impartiality — are related to these rules. I want to show what attitude rational persons would take toward certain rules considered as part of a public system that applies to all rational persons. If I can show that all impartial rational persons would favor adopting a public system that contains the moral rules, I will consider myself to have justified morality and to have shown that all of the rules contained in this public system are genuine or justified moral rules.

Notes

1. The original *Encyclopedia of Philosophy* (New York: Macmillan —Free Press, 1967) has no entry on impartiality. Neither the *Encyclopedia of Ethics* (New York: Garland, 1992) nor the *Supplement to the Encyclopedia of Philosophy* (New York: Macmillan, 1996) would have had an entry on impartiality if I had not proposed having one.

2. I am particularly aware of this tendency to substitute a technical term for an analysis of impartiality, for I did exactly this in *The Moral Rules* (New York: Harper and Row, 1970), my first book on the nature and justification of morality. In that book, I used the technical phrase "publicly advocate" as a substitute for the kind of impartiality required of morality. In that book, there is not even an index reference to impartiality.

3. Unless explicitly noted, in the remainder of this book when I talk about the impartiality required by morality, I shall be talking about rational persons.

4. Paragraph 17. To be fair to Mill, in paragraph 9 of chapter 5 of *Utilitarianism*, he explicitly states, "Impartiality . . . does not seem to be regarded as a duty in itself, but rather as instrumental to some other duty." In general, what Mill says in chapter 5 is far better than what he says in the previous four chapters of *Utilitarianism*.

5. I find it odd that many act consequentialists do not distinguish between these two cases. It is a wonderful example of being captivated by a simple theory.

6. Not all rational persons would accept this. Infanticide is not incompatible with hold-

ing that the moral rules should be impartially obeyed with regard to all those in the minimal group. Prior to the possibility of safe abortion, infanticide was widely practiced.

7. Allowing abortion for rape or incest, or to save the life of the mother, need not involve regarding fetuses as not belonging to the group that the moral rules impartially protect. See Judy Jarvis Thomson, "A Defense of Abortion," *Philosophy and Public Affairs* 1, no. 1 (fall 1971): 47–66.

8. In a widely discussed article, "Why Abortion Is Wrong," *Journal of Philosophy* 86, no. 4 (April 1989): 183–202, Don Marquis claims that what makes abortion wrong is that it deprives a being of "a future like ours." Marquis is aware that this is at most a sufficient condition for the wrongness of killing, for he is aware that it is also wrong to kill terminally ill patients who do not want to be killed even though they do not have a future like ours. Marquis's article is so persuasive for he oversimplifies in the same way that most philosophers in the consequentialist and realist tradition oversimplify. Marquis is correct that one of the reasons that rational persons regard killing as wrong is that it deprives people of a valuable future. But rational persons have other reasons for holding that killing is wrong or for claiming that there is a moral rule prohibiting killing. That killing deprives a being of a future like ours is not a property that makes killing wrong, but one feature of some killing that leads rational persons to advocate having a rule prohibiting killing. By skipping this intermediate step, Marquis writes as if he has discovered a feature of killing that makes it wrong independent of the attitude of rational persons. Once one realizes that saying that killing is wrong is simply another way of saying that all rational persons favor a moral rule prohibiting killing, it becomes clear that rational persons disagree about the scope of morality, that is, about who is impartially protected by the moral rules. Thus, the controversy about whether it is morally acceptable to have an abortion remains a controversy.

9. To hold that some animals should be impartially protected means that it is unjustified to sacrifice such an animal for the sake of a human being, unless it would be justified to sacrifice another human being. I do not think that many people hold such a view.

10. As mentioned in note 2, in the first publication of my moral theory, I invented the technical phrase "publicly advocate" and characterized public advocacy in such a way that it provided a test of moral impartiality. I did not completely recognize what I was doing and, in fact, used public advocacy as a replacement for the kind of impartiality required by morality. It was recognition of my own mistake that made it clear to me that very similar mistakes were being made by those who used the other tests of moral impartiality that I shall examine.

11. See Kurt Baier, *The Moral Point of View* (Ithaca, N.Y.: Cornell University Press, 1958).

12. Universalizability is sometimes put forward as if it is a necessary feature of moral judgments, not because it is required for impartiality, but because it is logically required for the correct use of such terms as "good," "wrong," and "ought." See R. M. Hare, *The Language of Morals* (Oxford: Oxford University Press, 1952), and *Freedom and Reason* (Oxford: Oxford University Press, 1963).

13. See John Rawls, *A Theory of Justice* (Cambridge, Mass.: Harvard University Press, 1971).

14. These different tests for moral impartiality are sometimes not regarded merely as tests of, or methods for achieving, moral impartiality; they come to be taken as replacements for it. Often it is not explicitly recognized that these tests should be regarded as providing a way of determining if one is being impartial in the way required by morality. Rather, it is often simply claimed that a moral judgment must satisfy one or the other of these tests if it is to count as a legitimate or genuine moral judgment.

PART II

THE MORAL SYSTEM AND ITS JUSTIFICATION

Chapter 7

Justifying the Moral Rules
The First Five

In this chapter and the next I try to formulate in a precise and systematic way those moral rules that are implicitly or explicitly used when a person is making some moral decisions about how to act and making some moral judgments about how others have acted. These decisions and judgments are those that involve the kinds of actions that are required or prohibited. The seven moral rules presented as paradigms in chapter 5 are explicit rules that involve these kinds of actions, and in the next two chapters all seven of these rules will be discussed. However, these explicit rules do not account for all of the decisions and judgments about kinds of actions that are morally required or prohibited, so there must be some additional moral rules that are implicit. I shall make these rules explicit and attempt to provide a complete and nonredundant list of moral rules. I intend for this list to account for all of those kinds of actions and omissions that rational persons regard as making one liable to punishment.

Morality consists of more than moral rules; there are also implicit and explicit moral ideals. Acting on moral ideals often results in favorable moral judgments, but when a person is expected to act on a moral ideal and fails to do so, this may result in an unfavorable moral judgment. However, failing to act on a moral ideal never warrants punishment, whereas violating a moral rule often does. That is why it is far more important to be precise about the moral rules. A misunderstanding concerning the rules is far more likely to lead to someone suffering undeserved harm than is a misunderstanding about the moral ideals. This chapter and the next are devoted to making all of the moral rules explicit and to providing precise formulations of them. In chapter 9, I shall provide an explicit account of the morally relevant features that determine what counts as the same kind of violation. I shall also show how one determines whether this kind of violation is justified or unjustified and, if justified, whether it is strongly or weakly justified. A proper understanding of this two-step procedure for justifying a violation of a moral rule is essential for understanding the moral system to which these rules belong.

In this chapter and the next, in addition to providing explicit and precise formulations of the moral rules, I shall attempt to provide a philosophical justification of them. I shall do that by showing that rational persons who use only those beliefs that are shared by all moral agents, or rationally required beliefs, will adopt the same attitude toward the moral rules. This attitude is that everyone should obey these rules toward all those protected by them unless they can publicly allow that kind of violation. When I refer to these rules as moral rules, I am considering them as part of a moral system, that is, as part of a public system that applies to all moral agents. Showing that rational persons would take the moral attitude toward the moral rules, that is, favor obedience to them unless the procedure for a justified exception has been satisfied, is sufficient for justifying them. This justification involves only uncontroversial facts about human nature and the concepts of morality, rationality, and impartiality that were provided in previous chapters.

I am attempting to provide both an explicit statement and a justification of those rules that account for the most important moral judgments. In order to account for these judgments in the most systematic way, some of the explicitly stated moral rules mentioned in chapter 5 may have to be slightly modified. Further, some implicit rules will have to be explicitly formulated. These formerly implicit rules will be justified in the same way as the explicit rules of common morality. Although there will be some revisions and additions to the explicit list of commonly accepted moral rules, there will be no surprises. In this chapter and the next I am performing two tasks: one, providing precise and explicit formulations of the commonly accepted moral rules, and two, justifying these rules, that is, showing that all qualified rational persons would favor adopting the moral attitude toward them.

Once a precise and explicit statement of the moral rules is provided, the following will be clear. First, these rules are involved, at least implicitly, in all moral decisions and judgments involving kinds of actions that are required and prohibited. Second, all impartial rational persons would favor including these rules as part of the moral system. To show that all rational persons take the moral attitude toward the moral rules is to show that the rules are justified. Because I think that these rules are, at least implicitly, the commonly accepted moral rules, I often simply call them *the moral rules*. Because I think that the attitude that all rational persons with no controversial beliefs would take toward the moral rules is, at least implicitly, the attititude that is commonly taken toward them, I often simply call it *the moral attitude*.

Since I have not performed an empirical investigation involving all the rational persons in the world, it might seem that I could not reach any significant conclusions about the attitudes of all rational persons on any topic, including their attitudes toward certain rules. However, I am concerned with rational persons only insofar as they are rational, thus I can employ the conclusions of chapters 2 and 3 on the nature of rationality. However, nothing in those chapters makes it obvious that there are any rules toward which *all* rational persons will take a certain attitude. Indeed, if the beliefs that rational persons can use are not limited to rationally required beliefs, then all rational persons may not take the same attitude toward anything. Rationally allowed beliefs vary enormously and people's attitudes are usually determined by their beliefs, so if rationally allowed beliefs can be used it is unlikely that all rational persons will agree in attitude toward the moral rules or anything else. Justifying the moral rules only requires showing that rational persons who use only rationally re-quired beliefs would adopt the moral attitude toward them.

Of course, in all actual situations of deciding how to act or in making judgments about the actions of others, rationally allowed beliefs are not only relevant, they are necessary. That moral agents are sometimes justifiably ignorant of the consequences of their actions or of some other morally relevant feature sometimes totally excuses them from moral judgments. But in formulating and justifying any part of the moral system that applies to these situations, only beliefs that are rationally required can be used. This limitation is necessary, since a moral system is a public system that ap-plies to all moral agents and as such must be known, understood, and acceptable to all moral agents. A moral agent can never be justifiably ignorant of what morality, or the moral system, requires, prohibits, encourages, and allows.

I shall examine the conceptual relationship between holding rationally required beliefs and the rationality of advocating a certain attitude toward a particular set of rules considered as part of a public system that applies to all rational persons. I shall examine this relationship both when one is impartial with regard to the minimal group and when one is not.[1] I have specified what a public system is, and what it is to be both rational and impartial independently of showing anything about one's at-titudes toward a certain set of rules. Therefore, showing that all impartial rational persons will take the appropriate moral attitude toward a particular set of rules con-sidered as moral rules is of some significance. How significant the conclusion is de-pends on the adequacy of the accounts of the concepts of morality, rationality, and impartiality presented in prior chapters. Insofar as one regards those analyses as cor-rect, just so far will one acknowledge the significance of the relationship between morality, rationality, impartiality, and taking a certain attitude toward a certain set of rules, considered as moral rules.

Showing all rational persons *could* favor including these rules in a public sys-tem that applies to all rational persons is sufficient to weakly justify them. Showing that when they use only rationally required beliefs all impartial rational persons *would* favor including these rules in a public system that applies to all rational per-sons is sufficient to strongly justify them.

Do Not Kill

I shall start by considering what attitude all rational persons would take toward the first of the commonly accepted moral rules discussed in chapter 5, "Do not kill."[2] One attitude that they need not hold is wanting to obey the rule themselves. How-ever, at first glance it would seem that they all would want all other people to obey the rule. But simply to say that all rational persons never want anyone to be killed, at least not by anyone other than themselves, does not seem necessary. One can be perfectly rational and not be concerned with the death (or permanent loss of con-sciousness) of persons of whom one has no knowledge. One can even be uncon-cerned with the death (or permanent loss of consciousness) of people about whom one does have knowledge. All rational persons need not adopt the attitude toward the rule "Do not kill" that all other people are to obey it.

They might all adopt the following attitude, however: "All other people are to obey the rule with regard to me." Since rational persons are necessarily concerned with their own preservation, this seems quite plausible. However, as pointed out in chapters 2 and 3, rationality and self-interest are not the same; a rational person might be as concerned with the preservation of some others as with his own preservation. A person is not acting irrationally if he sacrifices his life to save the lives of others, even of those he does not know, though, of course, he is not acting irrationally if he does not. Nonetheless, although a rational person can sacrifice his life for others, he must also want to preserve his own life, so it seems that all rational persons would hold this attitude toward the rule.

The attitude can be modified in a way that makes clear that a rational person need not be concerned only with his own preservation. All rational persons might hold this formulation: "All other people are to obey the rule with regard to everyone for whom I am concerned, including, of course, myself." If a rational person were concerned only with himself, he would want the rule obeyed only with regard to himself; if he were concerned with his family as well, he would want the rule obeyed with regard to them; if he were concerned with all rational persons, he would want it obeyed with regard to everyone. Even though rational persons can differ in the breadth of their concern for people, it seems as if they would all want the rule to be obeyed by all others with regard to those for whom they were concerned. I am claiming only that a rational person need not want to obey the rule himself, or to have it obeyed toward those for whom he was not concerned. I do not deny that a rational person could want it obeyed by all, including himself, toward all.

It may now seem that all rational persons would hold the following attitude toward the rule "Do not kill": "All other people are to obey the rule with regard to everyone for whom I am concerned, including, of course, myself." However, if this attitude does not allow for exceptions, a rational person would not hold it. As pointed out in chapters 2 and 3, there are circumstances in which it is not irrational to want to die, or even to be killed, such as when one is faced with torture or some incurable and extremely painful disease. A rational person would therefore not take an absolute attitude toward the rule "Do not kill." The following attitude allows for exceptions: *All other people are to obey the rule "Do not kill" with regard to everyone for whom I am concerned, including myself, except when those people want (or would want if they were fully informed) not to have the rule obeyed with regard to themselves.*

It must be recognized that the claim that all rational persons would take this attitude toward the rule is not incompatible with there being some further attitude that some or most rational persons might take toward the rule. I am trying to formulate an attitude that a rational person must take toward the rule, and so I must be extremely careful not to include anything on which rational persons might disagree. It seems that a rational person must want all other people to obey the rule "Do not kill" with regard to anyone for whom he is concerned, except when that person does not want to have the rule obeyed with regard to himself. The "except clause" does not mean that a rational person would necessarily want someone to kill a person for whom he is concerned (including himself) if that person wants to be killed. It means simply that when someone they care for wants to be killed, rational persons may differ on whether or not he should be killed. The "except clause" does not mean that all rational persons want the rule not to be obeyed in these cases, but only that they need not want it to be obeyed.

It may now seem that this is an attitude that all rational persons would adopt. However, the following situation shows that a rational person would not take this attitude toward the rule "Do not kill." Suppose someone for whom I am concerned is not sufficiently concerned for me, in fact, he is going to kill me. Most rational persons would not want someone to obey the rule "Do not kill" with regard to their killer, if killing him was the only way to keep themselves from being killed. To avoid the objection that if I am fully informed I would not be concerned for someone who is going to kill me, I present the following example. I will die unless I receive an organ transplant of a vital organ. Someone for whom I am concerned is the only person who has a suitable organ, but to remove it from him would kill him. If I could not kill him myself, to take the proposed attitude would commit me to wanting no one else to do something that is necessary to prevent my death. A rational person need not take this attitude, for a rational person can be an egoist.

As presently stated, the proposed attitude is that no one else is to break the rule with regard to those for whom I am concerned unless they do not want to have the rule obeyed with regard to them. But I have already shown that it is rational for me to want someone to break the rule with regard to this person, even though he may not want to have the rule broken with regard to himself.[3] There is also another kind of objection. Some person for whom I am concerned may want the rule to be broken with regard to himself, but I do not want it to be broken with regard to him, for I want him to stay alive or conscious. In order to meet these objections, I shall substitute the word "I" for the words "those people" in the except clause and make the other changes required by this substitution. The resulting attitude is one that all rational persons would adopt.

The Egocentric Attitude toward the Rule "Do Not Kill"

I call this final attitude *the Egocentric Attitude*. All rational persons would take this attitude toward the rule "Do not kill." Its final formulation is: *All other people are to obey the rule "Do not kill" with regard to everyone for whom I am concerned (including myself), except when I want (or would want if I were fully informed) the rule not to be obeyed with regard to them.* All that I am maintaining here is that because all rational persons desire to avoid death (or permanent loss of consciousness) they must take this attitude. I am not maintaining that there is no other attitude that all rational persons would take (I shall provide one); I am only maintaining that it would be irrational not to take the egocentric attitude as I have formulated it. Even if some rational persons considered this attitude to be incomplete, claiming that it needed to be supplemented by something not quite so egocentric, they would still want everyone to obey the rule "Do not kill" in the way specified by the egocentric attitude.

Do Not Cause Pain

Having formulated an attitude that all rational persons would take toward the rule "Do not kill," it seems clear that all of them would also adopt this same attitude to other moral rules. All rational persons would take the same attitude toward the rule "Do not cause pain." I use the term "pain" to include not only physical pain, but also all kinds of mental suffering, such as anxiety, displeasure, and sadness. I have not forgotten about masochists, whom I admitted in chapter 2 need not be irrational. If a person genuinely enjoys having others inflict pain on himself, he may be suffering from a mental disorder, but he need not be irrational. Having admitted this, how can I affirm that all rational persons, which includes some masochists, would take the proposed attitude toward the rule "Do not cause pain"?

The difficulty with the masochist is that since he enjoys pain it seems he would not want others to obey the rule "Do not cause pain" with regard to himself. However, a masochist may have nonmasochistic friends and would take the attitude for their sakes. More importantly, masochists do not enjoy all pain, nor do they enjoy pain in all circumstances. Hence, if rational, a masochist would accept the stated attitude toward the rule "Do not cause pain," for it includes the except clause. Thus others need not obey the rule toward him when he wants them not to obey it. If they know in a particular circumstance that he would enjoy having pain inflicted, then he is not committed to wanting that they not cause him pain. The masochist will supposedly make much greater use of the except clause.

It may seem absurd to worry about masochists, to attempt to provide an attitude toward these rules that everyone, including those with mental maladies, would take. But the goal is to provide an attitude that *all* rational persons would take, and though masochists may be mentally ill, they need not be irrational. As long as they are aware that most people do not generally enjoy being inflicted with pain, then, being rational, they should take the same attitude as all other rational persons. This shows that by rational persons I do not mean persons with a certain basic goodness, or normalcy, or any other vague but suspicious question-begging characteristic. Even rational masochists will, without giving up their masochism, take the same egocentric attitude as other rational persons toward the moral rule that prohibits causing pain. This shows that in making a connection between being rational and taking a certain attitude toward the moral rules I mean by being rational exactly what I said I did in chapters 2 and 3.

Although I formulate this rule as "Do not cause pain," and in the discussion of it have concentrated on physical pain, I should repeat here that I regard this rule as prohibiting the causing of not only physical pain but also mental pain or suffering, as discussed in chapter 2. This mental suffering is not only of the kind that is normally called mental pain, that is, the kind that comes from being subjected to sudden verbal abuse; it also includes the feelings of sadness, displeasure, and anxiety. Any formulation of the rules involves a choice with regard to their generality.[4] If the formulation is too general, as in utilitarianism, where there is only a single rule, it obscures the fact that there may sometimes be a disagreement on the importance of different rules. If the formulation is not general enough, it may be impossible to state all of the rules. I have adopted a level of generality that allows a complete and nonredundant set of rules to be stated. Thus one rule may be taken as prohibiting causing several distinct evils, but enough harms are distinguished that it is clear that rational persons can disagree in their rankings of the seriousness of the different harms.

Do Not Disable

Having shown that all rational persons would take the egocentric attitude toward the rules "Do not kill" and "Do not cause pain," it requires no additional argument to show that all rational persons would take this same attitude toward the implicit moral rule "Do not disable." As I use the term, to disable someone is to take away or diminish any of her voluntary abilities, namely, abilities to do a kind of voluntary act.[5] Voluntary abilities are composed of physical abilities, mental abilities, and volitional abilities.[6] Cutting off a person's hands causes a physical disability, in that it takes away his ability to do many kinds of physical activities. Destroying parts of a person's brain can cause a mental disability, in that it can take away his ability to add and subtract numbers. Causing someone to have a phobia, such as claustrophobia, is causing a volitional disability. To take away someone's ability to do any kind of voluntary act is to disable him. As with pain, there are degrees of disability, but no rational person wants to be disabled in any degree without an adequate reason. All rational persons would take the egocentric attitude toward the rule "Do not disable," just as they did toward the two previous rules.

Do Not Deprive of Freedom

Adopting the egocentric attitude toward the rule against disabling, makes it clear that there is another implicit rule toward which all rational persons would also take this attitude; namely, a rule prohibiting limiting or preventing the exercise of one's abilities. In fact, it is sometimes unclear whether one is being disabled or simply being prevented from exercising one's ability. This is especially true when the disabling, if it is to be called that, is temporary. This is related to the difficulty of deciding whether it is because one lacks the power or because one lacks the liberty that one is unable to do something. However, the status quo can be used when deciding whether it is one's power or one's liberty that is being taken away. If a change is made in the person, it is taking away power; if a change is made in the circumstances, it is taking away liberty. Undecidable cases are unimportant, because there are rules prohibiting taking away both.

I am attempting to account for common moral judgments. It is quite clear that unless one has a justification, preventing a person from acting is morally unacceptable. Even if there is disagreement about whether a person is being disabled or simply being prevented from exercising her abilities, there is no doubt that one of the two rules is being broken. Hence no act will unacceptably be allowed simply because it is difficult to classify. A rational person takes the same egocentric attitude toward limiting or preventing the exercise of her abilities as she takes toward diminishing or removing them. It is not important for her to decide if a given act fits under one or the other of these rules; all that is necessary is that it is clear that it falls under one or the other. A rational person need make no important distinction between someone who intends to cut off her arm and someone who intends to tie it in such a way as to make it permanently unusable.

Although it is clear that all rational persons will take the same egocentric attitude toward this fourth rule as they did toward the previous three, it is not so clear how to formulate it clearly and precisely, using traditional and easily understood terms. In the past I thought it important to distinguish between freedom and opportunity. Being deprived of freedom is usually being deprived of an indefinite number of opportunities. Being deprived of an opportunity is usually being deprived of the freedom to do some particular thing. This may be why some people claim that taxation is a deprivation of freedom, for taking away a person's money deprives him of the opportunity of doing many different things. However, even if a person is being deprived of only one opportunity, when the deprivation is due to coercion, it is usually said that the person has been deprived of freedom rather than opportunity.[7] Thus, although freedom and opportunity are distinct, it is not misleading to formulate the rule simply as "Do not deprive of freedom."

To deprive someone of freedom, as when you put him in a cell or tie him to a chair, prevents him from doing an indefinite number of things. To deprive someone of an opportunity, as when you do not allow him to participate in a game, prevents him from doing a specific thing. How many opportunities one must deprive a person of before it is appropriate to talk of depriving him of his freedom is more a problem of language than of morality. (In Chinese the distinction between freedom and opportunity is so great that the same word is never used to refer to both; in other languages there may be no distinction between the two.) This rule prohibits all actions that interfere with the exercise of a person's voluntary abilities, so it prohibits taking away his resources for acting, such as taking away his money, as well as depriving him of freedom in a more direct way, such as locking him in a cell. All rational persons would take the egocentric attitude toward the rule "Do not deprive of freedom" when this rule is interpreted as prohibiting causing any kind of limitation of the exercise of one's voluntary abilities.

I now realize that the deprivation of freedom to act is only one kind of deprivation of freedom; there is also the deprivation of freedom from being acted on. The English language allows both of these kinds of actions to be covered by the rule "Do not deprive of freedom." Because I would like to end up with ten rules, I shall interpret the rule "Do not deprive of freedom" as prohibiting both interfering with the exercise of one's voluntary abilities and taking away control over what is done to oneself, including both what touches one's body and what goes into it.

All rational persons would take the same egocentric attitude toward a rule prohibiting taking away control over what is done to one as they would to a rule prohibiting limiting the exercise of one's abilities, so both are included in the rule prohibiting the deprivation of freedom. To be made to see, hear, and so on, especially when one clearly states that she does not want to see, hear, and so on, is to be deprived of freedom. The rule prohibiting the deprivation of freedom prohibits (1) increasing the external limitations on exercising one's voluntary abilities, (2) decreasing the resources for exercising one's voluntary abilities, and (3) taking away control over what is done to oneself.[8] Although this rule may seem more complex than the previous three rules, like the previous three rules, the formulation of this rule should be easily understood. It is a natural part of what is meant by depriving of freedom to take away control over what is done to oneself, including one's body. Thus, it is not misleading to interpret the rule prohibiting depriving of freedom as including both depriving of freedom to act and depriving of freedom from being acted upon. Even given this very wide interpretation, there is no doubt that all rational persons will take the same egocentric attitude toward this rule that they took toward the previous three rules.

Do Not Deprive of Pleasure

The next implicit rule has often not been distinguished from the explicit rule "Do not cause pain." I formulate it as "Do not deprive of pleasure." This formulation is intended to make clear the distinction between causing pain and depriving of pleasure. To trample on flowers in order to prevent someone from enjoying them is to deprive of pleasure; it is not to inflict pain. To torture someone, physically or mentally, is not to deprive of pleasure, but to inflict pain. Sometimes an act does both. Female circumcision, which involves genital mutilation, not only prevents the young women on whom it is inflicted from ever experiencing the pleasure of a sexual orgasm, but also causes pain, both present pain, directly from the operation, and future pain as the result of the scars that occur.[9] Although inflicting pain is almost always worse than depriving of pleasure, a rational person would take the same egocentric attitude toward the rule "Do not deprive of pleasure" as she did toward the previous four rules.

This rule may seem somewhat vaguer than the rest, for what gives pleasure to one person may not give pleasure to another. Indeed, what gives pleasure to a person at one time may not give pleasure to her at some other time. But, as pointed out in chapter 2, some kinds of smiles, together with other facial and bodily expressions, provide a criterian of pleasure, so that there is usually no difficulty in knowing what gives a person pleasure, or what she enjoys doing or having done to her, such as playing golf or having her back scratched. The rule against depriving someone of pleasure tells one not to do that which will cause a person to stop feeling like smiling or not to feel like smiling in the future. A rational person would take the same egocentric attitude toward this rule as toward the previous four rules. Everyone is to obey this rule toward him and his friends unless he wants them not to obey the rule.

Final Statement of the Egocentric Attitude
toward Five Moral Rules

All rational persons would take the egocentric attitude toward five rules:

1. Do not kill.
2. Do not cause pain.
3. Do not disable.
4. Do not deprive of freedom.
5. Do not deprive of pleasure.

The egocentric attitude that all rational persons would take toward these five rules, stated with its final modifications, is *All other people are to obey the rule with regard to all for whom I am concerned (including myself), except when I want (or would want if I were fully informed) not to have the rule obeyed with regard to them.* The except clause does not imply that all rational persons want the rule not to be obeyed when the clause applies, but only that they need not want it to be obeyed.

A rational person takes the egocentric attitude toward the five rules because he wants to protect himself and those he cares for from the harmful consequences of these rules being broken with regard to him and those he cares for. These consequences, death, pain, disability, loss of freedom, and loss of pleasure, are the five harms or evils discussed in chapter 4. All rational persons want to avoid them. The rules can be formulated in order to make this point explicit:

1. Do not cause death (permanent loss of consciousness).
2. Do not cause pain (or other mental suffering).
3. Do not cause loss of ability (mental, physical, or volitional).
4. Do not cause loss of freedom (to act or to be acted upon).
5. Do not cause loss of pleasure (or opportunities for pleasure).

Stated in this way it becomes clear why all rational persons take the egocentric attitude toward the rules. Realizing that harms can be suffered because of the actions of others, all rational persons take this attitude toward the rules because they all want to protect themselves and those they care about from suffering any harm. Taking the egocentric attitude toward the five rules under discussion (no matter how stated), is not rationally required because rational persons somehow simply want others to act according to certain rules. This attitude toward these rules is rationally required because it is an attitude required by those who want to avoid the consequences that all rational persons want to avoid.

Rationality does not contain a queer implicit notion that requires rational persons to want all others to act according to these rules. The rules under discussion are rules that prohibit causing the kinds of consequences that all rational persons want to avoid. A rational person wants to avoid these consequences as much when they are brought about by natural causes as when they are brought about by the actions of persons. A rational person wants to avoid death, pain, disability, loss of freedom, and loss of pleasure, whether these are caused by an avalanche, or a person, or a mosquito. It is not surprising that for someone who believes in an omiscient, omnipotent, and omnibenevolent God, the problem of evil arises in those cases where these harms or evils are brought about, not through the voluntary actions of persons, but simply in the course of nature, by the creator of nature, God.

All of these rules can be broken unintentionally, that is, a person can bring about the consequences that the rules prohibit causing without intending to do so. A drunken driver can break all five rules, even though he has no intention of doing so. Rational persons are primarily concerned with avoiding suffering harm, whether or not these harms are brought about intentionally. They want others to avoid doing those actions that they should know will cause, or significantly increase the probability of, their suffering these harms. Rational persons not only want others to refrain from intentionally disobeying these rules, they also want them to take care not to break them unintentionally. The egocentric attitude toward these rules not only prohibits intentional violations but also prohibits those kinds of thoughtless or reckless actions that lead to the same undesirable consequences.

Although these rules are primarily concerned with the actions of others, rational persons will also use them to judge the intentions and motives of others. They do not want others to intend to break these rules toward anyone for whom they are concerned. Nor do they want the belief that someone for whom they are concerned will suffer one of the harms to be motive for anyone. Rational persons know that people usually do what they intentionally set out to do, so their attitude toward the rules is that they also prohibit intentional actions undertaken to violate the rules, whether or not the action is successful. They will count a person's shooting to kill, but missing, as a violation of the rule against killing, but they can punish the act less than a successful killing.[10]

Replacement of the Egocentric Attitude

Although the attitude described above is one that would be taken by all rational persons, it is not considered the appropriate attitude to be taken toward these rules considered as moral rules. The egocentricity of the attitude must be eliminated. The moral attitude toward a moral rule is not to want it to be obeyed only toward those for whom one is concerned. I pointed out in the preceding chapter that morality requires that the moral rules be obeyed impartially with regard to a group that includes at least all moral agents. The problem is how to replace the egocentric attitude toward the five rules under discussion with the appropriate moral attitude while at the same time keeping it an attitude that would be taken by all rational persons.

In a very important sense, this problem cannot be solved. No adequate account of rationality, according to which no rational person ever wants to act irrationally, can require all rational persons to favor impartial obedience to these five rules. All rational persons have rationally allowed beliefs, based on some combination of their present circumstances and their training or education, such that it would not be irrational for them not to favor impartial obedience to these moral rules. Or they may have such a special interest in some members of the minimal group or be so unconcerned with some other members, that it is rationally allowed for them not to favor impartial obedience to the moral rules. Indeed, if rationally allowed beliefs can be used, then even the egocentric attitude toward these five rules need not be held by all rational persons. A rational person might hold some religious belief that was in conflict with taking the egocentric attitude toward these rules, and he might give priority to the religious belief.

The problem caused by rationally allowed beliefs was anticipated at the beginning of this chapter, and it was eliminated by limiting the beliefs that rational persons can use to those that are rationally required. The problem caused by lack of impartial concern can be eliminated by requiring that the attitude adopted toward the rules be such that it would be rational for all persons to accept it. The first requirement, limitation to rationally required beliefs, is closely related to the feature of morality that all moral agents know and understand it. The second requirement, that the attitude be one that it would be rational for all those to whom it applies to accept, is intimately related to the feature of morality that all rational persons can accept it. Satisfying both of these requirements is necessary and sufficient for considering these rules as moral rules, that is, as part of a public system that applies to all rational persons. Since I am primarily concerned with showing what attitude all rational persons would take toward these five rules when considered as a part of such a system, these two requirements are not arbitrary constraints.

The appropriate moral attitude toward the rules must not only not involve any beliefs that are not shared by all rational persons, it must also not involve, either explicitly or implicitly, any egocentric references. The attitude that everyone obey the rule toward oneself and those for whom one is concerned is clearly not the appropriate moral attitude toward the rules. However, since one is considering these rules as moral rules, there is no need for an additional constraint on the appropriate attitude. Considering a rule as a moral rule requires that it can be part of a public system that applies to all rational persons. An egocentric attitude, that is, one that contains either explicitly or implicitly egocentric references, is not one that would even be understood by all rational persons, let alone be rational for them to accept; hence it could not be part of a public system.

Of course, in one sense, it has already been shown that an egocentric attitude is one that it would be rational for all persons to accept, for they all want the rules obeyed with regard to themselves and those for whom they are concerned. But insofar as this attitude is regarded as guiding their behavior, they do not accept the same attitude, for different persons are concerned with a different group of people. Although these attitudes may be expressed in the same words, one person's attitude toward the rules is not the same as another's if they are concerned with a different group of people. This being the case, there is no reason for a person to expect that someone for whom he is not concerned and who is not concerned with him will accept his egocentric attitude toward the rules. There will be no reason for a person to expect that others will accept his egocentric attitude because doing so restricts their freedom to harm him without providing any compensating protection to them from being caused to suffer harms by him.

Unless she has an impartial concern for all persons, a rational person cannot advocate that her egocentric attitude be part of a public system that applies to all rational persons. Each rational person will demand that the attitude be modified at least so as to require impartial obedience with regard to herself and those for whom she cares. When considering the rules as moral rules, one must put forward an attitude toward them that allows them to be part of a moral system, which is a public system that applies to all rational persons. This means that the attitude that one advocates toward these rules can also be part of a moral system. Thus the attitude that a rational person must adopt is that the rules be impartially obeyed with regard to at least all in the minimal group.

A rational person also knows that all other rational persons want her and her friends to obey the rules. Thus insofar as the attitude adopted must be one that it would not be irrational for all other rational persons to accept, she must advocate that the rules be obeyed by everyone, including herself and her friends. The condition that all other rational persons could accept the same attitude means that a rational person cannot adopt any attitude toward the rules, except one like that which would be adopted by a rational person who has an impartial concern for all persons. Thus it seems that if one is concerned only with the attitude taken by a rational person that is considering these rules as moral rules, that is, rules that are part of a public system applying to all rational persons, all rational persons will adopt the appropriate moral attitude toward these rules. Indeed, considering these rules as moral rules, by itself, restricts the beliefs that one can use to those that are shared by all rational persons. It also guarantees that one will take an attitude that is impartial with regard to the minimal group.

Considering These Rules as Moral Rules

Considering these rules as moral rules imposes a strong restriction on the attitude that rational persons must take toward these rules. This restriction includes the limitation that only rationally required beliefs be used, for considering these rules as rules in a public system that applies to all moral agents means that one cannot use any belief that is not shared by all moral agents. When one considers these rules as moral rules, then one favors impartial obedience toward the rules by all moral agents, including oneself. This allows for a conflict between the attitude a rational person takes toward these rules when considering them as moral rules and the attitude that he takes toward them when considering them as a guide to his own conduct. The former attitude is what he states as the appropriate way to regard these rules, but often this is not the same way that he regards them when considering them as a guide to his own actions. That these two attitudes are often different means that the attitude that rational persons take toward these rules when considering them as moral rules is often not sincere. This explains why hypocrisy is so common.

It has now been shown that if a person is considering these rules as moral rules, that is, as rules in a public system that applies to all moral agents, the attitude that he will adopt will be an impartial rather than an egocentric attitude. The goal of replacing the egocentric attitude with an impartial one may now be considered to have been accomplished. However, it may be interesting to consider whether this goal can be accomplished simply by limiting the beliefs that can be used to rationally required beliefs. This constraint might seem sufficient to make rational persons replace their egocentric attitude with the more appropriate impartial attitude toward these rules. Rational persons not only personally desire to avoid the evils caused by violations of these rules, they also desire everyone for whom they are concerned to avoid these evils. Being limited to rationally required beliefs means that they do not know for whom they are concerned. Since they may be concerned for all in the minimal group, it seems that the attitude they would take toward these rules is that they be obeyed impartially with regard to all.

But need a rational person, simply by being limited to using only rationally required beliefs, take the attitude that the five rules under discussion be obeyed by all, including herself? She need not, for she can still take the egocentric attitude. It is true that she knows that all rational persons desire to avoid the evils that these rules prohibit causing, so she knows that rational persons do not want her to inflict unwanted evil on them. She is aware that taking any attitude toward the moral rules other than that they be obeyed by all rational persons, including herself, with regard to all is not going to be accepted by all rational persons. But if she does not care whether or not her attitude would be accepted by all rational persons, then this need not determine what attitude she takes. I conclude that simply limiting a person's beliefs to those that are rationally required is not sufficient to guarantee that she will take the moral attitude toward these rules. However, adding that her attitude would be accepted by all rational persons, or that she is impartial with regard to the minimal group, does result in her taking the moral attitude.

The limitation that only rationally required beliefs be used shows the close connection between being impartial with regard to the minimal group and considering the rules as moral rules. I have tried to show that the limitation to rationally required beliefs, together with impartiality with regard to the minimal group, results in one adopting the same attitude as one who is considering these rules as moral rules. One might even adopt as the test of one's considering a rule as a moral rule that one is using only rationally required beliefs and is impartial with regard to all persons. Conversely, one can adopt as a test of one's impartiality with regard to the rules that one is considering them as rules in a public system that applies to all rational persons, that is, as moral rules.

If the argument of the previous paragraphs is correct, when one is limited to rationally required beliefs, impartiality with respect to these rules results in the same attitude as considering them as moral rules. It is also interesting that when limited to rationally required beliefs, adopting an attitude toward the rules that could be accepted by all rational persons necessarily leads to an impartial attitude toward these rules. The close connection between considering these rules as rules in a public system that applies to all moral agents and taking the appropriate moral attitude toward them shows that there is more in the writings of those who regard the moral law as the natural law than they are usually given credit for. For natural law is commonly regarded as that law which is known by and agreeable to all rational persons. The defenders of the natural law account of morality unfortunately lacked adequate accounts of rationality and impartiality.

I have now shown that once rational persons are limited to using only rationally required beliefs, one can replace the egocentric attitude toward the rules by an appropriate moral attitude, either by adding the constraint that the person also be impartial, or the constraint that the attitude be one that would be acceptable to all rational persons. I have argued that it does not make any difference which of these constraints one chooses, as both of them, independently, would result in all rational persons taking the appropriate moral attitude toward these rules. I admit that a rational person need not accept either the limitation to rationally required beliefs or to either one of the additional constraints. However, the limitation to rationally required beliefs was shown to be necessary to provide any agreement at all among all rational persons, even on the egocentric attitude. Further, since morality must be understandable to all rational persons, this limitation is necessary in order to ensure that the moral system will be understandable to all rational persons.

The constraint that a person's attitude be one that is acceptable to all rational persons is also necessary in order for one to consider these rules as moral rules, that is, as rules of morality. For morality is a public system that applies to all rational persons, and this requires not only that all rational persons understand it, but also that it not be irrational for them to accept it. These two constraints, the limitation to rationally required beliefs and the requirement that the attitude be acceptable to all rational persons, guarantee that one is considering these rules as moral rules. The constraint that one be impartial is also a natural constraint when talking about the moral rules, for it is universally acknowledged that morality requires impartiality with respect to the moral rules. This constraint, together with the limitation to rationally required beliefs, also seems to result in every rational person taking the appropriate moral attitude toward these rules.

Accepting either combination of constraints discussed above is equivalent to considering these rules as moral rules and will lead to taking the appropriate moral attitude toward these rules. Whether one combines the limitation to rationally required beliefs with the constraint that the person also be impartial, or the constraint that the attitude be one that would be acceptable to all rational persons, makes no difference. One's attitude toward these rules will be like that of a rational person who is considering these rules as moral rules. In what follows I will sometimes talk of an impartial rational person's attitude toward these rules and sometimes about a rational person attitude toward the moral rules. If what I have said above is correct, it should make no difference which I say, for they are equivalent ways of saying the same thing.

Since the moral attitude is derived from the egocentric attitude by removing its egocentricity, the moral attitude should be statable by changing the egocentric attitude appropriately. The egocentric attitude is *All other people are to obey the rule "Do not kill" with regard to everyone for whom I am concerned (including myself), except when I want (or would want if I were fully informed) that the rule not be obeyed with regard to them.* Removing all egocentricity yields *All people (including myself) are to obey the rule "Do not kill" with regard to everyone, except when a fully informed, impartial rational person can want the rule not to be obeyed.* "[F]or whom I am concerned (including myself)" is simply eliminated. "I want (or would want if I were fully informed)" is replaced by "a fully informed impartial rational person can want," because impartial rational persons do not always agree. As before, the except clause means only that when a fully informed, impartial rational person can want the rule not to be obeyed, not everyone agrees that it should be obeyed; it is not that they agree that it should not be obeyed. But if a fully informed, impartial rational person can want the rule not to be obeyed, this is sufficient to make that violation of the rule compatible with taking an impartial attitude toward it.[11]

Reformulating the Moral Attitude

Using "Do not kill" as the specimen rule, I shall now try to formulate the moral attitude more precisely. The present formulation, *All people (including myself) are to obey the rule "Do not kill" with regard to everyone, except when a fully informed, impartial rational person can want the rule not be obeyed* makes it clear that the moral attitude does not encourage blind obedience to the moral rules. On the contrary, it allows that quite often they need not be obeyed. Less often, all impartial rational persons may even favor their not being obeyed. Not only are there justified violations of the moral rules, there is even unjustified keeping of them. For an impartial rational person does not have a fetish for neat, uncluttered obedience to rules, but desires, insofar as possible, to avoid the unwanted evil consequences that usually result from violation of the moral rules. Sometimes, violating a moral rule has the foreseeable consequences that significantly more evil will be prevented by the violation than is caused by it. This possibility must be taken into account in formulating an attitude toward the rules that would be taken by an impartial rational person.

Since these rules are being considered as moral rules, which means as part of a public system that applies to all rational persons, all violations must be such that they can be publicly allowed. A publicly allowed violation is a violation that is understood and can be accepted by all rational persons. In order to make this point explicit, I shall rephrase the except clause, replacing "except when a fully informed impartial rational person can want that the rule not be obeyed" with "except when a fully informed impartial rational person can publicly allow the violation." The moral attitude is now *All people (including myself) are to obey the rule "Do not kill" with regard to everyone, except when a fully informed, impartial rational person can publicly allow the violation.*

What Counts as Depriving of Freedom or Pleasure?

In order to fully understand a moral rule, one must understand what counts as obeying the rule and what counts as violating it. What counts as violating the rules that prohibit depriving someone of freedom or pleasure is not as obvious as it seems, so these rules need further clarification. Acting in a way that one intends to result in a person losing freedom or pleasure always counts as depriving him of freedom or pleasure, but acting in a way that one knows will result in a person losing freedom or pleasure does not always count as depriving him of freedom or pleasure. It often is even less clear what counts as depriving of freedom or pleasure when one does not even know that one is acting in a way that results in a person losing freedom or pleasure.

Some thoughtless actions do count as depriving someone of pleasure, such as talking very loudly during a concert with the result that another person can no longer enjoy it. This is true even if one does not intend this result or even know that one's action has this result. Even actions that do not count as thoughtless because a person is justifiably ignorant that his action would have this result can count as depriving a person of freedom or pleasure. In this latter case, he may be totally excused for violating the rule, but being excused for violating a rule does not mean that he did not violate the rule. I am now concerned with determining what actions or inactions count as violations, not with whether those violations are excused or justified.[12]

The following examples make it clear that sometimes when A does something that results in B's having less freedom or pleasure than B would have had if A had not performed that action, A's action does not count as depriving B of freedom or pleasure. If someone is waiting in line to buy some tickets for a concert, he is not violating the rule that prohibits depriving someone of freedom or pleasure if he buys the last ticket and this results in no one else standing behind him in the line being able to go to the concert. Nor is he depriving someone of pleasure if he buys the last bag of popcorn. If he were doing something that deprived others of freedom or pleasure, he would need a justification or excuse for buying the last ticket or the last bag of popcorn in order to avoid moral condemnation of his action. But if he is not intentionally depriving them of freedom or pleasure, he does not need any such justification or excuse. He can buy the last ticket or the last popcorn simply because he wants to and not thereby be doing anything morally unacceptable.[13] Failing to act also does not count as depriving someone of pleasure or freedom unless that failure to act is a violation of one of the second five moral rules (to be discussed in the following chapter).[14]

Of course, if someone intentionally acts, or fails to act, in order to make it impossible for another to see the concert, for example, buys up all the remaining tickets, he is acting immorally. However, this case differs from the previous examples where the person is not intentionally seeking to deprive people of freedom or pleasure, but only knowingly or unknowingly acting in a way that results in their having less freedom or pleasure. What is it that determines if an action counts as depriving of freedom or pleasure, as in the case of talking too loudly at a concert, or does not count, as in buying the last ticket? It may seem as if it is determined by whether one's action counts as causing the person to have less freedom or pleasure. However, the opposite it true: what counts as causing a person to have less freedom or pleasure is determined by what counts as depriving someone of freedom or pleasure. Further, what counts as depriving someone of freedom or pleasure is determined by the interpretation of the moral rules prohibiting depriving of freedom or pleasure.

What Counts as Causing Death, Pain, or Disability?

Determining what counts as causing death, pain, or disability is done in the same way as determining what counts as depriving of freedom or pleasure. Intentionally acting to bring about the result that a person suffers a harm is always a violation of a moral rule, but not all actions that the agent knows, though does not intend, to result in some person suffering one of these evils count as violations of a moral rule.[15] In the morally relevant sense, a person causes an evil by her action only when her action can correctly be said to be a violation of one of these moral rules. This is just the reverse of what might have been expected, that a person can be said to have violated one of these moral rules only when her action causes someone to suffer an evil. In problematic cases, what counts as causing an evil is determined by whether or not one of these rules has been broken rather than the reverse. Whether or not a person is regarded as needing an excuse or a justification in order to avoid moral condemnation is what determines whether or not she is regarded as having caused the evil. There is no scientific sense of "cause" that can be used to settle whether or not some particular act counts as causing an evil. This accounts for some of the disagreement about whether someone, for example, a photographer whose actions result in a celebrity suffering some displeasure is causing that celebrity to suffer that harm.

The Interpretation of Moral Rules

Although societies play a crucial rule in interpreting the moral rules, it is not an arbitrary matter whether or not one is violating one of these moral rules. It has already been pointed out that acting in a way that one intends to result in a person suffering an evil always counts as violating one of these rules. Further, there are some cases where, even if unintentional, everyone counts an action as a violation of one of these rules. For example, driving a car and skidding on a slippery patch of road and thereby hitting someone counts as causing the harm that the victim suffers. This is true even if hitting the person was not only unintentional but is also unforseeable and not due to any negligence on the driver's part. If the latter is true, then although the driver violated the relevant rule, he is totally excused. What counts as a totally excusable violation of a moral rule, and what counts as no violation of it at all is determined by the interpretation of the rule. It is this interpretation that determines whether or not one has caused the harm and thus needs an excuse or justification, or has not done anything that even needs an excuse or justification.

Every society will interpret the rules in such a way that intentionally acting so as to bring about the result that someone suffers a harm is a violation of the rule. Strong interpretations are those to which all rational societies agree. Weak interpretations are those in which different rational societies have different interpretations of the rules, so that an action that counts as a violation of a moral rule in one society will not count as a violation in another. Determining the interpretation of a rule has some similarity to determining the justification of a violation of a rule. There is a close parallel between strong justifications and strong interpretations, those on which all impartial rational persons agree. However, unlike weak justification, where each individual decides for himself how he morally ought to act, each individual does not determine whether or not to act on his own weak interpretation. Rather, each society puts forward its own interpretation of the rules, and that is the correct interpretation of that rule in that society.[16] However, if a rational person disagrees with that interpretation of the rule, he can try to get society to change its interpretation.[17]

Rights

When members of a society disagree about the interpretation of a moral rule, it is important that the disagreement be resolved. Otherwise there will be significant conflicts and more evils will be suffered than if all accepted the same interpretation. Surprisingly, this is true no matter what interpretation they adopt, as long as it is one that an impartial rational person could advocate.[18] In many societies this interpretation is expressed in statements about rights, but often the rule itself is transformed into a statement about rights. It is commonly said that everyone has the right not to be killed. This also seems to be true of the right not to be caused pain, not to be disabled, not to be deprived of freedom, and not to be deprived of pleasure. These rights are claimed to be not merely legal rights but are said to be moral rights.

One of the clearest ways to see the intimate relationship, perhaps even one of identity, between violating one of these general rights and breaking one of the general moral rules, is to consider the question "Who can violate rights?" (My daughter, Heather, is the one who lead me to consider this question.)[19] It then becomes obvious that only moral agents can violate rights. One's rights are violated when a moral agent breaks the relevant moral rule with regard to a person without his consent. For example, a physician violates a patient's right not to be caused pain by breaking the moral rule prohibiting causing pain with regard to the patient without his consent. Paternalistic behavior by physicians always involves violating rights in this sense.[20] With regard to the general rights mentioned above, talking about violating someone's rights and talking about breaking a moral rule with regard to someone without his consent may be simply two ways of talking about the same thing.

When José causes pain to Maria it is appropriate to say either (1) that José has violated Maria's right not to be caused pain or (2) that José violated the moral rule prohibiting causing pain with regard to Maria without her consent. I prefer the latter way of talking, because it allows a conceptually clearer, more precise, and more fruitful way of discussing the moral aspects of causing pain or any other evil. For example, it is not clear if someone violates another's right not to be killed if she kills him in self-defense, for by attempting to kill her, he may have forfeited that right. But it is clear that she has broken the moral rule prohibiting killing and it is a relatively straightforward question to determine if her violation is justified. All impartial rational persons would favor that killing be publicly allowed in self-defense. Talking about having general rights not to be caused to suffer any of the evils is of limited usefulness, for the same points can be made more clearly and precisely by talking about the general moral rules. When a fully informed, impartial rational person can publicly allow a violation of a moral rule, that same person can hold that it is morally justifiable to violate or override a person's rights, or claim that the person has forfeited his right.

Although the rights not to be killed, disabled, and so on, do not add anything to the moral rules, other rights play a significant role in explaining how the first five rules should be interpreted. As mentioned in the previous sections, there are sometimes disagreements as to whether an action that results in someone suffering an evil counts as breaking a moral rule. I have already pointed out that if one violates one of the second five moral rules (to be discussed in the next chapter), then if an evil results, this counts as violating one of the first five rules. If a person deceives, breaks a promise, cheats, neglects her duty, or breaks the law, and as a result someone suffers an evil, she has caused that evil. Since one of these second five moral rules prohibits breaking the law, the law can determine whether or not one has violated one of the first five moral rules. Thus the law sometimes determines whether or not one has caused someone to suffer an evil. When someone suffers a harm as the result of an unintentional action or failure to act by another, legal terms such as "reckless" or "negligent" are used to indicate that the agent is regarded as having caused the harm.

Suppose one parks in front of another person's house and the law prohibits parking in front of another person's house. Then, if the owner of the house is upset because of one's parking there, one has broken the moral rule prohibiting causing pain. If the law does not prohibit parking in front of another person's house and the owner of the house is upset because of one's parking there, then one has not broken the moral rule prohibiting causing pain. In this case, the law determines whether one caused the owner pain. The law can also be said to determine whether one has violated the owner's right not to be caused pain. This is a violation of a moral right and not merely of a legal one, even though it is the law that grants him the right not to have someone park in front of his house.

Sometimes when no law is violated and none of the other second five rules is violated, it still has to be decided whether the evil suffered by one person has been caused by another. Rights are most significant in these kinds of situations. Consider the situation mentioned earlier where one person in a concert talks very loudly with the result that someone else is deprived of pleasure. In this situation the first person is regarded as having broken the moral rule prohibiting depriving of pleasure because he did not have the right to talk loudly during the concert and the second person did have the right to listen to the concert. Now consider the situation where a person buys the last ticket to the concert with the result that the other people behind him in line cannot see the concert. In this situation, he has the right to buy the ticket and they do not have any right to see the concert. In this situation, he did not break the rule prohibiting depriving people of freedom or pleasure. If one is not violating others' rights, then even if what one does results in their suffering some evil, one has not caused that evil and has not violated a moral rule.

How can one decide whether or not Maria, who is annoyed by José looking at her, has been caused to suffer this harm by José, that is, whether José has violated the moral rule that prohibits causing pain with regard to Maria? If people have some kind of right to privacy, then it will be relevant to determine the circumstances in which José is looking at Maria. Suppose José is standing on a street corner looking at all the women who pass without making any overt moves to approach them. Then even if Maria is annoyed at being looked at, it is not correct to say that José had broken a moral rule with regard to Maria. José has the right to look wherever he wants in public, and Maria has no right to walk on the street unlooked at. However, if José is peering through Maria's window blind, then the right to privacy yields the conclusion that Maria's annoyance at being looked at is caused by José, that José has violated a moral rule with regard to Maria. José has no right to peer through Maria's window blind, and Maria has a right to be in her room unlooked at. The right to privacy helps determine when an action counts as a violation of a moral rule.

Another example. Suppose a photographer is following a famous person around, constantly taking pictures of him. He is annoyed and asks her to stop. She claims that his annoyance is his own problem, that she has the right to take any pictures she wants as long as he is in a public place and that he has no right to be in a public place unphotographed. He claims that he has a right to be left alone, even in public places, and that she has no right to photograph him whenever she wants. He claims a right to privacy and denies her right to photograph him. She claims a right to photograph and denies his right to privacy. He is claiming that she is violating the moral rule that prohibits causing pain, and she is claiming that she is not. Who is correct depends upon the society. All societies that have the relevant concepts and practices agree that one has no right to talk loudly in a concert and that one does have a right to listen to a concert, but even these societies can differ on whether or not the photographer is violating the rights of the famous person.

Since morality is an informal public system, everyone in the society will agree on most cases. In the clear cases, these rights are not only recognized by everyone, they will be enforced by law as well, and so will also be legal rights. The unclear cases are those where there is an unresolvable moral disagreement, so that each society must transfer the question to the legal or political system. When a particular society must use the formal legal system to determine one's rights, for example, how much of a right one has to be left alone and how much of a right one has to photograph people, these rights will generally be regarded as legal rights, but not moral rights. Except for the rights not to have the moral rules violated with regard to oneself, including their strong interpretations, I do not claim that there are any universal moral rights. I regard rights like the right to privacy as the way that a society determines what counts as a violation of one of the first five moral rules. But since each society has its own right to privacy, even if a society has a right to privacy, it may not provide the same interpretation of the moral rules as another society with a slightly different right.

Rights that simply restate the moral rules, such as the right not to be killed, involve issues that are more clearly discussed by talking about moral rules. It is clearer to say that there is a moral rule prohibiting killing than that one has a right not to be killed. Saying that one's rights should be protected says no more than saying that the moral rules should be enforced. To say that one is justified in violating someone's right not to be caused pain is to say that one is justified in violating the moral rule prohibiting pain with regard to this person without his consent. Sometimes it is said that a person has a right, for example, a child has the right to be fed, when it would be clearer to say that someone else would be violating her duty if she did not feed him. I do not claim that the translations that I have offered are completely adequate, but I do claim that with regard to the rights that simply correspond to the moral rules, nothing is involved that cannot be dealt with by talking only of the corresponding moral rules.

However, rights such as the right to privacy or the right to a clean environment are not similarly superfluous. They are useful as aids in determining, for a given society, what is regarded as a violation of one of the first five moral rules.[21] They account for what is true about the ethical relativist's claim that different societies have different moral rules. Although the moral rules are completely universal, when they are not intentionally violated and there is no violation of any of the second five rules, what counts as a violation is interpreted differently by different societies. Some of this interpretation is expressed by the rights that different societies claim for their members. Unlike the moral rules, which are unchanging, rights can change and develop as the interpretation of the moral rules changes. I recognize that there are differences in the interpretation of the moral rules and that this results in some differences in what counts as a violation of one of these rules. However, these differences are trivial in comparison to the overwhelming agreement in most cases on what counts as a violation of each rule.

Punishment Is Part of the Moral Attitude

Although all rational persons, if impartial, will adopt the moral attitude toward the moral rules, not all rational persons are impartial, and hence not all will obey the rules as the moral attitude requires. Although impartial rationality requires adopting the moral attitude, rationality does not require acting on this attitude. Rationality always allows, but it does not always require, acting morally. It is the mark of a false theory to "prove" that it is irrational to act immorally. I have tried to show only that all rational persons will take the moral attitude toward these rules when they consider them as moral rules, that is, as part of a public system that applies to all rational persons. But all rational persons are aware that their agreement on the moral attitude does not guarantee that no one will violate a moral rule except when a fully informed, impartial rational person can publicly allow its violation. A rational person need not be a hypocrite, but all rational persons are aware of the possibility of hypocrisy. Awareness of the possibility of unjustified violation of the rules requires consideration of an impartial rational person's attitude toward such violations.

All rational persons want to discourage the breaking of these rules, at least with regard to those for whom they are concerned. They know, however, that the moral attitude toward the rules requires impartial treatment of all those who unjustifiably break the rules with regard to anyone. A rational person, insofar as she is impartially concerned with protecting everyone from suffering the evils caused by violations of the moral rules, will support measures that will discourage anyone from unjustifiably breaking these rules. If this were her only consideration, and she believed that harsher measures were better at discouraging violations, she might recommend the harshest measures to be used against anyone unjustifiably breaking the rules. However, being impartial she is also concerned with those who unjustifiably break any of the rules. To adopt as part of the public system the harshest possible measures against anyone who breaks the rule might result in excessively harsh measures toward those who break the law. They would be excessive because greater harm would be inflicted on violators than would be justified by the amount of harm prevented by such punishments.

An impartial rational person is as concerned with those who violate the rules as with those who are victims of the violation. The punishment adopted must be harsh enough to discourage serious unjustified violations of the rules, not only intentional ones, but also those done thoughtlessly. An impartial rational person will be prepared to do more to prevent those violations of the rules that cause the greatest amount of harmful consequences. Hence she will, as an impartial rational person, adopt harsher measures for the violation of the rule prohibiting killing than for violation of the rule prohibiting the deprivation of pleasure. The harshness of the measures for violations of rules that prohibit causing pain, disabling, and deprivation of freedom will vary with the amount of pain, disability, and loss of freedom. In some cases, the amount of pain, disability, or loss of freedom may demand measures as harsh as that against killing; in others, as little as that against the deprivation of pleasure.

Since one of the major goals of the moral system is to discourage everyone from unjustifiably breaking the rules, the kinds of measures adopted to discourage violations of the rules must be those that will best serve to discourage all rational persons from unjustifiably breaking the rules. Only the infliction of an evil on the violator is this kind of measure, for, as was shown in chapter 4, only the infliction of an evil serves to discourage all rational persons from performing an unwanted act. The question arises, "What evil?" Perhaps the same one that the violator inflicted on some person. If he killed, let him be killed; if he caused pain, let him have pain inflicted upon him; if he disabled, let him be disabled; and so on. Although this formula might appeal to a rational person's aesthetic sense, or sense of fitness of things, it is not supported by the best reasons.

The point of inflicting evil on violators is not to establish some aesthetic fitness, but to prevent further violation of the rules. An eye for an eye may have some appeal, but unless it can be shown that a public system that includes such retribution prevents violations better than a more lenient public system, no impartial rational person will accept it. Of two public systems that inflict evil on violators and are equally good at discouraging violations, an impartial rational person will choose that which inflicts the lesser evil. For her goal is to have no more evil inflicted than is necessary to prevent violations. Even a rational person who is not impartial wants those he cares about protected as much as possible from those he does not care about, and to have as little evil as possible inflicted on those he cares about when they break the rules with regard to those he does not care about. An impartial rational person is equally concerned with all.

Since the overall goal of morality is lessening the amount of evil suffered, an impartial rational person will decide between public systems that discourage violators equally well, by picking that which is most lenient, that is, inflicts the least evil. Between all those public systems that are equally lenient, she will pick the one that most discourages violations. Being impartial and rational is not sufficient for picking the appropriate punishment; one must also be fully informed, and this requires trying to find out what effect adopting public systems with different sets of punishments would, in fact, have in discouraging future violations. This cannot be known a priori and in fact, may differ in different societies with different cultural traditions. Further, between punishments that are harsher and better at discouraging violations and punishments that are less harsh but not as good at discouraging violations, impartial rationality may allow either choice.

The primary morally relevant feature that should determine which set of punishments are adopted is the overall amount of evil suffered; all impartial rational persons prefer a policy that results in less overall evil. If there were no other morally relevant feature, the only dispute would be about which set of punishments results in the least amount of evil. Although this dispute is partly factual, it also depends on different rankings of the evils. However, there is another morally relevant feature, since the evils inflicted by punishments are inflicted because a person has violated a moral rule. An impartial rational person may be prepared to allow more evil to be inflicted on violators to prevent a lesser amount of evil for victims because she gives greater weight to the morally relevant consideration that the evil is inflicted as a punishment for violating a moral rule. However, some rational persons may prefer a public system that results in the least number of people suffering the most serious evils, without even considering whether it is victims or violators that will be suffering.

A moral system allows evils to be inflicted on those who unjustifiably violate the rules in order to discourage future violation of the rules. Thus the public system will allow punishment only for those violators who are capable of guiding their actions by the rules. Except under special circumstances, it will not allow inflicting evil on

those who violate the rules through no fault of their own, such as excusable ignorance of the consequences of their actions or inability to act according to their
knowledge. The special circumstances are those where knowledge that evil will be
inflicted if harm results from one's actions with no excuses allowed, results in significantly less evil being suffered. This is the justification of strict liability laws. Absent
these special circumstances, morality does not allow inflicting evil on those who are
not responsible for their violations, because, by hypothesis, allowing such infliction
of evils will do nothing to discourage violations. Limiting punishment to the kinds
of cases that discourage future violations is simply choosing a system that equally
discourages violations but is more lenient than another.

Using the Moral Attitude to Distinguish
Moral from Nonmoral Rules

This seeming digression on an impartial rational person's attitude toward those who
unjustifiably violate the rules provides an important feature of an impartial rational
person's attitude toward the moral rules. In order for there to be an important distinction between moral rules and all other rules or precepts, all and only rules toward
which all impartial rational persons adopt the appropriate moral attitude can and
must count as moral rules. But as presently formulated, there seems to be no reason
for an impartial rational person not to adopt the moral attitude toward any rule or precept that he would like all people to obey. That is because the attitude as presently
formulated contains nothing about what is to be done to those who unjustifiably violate a rule. If unjustifiably violating a rule does not involve any punishment, one
might as well adopt the moral attitude toward a rule like "Smile when greeting people," or even a rule that it is impossible to obey impartially, like "Promote pleasure."

In order to distinguish the moral rules from all other rules, the appropriate moral
attitude must include an impartial rational person's attitude toward those who unjustifiably violate a moral rule, that is, those who violate it when no impartial rational
person would publicly allow that violation. Since all impartial rational persons want
to discourage everyone from violating the five rules under discussion, they would all
adopt the attitude that those who unjustifiably violate these rules be liable to punishment. Failure to include this feature as part of the public system would lessen the
protection from violations that all impartial rational persons want.

Adding the liability to punishment to an impartial rational person's attitude toward each of the moral rules results in the following formulation: *All people (including myself) are to obey the rule "Do not kill" with regard to everyone, except when
a fully informed, impartial rational person can publicly allow the violation. Anyone
who violates the rule when no impartial rational person can publicly allow such a violation may be punished.* This is the third formulation of the moral attitude. Only
those rules toward which all impartial rational persons would adopt this attitude
count as justified general moral rules. It is clear that all impartial rational persons
would adopt this formulation of the moral attitude toward the five rules discussed in
this chapter. Thus five general moral rules have been justified, or it has been shown
that at least five rules are justified general moral rules.

One point of including an impartial rational person's attitude toward unjustified violations in the moral attitude is to distinguish moral rules from all others, in order to make clear that "Promote pleasure" is not a moral rule. Thus it is no surprise that no impartial rational person would adopt the most recent formulation of the moral attitude toward the rule "Promote pleasure." Unlike the five moral rules, this rule cannot possibly be obeyed all of the time. Nor is it likely that it can ever be impartially obeyed with regard to everyone. Thus an impartial rational person would either have to adopt the attitude that everyone be publicly allowed to violate the promote-pleasure rule whenever and with regard to whomever he feels like doing so, or else to hold that everyone is liable to punishment all of the time. To do the former would make it pointless to adopt the moral attitude toward the rule; to do the latter would be to increase everyone's chances of suffering evil. I conclude that no impartial rational person would adopt the moral attitude toward the rule "Promote pleasure."

The same considerations show that "Prevent evil" is also not a moral rule. It might seem more plausible that some impartial rational persons might adopt the moral attitude toward this rule. However, the impossibility of impartially obeying the rule all of the time with regard to all moral agents, makes clear that no impartial rational person would adopt the moral attitude toward it. The addition to the impartial rational person's attitude that unjustified violations may be punished even eliminates as moral rules modifications of the above rules that can be impartially obeyed all of the time. Consider the rule "Offer to promote pleasure for the first person you see each day." This rule may not have the simplicity required of general moral rules, but even ignoring this, not all impartial rational persons would adopt the moral attitude toward it. An impartial rational person need not hold that the increase in the chances of having one's pleasure promoted is greater than the risk of suffering punishment.

The same point holds even when "prevent pain" is substituted for "promote pleasure" so that the rule is now "Offer to prevent pain for the first person you see each day." Either the rule is pointless because all impartial rational persons would publicly allow violating it whenever one felt like doing so, or, given the liability to punishment, an impartial rational person need not hold that adopting the rule decreases the chances of people suffering evils. Even if some impartial rational persons would adopt the moral attitude toward some of these contrived moral rules, not all of them would. It is not irrational not to take the moral attitude toward them. General moral rules are those toward which all impartial rational persons would adopt the moral attitude; it would be irrational not to take the moral attitude toward these rules.

The Punishment Provision

Including in the moral attitude the provision that unjustified violations may be punished has made it into a test that excludes all rules that are not moral rules and includes all rules that are. Since it serves such an important task, it is worth examining this provision in some more detail. I have said that all impartial rational persons adopt as part of their moral attitude that unjustified violations *may* be punished. I said that unjustified violations may be punished, rather than that they are to be punished because the latter would have needed to be qualified. Situations may arise in which punishing unjustified violations would cause significantly more evil than would result from failure to punish, for example, in political situations when attempting to punish might prevent the end of a civil war. Although all impartial rational persons would favor liability to punishment for unjustified violations of moral rules, they need not always favor actual punishment, even if punishment is determined in the way that was outlined earlier in this chapter.

An impartial rational person does not advocate that unjustified violations be punished in order to achieve some metaphysical fitness in the nature of things. Her primary goal is to minimize the amount of evil suffered, which is generally best served by punishing unjustified violations. But if it is not, an impartial rational person is not committed to punishment. That is why an impartial rational person advocates only that those who unjustifiably violate the rules *may* be punished rather than that they are to be punished. There are also further reasons. To advocate punishment requires someone to do the punishing. Who this someone should be and how he should go about his job is more properly a subject for political philosophy than for moral philosophy. Some things, however, should be said. First, it will usually be the responsibility of the government to punish. However, setting up a system that results in punishing all unjustified violations may cost more than it is worth. The potential for a significant loss of freedom may be considerably greater than the added protection against unjustified violations. People in law enforcement, like all people, are fallible and it may not be worth the risk of harm to have most minor violations punished.

On a more personal level, parents are generally considered to have the responsibility to punish their children for less serious violations. A parent may know that punishing his child for an unjustified violation will do more harm than good, even when the child has become a moral agent. Thus though the child has put himself in a position where he may legitimately be punished, it does not follow that he should be. If punishment is the best way to discourage future violations, without undue suffering of harm, children should usually be punished for unjustified violations, but there are times when they should not be. To insist that unjustified violations demand punishment, regardless of the consequences, is to allow one's desire for retribution to overwhelm achieving the kind of public system that applies to all moral agents. No impartial rational person would publicly allow retribution when publicly allowing it would result in more suffering of harm than not allowing it.

Summary

The justification of the moral rules that has been presented in this chapter may be considerably weaker than what has been generally sought. Many would like it to have been shown not only that impartial rationality requires taking the moral attitude toward the moral rules but also that rationality requires acting in the way specified by that attitude. I would have liked to be able to show it. In chapter 13, I shall try to explain further why the most that can be done is to show that rationality always allows acting morally, but I shall provide the best reasons I know of for acting in this way.

In the present chapter, I have been concerned only with showing that impartial rationality requires the moral attitude toward certain rules, and that rationality requires this same attitude toward these rules when considered as part of a public system that applies to all rational persons, that is, as moral rules. It is impossible to justify acting morally in as strong a sense as it is to justify taking the moral attitude toward the moral rules.

The moral attitude is presently formulated as follows: *All people (including myself) are to obey the rule "Do not kill" with regard to everyone, except when a fully informed, impartial rational person can publicly allow the violation of the rule. Anyone who violates the rule when no impartial rational person can publicly allow such a violation may be punished.* Only those rules toward which impartial rationality requires the moral attitude count as justified general moral rules. This discussion of the justification of the moral rules has therefore served a dual function: it has justified the moral attitude toward some commonly accepted moral rules, and it has also furnished a criterion for determining if a rule is a justified general moral rule. In the following chapter I shall not only examine the other rules toward which impartial rationality requires the moral attitude, I shall also examine the moral attitude in greater detail.

Notes

1. What I say about impartiality with regard to the minimal group does not change at all if any additions are made to the minimal group. I am now specifying only the group with regard to which morality requires impartiality; I am not specifying the respect in which morality requires impartiality with regard to this group, for that is what I hope to show. I want to show that a rational person who is impartial with regard to the minimal group (including any additions) and regards the moral rules as part of the moral system would advocate being impartial with respect to obeying the moral rules. Unless it is apparent from the context, whenever I use the phrase "the minimal group" one can substitute "the minimal group including any additions." I will occasionally use "all moral agents" instead of "the minimal group," but this is purely stylistic, and one can still substitute "the minimal group including any additions."

2. This rule could be stated more precisely as "Do not cause permanent loss of consciousness," but it seems unnecessarily confusing to give up the traditional formulation to include those rare cases where one causes permanent loss of consciousness without killing. Nonetheless, for rational persons permanent loss of consciousness is equivalent to being dead, and a rational person is unconcerned with whether or not he dies if he has suffered permanent loss of consciousness.

3. This example should make it quite clear that I have not included morality in my account of rationality, for clearly it would be immoral to have someone killed so his heart could be used as a transplant for me.

4. The appropriate generality may depend on the language in which the rule is stated. English allows for very general rules, but other languages may not. It does not matter how many rules there are, as long as there are not too many to list. It is essential that there be no harms that the moral rules do not prohibit causing.

5. Thus as I use the term, to "disable" a person is not necessarily only to cause a disability. One violates the rule prohibiting disabling with regard to a great athlete by causing her to lose some ability, even though she may not be disabled by one's action. It would be more precise to formulate the rule as "Do not cause a loss of ability." However, most serious violations

of this rule will cause disabilities, so it does not seem misleading to formulate the rule as "Do not disable."

6. For a full explanation of voluntary abilities and related concepts, see chapter 6 of Charles M. Culver and Bernard Gert, *Philosophy in Medicine* (New York: Oxford University Press, 1982), and Bernard Gert and Timothy Duggan, "Free Will as the Ability to Will," *Nous* 13, no. 2 (May 1979): 197–217, reprinted in *Moral Responsibility*, edited by John Martin Fisher (Ithaca, N.Y.: Cornell University Press, 1986).

7. This shows that the philosophical concept of freedom cannot be derived from the normal use of the term "freedom" in the English language.

8. As noted in chapter 2, in many languages it may not be possible to include all three of these in one rule. It may be stretching to include them all in one rule in English. But nothing turns on this as long as it is clear what the rule prohibits.

9. See Loretta M. Kopelman, "Female Circumcision/Genital Mutilation and Ethical Relativism," *Second Opinion*, no. 2 (October 1994): 55–71.

10. This is due to the lottery nature of punishment. A system of punishments should aim at lessening the harm suffered. Making a punishment for a failed attempt less than that for a successful attempt provides people with a reason not to make a second attempt after the first one has failed. This is especially important when death would result from a successful attempt.

11. "Fully informed" does not mean omniscient. As stated in chapter 2, to be fully informed means that the person "must have all of the relevant information that is possessed by all other rational persons at that time." I regard this as close to the ordinary meaning, as when it is said that a patient must be fully informed before her consent counts as valid or informed consent. "Fully informed" is included in the moral attitude to rule out counterexamples that would result if an impartial rational person was unaware of some foreseeable relevant information.

12. If an action counts as a violation, one may still be required to provide some compensation to the victim, even if the violation is completely excused or justified. This will depend on many factors, including the innocence of the victim, but it is a complex matter, and impartial rational persons may disagree on what is owed.

13. But if there are serious shortages of items necessary to continue living, a person who does not need such an item may be considered by some to be depriving people of necessities if he buys the last item simply because he wants it.

14. If someone does not give a person a ride to the concert, he is not depriving that person of the pleasure of hearing it unless by not doing so he has violated a moral rule such as breaking his promise to give that person a ride.

15. As with the rules prohibiting depriving of freedom and pleasure, failing to act does not count as a violation of the rules prohibiting killing, causing pain, and disabling, unless such a failure is also a violation of one of the second five rules. When failing to act is a violation of one of the second five rules and the result is that some person suffers harm, then the act counts as causing that harm and also as a violation of one of the first five rules. It is only in these circumstances that failing to act counts as causing an evil.

16. That societies interpret moral rules differently is used to support ethical relativism. However, all of these interpretations are of the same rules and there is a significant limitation on legitimate interpretations. Ethical relativism claims that there is not even any limitation on what rules are moral rules.

17. This is now happening in the United States, where some philosophers are trying to change the interpretation of the rule against killing. They want to count discontinuing treatment when a competent, fully informed patient has rationally refused to continue treatment and when one knows that discontinuing the treatment will result in the patient's death, as

killing the patient. They want to do this in order to minimize the difference between such discontinuing of treatment for a patient and actively killing a competent, fully informed patient who rationally requests to be killed. For a more detailed account of killing, see Bernard Gert, Charles M. Culver, and K. Danner Clouser, *Bioethics: A Return to Fundamentals* (New York: Oxford University Press, 1997), chap. 12.

18. This extremely significant point is one of the arguments that Hobbes uses to show the need for a sovereign. See my article, "Le Droit de nature," in *Le Pouvoir et le droit: Hobbes et les fondements de la loi*, compiled by Louis Roux and François Tricaud (Saint Étienne: Publications de l'Université de Saint-Étienne, 1992): 27–48.

19. See Heather J. Gert, "Rights and Rights Violators: A New Approach to the Nature of Rights," *Journal of Philosophy* 87, no. 12 (December 1990): 688–694.

20. Violating of rights thus has no closer relationship to depriving of freedom than it has to the violating of any of the other moral rules. Failure to see the close relationship between violating a person's rights and violating a moral rule with regard to a person without his consent has caused some confusion concerning the proper analysis of paternalism. See chapter 7 of Gert, Culver, and Clouser, *Bioethics*.

21. Rights are also used to determine what counts as a violation of the rule concerning deception. The right to know can be regarded as determining when withholding information counts as deception. Appreciation of this point is the result of conversations with my daughter, Heather.

Chapter 8

Justifying the Moral Rules
The Second Five

The five rules that were discussed in the last chapter do not account for all of the moral judgments that are made about what is morally required and prohibited. Although all of these rules, "Do not kill," "Do not cause pain," "Do not disable," "Do not deprive of freedom," and "Do not deprive of pleasure," are justified general moral rules, they are not the only rules toward which all impartial rational persons would take the moral attitude. In fact, these rules include only two of the original seven explicit moral rules listed in chapter 5. Three of the general moral rules justified in the previous chapter, "Do not disable," "Do not deprive of freedom," and "Do not deprive of pleasure," were not even listed as explicit moral rules. However, this is not in any way disturbing, for disabling a person or depriving him of freedom or of pleasure is considered by all to be immoral unless justified. These rules were always implicit moral rules. Further, these three rules share all the other relevant characteristics of "Do not kill" and "Do not cause pain," except having been listed as explicit moral rules.

Moral rules are part of a system that explains moral judgments. They are a convenient way of talking about the kinds of actions that need an adequate justification or excuse in order not to be immoral. The seven rules that are paradigms of explicit moral rules are rules of this kind. Five of these rules remain to be discussed: "Do not lie," "Keep your promises," "Do not cheat," "Do not commit adultery," and "Do not steal." In this chapter I shall discuss each of these rules, reformulating them if necessary, so that there is no doubt that they count as general moral rules. I intend to provide a nonredundant list of rules that accounts for all moral judgments about what is required or prohibited. Since there is no point in having redundant rules, I shall attempt to formulate these rules so that omitting any rule would result in some moral judgments about required or prohibited kinds of actions not being accounted for.

The five remaining paradigm-explicit moral rules shall be examined in order to determine whether all impartial rational persons would adopt the same attitude toward them as they did toward the five rules discussed in the last chapter. If they would, then these rules are also justified general moral rules. I shall also attempt to discover (1) whether any other rules need be added to this group of rules in order to account for some common moral judgments and (2) if these rules can also be justified. There will also be some discussion and reformulation of the moral attitude toward the moral rules. Finally, I shall consider why a rational person would be concerned with rules at all. Since a rational person need only avoid suffering evils without an adequate reason, and all reasons are beliefs that someone will avoid an evil or gain a good, it is not evident why a rational person, even if impartial, would take the moral attitude toward the moral rules.

Do Not Deceive

I shall start by examining a rational person's attitude toward the rule "Do not lie." Being lied to does not necessarily cause an evil in the way that all violations of the first five rules do. No rational person wants to be killed, to be caused pain, to be disabled, or to be deprived of freedom or pleasure, but why must rational persons have an aversion to being lied to? It may be true that most people dislike being lied to most of the time, but why should they? What is there in human nature or the human social situation that makes this aversion rationally required?

For present purposes, lying can be defined as making a false statement in order to lead someone to have some related false belief. This definition makes clear that if it is rationally required to want others not to lie to one, it is not because a false statement is being made, but because one is intentionally being led to have a false belief. What is important to a rational person is that he is intentionally being led to have a false belief, not that it is being done by making a false statement. A rational person would want to avoid intentionally being led to have a false belief by silence, by gestures, even by a true statement made in a certain tone of voice. Indeed, a rational person does not want to be led to have a false belief unintentionally, for example, by careless remarks. Thus, I shall change the rule "Do not lie" to "Do not deceive" in order to make clear that, like the previous rules, it prohibits both intentional and unintentional actions that cause someone to have a false belief.[1]

The rule concerning deception may be interpreted differently in different societies. As with the previous five rules, rights sometimes determine what counts as deception. If a patient has a right to know whether his examination revealed any serious medical problem, then silence by his physician can be a violation of this rule. However if a person has no right to know what his neighbor is doing Saturday night, then anything short of a false statement may not be considered a violation of the rule. Because lying, that is, intentionally making a false statement in order to get someone to have some related false belief, is unambiguously a violation of the rule prohibiting deception, many have preferred to state the moral rule in terms of lying rather than deceiving. But it is not as if it is often unclear what counts as deceiving, but always clear what counts as lying. Whether some common social remark that is clearly false, such as "You look the same as you did twenty years ago," counts as a lie and hence as violating the rule prohibiting deception is also subject to different interpretations.

The question I am now concerned with is, "What is a rational person's attitude toward the rule 'Do not deceive'?" "Does a rational person want himself and those for whom he cares to be protected from deception?" Obviously so, for being deceived generally increases the chances of suffering evils and decreases the chances of gaining goods. Thus all rational persons who are limited to rationally required beliefs would take the egocentric attitude toward the rule "Do not deceive." Changing this attitude toward the rule to the moral attitude requires that one consider the rule as a moral rule or else requires adding the constraint that one be impartial. Given either of these requirements, all rational persons would want everyone to obey the rule prohibiting deception unless an impartial rational person could publicly allow the violation. Thus, by a process whose details need not be repeated here it can be shown that impartial rational persons would adopt the same moral attitude toward the rule "Do not deceive" that they adopt toward the first five rules.

That an impartial rational person's attitude toward the moral rules does not require absolute obedience but, on the contrary, allows for justified exceptions is probably even more important with regard to the rule prohibiting deception than it is with regard to the previous five rules. There are some situations in which all impartial rational persons would publicly allow violation of this rule, so that some deception is strongly justified. All impartial rational persons will publicly allow deception when it is done with the consent of the deceived and for their benefit. Thus, magicians are not doing anything that it is morally problematic at all in performing their shows, for their deception is with the consent of and for the pleasure of the deceived.[2] This shows that although it is sometimes clearly morally acceptable to deceive, the rule prohibiting deception, like the previous rules, is to be taken literally.

Many cases of deception to prevent death and other serious harms to innocent parties will be strongly justified. When the person being deceived and the innocent person being benefited are the same, the deception may be an example of justified paternalism. When the harm that is prevented is less serious, impartial rational persons may disagree on whether the deception is justified. In what situations paternalistic deception, such as telling "white lies" to prevent a person from unpleasant feelings, is justified is a controversial matter. But it is not controversial that some deception is justified, and that the procedure for determining if the deception is justified is the same as for violations of the previous rules. Whenever an impartial rational person can publicly allow a violation, that violation is at least weakly justified. Thus all impartial rational persons will adopt the same attitude toward the rule "Do not deceive" that they adopted toward the previous five rules.

Keep Your Promises

The rule "Keep your promises" is unique, so far, in that it is the only rule to be stated positively. However, the negative formulation "Do not break your promises" leads to exactly the same moral decisions and judgments, so that there is no need to change any arguments. This equivalence of negative and positive formulations is not trivial. It is not repeatable with any of the previous rules. "Do not deprive of pleasure" does not even seem to have a plausible equivalent positive formulation. Both "Prevent the loss of pleasure" and "Promote pleasure" demand positive action, whereas the original negative rule does not. The rule prohibiting depriving of freedom can be obeyed by doing nothing; the same is not true of any positive formulation, such as "Prevent the loss of freedom" or "Promote freedom." The positive actions taken by countries as well as individuals in order to follow these positive guides make it quite clear that they involve far more than does obedience to the original rule.

"Do not disable" has the same relationship to "Prevent disabilities" as the previous rules had to their positive formulations. "Do not cause pain" and "Do not kill" require no action, but the positive formulations "Prevent the causing of pain," "Relieve pain," "Prevent killing," and "Preserve life" always require acting. There is no clear positive formulation of "Do not deceive," but taking "Do not lie" as the rule makes "Tell the truth" seem a plausible equivalent positive formulation. However, this plausibility is short-lived. For "Tell the truth" demands saying something, whereas "Do not lie" allows silence. The moral rules prohibit certain kinds of actions; they do not require positive action, except in those cases where there is no difference between requiring action and prohibiting it. There is no difference, except in style, between saying "Keep your promises" and "Do not break your promises." Acting in accordance with or violating either one necessarily involves acting in accordance with or violating the other.

"Tell the truth" is normally taken to mean the same as "Do not lie," only because it is usually addressed to a person who is talking or about to talk. However, when it is addressed to someone who is supposedly concealing some information, "Tell the truth" tells the person addressed not to keep silent. "Tell the truth" might sometimes even be interpreted as "Do not keep secrets." The point of the rule "Do not deceive" however, is to prohibit certain kinds of talk, such as lies, not to require that one talk. Although "Keep your promises" is phrased positively, its point is negative, prohibiting the breaking of promises. Unlike all of the previous rules, this rule presupposes that some previous action has taken place, that a promise has been made. That is why it can be phrased positively; once a promise has been made, keeping it and not breaking it are equivalent.[3]

The previous six rules presuppose no prior contact with other people. They can be broken with regard to people with whom one had no previous contact, either direct or indirect. The rule concerning promises obviously can be broken only with regard to people to whom promises have been made. If a person has not made any promises to anyone, then she cannot break this rule. The fact that the rule concerning promises presupposes some action on the part of the person who is subject to the rule has led some philosophers to consider this rule to be significantly different from all of the previous rules.[4] However, there is no morally significant difference between this rule and the one prohibiting deception. The action that is presupposed before this rule can be broken is an action that any moral agent who is a member of any society would have performed many times. Promising is a universal feature of human societies.

The Nature of Promises

For "Keep your promises" to be a general moral rule there must be promises in every society. It is only the view that promising involves the adoption of some societal convention, as marriage does, that leads some to the mistaken claim that there are societies without promises. Any society composed of persons who are subject to the previous moral rules will have a practice of promising. Every society demands some degree of cooperation among its members, some division of labor, some postponements of rewards. This, in turn, requires some practice whereby society can arrange for this cooperation, division of labor, and postponements of rewards. This practice will necessarily involve promising, including mutual promises or making contracts. Any person who is a member of a society will not only have the opportunity to make a promise, it is almost inevitable that she will make some. Thus this rule has the required universality.

The practice of promising, contrary to some philosophical analyses, need not involve any societal conventions. In any society where people have the ability to express their intentions, they have the ability to make promises. Although most societies have evolved verbal (and legal) formulas that help to distinguish promises from other statements of intentions, these formulas are not necessary. Saying "I promise" does make it clear to the person to whom one is promising that he can count on one's doing what was promised, but it is not necessary to say "I promise" for a statement of intention to be a promise. Promising need only involve stating one's intention to do something in certain kinds of circumstances. The clearest case is one in which the intention is expressed hypothetically, such as "I will do X, if you do Y," when both parties know that X is an action you want me to do and that Y is an action I want you to do. This is merely one clear example of a statement of intention becoming a promise without the use of any verbal formula.

José promises Maria to do X may be defined as (1) José states his intention to do X to Maria, (2) both José and Maria believe (2a) that Maria wants José to do X and (2b) that the point of José's stating his intention to Maria is to lead her to count on José's doing X. A statement of intention in these circumstances will quickly come to have the features that many philosophers have listed as part of the practice of promising. Since circumstances are not always clear, it is not surprising that verbal formulas have arisen which make it explicit that José intends Maria to count on his doing what he says he intended to do. The close relationship between promising and stating one's intention to do something for someone that both know she wants done can be seen by noting that in order to make sure a statement of intention is not taken as a promise one may have to say, "But don't count on my doing it."

Promising and Deceiving

This account of promising shows how closely related the rule prohibiting breaking promises is to the rule prohibiting deception. It may even seem plausible to say that the rule concerning deception tells one not to lie about the past or present; the rule concerning promises, not to lie about the future. But saying this ignores the fact that one can lie about the future when this involves no promise. Further, although a lying promise breaks the rule against deception, a promise can be broken even when there was no deception when the promise was made. There need not even be any deception in the future, for a person can openly change his mind and state that he will not keep his promise. He may also fail to keep his promise because he forgot. This rule prohibits not only intentional breaking of promises but also breaking them due to negligence. Perhaps more clearly than any other rule, this rule shows that the moral rules are not limited to the prohibition of intentional actions. Someone who breaks his promise because he did not take sufficient care to remember it, or to be in a situation where he could keep it, violates the rule requiring promises to be kept.

This account of promises also makes clear that all rational persons would take the egocentric attitude toward the rule "Keep your promises," and that all impartial rational persons would adopt the moral attitude toward it. The necessity of promises for any cooperative enterprise, large or small scale, and the harm that everyone would suffer if people could not generally depend on others keeping their promises, makes it clear why a rule requiring the keeping of promises is one of the paradigm moral rules. No rational person would want to have promises broken with regard to herself or those for whom she is concerned. Like being deceived, having a promise broken increases one's chances of suffering an evil and decreases one's chances of gaining goods and of obtaining other things that one is seeking. Using only rationally required beliefs, an impartial rational person would adopt the same attitude toward the rule "Keep your promises" as she did toward the previous six moral rules. A rational person considering this rule as a moral rule, that is, as part of a public system applying to all rational persons, would also take the same attitude.

Do Not Cheat

Cheating is often taken as a paradigm of an immoral act, thus it is somewhat surprising that the concept of cheating has been almost completely neglected by philosophers. The failure to examine the concept of cheating may lead to two objections against including "Do not cheat" in a list of general moral rules. It may be objected that it is unnecessary, because cheating, like lying, is simply a subclass of deception. Or it may be objected that cheating is a special case of breaking one's promise. Both of these objections are plausible. Most cheating does involve deception, but it is not clear if this is necessary. Also, cheating seems very similar to breaking a promise; seems, in fact, to be the breaking of an implicit promise. In order to reply to these objections, an analysis of the concept of cheating is necessary.[5]

Cheating in its basic form takes place only in a public system, such as a game which is a voluntary activity with a built-in goal. The rules of this activity can be drawn up explicitly, as in most games, or can simply grow out of custom, as in generally agreed-upon practices in buying and selling. Cheating involves the violation of the rules of this activity in order to gain this built-in goal, but not merely this. It is a violation for which the activity, at least initially, includes no explicit penalty except perhaps expulsion from the activity. Cheating usually involves violating a rule of the public system that no one is permitted to violate and remain in the activity governed by that system. This may be all that is meant by those who regard cheating as breaking an implicit promise. Since cheating is violating the rules of an activity in order to obtain the built-in goal or benefit of participating in that activity, it will usually not be successful if the other participants in the activity discover that one has cheated. This explains why cheating almost always involves deception. People who know that a person has cheated are generally not going to allow him to benefit by breaking a rule of that activity.

Although cheating is closely connected to both breaking a promise and deceiving, it is distinct from both and hence a distinct rule prohibiting cheating is necessary. Promises are always made to a particular person or group of persons. This is true even of genuine implicit promises. An implicit promise is sometimes characterized by saying "Silence gives consent." Someone is made an offer and, by not refusing, implicitly promises to carry out his part of the bargain. A person can cheat, however, never having come into contact with anyone who can claim that a promise, implicit or explicit, was made to him. Cheating depends on a social setting rather than on personal interaction; it is not obeying the rules of an activity when everyone participating in that activity is expected and required to do so.

Entering a game may sometimes involve making a promise to the other players that one will abide by the rules of the game, but usually this does not happen. Claiming that there must always be an implicit promise even when there is no communication between the players, because cheating is the breaking of a promise, is simply begging the question. It has no more force than the claim that cheating at solitaire is breaking a promise to oneself. The close surveillance of some tests and exams is a strong indication that no one regards the test takers as having implicitly promised not to cheat. Although there are similarities between breaking a promise and cheating, the rule requiring promises to be kept is not sufficient to prohibit every action that counts as cheating.

The account of cheating provided above also explains why a person who cheats generally will try to conceal his cheating from others. Most people participating in an activity will not allow a cheater to gain the built-in goal of that activity when he has not abided by its rules. However, when all of the people participating in an activity are employees of one person, this person can take advantage of his position outside of the activity to cheat without even bothering to conceal it from the others. The boss who plays golf with his subordinates may sometimes cheat quite openly. He may not count missed strokes, or he may remove the ball from the rough without taking a penalty. Of course, if he cheats too much, it might be said that he is not really participating in *that* activity or playing *that* game. But in a sense, cheating just is "not playing the game," and so this is not a serious objection. One need only notice the reactions of the people being cheated to realize that they do not consider themselves to be playing a different game. This analysis also explains why cheating at solitaire is possible even though one plays that game by oneself, and so it is not a moral matter.

Cheating is not reducible to either the breaking of a promise or deceiving, though all three of them might be classified as a violation of trust or faith. However, this would be to use "violation of faith" in a technical sense and would therefore not be generally understood. The rules must be stated in ordinary terms, so that everyone understands them. Although cheating may seem different from the other kinds of actions prohibited by the rules, it is like them in all the relevant respects. Like deceiving and breaking a promise, cheating may even be justified. Justified cheating may seem to be a contradiction, but although examples of justified cheating may be rare, they are certainly possible. Playing cards with someone who will kill one's family if he wins certainly justifies cheating. (If he will kill them if he loses, letting him win is not cheating.)

The rule against cheating does have one characteristic that none of the other rules have. One cannot break this rule unintentionally. There seems to be no such thing as unintentional cheating. With the first five rules, it is clear that violations can occur unintentionally. To act in a reckless or thoughtless way with the result that someone suffers one of the evils that these rules prohibit causing, generally counts as a violation of the relevant moral rule. The same is true with the rule concerning promises; simply forgetting about a promise counts as breaking it unintentionally. That only intentional actions count as violations of moral rules is clearly mistaken. People are often appropriately held morally responsible for careless or thoughtless actions that result in others being harmed.

Although it is not clear what, if anything "unintentional deception" normally refers to, a natural referent can be found without too much difficulty. Impartial rational persons adopt the moral attitude toward the rule prohibiting deception because being deceived generally has bad effects. A rational person is as concerned with natural deception as with intentional deception. Were ice to falsely appear as if it would support the weight of a person, an impartial rational person would favor a sign warning of this. A rational person wishes to avoid being deceived by nature as much as by a person, for it is the consequences of deception that she wishes to avoid. In adopting the moral attitude toward the rule prohibiting deception, some actions not intended to deceive would naturally count as unintentional deception, for example, telling jokes to naive people who will be misled by them or passing on gossip that one has good reason to believe not true. Such actions count as violations of the rule prohibiting deception.

It is much more difficult to find a natural referent for "unintentional cheating." However, since cheating is failing to abide by the rules of the public system of some voluntary activity in which one is engaging, the following is a plausible example of what might be called unintentional cheating. A person playing a card game, breaks a rule unintentionally, discovers it later, but tells no one about it. I do not claim that this is now called unintentional cheating. I am not even sure that it would actually be called either cheating or unintentional. Even though there is no intentional breaking of the rules, there is an intentional concealing of a past violation, and in some games, people are required to reveal that they have broken the rules. Concealing past violations would either be prohibited by the rule against cheating or by the rule against deception.

Further, people are expected to take reasonable care that they do not unintentionally violate the rules. The violation of those rules that would clearly be cheating if intentional generally goes against the interests of all the other participants in the activity. Thus the rule against cheating must be understood as requiring reasonable care that one does not violate the rules of any voluntary activity in which one is participating. This, of course, requires that one not enter any activity unless one knows the rules by which it is governed. Although its significance is so small as not to warrant calling it a moral matter, the attitude of people toward someone who enters a game not knowing the rules is close to moral condemnation. Expulsion is not unjustified.

Cheating as a Model for All Immoral Behavior

The concept of cheating is extremely interesting and important. Although philosophers have largely ignored it, an investigation of cheating is helpful in understanding the nature of morality, for cheating provides in miniature the nature of immoral action. Cheating in its basic form involves violating the rules of the public system in which one is voluntarily participating in order to gain an advantage over others in gaining the built-in goal of that activity.[6] The close parallel between cheating and breaking any moral rule can be seen by simplifying and redefining cheating, using the terminology that has already been introduced. Cheating is violating the rules of a voluntary public system. This redefinition of cheating shows how closely it parallels violating a moral rule. Removing "voluntary" from the redefinition and including all rational persons in the class of people to whom the public system applies provide an account of an action that needs moral justification.

Assuming, as is ordinarily the case, that one does not have an adequate reason for cheating, there is an extraordinary similarity between cheating and immoral action in general. This similarity helps to explain why cheating seems the paradigm case of an immoral action. Indeed, although cheating has not been explicitly discussed by philosophers, many have taken cheating to be the model for all immoral action. Although they are not generally aware of it, all those who make fairness central to morality are using cheating as the model of immoral action. Similarly, cheating provides the model of immoral action for social contract theorists. Their talk of promises, especially implicit promises, becomes more plausible if breaking an implicit promise is regarded as a way of referring to breaking the rules of a voluntary public system, that is, as cheating. Their effort to view society as a voluntary association also becomes more understandable.

However, despite the close parallel between cheating and immoral action in general, using cheating as the model of immoral action has had bad effects, such as overemphasizing the notion of consent. This has resulted in the view that one can perform an immoral action only with regard to those who are participating in the same voluntary public system. Coupled with the view that only people in the same society are participating in the same voluntary public system, the conclusion follows that one can be immoral only with regard to someone in one's own society. The immoral consequences of this view come out with great vividness in Stephen Toulmin's book *The Place of Reason in Ethics*.[7] In considering an island composed of two communities, C_1 and C_2, he seems to hold that nothing the members of C_1 might do to the members of C_2 or vice versa, can be immoral (135). This same point has been taken up by Gilbert Harman in his book, *The Nature of Morality*, who holds that only those who accept the same standards can regard one another as immoral.[8]

Taking cheating as the model for all immoral action thus leads some people to accept ethical relativism.

Another serious fault with using cheating as the model of immorality is the trivialization of morality. Cheating generally results only in the less significant harms that the moral rules prohibit causing. Thus Toulmin holds that morality is designed to prevent "causing to other members of the community some inconvenience, annoyance, and suffering" (132). There is no mention of death or disability. Although cheating should not be taken as the model for all immoral action, it is clear that cheating is a kind of action that needs moral justification. All impartial rational persons will take the same attitude toward the rule prohibiting cheating as they do toward the previous seven rules. "Do not cheat" is the eighth justified general moral rule.

Fairness

I have already pointed out that those who make fairness central to morality, or who put forward a social contract theory, have taken cheating as the model of immoral action.[9] Although "fair" is now often used as a synonym for "morally acceptable," in its basic sense, fairness is playing by the rules. To enlarge the concept by applying it to the making of the rules is to invite confusion. It is not even clear what it means to talk about having fair rules for a game. The clearest example of a game not being fair is one in which some persons are not playing by the rules, as when the dice are loaded or the cards are marked, so that a player has an advantage that he is not supposed to have by the rules of that game.

Basketball gives an advantage to those who are taller, but there is nothing unfair about that. That advantage can be minimized by various rule changes, but that would not make the game fairer, only less advantageous to those who are taller. Of course, if a game is supposed to be a test of some skills, and it has rules that provide an advantage to some players independent of their having those skills, it will not be as good a test of those skills as another game that does not provide such an advantage. But that does not make one game less fair than the other. Only when some players are given an advantage unrelated to the normal or standard rules of the game can a game be correctly viewed as unfair.

To talk about a person being fair presupposes that she is participating in some practice with rules that everyone is required to follow. A person in charge of hiring counts as acting fairly if she hires people in accordance with the stated criteria for hiring. It is a mistake to regard the criteria for hiring as fair or unfair, unless there is a practice that governs the setting of criteria for hiring. Fairness is not a basic concept, and it is a mistake to use it as such. It presupposes some practice that cannot itself be accurately described as fair or unfair. The practice that is presupposed by most who use the concept as basic is the concept of morality, that is, a public system that applies to all rational persons. Fairness is an important concept within morality; it is not a concept on which morality can be based. Part of the confusion about fairness stems from failing to distinguish it from impartiality. Impartiality is more fundamental than morality and is necessary for analyzing the concept of morality, but unless one is impartial with regard to the appropriate group in the appropriate respect, acting impartially need not be acting morally. Only if a person is acting impartially with regard to an appropriate group in an appropriate respect must he be regarded as acting fairly, but here acting fairly is simply acting morally.

Whether or not a person is acting fairly is most easily determined with respect to games, for most games have clear and explicit rules and there is usually no doubt about whether or not a person is abiding by these rules. But there are many social practices where the rules governing that practice are not quite so clear. A person who benefits from a practice, but does not do what is required for that practice to be maintained, is often regarded as acting unfairly. He is not abiding by the rules that everyone who benefits from the practice is expected to follow. This is almost explicit in the case of adultery. What is sometimes referred to as the problem of the free rider arises, in part, because not all activities have clear and explicit rules. People who regard others as not bearing their fair share of the burden believe that there are clear, if implicit, rules governing that activity and regard the free rider as violating these rules. Often, however, calling someone unfair is often simply a way of expressing moral disapproval, even though there is usually a suggestion that this involves not playing by the socially accepted rules.

Adultery

"Do not commit adultery" is a general moral rule only if all societies have the institution of marriage that this rule presupposes. If a society has no institution of marriage, no one can be married and so no one can commit adultery. However, it is extremely unlikely that any society has no institution of marriage, so I shall assume that the rule could apply to all people in all societies and hence can be a general moral rule. For purposes of this discussion, adultery will be defined as sexual intercourse by a married person with someone other than his or her spouse. It is not immediately apparent why sexual intercourse by a married person with someone other than his or her spouse is immoral, for it is not immediately apparent that this kind of activity increases the likelihood of people suffering some harm. It would be apparent if adultery generally caused marital problems, or if the spouse of the person committing adultery generally suffered, and such consequences do seem to follow when adultery is viewed as contrary to the point of marriage. However, it is not clear that all societies have an institution of marriage such that adultery is contrary to the point of marriage. While contemporary Western societies do seem to have this kind of marriage, other societies may not, and so a rule against adultery may not be a general moral rule.

This does not mean that adultery is not immoral in those societies that do have such an institution of marriage, for the immorality of adultery may not depend upon there being a general moral rule against adultery. It may be that in any society with the appropriate institution of marriage adultery violates some other general moral rule. But this would mean that adultery was not immoral in societies that did not have this kind of institution of marriage. This view seems quite plausible because it is reported by anthropologists that the Eskimos seem to openly accept sexual activity between married persons and those who are not their spouses. Such activity does not seem to cause marital problems or to cause the spouse to suffer. If the anthropologists are correct, the Eskimos do not have the same kind of institution of marriage as that in contemporary Western societies.

Adultery in Western societies is immoral because marriage in these societies involves participating in a practice requiring one to be an exclusive sexual partner in order to gain the goal of exclusive possession of a sexual partner. Of course, marriage in these societies is supposed to involve much more than this and usually does, but exclusive sexual activity is central to it. Adultery involves gaining the goal of marriage, an exclusive sexual partner, without abiding by the standards of that practice, being an exclusive sexual partner. That adultery is a form of cheating is, in fact, reflected in ordinary talk about adultery, for those committing adultery are said to be cheating on their spouses. In those societies that have an institution of marriage like that described above, adultery is immoral, for adultery is cheating and cheating, like violations of all other moral rules, is immoral unless an impartial rational person can publicly allow it.

Further arguments can be made against adultery. It generally involves deceit. It may also sometimes involve the breaking of an implicit promise. Although all of this is true, the same kind of thing can be said about most kinds of cheating. In fact, the similarity of the arguments against adultery and cheating supports the view that given the nature of the institution of marriage in contemporary Western societies, adultery is cheating. Nothing has been said that shows that this kind of institution of marriage is good or bad; all that has been shown is that in societies that have a certain institution of marriage, adultery is cheating, and hence is prohibited by a general moral rule. I have no arguments either that this kind of institution of marriage should be abandoned or that it should be adopted by all societies. But given the close popular association between morality and sexual activity, it is important to clarify their relationship.

Sex and Morality

Sexual relationships are important to all people in all societies. Sex seems to many to be an issue about which there ought to be a moral rule. However, philosophers, in contrast with the general public, who often regard morality as concerned primarily with sex, have almost completely ignored sexual matters.[10] To say that adultery is immoral because it is cheating may seem to many people a thoroughly implausible answer. Adultery is wrong, they might say, because any sexual relationship between two people who are not married is wrong. Some hold that premarital sexual intercourse is also wrong and premarital sex is not an instance of cheating. Those who favor nonmarital sex are sometimes accused of holding a "new morality." Those who uphold the traditional standards of sexual behavior and those who uphold the new are often thought to be having a fundamental moral dispute. This is a mistake. Whatever side one takes on this issue should not affect in the slightest one's attitude toward any of the moral rules discussed in this chapter and the previous one.

This extremely important point cannot be overemphasized. Some defenders of tradition equate sexual freedom with moral anarchy. They agree with some advocates of the "new morality" who hold that showing that a moral rule prohibiting sexual freedom is unjustifiable proves that no moral rules are justifiable. Both think that there is a rule governing sexual behavior that shares all the features of the other general moral rules. That they are mistaken can be seen by trying to formulate an independent moral rule concerning sexual behavior, toward which all impartial rational persons would adopt the moral attitude. Of course, rape is immoral. But it is immoral not because it is concerned with sexual matters, but because it necessarily involves a violation of one or more of the first five moral rules. Rape necessarily involves the deprivation of freedom and almost always the infliction of pain. Denying that there are any independent moral rules concerning sex does not involve denying that rape is universally immoral and that adultery is immoral in any society with the appropriate institution of marriage.

Whether premarital or nonmarital sex is immoral depends on the institutions and laws in the society concerning these matters. I am now talking about nonmarital sex between mutually consenting adults. Unless nonmarital sexual relations between consenting adults causes harm to someone, no impartial rational person would favor a rule prohibiting such activity. On the contrary, given that sex can provide some of life's more enjoyable moments, it would seem that depriving people of this pleasure is itself immoral unless it can be shown that such deprivation is necessary for avoiding greater evil. However, sexual activity is often accompanied by strong feelings, and there is a significant probability that someone will be harmed if sexual activity is engaged in without thinking about the probability of someone being hurt. To justify depriving people of the pleasures of sex it has to be shown that there is a significantly increased risk of harmful consequences, but for certain kinds of sexual activity it may be easy to show that.

Further, it is now undeniable that engaging in sexual activity with another person often involves increasing the probability that this person will suffer some physical harm. There are many sexually transmitted diseases, AIDS being the most recent and the most deadly. Further, for women there is the problem of an unwanted pregnancy with all of its attendant evils. Not to think about the possible harmful consequences of sexual activity with another person is thoughtless, and any evils that result from such activity are often correctly regarded as caused by that thoughtless action. In addition, given the importance of sexual activity to one's life, it would be imprudent not to think very carefully about the consequences before engaging in such activity. Sexual activity not involving another person, such as masturbation, is not a moral issue at all. Regarding it as such is the result of confusing morality and religion.

Stealing

Eight general moral rules have now been justified, and only one of the original seven explicit rules listed in chapter 5, "Do not steal," remains to be considered. It does not require a new argument to show that all impartial rational persons will adopt the same attitude toward the rule "Do not steal" as they did toward the previous eight rules. A rational person does not want to have anything he owns or anything owned by those he cares for stolen. To steal something from someone deprives him of pleasure or freedom. Using the same arguments that were used in justifying the previous eight rules, it seems that all impartial rational persons would adopt the moral attitude toward the rule prohibiting stealing.

However, insofar as stealing results in the deprivation of pleasure or freedom, no distinct moral rule prohibiting it is needed. There is no point in including in the list of general moral rules a rule that does not prohibit any action in addition to those already prohibited by the other rules. To show that an independent rule against stealing is needed, it must be shown that such a rule prohibits some actions not prohibited by any of the other rules. It may seem that stealing from the estates of the rich who will not even miss their money, or from companies who will simply add a penny to everyone's bill, are examples of stealing that do not result in anyone being deprived of freedom or pleasure. There are even more elaborate cases, such as using computers to transfer fractions of a cent from the accounts of others to one's own account, which do not seem to be prohibited by the rules against depriving of freedom or pleasure. Thus the rule against stealing does seem needed to account for the immorality of these actions.

But this kind of stealing makes clear that stealing requires practices that are not present in all societies. Just as not all societies may have the practice of marriage that makes adultery immoral, so the immorality of stealing may require the kind of practice of owning property that not all societies may have. Just as the immorality of adultery in a society with the appropriate kind of institution of marriage is not put in doubt by the discovery of a society without it, so the immorality of stealing in a society with the appropriate practice of ownership of property would not be put in doubt by the discovery of a society without such a practice. Thus the immorality of stealing cannot depend on there being an independent general rule against stealing. When adultery is immoral, this is accounted for by showing that adultery is prohibited by the rule prohibiting cheating; however, none of the previous eight rules seems to cover all cases of stealing. Thus it seems that another rule is needed in order to account for the immorality of stealing.

Before that can be done, however, an analysis of the concept of stealing must be provided. Stealing involves taking that which is owned by another. The concept of ownership depends upon the concept of law. Whether one owns something and under what conditions is determined by the law. Stealing is not merely taking that which is owned by another; it is taking it unlawfully. Thus every case of stealing will be a case of breaking the law, or will be parasitic upon it, such as children in a family "stealing" each others' toys or special snacks. Including as a general moral rule, the rule "Obey the law" guarantees that stealing without adequate justification is immoral, without making the rule prohibiting stealing an independent rule. Having the rule "Obey the law" as a general moral rule not only prohibits stealing, it also prohibits many other activities that are considered immoral by people in a society. Those who break the law when a fully informed, impartial rational person cannot publicly allow such a violation are usually regarded as acting immorally. Including "Obey the law" as a general moral rule accounts for these actions being regarded as immoral without making individual laws into moral rules.

An Account of Law

If "Obey the law" is a general moral rule, an account of law must be provided such that every society has laws, for a general moral rule must be applicable to all rational persons in all societies. It is impossible to give an adequate account of laws in a few paragraphs. It may even be that requiring that every society have laws makes it impossible to give an account of laws that even hints at the complexities that laws have in sophisticated societies. However, all that it is necessary to provide is a set of characteristics that are sufficient for calling something a law. In complex societies laws may have characteristics that I do not mention. It may even be that some will regard these unmentioned characteristics as necessary features of laws and will regard societies that do not have rules with these features as prelegal societies. However, I claim that there are no prelegal societies, that every society has laws in the relevant sense, and therefore that "Obey the law" can properly be regarded as a general moral rule.

Laws are rules. Disobeying the law will be similar to cheating in that both involve violating rules. The important difference between laws and those rules the violation of which is cheating is that cheating generally involves violating the rules of a voluntary activity, one that a member of the society can choose to participate in or refrain from. One can usually choose whether to be subject to the rules or standards, the violation of which is cheating, and so these rules do not normally apply to everyone in the society. One cannot usually choose to be subject to the law; whether or not one is subject to a law is often determined by the law, and so laws often apply to all members of the society. This difference between laws and rules the violation of which is cheating, is related to another difference. Violating a law normally has an explicit penalty; cheating usually has no explicit penalty other than expulsion from the activity.

I define a law as follows: *A law is a rule that is part of a system of rules (a legal system) that is known to all rational persons in the society to which the system applies and that, directly and indirectly, significantly influences their behavior.*[11] *Some of these rules apply to members of that society whether they wish to be subject to them or not, and some of them have explicit penalties for violation.*[12] A law *directly* influences one's behavior when one's behavior is affected primarily by one's knowledge that there is such a law or that others know that there is such a law. It *indirectly* influences one's behavior when it influences one's behavior independently of any such knowledge, such as by creating or sustaining an attitude among those subject to it to avoid certain kinds of actions.

This account says nothing of the origin of laws. Laws are not necessarily those rules that are instituted by authorized legislators; a law as I have defined it may arise from custom. Although laws guide the conduct of those subject to them, conditions may have changed since the law was enacted so that it may no longer serve a useful purpose. Indeed, a law need never have served to benefit society; to claim that it must have done this at least initially would exclude as laws far too many laws. Even the weaker qualification that laws must be believed to be for the benefit of society excludes too many laws to be included as part of an account of what a law is. Although my account of a law is purely descriptive, laws generally have the result of producing order and stability in society, of allowing greater predictability of the actions of the members of the society. Laws enable people to plan their lives with greater assurance.

The rule "Obey the law," unlike the previous eight rules, presupposes the institution of a society with a system of rules that applies to all of its members. The first six rules apply even in what might be called desert island situations. Coming upon a stranger who is minding her own business, one should neither kill her, cause her pain, nor disable her. Nor should one deprive her of freedom or pleasure or deceive her. Unlike the previous six rules, the seventh rule concerning promises presupposes some ongoing social interaction. It requires a social situation so that promises can be made. Once a promise has been made, however, the rule concerning promises applies independently of there being any official enforcement of promise keeping. The situation with cheating is the same; if appropriate activities evolve, one ought not cheat when participating in them. Thus the first six rules apply even when there has been no prior contact between individuals, and the next two rules presuppose only what I call an informal social situation. Only the rule concerning the law requires the establishment of a political system with rules governing all members of the society.

Each of the first eight general rules is normally violated with regard to particular persons, such as the person killed, deceived, and so on. The moral attitude of rational persons is developed from their egocentric attitude, that is, their aversion to having themselves or those they care for suffering any evils because of a violation of the rule with regard to them. Each of the first eight rules prohibits something that may be done to oneself or those for whom one cares. When the condition of impartiality is added, or the rules are being considered as moral rules, rational persons will adopt the moral attitude toward the rule. The present formulation of this attitude is *All people (including myself) are to obey the rule "Do not . . ." with regard to everyone, except when a fully informed, impartial rational person can publicly allow the violation of the rule. Anyone who violates the rule when no impartial rational person can publicly allow such a violation may be punished.*

This formulation, however, does not seem appropriate when applied to the rule "Obey the law" because normally one does not obey or disobey the law with regard to anyone, one merely obeys or breaks the law. Further, it is not possible to formulate the egocentric attitude toward this rule in the way it was formulated for the previous eight rules because one does not normally disobey the law with regard to particular persons, for example, those for whom one is not concerned. Although particular persons often suffer some evil because of a person's breaking of the law, an impartial rational person's attitude toward "Obey the law" cannot be built up by adding constraints to the egocentric attitude in the same way that was done for the previous eight rules.

A similar problem, though not as acute, arises with the rule "Do not cheat." Although when one cheats, one normally cheats someone, sometimes there may be no person who has been cheated. Cheating provides a kind of bridge between personal and social moral rules. For violations of the first seven moral rules, there is necessarily some one or more individuals with regard to whom one is breaking the rule. For the eighth rule, this will usually be true, but not necessarily so. Cheating has an impersonal aspect; the paradigm-example is the violation of the standards governing a voluntary activity. Violations can occur, and yet, even when all the facts are known, it may be impossible to pick out any individual of whom one could correctly say that he had been cheated. Thus it seems that the present formulation of the moral attitude makes it sometimes inappropriate for the eighth and ninth rules.

However, the first part of the formulation "All people (including myself) are to obey the rule with regard to everyone" can be replaced by "Everyone (including myself) is always to obey the rule." Replacing "with regard to everyone" by "always" and changing the word order make it appropriate to take the moral attitude toward the rule "Obey the law." (For aesthetic reasons I am also replacing "All people are" by "Everyone is.") The new formulation of the moral attitude is *Everyone (including myself) is always to obey the rule, except when a fully informed, impartial rational person can publicly allow violating it. Anyone who violates the rule when no impartial rational person can publicly allow such a violation may be punished.*

When considering only one society, it is plausible to substitute "law" for "rule" in the moral attitude and thus have an attitude toward particular laws that parallels the moral attitude toward each of the general moral rules. This parallelism between particular laws and each of the general moral rules is not accidental. Adopting the moral attitude toward a rule is similar to advocating that the rule be made a law. Further, many laws are simply specifications of some general moral rule, for example, the laws prohibiting killing, various kinds of deception, and breaking contracts. Indeed, the criminal law is almost entirely an interpretation and enforcement of the moral rules. Although the law is often talked of as the embodiment of impartial rationality and particular laws often embody the moral rules, this is not always true. Unfortunately some laws not only do not embody impartial rationality, they are so bad that all impartial rational persons would publicly encourage that they not be obeyed. However, the moral attitude allows for justified exceptions, so that bad laws are not an obstacle to all rational persons taking the moral attitude toward the rule "Obey the law."

Is "Obey the Law" a Justified General Moral Rule?

Contrary to what has just been said, some have claimed that impartial rational persons would not take the moral attitude toward the rule "Obey the law," or would take it only with regard to those laws that embody a moral rule.[13] However, it is quite clear that traffic laws, as well as many other legal regulations, are required for the kind of order, stability, and predictability that is required for large numbers of people to live together successfully. Further, the moral attitude allows the possibility that disobeying the law can be justified, sometimes even strongly justified. Thus adopting the moral attitude toward the rule "Obey the law" is not advocating an end to all civil disobedience. Civil disobedience usually occurs only when one believes that the law is unnecessarily causing significant evil. It is only justified when one has some reason to believe that disobeying the law will do something toward lessening that evil. Adopting the moral attitude toward the rule "Obey the law" only commits one to holding that, unless an impartial rational person can publicly allow the law to be ignored or broken, one should obey it.

Hobbes showed quite convincingly that, except for clearly immoral laws, everyone obeying the law is more likely to result in people suffering less harm than everyone disobeying the law and following their own rules. Even if their own rules would have made better laws, people are still more likely to suffer less harm by obeying existing laws.[14] Universal obedience to a mediocre law is better than each person doing what he thinks is best, even if he is right that what he thinks would be a better law would be a better law. In those cases where the law is so bad that it is not better for everyone to obey it, the except clause of the moral attitude comes into play. Given the flexibility of the moral attitude, there is no reason why all impartial rational persons would not take the moral attitude toward the rule "Obey the law." Taking such an attitude neither rules out justified civil disobedience nor discourages any legal attempts to improve the laws. It only rules out disobeying the law when this cannot be publicly allowed.

Although it is not possible to develop the moral attitude toward the rule "Obey the law" in precisely the same way that it was developed for the preceding rules, not much modification is needed. All rational persons know that they and those for whom they care may suffer some evil when the law is broken. Thus all rational persons would take the following egocentric attitude toward the rule "Obey the law": *I want all others to obey the law when not doing so increases the likelihood that anyone for whom I am concerned (including, of course, myself) will suffer an evil, unless I have (or would have if I were fully informed) a rational desire that they not obey the law in those circumstances.*

When, in order to eliminate the egocentricity, the constraint of impartiality is added, or the constraint that the rule be considered as a moral rule is adopted, it may seem that all impartial rational persons would adopt the moral attitude toward the rule "Obey the law." However, these constraints do not result in their adopting the moral attitude toward the simple rule "Obey the law," but rather toward the more complex rule "Obey the law whenever not doing so increases the likelihood of anyone suffering an evil." Reflecting on how easy it was to think that one could go from the egocentric attitude toward the rule "Obey the law" to the moral attitude toward it makes it clear that the same problem arises with regard to the rules prohibiting deception, breaking promises, and cheating, that is, those rules that do not prohibit directly causing one of the evils. The problem discovered is not one that is peculiar to the rule "Obey the law" but affects all the rules that can be broken on a particular occasion without increasing the likelihood of anyone suffering an evil.

This problem did not seem to arise in discussing the rules concerning deception, promises, and cheating because it seemed as if every unjustifiable violation of any of these three rules must result in increasing the likelihood of someone suffering some evil or being deprived of some good. Of course, this is not true. Unjustified deception may result in someone getting some undeserved good, while no one suffers in any way from that particular act. A promise may be unjustifiably broken even though no one suffers because of it. Unjustified cheating seems so obviously immoral that no one even considers that unjustified cheating can occur without anyone suffering any evil because of that particular act. However, just think of someone who cheats on an exam not graded on a curve because it is easier to do so, even though he would have passed without cheating if he studied. The question thus arises whether it has been shown that all impartial rational persons would adopt the moral attitude toward the rules under consideration in this chapter or only, as with the rule "Obey the law," toward some related but more complex rule.

This question arose in the discussion of the rule "Obey the law," not merely because it necessitated a change in the wording of the moral attitude. Far more important, I think, is that "Obey the law" seems to be a much less likely candidate for a general moral rule than any of the rules discussed previously. Suspicions about this rule force one to be more careful in examining its justification. And these suspicions seem to have been warranted. All that seems to have been shown is that impartial rational persons will adopt the moral attitude toward the rule "Obey the law whenever not doing so increases the likelihood of anyone suffering any evil," not to the simpler rule "Obey the law." Now it seems that the same inadequacy is present in the justification of the three previous rules. To justify these rules as originally formulated it must be shown that all impartial rational persons would adopt the moral attitude toward the original simple rules without the qualification about the particular violation resulting in increased chances of someone suffering some evil.

With regard to the four rules discussed in this chapter, would all impartial rational persons adopt the moral attitude toward the original simple rule or only toward the corresponding complex rule? This question can be put in the following way. Does one need to justify all deceiving, breaking of promises, cheating, and breaking the law, or does one need only to justify doing these acts when they increase the likelihood of someone suffering an evil? The simple rules, not the complex ones, are part of common morality, so there is now doubt that this part of common morality has been justified. Of course, all impartial rational persons will sometimes publicly allow violations of each of the last four rules in their original formulations, but if all rational persons would always publicly allow a violation when no one will be hurt by the particular violation, why not simply make that condition part of the rule? This makes it essential to consider the following question: "Is a rational belief that a particular violation will not cause anyone to suffer any evil sufficient for all fully informed, impartial rational persons to publicly allow such a violation?"

The Importance of Fallibility

Consider deception about one's past for the purpose of impressing other people, or breaking a deathbed promise about which no one else knows, or cheating on an exam in which everyone's grade is completely independent of what others do on the exam, or breaking a speeding law when no one else is on the road. Suppose that a fully informed, impartial rational person did not adopt the moral attitude toward the rules prohibiting deception, breaking a promise, cheating, and breaking the law in their original simple formulation. This means that she holds that anyone who justifiably believes that no one will be hurt by her particular act of deception, breaking a promise, cheating, or breaking the law may do so without being considered to be doing anything morally unacceptable, even if, contrary to justified expectations, some harm does result from those acts.

Given the fallibility of people, it is inevitable that harm will sometimes result from deception, breaking a promise, cheating, and breaking the law even though the person deceiving, breaking a promise, cheating, or breaking the law has rational beliefs that no harm will occur. Since the person did not believe that harm would result from his action, let alone intend that harm to result, not holding the moral attitude toward the rules as originally formulated means that when such harm occurs, the person is not to be regarded as having caused it. Thus the person is also not to be regarded as having broken one of the first five moral rules. To hold that a person did cause the harm, means that one is still taking the moral attitude toward the rules in their original formulation. Failing to take the moral attitude toward the original simple formulation of the rules means that when deceiving, breaking a promise, or cheating is discovered, but the person has a rational belief that no one would be harmed by that act, no penalties at all are to be administered, not even a scolding, even when some people are actually harmed.

The fallibility of persons is one of the presuppositions of morality. It is well known that people are more likely to be mistaken if holding the false belief makes it possible for them to do what they want to do. It is overlooking the fallibility of persons that results in the view that fully informed, impartial rational persons would not adopt the moral attitude toward the moral rules in their original simple formulation. Overlooking fallibility is also one factor in the popularity of various implausible forms of consequentialism, such as those that take the actual consequences of an action to be what is morally relevant. R. M. Hare, with his customary clarity, illustrates this point when he discusses a plausible violation of a simple general moral rule. His use of an omniscient archangel to show that in this case one should adopt an act-utilitarian position and completely neglect the commonly accepted simple general moral rules shows quite clearly that he does not recognize that morality applies only to the behavior of fallible beings.[15]

Regarding oneself as infallible when one is considering violating a moral rule in its original simple formulation is arrogance and is responsible for much evil being suffered. A similar arrogance, which is probably responsible for even more evil, is regarding oneself as infallible when believing that the beneficial consequences of one's own violation of a rule are greater than the harm caused by that violation. It is not only consequentialists that fail to recognize that the fallibility of persons is an essential presupposition of morality; Kant also thinks that morality applies to an omniscient God. Indeed, the failure to recognize that the fallibility and the vulnerability of people are essential both for explaining and justifying common morality is almost universal in the philosophical tradition. Apart from Hobbes, none of the major moral philosophers recognizes the importance of these features for understanding and justifying morality.

Fallibility about the consequences of a particular action are easily overlooked. With regard to the kinds of actions being discussed in this chapter, deceiving, breaking promises, cheating, and breaking the law, it is sometimes extremely plausible that no one will be hurt by a particular violation, especially if the violation is kept secret. One of the standard objections to those forms of consequentialism that take actual consequences to determine the moral acceptability of an act is that they have the result that the very same violation of a moral rule will be morally acceptable if kept secret, but be morally unacceptable if one talks about it or even if it is discovered. Requiring that a justified violation be one that an impartial rational person can allow everyone to know that they can violate in the same situation, makes more salient the harmful consequences of the violation being discovered. It also makes clear that whether or not a violation of the rule is actually discovered has no relevance to its moral acceptability.

It is recognition of the limited knowledge of persons and their fallibility that explains why no impartial rational person would publicly allow deceiving, breaking a promise, cheating, or breaking the law, simply on the grounds that the violation will cause no harm. This fallibility also explains why all impartial rational persons would choose the original simple formulation of the rules that prohibit deceiving, breaking promises, cheating, and breaking the law, rather than the more complex formulations of these rules that prohibit these activities only when they cause harm or increase the likelihood of causing harm. Indeed, fallibility explains why morality has rules at all. If all persons were omniscient, that is, knew all of the consequences of their actions, then they would have no need for rules. An impartial rational person would then favor everyone simply acting so as never to increase the amount of evil in the world and be unconcerned whether these actions were violations of the moral rules.

Consequentialism, of which utilitarianism is a particular form, is the right kind of moral system for a society of omniscient persons. But there are no omniscient persons. It is irrational to hold that any person, including oneself, knows all of the consequences of their actions. (Indeed, it is not even clear if the concept of omniscience makes sense with regard to moral agents, for moral agents cannot know all of their own future decisions.) Consequentialism remains so popular with philosophers because they often present their examples in such a way that there is never any doubt about what the consequences of the action will be. Indeed, the cases are sometimes presented as if there were no actual consequences other than those explicitly listed by the author. It is an extremely odd position: the actual consequences are what count, but only the actual consequences that are listed by the philosopher presenting the example.

It is not only that people are fallible with regard to the short- and long-range consequences of their own actions; people who are affected by the violations are also fallible and have limited knowledge. Since persons are not omniscient, if others did not generally follow the moral rules, no one could be sure when the rules would be obeyed. In order to make plans people need to know that other people will obey the rules in the way specified by the moral attitude, especially with regard to the rules considered in this chapter. If everyone knew that they were allowed to deceive, break a promise, cheat, or break the law whenever they justifiably believed that their particular act of deceiving, and so on would cause no harm, then no one would be able to depend on people obeying these rules with the consistency that is needed for social stability. Taking the moral attitude toward the rules in their original formulation makes one more aware of the harms that can result from the violation if one is mistaken — for example, if people discover the deception or cheating. It helps to counter the biases that everyone has toward friends and family.

The order and stability provided by people obeying the moral rules unless they are prepared for everyone to know that everyone is allowed to break the rule in the same circumstances explain why the moral attitude requires that an impartial rational person be able to publicly allow the violation. Recognizing the dangers posed by the fallibility of others serves as an important reminder that one's own fallibility also poses a danger. A person's holding that her own superior knowledge and intelligence allow her to violate rules in circumstances in which she would not favor their being publicly allowed demonstrates her arrogance. Arrogance, properly understood, just is thinking that it is morally acceptable for one to violate a moral rule in circumstances when one would not want everyone to know that such a violation is allowed. Arrogance is incompatible with moral impartiality. Violations of moral rules when no impartial rational person can publicly allow those kinds of violations result in more evil being suffered than everyone acting on the moral attitude toward these rules.

The moral system also results in less evil being suffered than a system that does not allow any exceptions to the simple general moral rules. In some emergency situations it is clear that violating a moral rule, for example, against deceiving, is justified. It is not merely that less evil will be suffered if the rule is broken than if it is not broken, such as lying in order to save an innocent life, there will be less evil even if everyone knows that a violation of the rule is allowed in these circumstances. The fallibility of persons is not so great that they can never justifiably believe that it is better to break a moral rule than to keep it. But if they are not prepared for everyone to know that they are allowed to violate the rule in the same circumstances, then they are making a special exception for themselves and that is not morally acceptable. The most intelligent persons are sometimes mistaken in their beliefs about the future, even when they have good reasons for their beliefs. This is especially true when the belief concerns an action that would benefit friends or family, but it is not the kind of action that they would be willing for everyone to know that they are allowed to do.

Justifying the Moral Rules Again

The rational belief that a particular act of cheating does not cause any harm is by itself not sufficient for an impartial rational person to publicly allow everyone to commit such a violation. The situation being considered is one in which an impartial rational person justifiably believes that no one will suffer because of her particular act of cheating. To publicly allow cheating in this situation is equivalent to advocating eliminating those practices that depend on people abiding by the rules. Although a particular act of cheating may have no bad consequences, if everyone knows that they are allowed to cheat when their particular act of cheating causes no harm, that knowledge may have serious harmful consequences. If the practices serve useful purposes that rational persons wish to protect, they must discourage people from cheating even when individual acts of cheating would cause no harm. This requires liability to punishment, and thus all impartial rational persons would indeed adopt the moral attitude toward the original rule "Do not cheat" in its original simple formulation.

This same argument works for the rule "Obey the law." If the law is a bad one, then the moral attitude may allow for it to be justifiably broken. But if the law is a good one, or even one about which impartial rational persons disagree, then the fact that an individual violation would do no harm is not sufficient to allow an impartial rational person to advocate that it be publicly allowed to violate that law. Except for clearly bad laws, general obedience to law is necessary to the order and stability that is essential for any society to function well. For everyone to know that they are allowed to violate a law simply on the grounds that no one will be hurt by that particular violation would eliminate this general obedience to the law and so have harmful consequences. No impartial rational person can advocate that the rule be violated simply on the basis of a rational belief that the particular violation causes no harm. Therefore all impartial rational persons will adopt the moral attitude toward the rule "Obey the law" in its original simple formulation.

That one knows that a particular violation of the law will cause no harm is not sufficient to show that all impartial rational persons would publicly allow it. Moral impartiality does not allow making special exceptions for oneself. It is the consequences of everyone knowing that they can break the law in those circumstances that determine whether or not one can publicly allow that violation. Appreciation of the impartiality required by the moral attitude is sufficient to show that all impartial rational persons will take the moral attitude toward the rule "Obey the law." Therefore it is a justified general moral rule. This argument also shows that it would be misleading to revise the rule to read "Obey good or just laws" as if such laws should always be obeyed and bad laws never obeyed. There are occasions on which an impartial rational person would publicly allow a violation of a good law and occasions on which no impartial rational person would publicly allow a violation of a bad law.

It is not necessary to go through the argument again to show that all impartial rational persons would adopt the moral attitude toward the general moral rules "Do not deceive" and "Keep your promises" without qualification. The undesirable consequences of the erosion of trust that would result from publicly allowing violations of these two rules simply because one justifiably believes that such a violation will cause no harm should be evident. That particular violations cause no harm is no guarantee that widespread violations will cause no harm. Indeed, with regard to the four rules under discussion in this chapter, it is clear that widespread violation of the rules will cause harm even though particular violations may not. This explains why it would have bad consequences if all violations that a person justifiably believes will cause no harm are publicly allowed. Not only is everyone's knowing this likely to lead to widespread violations, it will make people less likely to trust each other.

Independence of Each Moral Rule

It has now been shown that an impartial rational person would adopt the same attitude toward the rule "Obey the law" as toward the previous eight rules. Since stealing always involves breaking the law, stealing is immoral even if the rule against stealing is not a general moral rule. For all practical purposes one can treat "Do not steal" as a general moral rule, but I have attempted to make all the moral rules logically independent of one another. Someone who breaks one of these rules does not necessarily break any of the others, though the breaking of one may generally in-

volve the breaking of another one, for example, cheating almost always involves deceiving. The rule "Obey the law" does not eliminate the need for the rule "Do not
kill" even though most, if not all, societies have laws against killing. Even if there
were no laws against killing, deceiving, and so on, it would still be immoral to kill or
to break any of the other moral rules unless an impartial rational person could publicly allow such a violation. The rule "Obey the law" does not in any way render superfluous any of the previous rules, and it covers actions that are not covered by any
of the previous rules.

All seven of the explicit moral rules listed in chapter 5 have now been considered. Four of them, "Do not kill," "Do not cause pain," "Keep your promises," and
"Do not cheat," were found to be justified general moral rules. "Do not lie" was also
found to be a justified general moral rule, but was changed to "Do not deceive" to
broaden its scope. "Do not steal" was seen to depend on the notion of law and was
justified as a particular moral rule that can be derived directly from the justified
general moral rule "Obey the law." Similarly, "Do not commit adultery" was justified as a particular moral rule that can be derived directly from the justified general
moral rule "Do not cheat" in any society with the appropriate institution of marriage. In addition to these six rules, three other justified general moral rules were
made explicit, "Do not disable," "Do not deprive of freedom," and "Do not deprive
of pleasure." These nine justified general moral rules account for most moral judgments about what is morally required or prohibited, but an additional rule seems
necessary to account for the remainder.

The Nature of Duties

The rule "Do your duty" provides for those actions in society not covered by the rule
"Obey the law" and yet do not fall under any of the previous eight rules. As I use the
term "duty," duties are primarily connected with jobs, offices, roles, positions, and so
on.[16] All societies have a division of labor, many different jobs or offices need to be
filled, each with specific duties. A teacher has certain duties, so does a night watchman. The recording secretary and the treasurer have specified duties that are
spelled out by the rules of the organization in which they hold office. Parents have
duties, but children generally do not, unless duties have been assigned by their parents. Some of these duties are specified very precisely, some are extremely vague.
Judges and umpires are required to make their decisions impartially; it is their duty
to do so. Failure to do so by favoring one side is to violate the rule "Do your duty."
Duties are not limited to requirements to do specific things, as a night watchman
must make his rounds: often one has a duty to do things in a certain way. A judge
must not only show up for trial, she must also make her decisions impartially.

Although duties usually go with particular offices, jobs, roles, and so on, some
claim that there are more general duties. Sometimes it is said that all citizens have a
duty to vote and to participate in political discussion, but this seems hyperbole.[17]
Some also would say that it is the duty of every citizen to uphold the law. Although it
may not be incorrect to say this, it is usually said only in special circumstances,
when it is known that a large number of citizens do not like the law, for example, to

white southerners when the first civil rights laws were passed. This seems to be an appeal to the duty of citizens to obey the law of the land. Stealing, however, is not normally regarded as a failure to do one's duty, but simply as violating the law. Even when the appeal is made to all citizens to do their duty to obey the law, it is violating the law that is condemned; no further reference is usually made to the failure to do one's duty as a citizen. In this context, "It is your duty" means little more than "It is morally required." It is this use that philosophers have taken over when they maintain that people have a duty to obey the moral rules.

I do not use the term "duty" in this extended technical sense. People have duties in the normal sense because of some specific circumstances, such as their job, their profession, or their relationships. It is that use which is captured by the title of Bradley's famous essay, "My Station and Its Duties."[18] Confusion about the proper meaning of "duty" explains why some philosophers accept ethical relativism. They use "duty" in its normal sense where duties are dependent on one's role in a society, but then they switch senses and use "duty" in the philosophers' sense as equivalent to "moral requirement." It is not surprising that they conclude that all moral requirements are dependent on one's society. Extending the term "duty" to cover everything that one is morally required to do is both pointless and leaves no term available for a rule equivalent to "Do your duty."

Although duties are generally voluntarily incurred, they are not always so. A soldier who is drafted has no fewer duties than one who enlists. Children can be given duties by their parents. Duties can arise also from circumstances; in any civilized society, if a child collapses in one's arms, one has a duty to seek help; one cannot simply lay him out on the ground and walk away. This duty is not appropriately described simply as the duty to aid those in distress, for people do not have a duty to send money to others who are starving in far-off lands or even in nearby cities. It is, of course, morally good to do this, but people have no duty to be morally good. Some people do have duties to relieve pain for others; nurses have a duty to relieve pain for their patients. Their behavior, were it not their duty, would count as acting on a moral ideal. That the same action can change from a moral ideal to a duty may explain why the failure to provide a clear and explicit account of the normal use of "duty" has resulted in many philosophers not appreciating the significance of the distinction between moral rules and moral ideals.

Although most duties arise from social roles, it has already been noted that circumstances may sometimes also give rise to duties. In civilized societies one has a duty to help when (1) one is in physical proximity to someone in need of help to avoid an evil such as death or serious disability, (2) one is in a unique or close to unique position to provide that help, and (3) it would be relatively cost free for one to provide that help. These are the features of the kind of example usually presented to show that there is a general duty to help those in distress; for example, one is on the beach alone and sees a small child drowning in shallow water whom one can rescue with no danger whatsoever to oneself. The duty to help does not have precise limits, and it is sometimes impossible to say when a person has a duty to help or simply has a special opportunity to do something morally good. In the latter case one may be criticized for failing to avail oneself of that opportunity, but one cannot be punished. People ought to prevent evil, but, unless they have some special role or are in special circumstances, they have no duty to do so. It is neither a general moral rule nor a duty to prevent evil; it is a moral ideal.

Some may maintain that it is one's duty to keep one's promises, so that this rule eliminates the need for the rule "Keep your promises." It could be said that people have a duty to play fairly, and so the rule against cheating is superfluous. It has also been maintained that people have a duty to tell the truth, so that the rule against deception can also be eliminated. But these claims are all based on using "duty" in the extended philosophical sense. The question "Why should I give the book to him?" can be answered by citing several different rules, all of which are on a par. An obvious answer would be "You promised to give it to him," and the circumstance that makes this reply appropriate is simply the fact that you did promise. One can also imagine circumstances where the appropriate reply is "It is your duty as president of the organization to give the book to the winner of the contest." Sometimes the reply "Because the judge ruled that the book was legally his" is the appropriate one. One can even imagine circumstances in which the reply "Because it would be cheating not to" is an appropriate reply.

Trying to reduce all of these replies to "It is your duty" is pointless, for this reply carries no more weight than the replies that it is supposed to replace. The rules prohibiting deceiving, breaking promises, cheating, and breaking the law are justified as directly as the rule requiring that people do their duty. However, it is one of the standard practices of philosophers to try to reduce the moral rules to a single one, or failing that, at least to some smaller number than is generally accepted. One of the aims of social contract theorists was to reduce the rule "Obey the law" to "Keep your promises." Although had they been aware of the nature of cheating and the rule prohibiting it, they might have used it instead. There is no point in trying to reduce the number of rules when doing so requires changing the meaning of the remaining rules so that they do not mean what is generally meant by them, for example, using the term "promise" or "duty" in a wider than normal sense. "Do your duty" is a general moral rule that is on a par with the other rules, not one that includes the others within it.

Do Your Duty

The reasoning used to show that all impartial rational persons would adopt the moral attitude toward this rule is identical to that used to justify the rule "Obey the law." All rational persons know that they or someone for whom they are concerned may suffer some evil when a person fails to do his duty. Thus all rational persons want all other persons to do their duty when their not doing it increases the likelihood that anyone for whom they are concerned will suffer some harm. When the egocentricity is removed from this attitude and it is put in a form that is acceptable to all impartial rational persons, it results in the moral attitude being taken toward the rule "Do your duty whenever your not doing it increases the likelihood of someone suffering an evil." But it has been shown with regard to the previous four rules that allowing people to know that they can break them whenever they justifiably believe that their particular violation would result in no harm is likely to result in increased harm being suffered. Similarly, allowing everyone not to do their duty whenever they justifiably believe that this particular violation would result in no harm is likely to destroy valuable activities that depend upon consistent obedience to the rule. Thus all impartial rational persons would adopt the moral attitude toward the simple rule "Do your duty."

In these days of totalitarianism, doing one's duty has been used to justify the grossest immorality. Business executives often try to justify their acting in accordance with immoral company policy by claiming that their duty is to increase profits. However, the term "duty" is not synonymous with "what one is paid to do." Understanding what the term "duty" means requires knowing that one's action is not an unjustifiable violation of a moral rule. A job involves duties only to the extent that it does not require the kind of action that is always an unjustifiable violation of a moral rule. No one has a duty to unjustifiably violate a moral rule. Doctors do not have a duty to prolong the lives of competent patients who rationally refuse treatment. Professional killers do not have a duty to kill their innocent victims, though they may have been paid a sizable sum to do that.

Although the rule "Do your duty" can conflict with other moral rules, the conflict must be one in which the kind of action one has a duty to do is such that some impartial rational persons would sometimes publicly allow doing your duty even though it involves violating that other moral rule. Full understanding of the meaning of the term "duty" and hence of the rule "Do your duty" depends on knowledge of the moral system.[19] If no impartial rational person would ever publicly allow breaking the other rule in order to do the kind of action that one claims it is one's duty to do, then one does not have a duty to do it. Even with this proper understanding of duty, an impartial rational person is not advocating blind devotion to duty; indeed, she is not advocating blind obedience to any of the moral rules. All that is being maintained is the completely uncontroversial view that when a fully informed, impartial rational person cannot publicly allow disobeying "Do your duty" or any of the other nine justified general moral rules, the rule should be obeyed.

Impartiality and Rules: The Inadequacy of Consequentialist Moral Systems

I have now made explicit ten rules toward which all impartial rational persons who use only rationally required beliefs will take the moral attitude. However, even if it is granted that all impartial rational persons would adopt the moral attitude toward all of the rules under discussion, it may be asked why they need be concerned with rules at all. A rational person need not be concerned with rules, only with consequences. The only beliefs that count as basic reasons for acting are beliefs about the consequences of that act. The only difference that adding impartiality to rationality should make is that the person will be equally concerned with the consequences for everyone. Why should an impartial rational person be concerned with anything other than the consequences, direct or indirect, of a particular action? Why should a rational person be concerned with whether his action is a violation of a moral rule? This is not the same as asking why a rational person should be impartial. Everyone agrees that morality requires impartiality, but why does it require impartiality with respect to obeying the moral rules? It seems as if a rational morality would require impartiality solely with respect to consequences.

Not all impartial rational persons would pick that moral system which results in the least amount of evil being suffered independently of how those evils were distributed. That all rational persons would prefer one day of continuous pain to a thousand hours of pain one hour a day does not mean that all impartial rational persons would favor causing one day of continuous pain to one person in order to prevent a thousand persons from suffering one hour of pain. Even if no violation of a moral rule is involved, an impartial rational person need not favor relieving the pain of a thousand people suffering one hour of pain rather than relieving the pain of one person who is suffering continuously for a day. An impartial consequentialist may hold that one person suffering one day of continuous pain is worse than one thousand persons suffering one hour of the same intensity of pain. Consequentialism may include a concern for distribution. Consequentialism need not differ from deontology with regard to taking distribution considerations into account.

The fundamental dispute between consequentialists and deontologists is that the former hold that ultimately only the consequences of an act are morally relevant while deontologists believe that rules are an essential feature of morality. Both deontologists and consequentialists are in favor of impartiality; they may even be impartial with regard to same group. Consequentialists and deontologists differ essentially only in the respect with which one should be impartial with regard to this group. A consequentialist moral system is one that requires acting so as to bring about the least amount of evil or the greatest balance of good over evil.[20] That an action is in accordance with a rule, disobedience to which is generally harmful, does provide a reason for performing that action, but only because not acting in accordance with the rule is more likely to have harmful consequences than obeying the rule. Moral rules are simply regarded as maxims warning one of kinds of acts likely to bring about evil consequences, but they play no essential role in moral reasoning.

The distinguishing mark of a consequentialist moral system is that it takes the foreseeable consequences of a particular act as the only ultimate determinant of its moral rightness or wrongness.[21] Insofar as consequentialists recognize other morally relevant features, they regard them simply as aids to help one determine the foreseeable consequences of the particular act. A consequentialist system can consider the foreseeable consequences of that act on whether other people will perform similar acts and thus give some weight to the following of beneficial rules, but it must limit consideration to the foreseeable consequences of that particular act. Otherwise a consequentialist system is consequentialist in name only, and is really a kind of deontological system. A consequentialist system cannot take into account that cheating is a kind of act that needs justification unless this is involved in determining the foreseeable consequences of a particular act of cheating. For example, a person who is considering cheating should consider it morally relevant whether other people are likely to find out that he has cheated, for this changes the likelihood that they will be affected by that particular act of cheating.

A consequentialist system cannot take into consideration contrary-to-fact conditionals, such as what would happen if everyone knew they were allowed to cheat in these same circumstances. This does not involve a consideration of the foreseeable consequences of the act under consideration, direct or indirect; it is a consideration of the consequences of a purely hypothetical situation. Indeed, it involves considering the consequences of something that is not going to happen, namely, everyone knowing that this kind of violation is allowed. This is not an impartial concern with consequences but a concern about impartially following a rule. A deontological system recognizes that the kind of impartiality required by morality requires a concern for the consequences of this kind of hypothetical situation. No consequentialist system can require impartiality with respect to obeying the moral rules. Since this kind of impartiality is required by morality, no consequentialist system provides an adequate characterization of morality.

Some Problems with Rule Consequentialism

The recognition that morality requires impartiality with respect to rules, not with respect to consequences, has led to a view that has been called "rule consequentialism." On this view, consequences are used to determine only what rules are moral rules, but once the rules are determined, they, and not the consequences of the particular act, are used to determine the moral rightness of that act. It is not a serious objection to rule consequentialism that it is not a consequentialist system. It simply means that rule consequentialists realize that a consequentialist moral system does not have the best consequences. However, if rule consequentialism is to be taken as a moral system, it must be clear what it takes the rules to be like. There are two alternatives: either the rules have exceptions or they do not. If they have no exceptions, they must be so long and complex that they cannot possibly be formulated, let alone taught, and are certainly not the rules that are part of common morality. If they have exceptions, then they are likely to be identical to the ten general justified moral rules and the important issue is, how does the rule consequentialist determine when a violation of one of these rules is justified?

On the first alternative, when there are no exceptions, the rules cannot be part of an informal public system that applies to all rational persons. Given that there are unresolvable moral disagreements among equally informed, impartial rational persons, there will be indefinitely many different sets of rules. All individuals will have their own set of moral rules, which means that morality would not apply to all moral agents. One cannot morally judge another person by one's own particular set of moral rules when that person is justifiably ignorant of those rules. To claim that the exceptionless rules are those that God or an omniscient archangel would pick has the result that no one knows the rules and morality would not be a public system either. Thus having rules with no exceptions results either in extreme individual ethical relativism or in a universal and uniform moral system that is known to no human being. Although philosophers have held both of these views, both are such clearly inadequate accounts of morality that it is only their lack of clarity that has allowed them to be taken seriously.

On the second alternative, there will be justified exceptions to the rules, but if these exceptions are made solely on the basis of the consequences of the particular act, rule consequentialism collapses into act consequentialism. Of course, rule consequentialism will make more salient the effects of the violation on the rule, but if consequences are still limited to the foreseeable effects of the violation, it remains an act-consequentialist moral system. This kind of system has already been shown to be inadequate. Determining justified exceptions to general moral rules by a procedure that considers the consequences of the hypothetical situation in which everyone knows they are allowed to violate the rule works quite well. However, such a view is no more a consequentialist view than a false friend is a friend. (I call this fallacy, the fallacy of ignoring the modifier.) Rather, this kind of "rule consequentialism" is a deontological system that is closely related to a correct account of moral reasoning. However, if is to be completely adequate, it must also include all of the other features of morality that I have shown to be essential to it, including the realization that morality is an informal public system.

Some consequentialists may claim that I have misrepresented what they are saying. They are not putting forward a system that is intended to serve as a moral guide. Rather, consequentialism is a theory that explains and justifies our common moral system or some superior alternative to it. On this interpretation of consequentialism, that moral system should be adopted which, allowing for distribution considerations, results in the least amount of evil suffered. However, given the fallibility of persons and the need for morality to be public, the moral system should be deontological not consequentialist.[22] If this is consequentialism, then it is simply claiming that the point of morality is to lessen the amount of evil suffered by members of the protected group. I agree that this is the point of morality, but still think it important to correctly describe the nature of morality.

Even on this most charitable interpretation of consequentialism, it seems to hold that the content of the moral rules and ideals might be continually changing as more is discovered about the consequences of adopting different moral systems. I hold that moral rules and ideals do not change, although their interpretations might, for I not only regard morality as firmly rooted in human nature but also realize that morality must be known to all moral agents. I do recognize that as more is discovered about the consequences of different kinds of actions, that will change the violations that fully informed, impartial rational persons will publicly allow, but this fits in well with the informal nature of morality. One of the attractions of consequentialism is that it seems to provide a decision procedure that yields a unique answer to every moral question. If so, then it does not recognize that morality is an informal public system. Consequentialism does not even seem to recognize that disputes about which moral system results in the least amount of evil suffered by the impartially protected group may be unresolvable, because disputes about the rankings of the evils and about who is part of the impartially protected group are unresolvable.

That morality must be known to all to whom it applies affects the way that it is taught to those to whom it is about to apply: children. Such teaching is not like teaching history or science, which involves providing some completely new information. Teaching morality is more like training children to pay attention to what they already know, such as that their actions can result in other people suffering harms. It also involves pointing out to them that all people, including themselves, are fallible and vulnerable. Once they are old enough to understand the consequences of their actions, it should be apparent to them that unjustified violations of the moral rules increase the likelihood that people will suffer harm. Morality should be taught to everyone, adherence to it should be endorsed by all members of society whose endorsement counts, and everyone should be urged to follow it. The requirements of the moral rules apply to all rational persons.

Summary

There are ten justified general moral rules:

1. Do not kill.
2. Do not cause pain.
3. Do not disable.
4. Do not deprive of freedom.
5. Do not deprive of pleasure.
6. Do not deceive.
7. Keep your promises.
8. Do not cheat.
9. Obey the law.
10. Do your duty.

I think that this is the most natural formulation of all of these rules.[23] No technical terms are used in any of these formulations, but, as discussed earlier, some of the ordinary terms have been given slightly wider senses. The first rule prohibits causing the permanent loss of consciousness; the second rule prohibits causing mental suffering as well as physical pain; the third rule prohibits causing any loss of ability; the fourth rule not only prohibits interference with the exercise of one's abilities, it also prohibits unauthorized touching of a person; and the fifth rule prohibits depriving of pleasure and of opportunities for pleasure. Taken in these ways, these rules account for all moral judgments about the kinds of actions that are morally prohibited and required.

Toward each of these rules the following attitude would be taken by all impartial rational persons who use only rationally required beliefs. *Everyone (including myself) is always to obey the rule "Do not . . .," except when a fully informed, impartial rational person can publicly allow violating it. Anyone who violates the rule when a fully informed, impartial rational person cannot publicly allow such a violation may be punished.* This same moral attitude would be taken by all rational persons when they consider these rules as moral rules, that is, as public rules that apply to all rational persons.

The proper accounts of rationality and impartiality, and of morality as a public system, are essential for justifying the general moral rules. These accounts result in a moral attitude that provides formal criteria of justified general moral rules that have precisely the content that those opposed to formal criteria usually want. Those rules toward which all impartial rational persons would take the moral attitude are justified general moral rules. The ten rules listed at the beginning of this summary are rules toward which all impartial rational persons would take the moral attitude and so have been shown to be justified general moral rules. These rules have just the content that everyone takes the justified general moral rules to have. The perennial debate between formalists and those who demand content can now be seen to be like most other debates in philosophy: both lacked an adequate account of some more basic concepts. Adequate accounts of rationality and of impartiality, and of morality as a public system make it possible for these differences to be reconciled.

A rule has all of the characteristics that all moral rules are believed to have (those listed in chapter 5), if and only if it is one toward which all impartial rational persons would adopt the moral attitude. This shows that all of these characteristics fit together and are not merely an ad hoc collection of features that happen to have become associated with the moral rules. Showing that all impartial rational persons would adopt the moral attitude toward these rules shows that these rules have all of the characteristics that justified general moral rules are believed to have and so shows that some rules are justified general moral rules. Showing which rules are those toward which all impartial rational persons would adopt the moral attitude not only identifies which rules are justified general moral rules, it also justifies these rules. In an important sense, therefore, discovering what rules are justified general moral rules is justifying those rules.

Justifying the moral rules does not eliminate all moral disagreement, but it does set limits to such disagreement. These limits depend upon restricting those beliefs that can be used in describing or justifying the moral system to rationally required beliefs. This is the only way to guarantee that every moral agent understands the moral system. But since morality is an informal public system, that there is a universal morality does not mean that fully informed, impartial rational persons never disagree about moral matters, only that there is a universally agreed upon framework for discussing them. This universal framework will yield some universally accepted judgments, but it will not settle almost any controversial moral issue such as abortion or environmental issues. However, disagreement among impartial rational persons about what morally ought to be done always occurs within a larger framework about which there is no controversy. This lack of controversy may explain why the overwhelming agreement on most moral matters is so often overlooked.

Notes

1. My colleague Walter Sinnott-Armstrong has suggested that false beliefs should be added to the list of basic evils. If so, the rule concerning deception would fit more naturally with the first five rules than with the second five. Although I have no objection to including false beliefs in a list of things that all rational persons want to avoid, I do have some mild objections to including it in the list of basic evils. It does not seem to me that false beliefs are in the same category as the five basic evils or harms. I agree that people do not want to be led to give up a true belief, but that is because giving up a true belief decreases one's chances of obtaining goods or avoiding evils. But if the choice is between having a false belief and having no belief, having the false belief is worse only if it is likely to interfere with gaining knowledge or would lead one to do something that would make it more likely that one suffered one of the other harms. If all of this is true, then there is no need to include false beliefs as a basic evil. False beliefs are to be avoided because they increase the risk of suffering one of the five

basic harms or decrease the chances of obtaining a good. Also, since knowledge is an ability and hence a basic good, I see no need to include truth as a distinct basic good.

2. This is identical to the situation in which physicians normally violate the rule against causing pain, viz., with the consent of their patients and for their benefit. There is nothing morally problematic about this at all.

3. Chris Deabler has called to my attention that Jürgen Habermas explicitly notes the positive formulation of this rule. However, Habermas does not seem to realize that this rule (and also the rule concerning doing one's duty) can be stated positively because the positive formulation and the negative one are equivalent. Jürgen Habermas, *Justification and Application*, trans. by Ciaran Cronin (Cambridge, Mass.: MIT Press, 1993): 67.

4. For example, see John Rawls, "Two Concepts of Rules" *Philosophical Review* 44, no. 1 (1955): 3–32.

5. Note to translators: Teaching a course in Argentina on my book showed me that there may be no word in some other languages that corresponds closely enough to the English word "cheat" to allow that word to cover all that I include under cheating. What I mean by "cheat," though including somewhat more than what is normally included, is close enough to its normal meaning that I do not regard myself as having invented a special technical sense of the term. If another language does not have a word that corresponds to the English word "cheat," I would prefer that the list of justified general moral rules be enlarged, rather than some technical term be invented that includes everything that is covered by the rule prohibiting cheating. It is not important that there be only ten rules. Since it is a condition of being included as a justified general moral rule that all impartial rational persons who understand the rule will take the moral attitude toward it, the list of rules will not grow to unmanageable proportions. It was the discussion of cheating that made me aware of this problem, but the same point applies to other rules as well, especially the rule that prohibits depriving of freedom.

6. This may be why students do not normally regard cheating on exams in the same way that they regard cheating in a game. Taking exams, except at the more advanced levels, is not a voluntary activity. In fact, cheating on an exam is in essential respects like cheating on one's income tax; it is more like breaking the law than it is like the paradigm cases of cheating. Unless they are explicitly graded on a curve, most students do not realize that cheating affects other students in a disadvantageous way. The other participants in an activity are normally regarded as victims of the cheating, but many mistakenly think that when no one is directly hurt by breaking a law, it has no victims.

7. See chapter 10, sec. 2, "The Notion of 'Duty"; Cambridge: Cambridge University Press, 1949.

8. Oxford: Oxford University Press, 1974.

9. It should be obvious that John Rawls is a paradigm-case of such a philosopher, and thus his retreat from a universal to a societal basis for morality is not at all surprising.

10. Thus philosophers have almost nothing to say about the moral acceptability of premarital or, more generally, nonmarital sex.

11. Knowing the legal system does not require knowing every law in the system. No person in any society knows every law, but all know there is a legal system, and they know many of the rules of that system. Although it may be an ideal for a legal system to be a public system, it is never such, for it always has some rules that some people to whom it applies do not know or understand. That is why ignorance of the law is often no excuse for violating it. If the legal system is bad, it may even have laws that it would be irrational for some citizens to use for guiding their own behavior or judging the behavior of others. Further, legal systems, unlike a moral system, are usually formal systems, in that they have procedures for dealing with

disagreements and authorities who have some special role in that procedure. Because primitive legal systems may not have such procedures and authorities, some people falsely consider them to be moral systems. (See chapter 14 for a fuller discussion of this topic.)

12. These rules may also apply to visitors to the society.

13. See Michael Davis, "Gert, Smith, and the Duty to Obey the Law," *Southern Journal of Philosophy* 20, no. 2 (1982): 139–152.

14. See my article, "Le Droit de Nature," *Le Pouvoir et le droit: Hobbes et les fondements de la loi*, compiled by Louis Roux and François Tricaud (Saint-Étienne: Publications de l'Université de Saint-Étienne, 1992): 27–48. A similar point is made by Russell Hardin in his book *Morality within the Limits of Reason*.

15. See R. M. Hare, *Moral Thinking: Its Levels, Methods and Points* (Oxford: Oxford University Press, 1981).

16. The term, "duty," has no equivalent in Spanish. *Deber*, the noun, is sometimes translated as "duty," but it is not limited to that which is required by one's job, profession, etc.; rather it closely resembles the technical philosophical use, meaning "what one morally ought to do." In Spanish the closest word to the ordinary English use of "duty" seems to be *responsibilidad*, but it seems somewhat narrower than what is normally meant by "duty." There may also be no equivalent to "duty" in other languages as well. However, every language is able to refer to those societally based requirements that are referred to in English by the term "duty," even if this may involve several different terms.

17. In *A Theory of Justice* (Cambridge, Mass.: Harvard University Press, 1971), John Rawls puts forward similar duties.

18. See F. H. Bradley, *Ethical Studies* (Oxford: Oxford University Press, 1876).

19. The key terms in all of the moral rules are also completely understandable only with knowledge of the moral system. Fully understanding what "kill" means depends upon knowing the moral system. One cannot know whether one person killed another, that is, caused another to die, unless one knows whether the person needs an excuse or justification for his action or lack of action. Indeed, whether not feeding a person counts as killing him and so needs to be justified or excused may depend upon whether or not one had a duty to feed that person. Nonetheless, "kill," unlike "murder" is primarily a descriptive word. There is both justified and unjustified killing; for example, killing in self-defense is justified, killing to prevent being identified as a thief is not. "Duty" is primarily also a descriptive word, for one can be justified or unjustified in doing one's duty.

20. Although many consequentialists, following Mill, do not distinguish between morally required actions and those that are morally encouraged, they can make such a distinction. They can claim that morally required actions are those that would have the best consequences if done and also have the best consequences if doing them were enforced; whereas morally encouraged actions are those that would have the best consequences if performed, while enforcing the doing of them would not have the best consequences. But this seems to make kinds of action, or moral rules, an essential feature of moral reasoning, and so this distinction seems to be incompatible with an act-consequentialist view.

21. I use foreseeable rather than actual consequences in order to provide the most plausible account of act-consequentialism.

22. G. E. Moore in *Principia Ethica* (Cambridge: Cambridge University Press, 1903), probably holds this view; Russell Hardin in *Morality within The Limits Of Reason* certainly does.

23. Although it might be clearer to change the positively formulated rules to a negative formulation — "Do not break promises," "Do not disobey the law," and "Do not neglect your duty"— several considerations favor the positive formulations of these rules. First, the positive

formulations are far more natural. Second, using the positive formulations shows that the claim that moral rules are prohibitions is not merely a verbal claim. Third, the positive formulations make clear that some of the moral rules presuppose social practices. Related to this third consideration is a fourth: The terms "oblige" and "obligation" have their normal use primarily in connection with the three positively stated moral rules, namely, "Keep your promises," "Obey the law," and "Do your duty." Formulating these rules positively allows this linguistic point to be made more clearly.

Chapter 9

Justifying Violations

As pointed out in chapter 5, moral rules have justified exceptions. In the two previous chapters it was shown that the attitude of all impartial rational persons toward the justified moral rules includes an except clause. In this chapter I shall examine this moral attitude in greater detail, making clear what violations may be punished, what is meant by the except clause, and providing an explicit account of the morally relevant features that determine what counts as the same violation. I shall then explain how to determine whether this violation is justified or unjustified and, if justified, whether it is strongly or weakly justified. This account of the two-step procedure is necessary in order to fully understand the moral attitude toward the moral rules. Since a complete understanding of the moral rules requires an understanding of the proper attitude toward them, an account of how violations of the moral rules are justified is essential for a complete understanding of these rules.

As shown in the previous two chapters, rarely is there a dispute about what counts as a moral rule, that is, about what general kinds of action need to be justified — but there is sometimes a dispute about the interpretation of a rule, that is, whether a particular act counts as a violation of that rule. There are also some serious disputes about the scope of moral rules, such as whether fetuses are in the impartially protected group. Most actual moral disputes are about what counts as a justified violation of a moral rule. However, everyone agrees that if one exception to a moral rule is justified, all exceptions of the same kind are also justified. It is, therefore, extremely important to make clear what counts as an exception of the same kind. This chapter is the first detailed attempt to provide a method for determining what counts as an exception of the same kind. I try to provide an explicit account of all of the features that determine how an exception is classified as an exception of the same kind as another exception. These features, which I call the *morally relevant features*, are the features used in the first step of the procedure to determine whether a particular violation of a moral rule is justified.[1]

These morally relevant features have not been discussed by philosophers in any systematic way; indeed, they have hardly been discussed at all. What is most surpris-

ing about them is how varied they are. Some philosophers, such as consequentialists, hold that the only morally relevant features are the consequences of that action
and its alternatives. But most people realize that it is morally relevant whether a person has given consent for a moral rule to be violated with regard to him. For example, whether a patient has given valid consent to a painful operation is often decisive
in determining whether it is justified to proceed with that operation. It is also
morally relevant whether the violation of a rule is part of a legitimate punishment or
whether the violation occurs in a emergency situation. It should be evident from
these three examples of morally relevant features how varied they are; some of them
are not even reasons for acting.

Justifying violations of the moral rules is similar to justifying the moral rules
themselves. It consists in showing that all suitably qualified impartial rational persons can or would publicly allow this kind of violation of the moral rules. However,
there is a difference. All suitably qualified impartial rational persons agree on the
moral rules, that is, on what kinds of actions need to be justified, but they do not always agree on what kinds of violations should be allowed. Nonetheless, all rational
persons agree on the procedure by which a violation can be justified. This procedure must be such that it can be part of a public system that applies to all rational
persons, which means that it must be understandable to all rational persons and not
irrational for them to use it in making decisions about how to act and judgments on
the actions of others.

Strongly and Weakly Justified Violations

In chapter 2, I pointed out that only those actions that would be irrational if one did
not have a reason for them needed to be justified. By providing reasons that showed
that an action was either rationally allowed or, less frequently, rationally required,
such actions could be justified. Rational justification consists in providing reasons
that are adequate to make an otherwise irrational action rational. If the reason is
such that all rational persons would favor acting on it, the action is strongly justified,
and it is irrational not to act on that reason in that situation. If the reason is such that
all rational persons can favor acting on it, but also that all rational persons can favor
not acting on it, it is only weakly justified, and it is rational either to act on the reason or not to act on it.[2] If the reason is such that no rational person would favor acting on it, it is an inadequate reason, and it is irrational to act on it in that situation.
Given the hybrid nature of rationality, no reason concerning the interests of others
will be such that all rational persons would favor acting on it. Only reasons concerning one's own interests can ever be irrational not to act on, and that is only when
one's own interests are the dominant interests involved.

When one is concerned with moral justification, egocentricity is no longer involved. However, moral justification is similar to rational justification in that only
those actions that would be immoral if one did not have a reason, that is, that are violations of the moral rules, need to be morally justified. It is also similar in that violations can be either strongly justified or weakly justified. When all impartial rational persons would publicly allow a violation, it is a *strongly justified* violation. No

impartial rational person would condemn or punish such a violation, such as breaking a trivial promise in order to save a life. Not only are such violations not immoral, obeying the rule in these circumstances would be morally discouraged, that is, no impartial rational person would favor obeying the rule. A strongly justified violation does not count at all against one having the moral virtue associated with a particular rule; on the contrary, a strongly justified lie counts in favor of one having the virtue of truthfulness, not against it. It is even tempting to deny that a moral rule has been broken, but this temptation should be resisted because it results in confusion.

When impartial rational persons differ on whether or not they would publicly allow a violation it is a *weakly justified* violation. A possible example might be deception in order to avoid hurting someone's feelings. Impartial rational persons who would not themselves violate a rule in a situation where a violation is weakly justified may disagree on whether to punish such a weakly justified violation. Weakly justified violations generate two related but different genuine moral perplexities; not only is it often difficult to decide whether or not to violate the rule, it is often even more difficult to decide what to do when someone else violates it. When no impartial rational person would publicly allow a violation, it is a morally unjustified violation. A clear example is killing people in order to get their money. All impartial rational persons would favor allowing such violations to be punished.

One kind of strongly justified violation occurs when, with her valid consent, a physician inflicts harm on a patient in order to prevent her suffering a significantly greater harm. Most doctors do this daily; it is not in the least morally problematic. An unjustified or weakly justified violation, depending on the details of the case, occurs when, *without* her valid consent, a physician inflicts harm on a patient in order to prevent her suffering a significantly greater harm. This kind of paternalistic action, such as deceiving a patient for her own benefit, used to be fairly common in medicine. Since most paternalistic behavior is unjustified or weakly justified, it is not surprising that there is controversy concerning it. Valid consent is a morally relevant feature that can change a weakly justified violation, often even an unjustified violation, into a strongly justified one. Morally unjustified violations include most criminal actions, as most criminals harm others simply in order to gain some benefit for themselves.

Final Revision of the Moral Attitude

The moral attitude, as presently formulated is *Everyone (including myself) is always to obey the rule "Do not . . .," except when a fully informed, impartial rational person can publicly allow violating it. Anyone (including myself) who violates the rule when a fully informed, impartial rational person cannot publicly allow such a violation may be punished.* This attitude seems to allow for punishment only when a violation is unjustified; however, some impartial rational persons may favor punishment for weakly justified violations. If no weakly justified violations may be punished, that means that any violation that any impartial rational person favors must be allowed by all. This would have undesirable consequences, especially with regard to the rule "Obey the law," for it would mean that no weakly justified violation of the law could be punished, and that would make it impossible to enforce laws about which there is moral disagreement.

Morality is an informal public system, which means that there will be moral disagreements among impartial rational persons. Among these disagreements are disagreements about the scope of morality, that is, about who is in the impartially protected group. There can also be disagreements about how much those not in this group should be protected. Impartial rational persons can disagree about whether there should be any laws against cruelty to animals and about how protective those laws should be. Those impartial rational persons who think there should not be any such laws or that the laws are too protective might publicly allow violations of these laws when obeying them would stop scientists from using animals in some important experiments that may prevent serious harms to rational persons. If some impartial rational persons would favor violating these laws, and it were not morally justifiable to punish weakly justified violations, then the laws would have little or no force. Even if those who thought that animals should be protected were in the vast majority, they would still be unable to enforce laws that were justifiably enacted.

Similarly, those impartial rational persons who think some animals, such as chimpanzees and dolphins, should be in the impartially protected group may hold that there should be stricter laws protecting these animals or that the existing laws protecting them should be enforced more strictly. These impartial rational persons might publicly allow violations of the law in order to prevent these animals from being used in experiments designed to prevent serious harms to rational persons. They need not publicly allow killing, causing pain, or disabling in order to prevent these animals from being used in these experiments, but they might publicly allow civil disobedience to stop such experiments. If some impartial rational persons would favor violating these laws, and if it were not morally justifiable to punish weakly justified violations, then the laws would have little or no force. Even if those who thought that these animals should not be protected from being in these experiments were in the vast majority, they would still be unable to enforce laws that were justifiably enacted. Thus it would be impossible for a moral democracy to enact laws on any controversial matter because such laws could not be morally enforced.

These consequences are not acceptable, so it must sometimes be morally acceptable to punish weakly justified violations of a moral rule. This should not be too surprising, for, as was pointed out in the previous chapter, societies determine the interpretations of the moral rules, and even though some people in the society prefer a different interpretation, they are governed by the societal interpretation. Governments often enact laws about which equally informed, impartial rational persons disagree; if they could not enforce these laws against the minority that disagrees with them, it would be impossible to govern. They could not enforce a draft, or perhaps even taxes, if any fully informed, impartial rational persons would publicly allow violating the law. Although disagreeing with a law is often not sufficient to even weakly justify violating it, there are enough cases where some impartial rational persons could favor violating a law that a government must be allowed to punish weakly justified violations of a moral rule.

Although the moral attitude must therefore allow punishment for weakly justified violations, it does not require punishment for weakly justified violations; indeed, it does not even require punishment for unjustified violations. Rather, the moral attitude allows for punishment of violations, unjustified or weakly justified, when an impartial rational person can publicly allow it. But no impartial rational person can publicly allow punishment for a strongly justified violation, for this is the kind of violation that all rational persons would publicly allow. In order to allow weakly justified violations to be punished, the final version of the moral attitude is as follows: *Everyone (including myself) is always to obey the rule "Do not . . .," except when a fully informed, impartial rational person can publicly allow violating it. Anyone (including myself) who violates the rule when not all fully informed, impartial rational persons would publicly allow such a violation may be punished.*

Advocating That Violations Be Publicly Allowed

Since the moral attitude allows breaking the rule only when a fully informed, impartial rational person can publicly allow breaking it, it is important to examine what is involved in advocating that a violation be publicly allowed. An impartial rational person can publicly allow a violation only if all rational persons understand and are able to accept what she is advocating. This means that if an impartial rational person favors publicly allowing a violation of a rule it must be possible to provide a description of the violation that is understood and can be accepted by all rational persons. For example, all rational persons can understand and accept a violation in which a fully informed rational person has freely and voluntarily consented to the rule being violated with regard to her and the violation will prevent significantly more harm than it causes. All impartial rational persons would publicly allow the kind of violation of a rule that fits this description.

Most medical interactions are of this kind: a patient consents to his doctor giving him painful rabies shots because he knows that failure to have them will result in significantly greater pain and death. In fact, given the extremely horrible nature of death by rabies, if the patient refuses the rabies shots with no reason other than his irrational fear of present pain, all fully informed, impartial rational persons would still publicly allow giving it to him. However, when the harm a person would suffer if one did not break the rule with regard to him is not of this magnitude, then impartial rational persons may disagree about whether they would publicly allow breaking the rule with regard to him when he does not consent to it. If the harm prevented is not indisputably significantly greater, then no impartial rational person would publicly allow a violation without the consent of the patient. This is why informed consent is so important in the moral practice of medicine and why paternalistic action is often controversial.

The Same Kind of Violation

Before a fully informed, impartial rational person can decide whether to publicly allow a violation of a moral rule, she must determine what kind of violation she is publicly allowing. The only considerations that she can use in determining the kind of violation are those that are understood by all rational persons. Otherwise some rational persons would not understand what kind of violation this particular violation is, and so would not understand why it is justified. Specific facts count as morally relevant considerations only insofar as they are instances of more general facts that would be understood by all rational persons. This does not mean that the details of a situation cannot be considered; on the contrary, it is crucial that the specific details be considered, but only those specific details that can be reformulated in a way that can be understood by all moral agents. A fully informed, impartial rational person who favors publicly allowing a violation is not advocating publicly allowing this particular violation in all of its individuality; rather, she is advocating publicly allowing all violations of the same kind. It therefore becomes extremely important to determine what counts as the same kind of violation.

Some philosophers have qualified their claims that certain kinds of violations are justified by adding a *ceteris paribus* clause. But as others have noted, often it is this clause that is doing most of the work. Everyone recognizes that saying that this kind of violation is justified *ceteris paribus* is usually intolerably vague. What is needed is an explicit list of morally relevant features. However, if this list is to be part of the public system, the morally relevant features must be formulated at a level of generality that can be understood by all moral agents. But even this level of generality would allow there to be an indefinitely long list of morally relevant features, for example, headaches, stomach pains, and extreme anxiety, could be counted as distinct categories of morally relevant features. Thus counting each distinct kind of pain and disability as a distinct morally relevant feature would result in such a long list that it would be impossible to make the list explicit. However, it is possible to provide an explicit list of general questions to which all of the answers are morally relevant features of the violation.

The point of providing an explicit list of questions is to make clear what kinds of considerations should be used to determine when two violations count as the same kind of act. If a rational person regards which kind of pain is being suffered to be morally relevant regardless of who is suffering that pain, then which kind of pain is being suffered is morally relevant. Nonetheless, there is no need to include in the list questions concerning each of the kinds of pain. The same is true of questions about kinds of disabilities, losses of freedom, and losses of pleasure. Indeed it is not even necessary to have distinct questions about pain, disability, loss of freedom, and loss of pleasure. All of the different harms or evils can be taken as providing answers to the same question, with the understanding that different amounts and kinds of harms or evils are sufficient to make two violations different kinds of acts. The different kinds and amounts of harmful and beneficial consequences have always been explicitly considered to be morally relevant features. I still consider them to be so, but I see no need to explicitly list questions about all of the individual evils and goods. It is important, however, to have explicit questions to which the other morally relevant features are answers, for many of these features have often been overlooked in discussions of which violations are justified.

Morally Relevant Features

A morally relevant feature of a moral rule violation is a feature that if changed could change whether some impartial rational person would publicly allow that violation. If all of these features are the same for two violations, then they are the same kind of violation, and if an impartial rational person would publicly allow one of them, then she must also publicly allow the other. If one favors publicly allowing a particular violation but does not publicly allow another that seems similar, then, as an impartial rational person, one must show how the two violations differ with regard to at least one of these morally relevant features. It does not follow that two different impartial rational persons who regard a violation as of the same kind must agree on whether or not to publicly allow that violation. For impartial rational persons may differ in what they believe about the consequences of that kind of violation being publicly allowed or in their ranking of these consequences.

The answers to the ten questions that I am about to present provide features that might affect whether or not some impartial rational person would publicly allow the violation. The answers to this list of questions seems to me to include all of the important morally relevant features, but I have thought this before and have been mistaken, as shown by the fact that the list of questions in the most recent previously published version of my moral theory did not contain the last three questions. Although there is no doubt that all of the answers to the questions on the list are morally relevant, it is quite likely that there are morally relevant features that are answers to questions that are not on the current list. I welcome suggestions about questions that would have such answers. Any feature that can change whether some impartial rational person would publicly allow some violation such that all rational persons can understand it counts as a morally relevant feature.

The answers to the following questions are all morally relevant features.

1. *What moral rule is being violated?*

It is quite clear that stronger reasons are needed for violating the rule prohibiting killing than for the rule prohibiting depriving of pleasure. What may not be so obvious is that, when the consequences of the particular act are the same, it may be justified to cause pain, when it would not be justified to deceive. For example, when the probability of success is the same, it may be justified to harass a patient into continuing a treatment that it is irrational to refuse, such as physical therapy after a stroke, whereas it would not be justified to deceive that patient for the same purpose. This is because even when violations of the two different rules are the same in all of their other morally relevant features, the consequences of everyone knowing that a violation of the rule prohibiting deception is allowed may be far worse than everyone knowing that a violation of the rule prohibiting causing pain is allowed. This shows the importance of the two-step procedure that is required by the moral system but neglected by both Kant and consequentialists.

2. A. *What harms are being caused by the violation?*
   B. *What harms are being avoided (not being caused) by violating the rule?*
   C. *What harms are being prevented by the violation?*[3]

The kinds of harms, their severity, the length of time they will be suffered, and their probability of occurrence must be specified. If more than one person is involved, the distribution of these evils among these persons must also be specified. There are different kinds of evils, such as death, pain (and even kinds of pains), and so on. That impartial rational persons may rank these harms differently accounts for much of the moral disagreement that occurs when there is genuine agreement on the facts. However, in two decades of participating in medical consultations, I have found that most moral disagreements are the result of different beliefs about the facts, especially different beliefs about the probability of various evils occurring, rather than the result of differences in the ranking of evils. However, if two people agree on what evils will be caused, avoided, or prevented by a particular act, including kind, severity, duration, probability, and distribution, and even if they agree on the rankings of those evils, and on the goods (benefits) being promoted (see question 5 below) they still may not agree on what kind of act it is. For, although no one doubts that the evils being caused, avoided, and prevented, and the goods being promoted, are morally relevant, there are other morally relevant features in addition to these consequences.

Some consequentialists, such as G. E. Moore, take the counterintuitive view that it is the actual consequences, even if unforeseeable, that are morally relevant. Some Kantians seem to hold that only intended consequences have moral relevance. Contrary to both of these views, it is the foreseen and foreseeable goods and evils that are most relevant to the making of most moral judgments, and foreseen consequences that are most relevant to the making of most moral decisions. Actual consequences that are unforeseeable play no role in moral judgments, although they may appropriately be considered in determining the punishment of someone who committed an unjustifiable or weakly justifiable violation of a moral rule.[4] Further, actual consequences may require an excuse, even though their being unforeseeable provides that excuse. Whether one intends to cause some harm, or only does so knowingly (see question 9 below) may affect not only a moral judgment that is made on an act, but also a decision about how to act.

Thus, actual, foreseeable, foreseen, and intended consequences can all be morally relevant. But of these four kinds of consequences, actual consequences have the least moral relevance; intended consequences are in third place, while foreseen and foreseeable consequences are the most relevant. What counts as foreseen and intended consequences is completely determined by what the agent foresees and intends, while the agent has no special status at all in determining the actual consequences. Foreseeable consequences are neither completely determined by the agent nor are they completed unrelated to the agent. Since foreseeable consequences are the kind of consequences that are most relevant to the making of moral judgments, it is important to be as clear as possible about what consequences count as foreseeable. Foreseeable consequences are determined by the knowledge and intelligence of the agent; they are what he can be expected to foresee. What most people with similar knowledge and intelligence would foresee in a situation is foreseeable.

Determining what counts as foreseeable consequences is similar to determining what counts as an irrational belief. It is irrational for a normal adult to believe in Santa Claus; it is not irrational for a normal five-year-old to believe in him. The adult has a level of knowledge and intelligence such that it would be obvious to almost everyone with similar knowledge and intelligence that believing in Santa Claus is inconsistent with what they know and believe. The five-year-old has a level of knowledge and intelligence such that it would not be obvious to almost everyone with similar knowledge and intelligence that believing in Santa Claus is inconsistent with what they know and believe. Similarly, it is foreseeable to a normal adult that playing with matches can cause a serious fire. This is not foreseeable to a normal five-year-old. Most people with the knowledge and intelligence of a normal adult would foresee the consequences of playing with matches. It is not the case that most people with the knowledge and intelligence of a normal five-year-old would foresee this.

Although it will usually be clear whether or not the consequences of an action were foreseeable to the agent, sometimes it will not. Fully informed, impartial rational persons can, within limits, disagree about whether the consequences of an action were foreseeable to the agent. It is often important whether the consequences of an action were foreseeable to the agent, for if they were not he may be excused, and if they were he may not be. Lack of clarity or disagreement about whether or not the harmful consequences were foreseeable to the agent may result in a partial excuse. That foreseeable consequences are agent-relative makes clear that two people can cooperate in performing the same action and yet some of the consequences of that action be foreseeable to one of them and unforeseeable to the other. Even though foreseeable consequences are relative to the knowledge and intelligence of the agent, they are still objective factors.

3. *What are the relevant desires and beliefs of the person toward whom the rule is being violated?*
    A. *What are the relevant desires of the person toward whom the rule is being violated?*

There are several possibilities. (1) The person has a rational desire that results in his wanting the rule to be violated; for example, a patient desires to live and wants the painful treatment because he believes it necessary to save his life. (2) The person has a rational desire that results in his not wanting to have the rule violated; for example, a defendant desires not to be deprived of freedom so he does not want to be convicted and to spend the next year in prison. (3) The person has desires that are relevant to her not wanting the moral rule violated, but these desires are not rational; for example, a young woman desires to die because her fiancé has been killed in a motorcycle accident so she does not want doctors to prevent her suicide attempt from succeeding. (4) The person has no desires at all that are relevant to the moral rule violation; for example, a person is so demented he does not have any desires that would be affected by the proposed violation of the moral rule.

The relevant rational desires of a person are morally relevant even if, because of the lack of relevant rational beliefs, he does not see the connection between his rational desires and the moral rule violation. For example, a patient who has a rational desire to live even if this means enduring significant pain may not want a painful operation because he does not realize that it is necessary to save his life; another patient has a rational desire to die rather than to endure significant pain and so does not want a painful operation even though he knows that it is necessary to save his life. At least some, if not all, impartial rational persons would publicly allow treating these two patients differently, even though neither wants to have the operation.

> B. *What are the relevant beliefs of the person toward whom the rule is being violated?*

Again there are several possibilities. (1) All of his beliefs about how he will be affected by the violation are rational and based on adequate evidence. (2) Some of his beliefs about how he will be affected by the violation are rational and based on adequate evidence, but others are either irrational or would be irrational if the person had a higher level of intelligence or knowledge. (3) He has no beliefs about how he will be affected by the violation, or all of his beliefs are irrational or would count as irrational if he had a higher level of intelligence or knowledge.

As shown by the contrast between the two patients who do not want a life-saving operation, what a person knows about the consequences of his decision may influence whether impartial rational persons would publicly allow violating a moral rule with regard to him. The relevant beliefs of a person, including whether they are irrational, or would be if the person had a higher level of knowledge or intelligence, may determine whether a person is competent to make a rational decision. The irrationality of a patient's desires may also determine whether a person is competent.[5] The competence of a patient to make a rational decision is often used by physicians when they decide whether to violate a moral rule with regard to that patient for his own benefit, but without his consent — that is, whether or not to act paternalistically.[6]

Questions 3A and B are relevant not only in determining competence but also in determining other aspects of informed consent. Whether a patient has given valid (informed) consent to a medical procedure is dependent on her relevant rational desires and beliefs.[7] It is generally acknowledged that whether or not a patient has given valid consent to a medical procedure is morally relevant in determining whether one should perform that procedure. A consent counts as valid only if the patient has the relevant rational desires and beliefs. As with the other morally relevant features, this feature is morally relevant only insofar as the agent knows, or at least justifiably believes, that the person has the relevant rational beliefs and desires. That is why actual consent is morally relevant in many medical situations; only by obtaining a patient's valid consent can a physician know that the patient has the relevant rational beliefs and desires.

> 4. *Is the relationship between the person violating the rule and the persons toward whom the rule is being violated such that the former has a duty to violate moral rules with regard to the latter independent of their consent?*

That the answers to this question are morally relevant features accounts for the fact that, in most societies, the relationship that parents have with their children is morally relevant. When considering the violation of a moral rule, it is morally relevant whether it is the parents of the children who are violating the rule with regard to them.[8] Parents' violations of the rule against depriving of freedom with regard to their children, for example, making them do their homework, does not count as the same kind of violation as a violation of the same rule by an adult toward a child with whom he has no special relationship. This is true even when the evils caused, avoided, and prevented and the relevant desires and beliefs of the child are the same.

That the answers to this question are morally relevant features also explains why the relationship between governments and their citizens is morally relevant. When a government deprives one or more of its citizens of some freedom, that is not the same kind of act as one citizen depriving another one of the same amount of freedom, even when the evils caused, avoided, and prevented and the rational desires and beliefs of the person being deprived of the freedom are the same. Of course, both acts of deprivation may be morally unjustified, but since they are not the same kind of act, it may be that one of them is justified and the other not. This feature makes it possible that appropriate members of the government may be justified in inflicting an evil on a citizen when people without this special relationship are not justified in inflicting that evil in what may otherwise count as the same kind of situation. Different answers to this question provide morally relevant features that are essential for distinguishing punishment from revenge. Without these morally relevant features, revenge and legitimate punishment would count as the same kind of violation.

5. *What goods (including kind, degree, probability, duration, and distribution) are being promoted by the violation?*

Except for trivial violations of a moral rule, or outlandish philosophical examples, the answers to this question are morally relevant features only when the answer to the previous question is positive or when one has the valid consent of the person toward whom the rule is being violated. I regard the kind of situation, when there is a violation by someone who has a duty to violate the moral rules with regard to the person toward whom the rule is being violated, a political one.[9] When dealing with individuals who do not have this kind of special relationship, negative utilitarianism, a consequentialist view that counts only evils as morally relevant, accounts much better for common moral judgments than classical utilitarianism, a consequentialist view that treats goods and evils as equally relevant. However, when dealing with governments, the reverse seems to be true. The major classical utilitarians, Bentham and Mill, were primarily concerned with the actions of governments.

It is the failure to appreciate, or perhaps even to notice, the moral significance of the close relationship between questions 4 and 5 that is a major factor in accounting for many contemporary consequentialists converting a plausible moral system applied to government into an implausible system applied to individuals. I have already shown that no consequentialist system adequately accounts for many moral judgments. However, recognition of the relationship between questions 4 and 5 explains the strong points of both negative and classical utilitarianism. It should be explicitly noted that this question concerns only the promotion of goods; depriving of a good is the same as causing an evil and so is included in question 2.

6. *Is the rule being violated toward a person in order to prevent her from violating a moral rule when the violation would be* (1) *unjustified or* (2) *weakly justified?*

This question allows one to distinguish between deception by those involved in some kinds of undercover police work and deception by those seeking to gain additional anthropological or sociological knowledge, even when the other morally relevant features are the same. Whether or not the action is an attempt to prevent a violation of a moral rule can also be used to distinguish between justified and unjustified spying (and other activities) by one government with regard to another. These activities, and other violations of the moral rules, which are unjustified when employed by an aggressor nation, may be justified when employed by a nation responding to aggression. Of course, a positive answer to this question does not justify all violations of moral rules; it must still be the case that an impartial rational person can publicly allow this kind of violation.

I have already discussed the fact that impartial rational persons may publicly allow enforcement of laws even when the violation is weakly justified. Although law enforcement is often thought of as involving the punishment of violations of the law, it can also involve prevention of such violations. It may be morally allowed for police to deprive of freedom, such as preventing some public activity, in order to prevent a weakly justified violation of the law, when it would not be morally allowed for them to deprive people of that same freedom if no law was being violated. However, it is plausible that more serious violations of a moral rule might be justified in order to prevent completely unjustified violations than to prevent weakly justified violations. There is a problem with evaluating this plausible claim because it is extremely difficult to describe two different violations that differ only in the feature that one is a completely unjustified violation and the other is a weakly justified violation.

7. *Is the rule being violated toward a person because he has violated a moral rule* (1) *unjustifiably, or* (2) *with a weak justification?*

This is a crucial question when discussing punishment. It would be inappropriate to call the infliction of an evil "punishment" unless the person is being inflicted with the evil because of an unjustified or weakly justified violation of a moral rule. The infliction of an evil also is not punishment if the person inflicting the evil does not have a duty to do so, which is why a positive answer to question 4 is presupposed when justifying punishment. It also seems morally relevant whether the violation is weakly justified or completely unjustified, but the claim that impartial rational persons may inflict greater penalties for the latter kind of violation even if all the other features are the same is difficult to evaluate for the same reasons cited in the discussion of the previous question.

A positive answer to question 7 together with a positive answer to question 4 explains why the infliction of an evil that is justifiable as a punishment may not be justifiable when it is not a punishment but all of the other morally relevant features are the same. The answers to this question are also relevant when considering the infliction of an evil that is not appropriately called "punishment," for example, harms that are inflicted as responses to immoral acts of war. However, this kind of infliction of harm, like standard punishments, must have prevention of future violations as its justification or it is simply an unjustified act of revenge.[10]

8. *Are there any alternative actions or policies that would be preferable?*

The answers to this question are so obviously morally relevant features that I can only explain not explicitly including it in previous editions as a result of my having been blinded by the obvious.[11] In fact, I used the answers to this question when discussing alternative systems of punishment, which confirms my view that I am simply making explicit those features of the moral system that are implicitly used when making moral decisions and judgments. The presence or absence of an alternative action or policy that impartial rational persons would prefer to the action being considered is clearly morally relevant. Many paternalistic actions that might be justified if there were no nonpaternalistic alternatives are not justified if there is a preferable alternative, such as taking time to persuade citizens or patients rather than deceiving them. Explicit awareness of this feature may be useful in leading people to try to find out if there are any alternative actions that would either not involve a violation of a moral rule or that would involve causing much less evil.

The inadequacy of most of the discussion of legalizing physician-assisted suicide is an example of the failure to consider this morally relevant question. It seems to be admitted by proponents of legalizing physician-assisted suicide that doing so has some risks, such as increasing pressure on terminally ill patients to die sooner and various other kinds of abuse. However, they claim that these risks are significantly outweighed by the benefits of legalizing physician-assisted suicide, such as the elimination of months or years of terrible pain and suffering. If there were no alternative method of eliminating these months or years of terrible pain and suffering, then they would have a strong argument. However, since patients are already allowed to refuse not only any medical treatment but also food and fluids, legalizing physician-assisted suicide does not prevent any significant pain and suffering. If patients are educated about the possibility of refusing food and fluids, which contrary to popular opinion is relatively painless, they can arrange the timing of their death as quick or quicker than with physician-assisted suicide. The presence of this alternative changes the force of the argument.[12]

An action or policy counts as an alternative action or policy if it is either foreseen or foreseeable to the person acting and it would be rational for him to attempt to perform that action or adopt that policy. Alternative actions or policies, like foreseeable consequences, are related to the situation and characteristics of the persons involved. However, what in hindsight was an alternative action or policy might not have been an alternative at the time of acting, for what is foreseeable at a later time may not have been foreseeable earlier. Equally informed rational people can, within limits, disagree on what the foreseeable consequences were at a time, and so disagree about what the alternatives were at that time. This is a disagreement about the level of intelligence and knowledge of the people involved and about what people with this level of intelligence and knowledge can be expected to foresee. The stan-

dard test is whether most people with similar knowledge and intelligence in that situation would have foreseen this alternative. When there is no agreed-upon method
for deciding this, there may be an unresolvable moral disagreement.

9. *Is the violation being done intentionally or only knowingly?*

There are many other questions, such as: Is the violation being done (A) voluntarily
or because of a volitional disability? (B) freely or because of coercion? (C) knowingly or without knowledge of what is being done? (D) Is the lack of knowledge excusable or the result of negligence?[13] A different answer to any of these questions
may change the moral judgments that some impartial rational people may make on
violations that are alike in all of their other morally relevant features. However, my
primary goal in listing questions is to help those deciding whether to commit a given
kind of violation, thus I have not included those questions to which the answers are
of value solely in judging violations that have already been committed, for they cannot be used in deciding how to act. The answers to questions 9 A, B, C, and D cannot help one decide whether to commit a violation that has one of these features
rather than another. For example, a person cannot decide whether to do an action
freely rather than because of coercion. Hence these features are not useful in deciding how to act.

However, the answer to question 9 might sometimes be useful in deciding how
to act. Although one cannot usually decide whether or not to commit a violation intentionally or only knowingly, sometimes that is possible. A person might not publicly allow a violation that was done intentionally but might publicly allow another
that was not done intentionally, even though it was done knowingly and the two violations are alike in all of their other morally relevant features. For example, a nurse
may be willing to administer morphine to terminally ill patients in order to relieve
pain, even though she knows it will hasten their death, but, with no other morally
relevant changes in the situation, she would not administer morphine in order to
hasten the death of the patient. Many impartial rational persons would agree with
this decision of the nurse and publicly allow administering morphine in the first situation but not the second.[14] This question explains what is correct in the doctrine of
double effect, which states that in some cases where all of the other morally relevant
features are the same, it may be morally acceptable to do an act knowingly that is
not morally acceptable to do intentionally.

Usually this doctrine is used when one has to choose between harming two different individuals. Some claim that it is morally permissible to prevent harm for one
person, even if one knows that one's action will result in harm for another, but not
permissible to intentionally cause harm in an otherwise similar situation. A common example is a surgical procedure to save the life of the mother although the sur-
geon knows it will result in the death of the fetus versus intentionally killing the
fetus to save the life of the mother.[15] The distinction between an action being done
intentionally or only knowingly may also account for what many regard as a morally
significant difference between lying and other forms of deception, especially withholding information. Lying is always intentionally deceiving, whereas withholding
information may often be only knowingly deceiving. Nonetheless, it is important to

remember that almost all violations that are morally unacceptable when done intentionally are also morally unacceptable when done only knowingly.

10. *Is the situation an emergency such that no person is likely to plan to be in that kind of situation?*

I am talking about the kind of emergency situation that is sufficiently rare that no person is likely to plan or prepare for being in it. This question is necessary to account for the fact that certain kinds of emergency situations change the decisions and judgments that many would make even when all of the other morally relevant features are the same. For example, in an emergency when large numbers of people have been seriously injured, doctors are morally allowed to abandon patients who have a very small chance of survival in order to take care of those with a better chance. However, in the ordinary practice of medicine doctors are not morally allowed to abandon patients with poor prognoses in order to treat those with better prognoses, even if doing so will result in more people surviving. Public knowledge that this procedure is allowed in emergencies will not affect anyone's behavior nor should it cause anyone increased anxiety, whereas public knowledge that this procedure is allowed in the normal practice of medicine may have profound effects on people's behavior and anxiety levels.

Failure to realize that a situation is an emergency situation is a morally relevant feature explains why consequentialists often cite emergency situations in order to show that consequences are the overriding if not the sole morally relevant consideration. They do not recognize that what is morally acceptable in an emergency situation may not be morally acceptable in a nonemergency or normal situation. An impartial rational person might publicly allow breaking a moral rule in an emergency situation when he would not do so in a nonemergency situation, even when all the other morally relevant features are the same, including the foreseeable consequences. Physicians are sometimes allowed to deprive patients of their freedom and even to inflict pain without consent in emergency situations when they are not allowed to do so in nonemergency situations that have all of the same other morally relevant features. What is morally decisive is not the foreseeable consequences of the particular violation but the consequences of that kind of violation being publicly allowed.

Although I have provided a list of ten questions, it is clear that these questions generate far more than ten morally relevant features. I cannot even estimate how many such features there might be, for there is no precise way of determining what counts as a single feature. The point of the list of questions is to help guide the search for morally relevant facts. Everyone admits that the solution to most moral problems depends on discovering all of the relevant facts, but previously there has been no guide to help one determine which facts are morally relevant. I have shown that those facts which provide answers to any question on the list of ten questions may be a morally relevant fact. This list of questions is not a check list that one must explicitly go through when considering any violation of a moral rule, for it will often be obvious what the answer to some of these questions are. For example, question 7 never arises in making moral decisions in medicine.

I have not shown that the answers to the preceding questions provide the only morally relevant features. I do not know how I could show this any more than I could show that there are only ten moral rules.[16] However, like the rules, a feature cannot count as morally relevant unless it can be formulated in a way that is understandable to all moral agents. Nonetheless, it is quite likely that those who concentrate on discussing the features of particular acts have already discovered morally relevant features that I have left out, although they have not reformulated them in a way that is understandable to all moral agents. Only if a feature can be formulated so as to be understandable to all moral agents can it be part of a public system that applies to all rational persons. This is not merely a theoretical requirement; as a practical matter, requiring this level of generality is needed to ensure the kind of impartiality required by morality. Without this level of generality it would be possible to manipulate descriptions of violations in a way that would seem to allow a person to benefit his friends and family.

Requiring that the morally relevant features can be stated in terms that are understandable by all moral agents may make them seem too abstract and general. I have no objection, indeed I think it would be valuable, for others to describe the morally relevant features in a less general way, and to provide particular examples that show how a feature is morally relevant. Although all of these more detailed descriptions of features must be instances of the features that are answers to the ten questions in this section, providing examples and describing the features in greater detail may give them more force. For purposes of describing the moral system, however, the completely general characterization of the morally relevant features represented by the answers to the above list of questions is sufficient.

The Two-Step Procedure and the Morally Decisive Question

The answers to the ten questions given in the previous section provide a list of features that determine the kind of violation being considered. The crucial first step in moral reasoning about particular violations is determining what kind of violation a particular violation is. After all of the morally relevant facts have been described, using the list of questions to determine which facts are morally relevant, the next step is determining whether or not an impartial rational person can publicly allow this kind of violation. This determination is made by answering *the morally decisive question* "What effects would this kind of violation being publicly allowed have?" The answer to this question is morally decisive in determining whether the violation of the rule is justified or unjustified, and, if justified, whether it is strongly or weakly justified.

The answer to the morally decisive question does not contribute to determining what counts as the same kind of act, rather it presupposes that the kind of act has already been determined. It is impossible to answer the morally decisive question "What effects would this kind of violation being publicly allowed have?" without first having a clear answer to what counts as the same kind of violation. Moral reasoning involving the violation of a moral rule always requires this two-step procedure; the first, specifying the kind of violation, the second, determining the consequences of that kind of violation being publicly allowed. There are not two levels of moral thinking to be used in different situations, one for simple problems, the other for settling conflicts between general moral rules and ideals, as Hare proposes.[17] Rather, both steps of this two-step procedure are required whenever violating a moral rule is being considered. Collapsing these two steps into one may be another mistake of consequentialism.

Consequentialists are right that only consequences count, but this is only at the second stage of moral reasoning when considering the consequences of publicly allowing the violation. But at this stage, it is not the consequences of the particular act that are being considered, but the consequences of a contrary-to-fact hypothetical situation, namely, the consequences of everyone knowing that this kind of violation is allowed. Consideration of the consequences of this purely hypothetical situation is necessary for the kind of impartiality required by morality, for one is acting impartially in violating a moral rule only if one would be willing for everyone to know that they also are allowed to violate the rule in the same circumstances. At the first stage, determining the kind of violation, the consequences of the act and its alternatives are not the only morally relevant features; there are many nonconsequentialist features, for example, the relationship between the parties involved.

Causes of Disagreement: Facts, Ideology, and Rankings

Agreement on what counts as a morally relevant feature is not the same as agreement concerning what morally relevant features any particular violation actually has. Although everyone agrees that the amount of pain being caused, avoided, or prevented is a morally relevant feature, people often disagree about how much pain will be caused, avoided, or prevented by a particular violation of a moral rule. Most moral disagreements are disagreements about the facts of the case, which leads people to disagree about whether or not a particular violation is of the same kind as some other violation. This is a disagreement in the first step of the two-step procedure. However, even if two persons agree that two violations have all the same morally relevant features so that they agree that they are the same kind of act, they may still disagree on whether or not to publicly allow such a violation. Impartial rational persons may differ, not only in their ranking of the goods and evils involved but also in their belief about what would happen if everyone knew that this kind of violation was allowed. This is a disagreement in the second step of the two-step procedure.

When there is agreement on the facts of the case, that is, on the kind of violation, all disagreement between impartial rational persons on whether a kind of violation should be publicly allowed is a disagreement in the second step. If no impartial rational person would prefer the consequences of this kind of violation being publicly allowed to the consequences of it not being publicly allowed, it is *unjustified*. If all impartial rational persons would prefer the consequences of this kind of violation being publicly allowed to the consequences of it not being publicly allowed, it is *strongly justified*. If impartial rational persons disagree on whether they prefer the consequences of this kind of violation being publicly allowed to the consequences of it not being publicly allowed, it is *weakly justified*. Weakly justified violations can result either from differences in rankings of the goods and evils or from differences in beliefs about the consequences of everyone knowing that this kind of violation is allowed.

Differences about what the effects of this kind of violation being publicly allowed are, are based on differences in views about human nature or the nature of human societies. For example, one person may believe that publicly allowing trivial deception in order to avoid minor anxiety or displeasure for the deceived would result in a substantial decrease in the amount of anxiety and displeasure suffered, while another believes, on the contrary, that this kind of violation being publicly allowed would result in increased anxiety because of additional uncertainty about whether one was being deceived. The latter person might also believe that there will be an increase in nontrivial deception, some of which will have harmful effects not anticipated by the person who is deceiving.

Although these different views of human nature seem to be disagreements about matters of fact, since the facts are not available and most likely will never become available, the resulting dispute should be regarded as *ideological*. An ideological dispute is best thought of as a dispute about human nature or the nature of human society that cannot be resolved and that results in disagreement on public policy. A disagreement about whether to publicly allow a particular kind of violation that is based on a disagreement about the consequences of publicly allowing the violation versus the consequences of not publicly allowing it is almost always an ideological disagreement, for there is no way of settling the seemingly factual differences on which the disagreement depends. Ideological disputes always have a significant political dimension and often involve different views about the way the government should act. Common examples of ideological disputes are disputes about the effects of publicly allowing the government to restrict freedom to improve the welfare of its citizens.

I do not count a dispute as ideological if it is based solely on a disagreement in the rankings of goods and evils. Different rankings provide another explanation for disagreement on whether to publicly allow a kind of violation. A straightforward difference in the ranking of the consequences that are believed to result from the violation being publicly allowed can occur even when there are no ideological differences. However, ideological differences are so closely related to differences in rankings that it is not clear which of the two is most responsible for the disagreement. A person who ranks freedom higher than another is less likely to believe that people will misuse additional freedom, while a person who believes that people will misuse additional freedom often ranks freedom less highly. Indeed, it is extremely unlikely that ideological differences and differences in rankings are ever completely distinct.

Providing a procedure for determining whether some violations of the moral rules are unjustified or strongly justified is not providing a mechanical decision procedure for settling moral questions. Although some actual moral disputes about violations can be settled by simply applying the moral attitude to the moral rules and getting clear about the facts, many violations will be weakly justified. Although this means that fully informed, impartial rational persons will continue to disagree, the two-step procedure is still useful in several ways. First, it provides guidance about what facts are morally relevant, helping one to know what facts to look for when attempting to make a moral decision. Second, it helps to show what disagreement about facts, for example, a disagreement about the probability of benefit from an action or policy, is responsible for the moral disagreement. Hence, if there is a change in the facts, it may facilitate future agreement. It may even prompt a new proposal that results in a different set of facts. Third, when there is agreement on the facts, it helps people pinpoint the source of their disagreement, a difference in ranking or an ideological difference, thus improving the chances of later agreement. Finally, the recognition that impartial rational persons can agree on all the facts and yet disagree about what ought to be done promotes tolerance of different moral decisions and judgments.

This explicit account of the moral rules, the morally relevant features, and the two-step procedure for justifying violations is intended to provide a limit to genuine moral disputes. As in all informal public systems, all impartial rational persons will usually agree about what morally should be done. However, when there are disagreements, even a completely correct application of the moral system will not settle all issues. Impartial rational persons must often decide on their own whether they would publicly allow the violation. Therefore, I have not provided anything that functions like an ideal observer, or Aristotle's practically wise person, to whom one can take any moral problem and he will pronounce what ought to be done. The cases that can be answered clearly by what I have said are those cases in which most people have no doubt about what is morally right. Applying the justification procedure to a controversial case will almost always result in the violation being weakly justified, that is, with impartial rational persons disagreeing about whether it should be publicly allowed. But morality is an informal system, so that controversial cases, although they are the most discussed, are only a small percentage of cases in which moral decisions about whether violations should be publicly allowed are made.

Morality Must Be Public

In the previous two chapters I made explicit the ten rules toward which all impartial rational persons who use only rationally required beliefs will take the moral attitude. Everyone to whom these rules apply not only knows them, each also knows that they must be followed impartially. This involves knowing the appropriate moral attitude toward these rules, the morally relevant features, and the two-step procedure for justifying violations. Most people do not have explicit knowledge of the rules, the moral attitude, and the two-step procedure; they know them in the same way they know the grammar of their language. Everyone knows that certain kinds of actions, such as killing and cheating are immoral unless justified. They also know that all exceptions to the rules must be impartially determined, so that a person who favors a violation being publicly allowed must publicly allow all violations with the same morally relevant features. As a public system applying to all rational persons, all of morality must be known to and acceptable to all rational persons. Not only the rules, but also the morally relevant features and the two-step procedure for justifying violations must be understandable by and acceptable to all rational persons.

A moral system must be a public system because everyone agrees that morality applies to all those who understand it and can use it as a guide for their conduct. Since morality applies to all rational persons, all rational persons must understand it and be able to use it as a guide for their conduct. Morality cannot be a public system that applies to all rational persons if it is not known to and cannot be accepted by all rational persons. Thus a moral system cannot depend on any beliefs that are not known to all rational persons; the moral rules must be formulated in a way that is understandable to all rational persons; and the morally relevant features must be formulated in the same way. That morality is a public system that applies to all rational persons also explains why the two-step procedure for determining justified exceptions to the rules requires that an impartial rational person can publicly allow that kind of violation.

The public character of morality is also closely related to moral impartiality. Morality requires one to be impartial with regard to at least all other moral agents with respect to following the moral rules. Moral impartiality with respect to the moral rules requires that there be no special exceptions for anyone. Moral impartiality requires every rational person to justify violations following the same two-step procedure. The violation must be describable by means of the universally understood morally relevant features, and it must be possible for a fully informed, impartial rational person to publicly allow that kind of violation. Requiring the violations to be publicly allowed guarantees that the moral system retains the proper kind of impartiality. Requiring only that everyone be allowed to violate the rule, but not that the violation be publicly allowed, might result in a moral system in which those who know the violation is allowed will benefit and those who do not know, will be at a disadvantage. This would be incompatible with morality being a public system that applies impartially to all rational persons.

Fallibility and Vulnerability

In the real world, it is the vulnerability and fallibility of persons that make impartiality with regard to the rules so important. It may be impossible to even imagine that moral agents have beliefs about everything that is morally relevant and yet are infallible, that is, that they never make mistakes about the consequences of their actions, including the effect that their actions would have on their own character and the character of others. However, if it can be imagined that everyone knows that everyone else is infallible, there would be no point in being concerned with whether anyone unjustifiably violated any of the moral rules. Indeed, there would be no point in having any rules. Assume both that such infallible yet vulnerable people could be moral agents and that, contrary to fact, praise and condemnation were still appropriate. They would then be praised for acting in ways that result in the least amount of harm (or the best balance of benefits and harms), and it would be irrelevant whether or not that action was in accord with or in violation of one of the moral rules. That no one is infallible and everyone knows that no one is infallible is why the moral rules, especially the second five, are needed and why all impartial rational persons favor obedience to these rules unless an impartial rational person can publicly allow such a violation. It is the fallibility of persons that makes a general increase in unjustified violations of the moral rules lead to an increase in the overall amount of evil consequences being suffered.

Although vulnerability is essential for morality or anything that has the same kind of point as morality, fallibility, although essential for what is normally regarded as morality, is not needed for a kind of guide that has the same point as morality. Just as the first five rules are more fundamental than the second five, so vulnerability is more fundamental than fallibility. But fallibility is not only essential when considering violations of the second five rules, it is also essential when considering violations of the first five rules. It is impossible to overestimate the amount of evil caused by those who unjustifiably violate the first five rules for what they take to be better consequences in the future. Common morality is designed for beings who are not only vulnerable but also fallible. That is why it is so misleading to talk about morality with regard to God, who is supposed to be both invulnerable and infallible. Hobbes was one of the few philosophers to appreciate this point. There can be no adequate account of morality without taking into account these fundamental features of the nature of moral agents, their vulnerability and fallibility.

Kant's Categorical Imperative versus Publicly Allowing a Violation

Kant does not provide a list of questions that allow one to describe an act by using only its morally relevant features. Thus he cannot provide an objective description of the kind of act about which one is making a moral judgment. He seems to hold that the kind of act is determined by the actual maxim used by the person who is acting. This may explain why Kant mistakenly holds that moral judgments can be made only on intentional actions. But if one ignores that Kant has misdescribed the first step of the two-step procedure for determining justified exceptions, the first formulation of the categorical imperative, "Act only according to that maxim whereby you can at the same time will that it should become a universal law," provides a plausible formulation of the second step. It may plausibly be interpreted as stating that morality allows doing only those kinds of acts that an impartial rational person can publicly allow. This interpretation of the categorical imperative, by showing how it guarantees the kind of impartiality required by morality, explains why it has been so widely, but mistakenly, accepted as capturing the essence of morality. It also explains why many who reject Kant's metaphysics still think so highly of this aspect of his ethical theory.

However, apart from providing some approximation to the correct account of moral impartiality, Kant's ethical theory is almost completely misleading. Part of the explanation for this is that Kant regards all empirical facts about the world, including all facts about human beings, as irrelevant to explaining the nature of morality. Kant holds that such facts are useful only in applying the moral system to particular cases. In particular, he does not realize that it is the rationality (in the normal sense), vulnerability, and fallibility of moral agents that explain why morality has the nature it has. Kant's metaphysical account of "reason" cannot explain the categorical demands of morality, for on his account of rationality it is quite sensible to ask "Why be rational?" Further, as Mill points out, the categorical imperative divorced from the correct account of reason allows rules of conduct that everyone would regard as immoral. Kant's supposedly metaphysical foundation of morality is so far off the mark that it is surprising that his description of morality resembles common morality at all. What resemblance there is may be explained by noting that Kant, like Mill, started by trying to justify common morality, so perhaps it is not so surprising that something of it remains.

Without using, at least implicitly, the correct accounts of rationality, impartiality, and those empirical facts that everyone is rationally required to believe, the categorical imperative is inadequate for distinguishing morally acceptable acts from morally unacceptable ones. Even with the correct account of rationality, the categorical imperative permits far too many paternalistic actions to count as morally acceptable. Kant can show that the categorical imperative prohibits paternalistic deception, but he cannot show that it prohibits paternalistic causing of pain. For the categorical imperative classifies as morally acceptable any kind of act that a rational person can consistently put forward as a maxim for every rational person to act on. A rational person, in Kant's sense, cannot only allow but can even will that everyone cause pain to a person in order to save that person's life, even if that action requires overruling that person's rational (in the normal sense) refusal. Kant explicitly claims that the categorical imperative rules out suicide because of pain, so that it seems quite likely that he would actually endorse the paternalistic overruling of competent patients' rational (in the normal sense) refusals of life-prolonging treatment.

Further, the first formulation of the categorical imperative does not prohibit causing significant pain to one person to produce great pleasure for very many others. Another formulation of the categorical imperative, which requires that one always treat a person as an end in himself and never merely as a means, does prohibit this, but it also prohibits causing significant pain to one person in order to prevent even greater pain and death for thousands or even millions of others. However, this latter kind of action is at least weakly justified, and if the harm prevented is great enough, may even be strongly justified. That one formulation of the categorical imperative allows causing pain to produce pleasure, while another does not even allow causing pain to prevent much greater pain, shows that the different formulations of the categorical imperative are not equivalent. Further, there is no consistent interpretation of any formulation that does not have a clear counterexample. If the categorical imperative is interpreted literally, as ruling out as morally unacceptable any act done on a maxim that one could not will to be acted on by everyone, it would label as morally unacceptable many acts that clearly are not immoral, such as acting on the maxim "In order to avoid embarrassment never be the first to arrive at (or the last to leave) a party." Further, Kant never even considers that fully informed, impartial rational people can disagree in what they would will everyone to act, so that he cannot allow or explain moral disagreement. He does not realize that morality is an informal public system.

Kant also seems to have conflated the concept of universality, applying to all rational persons at all times and places, and the concept of absoluteness, not having any exceptions. Thus, even if the categorical imperative did generate general moral rules it would still be inadequate, for Kant never provides any way of deciding when one can justifiably violate these rules. However, given some of Kant's examples, the categorical imperative might be taken as presupposing the general moral rules and as providing a method of identifying justifiable exceptions to these rules. On this (implausible) interpretation of Kant, a violation of a moral rule is justifiable only if one can will that everyone violate that rule in the same circumstances. Kant intends to rule out people making special exceptions for themselves, for he recognizes that when considering violating a moral rule, morality requires impartiality. However, just as Rawls makes the veil of ignorance thicker than is necessary for impartiality, so Kant's categorical imperative requires more than is necessary for impartiality. Rawls wants unanimity as well as impartiality, and Kant wants violations of the categorical imperative to involve contradictions.[18] Just as the veil of ignorance is not necessary for impartiality, the blindfold of justice is sufficient, so the requirement that one will that everyone violate a rule is not necessary for moral impartiality; it is sufficient that one never violate a rule unless one can publicly allow such a violation.[19] Regardless of what Kant intended, the value of his categorical imperative is solely in its recognition, poorly expressed, that morality is a public system that applies to all rational persons and that impartiality with respect to obeying the moral rules is an essential feature of it.

Kant can be given an interpretation that not only captures the spirit of his view, but also provides a fairly adequate account of that part of morality represented by the moral rules. First Kant must be provided with the proper understanding of rationality. Then the terms "maxim" and "law" must be replaced by the phrase "public system." Making these changes results in the first formulation of Kant's categorical imperative becoming "Act only on that public system whereby you can at the same time will that it should apply to all rational persons." Understood in this way, the categorical imperative does indeed rule out all immoral actions. It does not account for the moral ideals, but since the categorical imperative is only supposed to deal with moral requirements, this is to be expected. This reformulation suggests that Kant shares an error with almost all other philosophers who have tried to provide a justification or foundation for the moral rules. He thinks that it is appropriate to consider each rule separately rather than see them as part of a public system that includes not only the rules but also a procedure for justifying violations of the rules.

Summary

It is morally justifiable to violate a moral rule only when a fully informed, impartial rational person can publicly allow such a violation. Deciding whether to publicly allow such a violation involves a two-step procedure. The first step is using the list of ten questions to discover the morally relevant facts that determine the kind of violation, and the second step is comparing the consequences of that kind of violation being publicly allowed to the consequences of it not being publicly allowed. Both steps must be taken before deciding whether or not to publicly allow that kind of violation. Understanding the moral rules requires understanding how to apply the two-step procedure for determining justified exceptions. Such understanding requires knowing when and how violations of the rules can be justified, which requires recognition of the morally relevant features that determine what counts as the same kind of violation. A moral rule cannot be properly understood independently of understanding how it interacts with other elements of the moral system, and any attempt to do so involves a distortion, not only of the rule but of morality itself.

All impartial rational persons who use only rationally required beliefs will take the moral attitude toward each of the general justified moral rules. The final formulation of this attitude is *Everyone (including myself) is always to obey the rule "Do not . . . ," except when a fully informed, impartial rational person can publicly allow violating it. Anyone who violates the rule when not all fully informed, impartial rational persons would publicly allow such a violation may be punished.* The except clause of the moral attitude does not mean that all impartial rational persons favor violating a moral rule whenever a fully informed, impartial rational person can publicly allow violating it. Rather, it simply means that when a fully informed, impartial rational person can publicly allow a violation of a moral rule and also can favor not publicly allowing that violation, some fully informed, impartial rational persons will favor violating the rule and some will not.

The final sentence of the moral attitude, concerning liability to punishment, makes clear that an impartial rational person can favor liability to punishment for a violation of a moral rule even when some impartial rational person can publicly allow such a violation. Only if all impartial rational persons would publicly allow such a violation would no impartial rational person favor liability to punishment. When the violation is only weakly justified, that is, when impartial rational persons disagree on whether to publicly allow the violation, then they also may disagree on whether the person violating the rule may be punished. An impartial rational person need not exempt from liability to punishment another impartial rational person who has violated a rule because the latter would publicly allow such a violation. Acting according to one's conscience, that is, according to one's public attitude, does not exempt one from morally justified punishment, even though it does exempt one from justified moral condemnation.

Evils are ranked in too many diverse ways, and there are too many ideological differences for all impartial rational persons to permit any violation that some impartial rational person would publicly allow. The diversity of rational rankings of evils and ideological differences explain why morality is an informal public system that has no experts whose decisions must be accepted. Any moral decision or judgment based on a rational ranking of evils and a correct application of the two-step procedure is justifiable. This may explain why there is sometimes a divergence between moral judgments and legal judgments. That some fully informed, impartial rational persons would publicly allow a violation does not require those in charge of enforcing the law, also acting as impartial rational persons, to publicly allow such a violation. When the government would favor not publicly allowing a violation, it may be morally justified in punishing those who commit these weakly justified violations.

That morality is a public system that applies to vulnerable persons explains the content of the moral rules, especially the first five. That morality is a public system that applies to fallible persons explains both the need for moral rules, especially the second five, and why impartiality with respect to obeying the moral rules is an essential feature of morality. That morality is a public system that applies to all rational persons explains why the morally relevant features must be known to all rational persons and why ignorance of any part of the moral system does not count as an excuse.

That morality is an informal public system explains why, although there is agreement on most moral matters, some moral disagreements are unresolvable. That morality is an informal public system that applies to vulnerable and fallible persons explains why applying morality to an omnipotent and omniscient God is both confused and confusing.

Both deontologists and consequentialists fail to recognize that fallibility is presupposed by morality. The debate between them can be resolved by explicitly recognizing what they both overlook. Deontologists are right about the need for rules; consequentialists are right that morality has a point or purpose. Both fail to see that it is the fallibility of persons that explains why rules are needed in order to accomplish the point of morality. Deontologists recognize that general moral rules are an essential feature of morality, but they overlook that moral rules have exceptions and that a rational person will always determine if an exception is justified by reference to the point of morality. Consequentialists recognize that morality has a point, but they overlook that achieving the point of morality requires not only the use of rules but also that justified exceptions must be limited to those that can be publicly allowed. Recognizing that morality is an informal public system that applies to rational, vulnerable, and fallible moral agents is thus useful not only in resolving moral disputes but also in resolving philosophical disputes about morality.

Notes

1. Although I shall usually talk about the morally relevant features as determining what counts as the same kind of violation, I shall sometimes talk about them as determining what counts as the same circumstances or the same kind of situation. Nothing turns on which expression is used.

2. I often describe a weakly justified action by saying that some rational persons would and some rational persons would not favor acting on it.

3. Often it is only the risk of harm that is being caused, avoided, or prevented, and the seriousness of the risk is clearly morally relevant. Far more can and should be said about the role of risk and probability in making moral decisions and judgments, but I leave this topic to others more qualified to deal with it.

4. This is due to the lottery nature of punishment. Whether or not one is actually punished, and how much punishment one receives, is often appropriately determined by factors outside of one's control. Both unjustified and weakly justified violations of a moral rule subject one to the lottery nature of punishment. Although this does not justify inflicting greater punishment than is authorized by the law, the law can take into account the actual, although unforeseeable, consequences of the violation.

5. For a fuller discussion of competence, see Bernard Gert, Charles M. Culver, and K. Danner Clouser, *Bioethics: A Return to Fundamentals* (New York: Oxford University Press, 1977), chap. 6.

6. For a fuller discussion of paternalism, see Gert, Culver, and Clouser, *Bioethics*, chaps. 9 and 10.

7. For a fuller discussion of consent, see Gert, Culver, and Clouser, *Bioethics*, chap. 7.

8. In some societies, other family members such as aunts and uncles have a similar relationship. In more limited contexts, teachers and coaches may also have such a relationship.

9. Thus I agree with the feminist view that relationships in a family should be thought of as political.

10. Hobbes was completely clear about this point. See *Leviathan*, chap. 15, para. 19, the seventh natural law. See also *De Cive*, chap. 3, sec. 11, the sixth natural law.

11. My colleague Jim Moor, who is applying a variation of this moral system to ethical problems arising from the use and development of computers, pointed out the need to have this feature explicitly listed as a morally relevant feature.

12. See James L. Bernat, Bernard Gert, and R. P. Mogielnicki, "Patient Refusal of Hydration and Nutrition: An Alternative to Physician Assisted Suicide or Voluntary Euthanasia," *Archives of Internal Medicine* 153 (December 27, 1993): 2723–2728; and Gert, Culver, and Clouser, *Bioethics*, chap. 12.

13. For a fuller account of intentional, voluntary, and free actions, see Bernard Gert and Timothy Duggan, "Free Will as the Ability to Will," *Nous* 13, no. 2 (May 1979): 197–217, reprinted in *Moral Responsibility*, edited by John Martin Fisher (Ithaca, N.Y.: Cornell University Press, 1986).

14. See Bernard Gert, "Transplants and Trolleys," *Philosophy and Phenomenological Research* 53, no. 1 (March 1993): 173–179.

15. I am not endorsing this way of thinking about abortion. As indicated by the discussion of the scope of morality in the chapter on impartiality, there is an unresolvable disagreement on whether a fetus is included in the group impartially protected by morality.

16. I have already pointed out that in languages other than English, there may be more than ten moral rules.

17. See R. M. Hare, *Moral Thinking: Its Levels, Method and Point* (Oxford: Oxford University Press, 1981).

18. Marcus George Singer in chapter 4 of his *Generalization in Ethics* (New York: Knopf, 1961) vainly tries to save Kant by inventing the notions of "invertibility" and "reiterability."

19. My colleague Walter Sinnott-Armstrong has pointed out to me one place in which Kant does use "allow" rather that "will" in formulating the maxim to be made into a universal law. This suggests that Kant did not see any important distinction between "willing that everyone act in a certain way" and "allowing everyone to act in a certain way." See Immanuel Kant, *Critique of Practical Reason*, translated by Lewis White Beck (New York: Bobbs-Merrill, 1956), 27.

Chapter 10

Moral Ideals

Moral ideals seem to embody the nature of morality more than moral rules, for following moral ideals is acting so as to achieve the point of morality, the lessening of evil or harm being suffered. A person can act in accordance with moral rules, that is, not violate any of them, without any contact with other people, but following moral ideals involves helping other people. It never seems out of place to praise someone for justifiably following moral ideals, but it would be odd to praise a hermit for justifiably obeying moral rules. Thus it may seem surprising that the account of morality presented so far has been far more involved with describing and justifying the moral rules than with describing and justifying moral ideals. But even John Stuart Mill, who is the leading representative of the view that the goal of morality is the greatest good, makes the following statements: "The moral rules which forbid mankind to hurt one another (in which we must never forget to include a wrongful interference with each other's freedom) are more vital to human well-being than any maxims, however important, which only point out the best mode of managing some department of human affairs. . . . It is their observance which alone preserves peace among human beings; if obedience to them were not the general rule, and disobedience the exception, everyone would see in everyone else an enemy against whom he must be perpetually guarding himself. . . . [A] person may possibly not need the benefits of others, but he always needs that they not do him hurt."[1]

The Role of Moral Ideals

The moral rules account for those decisions and judgments about what is morally required and prohibited; for a human society to continue to exist all people must generally act in accordance with them. The moral ideals account for those decisions and judgments about what is morally encouraged; for a human society to flourish, a significant number of people must follow them from time to time.[2] Morality contains both rules and ideals. This has been noted from the very first chapter, but emphasis on the moral rules has been so great that it may very well have been forgotten.[3] However the first chapter noted that moral judgments are judgments on actions, intentions, and so on, using some moral rule or ideal. Even the previous chapter, which was devoted to showing how violations of the moral rules must be justified, noted the role of the moral ideals.

This chapter is primarily concerned with attempting to distinguish the moral ideals from other ideals. No attempt shall be made to provide a complete and precise list of the moral ideals for, unlike the moral rules, it is not important that the ideals be listed completely and precisely. People can be punished for not following moral rules, so it is important for all of them to be stated clearly and precisely. Not following moral ideals does not warrant punishment, so no harm is done if there is no complete and precise list of them. Further, no one needs a list of moral ideals, for everyone knows that acting to lessen the amount of evil being suffered is following a moral ideal. But, since following a moral ideal can justify violating a moral rule, even for an individual and even without consent, whereas no other ideals can do so, it is important to make the distinction between moral ideals and other ideals as clear as possible. Confusion on this matter has had serious harmful consequences. It is therefore useful to provide an account of the general moral ideals and to explain how they differ from other ideals.

Justification of Moral Ideals

There is no need to provide a detailed justification of each moral ideal, so I shall justify them all at once. All moral ideals, "Preserve life," "Relieve pain," "Help the needy," "Prevent immoral behavior," and so on, concern lessening the amount of harm or evil suffered. Following a moral ideal by relieving pain directly lessens the amount of harm or evil suffered; following a moral ideal by preventing immoral behavior indirectly lessens the amount of harm or evil suffered. All rational persons favor everyone following those moral ideals that directly lessen the amount of evil or harm suffered with regard to themselves and those for whom they are concerned. With regard to those moral ideals that indirectly lessen the amount of evil or harm suffered, all rational persons favor everyone following those moral ideals when doing so results in less harm suffered by themselves and those for whom they are concerned. All rational persons who use only rationally required beliefs would hold this egocentric attitude toward all of the moral ideals. However, this egocentric attitude is not the appropriate attitude to take toward the moral ideals, so the egocentricity must be eliminated.

The egocentricity is eliminated in the same way it was for the moral rules, by requiring rational persons to be impartial or else to consider these ideals as part of a public system that applies to all rational persons. All impartial rational persons favor everyone following the moral ideals unless an impartial rational person would favor not following them in those circumstances. The same is true of rational persons who regard these ideals as part of a public system that applies to all rational persons. This means that impartial rational persons or rational persons considering these ideals as part of the moral system will encourage following them whenever that does not in-

volve the violation of a moral rule. They will not encourage, indeed they will prohibit, following these ideals, when this involves an unjustified violation of a moral
rule. When following a moral ideal involves a weakly justified violation of a moral
rule, some impartial rational persons will encourage following the moral ideal and
some will not.

However, impartial rational persons will not require following these ideals impartially, for it is clear that with regard to even the minimal group this is not possible. Nor will they require following these ideals all of the time, for this is also impossible. Thus they would not favor punishment for failing to follow them. The
appropriate attitude toward justified general moral ideals is not the same as the
moral attitude toward the justified general moral rules. That attitude is *Everyone (including myself) is always to obey the rule "Do not . . .," except when a fully informed,
impartial rational person can publicly allow violating it. Anyone who violates the rule
when not all fully informed, impartial rational persons would publicly allow such a
violation may be punished.*

Toward the moral ideals the attitude would be significantly different. All reference to punishment would be eliminated and "always" would be replaced by "encouraged." The attitude that would be taken by impartial rational persons would be
*Everyone is encouraged to follow the ideal "Prevent . . .," except when a fully informed,
impartial rational person would not publicly allow following it.* As with the moral attitude toward the moral rules, the except clause of the attitude toward the moral ideals
does not mean that no one is encouraged to follow a moral ideal when any fully informed, impartial rational person would not publicly allow following it. Rather, it
means that fully informed, impartial rational persons can disagree about whether
they would encourage following it. Only when no fully informed, impartial rational
person can publicly allow following the ideal is following it not encouraged.

Since general moral ideals are part of common morality and common morality
is a public system that applies to all moral agents, the ideals must be stated in a way
that is understandable to all rational persons. The only beliefs that can be used in
formulating the general moral ideals are rationally required beliefs. Everyone knows
these moral ideals, and it is never irrational for a person to follow them as the public
system allows. That moral ideals are not prohibitions but, on the contrary, that following them always requires positive action explains why it is impossible to follow
general moral ideals either all of the time or impartially with regard to all those protected by morality. Unlike the moral attitude toward the moral rules, the attitude
that is taken toward the moral ideals does not distinguish them from all other ideals.
The attitude of impartial rational persons toward utilitarian ideals, namely, to promote benefits, is the same as the attitude that is taken toward moral ideals. However,
it is important to distinguish moral ideals from all other ideals, for moral ideals can
justify violations of the moral rules in situations when no other ideals can.

Direct and Indirect Moral Ideals

The most important moral ideals are those directly concerned with the lessening of
such evils as death (permanent loss of consciousness), pain, and disability. People

who contribute to or volunteer for the various relief agencies that aid the innocent victims of war, famine, floods, earthquakes, and other man-made and natural disasters are clearly following moral ideals. Those who work with the deprived peoples of the Earth, trying to help them deal more effectively with the evils they suffer, are also clearly following moral ideals. Since diseases, disorders, or maladies also cause so much death, pain, and disability, helping to cure or prevent diseases or maladies is also a way of following moral ideals. Among the major professions, medicine and nursing seem most devoted to following moral ideals, such as preventing death, relieving pain, and lessening disabilities. These moral ideals are the primary motives for many who enter into the professions of medicine and nursing, and so doctors and nurses are often regarded as morally good persons.

Although it may not be obvious, there are also moral ideals directly connected with the evils that are the concern of the fourth and fifth moral rules. These ideals, "Prevent the loss of freedom," and "Prevent the loss of pleasure," need not be related to violations of the moral rules. Freedom and pleasure may be lost by the operation of natural causes, as well as by the acts of other persons. For example, working to save the homes and prized possessions that are threatened by fire or flood is trying to prevent the loss of freedom and pleasure. Of course, it is also following a moral ideal to try to prevent the loss of freedom and pleasure when these are caused by other persons, such as burglars, so that police work should be regarded as concerned with moral ideals. Extraordinary amounts of evil are neither the result of natural causes, nor of particular unjustified violations of moral rules. They stem from social causes. Working to eradicate slums and poverty is generally following moral ideals.

War, justified or not, causes immense amounts of all of the evils. This is true of civil wars, guerrilla wars, terrorist wars, wars of independence, wars of liberation, and wars between nation-states. Wars may be the greatest cause of the evil now suffered by humankind. Working to prevent war and to achieve and preserve peace is acknowledged by all rational persons to be following moral ideals. "Blessed are the peacemakers" is a sentiment shared by all impartial rational persons. Given the immense increase in the destructive powers of the weapons of war, the prevention of war, especially nuclear war, may be the most important single goal of those following moral ideals.

Just as the moral rules might be summarized as "Do not cause harm or act so as to increase the probability of people suffering harm," so the direct moral ideals may be summarized as "Prevent harm or act so as to decrease the probability of people suffering harm." Each specific direct moral ideal can be generated by replacing "harm" with a different specific harm such as "pain" and "loss of freedom." Specific indirect moral ideals can be generated from each of the justified general moral rules by substituting "prevent" for "do not" and changing the wording slightly.[4] "Prevent killing," "Prevent the causing of pain," "Prevent disabling," "Prevent the deprivation of freedom," "Prevent the deprivation of pleasure," "Prevent deceiving," "Prevent the breaking of promises," "Prevent cheating," "Prevent the breaking of the law," and "Prevent the neglect of duty" can all be regarded as indirect moral ideals. Although following these ideals may not directly decrease the amount of harm or evil suffered, the indirect result of general following of them is a decrease in the amount of evil suffered.

However, just as there is unjustified obedience to a moral rule, so there can be unjustified following of a moral ideal. It is often unjustified to follow an indirect moral ideal, for the person causing the evil may be strongly justified in causing it, as in some cases of punishment. Even if the indirect moral ideals listed in the last paragraph are reworded to include the word "unjustified," as in "Prevent unjustified killing" and "Prevent unjustified cheating," it still may be unjustified to follow the ideal. For it may be that preventing an unjustified violation of a moral rule itself requires an unjustified violation of a moral rule. Even intentionally acting on the direct moral ideals, "Postpone death," "Relieve pain," and "Prevent disabilities," may sometimes be unjustified, for acting in these ways may unjustifiably violate a moral rule. It is unjustified to prevent a person from dying if he is competent and has rationally refused life-prolonging treatment. It takes judgment to live a moral life: simply obeying moral rules and following moral ideals does not guarantee acting in a morally acceptable way. Morality is a complex system, and any attempt to summarize it by a simple slogan or even to think that one part of that system can be understood independently of the rest is always going to be misleading.

Moral Ideals and Moral Worth

The moral ideals that are related to preventing unjustified violations of the moral rules can be followed in a number of different ways. One way is by clarifying common morality and making explicit the appropriate moral attitude toward the moral rules. Someone who tries to prevent those unjustified violations of the moral rules that arise from a misunderstanding of morality, as does the writer of this book, is justifiably following a moral ideal. However, doing this or even trying to persuade others to genuinely adopt the moral attitude toward the moral rules, as I do in chapter 13, indicates nothing about the moral character of the person doing the persuading. Nothing I say in this book is a reliable indication of my moral character. My response to the claim that I am preaching rather than doing moral philosophy, is that I am preaching what any rational person should preach. That all rational persons, even those that are not morally impartial, will preach that people adopt the moral attitude toward the moral rules helps to explain the popularity of the maxim "Practice what you preach." It also explains the prevalence of hypocrisy.

Following the moral ideals by providing clarification of morality or even by preaching that everyone adopt the moral attitude toward the moral rules does not usually have moral worth when doing so requires no sacrifice or risk as in writing this book. However, there are occasions in which preaching morality does have significant moral worth. Someone who speaks out openly against the immoral action of some powerful person or group of persons is following a moral ideal in a significant way. Someone who urges his country to stop acting in an immoral fashion often undergoes significant risk in so doing, and his action deserves moral praise. Even someone who does not undergo any risk but merely devotes a great deal of time and effort to encouraging people to act morally may deserve moral praise. Of course, much depends on the motive for the action, but this will be discussed in more detail in the next chapter and needs no special comment here.

The moral worth of an action is determined, not by the amount of evil prevented or relieved, but by how much it counts in judging the moral character of the person acting. A billionaire who gives a thousand dollars to a worthy charity prevents or relieves more evil than a person with an income only slightly above the poverty level who gives only one percent of that. However, it may be that the act of the poorer person has more moral worth. Indeed, simply obeying a moral rule when it would be unjustified to violate it may have more moral worth than most instances of following moral ideals, as when the cost to the individual for obeying the rule is very large. In such a case obeying the moral rule may indicate more about the moral character of the person than most cases of following a moral ideal. The relationship between moral ideals and moral worth is not a simple one, and some following of a moral ideal may even have negative moral worth, such as much too small a gift from a very wealthy person.

Negative Consequentialism and the Point of Morality

Whereas the moral rules require that people not cause anyone to suffer evil, the moral ideals encourage people to prevent or lessen the evil being suffered by anyone. Morality requires that everyone obey the moral rules impartially; it only encourages people to follow the moral ideals with regard to anyone they choose. When what is required by a moral rule conflicts with what is encouraged by a moral ideal, a decision must be made about whether or not breaking the rule is justified. These cases cannot be decided in the abstract, but each case must be treated by using the two-step procedure, including using the morally relevant features to describe the violation. Talking about the rules as being more important than the ideals, and hence as taking priority in cases of conflict, is extremely misleading.[5] It is also misleading to consider only the particular case, as negative consequentialism does, for the decisive consideration is the consequence of everyone's knowing that this kind of violation is allowed. Neglecting these consequences can even have bad results in the particular case, for one may overlook the serious harmful consequences of the violation being discovered, such as the patient discovering that the doctor lied to him.

Negative consequentialism seems to use a much simpler procedure than the two-step procedure required by the moral system, but because it often results in the same decisions and judgments it has mistakenly been taken as an adequate account of morality. However, since it does not require that an impartial rational person be able to publicly allow the violation of a moral rule it sometimes yields unacceptable moral decisions and judgments. When negative consequentialism conflicts with the two-step procedure, the latter clearly accounts for common moral intuitions better than the former. For example, the former would often allow cheating to prevent one's parents from feeling bad. On the standard consequentialist interpretation, negative consequentialism does not take into account either that morality is a public system or that morality requires impartiality with regard to rules not consequences. Interpreting negative consequentialism as requiring that an impartial rational person be able to publicly allow violations of moral rules, misleadingly gives that name to the account of morality that I have been providing.

All forms of consequentialism, including negative consequentialism, are so vague as to be almost totally useless as moral guides. They pretend to provide precise procedures for making decisions, indeed to provide unique answers to every moral question, but they do not provide such guides in even slightly controversial cases. Consequentialism provides no procedure for weighing foreseeable beneficial consequences against foreseeable harmful ones or even for weighing one kind of evil against another. It says nothing about how probabilities are to be considered, nor does it answer any questions about distribution or even about the scope of morality. It makes no mention of the morally relevant features. Although negative consequentialism has the excellent general principle of lessening the suffering of harm, this principle is useful only as a device to remind oneself of the point of morality, it is not a useful guide in individual cases of moral conflict. Negative consequentialism also leads to the false view that those who unjustifiably violate the second five moral rules when there is no foreseeable harm to anyone from that particular act are really not acting immorally.

Distinguishing Moral Ideals from Utilitarian Ideals

Because the goal of morality is the lessening of evil, moral ideals are a more significant part of the moral system than utilitarian ones. Except for governments, utilitarian ideals, that is, ideals that encourage the promotion of benefits or goods, do not normally justify the breaking of a moral rule. This point is obscured by the fact that most often what is called "doing good," such as doing volunteer work in a hospital, is not promoting goods, but rather preventing evils. Preventing the evils of death, pain, and disability are clearly moral ideals. But when one is considering preventing the loss of freedom and the loss of pleasure, the distinction between moral and utilitarian ideals is not quite so clear. There is not a precise distinction between the moral ideals "Prevent the loss of freedom" and "Prevent the loss of pleasure" and the utilitarian ideals "Increase freedom" and "Increase pleasure." In fact, increasing the freedom and pleasure of those who are regarded as "deprived persons" is following moral rather than utilitarian ideals. (I shall have more to say about "deprived persons" in chapter 14, when discussing morality and society.) However, this point does not count against the moral significance of the distinction between preventing or lessening evils, which includes both preventing or lessening the loss of goods and providing benefits to the deprived, and simply promoting goods for those who are not deprived.

Morality normally starts with the status quo. Moral rules prohibit changing the status quo by causing evil. Moral ideals encourage changing the status quo by lessening the amount of evil. This is the only kind of change encouraged by morality when not in a political situation. However, one of the goals of a political system is to promote benefits or goods for all of its citizens. Governments and parents are sometimes allowed to violate moral rules to follow utilitarian ideals, but this is a very limited exception. Morality does not discourage promoting goods as long as this does not involve unjustified violations of the moral rules, but it is not the goal of morality to promote the greatest good for the greatest number. Nor does morality demand that the goods of the earth be equally distributed among all its inhabitants. Moral ideals are not revolutionary except in those societies where there is significant immoral action by those in power or when there are great numbers of deprived persons. Unfortunately, in the world today and probably at all times in the past, there are many societies where moral ideals are revolutionary.

Moral Ideals and Impartiality

General moral ideals, like the general moral rules, make no mention of person, place, group, or time. This may lead some to the mistaken view that, in following general moral ideals, favoring some persons over others must be excluded as rigorously as when obeying the moral rules. The moral rules require obedience with regard to all persons impartially. It is not morally allowed to violate a moral rule with regard to a person one does not care about in order to follow a moral ideal with regard to someone one does care about, unless one would favor everyone's knowing that they can violate the rule in the same circumstances. For example, that one loves a person does not justify killing an innocent stranger in order to obtain an organ necessary to save her life. But when no violation of the moral rules is involved, the moral ideals do not require that one act impartially with regard to all persons; a person does not need to flip a coin to decide whether to rescue his own child first. When there is no violation of a moral rule, there is no need to act impartially.[6]

It is morally acceptable to choose to follow a moral ideal with regard to some group of persons with whom one has some special relationship. Officers of the NAACP have no need to justify concentrating their efforts in following moral ideals toward aiding African Americans. Contributors to the United Jewish Appeal need not justify concentrating their efforts toward aiding other Jews. Nor do members of the government of the United States need to justify being primarily concerned with aiding the deprived citizens of America. It is impossible, and therefore pointless, to try to follow moral ideals with regard to all persons impartially. Furthermore, it is a mistake to think that people need to justify choosing the persons or groups with regard to whom they will concentrate their efforts. It is usually not even morally better to exclude personal preferences. A possible exception to this is choosing an alternative that will result in significantly greater relief of evil regardless of any relationship to oneself.

The view that moral ideals should be followed impartially may amount to no more than the view that they should be followed impartially with regard to all those with whom one comes into personal contact. But it is doubtful if anyone actually holds that a person is morally required to give equal amounts to every beggar that asks for money. Further, following moral ideals with regard to those with whom one comes into personal contact is in no way morally preferable to following moral ideals with regard to those related by race, religion, or similarity of genetic disability. What gives it an air of being morally preferable is that choosing to follow moral ideals impartially with regard to everyone with whom one comes into personal contact may seem to be less likely to lead to unjustifiable violations of a moral rule in order to follow a moral ideal. However, in the present world, when people can so easily cause harm to those with whom they will never come into personal contact, this is no longer true. It is best simply to distinguish between moral rules and moral ideals and realize that morality requires impartiality only with respect to obeying the moral rules.

Impartiality and Equality as Moral Ideals

Although impartiality is not required when following moral ideals, it might be thought that impartiality is itself a moral ideal. Someone might claim that, even though no one is morally required to be impartial except when contemplating the violation of a moral rule, acting impartially is itself a moral ideal. However, once one understands that the concept of impartiality must be specified with regard to group and respect, this claim can be seen to be confused. Even when talking about impartiality with regard to the minimal group, no impartial rational person would favor everyone striving to be impartial in all of their actions. Such impartiality is impossible. Although it is plausible to claim that one is acting on the highest moral ideal when one chooses that action, policy, or life plan which prevents or relieves the greatest amount of harm, such a choice is always made from among a very limited set of alternatives. Trying to act so as to benefit every moral agent impartially is quixotic. It is far less likely to result in lessening harm than acting to relieve or prevent harm with regard to some related group with no thought at all about the billions of people who will not benefit from one's action.

Just because acting impartially when contemplating the violation of a moral rule is likely to result in less harm being suffered does not mean that acting impartially in any other situations is likely to have the same results. If it will not have these results, then there is no reason to encourage such behavior. Indeed, as discussed in the previous section, it is extremely unlikely that striving to be impartial in all of one's actions will have the most beneficial results. Moral impartiality is important because it makes one less likely to unjustifiably violate a moral rule. But except for moral impartiality or when impartiality is required by one's job or role, impartiality is not usually something that rational persons, even impartial rational persons, need value. Only a confused idea of impartiality even makes it plausible to regard impartiality as a moral ideal.

Closely related to the confused idea of impartiality is the confused idea of equality. Many people seem to hold that equality is a moral ideal or that it is a moral ideal to promote equality among people. If this means that it is a moral ideal to promote acting impartially with regard to all people with respect to the moral rules, then the moral ideal of equality is the same as the moral ideal of promoting moral behavior. However, it is doubtful that this is what most people mean by promoting equality. What they may mean is that it is a moral ideal to make opportunities or incomes more equal. If equality means providing aid to those who are deprived, then of course it is acting on a moral ideal, but equality is not needed for this kind of action, lessening harm is sufficient. If equality means taking away opportunities or income from those who have more, regardless of the benefit to those who have less, then it is not only not a moral ideal, it is an unjustified violation of the moral rules.

It is not even clear why any rational person would want to encourage equality among people, unless this means attempting to aid the deprived. If people are not deprived, only an overestimation of the amount of pain suffered due to envy provides an adequate reason for taking equality as a moral or political ideal. It is not equality but the lessening of the suffering of its members that should be the most important goal of every political system. However, there will often be disagreement whether an action or policy counts as lessening harms or as promoting benefits. Further, promoting some significant goods may even take precedence over relieving some relatively trivial evils. Disagreements on these matters may lead equally informed, impartial rational persons to disagree about whether one political system is better than another. Impartial rational persons favor a political system that lessens harm more than another system. They need have no preference for a society that promotes equality unless this results in lessening harm. Except when concerned with aiding those who are deprived, it seems quite likely that the loss of freedom and other harms involved in promoting equality is not justified by the harms prevented or relieved. Even more than impartiality, the idea of equality is so confused that it serves no useful purpose to put it forward as a moral ideal.

Loyalty as a Moral Ideal

It is interesting that not only are impartiality or equality regarded by some as a moral ideal, but their opposite, loyalty, is also taken by some to be a moral ideal. Loyalty involves giving special consideration to a person or group of persons, providing them with benefits or services that one does not provide impartially to everyone. It means having more concern for some rather than having equal concern for all. Loyalty to a person or group of persons does not aim at equality for them except accidentally; rather, it aims at giving them benefits not available to all. Loyalty to some members of a group in a certain respect is incompatible with being impartial with regard to the whole group in that respect. Loyalty to one's friends who have committed some crime may be incompatible with moral impartiality, for it may require one to lie to prevent their being found guilty and punished. Loyalty must be limited for it to be regarded favorably by impartial rational persons. Loyalty is only appropriate when one's actions do not involve unjustifiably violating a moral rule; impartiality, not loyalty is appropriate when contemplating the violation of a moral rule.

Loyalty has a close relationship to gratitude, for often the group or individual to whom a person is loyal has provided benefits to him. Indeed, when calling for loyalty an individual or group sometimes explicitly points out the benefits that have been provided to the person. Sometimes, the promise of future benefits is made in order to encourage loyalty, but insofar as the actions are done because of the promise of future benefits, it does not seem correct to describe the resulting actions as done from loyalty. Loyalty is often given in gratitude for past benefits, indeed, it is often a kind of gratitude. It is also compatible with the intention to gain future benefits, but a person is not loyal to a group if he ceases to act loyally when the group can no longer provide benefits. Similarly, a person's seemingly grateful actions do not show gratitude if he ceases to do them when he no longer expects benefits from his benefactor. Genuine loyalty, like genuine gratitude, does not depend on future benefits.

When a person has no duty to be impartial and is not contemplating a violation of a moral rule, then loyalty is generally more appropriate than impartiality.[7] Loyalty to family, friends, country, or colleagues is admirable as long as it does not involve an unjustified violation of a moral rule, including the rule requiring doing one's duty. Morality may even encourage appropriate loyalty, but loyalty does not need much encouragement. On the contrary, inappropriate loyalty provides a powerful motive for immoral behavior. Loyalty to family, friends, country, or colleagues provides such powerful motives that many people who would not act immorally for reasons of self-interest are prepared to act immorally out of loyalty. How powerful loyalty is can be seen by the overwhelmingly negative attitude toward whistleblowers held by members of the affected group even when it is absolutely clear that blowing the whistle on the immoral actions of others in that group was the morally right thing to do. Learning the limits of loyalty is one of the most important lessons that otherwise moral people can learn from a clear, precise, and explicit account of morality.

Religious and Other Ideals

All of the major religions of humankind not only urge their adherents to follow moral and utilitarian ideals, they also put forward ideals concerning character traits and personality traits. At its best, religion puts forward universal ideals of virtue, such as the ideal of loving-kindness, which involves acting on the moral ideals because of love of others. Although the highest ideals of the major religions involve the moral ideals, this is generally obscured because these ideals often are not distinguished from ideals that are peculiar to the particular religion. The harm done by this failure to distinguish universal moral ideals from ideals that depend essentially on belief in a particular religion cannot be overestimated. This failure has also contributed to the mistaken view that religious ideals that could not even be part of a public system that applies to all rational persons sometimes justify violating the moral rules.

Whenever the ideal that a religion supports rests essentially on a revelation, or scripture, or anything that is not known to all rational persons, impartial rational persons cannot publicly allow a violation of a moral rule in order to follow it. It is never morally justifiable to follow these ideals when this involves violating the moral rules. Failure to realize this has resulted in the unjustified infliction of an extraordinary amount of evil. Even if all those who inflicted pain and suffering on others in order to get the victims to accept some religious beliefs were completely sincere; even if their motives were simply to help their victims avoid the pain of eternal damnation, still their actions were not morally acceptable. Neither sincerity nor good motives guarantees morally acceptable behavior. Understanding that morality is a public system that applies to all rational persons is absolutely essential for guarding against excessive religious zeal. Only such understanding guarantees that no one will claim moral knowledge that is not equally available to all.

Nations also have put forward ideals for which no impartial rational person can publicly allow a violation of a moral rule. The evils caused by pursuing these ideals, even when this involves unjustifiably violating the moral rules, may now outweigh the evils caused by the unjustified violations of the moral rules for nonuniversal religious ideals. Persons of various races and ethnic groups also have put forward ideals that no impartial rational person can publicly allow being followed when doing so involves violation of the moral rules. The amount of evil caused by racist and ethnic ideals may even rank with the amount of evil caused by religious and nationalistic ideals. Following these ideals need not lead to evil. Indeed, if one recognizes that pursuit of these ideals does not justify violation of the moral rules, then many positive benefits may come from following these ideals. The particularistic ideals put forward by religions, countries, and even ethnic groups, may be quite worthy ideals, when it is fully recognized that they do not justify the violation of moral rules.

Although morality cannot and does not provide a complete guide to life for all persons, for impartial rational persons it provides the supreme guide. Morality provides a guide to conduct such that all impartial rational persons would favor no one ever being allowed to violate its requirements for the sake of any ideal that is not part of the moral system. Impartial rational persons need not even encourage everyone to always act on moral ideals rather than less universal ideals or goals, but only ideals or ends that an impartial rational person can include in a public system that applies to all rational persons justify the violation of a moral rule. This means that only moral ideals, ideals of virtue, and, in special circumstances, utilitarian ideals can justify violating moral rules. It is a measure of the moral development of a religion, or of a country, that it subordinates its particular ideals to the requirements of morality. Indeed, every major religion has an interpretation that regards it as supporting a universal common morality. Almost every public figure in every civilized country claims that morality is their supreme guide and that neither they nor their country would never violate a moral rule for any partisan ideal or goal. Even though many of these claims are hypocritical, they show that everyone knows that when addressing oneself to all of humankind, morality has to be put forward as the supreme guide.

Fanaticism

A person who is willing to break a moral rule in order to promote some ideal or cause that could not be part of a public system that applies to all rational persons, is a fanatic. In fact, this is an acceptable definition of a fanatic. A religious fanatic is one who is willing to break a moral rule in order to do what he believes God commands, or his religion demands. A nationalistic fanatic is one who is willing to break a moral rule in order to advance the interests of his country. A racist or ethnic fanatic is one who is willing to break a moral rule in order to maintain the purity of his race or the advancement of his ethnic group . Even when an ideal is universal, but no impartial rational person would favor violating a moral rule to follow that ideal, it is fanaticism to violate a moral rule to follow the ideal. A scientific fanatic is one who is willing to break a moral rule in order to gain scientific knowledge; an aesthetic fanatic is one who is willing to break a moral rule in order to create great art.

The proper understanding of the oft misused saying "The end does not justify the means" is "No end justifies immoral means." However, what counts as "immoral means" depends to some degree on the end that is sought. Breaking a moral rule does not count as using immoral means if an impartial rational person can publicly allow such a violation to seek this goal. But even the goal of lessening the amount of evil or harm, which is the goal of morality, still has limits on how one may seek to achieve this goal. Because morality was developed by and for fallible people, even following moral ideals must be limited to actions that can be publicly allowed. It is usually not one's goal that determines whether one's action is morally acceptable; it is whether one is using morally acceptable means to achieve that goal. No matter how important a positive ideal is, morality does not allow following it if doing so involves violating a moral rule when no impartial rational person can publicly allow such a violation.

Personal Ideals

Personal ideals involve the goals that rational persons seek for themselves. Some of these are goals that all rational persons seek and some are not. Philosophers have historically concentrated on those goals that are common to all rational persons, and the following discussion shall be limited to these common goals. Generally speaking, these ideals can be divided into two distinct categories. For some the ideals are the personal goods such as abilities, resources, and pleasure. They seek as much as they can of one or more of these goods. For others, the ideals are the virtues; they seek to become a certain kind of person. All rational persons do desire some personal goods, and all rational persons do wish to have the personal virtues. In older and somewhat more colorful language, for some the ideal is a life of pleasure, for others a life of virtue. However, this colorful way of putting it is quite misleading, for as pointed out above, there are other personal goods in addition to pleasure, and virtue is not a homogeneous whole; the moral virtues differ from the personal ones in significant ways.

However, it might be claimed that all rational persons do share a common personal ideal, one which is very close to Aristotle's account of happiness. They all desire to be a person of virtue and to have a high degree of all the personal goods. However, this consensus about personal ideals is largely verbal. Not all rational persons rank the goods in the same way, and not all rational persons desire all of the moral virtues. Indeed many do not desire any of the moral virtues but only want to seem to have them. They are concerned only with themselves and their friends. The plausible claim that all rational persons regard happiness, in Aristotle's sense, as the *summum bonum* or greatest good, is thus misleading.

The *Summum Bonum* or Greatest Good

The lure of the *summum bonum* is almost irresistible. It is extraordinarily difficult to accept the view that there is no one thing, or some simple combination of things, that is the goal of all rational persons. Even those who realize the impossibility of formulating any intelligible account of a *summum bonum* continue to use the concept.

Perhaps this is due to thinking that denying that there is a *summum bonum* is the same as denying that there is any rational goal to human life. But there can still be rational *goals*. Rational persons do agree that all harms or evils should be avoided and that no goods should be. However there is great diversity in the ranking of these personal goods and evils. People have different personal ideals, even if all of those ideals are describable as wanting to have a personal good. Some persons may desire pleasure, in the ordinary sense of that term, others, abilities, and still others, freedom, resources, or power. And even within these broad categories rational people have different rankings. Some persons desire to increase their physical and mental abilities, an ideal often described as self-realization, and one much favored by philosophers; others are hedonists and desire only pleasure. Nothing is gained by trying to include all of these goals in a *summum bonum*, and it is misleading to do so.

Further, not all personal ideals involve attaining personal goods; some are concerned with becoming a certain kind of person, often a person with all of the virtues. Some virtues, which I call the "personal virtues," such as prudence, temperance, and courage, are desired by all rational persons, for having them primarily benefits the person who has them. These virtues, however, generally form only a small part of a person's personal ideals. The virtues that form the most significant part of some people's personal ideals are the moral virtues, such as honesty, kindness, virtues that primarily benefit others. For Plato and Aristotle all of the moral virtues went together under a name that has come to be called justice. Biblical thought added another virtue, sometimes called mercy or kindness. These two virtues, justice and kindness, were thought to comprise all of moral virtue by Hobbes and almost all thinkers after him. If justice is appropriately related to the moral rules and kindness to the moral ideals, this view is substantially correct. But even so, not all rational persons wish to have the moral virtues, though they are a personal ideal for many rational persons.

People rank the personal and moral virtues differently, some preferring the former and others the latter. They may even rank obtaining personal goods higher than attaining moral virtues, or vice versa. One can describe the preferences for different personal ideals as primarily a difference in emphasis. However, to do this would encourage the misleading view that all persons really want the same thing, only in somewhat different proportions. Moreover, it is also an error to hold that each person has his own *summum bonum* or matter of ultimate concern, even though it may be different from that of another person. Most rational persons have many personal goods they wish to obtain and several moral virtues that they wish to acquire. Although one may rank higher than any of the rest, it is rarely more important than all the rest put together. It is generally as misleading to talk about the *summum bonum* with regard to an individual person as it is to talk about it with regard to all rational persons. Pursuit of personal ideals clearly does not justify immoral behavior, but the failure to distinguish morality from other guides to conduct has obscured this, and so pursuit of quite worthy personal ideals has often led to immoral conduct.

Happiness and Pleasure

At least since Aristotle, happiness has been considered a goal that is sought by all rational persons. However, there are so many diverse views of happiness that even were it accepted as the goal sought by all rational persons this would not mean that all rational persons had the same personal ideal, except in a purely verbal sense. If happiness is to be something that all rational persons rank above everything else, both for themselves and for all those for whom they are concerned, then nothing will count as an acceptable account of happiness. If happiness is what all rational persons rank highest, Aristotle is certainly right that a happy life is not a life of pleasure. Not all rational persons prefer a life of pleasure to a life that has less pleasure but more of some other good. Indeed, some rational persons rank being a certain kind of person higher than any goods.

Although everyone agrees that there is a close connection between happiness and pleasure, the two are quite distinct. A life of pleasure may be a happy life, but it also may not be; nor is happiness remembered pleasure, for one may remember pleasure but not look back upon it with pleasure. One can regret pleasure, but not happiness. One way to relate happiness and pleasure is to regard a happy life as one that is remembered with pleasure, which a life of pleasure need not be, for one may come to regard it as a wasted life. In order for it to be even plausible that happiness is that which all people rank highest, happiness must be that which a rational person remembers or would remember with pleasure.[8] This seems close to what Aristotle meant by happiness, namely, a life that a rational person would view as successful. In order to guarantee that the moral virtues would be included in such a life, it could be taken as a life that an impartial rational person would view as successful. However, not even all impartial rational persons would agree with Aristotle's account of what such a life would be like.

On this account of happiness, to say "This is the happiest moment of my life" is to make a prediction, not in the literal sense that one is denying that she will ever have a happier moment. It is the prediction that one will remember that moment with great pleasure for the rest of one's life. Often the happiest times of one's life are those in which one is so absorbed in the activities of living and doing that at the time one often complained of having no time to enjoy life. This account of happiness is obviously incomplete, but it does have the virtue of partially explaining why happiness has been thought to consist of so many diverse elements. There are very many different kinds of things that rational persons, even impartial rational persons, can remember with pleasure. It is also plausible that a happy life, as that which is remembered with pleasure, might be preferred by all rational persons to anything else. It is interesting that the so-called utilitarian paradox, that one best achieves pleasure by not aiming for it, seems not to be true for pleasure but, on this account of happiness, does seem to hold for happiness. Happiness, in the sense just described, may be everyone's personal goal, but it is unlikely that anyone will find it by seeking it directly. One seems far more likely to find it by becoming a virtuous person.

Authenticity

As objective morality has fallen into disfavor, another trait of character has come to the fore as being the most significant trait of character for many people. The most popular name for this trait of character is authenticity. Authenticity is not to be understood merely as truthfulness, which would make it merely one of many specific moral virtues. Rather, authenticity seems as if it were designed to replace all of the moral virtues. On at least some accounts, authenticity requires only lack of hypocrisy. It is relatively easy to see how authenticity on this account seems to encompass all of the moral virtues. All persons who make moral judgments present themselves as accepting the moral system as an appropriate guide to behavior. Since authenticity excludes hypocrisy, an authentic person must act in the way that he presents himself, that is, as genuinely adopting morality as the supreme guide for his behavior. Such a person will have all of the moral virtues. I doubt that such thoughts prompted those who advanced authenticity as a universal personal ideal, but it seems compatible with much that has been written on the matter.

In much talk about authenticity there is great emphasis on the fact that everyone was thrown into a world on which they all depend and will soon leave, willingly or not. This emphasis fits in nicely with the view of authenticity presented above. Acknowledgment that one is mortal and dependent on others may lead one to view oneself as like other persons in most important respects, and thus may result in one's attaining the virtue of humility. Humility may be essential for genuinely adopting morality as one's supreme guide to conduct. Recognizing that one will die and the world continue, just as it has for all the people who have gone before and will do for all of the people who come after, is a powerful antidote to arrogance. The same is true of acknowledging one's dependence on other people and on society in general. Interpreted in this way, authenticity is a worthy personal ideal, for it may lead to humility.

However, authenticity is not always understood in this way. Authenticity most closely resembles the ancient Greek doctrine of living according to one's nature. The Greeks, of course, regarded a person's essential nature as that of a rational being, and so living according to nature was interpreted very much like living rationally, but with no distinction made between living as rationality requires and as impartial rationality requires. Today, however, a person is no longer regarded as essentially a rational being. Thus authenticity requires a person to follow his nature without telling him what that nature is. Perversion of the concept was inevitable. Authenticity was taken as requiring only that one act naturally, interpreted as acting as one feels, free from the artificial constraints imposed by society. No distinction was made between the constraints imposed by morality and those imposed by arbitrary social conventions, so on this view an authentic person would believe that he should violate the moral rules whenever he felt like doing so. The "hero" of Gide's *The Immoralist* is someone who adopted the confused concept of authenticity as a personal ideal.

Tolerance

Most of what has been said about the moral ideals does not apply to tolerance, yet tolerance is regarded by some as one of the most important moral ideals. Tolerance is not a moral ideal. It is required by the moral rules. Tolerance, properly understood, does not involve doing anything; rather, it consists in not doing certain things. To be intolerant is to violate any of the moral rules, particularly the first five, with regard to someone because of some morally indifferent characteristic he possesses. A tolerant person will not kill, cause pain to, disable, or deprive of freedom or pleasure any person because of the color of her skin, her place of birth, or her morally acceptable religious beliefs. An intolerant person is necessarily an immoral person, for he violates a moral rule unjustifiably. Legislation enforcing tolerance is simply legislation enforcing the moral rules. Such legislation is quite different from legislation that seeks to enforce the following of some moral or utilitarian ideal, such as requiring that one benefit some disadvantaged group. Impartial rational persons can disagree on whether or not this kind of legislation should be enacted.

Those who say that you cannot make people moral by legislation fail to distinguish the moral rules from moral ideals. Every civilized society enforces the moral rules. The criminal law is designed for precisely this purpose. In civilized societies the violation of every moral rule is punishable by the criminal law. This is even true of the rule "Obey the law," for even if the original law broken was not part of the criminal law, continuing violation may become a matter of the criminal law. You cannot make people follow a moral ideal by passing a law, for the passing of such legislation makes what would have been an action encouraged by a moral ideal into an action required by a moral rule. This seeming paradox is no argument against such legislation, but it may explain why some hold the view that morally good actions should not be enforced by legislation. Of course, legislation should not be used to force people to follow personal ideals, such as those regarding sexual behavior, when these ideals are not related to the moral rules and ideals. This kind of legislation is based on the mistaken view that morality prohibits even nonharmful deviant sexual practices.

Neither morality nor tolerance requires one to give equal consideration to all views. Some views do not deserve serious consideration. But the expression of absurd views, even of immoral views, though not to be encouraged, should usually not be suppressed. Freedom of speech and related freedoms are not moral ideals; they are required by the moral rules. The only justifiable limitation of freedom of speech is provided by the moral ideals, and involves the prevention of significant harm. The only justification for violating a moral rule with regard to someone who expresses an immoral view is to prevent people from suffering sufficient harm that an impartial rational person would publicly allow such a violation.[9] Dislike for, even disgust with, the views being expressed, does not justify violating a moral rule with regard to the person expressing the view. Similarly, dislike for or disgust with the personal preferences or habits of others, by itself, does not provide a justification for violating a moral rule with regard to them. Cleanliness may be next to godliness, but unless it results in increasing the risk of others suffering some evil, it has little to do with morality.

Failure to distinguish the moral rules and ideals from those rules and ideals that are often confused with them allows some to violate the moral rules with regard to those whom they dislike or with whom they disagree. Regarding some morally indifferent behavior, such as homosexual behavior, as morally unacceptable enables intolerance, which is immoral, to masquerade as morality. This masquerade is no better when the intolerant are sincere than when they are not. In fact, when a person sincerely believes that morality supports his intolerant actions, he is likely to cause more evil than when he is aware of the masquerade. Homosexuality provides one of the best current examples of the harm caused by not distinguishing morality from religion. Even better examples were the extraordinary amounts of evil caused by those who sincerely believed that it was morally right to persecute those who held different religious beliefs. But even without religious sanction many confuse sexual deviance with immoral behavior. The enormous amount of evil still inflicted on those who refuse to conform to the nonmoral sexual customs of a society is not based solely on religion.

Religious tolerance is fairly well established now in most democratic countries. Very few would hold it morally justified to violate the moral rules with regard to anyone because of his religious beliefs. I do not think that this is due primarily to an increase in moral understanding, but to a decrease in the importance of religious beliefs. The fundamentalist sects are notoriously less tolerant of people holding different religious beliefs than are the more liberal denominations. I do not believe this reflects a difference in moral character or moral understanding. It reflects what is admittedly the case, that religious belief is much more important to members of fundamentalist sects. Very few people are tolerant of different views on matters they consider important. Many people are quite prepared to violate the moral rules with regard to those who express sufficiently unpopular views on political matters. But tolerance only demands not violating the moral rules with regard to the person expressing the views; it does not demand that one make no negative response to those views. The vigor of one's response to views one dislikes, particularly immoral views, is not restrained by tolerance. Tolerance simply demands that this vigor not express itself in an unjustified violation of a moral rule.

Politeness is important. Politeness is a character trait involving acting so as to avoid giving offense to others and even counts as a moral virtue. But politeness is a moral virtue only when properly understood.[10] Politeness can never require either unjustified violation of a moral rule or conflict with justifiably following a moral ideal. It is a misunderstanding of politeness to think it requires one never to challenge someone who has put forward immoral views. If people express racist or sexist views, it is following a moral ideal to try to clarify their thinking about morality. Since it often takes considerable courage to challenge the views of others in the service of morality, it is convenient for those who lack this courage to continue to hold the mistaken view that politeness requires them never to give offense to others.

The close connection between tolerance and morality makes it seem unlikely that anyone would seek to undermine the latter in order to promote the former. Yet this seems to be what those anthropologists who espouse ethical relativism are doing. These anthropologists wish to encourage tolerance of the customs and mores of the peoples they study. They hold, quite rightly, that it is morally unjustified for outsiders to come into a culture and try to change the way these people live. Although they do not express it in this way, they hold that one should not violate a moral rule with regard to these people in order to get them to change their own morally acceptable way of life. However, they sometimes support this perfectly correct view by maintaining that there are no universal moral rules; that morality is completely a matter of one's own culture. But if one's culture allows the violation of moral rules with regard to those who live differently, morality would provide no reason to be tolerant of the culture of different peoples.

The anthropologists' confusion has been discussed repeatedly. They have failed to distinguish the moral rules from the nonmoral customs of a society. They wish to maintain that no one should impose their nonmoral customs and practices, particularly sexual ones, on other cultures because doing so causes problems for those cultures, with an inevitable increase in suffering of harm. However, having failed to distinguish morality from those aspects of a culture which are peculiar to it, they do not have the concepts to express their views correctly. They advocate tolerance without realizing that in so doing they are making use of the universal public system of morality. It is ironic that these people, who are so morally sensitive and sophisticated, should argue for the correct moral view by attacking the idea of a universal morality. However, it seems that many anthropologists have become aware of this problem, and are now coming to realize the importance of universal values.[11]

Significance of Moral Ideals Being
Encouraged but Not Required

To hold that morality requires following the moral ideals results in an account of morality that is too idealistic. It is not only philosophically incorrect, it has bad practical consequences. An idealistic morality is too easy to dismiss as being all right in theory, but of no use in real life. To hold that morality requires everyone to follow moral ideals is a misguided attempt to encourage such action. It is more likely to provide an excuse for those who wish to dismiss morality as impractical or too difficult for ordinary human beings like themselves. Distinguishing clearly between the moral rules and moral ideals, and making clear that morality requires obedience only to the former, does away with this excuse. Since morality does not require people to follow moral ideals, the demands of morality are not too difficult for ordinary human beings. Even though the moral ideals encourage people to go beyond what is morally required, the basic reason for following the moral ideals is the same reason for obeying the moral rules, namely, to lessen the amount of harm suffered. No philosophical theory will have much force in persuading people to follow moral ideals.

The view that obedience is required only with regard to the moral rules does not result in a minimalist morality. To think that it does is to make the mistake that morality consists only of requirements. Morality also provides a guide for those who want to go beyond what is morally required. The moral ideals are an essential feature of the moral system, and although following them is not required, it is encouraged. Those who are inclined to follow the ideals usually will do so without the aid of a moral theory. Those who are not so inclined usually will not do so, regardless of their agreement with a particular moral theory. The primary practical function of a moral theory is preventing people from doing what is morally wrong because of a misunderstanding of morality. Lack of the proper understanding of morality can lead to morally wrong actions. This book has some slight chance of helping some people avoid an immoral action that they might otherwise have done; however, there is almost no chance that it will result in anyone doing a morally good action by following a moral ideal, which they would not have done without reading it.

Compassion

One may follow moral ideals because of compassion. However, misguided compassion may lead one to follow a moral ideal when this is the morally wrong thing to do. Although a correct understanding of morality may prevent this, even a perfect understanding of morality, without compassion, generally will not lead one to follow moral ideals. *To have compassion for others is to suffer because of their suffering.* Thus compassion may lead one both to avoid causing anyone to suffer and to relieve the suffering of others. There are degrees of compassion, and most people have more compassion for those they love than they do for others. But it is not unusual for everyone to have some compassion for all humankind, even if it is only a very small amount. To see others seriously hurt, especially children, even though one does not know them, is distressing to all people not suffering from some mental disorder.

A compassionate person is often thought to be the same as a kind person, but compassion need not lead to kindness. One who has great compassion, but only for a limited group, such as his family, may be ruthless in dealing with other people. Even one who has great compassion for all humankind will not necessarily be a kind person, for he may seek to relieve his suffering by trying to forget about others. This can be done in many ways: drink, drugs, searching for excitement and adventure, even complete dedication to some intellectual pursuit. A person may be so overcome by his compassion that he completely avoids those whose suffering causes him to suffer. If one's goal is merely to relieve oneself of the suffering of compassion, following moral ideals may not be the most satisfactory way of proceeding; one always has the sufferings of others clearly in mind. Nonetheless, there is some personal benefit to the compassionate person in following moral ideals, for she does get some pleasure in seeing some suffering being relieved or prevented.

Being morally good, however, is not primarily a matter of emotions or feelings, it is a matter of action; what is important is what one's compassion leads one to do. Emotions and feelings are morally important only insofar as they lead to morally good actions. It is a confusion to hold that a morally good person is really no better than one who always acts selfishly, as each is simply trying to minimize her own pain and to increase her own pleasure. Apart from the fact that this is not even true, it is beside the point. If one does not unjustifiably violate moral rules, then it is morally insignificant what one's motive for following the moral ideals is, as long as it does not depend on others' being aware of what one is doing. Compassionate persons can relieve their compassion in many different ways. A person does not deserve moral praise because she is compassionate, but because her compassion leads her to justifiably follow moral ideals.

It is not uncommon, however, for compassion to lead one to act in a morally unacceptable way. In a well-known article, "It's Over, Debbie," a doctor tells how his compassion for a terminally ill patient, not his own, who was in serious pain, led him to kill that patient.[12] In this case, the patient seems to have requested to be killed, but a similar compassion may lead others to kill competent patients who have not requested to be killed. Even in the case of Debbie, the patient was killed with no waiting period, no determination of whether or not she was depressed, no confirmation of her diagnoses, no discussion of alternatives, and so on. No impartial rational person would publicly allow one person to kill another in these circumstances. The compassionate doctor demonstrated arrogance in killing Debbie, for he would not favor everyone's knowing that they are allowed to kill someone in the same circumstances. It is understandable how "compassion" comes to be used as a term of praise, but it is incorrect to use the term in that way.

Love

Compassion should be distinguished from love. One may have compassion for someone without loving her; however, love is so intimately related to compassion that a person is not even regarded as genuinely loving another unless she also feels compassion for him. Since love without compassion is not regarded as genuine love, I shall regard love as always being accompanied by compassion. Thus although the emotion of love is, in itself, pleasant, it contains a liability to the unpleasantness of compassion. *To love someone is to take pleasure in her pleasure.*[13] This is what is common to all forms of love: of parents and children for each other and of men and women for their spouses. To talk of one person's loving another means that she gets more pleasure from seeing that person pleased than she does from seeing others pleased. Love is also accompanied by desires to be with, to touch, and more generally to please the loved one. These desires cannot always be satisfied, so love contains a liability to significant displeasure. Love is also accompanied by thoughts of the loved one, and persons can even discover that they love someone by coming to realize how often that someone is in their thoughts.

The expressions of love I call the acts of love. In the acts of love, I include some sexual acts, for sexual acts are among those in which people can express their love most directly and loving sex is one of the most pleasant activities there is. But there are many other ways in which people can express their love. Parents express their love for their children when they bring them toys; their reward is to see the look of delight on their faces. The spontaneous attempt to give someone pleasure is the surest sign of love. People often treasure this far beyond the particular pleasure they have received. To be loved is to have someone take pleasure in your pleasure. To love someone who loves you is one of the most glorious things that can happen, for pleasure builds on pleasure as is possible in no other way. This is not merely true of love between a man and a woman, but also of love between parents and children or indeed between any two people. This is why it is truly a loss to be unable to love. To be unable to love is to be unable to enjoy the pleasures of others. This means the loss of a significant amount of pleasure.

Love is not behavior, although like all emotions behavior is an essential part of its criterian. Love is an emotion that involves feeling like behaving in those ways that serve as its criterian. It is because those ways of behaving show that one gets pleasure from pleasing the other that love can be defined as a feeling of pleasure at the pleasure of another. If Olga loves Ivan she will naturally act in ways that please him; indeed, Olga can suddenly discover that she is in love with Ivan by recognizing that she gets pleasure from pleasing him. She may find herself going to considerable efforts to please him and not considering them a sacrifice at all. Falling out of love is discovered in the same way. Olga discovers that she no longer gets pleasure from pleasing Ivan, that efforts to please him really are efforts. The proposed definition of love also explains why some babies are said to be lovable; it is almost impossible not to take pleasure in their pleasure. Of course, love involves more than simply getting pleasure from the pleasure of another, but all of the other characteristics of love mentioned above, such as thinking about the loved one, are related to this essential feature.

Jealousy and Envy

Unselfish love, that is, delight in the pleasure of another regardless of who causes it, is the most satisfactory kind. Unlike selfish love, which delights only in the pleasure that one causes oneself, it cannot give rise to jealousy. Jealousy involves displeasure caused by the thought that the person one loves is being pleased by someone other than oneself. One who loves another selfishly may actually seek to deprive her of pleasure that is caused by someone else. But it is not only love between men and women that can be selfish. A parent may selfishly love his children. It is even possible for a person to love God selfishly, though this would probably manifest itself in annoyance at others who seek to please God, rather than toward God himself. The most common cause of jealousy is that the person one loves loves another, that is, gets pleasure from the pleasure of another. Jealousy involves wanting to keep the love of another and anger at the thought of losing it to someone else. Although the thought of losing the love of someone to another may lead to fear, fear is not an essential feature of jealousy.[14] It is not insignificant that we talk of jealous rage but not of jealous terror.

A jealous love is a possessive love, a desire to have and to hold, and the thwarting of that desire is what causes the jealousy. When a man is loved by the woman he loves, then it is very plausible that his annoyance at her being pleased by another will be very closely related to his annoyance that he is going to lose her love. This may be why jealousy also has a wider sense in which it involves feeling displeasure at the thought one might lose anything one values to another, not merely the love of a person, but also a position of power. If a person receives pleasure from something, then he is very likely to be annoyed if it is taken from him, and if he values that pleasure very highly, then he is likely to be very angry about losing it. Of course, he may also fear losing it, and that fear may even contribute to his anger, but it is the anger, not the fear, that is an essential feature of his jealousy.

If a man loves a woman selfishly and some other man pleases her, the first man is said to be jealous of the second. But the phrase "jealous of the second" is misleading. It should be "jealous because of the second." The second causes the jealousy of the first by pleasing the woman he selfishly loves. Exactly the same is true when brothers and sisters are said to be jealous of each other; rather, all love their mother selfishly, and each is displeased when she is pleased by any of the others. Husbands and wives are jealous of each other, not of their spouses' lovers. But because one often envies the person who causes him to be jealous, jealousy and envy are often confused. One can only be jealous of someone whom one selfishly loves, though one's jealousy may be caused by another because he pleases her. He is important only because of his relationship to the woman one selfishly loves. It is the fact that she is pleased by any other, not any particular other, that causes one's jealousy.

Envy is different. To envy someone is to be displeased because of his having something that one desires but does not have. One can envy a man because he pleases some beautiful woman, but unless one loves her, one is not jealous because of that. Similarly, a child of one family can envy a child of another because that child's mother is pleased by her child, but he cannot be jealous because of that child. He can only be jealous if his own mother is pleased by that child. Envy is not primarily related to love as jealousy is; envy is more often caused by another's money, fame, or talents. Jealousy, in its primary sense, does not seem as bad as envy because in order to be jealous, one must at least love someone. But both jealousy and envy can lead to hate. To hate someone is to be displeased because of his having some good, whether or not one desires that good oneself. Even worse, hate may come to include pleasure because of that person's suffering some evil. Hate may thus be opposed not only to love but also to compassion.

To have the disposition to feel jealousy or envy significantly more than most is to be a jealous or envious person. To have a greater disposition than most to suffer because of the suffering of others is to be a compassionate person. I call these kinds of dispositions personality traits. It is not only unpleasant to be a jealous or envious person, for one has unpleasant feelings more often than others without such traits, but these traits often leads one to act in morally unacceptable ways. Jealousy and envy need not lead a person to act in these ways, for she may not allow herself to act on these emotions. Nonetheless, personality traits have such a large influence on character traits that often people do not distinguish them, using the same word, such as "compassionate," to refer to both. However, it is important to distinguish personality traits, which are dispositions to feel, from character traits, which are dispositions to act. It would be much clearer if "compassionate" were used to refer only to the personality trait and "kind" were used to refer to the related character trait. Personality traits and character traits and their relationship will be discussed in more detail in the following chapter.

Extended Use of "Love"

Although love is primarily a matter of taking pleasure in the pleasure of another, it so naturally becomes a matter of taking pleasure in any good obtained by another that often no distinction is made. A person is said to love someone whenever she is pleased by his obtaining some good. Love in the basic sense is always love for individuals, for only an individual can feel pleasure. But in the natural extension, a person can be said to love a country, and perhaps any other group or organization, when he is pleased by their achieving some good. When the country one loves is one's own, then love of country becomes pride in country. When this pride is felt only when the successes of the country are not obtained by immoral actions, that pride can properly be said to be a feeling of patriotism. When pride is felt for successes even when obtained by immoral actions, then the feeling is appropriately said to be a feeling of nationalism. Love of country, like all other love, needs to be restrained by morality. Without such restraint it leads to serious immoral actions.

Self-love can also be understood as a natural extension of love. A person who enjoys her successes, who is pleased when she achieves her goals, would be one who should be described as having self-love. Such a person not only need not be selfish, she is likely to be a loving and kind person. To love oneself is not incompatible with loving others; on the contrary, it is very doubtful that someone who does not love herself will love others. Just as self-love may increase the probability of loving another, so love of one may make it more likely that one will love others. One of the most delightful features of love is that the pleasure one receives from loving another may increase rather than decrease when both love someone else besides. A husband and wife's love for each other often increases after they have a child whom they have come to love.

Concern or Caring

This short digression on love and related emotions is not entirely beside the point. I admit that it is primarily due to my dissatisfaction with other accounts of love, but clarity about the distinction between love and compassion makes it easier to understand the distinction between what I call "being concerned with" or "caring for" a person and what I call "taking an interest in" a person. A person can be concerned with or care for another person without either loving him or having compassion for him. To care for or be concerned with a person means only that *the belief that doing something will help a person to avoid suffering some harm is a motive for doing that thing.* The strength and breadth of one's concern is measured by how often and how strongly that motive explains one's actions. Compassion for people naturally leads one to care for them, but it is not the only cause. The degree of concern will certainly be affected by the way one has been brought up. To be a kind person requires more than caring for people; one must not care for some at the expense of others. Caring can lead to unjustifiable violations of a moral rule; kindness cannot.

To take an interest in a person means that *the belief that doing something will help a person gain some good is a motive for one's doing it.* Just as one can care for a person without feeling compassion, so one can take an interest in a person without loving him. Distinguishing between love and compassion, and between compassion and caring, explains why it is incorrect to say that morality requires one to "love thy neighbor as thyself." There are several different mistakes involved. First, morality only requires one to act in certain ways; it does not require one to have any feelings toward anyone. Even if it did, the feeling would be compassion, not love. Second, morality does not even require that a person act as if she is as concerned with her neighbor as herself. Morality neither requires nor encourages regarding one's own benefits and harms and that of others impartially. Morality requires only that one avoid unjustifiably breaking the moral rules with regard to one's neighbor. Even the moral ideals only encourage being concerned with the evil suffered by one's neighbor; they need not encourage being as concerned with his evil as with the evil suffered by oneself.

It is because the moral ideals do encourage being concerned with one's neighbor that the question "Who is my neighbor?" need not indicate any lack of the proper moral attitude, but only a realistic sense of one's limitations in acting on the moral ideals. "Love thy neighbor as thyself" cannot be taken to be what morality requires, even if "love" is changed to "compassion," not even if "compassion" is taken as "concern." Even understood as "Be as concerned with your neighbor as with yourself" is not only not a statement of what morality requires, it is not even the best way of encouraging action according to moral ideals. People should be encouraged to follow moral ideals, but presenting such an extreme statement of what morality encourages only leads people to dismiss morality as utopian. Morality demands only that one avoid unjustifiable violations of the moral rules; when this demand is met, it encourages any action on the moral ideals.

Some people seem to prefer the loftiest kinds of statements when talking about morality. They can repeat these to each other, feel some sort of warm glow, and then forget all about them as they go about their daily lives. If someone presents some statement that does not demand very much, they often dismiss it as cynical. They dismiss it because it presents demands that can actually be followed by all persons. "Love thy neighbor as thyself" is one of their favorite sayings. No one feels compelled to live by it; obviously only the saintly can even approach it. "Live and let live," on the other hand, is often regarded as merely advocating the easy way out. But "Live and let live" is an excellent statement of what the moral rules demand. Do not interfere with others; do not cause them any harm. Morality does encourage going beyond the moral rules and following the moral ideals, so one can change the slogan to "Live and help live." These maxims do not have the emotional appeal of the more lofty statements, but as maxims that all persons can actually live by, they state a realistic way of presenting morality as the most important guide in the conduct of one's life.

Morality should not be presented as providing a guide that all rational persons aspire to follow, though with no hope of ever being able to do so. Morality is an informal public system that applies to all moral agents. This system requires that every rational person not violate a moral rule unless an impartial rational person can publicly allow that kind of violation. This requirement holds no matter what one's personal goals in life are. But morality consists of more than requirements; it also encourages people to help others, to prevent and relieve the harms they are suffering. The moral ideals provide a positive guide to life; they embody the point of morality, the lessening of evil, more clearly than the moral rules. Nonetheless, it is only with respect to the rules, not the ideals, that morality requires obedience. Neither the moral ideals nor morality itself has a final goal. As long as human beings continue to live, the elimination of evil and harm can never be reached. Morality does not have the elimination of all evil as its goal, only its lessening, and even this can only be done in a way that is publicly allowed. The task of morality is neverending, but the guide provided by morality can be followed by everyone.

Notes

1. *Utilitarianism*, chap. 5, para. 31. See also Mill's remarks on the importance of security in para. 24 of chap. 5. Note echoes of Hobbes.

2. I am talking about general moral ideals, those ideals that have the same generality as the justified general moral rules.

3. This is one explanation for the complaint that what I present is a minimal morality. It is true that all that morality requires is acting in accordance with the moral rules, but only those who mistakenly believe that morality consists solely of requirements would conclude from this that my account of morality is a minimal one. Of course, some people may use the phrase "moral requirement" so loosely that any action that can be criticized on moral grounds is a violation of a moral requirement, so they regard my account of moral requirements as too limited. However, although I think a person may sometimes be appropriately criticized for not following a moral ideal, I limit the phrase "moral requirement" to the kinds of actions that it is appropriate to enforce by punishing violations.

4. The positively stated moral rules must be reformulated as negative rules for this to be literally true of these rules.

5. Rawls seems to make such a claim when talking about the difference between what he calls the negative and positive duties. See *A Theory of Justice* (Cambridge, Mass.: Harvard University Press, 1971), 114.

6. It should be clear that I am talking about impartiality with regard to the minimal group, with or without additions.

7. This is also John Stuart Mill's position. See *Utilitarianism*, chap. 5, para. 9. "Impartiality, however, does not seem to be regarded as a duty in itself, but rather as instrumental to some other duty; for it is admitted that favor and preference are not always censurable, and, indeed, the cases in which they are condemned are rather the exception than the rule. A person would be more likely to be blamed than applauded for giving his family and friends no superiority in good offices over strangers when he could do so without violating some other duty; and no one thinks it unjust to seek one person in preference to another as a friend, connection or companion."

8. I am using "remember" in its basic sense, in which what one remembers is correct. So in saying that a person remembers his life, I means he remembers it correctly.

9. My colleague Susan Brison has argued that hate speech does cause sufficient harm to its victims that its prohibition may be justified. This is a very plausible view, and I would regard the prohibition of some hate speech as at least weakly justified.

10. For excellent examples of the proper understanding of politeness, and of etiquette in general, see the newspaper columns of Miss Manners by Judith Martin. She is clear that morality is often enforced by law, but that less serious violations of the moral rules are usually regarded as a breach of etiquette.

11. See my article "Universal Values and Professional Codes of Ethics," *Anthropology Newsletter* 36, no. 7 (October 1995): 30–31.

12. *Journal of the American Medical Association* 259 (1988): 272.

13. This definition of love, although it sounds as if it were derived from introspection, is developed from the public criterian both behavioral and circumstantial, that are used to teach

the term "love." For example, a young child is often told "Mommy loves you so much," just at the time when Mommy is hugging, kissing, and cuddling him. And when the child runs to his father and jumps up into his arms he often hears "You love your Daddy." As the child grows she is taught that other behavior also serves as criterian of love, "You must love your mother very much to spend so much time making this present for her." It is the natural expressions of love that are its criterian and from which the definition of love is derived. The same is true of the definitions of all of the other psychological terms defined in this chapter and elsewhere in this book. For a further explanation of this way of determining the meaning of psychological terms, see my articles "Psychological Terms and Criteria," *Synthese* 80 (1989): 201–222, and "Criterian and Human Nature," in *Wittgenstein: Eine Neubewertung, Toward a Re-Evaluation*, vol. 2, edited by Rudolf Haller and Johannes Brandl (Wien: Verlag-Hölder-Pichler-Tempsky, 1990): 106–114.

14. Thus Jerome Neu is wrong when he defines jealousy as fear of loss to another. See Neu, "Jealous Thoughts," in *Explaining Emotions*, edited by Amelie Rorty (Berkeley: University of California Press, 1980).

PART III

VIRTUE, METAETHICS, AND POLITICAL PHILOSOPHY

Chapter 11

Virtues and Vices

Moral philosophy used to be primarily concerned, not with particular acts, but with those traits of character that were virtues and vices. Hobbes says "the science of virtue and vice, is moral philosophy."[1] However I have defined morality without even mentioning virtue or vice. Nonetheless, I realize that no account of morality is complete without an account of virtue and vice. Moreover, as a practical matter, children should be taught morality by means of the moral virtues. It is only in theoretical contexts that the moral and personal virtues are derived from more basic concepts, although this theoretical understanding is helpful in teaching the virtues. The basic concepts, especially that of rationality, discussed in previous chapters shall be used to provide accounts of both moral and personal virtue and also to explain the distinction between them. Failure to make this distinction is another explanation for the false philosophical view that morality is primarily a general guide for an individual seeking the best life. I shall also provide accounts of particular virtues and vices, both moral and personal.

Training Children to Act Morally

All impartial rational persons agree that children should be trained to act morally.[2] They want the most effective training because this offers the most protection for everyone from unjustified violations of the moral rules, but they also want the training to inflict as little evil as possible. In this respect impartial rational persons' attitude toward the training of children parallels their attitude toward punishment. As with punishment, some impartial rational persons will place more emphasis on the one goal, others, on the other, but some points will be agreed to by all. If a lesser punishment is as effective in training as a greater, all impartial rational persons will favor using the lesser.[3] If it is as effective to train children by rewarding them for making morally right decisions in tempting or difficult situations as it is to punish them for making morally wrong choices, then all impartial rational persons would

277

favor training by reward. However, it is extremely unlikely that children can be trained to act morally if they are never punished for unjustifiable violations of the moral rules.

Although impartial rational persons want no harm inflicted on children unless it is necessary to train them to act morally, they may allow it when it is necessary. As impartial persons they are not merely concerned with the children being trained, they are equally concerned with the people who will be affected by the behavior of the children when they grow up. The best way to train children is to set a good example, such as refraining from immoral actions and acting in morally good ways, for acting in these ways not only involves no infliction of evil, it results in less evil being suffered overall. Children should also be taught how to determine what is morally acceptable and what is morally unacceptable. Since some moral issues are extremely complex, it is crucial to explain to children why it is not always morally acceptable to act so as to achieve the point of morality directly. Sometimes it is wrong to prevent a person from suffering a harm. It is also important to point out that although some moral disagreement is both legitimate and unresolvable, morality often provides clear guidance on how to act.

Impartial rational persons do not want children to be trained to follow the moral rules or ideals blindly; they want them to obey the rules and follow the ideals as an impartial rational person would. They know that there are occasions when all impartial rational persons would publicly allow a violation of a moral rule or would not encourage following a moral ideal. They also want children to act morally even when they believe that no one will find out about their actions. They know that life provides many occasions when a person has opportunities both to act immorally and to do something morally good with little chance that anyone will discover it. Impartial rational persons' primary concern with motives is with their reliability. Nonetheless, being equally concerned with the children, they want them not only to act morally but also to enjoy acting in that way. Insofar as the motives from which they act are equally reliable, impartial rational persons prefer them to be embedded in pleasant emotions like love rather than unpleasant ones like guilt. To have the moral virtues is to have those traits of character that all impartial rational persons want everyone to have.

Having the moral virtues requires judgment because it involves obeying the rules and following the ideals in the way that an impartial rational person would, not simply always obeying the moral rules and following the moral ideals as much as possible.[4] Impartial rational persons sometimes disagree on how one ought to act, and, since such persons have the moral virtues, it follows that virtuous persons will sometimes act in different ways.[5] This is why one cannot simply set out detailed descriptions of how a virtuous person would act in all specified situations. In discussing virtue and vice, even more than in discussing the other aspects of morality, one must keep in mind the raising of children. To bring up children so that they will have a good moral character requires both training and teaching. They must not only be provided with the right precepts and role models, they must also be taught to understand what morality is and why it is that way. All impartial rational persons advocate that children be brought up to have the moral virtues. This follows directly from the view that all impartial rational persons favor all persons acting morally.

Some Presuppositions

The preceding discussion of virtues and vices presupposes that examples, teaching, and training can affect not only the way a child behaves but also how she feels about behaving in that way. It does not presuppose that children are a blank slate on which the proper examples, teaching, and training will inevitably engrave the virtues. It is now almost universally recognized that there are genetic predispositions that have a significant influence on how one behaves. It is obvious, but true that the same training can affect different persons differently. Luck also plays some role in the development of a person. For example, does a temptation present itself before or after a person has acquired the ability to resist it? Although luck rarely is decisive in determining one's character, unless one counts a person's genetic inheritance and early training as matters of luck, it always plays some role. But although genetic inheritance and early training may have a decisive role in whether one acquires the virtues, in normal cases these factors merely leave open the possibility for acquiring them. What is often decisively determined by genetic inheritance and early training is personality.

Personality Traits

There is no clear distinction in ordinary language between what I call personality traits and what I call character traits. As I use the phrase "personality traits," it refers to dispositions to have certain kinds of emotional responses in certain general kinds of circumstances, not habits of behaving in standard ways in those circumstances. This distinction is often overlooked both because a person's emotional response has such an important effect on the way she acts and because what a person feels is often judged by the way she acts. Since a person normally acts according to her feelings, words that refer primarily to personality traits are often mistakenly thought to apply primarily to habits of acting. To describe someone as shy is often taken as meaning that she habitually avoids meeting new people, but as a personality trait, shyness is the disposition to suffer anxiety at meeting new people, rather than the habit of avoiding them. This can be seen from the fact that it can be correctly said of someone who acts like a politician at election time that she is really shy, but that she manages to overcome it.

I take the following terms to be typical of terms used to describe a person's personality traits: "shy," "gregarious," "optimistic," "pessimistic," "timid," "fearless," "envious," and "compassionate." Not all dispositions to have emotional responses are personality traits, only those that are dispositions to the kinds of general circumstances that all rational persons are likely to confront. The disposition to feel anxiety when confronted with snakes is not a personality trait because it is not a circumstance that every rational person is likely to confront. Shyness and gregariousness, which is a disposition to feel pleasure when confronted with new people, are personality traits because being confronted with new people is a circumstance that everyone is likely to confront. Both optimism, having the disposition to feel hope when confronted with a challenge, and pessimism, having the disposition to feel despair when confronted with a challenge, are personality traits, for everyone is confronted with challenges. Timidity is the disposition to feel anxiety when confronted with small dangers, and fearlessness is the disposition not to feel anxiety even when confronted with large dangers. Both are clearly personality traits.

The disposition to feel anger whenever the computer goes down is not a personality trait, because many people are not involved with computers. However when one is more disposed than most to feel angry whenever one's desires are frustrated or one's plans are disrupted, then one is irascible. It is a personality trait because everyone is likely to have some desires frustrated or some plans disrupted at some time. The disposition to feel compassion when confronted with the suffering of others is a personality trait because it is likely that every rational person will confront the suffering of others. Similarly, the disposition to feel envy is a personality trait because the circumstances that can give rise to envy are ubiquitous. All of these personality traits have important effects on how one acts, but some, like being compassionate, are closely related to specific character traits, like kindness, while others, like shyness, are not. The above list contains only a small sample of personality traits, and personality traits are far more complex than I have indicated. However, I am primarily concerned with character traits and am discussing personality traits primarily to clarify the nature of character traits, including distinguishing them from personality traits.

Character Traits

Character traits, like habits, are dispositions to behave, but they differ from habits in several ways, one of the most salient being that they involve a much wider range of actions. Habits are dispositions to behave in specific physical or mental ways, for example, a person may habitually put on her right shoe before her left, or always add a column of numbers starting from the bottom. Traits of character are dispositions to respond to situations that are general enough that they are likely to be encountered by everyone. Unlike habits, there may be no specific physical or mental activities that necessarily accompany this kind of response. For example, imprudence is a disposition to respond to a situation that may have significant future consequences without considering these consequences adequately. Ways of acting in response to danger, the suffering of others, or temptations to act immorally, are all character traits.

Most facts about character formation cannot be discovered by philosophical analysis but require empirical investigation. However, that character traits are dispositions to respond that have been at least partially formed by the free, intentional, voluntary acts of the person who has those character traits is an essential feature of their nature.[6] Dispositions to respond, although affected by both personality traits and by teaching and training, are not appropriately regarded as character traits until they are strengthened or weakened by the actions one performs. Rational persons are held responsible for their intentional, free, voluntary actions, including their responses to general situations. The pattern of such responses is the criterion of one's character. This means that each person is to some degree responsible for her own character.

A person's character consists of a number of traits, each trait concerning a range of actions. A failure to distinguish character from personality has led philosophers and others to the view that a person's character is relatively unchangeable after the age of five. But a child of five does not yet have a character, for his dispositions to respond have not been formed to any significant degree by his own free, intentional, voluntary acts. People's personalities are not something for which they are usually held responsible. This can be seen from the fact that children have well-developed personalities before they reach an age at which they are held responsible for anything. Personality traits are primarily genetic or formed by very early training, for babies and very young children have personality traits. Although a person may try to change her personality traits by free, intentional, voluntary acts, for example, engaging in some form of psychotherapy, most persons do not. Character traits, though strongly affected by personality traits, can be influenced well into adulthood by the way that one acts.

Teaching children to be virtuous involves not only training them to act virtuously but also to enjoy acting in that way. Children who are taught and trained in the appropriate ways will usually not only come to have a disposition to act virtuously, they will also come to enjoy acting in that way. The kinds of punishments and rewards that are most effective in affecting the way children feel about acting in a way that exemplifies character traits are often very mild, often only a frown or a smile. A child who is praised for responding to the suffering of others by trying to help is more likely to come to enjoy responding in that way, and hence to develop the virtue of kindness. Simply expressing approval to a child who tells the truth when there is a temptation to lie and disapproval when she lies, may result in her coming to view unjustified deception as not even an option. Training to develop virtuous character traits almost always involves training a person to come to enjoy acting in that way. Children should be raised to enjoy acting morally, not only because it increases the likelihood of their acting in this way, but also because the children will feel better when acting morally. Aristotle would not even consider a person to have a virtuous character trait unless she enjoys exercising that trait, for Aristotle held that virtues must contribute to a person's flourishing.[7]

Some personality traits that are used to explain character traits are so closely related to them that often they are not distinguished. For example, most people who call a person "compassionate" do not distinguish that from calling her "kind." However, it is sometimes important to distinguish between persons who suffer because of the suffering of others, which is being compassionate, and those who act so as to relieve the suffering of others, which is being kind. Only by making this distinction can one recognize that a compassionate person need not be a kind one, nor need a kind person be compassionate. Failing to distinguish clearly between personality and character may also result in people being mistakenly praised for their personality or, even more seriously, being wrongly condemned for undesirable personality traits. The praise can be mistaken because their compassion does not lead to kindness, and the condemnation is wrong because despite their lack of compassion their actions exemplify kindness. However, personality has an extraordinary impact on character, and, insofar as personality traits can be influenced by training, children should be nurtured so that they develop a personality that is most conducive to their achieving a moral character.

Although personality traits often explain why people act as they do, persons are also capable of guiding their actions by reasons. Reasons can lead a person to respond to a situation differently than the way she feels like responding. A sadistic person need not be cruel or even callous although she enjoys seeing people suffer, for preventing the suffering of others may serve as a motive for acting that is stronger than enjoying their suffering. Indeed, a person can come to enjoy being kind because it demonstrates her ability to act on reasons and thus transcend her personality. Beliefs that are reasons are often motives simply because they are reasons, for many people have as a personal ideal to be a person who acts on good reasons. As discussed in the previous chapter, many people have as a personal ideal being virtuous persons. Having as a personal ideal being a virtuous person may lead people to act in virtuous ways even though they do not have an associated personality trait. They know that dispositions to respond are usually strengthened by acting on them, so they act virtuously in order to strengthen their disposition to act in virtuous ways. Paradoxically, they first act virtuously in order to become virtuous rather than because they are virtuous.

Character traits are not generally used in explanations of behavior, for they simply are habitual ways of responding to situations general enough that they are likely to be encountered by everyone. Of course, a particular action can be explained by citing a character trait, but this simply fits it into a general pattern of behavior, such as that she kept her promise because she is a very dependable person. Those character traits that all rational persons, or all impartial rational persons, judge in the same way, like courage and cruelty, are called virtues and vices. But not all character traits are virtues or vices; some character traits like ambition are such that rational persons disagree about whether they should be cultivated. Rational persons can agree on the description of ambition and still disagree on whether they want themselves or their children to have such a character trait. With regard to the virtues and vices, rational persons agree that they want all the personal virtues themselves and want everyone else to have all the moral virtues.

Virtues and Reasonable Expectations

Not everyone either has a moral or personal virtue or else has the corresponding moral or personal vice. Many people are neither truthful nor deceitful, courageous nor cowardly, prudent nor imprudent. In order to explain this fact, the analysis of virtue and vice must take into account both what it would be reasonable to do and what it would be reasonable to expect a person to do. Being reasonable is simply not being unreasonable and being unreasonable involves believing or acting contrary to what a rational believer or agent acknowledges to be clearly the best reasons. Since people sometimes disagree about what it would be reasonable to do or to expect a person to do, there will be differences in the assignment of a virtue or a vice to a person. But, as in all other areas of morality and rationality, there are limits to these differences. It is not reasonable to expect a person to act in a certain way if almost no one in that situation acts in that way; it is reasonable to expect a person to act in a certain way if almost everyone in that situation acts in that way.

If a person acts significantly better than it is reasonable to expect, he has a virtue; if he acts significantly worse, he has a vice. If he simply acts as it is reasonable to expect, he has neither the virtue nor the vice. Moral virtue, in general, involves justifiably following the moral rules and ideals significantly more than most people do; moral vice involves acting contrary to the guide provided by morality significantly more than most people do. Personal virtues involve acting in accord with one's rational goals or plans significantly more than most people do; personal vices involve failing to act in accord with one's rational goals or plans significantly more than most people do. However the personal vices do not usually involve acting irrationally, only unreasonably.

Having a particular moral virtue involves justifiably following the related moral rule or ideal significantly more than most people do; having a particular moral vice involves unjustifiably acting contrary to the related moral rule or failing to justifiably follow the related moral ideal significantly more than most people do. Having a particular personal virtue involves acting reasonably in a general kind of situation, or in the face of some general kind of temptation, significantly more than most people do; having a particular personal vice involves acting reasonably in a general kind of situation, or in the face of some general kind of temptation, significantly less than most people do. What counts as acting reasonably will depend in part on the rankings of the goods and evils by the person acting. Acting contrary to one's clear rankings of goods and evils is acting unreasonably even though that way of acting is not irrational. Acting reasonably thus involves more than not act irrationally; it also requires not acting unreasonably.

Moral Virtues and Vices

A clear account of the moral system is necessary for a proper understanding of the moral virtues and vices, for a particular moral virtue involves following some part of the moral system significantly more than most people do; and a particular moral vice involves acting contrary to some part of the guide provided by morality significantly more than most people do. Although it is not discussed in most philosophical accounts of the virtues and vices, the same person may have both moral virtues and moral vices. What this shows is that character traits are not always, probably not even primarily, formed on the basis of rational deliberation. If they were, all of the moral virtues would go together, for the reasoning that is persuasive with regard to one moral virtue should be persuasive with regard to them all. For most people heredity and early training that explains their personality traits also explains their particular moral virtues and vices. Understanding the relationship between the moral virtues and vices and the moral system is neither necessary nor sufficient for developing the virtues; however, it is necessary for properly understanding them.

The moral virtues and vices involve free, intentional, voluntary actions related to the moral rules and ideals. Associated with each of the second five moral rules is a moral vice, that is, a disposition to respond to a conflict between a moral rule and one's interests or inclinations, in a way that involves unjustifiable violation of that rule. Associated with the rule concerning deception is deceitfulness; with promises, untrustworthiness; with cheating, unfairness; with obeying the law, dishonesty; and with doing one's duty, undependability. The linking of a particular moral vice with a specific moral rule is somewhat arbitrary, so undependability might also be linked with the rule prohibiting breaking promises. However, this pairing makes discussion easier and does not distort the understanding of the vices, even though a more careful examination of the terms referring to the moral vices might reveal more complexity.

All the moral vices connected with the second five rules have corresponding virtues. In fact, except for truthfulness, which corresponds to the vice of deceitfulness, the names of all of these other virtues can be derived from those of the corresponding vices simply by removing the prefix. Since these moral virtues are dispositions to follow the moral rules as the moral attitude specifies, all impartial rational persons favor everyone having these moral virtues. The account of morality makes it obvious why the moral virtues connected with the second five rules, truthfulness, trustworthiness, fairness, honesty, and dependability, are those traits of character that all rational people want others to have and at least pretend to want for themselves. Rational persons favor others acquiring the moral virtues in order to lessen their own risk of suffering harm. However, since they know that other rational persons also want them to act morally, they must, at least, pretend to cultivate these virtues in themselves. This explains the truth of La Rochefoucauld's saying "Hypocrisy is the homage that vice pays to virtue."

The moral virtues and vices connected with the second five moral rules lie on a single scale. As a person becomes less truthful, she becomes more deceitful, less trustworthy, more untrustworthy, and so on. A person may be completely dependable, generally dependable, fairly dependable, somewhat dependable or undependable, fairly undependable, generally undependable, or completely undependable. The virtue and the vice are such that as a person moves away from one end of the scale, she necessarily moves toward the other. But most people are somewhere in the middle, and it would be incorrect to claim that they have either the virtue or the vice. A person has a particular moral virtue or vice only if, given similar circumstances, the frequency with which she unjustifiably breaks the corresponding moral rule is significantly less than others or significantly greater. In fact, the second five moral rules can be restated in terms of either the virtues or the vices. The rules might be either "Be truthful, trustworthy, fair, honest, and dependable" or "Do not be deceitful, untrustworthy, unfair, dishonest, or undependable." The importance of this close association between the second five rules and the moral virtues and vices will be demonstrated in chapter 13 when I discuss the question "Why be moral?"

Although most of what are normally listed as the moral virtues and vices are related to the second five moral rules, some moral virtues and vices are not. Cruelty is a moral vice that is related to the first five rules. It is most obviously related to the rule prohibiting the causing of pain, but it does not seem restricted to this rule. Rather, cruelty can manifest itself in unjustifiable violations of any of the first five rules, that is, any unjustifiable infliction of a harm on someone. Of course, some people are more cruel than others; whereas some people kill and torture unjustifiably, others may only deprive of pleasure unjustifiably. There do not seem to be distinct vices related to each of the first five moral rules, there are only degrees and kinds of cruelty.

Unlike the moral vices connected to the second five moral rules, a decrease in cruelty does not necessarily lead to an increase in what might be taken as the corresponding moral virtue, kindness. Between kindness and cruelty sits indifference. Unlike the moral virtues connected to the second five rules, honesty, fairness, and so on, kindness does not consist in obeying the moral rules. Rather, kindness is a disposition to follow the direct moral ideals, to act so as to relieve the suffering of others, when this does not involve unjustifiably violating a moral rule. This explains the presence of indifference. Kindness is not simply lack of cruelty as honesty is lack of dishonesty. Nor is cruelty simply lack of kindness as dishonesty is lack of honesty. Lack of kindness is indifference; when regarded as a moral vice it is known as callousness and is regarded as close to cruelty. There are no moral virtues related to the first five rules, for no one is thought to deserve praise simply for never unjustifiably causing harm to others. Indeed, if a person never unjustifiably causes harm, but also never acts to prevent or relieve it when he has an opportunity to do so, he simply may be regarded as callous.

Although this list of six moral virtues and seven moral vices is not complete, it is sufficient to confirm a general description of the moral virtues and vices. Any character trait that involves unjustifiably violating the moral rules or that involves failing to follow the moral ideals when this can be done justifiably is a moral vice. Any character trait that involves justifiably obeying the moral rules or justifiably following the moral ideals is a moral virtue. However moral virtues and vices also can be characterized without mentioning the moral rules or ideals. They can be defined in terms of the attitudes of all impartial rational persons. A moral virtue is any trait of character that all impartial rational persons favor all persons possessing.[8] A moral vice is any trait of character that all impartial rational persons favor no person possessing. But regardless of how the moral virtues and vices are defined, they all have a direct conceptual relationship to moral rules and moral ideals.

Of the four traditional cardinal virtues, justice, prudence, temperance, and courage, only justice is properly classified as a moral virtue.[9] Neither prudence, temperance, or courage has any direct conceptual relationship to either the moral rules or the moral ideals. Justice as a cardinal virtue differs from the other moral virtues related to the moral rules, for it has no special relationship to a particular moral rule; a just person does not unjustifiably violate any of the moral rules. In this sense, justice is not merely one moral virtue among many; it contains all the moral virtues related to the moral rules. Since justice has no conceptual relationship to the moral ideals, it is possible for a person to be just but callous. Thus, although justice is necessary to moral goodness and an unjust person is an immoral person, being just is sufficient only for not being immoral; it is not sufficient for moral goodness. Moral goodness requires not only justice but kindness.

Motives and the Morality of an Action

To regard an action as morally acceptable if it is what a virtuous agent would do in the circumstances creates no problems when the moral virtues are analyzed in terms of the moral system. However, to regard the moral virtues as more basic than the moral system involves not accepting such an analysis. Thus one must find some other way of determining what a virtuous agent would do. One plausible way of determining this is by discovering the motive of the action and determining if it is the kind of motive that would lead a morally virtuous person to act. Taking the virtues as more basic than the moral system may therefore result in holding that it is not the moral system, but the motive that determines the morality of the action. If a person deceives in order to ingratiate himself or those he represents, then his action is immoral even if no harm is done, but if he deceives in order to save someone from suffering severe anxiety, then his action is not immoral. Similarly, stopping treatment for an incurable cancer patient who had made a valid refusal of treatment is immoral if done in order to benefit oneself, but not if done in order to prevent the victim's suffering.

Persuasive as these claims sound, they are false. The motive cannot determine the morality of the action, for people can act immorally from the best motives. Failure to see this may be due to the failure to distinguish between the moral judgment that is appropriately made about a person who acts from certain kinds of motives and the moral judgment that should be made about the act itself. What does determine the moral acceptability of an action is whether impartial rational persons can publicly allow that kind of violation. If a violation can be publicly allowed, then it is not morally wrong no matter what the motive; if it cannot be publicly allowed, then it is immoral, regardless of the motive. This point may not be properly appreciated because certain kinds of motives usually lead people to unjustifiably violate moral rules whereas other kinds of motives generally lead only to violations that can be publicly allowed.

There is a strong correlation between, on the one hand, acting from one kind of motive and being able to publicly allow that kind of violation and, on the other, acting from another kind of motive and no impartial rational person's being able to publicly allow that kind of violation. These correlations explain the plausibility of holding that an act done from the former kind of motive is morally acceptable and an act done from the latter kind of motive is morally unacceptable. But although the correlations are strong, they are not perfect. When a motive that normally leads to a kind of action that is morally acceptable leads to a particular action that cannot be publicly allowed, it is clear that the motive does not determine whether the action is morally acceptable. Whether an impartial rational person can publicly allow such a violation is what determines the morally acceptability of the action. The motive, at most, determines the moral worth of the action, that is, how much it indicates about the moral character of the agent.

That it is a mistake to determine the moral acceptability of an act on the basis of the motive of the agent is shown by the fact that paternalistic actions, if they are genuinely paternalistic, are always done from a motive to benefit the person toward whom one is acting paternalistically. But paternalism also involves violating a moral rule with regard to that person, so it needs to be justified. Since some paternalistic actions are not justified, it is clear that good motives are not sufficient to make an act morally acceptable. Even compassion, if it is not governed by the moral attitude, can lead to immoral action. Violating a moral rule with regard to people without their consent but for their benefit may be motivated by genuine compassion, but if one could not will that everyone know that they are allowed to violate the rule in the same circumstances, it is morally unacceptable. Paternalistic behavior shows quite clearly that what determines the moral acceptability of an act is not the motive from which it is done, but rather whether the action is one that an impartial rational person can favor being publicly allowed. Even violating a moral rule with regard to someone with her consent, when no impartial rational person can favor such a violation being publicly allowed, is an act of arrogance.[10]

Moral Virtues: Behavior or Behavior plus Enjoyment

Some philosophers do not regard it as sufficient for having a moral virtue that a person have a disposition to behave in morally acceptable ways; he must also have a disposition to enjoy acting in these ways. Some people incorrectly think that this is a disagreement between Aristotle and Kant on the nature of the virtues. Aristotle is taken as holding that moral virtues do not involve merely a disposition to act in morally acceptable ways but also a disposition to enjoy acting in those ways. Kant, on the other hand, is sometimes mistakenly taken to hold that the moral virtues are limited to dispositions to act in morally acceptable ways and that enjoying acting in those ways actually detracts from having the virtues. If this were actually the dispute, Aristotle would be correctly regarded as having the better view, for there is no question that impartial rational persons prefer everyone not only to act morally but also to enjoy doing so.

It is clearly preferable for children to be brought up to enjoy acting morally rather than to act morally in a grudging way. Not only are those who enjoy acting morally more likely to act morally but it will be more enjoyable for them to do so. However, this does not settle the question about whether enjoying acting as the moral virtue requires is essential for having the virtue or is only a bonus. It might be thought that no one could reliably act as a moral virtue requires without enjoying acting in that way. But whether this is true is clearly an empirical matter, not one that can be decided by philosophical analysis. If it is not true, it seems that the trait of character that simply involves reliably acting as the moral virtue requires should be described as a moral virtue. If one mistakenly regards the moral virtues as necessarily contributing to a person's flourishing, then one will take enjoying acting morally as essential to the moral virtues. But one need not make this mistake in order to regard a virtue as necessarily involving the disposition to enjoy acting virtuously.

If the moral virtues are thought of as traits of character that all rational persons want other people to have, then the moral virtues will not require enjoying acting as the virtues requires, only having a reliable disposition to act in those ways. On the other hand, if the moral virtues are thought of as those traits of character that all impartial rational persons want everyone, including themselves, to have, then the moral virtues seem to require enjoying acting as the virtue requires. The former way of describing the moral virtues distinguishes them quite sharply from the personal virtues. The latter way of describing them is much closer to Aristotle's view, for he viewed the moral virtues on the model of the personal virtues.[11] Although either of these ways of characterizing the moral virtues identifies the same virtues, the latter way is more accurate.[12] This latter way does make enjoying acting as the moral virtue requires an essential feature of having the virtue, for all impartial rational persons would prefer everyone to enjoy acting as the moral virtue requires. However, in English there are no words, other than the names of the moral virtues, that characterize a person who acts as a moral virtue requires but does not enjoy acting in that way, so I will also regard such a person as having the moral virtue.

Personal Virtues: Behavior or Behavior plus Enjoyment

With regard to the personal virtues, there is less of a problem, for personal virtues are those traits of character that all rational persons want for themselves. All rational persons clearly prefer having a trait of character that they enjoy exercising rather than one that they find unpleasant to exercise. A person who has a very high cholesterol count would prefer coming to enjoy eating fresh fruits and vegetables rather than continuing to enjoy pepperoni pizzas and cheeseburgers but not eating them because of fear of a heart attack. Using Aristotle's terminology, all rational persons would prefer to be temperate rather than merely continent. Of course, if they could not be temperate, they would prefer being continent to being incontinent. However, this does not settle the verbal question about whether someone who has a reliable disposition to act as the personal virtue requires has a virtue if he does not enjoy acting in that way. Although all rational persons would prefer enjoying acting as the personal virtue requires rather than simply acting in that way without enjoying it, this does not settle the question. Since personal virtues are the traits of character that all rational persons want to have for themselves, it is clear that they all prefer having a personal virtue that involves enjoying acting as the virtue requires, rather than simply acting as the virtue requires. Nonetheless, as with the moral virtues, the English language does not distinguish between a trait of character that consists simply of a reliable disposition to act as a personal virtue requires and a trait that also involves enjoying acting in that way, so I will regard both as personal virtues.

Can Virtues Conflict?

An adequate understanding of the virtues should explain why it is a mistake to think that there is any situation where exercising any moral or personal virtue conflicts with exercising any other virtue. Truthfulness involves not unjustifiably violating the moral rule prohibiting deception, but truthfulness as a moral virtue also involves not following this rule when doing so would be unjustifiable. To tell the truth when it is unjustifiable to do so is to be boorish, insensitive, or tactless. Even when only some impartial rational persons would publicly allow deception, deception is not incompatible with truthfulness. Similarly, causing suffering is not incompatible with kindness in situations where impartial rational persons can publicly allow causing that suffering. Since all impartial rational persons want to have all of the moral virtues and all of the personal virtues themselves, no virtue can conflict with any other.

However, especially in the practice of medicine, one sometimes has painful news to tell. There are times when not telling this news, a grim prognosis, counts as deception as clearly as making a false statement. When telling the bad news clearly will result in suffering, it seems as if being truthful requires that one be unkind, whereas kindness requires that one be deceitful. If truthfulness demands telling and kindness demands not telling, there does seem to be a conflict between the virtues. To claim that one can tell, but tell in such a way that minimizes the suffering of the patient, thus satisfying the demands of both truthfulness and kindness, is too easy a way out. Although one can and should minimize the suffering of the patient by telling in the least painful way, it will still often be the case that significantly more suffering will occur if you tell, no matter how, than if you deceive either by not telling or by making a false statement.

Characterizing the different moral virtues as character traits that involve responding to different situations in ways that impartial rational persons could allow suggests that the virtues cannot conflict with one another because they are called for in different situations. This suggestion, however neglects the fact that the same situation, such as having bad news to tell, can call for the exercise of two virtues such that if one of these virtues is exercised, it seems to rule out the exercise of the other virtue. Having bad news to tell seems to be a situation where both truthfulness and kindness are called for, yet it does not seem possible to exercise both. A similar problem can occur with the personal virtues; one might be in a dangerous situation that calls for both courage and prudence and yet it seems impossible to exercise both. If one acts in one way, it will be appropriately described as courageous but not as prudent, and if one acts in the other it will be appropriately described as prudent but not as courageous.

Does this show that truthfulness and kindness can sometimes come into conflict so that truthfulness requires unkindness and kindness sometimes requires deceitfulness? Does the same problem arise for courage and prudence? If so, then it cannot be correct that all impartial rational persons want all of the personal and moral virtues and want to avoid all of the personal and moral vices. Thus for virtues to be traits of character that all impartial rational persons want, it must be shown that the virtues do not conflict in the situations described above. On one interpretation of the doctrine of the unity of the virtues, all fully informed, impartial rational persons want to have all of the virtues. On that interpretation, the doctrine is true. On a more traditional interpretation of this doctrine, it claims that in order to have any of the virtues one must have them all. On this interpretation of the doctrine of the unity of the virtues, it is false. It is not only false that one cannot have the personal virtues without having the moral ones, it is also false that one cannot have one of the moral virtues without having them all, or cannot have one personal virtue without having them all.

Exercising a Virtue versus Exemplifying It

In order to show that virtues do have the kind of unity such that a fully informed, impartial rational person wants to have them all, a distinction must be made between having or exercising the virtue and *exemplifying* it. To exemplify a virtue is to act in such a way that one's action can be used as a paradigm of that virtue in the way that risking danger to accomplish some goal can exemplify courage. To want a virtue is not necessarily to want to *exemplify* it in every situation. In some situations rational persons may prefer to exemplify different virtues; in the same situation one impartial rational person may prefer to exemplify truthfulness and another one prefer to exemplify kindness. But exemplifying one virtue never requires exemplifying another vice; indeed, exemplifying one virtue never requires even having or exercising another vice. The view that exemplifying one virtue sometimes requires exemplifying or exercising another vice may arise from the fact that rational persons, even impartial rational persons, sometimes disagree about what ought to be done.

One person may hold that retreating counts as prudent while another person holds that it would be cowardly to retreat. One person may hold that withholding the truth counts as kind while another person holds that it would be deceitful not to tell. However, this does not show a real conflict between the virtues. To each of the persons involved there is no conflict of virtues; the one who thinks it prudent to retreat does not regard retreating as cowardly, and the one who thinks it cowardly to retreat does not regard retreating as prudent; the one who thinks it kind to withhold does not regard withholding as deceitful, and the one who thinks it deceitful to withhold does not think that withholding is kind. Rather, they disagree about whether this avoidance of danger is supported by the best reasons or whether preventing this suffering counts as a morally adequate reason for not telling this patient the truth. This is a disagreement about whether a particular act of avoiding danger counts as prudent or cowardly, or whether a particular act of withholding counts as kind or as deceitful. This disagreement is compatible with complete agreement that genuine prudence does not require cowardice, and genuine kindness does not require deceitfulness.

If prudence is taken as a virtue, then there can be no such thing as cowardly prudence. If kindness is taken as a virtue, then there can be no such thing as deceitful kindness. One is not exercising kindness when it is morally unjustifiable to deceive in order to prevent a person's suffering. To regard deceitful kindness as kindness is like regarding a false friend as a friend or a rubber duck as a duck; it is to commit the fallacy of *ignoring the modifier*. To know that it would be morally wrong not to tell the patient and yet to be unable to bring oneself to tell him is not kindness, at least not kindness if it is to be regarded as a moral virtue. Rather, it is a manifestation of the personality trait of compassion, and the examination of paternalism has shown that compassion can easily lead to arrogance. It is, of course, true that a person with compassion is more likely to be kind than a person without compassion, but confusing kindness with compassion is as much a mistake as confusing courage with fearlessness. Only by distinguishing between the virtues and the personality traits that are closely related to them is it possible to have a coherent account of the virtues.

Someone who does not retreat when retreating is supported by the best reasons is not courageous but rash. Someone who claims that it is not being truthful to withhold, even when all impartial rational persons would favor withholding, is confusing the virtue of truthfulness with compulsive truth telling. A truthful person never deceives when it is morally unjustifiable to deceive; but when it would be morally wrong not to deceive, a truthful person deceives. Although this sounds paradoxical, it is clear that if truthfulness is to be a moral virtue it must never require doing what is morally wrong. Someone who tells an unpleasant truth in a situation when all impartial persons would publicly allowing deceiving, is not truthful but tactless. The names of the virtues may sometimes mislead, but recognition that all fully informed, impartial rational persons want everyone to have all of the virtues both helps one to avoid confusion and to provide an adequate analysis of them.

Virtues and Rationality

Any account of the virtues or of rationality that makes it impossible for all impartial rational persons to want everyone, including themselves, to have all of the virtues is inadequate. Recognition that having or exercising any moral or personal virtue can never require having or exercising any moral or personal vice provides some help in coming to a proper understanding of both the moral and personal virtues and vices. It makes clear that the virtues are not properly regarded as involving distinctive ways of responding to the same situation, such that one virtuous way of responding is incompatible with some other virtuous way of responding. Certainly, no virtuous way of responding can ever require acting in what would be correctly described as exercising a personal vice; for example, kindness cannot require cowardice, and prudence cannot require deceitfulness. If having or exercising any of the virtues were ever incompatible with having or exercising any other virtue, it would be impossible for an impartial rational person to seek all the virtues. As noted above, this is not an acceptable conclusion.

Realizing that all of the virtues are compatible shows the inadequacy of some ways of defining courage and prudence. Suppose that courage is defined as the trait of acting so as to overcome the present danger regardless of the possible harmful consequences to oneself and that prudence is taken as the trait of acting so as to minimize the possible harmful consequences to oneself. Although these accounts have some plausibility, given what was said in the previous paragraph, both cannot be correct. If they were, sometimes when faced with danger, one could not be both courageous and prudent, but would be forced to choose between being courageous and imprudent or being prudent and cowardly. Accounts of other moral and personal virtues and vices lead to similar problems; they allow for situations such that exercising one virtue requires exercising another vice. But the virtues cannot conflict, so these accounts must be false.

A trait of character is a virtue only if all impartial rational persons want everyone, including themselves, who have all of the other virtues to have that trait of character as well. Thus not only must all virtues be compatible but a virtuous action must always be rational. If a virtuous action were ever irrational, then not all impartial rational persons would want to have all the virtues. The simplest and most direct way to guarantee that all virtuous action is rational is to include as part of the definition of any virtue that it requires acting rationally. This is true not only of the personal virtues like courage and temperance but also of the moral virtues such as kindness and truthfulness. Obviously, this is not a sufficient account of a moral virtue, for it is also rational to exercise a moral vice; it is not irrational to act immorally, even to do so habitually. It is plausible to maintain that the moral virtues require one to act on the best reasons, but although acting on the best reasons never clearly favors acting immorally, sometimes the reasons for acting morally will not be clearly better than the reasons for acting immorally. Moral virtues do require acting as an impartial rational person would publicly allow.

Personal Virtues and Vices

The relationship between the personal virtues and rationality is complex. Although all virtues, moral and personal, involve acting rationally, this only means that no virtue can allow acting irrationally; it does not mean that all virtues involve acting as rationality requires. If it did, then not having the virtue, or having the vice, would involve acting irrationally. However, as pointed out above, it is not irrational to have a moral vice. It may seem that it is irrational to exercise a personal vice, but then having a personal vice would be to have a mental disorder, for to have a condition that habitually leads to irrational actions is sufficient for having a mental disorder. Thus having a personal vice would not result in intentional, free, voluntary actions, for no one intentionally, freely, and voluntarily habitually acts irrationally.

That a personal vice is a mental disorder is not an implausible view. Having a personal vice is suffering from weakness of will and weakness of will is closely related to a mental disorder. But it would also have the result that no one should be held responsible for exercising a personal vice, and this does not seem quite as plausible, especially when the exercise of a personal vice, for example, intemperance, leads to a morally unacceptable action. To avoid this result one might claim that a personal virtue does not allow one to act contrary to the best reasons, and thus exercising a personal vice is only acting unreasonably, not irrationally. It is tempting to hold that a personal virtue does not allow one to act contrary to the best reasons, for this would make it impossible to have both a personal virtue and a moral vice. All moral vices sometimes involve acting contrary to the best reasons; for example, callousness involves ignoring the suffering of others when one has better reasons for helping them. But then no immoral person could be prudent, an odd result.

Unlike the moral virtues, the personal virtues are virtues that all rational persons personally want to have themselves, whether they are concerned only with themselves or are impartially concerned with all moral agents. No rational person wants to have the corresponding personal vices. One can, in fact, define the personal virtues as those character traits that all rational persons want for themselves, and personal vices as those that no rational person wants for herself. All rational persons want to have the three cardinal virtues personally, but they need not want that all other persons have them. Impartial rational persons favor all morally good persons having all the personal virtues, for this increases the chances that these persons will be more successful in preventing and relieving harm. No impartial rational person wants those who are cruel to acquire any of the personal virtues; on they contrary, they would prefer them to have the personal vices. As Kant points out, immoral people having the personal virtues would increase the chances of other people suffering evil consequences from unjustified violations of the moral rules. This makes it clear that prudence, temperance, and courage, are personal not moral virtues, and their opposites, imprudence, intemperance, and cowardice, are personal not moral vices.

The personal virtues are consistent with a wide range of personality traits, desires, and emotions; they require only that one not allow certain kinds of situations to make one act irrationally or unreasonably. It does not make any difference how many separate personal virtues one invents or discovers; all of them will be consistent with each of the others, for they will differ from one another only in the kinds of situation that provide the paradigmatic tests of the virtue. Courage is the trait of character that involves not allowing danger or fear to make one act irrationally or unreasonably. Prudence involves not allowing present concerns to make one neglect future consequences with regard to oneself or those for whom one is concerned when this would result in one acting irrationally or unreasonably. Temperance involves not allowing strong emotions or desires to make one act irrationally or unreasonably. Fortitude will be the virtue of not allowing continuing hardships to make one act irrationally or unreasonably. Perhaps patience can be defined as the virtue of not allowing long delays to make one act irrationally or unreasonably. Most of the personal vices can be defined by simply leaving out the "not" in the definition of the corresponding virtue. Cowardice involves allowing danger or fear to make one act irrationally or unreasonably. Intemperance is allowing strong emotions or desires to make one act irrationally or unreasonably.

This account of the personal virtues may seem to achieve the unity of the virtues that Plato and others have sought. The personal virtues are distinguished from one another by the situation that paradigmatically tests the virtue, so that danger or fear test courage, strong emotions and desires test temperance. Thus a person who always acts reasonably will have all of the personal virtues. However, that a person who always acts reasonably will have all of the personal virtues does not show that a person who always acts reasonably when tested in some situations will do so when tested in other ways. Different personality traits, as well as different role models and other features of one's teaching and training, not only make it possible to be both courageous and intemperate, they make that possibility a reality for many people. The character who always confronts danger reasonably, but behaves unreasonably, perhaps even irrationally, when angry or lustful, is almost a cliché in movies. That all impartial rational persons want everyone to have all of the virtues shows that it is possible to have them all, but that human beings are not completely rational beings explains why it possible for persons to have both personal virtues and vices.

However, even a person who has all of the personal virtues may not want to *exemplify* a particular virtue in every situation where it is tested. Situations that seem to call for prudence or courage to the exclusion of the other should not be seen as showing the incompatibility of the virtues, but only the impossibility of performing an action that exemplifies both of them. The same point can be made about the seeming conflict between truthfulness and kindness. One can exercise a virtue without exemplifying it, for *exemplifying* a virtue requires acting in a way that is paradigmatic, whereas *exercising* the virtue only requires intentionally acting in a way that is compatible with having the virtue. The view that virtues can sometimes conflict is partly the result of confusing the true view that sometimes one may not be able to exemplify two virtues at the same time, with the false view that in these cases both virtues cannot be exercised. Exercising courage, that is, acting reasonably in the face of danger, does not always require trying to overcome that danger, which is what is required for exemplifying that virtue. Realizing this allows for a much better understanding of the virtues. Rational persons can and do rank the evils differently, and as long as the ranking is rational, and the person acts reasonably according to his own rational ranking, then he is exercising a personal virtue. This can be shown by examining the three cardinal virtues and vices that are personal virtues and vices.

Prudence and Imprudence

For prudence to be a personal virtue, it must be a trait of character that, regardless of their personality, all rational persons want to have. Prudence cannot be a trait of character that appeals only to persons who enjoy safe activities, such as stamp collecting; it must also appeal to those persons who enjoy more dangerous activities, such as mountain climbing. Prudence should not be confused with timidity, which is a personality trait, not a trait of character. A prudent person is one who carefully considers the consequences of her actions when these are likely to be serious, and who does not take unnecessary risks in seeking to reach her goal or satisfy her desires. This does not mean that a prudent person takes no risks, but she does not take them unless they seem to be a good way to obtain what she is seeking. A person who enjoys action and adventure is not excluded from being a prudent person. For her, risks are enjoyable. If she takes care to prepare herself and has considered the evil risked in the light of the good to be gained, a prudent person may even be a lion tamer.

A prudent person is generally contrasted with a rash or impulsive person, who undertakes a course of action that is likely to have important consequences without adequately considering these consequences. This does not mean that a prudent person never acts on impulse, but she does not do so in cases where the consequences may be momentous. A prudent person is one who does not sacrifice what she considers to be a greater future good to a lesser present one through lack of concern for the former. But a prudent person also does not unnecessarily sacrifice present goods by focusing too narrowly on the future. Although one can fail to be prudent by worrying about the future too much, prudence is most clearly opposed to imprudence. A prudent person does not allow situations where the long-term consequences of her action for herself and those for whom she is concerned may result in significant evil or failure to achieve significant goods lead her to act unreasonably. Defined in this way, it is clear that prudence is a personal virtue. All rational persons favor taking into account the long-term consequences of their actions in order to avoid significant evils and loss of significant goods for themselves and those for whom they care.

A person can also be prudent in handling the affairs of others, even of others for whom he is not concerned. Many people have jobs or positions which require them to invest the funds of others prudently. If someone in one of these positions is so taken by an investment opportunity that he does not exercise due diligence in considering the serious risks if the investment does not work out, he is acting imprudently. He may also be failing to do his duty. It is when this failure to do one's duty is due to imprudence, rather than an attempt to profit from the misuse of the funds entrusted to him, that people talk of weakness of will. In this kind of situation, where the people who will suffer most are not people for whom the imprudent person is concerned, then it may only be unreasonable, but not irrational, for him to act imprudently. Such action can be punished, for it is plausible that it is as much a lack of concern for these others as a lack of prudence that was responsible for the imprudent action. But when a person habitually acts imprudently with regard to himself, it seems as if he must be suffering from some mental disorder. It is not appropriate to call a person imprudent if he simply lacks the intelligence to see the long-term consequences of his actions.

Temperance and Intemperance

Temperance can be taken as part of prudence, but there is a significant difference in emphasis. Whereas prudence primarily involves having appropriate concern for the future, temperance primarily involves avoiding losing control because of the present. A temperate person is one who responds reasonably when in the grip of some strong emotion or desire. Temperance does not require always overcoming the emotion or refusing to satisfy the desire, for described in this way, temperance is not a trait of character that would be desired by all rational persons. Rather, considered as a virtue, temperance simply requires that one not allow a strong emotion or desire to make one act irrationally or unreasonably. It is not always intemperate to satisfy a strong desire or express a strong emotion. Intemperance is a vice only if the indulgence of one's present desires or emotions leads one to act unreasonably or irrationally.

It is tempting to think of a temperate person as a person who comes to have less of those emotions and desires that might cause him to lose control. But a rational person may enjoy having strong emotions and desires, and if temperance is to be a personal virtue, all rational persons, regardless of their rationally allowed desires, must want to be temperate. Although all rational persons want to enjoy acting in the way that they do act, not all rational persons want to avoid the struggle involved in acting that way. Some people get great pleasure from overcoming danger, obstacles, and temptations. The kind of serenity that Aristotle puts forward as part of his account of the personal virtues need not be shared by all rational persons. Not every rational person would prefer ceasing to have those strong emotions and desires that tempt one to act unreasonably to continuing to have them and enjoying overcoming these strong emotions and desires. A temperate person can enjoy either resisting strong emotions and desires or enjoy having ceased to have them. What is common to all correct accounts of temperance is the disposition not to allow strong emotions or desires to make one behave irrationally or unreasonably. And in the fullest sense, it also involves enjoying acting in this way.

This account of temperance may not describe the ordinary view of temperance, but it is what temperance must be like if it is to be a personal virtue. Temperance is frequently regarded as abstention from or great moderation in the use of alcohol and tobacco and not indulging strong desires or emotions. This is unfortunate. There is a need for the concept of temperance as a genuine personal virtue, one desired by all rational persons, not merely by a genteel middle class. On the concept of temperance with which philosophers have traditionally been concerned, a temperate

person need not have weak desires or emotions. If one does not have any strong desires or emotions, one has little need of temperance. Temperance consists in having
the strength of character that allows one to resist acting on a strong desire or emotion when to satisfy it would be unreasonable.

The "cool moment" aspect of rationality (chapter 2) provides the clearest back-
ground for understanding the concept of intemperance. The "cool moment" aspect
of rationality concentrates on the irrationality of acting on a rational desire that in a
cool moment a person would decide was significantly less important than the desire
or set of desires she would frustrate by so acting. Although such an action may be irrational because one should know that it will result in one's suffering frustration
without an adequate reason, it need not be so. It may only be unreasonable to act
contrary to the rankings one has in a cool moment. Although the more important
desires a person sacrifices by failing to control her present emotions or desires often
concern her own self-interest, they also may, and often do, concern those of others. A
person who is quick to anger may decide in a cool moment that giving vent to her
anger results in the sacrifice of the greater interests of others. That is, in a "cool moment" she may be motivated by the fact that avoiding harm to others is a better reason than avoiding the unpleasantness of controlling her anger; nonetheless, when
she is angry, she may not be able to control her anger. She is unable to act reasonably
when in the grip of her anger. Such a person is intemperate.

When this is the case, philosophers have often talked of "weakness of will." That
lack of temperance is sometimes the cause of immoral action explains why some
have regarded temperance as a moral rather than a personal virtue. Although temperance, like all of the personal virtues, is often necessary for acting morally, this is
not sufficient to make temperance a moral rather than a personal virtue. One may
be a temperate person in all those situations where failing to control a strong emotion or desire adversely affects one's own interests or the interests of those for whom
one cares. But if a person is unconcerned with those who are hurt by one's failure to
control those emotions or desires, he may not even try to control them. Such a person is not intemperate, for it is not these strong emotions and desires that lead him
to act unreasonably, but rather lack of sufficient concern for others. Defining a temperate person as one who does not let her present desires or emotions make her act
unreasonably distinguishes between intemperance as a personal vice and callousness and cruelty, which are moral vices. When this distinction is made, it is clear
that all rational persons, even those that are immoral, desire temperance for themselves and those they care about. This shows that temperance is a personal virtue not
a moral one.

Courage versus Cowardice and Rashness

Although Aristotle's general account of virtue has some serious problems, he was correct in viewing courage as a mean between the extremes of rashness and cowardice.
However, all too often courage is simply contrasted with cowardice and rashness is
completely forgotten. This results in a tendency to equate courage with fearlessness,
and cowardice with timidity, even though fearlessness can lead to rash action as easily as, if not more easily than, it leads to courageous action. Equating courage with

fearlessness is an example of confusing character traits with personality traits. All rational persons want to be courageous, but not all rational persons want to be fearless. Whether fearlessness or timidity are due to heredity or to early childhood training, it is clear that children can be fearless or timid at ages far below those at which it is appropriate to ascribe any characters traits, especially virtues or vices, to them.

If someone is in a situation in which it would be reasonable to expect a person to be so affected by danger or fear that she would abandon the reasonable course of action, then if she does abandon it, the action does not count as showing her to be cowardly. However, it does count as showing that she is not courageous. Being courageous involves continuing with the reasonable course of action even in those situations in which it would be reasonable to expect a person to abandon it. A person counts as having courage to the extent that she continues with the reasonable course of action in situations where it would be reasonable to expect her to abandon it. The greater the expectation that a person will abandon the reasonable course of action, the more courage is shown when she continues it. Of course, this analysis also allows for persons to be courageous when faced with some kinds of dangers or fears but not with others. Physical courage might be distinguished from other kinds of courage if it turned out that some people regularly continued reasonable courses of action when faced with physical dangers that made it reasonable to expect that a person would abandon them, but did not continue reasonable courses of action when faced with public disapproval or economic loss.

Cowardice is shown when fear or danger leads one to abandon a reasonable course of action, or even to act irrationally, when it is reasonable to expect people to continue the reasonable course of action in that situation. If a person does continue her reasonable course of action in this kind of situation, then this does not show courage, but it is necessary for courage. Although courage is shown by continuing the reasonable course of action when this is not what it is reasonable to expect, it also requires continuing that reasonable course of action when it is reasonable to expect that fear or danger will not deter this kind of behavior. Courage necessarily excludes cowardice, even though it is not merely lack of cowardice.

Extreme cowardice, that is, abandoning a reasonable course of action, perhaps even acting irrationally, when faced with a low risk of evil, or a risk of a small evil, may cease to be a vice and become a pathological condition, such as a phobia. There is no sharp line between having a pathological condition and having a personal vice. This is true not only of cowardice, but also of intemperance and imprudence, indeed of all personal vices. It is often not clear whether an action exemplifies a genuine volitional disability or only a weakness of will. Even intemperance, which is sometimes simply described as weakness of will, may be a volitional disability. This close connection between the personal vices and pathological states may explain the ambivalent attitude many bear toward those who exhibit the personal vices. Should their actions be disapproved or they pitied? Probably the best way to determine whether the cowardice, intemperance, or imprudence of a particular person is a personal vice or a volitional disability is to see if it manifests itself primarily when the interests of others suffer, or whether it is equally present when the person's own interests will suffer.

A courageous person responds reasonably to danger or when she is suffering from fear. Since fear is an emotion, this may produce an overlap between temperance and courage, and there are circumstances in which some responses to fear would be called intemperate, even though generally they are called cowardly. It should be no surprise that there is an overlap between the various personal virtues and vices, since what distinguishes one personal virtue from another is only the circumstance in which one normally exemplifies the virtue. What distinguishes one vice from another are the circumstances in which one acts irrationally or unreasonably. Circumstances cannot always be clearly distinguished, so it should not be surprising that there are occasions in which it is equally appropriate to praise a person as either temperate or prudent, and others where she may be condemned for either intemperance or cowardice.

When faced with some significant present danger it is usually courage, not temperance or prudence, that is called for. Courage does not require always facing the danger and attempting to overcome it. Some dangers are severe enough to make a rational person modify her plans, or even to give them up entirely. If being courageous always required trying to overcome every danger, it would not be a personal virtue. No rational person would want to have such a character trait. If courage is to be a personal virtue, it must consist in not allowing fear or danger to make one act unreasonably or irrationally. A courageous person must be one who after consideration of the danger involved acts in the reasonable way. She attempts to overcome it, if this seems most likely to benefit herself or those she cares about, and abandons her plans if this seems most beneficial. Only when understood in this way can courage be considered a personal virtue.

Courage seems to have a more intimate connection with the moral ideals than either temperance or prudence. It is more natural to associate temperance with the moral rules, for, as noted previously, intemperance often results in violation of a moral rule. Although prudence is required if one is to act according to the moral rules or follow the moral ideals most effectively, it does not seem intimately connected with either the moral rules or the moral ideals. Courage, though sometimes required to obey the moral rules, is most often required in order to follow the moral ideals. It takes courage to speak out against the immoral behavior of powerful people or to rescue people from dangerous situations. It is no wonder that courage has often been considered a moral virtue, for it is so often required by those who want to follow moral ideals. It is no wonder that it is often valued so highly, for it is a rare commodity, and that which is rare is generally highly prized. The courage generally shown by parents when their children are in danger shows quite clearly that courage is not isolated from the values one has. Courage can be had when a person values something enough. It is not, I think, a lack of courage that explains why so few people show it in the pursuit of moral ideals. Rather, it is that so few people care enough about following moral ideals.

Personal Virtues as the Mean between Two Extremes

It is interesting, although perhaps not important, that the three cardinal personal virtues seem to fit Aristotle's account of a virtue as the mean between two extremes.

Prudence is the mean between impulsiveness, too little concern for the future, and being overcautious, having too much concern for the future. The prudent person does not allow concern for the consequences of her actions to inhibit her, but neither does she ignore these consequences. It is quite appropriate to advise someone to care not too much, yet not too little for the future. As a bit of practical advice, it might even be worthwhile to tell her to aim at erring in the direction of that extreme toward which she is not naturally inclined. All of which suggests what Aristotle says.

Temperance also is plausibly described as a mean between two extremes: the extreme of intemperance or overindulgence, not controlling one's present desires and emotions, and the extreme of asceticism or Puritanism, refusing to satisfy any strong desire or display any strong emotion. Since this latter extreme, which is a kind of generalized masochism, generally does not result in harm to others, it is rarely remarked upon. However, it is quite common, and probably responsible for the loss of considerable amounts of pleasure. Intemperance is sometimes taken as the sole opposite of temperance, as if it were impossible to err by controlling one's present desires and emotions too much. A rational person would advise those for whom she was concerned to steer the middle course between indulging all of their present emotions and desires and indulging none of them. Again, it would be practical to tell them to err in the direction of that extreme toward which they are not naturally inclined.

The extremes between which courage lies are cowardice and rashness. The former consists in letting fear or danger dissuade one from carrying out one's plans even though, all things considered, it is reasonable to attempt to overcome the danger and proceed as planned. Rashness consists in trying to overcome some danger when, all things considered, it is unreasonable to try to do so. However, when a person refuses to do something rash, it is usually said that she is acting prudently rather than courageously. Conversely, even when it is reasonable to try to overcome some danger, a person is generally praised for courage rather than prudence when she acts reasonably in the face of danger. Thus, although prudence and courage both lead to the same action, since they are exemplified by different actions, they are sometimes thought to be incompatible.

Although courage is sometimes shown by the overcoming of fear, it is not necessary to fear in order to be courageous. Someone who recognizes the danger that she faces, but does not fear it, is no less courageous when she reasonably decides to face it than the person who does so even though she fears it. The action of the person who fears might be praised more highly, as it is a more difficult act, but the person who does not fear would be admired more, as being the kind of person one would prefer to be. A courageous person has the proper respect for the dangers she faces; she does not let them overawe her, nor does she ignore them. To do the former is to give up an opportunity to obtain some goods; to do the latter is to increase one's chances of suffering evil. As in the case of prudence and temperance, a rational person would advise a timid person to err on the side of rashness, a fearless person not to fear erring on the side of cowardice. For this is more likely to result in their achieving the mean of courage.

Relationship between the Personal Virtues and Morality

Saying that prudence, temperance, and courage are personal rather than moral virtues does not mean that all rational persons want these virtues only for their own self-interest. Although a rational egoist may desire these traits simply in order to benefit herself, a rational person who desires to act morally wants them in order to enable her to act morally. Prudence, temperance, and courage are not only an aid to the person pursuing her own self-interest, they are an equal aid to the person who seeks to act morally. Although prudence, temperance, and courage are personal rather than moral virtues, not only do they not conflict in any way with moral action, they are essential for having the moral virtues. In real life, no one has the moral virtues without the personal virtues, for the personal virtues are necessary for reliable moral action. However, it is not uncommon for a person to have the personal virtues without the moral ones.

I am distinguishing between the personal virtues and the moral ones in order to make clear that the former have no necessary connection with being moral. A person may be prudent, temperate, and courageous and yet be thoroughly immoral. People may hesitate to call an immoral person prudent, temperate, or courageous, because to assign a personal virtue to a person is to praise him, and people hesitate to praise immoral persons. Unfortunately, there is no doubt that a person can have all the personal virtues without having any moral ones. Such persons are extremely dangerous, especially if they are not merely self-interested, but are leaders of some large national, racial, or religious group. However, it should not be forgotten that although the personal virtues should be distinguished from the moral virtues, realistically it is impossible for a person to have the moral virtues without also having the personal ones. This is one explanation of the mistaken inclination to regard the personal virtues as moral ones.

I have defined a personal virtue in a negative way and a personal vice in a positive way. A personal vice is allowing something like a strong emotion to make one act unreasonably, and the corresponding personal virtue is not allowing that thing to make one act unreasonably. However, I have also described a personal virtue as acting reasonably in certain kinds of situations and the corresponding personal vice as acting unreasonably in that kind of situation. It may seem that there is no difference in these two different ways of describing personal virtues and vices, but, in fact, the first way is far more precise. Acting unreasonably is acting contrary to what are clearly the best reasons. The first account of personal virtues and vices makes clear that the vice consists in allowing something in the situation to make one act contrary to what are the best reasons. If one never acts according to the best reasons when those reasons concern the interests of others, one does not have a personal vice, but a moral one. That the same unreasonable action can be explained by both a moral vice and a personal one is another explanation why the two are sometimes not distinguished from each other.

Virtues and the Nature of Persons

The attitude that a rational person takes toward the moral virtues, and hence toward the moral rules and ideals, as well as the attitude she takes toward the personal virtues, depends upon the nature of persons. If persons were not vulnerable, that is, could not be caused by others to suffer the evils that the first five rules prohibit causing, then these rules would be pointless. If they also could not be prevented from gaining goods, the second five rules would also lose their point, and if they could not be helped to avoid harms or gain goods, the moral and utilitarian ideals would lose their point. Thus there would also be no point in acquiring the moral virtues. Further, if people could not suffer any evil at all nor act to gain any goods, there would be no point in acquiring the personal virtues. That persons can be caused by others to suffer the evils that the first five moral rules prohibit causing is a fundamental fact that plays an essential role in any adequate account of morality. This can be seen most clearly by imagining a world in which impartial rational beings would not favor obedience to any of the first five moral rules.

In such a world, the beings must be such that they cannot be killed. If they die, they die from internal causes that cannot be affected by others or themselves. These beings would certainly have no need for a rule against killing, if they could even understand such a rule. Suppose further that these beings can suffer no physical pain. This is relatively easy to imagine, there now being some human beings who, due to a defect in their nervous system, feel no pain, others, who never suffer anxiety, sadness, or displeasure. These beings are so insensitive to the words or actions of others that they would have no use for the second rule, "Do not cause pain." Suppose also that these beings cannot disable each other or deprive each other of freedom. Imagine further that they desire and get pleasure from nothing but contemplating the mysteries of the universe and no one can deprive them of this pleasure. The third, fourth, and fifth rules now become pointless, and perhaps unintelligible.

It is not clear that the beings described in the previous paragraph are rational beings. According to the description, they do nothing except, perhaps, contemplate aloud. Nothing distinguishes this verbal behavior from a recording. These beings have no desires or aversions that can be affected by anyone. They show no purposive activity; in fact, they need show no activity at all. However, in order to make this imaginary world even slightly plausible, suppose that they do engage in verbal activity. But even this is limited. They cannot interfere with one another at all. They cannot deprive one another of pleasure by talking too loudly and destroying the pleasures of contemplation. These imaginary beings are completely independent of anyone else. They can neither be helped nor harmed in any way by anyone. Even if they are aware of others, they are completely indifferent to them. Such beings, which seem to be regarded as ideals by some religions, and even some philosophers, are certainly quite different from human beings. They can be regarded as rational beings only by providing them with a history. So imagine a group of beings like those that Shaw presents in *Back to Methuselah*, beings who hatch from eggs as something like normal but very wise adult human beings, and then become more and more independent of each other. Then allow for changes over many generations until the beings have the characteristics described above.

302 Virtue, Metaethics, and Political Philosophy

Even with such a history it is still not clear that such beings should be regarded as rational beings. Even if they were, it is quite clear that the first five moral rules would have no application in a world populated solely by such beings. These rules have application only to people who can be caused to suffer the evils that the first five moral rules prohibit causing. It is pointless to have a rule "Do not kill" when no one can be killed. Similarly it is pointless to say "Do not cause pain" when no one can suffer pain, or "Do not disable, deprive of freedom or deprive of pleasure" when it is impossible to do so. These beings are such that none of the first five rules has any point with regard to them. The questions that now arise are "Do any of the second five rules or the moral ideals have any point?" and "Is there any point in acquiring the virtues, moral or personal?"

In this world, the second five moral rules are justified, that is, all impartial rational persons adopt the moral attitude toward them, because general violation of them always results in an increase in the suffering of evils or a decrease in the gaining of goods. In the world being imagined no one can suffer any of the evils prohibited by the first five moral rules nor be prevented from gaining any goods. Hence this justification of the second five moral rules no longer holds. Is there any other justification for these rules? Not only does there seem to be no justification for the second five moral rules, but given this world of completely independent beings, there seems to be no justification for having any rules governing one's behavior toward others at all. It is pointless to have such rules if no one benefits from them. It is equally pointless to encourage behavior on the moral ideals if no one can be benefited. In the world now being imagined no one benefits from anyone following either moral rules or moral ideals. It follows immediately that there is no justification for the moral virtues, for all of the moral virtues are connected with the moral rules or ideals, and these are pointless in a world where no one can cause, relieve, or prevent any evil or any good for anyone.

The pointlessness of the second five rules, and consequently of the moral virtues associated with them, can be seen most clearly by slightly modifying this imaginary world of invulnerable beings. Imagine a slightly earlier stage of these beings. At this stage, they remember what it was like when they could be seriously harmed by others. Now in their joy at being free from the necessity to follow any rules, moral or otherwise, they take pleasure in deceiving, breaking promises, cheating, disobeying the law, and neglecting their duties. These beings therefore differ from the beings described in the previous example. They take pleasure in something other than mere contemplation of the world. Apart from this change, and any further changes that are required by this change, they are the same as the beings described in the previous example. No one ever suffers any evil as a consequence of deception, a broken promise, being cheated, a law being broken, or a neglected duty.

In this situation would an impartial rational being adopt the moral attitude toward the second five rules, or the acquiring of the associated virtues? There seems to be no reason why she would. No one has anything to gain from universal obedience to the second five rules or having the associated moral virtues. Of course, having read Kant, they may know that it is impossible for everyone to deceive all of the time, never to keep a promise, and so on. Being aware that universal deception, breaking promises, and so on is impossible, self-frustrating, or unintelligible, an impartial rational being in this imaginary world would favor sufficient obedience to the rules so that it is possible to break them. But since the whole point of establishing the rules is simply to provide the opportunity to violate them, no impartial rational being would favor everyone always obeying them.

Gaining Goods and Avoiding Evils Necessary for Virtues to Have a Point

The possibility of avoiding, causing, or preventing goods and evils to oneself or those for whom one is concerned is also what makes prudence, temperance, and courage worthwhile. Even a virtue such as patience lacks a point in a world without any possibility of suffering any evils or gaining any additional goods. All of the other personal virtues would become as useless as patience in a world without the possibility of suffering evils or gaining goods. If no one benefits from being concerned with the future, controlling one's desires, or facing any danger, then prudence, temperance, and courage lose their significance. It is the possibility of suffering evils and gaining goods, primarily the former, that gives a point to the acquiring of the moral and personal virtues. This may explain why some religious thinkers "solve" the problem of evil by claiming that evil is necessary for the cultivation of those character traits, including both the moral and personal virtues, that are now valued so highly. Of course, these character traits are valued so highly precisely because there is so much evil in the world, so this "solution" does not have much force.

Changing the original imaginary world so as to allow the beings to deprive each other of the pleasure of contemplation by talking very loudly makes most if not all of the virtues become possible. For example, these beings might carelessly talk too loudly when particularly excited by something they were contemplating. This might invite reprisals by others. The virtue of temperance would now be desirable. Since reprisals might provoke counterreprisals, prudence would also be called for. It may be inappropriate to talk of courage, but fortitude would be possible. It is now even possible to imagine some organization in which certain beings were designated as officials whose duty is to warn those who begin talking too loudly and to punish those who do not heed their warnings. It is not clear if the possibility of all the moral virtues could be generated in this simple world, but it is clear that some of them could be. The point of this example is to show that very little evil is required before some of the moral and personal virtues become possible again.

Adding the possibility of pain to this world by supposing that certain kinds of talk not only deprive of pleasure but actually inflict pain makes all of the moral and personal virtues become justified again. Perhaps this accounts, in part, for the view of the classical utilitarians that morality is concerned only with pleasure and pain. In the imaginary world under consideration, the utilitarians would not be so far wrong, but in the real world, their view is vastly oversimple. Not only is there the matter of life and death, but the ways in which one person depends on and can interfere with another are vastly more complex. Morality must be understood with reference to the real world, not with reference to some more simple imaginary world.

The Inadequacy of Kant's Categorical Imperative

Consideration of the above imaginary world shows the inadequacy of using the lack of formal universalizability as conceived by many philosophers, especially Kant, as the criterion of an immoral action. In this imaginary world, it is as impossible to completely universalize deception, promise breaking, and so on, as in the actual world. Whereas in the actual world it is immoral ever to do these things simply because one feels like doing so, in the imaginary world, it is not. No impartial rational being in this world would favor evils being inflicted on someone because she violated one of the second five moral rules simply because she felt like doing so. However, all impartial rational beings might favor punishment for a course of action reminiscent of an ordinary violation of the moral rules. These beings would favor not violating the moral rules all of the time; they might even favor punishing those who did.

Punishment would consist in depriving the violator of the pleasure of violating any of the rules. No one would pay any attention to anything she says or does, thus eliminating the possibility of deception; no promises would be accepted; she would not be allowed to participate in any voluntary activities; she would be declared exempt from all laws and be excused from all duties. For the only evil that can be inflicted on these beings is to deprive them of the pleasure of breaking the moral rules. The strangeness of this punishment makes it clear that there would be another kind of activity for which these beings might favor punishment. This would be any unauthorized activity designed to keep others from violating the moral rules. Any being who prevented others from violating the moral rules would, in this strange world, herself be acting immorally. She would be unjustifiably violating the one moral rule that retained its point in this world, the rule "Do not deprive of pleasure."

In the course of a moral argument one sometimes says, "What would happen if everyone acted like that?" but this question is primarily rhetorical. For one thing, it is not even clear what the question means. In the strange world under consideration, it is possible to ask someone who lies, "What would happen if everyone acted like that?" Part of the ambiguity in the question becomes clear if she should reply, "Do you mean 'What would happen if I and everyone else lied every time we spoke?' or 'What would happen if everyone lied whenever they felt like it?' It is only if you mean the first that lying becomes impossible, or self-frustrating. If you mean the second, then nothing much may happen at all." Note that asking whether an impartial rational person in this world would publicly allow random violations of the second five rules yields the correct answer. All of them would publicly allow it, and so in this strange world such violations would not be immoral.

When violations of the second five moral rules are immoral, it is not because they are not universalizable, but because no impartial rational person would publicly allow such a violation. In considering whether or not to publicly allow such a violation, an impartial rational person is not concerned with what would happen if everyone actually were to commit such a violation or even if it is possible for everyone to actually commit this kind of violation. It is only the consequences of everyone knowing that they are allowed to commit such a violation that is required for moral impartiality. If no impartial rational person would publicly allow the violation, it is unjustifiable; if all impartial rational persons would publicly allow the violation, it is strongly justifiable; if some impartial rational persons would publicly allow the violation, it is weakly justifiable, but punishment for the violation may also be justifiable.

Why should impartial rational persons care if the maxim of their action satisfies Kant's categorical imperative: "Act only according to that maxim whereby you can at the same time will that it should become a universal law"? Despite Kant's metaphysical claims, it is the mistaken belief that satisfying the categorical imperative is essential for impartiality that gives the categorical imperative its force. Further, as discussed earlier, Kant does not provide a guide for determining the appropriate maxim that should be subjected to the categorical imperative. Almost any action can be claimed to be based on a maxim that one would universalize. If a person takes advantage of a situation to steal from a person richer than her, even though she is not poor, she can claim that the maxim for her action is "In order to increase one's income, take advantage of all opportunities." It may be objected that she has left out the important aspect of her action, that it involves stealing, but although Kant explicitly wants this aspect to be included, he never provides a list of morally relevant features that determine the kind of action that one must test for universalizability.[13] Kant neglects the first stage of moral reasoning, determining the kind of action, and concentrates on the second stage, determining the universalizability of the maxim. He provides no guide for determining what features must be included in the maxim to which the categorical imperative is to be applied.

The difficulty in applying the categorical imperative is only one of the things wrong with it. It is simply false that a rational person is acting immorally whenever she acts on a maxim that she would not favor everyone acting on. Even if a rational person would favor no one acting in some way, acting in this way need not be immoral; it may only be imprudent or cowardly. Only when one's action can be correctly described as a violation of a moral rule must an impartial rational person be able to favor everyone being publicly allowed to act in this way. Advocating that everyone know that they are allowed to violate the rule in these circumstances is sufficient; there is no need to be able to will that everyone actually violate the rule in those circumstances. It is absurd to demand that every maxim a moral person acts on be one that she would, or even could, will to be a universal law. No one would think it is a moral requirement if they realized that it is not required for acting impartially. Even if an action is a violation of a moral rule, what makes it morally unacceptable is not that it cannot be universalized, but that it cannot be publicly allowed by any impartial rational person. Not surprisingly, only the latter is necessary for moral impartiality.

Kant's categorical imperative is of limited value for discovering or testing moral rules. It is not even adequate for testing what counts as a justifiable violation of a moral rule, although it is closer to the mark for this task. However, even when considering violations of a moral rule the categorical imperative is a misleading test of moral impartiality. Moral impartiality is not achieved by considering what would happen if everyone were actually to do a kind of action, but by considering what would happen if everyone knew that they were allowed to do that kind of action. However, unless an action is a violation of a moral rule, everyone already knows that they are allowed to do that kind of action. Thus the only kind of action for which moral impartiality is important is a violation of a moral rule. The kind of violation that no impartial rational person would publicly allow is the kind of action that if it were publicly allowed, would make it more likely that there will be an increase in the suffering of evil.

Humility and Arrogance

The words of the prophet Micah, "What doth the Lord require of thee, but to do justly, to love mercy, and to walk humbly with thy God," are a stirring testimony to the support that religion can give to morality, and to the dangers that attend such support.[14] For Micah, the Lord commands everyone to do what is morally right and love what is morally good, and thus he provides a powerful support for morality. The Lord also requires one to walk humbly with him, and Micah does not distinguish this requirement from the requirements of morality. One may be led to think that a person who does not fulfill this last requirement is to be condemned in the same way as one who does not fulfill the first two, leading atheism to be condemned as immoral. As Hobbes, however, clearly pointed out, there is no ground for calling the atheist unjust. Believing in God and acting morally do not necessarily go together; people can do either one without doing the other.

However, Micah's remark about walking humbly with God can be taken as extolling the virtue of humility. Humility, although of great importance, has been ignored in secular writings and misinterpreted in religious writings. It is not itself a moral virtue, for it has no direct conceptual connection with either the moral rules or the moral ideals. Rather, it incorporates a way of viewing the world and one's place in it that is necessary for a rational person achieving the moral virtues. Humility involves recognition of one's fallibility and vulnerability. Given the traditional relationship that humility has to belief in God, I shall call it a spiritual virtue, but as I understand humility, it is independent of whether one believes in God. Humility as it relates to morality involves a realization that one shares all the morally significant characteristics of all other moral agents, especially the characteristics of fallibility and vulnerability. It involves a recognition that morality applies to oneself in the same way that it applies to every other moral agent. It is the ground of moral impartiality, and as such may be the foundation of all of the moral virtues.

This analysis of humility fits the context of Micah's remark, and explains how humility is linked with justice and mercy. In this context, humility must be taken as very significant, for justice and mercy (which Hobbes calls charity and I call kindness) together comprise all the moral virtues. Its contrary is arrogance, the view that one is exempt from some or all of the moral requirements to which all other moral agents are subject. Not all immoral actions are due to arrogance; many are simply due to lack of sufficient concern with others. Arrogance is primarily responsible for those large-scale immoral actions that are done by the best and the brightest, and is also responsible for much unjustified paternalistic behavior. Arrogance consists in viewing oneself as not subject to the constraints that morality imposes on all rational persons. Humility consists in recognizing that, no matter who one is or what one has accomplished (for humility is not inconsistent with pride), morality still applies to oneself as it does to everyone else.

Humility and arrogance involve more than an attitude toward the constraints of morality; they involve a general attitude toward one's place in the world. Someone with humility recognizes that he is never a sufficient condition for his own successes. He realizes that an overwhelming number of events could have happened, which he had no part whatsoever in preventing, that would have made his successes impossible. He is keenly aware of his dependence not only on the physical world but also on the social world. He knows that he cannot even take complete credit for being the kind of person he is, that his family and school and society were indispensable factors in his being who he is and his being able to do what he does. He appreciates his dependence on others and realizes that in the most fundamental respects he is like everyone else. Hence he is never condescending to anyone and not only abides by the constraints that morality imposes on everyone, he does so willingly.

The arrogant person does not appreciate his dependence on others; he regards himself as a self-made person. Of course, no rational person can deny his dependence on the physical world, or even on the social world, but the arrogant person does not regard himself as dependent on them in the same way as others. He may hold that he has been singled out by God as worthy of special consideration, or he may simply ignore how much he owes to others. He arrogates to himself the credit that belongs to others. He does not recognize that in the most fundamental respects he is like everyone else. Rather, he regards himself as different from others, as not bound by the same rules that they are bound by. He is therefore unwilling to abide by the same constraints that morality imposes on everyone. Understanding humility and arrogance in this way helps one to appreciate why Micah appropriately links humility with justice and mercy.

Humility involves the recognition that one is subject to the same constraints of morality as every other rational person. Humility also involves the recognition that all moral agents are competent to engage in moral reasoning and should be afforded the full protection of morality. This account of humility explains why humility results in treating all moral agents with dignity and respect.[15] Arrogance involves the belief that one is not subject to the same public system that applies to all other rational persons. This accounts for the ordinary view about arrogance as well as explaining some otherwise very paradoxical relationships. On this account of arrogance it is quite clear why arrogance leads to immoral behavior. It is also quite clear why great wealth or power leads to arrogance. The arrogance of those with superior intelligence, great beauty or talent, or high social status is also easily understood. Less obvious, but made clear by this account, is why sincere and devout religious belief can lead to arrogance, as can any belief in the importance and righteousness of one's cause, political or scientific. Even the paradoxical arrogance born of despair is explained; one may believe that one has suffered so much that one is no longer subject to the constraints of morality.

Notes

1. *Leviathan*, chap. 15, para. 40. However, Hobbes, unlike most other philosophers, clearly distinguishes between moral and personal virtues. See *De Cive*, chap. 3, sec. 32.

2. It should be kept in mind that when I say that all rational persons, or all impartial rational persons, agree, I mean those persons who use only rationally required beliefs. As I pointed out earlier, if rationally allowed beliefs are included, it is impossible to reach any agreement. Religious beliefs are rationally allowed, but they can lead a rational person, even an impartial rational person, to make judgments that are incompatible with those she would make if she used only rationally required beliefs.

3. Oddly enough, perhaps as a result of cognitive dissonance, it seems that lesser punishments are often more effective than greater ones in training children.

4. See my article "Virtues and Moral Rules—A Reply," *Philosophia* 26, nos. 1–2 (July 1998): 1–6.

5. This is sometimes recognized by those who put forward a virtue theory of morality. For example, Rosalind Hursthouse, in her article, "Virtue Theory and Abortion," *Philosophy and Public Affairs* 20 (1991): 223–264, reprinted in *The Problem of Abortion*, 3rd ed., edited by Susan Dwyer and Joel Feinberg (Belmont, Calif.: Wadsworth, 1997); 150–159, explicitly "allows for the possibility that two virtuous agents faced with the same choice in the same circumstances may act differently" (150).

6. If it turns out that the paradigm examples of virtues and vices are not affected in any significant way by the free, intentional, voluntary actions of the persons who have them, then this would be equivalent to discovering that atoms could be split. Although this would not change the paradigm examples, not only would the present understanding of virtue and vice be dramatically altered but our whole understanding of morality would have to be changed.

7. Indeed many virtue theorists take this to be an essential feature of virtues. For example, in "Virtue Theory and Abortion" Rosalind Hursthouse is simply stating a standard view when she says, "A virtue is a character trait that a human being needs to flourish or live well." This standard view is the result of the failure to distinguish clearly between the moral and the personal virtues. It is a correct feature of the personal virtues, but unfortunately, it is not true of the moral virtues. One can be misled into thinking it is true only by adopting a radical ethical relativism. In any normal sense of flourishing or living well, a person can flourish or live well without obeying the moral rules impartially with regard to all moral agents. If he obeys them with regard to those for whom he is concerned, and that group is large enough, he can flourish or live well even though he consistently and unjustifiably violates the moral rules with regard to people outside of that group, and so does not have the moral virtues. The importance of distinguishing between the moral and personal virtues will be discussed further in this chapter and in chapter 13.

8. Since having either a moral virtue or vice requires being significantly different from others, it may be impossible to favor everyone having a moral virtue, even though it is possible to favor no one having a moral vice. What impartial rational persons favor is everyone having a character trait that now corresponds to a moral virtue, although if everyone had it, it would not be called a virtue any more.

9. See Thomas Hobbes, *De Homine*, chap. 13, sec. 9.

10. See "It's Over, Debbie: A Piece of My Mind," *JAMA* 259, no. 2 (1988): 272, for an excellent example of how a misunderstanding of morality can allow compassion to combine with arrogance to result in the morally unacceptable action of killing a suffering patient about whom one has almost no knowledge.

11. See *Nicomachean Ethics*, chaps. 2–5.

12. The former way is not quite correct, for a rational person need not want other people to have the moral virtues if this means he wants them to act morally with regard to everyone. This problem is parallel to a rational person's attitude toward the moral rules, which, before additional constraints were added, was an egocentric attitude, not the moral attitude.

13. See Immanuel Kant, *Critique of Practical Reason*, translated by Lewis White Beck (New York: Bobbs-Merrill, 1956), 27.

14. Book of Micah, chap. 6, verse 8.

15. To treat people with dignity and respect is to treat them as having the full protection of morality and as competent to engage in moral reasoning. This topic is also discussed in chapter 13, "Why Should I Be Moral?"

Chapter 12

Moral Judgments

As shown in the first chapter, all previous accounts of moral judgments are inadequate because they provide no clear distinction between moral and nonmoral judgments. These linguistic or metaethical accounts are unable to provide a clear distinction because they are primarily theories about the purposes of making moral judgments, not about the content of these judgments.[1] The various linguistic theories of moral judgments are thus not mistaken accounts of the nature of moral judgments, rather they are accounts of the way that many judgments, including moral judgments are used. Since nonmoral judgments, such as financial and prudential judgments, have many of the same functions as moral judgments, what the various linguistic accounts say about moral judgments applies equally well to many kinds of nonmoral judgments. Thus, all of these theories have something of value to say about the functions and purposes of making moral judgments, even if they do not distinguish moral judgments from nonmoral judgments.

In this chapter I am primarily concerned with those features of moral judgments that distinguish them from nonmoral judgments. It is no accident that previous accounts of moral judgments were not concerned with this task, for most previous accounts of morality described it solely in terms of its form or its function without mentioning its content. Only after providing a clear account of morality, identifying the moral rules, ideals, and virtues and distinguishing them from other kinds of rules, ideals, and virtues, is it possible to distinguish moral judgments from nonmoral judgments. Moral judgments are judgments that are made on the basis of these features of morality; they can, of course, be mistaken, but the paradigm cases of moral judgments are those that are correctly made by using the moral system. A judgment that is regarded by its maker as being completely unrelated to the moral system is not a moral judgment.

Linguistic Theories of Moral Judgments

All of the linguistic theories of moral judgments, that is, those theories that state the function of moral judgments, are correct; at least, they are all correct if they are understood as providing one of the purposes of making moral judgments. They are not correct if taken as providing the sole function of moral judgments, for moral judgments are used for a variety of purposes. In what follows, I shall briefly summarize several of the more prominent linguistic theories, trying to show that all of them do correctly describe one or more of the functions of moral judgments. One of my aims in doing this is to show that all of these theories are compatible with my account of morality as an informal public system that applies to all rational people. This account allows for judgments based on the moral system to serve a wide variety of functions.

The imperative theory regards moral judgments as a special kind of command and points to the fact that moral judgments are primarily used to tell people what to do or, more frequently, what not to do. This theory is most persuasive for moral judgments made to someone who is considering whether to act in a certain way. Judgments such as "You ought to do it" or "You shouldn't do that" do resemble commands in many ways. However they are more plausibly regarded as giving advice, for these judgments are often given in response to questions like "What should I do?" which are requests for advice. The moral judgments that are closer to commands are those containing the word "must," such as "You must give back the money now."[2] The imperative theory taken together with the account of morality as an informal public system that applies to all rational persons provides an adequate account of some uses of moral judgments.

The commending theory is most persuasive for moral judgments about people. Moral judgments like "She is a good person" and "He has a bad character" do resemble the kinds of evaluations we make of plays, paintings, tools, and so on. Although this theory acknowledges that moral judgments are made upon the basis of standards, it does not distinguish moral standards from nonmoral ones. It allows for the standards to be universal or relative to a culture, or even based on the preferences of an individual. Like the previous linguistic theory, this theory, taken together with the account of morality as an informal public system that applies to all rational persons, is an accurate account of the way that some moral judgments are used.

The emotive theory regards moral judgments as expressions of our emotions or feelings. This theory is most persuasive when we consider those moral judgments such as "But cheating is wrong!" which are not intended to provide new information to someone but rather to register our feelings about what is being done. Suppose one sees a good friend cheating or about to cheat. Telling her that cheating is wrong is clearly an expression of one's feelings, not an attempt to inform her of something she did not know, and it is probably also an attempt to influence her not to cheat. The emotive-imperative theory is an explicit recognition of the close connection between expressing one's feelings and trying to influence the way someone else behaves. When taken as an account of the function of some moral judgments, this theory is also compatible with the account of morality as an informal public system that applies to all rational persons.

Although all of these linguistic theories are compatible with an account of morality as an informal public system that applies to all rational persons, they were put forward by those who did not have such an account. The proponents of these theories regarded the existence of unresolvable disagreements in the moral judgments made by different people as showing that there was no moral system that applied to all people. They did not consider that a universal moral system might be an informal public system and hence allow for some unresolvable disagreements. It is remarkable that the existence of a relatively small number of unresolvable disagreements was taken as conclusive evidence against a universal morality, while the existence of the overwhelmingly greater agreement in moral judgments was not taken as any evidence in favor of a universal morality.

Given the motivation for these theories, it is not surprising that none of them adequately accounts for moral judgments made in response to questions like "Was Kant a good person?" or "Was lying the right thing to do in that situation?" These questions seem to be genuine questions, not requests for imperatives, commendations, or expressions of feeling. This focus on moral judgments as responses to questions has led some to regard moral judgments as statements of fact. Those who held this kind of theory usually did accept a universal morality, but there is no necessary connection between these two positions. The theory of moral judgments as stating facts is most persuasive when characterizing moral judgments that are made in the context of a philosophical or historical discussion. In these discussions, an account of the morally relevant features of a situation is provided and the judgment that is offered as a conclusion is very like stating a fact. The linguistic account that takes moral judgments as stating facts provides an accurate account of some uses of moral judgments. Like all of the previous linguistic theories, it is compatible with the account of morality as an informal public system that applies to all rational persons. Indeed, none of the current theories of realism, quasi-realism, antirealism and so on is incompatible with this account of morality, for, like the overtly linguistic theories, none of these theories is about morality either; they are only theories about the linguistic character of various kinds of judgments, including moral judgments.

The examples of moral judgments given in the preceding paragraphs contain the words "ought," "shouldn't," "good," "bad," "wrong," "right," and "must." However, it is not because they contain these words that they are moral judgments. In fact, less than five percent of the judgments containing these words are moral judgments, most are prudential or aesthetic, and so on, and most moral judgments do not even contain these words. Rather than simply tell someone that he ought to do something, we usually say something more specific; "You promised to do it" or "It is your duty to do it." Similarly, in making moral judgments about people, we do not generally say that they are good or bad but something more specific, that they are kind and trustworthy, or cruel and deceitful.[3] Moral judgments about actions also generally contain more specific terms than "right" or "wrong," as in "That would be cheating." It is primarily in philosophical discussions of morality that these general terms are used. In everyday life the general terms used in moral judgments are more likely to be the kinds of terms that do not usually appear in books on moral philosophy, terms such as "He's a prince," "What a rotten thing to do," or statements regarded as unfit to print at all.

Distinguishing between Moral and Nonmoral Judgments: Overridingness

Although the linguistic theories of moral judgments are primarily different accounts of the purposes of making moral judgments, some of them attempt to distinguish moral judgments from nonmoral judgments by adding additional features, such as using the attitude of the person making the judgment. One such additional feature is that a judgment counts as a moral judgment if and only if the person making it is not only willing to universalize his judgment but is also prepared to act on the resulting universal principle. Being so prepared is taken as the defining condition of moral judgments that distinguishes them from all other kinds of value judgments that are also universalizable. According to this view, what makes a judgment a moral judgment is that its maker regards it as one that cannot be overridden; that is, the maker is always prepared to act on his moral judgments regardless of any conflicting nonmoral judgments.[4]

Overridingness is supposed to distinguish moral judgments from prudential, aesthetic, and legal judgments, which can sometimes be overridden by moral considerations. A moral judgment, on the other hand, can never be overridden by nonmoral considerations, though it might be modified by other moral considerations. The claim that moral judgments are overriding either ignores the fact that many people take their religious judgments to override their moral judgments, for example, Kierkegaard's teleological suspension of the ethical, or it regards those religious judgments that are taken as overriding as moral judgments. Taking overridingness as the defining condition of moral judgments is incompatible with the view that morality has any objective content at all. If any judgment that a person takes as overriding is a moral judgment, then not only are judgments made by religious fanatics moral judgments, but so are the judgments of fanatical Nazis favoring the extermination of non-Aryans.

This view of moral judgments is a natural outcome of the account of morality as primarily intended to provide a guide for the individual person who adopts it. On this account, moral judgments express the motivation of the person who makes them, for a genuine moral judgment simply makes explicit a part of the guide the person has adopted for himself. This account of moral judgments denies that a hypocritical moral judgment can be a genuine moral judgment about the behavior of someone else when the person is not prepared to act on that judgment herself. Realizing that morality is a guide to behavior that rational persons put forward to govern the behavior of others, whether or not they plan to follow that guide themselves, makes it clear that a person need not be motivated to act according to his own moral judgments. A person making a genuine moral judgment really does want others to act on the judgment, even though he is not prepared to act on it himself. Such a judgment need not be a mere "inverted commas" moral judgment, simply stating what one's society regards as moral; rather it can be a judgment that one personally regards as morally correct.

If morality has the objective content that it has been shown to have, the view of moral judgments as overriding has a touching innocence. It assumes that everyone who makes moral judgments takes common morality as their supreme guide to conduct. It is as if someone who genuinely wants others to act morally, and makes the appropriate moral judgments, must also want himself to act in that way. Even if the overriding view is softened by allowing for weakness of will and regret that one did not act as one judges people morally ought to act, it is still too strong. It denies that there are any people who want others to act morally, but who do not care whether or not their own behavior is in accord with common morality. The mistaken account of morality as a guide one adopts for oneself has given rise to the mistaken view of moral judgments as necessarily expressing one's intention to act according to this judgment. But hypocrites not only make genuine moral judgments, they generally make correct ones, which is why people are urged not to be hypocritical, but rather to act on their moral judgments.

Although there is a distinction between moral judgments and judgments that merely seem to be moral judgments, this distinction is not based on whether or not the person is prepared to act on his judgment. Moral judgments must be based on a public system that applies to all moral agents. Someone may mistakenly regard his judgment that people ought to refrain from eating meat on Fridays or from working on Saturday as a moral judgment. He may act on that judgment himself, want everyone to act on it, and even regard it as overriding, but if he admits that this judgment is based on a code of conduct that is not known by all moral agents, it is not a moral judgment. If he regards his judgment as based on some revelation or scripture known only to members of a religion, then his judgment is a religious judgment, not a moral one. A basic moral judgment cannot be based on a system that some moral agents do not know or which it would be irrational for some of them to act on. Judgments based on the legal code of a society, especially if it is the kind of legal code present in relatively small societies, are often called moral judgments, for they are usually made about moral matters. But these judgments are best regarded, not as moral judgments, but as personal legal judgments, for they are based on the legal code of that society and could not be part of a public system that applies to all rational persons.

Moral Judgments versus Judgments on Moral Matters

Although moral judgments are made about actions, intentions, motives, persons, policies, and organizations, the moral judgments that are made about actions are fundamental. All of the other moral judgments rest on this foundation. I intend what I say about moral judgments to apply to intentions, motives, persons, policies, and organizations, but I shall identify the subject matter of moral judgments by talking primarily about actions. However, moral judgments about intentions, motives, persons, policies, and organizations are judgments about this same subject matter. Moral judgments are limited to the actions of those to whom the moral system applies, namely, moral agents. Moral judgments cannot be made about the actions of mosquitoes or monkeys. Of the actions of moral agents, moral judgments can be made only about those that affect beings that are protected by morality and are covered by some moral rule or moral ideal. All and only actions by moral agents affecting beings that are protected by morality and that are covered by some moral rule or ideal are "moral matters." A moral judgment must be about a moral matter. Since people disagree about the scope of morality, they will also disagree about whether or not judgments about actions that affect nonmoral agents are moral judgments. But if a being is protected by morality, then any action by a moral agent that is governed by a moral rule or ideal that affects this being counts as a judgment about a moral matter.

This allows for three kinds of disputes about whether a judgment is really a judgment about a moral matter. (1) The action may not be by a moral agent; (2) it may not be covered by a moral rule or moral ideal; or (3) it may not affect beings that a rational person regards as protected by morality. It is more than a theoretical possibility that people can be mistaken about whether or not something is a moral matter, that is, the proper object of a moral judgment. There can be a dispute about whether a child or a retarded adult is a moral agent. This dispute is closely related to the dispute about what counts as an excuse for violating a moral rule and is discussed in the section on responsibility standards in this chapter.

Those who deny that various sexual practices, such as homosexual behavior, are immoral are best understood as denying that homosexual behavior is covered by a moral rule or ideal. They claim that those who say that homosexual behavior is condemned by scriptures are not making a moral judgment but a religious or personal legal one. They hold that these people are mistaken even in thinking that they are making a judgment about a moral matter. For this kind of behavior is not covered by a moral rule or ideal, that is, a rule or ideal that is part of a public system that applies to all rational persons. The debate is complicated because those who claim that homosexual behavior is immoral may be claiming not that it is immoral per se, but that it is immoral only because it is contingently related to some other matter that is a moral matter, such as the increased risk of AIDS.

There is a genuine question whether or not judgments about some environmental matters are judgments about moral matters. Some people claim that independent of its effects on any sentient beings, it is wrong to destroy trees. It may be environmentally wrong to do so, or spiritually or religiously wrong, but if there is no effect on any sentient beings, then it is not a judgment about a moral matter. For a judgment about a moral matter must be about beings that a rational person regards as protected by morality. Of course, in the real world the destruction of trees, especially of whole forests, always has significant effects on sentient beings, especially when it is recognized that these sentient beings need not be human beings. So claiming that destroying trees is wrong can be a moral judgment, but it is a moral judgment only if it is related to its foreseeable effects on sentient beings.

Judgments about homosexual activity, like judgments about environmental matters, or about any other kind of behavior, are moral judgments only when they are judgments about moral matters. They must concern behavior by moral agents that is covered by a moral rule or moral ideal toward beings protected by morality. But these are not sufficient conditions for characterizing a judgment as a moral judgment, only as a judgment about a moral matter. Taking all judgments about moral matters to be moral judgments may be what leads many to mistakenly regard personal legal judgments about moral matters, that is, judgments about moral matters based on a society's legal code, as moral judgments. But moral judgments must not only be about moral matters, they must also be based on the moral system.

A moral judgment must be believed, at least when challenged, to be one that could be made by an impartial rational person on the basis of a public system that applies to all rational persons. Either it must be a judgment that itself is understood and could be accepted by all impartial rational persons, what I call a "basic moral judgment," or it must be related to a basic moral judgment in an appropriate way. One appropriate way is for the judgment to be restated as a basic moral judgment by replacing more specialized terms with more general terms, for example, "trigeminal neuralgia" by "severe facial pain." Another way is for the judgment to be deducible from a basic moral judgment together with what one believes to be true factual judgments. Moral judgments are mistaken if either the factual beliefs are false or the belief that the judgment could be made on the basis of a public system by an impartial rational person is false.

Moral judgments are not merely judgments made on moral matters, for people can make judgments on these matters without caring whether or not any impartial rational person using a public system that applies to all rational persons could make that judgment. In fact, people can make judgments on these matters that they know to be inconsistent with the judgment that would be made by any impartial person using a public system that applies to all rational persons. Indeed, such judgments are often made by racists and religious and nationalistic fanatics. They make judgments that they know could not be made on the basis of the moral system, but they do not care. Their judgments are based on their race, religion, or nation, which for them is overriding. It is important not to take overridingness as a criterion of moral judgments.

Unfortunately there has not been an adequate account either of a moral matter or of a moral judgment, so that the distinction between a moral judgment and a judgment on a moral matter has generally not been recognized. Some of the so-called analyses of moral judgments have not in fact been analyses of moral judgments, but merely analyses of judgments made on moral matters. Considered as an analysis of judgments made on moral matters, emotivism is extremely plausible, for many people's judgments on moral matters are simply expressions of their feelings that are aroused by consideration of the act they are judging. Many people do not even consider whether the judgment they are making is one that an impartial rational person could make, or rather they do not consider this unless their judgments are challenged. It is impossible to overestimate the amount of stupidity in the world. If emotivism is considered as an analysis of the unreflective judgments about moral matters, or what are taken as moral matters by many persons, it is probably correct.

The feelings that are aroused by consideration of an act about which a moral judgment is appropriate usually reflect the legal code of one's society. Ethical relativism is also largely correct if taken as an analysis of the way in which most people make judgments about moral matters, especially when considering unreflective judgments, that is, those made simply on the basis of the legal code of one's society. But not all judgments about moral matters are unreflective. After careful reflection, some people make judgments about moral matters that conflict with the legal code that expresses the dominant views in their society. Indeed, some people, though undoubtedly a very small number, make judgments about moral matters that conflict with the way they presently feel toward the act in question. There is often a considerable time lag between coming to see what the correct moral judgment about an act is and coming to feel toward that act the way one thinks one ought to feel.

If a person knows that no impartial rational person would agree with his judgment, then he is not making a moral judgment. But usually he does not know this. Usually he does not consider whether any impartial rational person could agree with his judgment. Sometimes one may even believe that some impartial rational person would agree with one's judgment, but further reflection convinces one that this is not the case. It is this latter case that is most appropriately called making a mistaken moral judgment. It is not surprising that people often make mistaken moral judgments. It is not always an easy matter to determine what judgments an impartial rational person could make. One must consider what judgment one could make if one did not know who the parties involved were, but knew only the morally relevant facts. Sometimes considering the act with the two parties reversed is helpful. But not always. A judge should not consider what judgment she would make if she were the criminal. What she must consider is what judgment she would make as an impartial rational person.

The distinction between moral judgments and judgments made about moral matters allows one to make a simple statement about moral progress. Moral progress occurs as judgments about moral matters become moral judgments. But this progress has practical significance only if these judgments are not hypocritical. It is generally not realized how many judgments about moral matters are not even intended to be moral judgments. Many people realize that no impartial rational person would agree with their judgments, but they do not care about this. They are not concerned with the possibility of agreement among all rational persons, only with the agreement among a very limited subset of them. In small simple societies, this often includes only the other members of the society. In large complex societies, it may not even include this many. Some people make judgments that could only be agreed to by people with a similar social status. Some people make judgments that could be accepted only by people of the same race or religion. Indeed, in large societies a person is usually considered highly moral if his judgments about moral matters could be agreed to by all members of his society. Since most of the moral matters that one makes judgments about concern only those people in one's society, it is easy to overestimate the extent of moral progress. A person whose judgments about domestic matters make him seem a most moral person often is seen not to be so when he makes judgments about foreign policy.

One of the lesser, but nonetheless significant, evils of war is the reversing of moral progress. People whose judgments about moral matters have been genuine moral judgments no longer make the same judgments. Especially when the moral rules are unjustifiably violated by their country, they make judgments that could not possibly be agreed to by any impartial rational person. They no longer care whether there could be agreement among all rational persons; they are concerned only with agreement among their fellow citizens. They even condemn as unpatriotic those who continue to make genuine moral judgments about such matters. Thus nationalism overwhelms morality, not only as the basis for action, but also as the basis for judgment about moral matters. Confusion about morality often allows nationalistic judgments to pass for moral ones, a confusion often not only supported by the leaders of the country but often shared by them. Sometimes, however, nationalism is explicitly put forward as superior to morality. "My country, right or wrong" is a slogan that war makes respectable even in most civilized societies. War often causes people to lose that decent respect for the opinion of humankind that morality demands.

"Morally Good" and "Morally Bad"

Whether a judgment is a moral judgment does not depend upon the words contained in it. A moral judgment can be made without actually saying anything at all; in some situations one can simply shrug one's shoulders. However, it may be useful to examine the kinds of moral judgments that have been the subject of so much philosophical writing. Although "good," "bad," "right," "wrong," "ought," and "should" are far more often used in making nonmoral judgments than in making moral judgments, examination of these words can be of some value in analyzing some moral judgments. For each of them does occur in moral judgments that can be used to represent a wide range of similar moral judgments. Showing how moral judgments using these words are related to the moral system may help to clarify the nature of particular moral judgments.[5]

An account of the use of "good" and "bad" in nonmoral judgments was provided in chapter 4, so that all that needs to be done now is to consider their use in moral judgments. Generally, an action is said to be morally good when it is not in violation of any moral rule and is encouraged by some moral ideal. However, strongly justified violations of a moral rule in order to follow a moral ideal are also normally considered to be morally good actions. The clearest cases of morally good actions are giving to or doing volunteer work for various charitable organizations such as UNICEF. Giving to museums, however, is generally following utilitarian rather than moral ideals. That supporting museums or opera companies is not following a moral ideal means only that doing so does not justify individuals' violating a moral rule; it does not mean that such support is not to be encouraged. Moral goodness is not the only kind of goodness, and a society in which no one follows utilitarian ideals would be an extremely unpleasant society.

Working for organizations like the American Civil Liberties Union is somewhat more complex. Insofar as these organizations seek to prevent the deprivation of freedom without themselves violating moral rules, they are clearly doing morally good actions. But sometimes such organizations follow moral ideals even when this involves violating a moral rule. If the violations were always strongly justified, there would be no problem, but sometimes they are only weakly justified. This latter situation makes it more difficult to characterize the actions. Although the organization always seeks to follow moral ideals, weakly justified violations are not always regarded as morally good. They are, not surprisingly, properly regarded as morally controversial actions, with those that favor the violation regarding them as morally good, and those who do not, regarding them as morally bad. Nonetheless, such organizations are usually morally good organizations, for much of what they do is morally good, even if controversial.

An unjustified violation of a moral rule is always morally bad, even if it is done in order to follow a moral ideal. The clearest cases of this in medicine are cases of unjustified paternalism, where a physician wants to prevent harm to her patient, but does so by violating a moral rule in a way that no impartial rational person could publicly allow. In science, a professor "giving" first authorship on a paper to a graduate student who did little or no work on it is often an example of acting on a moral ideal that involves an unjustified violation of a moral rule. The act is done in order to benefit the student, but it involves deceiving readers of the article and others who are evaluating the work of the student. The paradigm of a morally bad action is an unjustified violation of a moral rule, but failing to help someone avoid a significant harm when one is in a special position to do so and helping does not involve any significant personal sacrifice is often regarded as morally bad. Even when one has no duty to perform this kind of act, so that it does not involve breaking a moral rule, it is an indication of a bad moral character. In calling an action morally bad, the relationship with character is usually stressed.

Moral Judgments about Persons

A person is called just or righteous if he does what is morally wrong or bad significantly less often than most and does what is morally right significantly more often than most. Such a person, as Aristotle notes, will not be continually tempted to do what is morally wrong. In fact, it is doubtful that a person who was continually tempted would do what is morally wrong significantly less often than most. Although a just person may be tempted to do what is morally wrong from time to time, situations that would tempt most persons will most often not tempt her. Of two persons facing the same temptation, we may praise the morally right action of the person who is tempted more than we praise the morally right action of the person who is not, but we admire the character of the latter more. This is similar to two persons facing the same danger, where we praise the courageous action of the person suffering from fear more than we praise the courageous action of the person who is not, but admire the character of the latter more. When justice is combined with charity, or the just person is also kind, she is what I call a morally good person.

A morally good person is one who does morally bad actions significantly less often than most and does morally good ones significantly more often than most. In judging a person not only her actions but also her intentions and motives are relevant. A morally good person must intend to do morally good actions and intend to avoid morally bad ones. A person who unintentionally prevents harm to others and does not harm them simply because things do not turn out as she intends is not morally good. Although this kind of situation generally occurs only in slapstick movies, it is worth mentioning to avoid the false impression that it is the actual consequences of a person's actions that count toward her being judged morally good or bad. But actual consequences are important. A person who always tries to prevent harm but never does, is not generally thought of as morally good. Of such a person, it may be said that she means well; but, contrary to Kant, some results are necessary before she is regarded as morally good.

Good results, even if intentional, are not sufficient to make a person morally good; the appropriate motives are also important. A person who follows the moral ideals and obeys the moral rules, but does so solely or primarily from fear of punishment or desire of praise, is not usually considered a morally good person. A morally good person must do morally good actions and avoid doing morally bad ones for certain kinds of motives. These motives are not, as Kant maintained, limited to acting out of respect for the moral law; indeed, this motive is not even the primary motive for most morally good persons. The basic motive for morally good persons is concern for others. I will discuss the most important motives for being morally good in greater detail in the next chapter, on why one should be moral. For now it is sufficient to point out that a person is regarded as morally good if she intentionally does morally good actions and avoids morally bad ones, and her motive for doing this is one that can be depended on to operate even when she believes that no person will know about her action.

The use of "good," "bad," "better," and "worse" in moral judgments fits the general analysis of these terms used in judgments describing particular kinds of things. A good X is an X that all qualified rational persons would choose when they wanted an X for its normal function, unless they had an adequate reason not to. A bad X is an X that no qualified rational person would choose when they wanted an X for its normal function, unless they had an adequate reason to choose it. A morally good action is one that all qualified rational persons would choose to have performed, unless they had an adequate reason not to; a morally bad action is one no qualified rational person would choose to have performed, unless they had an adequate reason to choose it. A morally good person is one that all qualified rational persons would choose when they were selecting persons to be a member of their society, unless they had an adequate reason not to. A morally bad person is one no qualified rational persons would choose to be a member of their society, unless they had an adequate reason to choose him. Unless they had an adequate reason, all qualified rational persons would pick the morally better persons when choosing persons to be members of their society so that all qualified rational persons would select the morally good person over the morally bad one.

The above analyses make clear that moral judgments about actions and persons using the words "good" and "bad" fit the standard analysis of the use of "good" and "bad" in nonmoral judgments. In particular, the moral judgments of persons are very similar to judgments made of tools, and even more similar to judgments made of athletes. This similarity of judgments does not require that persons be regarded like tools, or even like athletes, performing a function of any sort. Nonetheless rational persons are primarily interested in the moral character of others because of the consequences for themselves and those for whom they are concerned. This is another consequence of the view that morality is a public guide that everyone wants others to follow.

Moral Standards

To call someone a morally good person, or even to call her a moral person, is to praise her. These praises are normally reserved for persons considered to be significantly better than persons usually are. I use the phrase "moral standards" to mean the standards used in determining how much moral praise or condemnation a person deserves. The higher the moral standard, the more morally right and good actions are required for a person to be praised as moral or morally good. The lower the moral standard, the more morally bad or wrong actions are required for a person to be condemned as immoral or morally bad. Rational persons who have higher expectations of how persons usually act will demand more of a moral person than someone who has lower expectations.

Since people's expectation of how persons do act determines how high or low their moral standards are, any narrowing of the range of acceptable moral standards must be accomplished by narrowing the range of acceptable expectations about how persons do act. This latter narrowing can be done, in part, by examining the way that persons actually act. If no person has ever lived a full life without committing some immoral actions, it is pointless to demand no immoral actions before we call a person moral. If the morally best person anyone has ever heard of spent only one-fourth of her time in following the moral ideals, it is absurd to demand that a morally good person devote half of her time to following the moral ideals. Moral standards should be determined, in part, by the findings of psychology, sociology, and anthropology. These sciences have relevance to morality by discovering how persons actually behave.

Even though moral standards are not determined by impartial rational persons, who have only rationally required beliefs, but by actual rational people with rationally allowed beliefs, it is tempting to claim that moral standards should be higher than they are. All impartial rational persons would favor people giving up at least some luxuries in order to provide others with necessities. They would certainly expect more people to be following moral ideals more often than they actually do. Almost no actual persons have an impartial concern for all; if any significant number did, moral standards would be much higher than they presently are. But to claim that the moral standards should be higher is somewhat misleading. Its most straightforward interpretation is that the moral judgments that are made of persons are usually wrong, for the wrong standards are being used. However, it is not clear that ceasing to call a significant number of people morally good will serve as any incentive for them to do more morally good acts. It is not inappropriate, however, to straightforwardly state that people should act on moral ideals more often than they do.

Moral Worth of Actions

Moral standards not only determine our moral judgments of people, but also those of particular actions. A judgment of the moral worth of an action is a judgment concerning how much the action indicates about the moral character of the person. Telling the truth when this has serious consequences for oneself is an action that has significant moral worth. Rescuing a child at great risk to oneself also has significant moral worth. Both of these actions are a strong indication of good moral character. A normal donation to charity involving no sacrifice has little moral worth, for it does not indicate much about the moral character of the person. Usually, to say that an action has moral worth means that it is an indication of a good moral character. An action that is a strong indication of bad moral character is not normally said to have negative moral worth, but rather simply to be morally bad. A morally bad action need not involve either the unjustified violation or the unjustified keeping of a moral rule, it can simply be a callous action, such as failing to act on a moral ideal in a situation when the normal expectation is that a person would do so.

I do not suggest that language is used with such precision, nor do I advocate, or even believe it possible, that it be used in this way in the future. However, I think the following may be of some value as a summary of the meaning of the phrases "morally good," "morally bad," "morally right," and "morally wrong" as applied to actions. *Morally good* actions are those that all impartial rational persons favor doing, but do not favor liability to punishment for not doing. *Morally bad* actions are those that all impartial rational persons favor not doing, without considering the question of punishment. *Morally right* actions are those that all impartial rational persons not only favor doing, but also generally favor liability to punishment for not doing. *Morally wrong* actions are those that all impartial rational persons not only favor not doing, but also generally favor liability to punishment for doing. The notions of morally right and morally wrong are connected with the notion of punishment, while the notions of morally good and morally bad are not usually connected with it. Despite this, it can be seen that "morally bad" and "morally wrong" can often be applied to the same actions, whereas "morally good" and "morally right" usually apply to quite different actions.

Responsibility Standards

Judgments about whether, or to what degree, a person is responsible for some action that falls under the scope of the moral system are judgments of blame and credit. In contrast with judgments of moral worth, which are usually made of morally good actions, judgments of responsibility are usually made of morally wrong actions. If a person is totally excused from responsibility for an action, then she gets no moral blame or credit for it; if she has a partial excuse, then she has to take some responsibility for the action, though not as much as someone who has no excuse. Talk about credit and blame usually occurs in situations where there is some question about whether or how much to hold a person responsible for their action or for the results of their action.

The standards that are used to determine how much credit or blame a person should get for a particular action are "responsibility standards." These standards are not used to make moral judgments, but to make judgments about what degree, if at all, a person should be subject to moral judgment, and perhaps even more importantly, judgments about what degree, if at all, a person should be subject to punishment. These standards are used in judging excuses. The standard punishment for a certain kind of violation of a moral rule, for example, attempting to kill a person, is designed for the person who is fully responsible. To judge that he is not completely responsible is to decide that his punishment should be somewhat less than the standard punishment. Which responsibility standards are adopted has significant consequences, because judging how much a person is to be blamed affects how much he is to be punished.

Blame and Credit versus Praise and Condemnation

The usual ways of talking about praise and blame have obscured the distinction between moral standards and responsibility standards. Praise is not the opposite of blame, but of condemnation, and is related to moral standards. Blame and its opposite, credit, are related to responsibility standards. It is easy to see how the confusion arose. To call a person morally good is to praise her. A person is praised as morally good only if she does morally good actions. But the amount of positive moral worth that her actions have depends upon her being responsible for them. If an action that normally has a certain amount of positive moral worth is one for which complete credit is not given, this will lessen the amount of moral worth. It will do so because by taking away some credit the action is no longer as strong an indication of the moral character of the person. Since the assignment of credit affects the assignment of moral worth, the two have not always been clearly distinguished. Similarly, how much a person is condemned for an immoral action will depend upon how much she is held responsible for it. Thus blame and condemnation are often not distinguished.

Praise and blame are mistakenly regarded as opposites because each is the dominant member of its pair. Judgments about moral worth are primarily made of morally right and morally good actions. All moral and morally good actions should be encouraged and ranking positive moral worth provides some extra incentive since rewards are not usually given for such actions. Degrees of punishment do provide a scale for ranking most immoral actions; hence there is little need for judging negative moral worth. Further, all immoral behavior should be discouraged; thus there seems to be little point in ranking negative moral worth. Judgments of responsibility are primarily concerned with morally wrong or morally bad actions, for there is little need to be concerned about assigning full responsibility for morally good actions; no one usually suffers if more credit is given than is deserved. It is important to be concerned about assigning responsibility for morally wrong actions, for someone suffers unjustifiably when she is blamed more than she deserves.

How much credit or blame a person deserves depends upon the strictness of the responsibility standards. The stricter the standards, the greater the excuse needed to reduce the amount of blame. Stricter responsibility standards may result in people taking more care not to act immorally, but they may also result in more punishment being inflicted on people. Whether or not these statements are true cannot be determined a priori, but only by a study of how people actually behave. Just as the proper amount of punishment is determined by seeing what comes closest to maximum deterrence with minimum infliction of evil, so the proper responsibility standards are those that most closely approach this ideal.

Just as with moral standards, psychology, sociology, and anthropology, are all relevant in determining the proper responsibility standards, for they may help determine what responsibility standards result in the least amount of evil suffered. But science cannot decide between two different standards that result in the same amount of evil being suffered. Some prefer stricter standards and fewer violations, although these are offset by an increase in the amount of punishment; others prefer more lenient standards, although the decrease in punishment is offset by an increase in violations. But of two standards, both equally effective in discouraging violations, the more lenient is the better. This is exactly parallel to determining the amount of punishment. It is unlikely that there is a unique determination of how much a given violation should be punished and people often disagree about how much a given person should be held responsible. This is why the question of what a person deserves has never been answered to everyone's satisfaction.

"Right" and "Wrong"

To show that the use of the words "right" and "wrong" in moral judgments is similar to their use in nonmoral judgments, an account of their use in nonmoral judgments must first be provided. In their nonmoral use, "correct" and "incorrect" mean the same as, and can even be substituted for, "right" and "wrong." In theoretical problems, an answer is right (correct) if all the people qualified to deal with this problem would agree on that answer. An answer is wrong (incorrect) if all qualified people would agree that it is not the answer. If there is unresolvable disagreement among qualified people, or if there is unresolvable disagreement about who counts as a qualified person, then there is no right answer to problem. However, lack of agreement on a right answer is completely compatible with complete agreement that almost all of the proposed answers are wrong. Thus lack of agreement on a right answer does not mean that anything goes, and such a lack of agreement is compatible with almost complete objectivity.

Disagreement about whether an answer is right may simply be a result of insufficient knowledge to settle the matter. This may be the result of a lack of knowledge of all the relevant facts or of appropriate techniques. However, in the absence of the agreement of all qualified people, continuing to maintain that a certain answer is right is doing no more than expressing one's feelings, unless one holds that some new technique or information will be found that will result in such agreement. A person who does not believe that any new information or techniques will lead all qualified people to agree with him should cease calling his answer right. If one cannot even describe a situation that will result in the agreement of all qualified persons, then calling an answer right or a statement true primarily expresses one's feelings. This is the point of the verifiability principle. The logical positivists claimed that when qualified rational persons cannot agree on an answer to a question, any answer that is given does not have cognitive meaning. Unfortunately the positivists also claimed that qualified rational persons would only agree on answers to empirical and mathematical or logical questions, as if all qualified rational persons would never agree that some particular decision about which course of action to take was wrong.

Answers to theoretical problems differ from answers to practical questions in that the rightness or correctness of the former are not regarded as determined by the conditions at a time. If an answer to a theoretical question is right, it is always right. Even if all qualified people at a given time agree that an answer is right, further knowledge may show that all of them were wrong. Of course, when all qualified people agree on an answer, it is called right, but this is always subject to revision if completely new information becomes available. On the other hand, the rightness or correctness of answers to practical questions are sometimes determined by the conditions at a time. Sometimes, when all qualified persons would make the same decision, the right decision can be known independent of its outcome. It is because of this kind of case that "right decision" does not mean simply "decision that has the best (actual) consequences."

Imagine a case in which all qualified persons would agree that a person who decides to stay in a burning building rather than to climb down the fire escape has made the wrong decision, the person herself included. Yet it may be that the desired result, saving her life, was in fact achieved by her staying put, and would not have been achieved had she climbed down the fire escape. For it may be that a small plane brushed the side of the building, tearing down the fire escape while she would have been on it, and the wind from the plane was strong enough to blow the fire out. Although she achieved the desired result by staying put, and would not have achieved it by climbing down the fire escape, this does not alter the fact that the decision to do the latter was the right decision, and the decision to do the former, the wrong one. Right decisions can have tragic results.

Decisions or courses of action are right when all properly qualified persons would favor them; wrong when no properly qualified person would favor them. However, unlike answers to theoretical problems, the rightness of a decision is often determined by conditions at the time the decision was made. However, sometimes, in nonmoral decisions what is regarded as right or wrong is determined after the fact, that is, only after seeing whether it leads to the desired result. But this is never true of moral decisions. When equally qualified persons would make different decisions, the one that leads to the desired result is often called the right one. That a person makes such a right decision, however, does not mean that she deserves credit for it, for she simply may have been lucky. However, if a person generally makes right decisions, she tends to be given credit for them, even if others cannot see why her decisions generally turn out right. Talk of intuition is common here, and a person who gets such a reputation often acquires a number of followers, for example, stock market analysts.

"Morally Wrong" and "Morally Right"

A morally wrong action is usually an unjustified violation of the moral rules. All qualified people, in this case all fully informed, impartial rational persons, agree that such an action is wrong. Any action that can be called "morally wrong" can also be called "morally bad," but not vice versa. "Morally bad" has a much wider application than "morally wrong." This should be clear from the fact that "morally bad" is often used to describe people, motives, and intentions, as well as actions, whereas "morally wrong" is usually restricted to actions. "Morally wrong" is used to emphasize the objective character of the judgment. A morally wrong action is one that *all* impartial rational persons would favor not doing. "Morally bad" is related to the nonmoral use of "bad," and is generally used to emphasize that the action is to be avoided or not to be done. A morally bad action is one that all impartial rational persons favor *not* doing.

"Morally wrong" is related to the nonmoral use of "wrong" in the making of practical judgments except that, as mentioned above, what is morally wrong is *always* determined by what all qualified persons would decide at the time of acting or deciding. A moral judgment of an action is never determined by an outcome that no qualified person would have foreseen. It is only the consequences that are foreseeable to the agent, not the actual consequences, that are relevant to most moral judgments. What an omniscient being would have known is irrelevant, only what was foreseeable to the moral agents involved is relevant to the moral judgment made on that action or decision. Morality is for fallible beings with limited knowledge, not omniscient ones.[6]

Whereas it is impossible to reach agreement on the actual consequences of an action, impartial rational persons often can agree that the foreseeable consequences of an action make it morally wrong. The objectivity of moral judgments does not depend on knowledge of the actual consequences of an action or decision when those consequences were not foreseeable at the time of the action or decision. In fact, since actual consequences continue infinitely into the future, no moral judgment that depends on them can be made unless there is an arbitrary decision made about how far in the future actual consequences will be relevant. Many consequentialists do not fully realize that "morally right" differs from other uses of "right" applied to actions or decisions in that "morally right" never simply means "action or decision that has the best (actual) consequences." "Morally right" is not redundant. Of course, even foreseeable consequences are not the only factor determining the moral rightness or wrongness of an action or decision; there are many other morally relevant features.

The account of "morally right" as applied to actions is more complex than the account of "morally wrong." Even ignoring justified violations, not all actions that are in accordance with the moral rules are morally right actions. Since all the moral rules are, or can be stated as, prohibitions, any action that is not a violation of a moral rule is in accordance with it. Counting all such actions as morally right would mean that an action like putting on my right shoe before my left is a morally right action. In the first chapter, I pointed out that this kind of action is not even subject to moral judgment. To call an action "morally right" normally indicates that it counts in favor of the positive moral character of a person. An action is appropriately called "morally right" only in those circumstances in which a person is considering doing a morally wrong action or in which a morally wrong action seems a genuine alternative.

These circumstances are of two kinds: (1) those in which a person has, or might be expected to have, a strong desire or motive to violate a moral rule unjustifiably, and (2) those in which a person has, or might be expected to have, difficulty in determining whether or not all fully informed impartial rational persons would publicly allow violating a moral rule. This results in two kinds of morally right actions. The first is where one ignores or overcomes some significant temptation. It is this kind of action that seems most straightforwardly related to one's character and counts in favor of one having the associated moral virtue. The second kind of morally right action is done in circumstances where it is difficult to determine what all impartial rational persons would favor. Talk of moral insight and judgment is common here. The temptations usually do not involve a conflict between different moral rules or between a moral rule and a moral ideal, but merely a conflict between a moral rule and some nonmoral consideration. Difficult determinations, however, almost always involve a conflict between different moral rules or between a moral rule and a moral ideal.

In the clearest cases of a morally right action of the first kind, a person's personal virtues are given credit for her doing the morally right action, such as when it takes courage to tell the truth. If the morally wrong action had been done, it would have been said that it resulted from a lack of the appropriate personal virtue, for example, that she lied because she did not have the courage to tell the truth. It is an immoral action of this kind that is appropriately described as proceeding from weakness of will. Not all morally right actions of this first kind are due to strength of will. Sometimes one is tempted to unjustifiably violate a moral rule because of self-interest or the interests of others, and it is not the personal virtues but the moral virtues that are put to the test. For example, a physician is tempted to withhold information from a patient in order to avoid the unpleasantness of telling him the bad news, but knows that this kind of deception is not justified. The two cases are similar in that there is no doubt about what the morally right action is; what makes it appropriate to call the action or (nonaction) "morally right" is that there is a significant temptation not to do it. Philosophers have usually regarded self-interest as most important temptation, but often one must overcome the motives provided by one's family, one's religion, or one's country. Even altruistic motives and compassion often tempt a person to act immorally.

When compassion, religion, or country provide the motives for immoral action, then the overcoming of temptation is complicated by the difficulty in coming to see whether all impartial rational persons could publicly allow the violation. It is often not easy to see what could be publicly allowed by impartial rational persons in the same situation. Morally irrelevant considerations are extraordinarily difficult to eliminate. That *one's* family or country will benefit and those one does not care for will suffer are considerations that almost invariably affect one's judgment. Distortion of the facts is almost inevitable. It is the recognition of the difficulty of being impartial in a case in which one is involved with any of the parties that accounts for the rule that judges disqualify themselves in such cases. Nonmoral considerations, such as that it is *one's* family that is involved, usually lead to following a moral ideal when this involves unjustifiably breaking a moral rule. One function of explicitly describing the situation using only the morally relevant features is that it may help to eliminate egocentric biases.

When, given all the morally relevant information, including the foreseeable consequences, all impartial rational persons would publicly allow violating a rule in order to follow an ideal, then doing so is morally right. When no impartial rational person would publicly allow violating a rule in order to follow a moral ideal, then breaking the rule is morally wrong. When fully informed, impartial rational persons disagree about whether to publicly allow breaking the rule, then breaking the rule is neither morally right nor morally wrong. Only if some further information is now available that would lead all impartial rational persons to agree, should one continue to maintain that the action is either morally right or morally wrong. If no information is now available that would result in the agreement of all impartial rational persons, then to maintain that the action is morally wrong is better expressed by saying that the action morally ought not be done. But as discussed in more detail later, in the section on "ought" and "should," there are still objective limits to when it is appropriate to say of someone that he morally ought to do something.

The account of "morally right" given above allows a more precise account of "morally wrong" than that given earlier. In that earlier account I said that a morally wrong action is usually an unjustified violation of the moral rules. Now it can be seen that an action that is in accordance with a moral rule when all impartial rational persons would publicly allow violating the rule in order to follow a moral ideal also counts as a morally wrong action. This class of morally wrong actions differs from unjustified violations of the moral rules in that only for the latter do all impartial rational persons favor liability to punishment. However, sometimes it is one's duty to violate a moral rule in order to do what usually counts as following a moral ideal, for example, a psychiatrist may have a duty to restrict the freedom of a person in order to prevent him from suffering a much greater harm. This no longer counts as a conflict between a moral rule and a moral ideal, but rather as a conflict between two moral rules. When moral rules conflict with each other, impartial rational persons do favor liability to punishment for doing the morally wrong action, for all of these cases involve an unjustified violation of a moral rule.

"Morally Indifferent"

Morally indifferent actions are not the same as weakly justified violations of the moral rules. Weakly justified violations are those that some impartial rational persons would publicly allow, while others would not. Although some impartial rational persons may be indifferent about these violations, some impartial rational persons would favor their being prohibited, while others would favor their being either allowed or encouraged. To call such actions morally indifferent is misleading, for this suggests that all impartial rational persons are indifferent about such actions. A morally indifferent action or decision should be one that all impartial rational persons agree that, morally speaking, it makes no difference which action is chosen. An example of such actions will be those in which all of the morally relevant features are the same, except that a different group of people will be benefited or harmed, such as a government decision to locate or close a facility in one city rather than another.

However, the largest class of actions that are normally described as morally indifferent belong in the class of actions that fall outside the scope of morality. But, just as "morally right" is not used of an action unless a morally wrong action seems a genuine alternative, so the phrase "morally indifferent" is normally used in describing an action only when denying, perhaps in anticipation, that the action is morally wrong. Although all of these actions are ones toward which all impartial rational persons would be morally indifferent, they are not actions or decisions about which everyone is actually morally indifferent, such as which shoe, left or right, is put on first. Rather, they are actions that many people regard as morally wrong, such as unusual kinds of sexual activity between consenting adults. To call such actions morally indifferent is to claim that all impartial rational persons would be indifferent to whether such actions were performed.

"Ought" and "Should"

"Ought" and "should" have often been considered to be the most important words to clarify for understanding moral judgments. Although the two words cannot always be substituted for each other (in fact, it seems as if only "ought to" rather than simply "ought" can be substituted for "should"), it makes no difference to my points which word is used. Thus I shall use the one that sounds to me most natural in the context, and I shall not be concerned about establishing conclusions about "ought" from premises about "should." Before I try to give an account of these words as they occur in moral judgments, I shall, as I did with the words "good," "bad," "right," and "wrong," try to provide an account of their use in nonmoral judgments. For, as the slightest examination of the use of these words shows, "ought" and "should" are most often used in nonmoral judgments, not in moral ones. In fact, examination of computer searches of random samples of English text shows that far less than 10 percent of the uses of "ought" or "should" are even remotely related to any moral context.

The following examples not only show some of the many nonmoral judgments in which "should" and "ought" occur, they also show that "ought to" and "should" are often interchangeable. "You should (ought to) see that movie." "You should (ought to) get some sleep." "I ought to (should) leave now." "You should (ought to) use a lighter shade of lipstick." "You should (ought to) have thought of that sooner." "She ought to (should) have an operation immediately." "She ought to (should) be up by now." "She should (ought to) have three teeth by now." "This bridge should (ought to) have four lanes each way." "All of us ought to (should) quit smoking." "I should (ought to) be studying for the exam now." "I know I should (ought to) have tried harder, but I didn't feel like doing it." "I know I should (ought to) be studying, but I don't feel like it." "There ought to (should) be more blue in that corner." "The lighting should (ought to) suggest a foggy night." "What should (ought) I (to) do now, wash the dishes, or make the bed?" "I don't know what I should (ought to) do." "You ought to (should) quit worrying so much about others and take care of yourself." "You ought to (should) look out for number one and let others take care of themselves." "If there is no other way to get out of it, you should (ought to) lie."

It is, or should be, clear after looking at the sentences in the preceding paragraph that no simple account of "should" or "ought" will be adequate. To regard statements containing "should" or "ought" as commands is plausible for some of the examples given above but obviously implausible for others. It is, in general, most plausible for those sentences starting with "you" and in the present tense. It is less plausible for sentences starting with "I," and has no plausibility for those sentences starting with "she," in the past tense, or which are interrogatives, that is, questions. Even some declarative sentences, for example, "She should have three teeth by now," are not imperatives in even the widest sense of that term. It also is, or should be, clear that some of these statements advocate that one not be morally good and even that one should act immorally.

"Ought" and "Should" in Practical Judgments

The discussion of "right" and "wrong" showed that they were used to describe answers either to theoretical questions or to practical questions. It should not be surprising that "ought" and "should" are also used in the same two contexts; although, as with "right" and "wrong," the description of their use in one context will be very similar to the description of their use in the other. However, "right" and "wrong" are more commonly used in theoretical judgments, whereas "ought" and "should" are most often used in practical judgments.

In nonmoral practical judgments, the basic use of the terms "ought" and "should" is to advocate a course of conduct. When they are addressed to a particular person, they must advocate doing an action that a rational person concerned with that person could advocate. To say to a person that she ought to do something is to imply that as a rational person concerned with her, you advocate doing that action. Further, you imply that there are reasons for her to do that action, and if the action involves any harm or risk of harm, you imply that they are adequate reasons. To say to a person that she ought to do something, when you do not think that any rational person concerned with her would advocate that course of action to her, is close enough to lying to be a violation of the rule "Do not deceive." In fact, if you said, "I think you ought to do it," and thought that the action was one that you as a rational person would not advocate to anyone for whom you were concerned, then you could properly be accused of lying.

Nothing said above should be taken as implying that in every situation there is only one course of action that it is appropriate to tell someone that he ought to follow. As pointed out in chapter 2, two persons can act in incompatible ways and both be acting rationally, so it follows that one person may maintain that Martin ought to do X, and another maintain that Martin ought to do Y, where X and Y are incompatible courses of action, yet both may be using "ought" correctly. Two people can disagree about what a person ought to do because they may disagree about what is really in his best interest. These disagreements often involve different rankings of the goods and evils and can usually not be resolved even when there is complete agreement on the facts. Even when two persons agree about what is in someone's best interest, they may disagree about the best way in which to obtain the desired goal. These kinds of disagreements can sometimes be settled; for example, it may be that one person knows the advisee better than the other, and upon acquainting the other with this additional information both agree upon the course of action they would advocate.

As stated above, agreement on all the relevant facts does not guarantee that rational persons will agree upon the course of action they maintain that a person ought to follow. Two people, for example, an economist and a banker, advising a young person with the ability to be either, may advise her to follow different careers even though they do not disagree on any facts and both are interested solely in the welfare of the person they are advising. When the disagreement cannot be resolved because the reasons for either course of action are no better than the reasons for the other, there is no right course of action and the course of action that one says ought to be followed will generally reflect his own individual ranking of the reasons. When aware of this kind of conflict, it is better to say, "I think you ought," rather than simply "You ought," because the latter suggests that everyone agrees and the former acknowledges that there is disagreement.

It should not be thought, however, that every practical judgment containing "should" advocates a course of action intended to benefit the person to whom it is addressed. Although saying "You ought to do X" implies that a rational person concerned with you could advocate your doing X, it does not imply that doing X will benefit you personally. It is not incorrect to tell someone that he ought to do something that will benefit someone else. People are often told what they ought to do in order to benefit someone for whom they are concerned. This is a perfectly acceptable use of "ought." If Maria cares for someone, it is appropriate to tell her that she ought to do something that will benefit him, even if her doing so will not benefit her personally. Further, even if Maria does not care for that person, but that person will avoid a great harm, it is appropriate to tell her that she ought to do what will benefit him, even if does not benefit her. A rational person can recommend that a person for whom he is concerned act in a way that does not benefit either her or anyone for whom she cares.

However, it is also a correct use of "ought" to advise a person not to be so concerned with others, but to look after his own interests. This is why it is a mistake to analyze "ought" in terms of better reasons. If the only interests involved are those of the person being advised, then to tell him that he ought to do X implies that there are better reasons for doing X than for alternative courses of actions. But when the interests of others are also involved, especially the interests of those for whom the person being advised has no concern, then using "ought" does not imply that there are better reasons for acting in his own interests rather than in the interests of others. It is correct to use "ought" either to advise the person to act in his own interests and against the greater interests of others, or to advise him to act in the interests of others and against his own lesser interests.

This creates the possibility of even greater disagreement among rational persons in advising someone about what he ought to do. For one course of action might benefit the individual personally; another might benefit those for whom he is concerned; and a third prevent great harm to others, but not benefit himself or those for whom he is concerned. Rational persons may therefore disagree about the course of action they advise someone to take, even though all agree that there are better reasons for acting in one way than in either of the others. One may advocate a course of action designed to benefit the individual personally; another may advocate a course of action designed to benefit those for whom he is concerned; a third may advocate preventing the greatest harm. But even in the latter two cases, it is correct to tell someone that he ought to do X, only if X is an action or course of action that a rational person concerned with him could advocate, and if it is one that you, in fact being concerned with him, do advocate. And although it is always appropriate to use "ought" to recommend a course of action that is supported by the best reasons, it is also sometimes appropriate, when the best reasons concern the interests of others, to use "ought" to recommend a course of action that is not supported by the best reasons.

In some situations every rational person knowing the same relevant facts and concerned with the individual or individuals involved will advocate the same course of action; for example, all qualified doctors will agree that someone in the patient's condition ought to have an operation immediately. It is incorrect to say that a person ought to do X, if, no fully informed, rational person concerned with him would advocate his doing X. Thus, unlike commands, statements containing "ought" or "should" can be incorrect. Of course, someone can make a mistake in *giving* a certain command; she may not mean to say what she did, or obeying the order may have consequences other than those intended, but a person can give a command to an individual for whom he has no concern. However, telling a person that she ought to do something implies that there are reasons (adequate if needed) to do that action, such that a rational person concerned for her could advocate her doing that action. If there are not such reasons, one was either mistaken in telling her she ought to do it, or one was deceiving her.

This analysis of the basic use of "ought" is easily expanded to account for statements in the first or third person, singular or plural, and in either present or past tense. Saying that you (I, she, we, they) ought to do X, means that there are reasons for your (my, her, our, their) doing X and that, as a rational person concerned with you (myself, her, us, them), I advocate that you (I, she, we, they) do X. Saying that you (I, she, we, they) ought to have done X, means that there were reasons for your (my, her, our, their) doing X and, as a rational person, concerned with you (myself, her, us, them) I would have advocated that you (I, she, we, they) do X. Sometimes one may be making an even stronger claim, namely that all fully informed, rational persons would advocate your (my, her, our, their) doing X, or would have advocated your (my, her, our, their) doing it.

I realize that it may sound somewhat strange to talk of advocating a course of action to oneself, but on reflection I think that this strangeness will disappear. It is not at all unusual for a person to tell herself that she ought to do such and such, that it is the only rational thing to do. Nor is it always the case that she always does what she thinks she ought to do. Indeed, this is the kind of situation that leads people to talk of weakness of will. The proposed analysis accounts as well for statements such as "I know I should have done it, but I just couldn't get myself up to doing it," as it does for the more straightforward statements like "You ought to have an operation."

Adapting the analysis to statements such as "This bridge ought to have four lanes each way" and "The lighting ought to suggest a foggy night" also presents no difficulties. Insofar as these statements are addressed to someone who is going to build the bridge or to control the lighting, they are to be understood in the same way as second-person, present-tense statements containing "ought to," such as "You ought to make the lighting suggest a foggy night." However, if they are not addressed to someone who is building the bridge or controlling the lighting they can also be understood in the following way: "I, as a rational person concerned with the people affected by the bridge (lighting), advocate that the bridge have four lanes each way (that the lighting suggest a foggy night)." Here, again, one may or may not be claiming that all fully informed, rational persons would agree with one's judgments. Whether one is claiming that or not will become clear from what one says if someone disagrees with what one says.

"Ought" in Theoretical Judgments

So far I have been concerned solely with the use of "ought" in nonmoral practical judgments. I shall now turn to the use of "ought" in nonmoral theoretical judgments; judgments such as "She ought to be up by now" and "She ought to have three teeth by now." "Ought" is used less often in judgments of this sort, and most philosophical accounts of "ought" have completely ignored its use in this kind of judgment. In these judgments, no action is being advocated, much less commanded; rather, something is claimed or asserted. Depending on the context, "She ought to have three teeth by now" can be taken as a prediction that she now has three teeth or as a claim that she deviates from the normal, generally, though not always, with the suggestion that this is a bad thing. If it is not known how many teeth she has, then the statement is most likely a prediction. If it is known that she only has one tooth, it is a claim that she has fewer teeth than would normally be expected, because of either her age or her family history.

The prediction and the claim are more closely connected than they seem at first glance. For the prediction is generally made on the basis of one's belief about how many teeth children of her age generally have. Of course, both the prediction and the claim can be made on somewhat narrower grounds than what is normal for children of her age. If, for example, everyone in her family has been an early teether, then "She ought to have three teeth by now" can be based on one's beliefs about the age that her brothers and sisters got their teeth. But one must have some reasons for one's prediction or claim, for the use of "ought," even in theoretical judgments, implies that one has reasons for one's judgment. If one says "She ought to have three teeth by now" and upon being asked why, does not have any reason, then one has misused the language. "Ought" should be used in nonmoral theoretical judgments only when one has beliefs that would lead some rational person to accept the judgment. Of course, sometimes a belief that leads one rational person to accept a judgment will not lead another one to accept it, but this consequence should already be expected.

Disagreement about whether to accept a particular "ought" judgment of this kind sometimes rests on disagreement about the beliefs that are used to support it. These disagreements can sometimes be settled by finding out the facts, but not always. Rational persons may differ in the weight they give to the support provided by certain facts. Sometimes, however, the facts are such that any rational person acquainted with them would accept certain "ought" judgments. Suppose we know that a child has always napped for one hour and then played quietly in her bed for another hour. Then, in the absence of any reason to believe anything is unusual today, her mother's remark made one hour and forty-five minutes after she went to sleep that she ought to be up by now would not be disputed by any rational person.

Nonmoral theoretical judgments like nonmoral, practical judgments containing "ought" sometimes make stronger claims, sometimes weaker ones. If one says "She ought to be up," then one must, at least, be claiming that one has some beliefs that would lead some rational persons to accept the judgment. The presence of new information can drastically change our assessment of a judgment. For example, in the case of the mother's remark about her child being up from a nap, information that the child had been given a sleeping pill just before she went to bed today would make us less likely to accept the mother's judgment. Since "ought" judgments are generally made on the basis of many beliefs, a change in one of them need not affect our assessment of an "ought" judgment, but sometimes, as in the example sketched above, it will.

Nonmoral theoretical judgments can be analyzed into a kind of nonmoral practical judgment like "I, as a rational person, advocate believing this prediction or claim." A rational person would advocate believing a prediction or claim only if it was supported by some belief that she accepted and that she thought provided adequate support for the prediction or claim. Although nothing is lost by analyzing nonmoral theoretical judgments into practical ones, a nonmoral theoretical judgment containing "ought" should always be distinguished from a nonmoral practical judgment containing the same words. However, there are occasions when a theoretical judgment is made with the tone of a practical one, and sometimes it is not clear which of the two is meant. "She ought to be up by now," said of a teenager rather than a baby, could be either a practical or theoretical judgment. There may be times when even the person who made it is not clear which she meant. So that if you asked her, "Do you mean that you think she's up, or that you think she ought to get up?" she may be unable to answer, or will reply "Both. I think she is up, but if she isn't I think she ought to get up."

This may be the time to emphasize again that I am not primarily concerned with providing an account of ordinary language. I am, at most, providing an account of an "idealized" ordinary language. By "idealized," I do not mean one that all rational persons would prefer, but only one that has more precision than ordinary language. However, that greater precision is accompanied by less flexibility, so for everyday use, ordinary language is more suitable than an "idealized" one. As will be apparent from the account of "ought" and "should" as they occur in moral judgments, even the distinction between making moral judgments and making nonmoral ones is not precise. Nonetheless I believe that a clear distinction can be made, and the analyses that I provide should enable one to understand the meaning of "ought" and "should" in both moral judgments and nonmoral ones.

"Ought" and "Should" in Moral Judgments

Moral judgments containing "ought" or "should" are practical judgments that are based on the moral system. In order to be correct they must be based on adequate information about the morally relevant features of the action and be judgments that an impartial rational person could make using an informal public system that applies to all rational persons. But not all practical judgments containing "ought" or "should" that are made on the basis of such a public system, or that one makes as an impartial rational person, are moral judgments; these judgments may also be prudential, aesthetic, or utilitarian judgments. To be a moral judgment, the "ought" judgment must also be about a moral matter. These judgments not only include advocating doing morally right and morally good actions and avoiding doing morally wrong and morally bad actions, they also include advocating doing and not doing actions about which impartial rational persons disagree, that is, weakly justified violations of moral rules.

The objectivity of a moral judgment containing "ought" is guaranteed by the fact that such a judgment must be one that any impartial rational person could make. In making the moral judgment "You ought to do X," one is implying that an impartial rational person concerned with you could advocate your doing X. However, one is not implying that one would advocate that everyone in morally similar circumstances do X. Unless the judgment involves violating a moral rule, one does not have to universalize a moral judgment containing "ought" in the strict sense suggested by Kant or Hare. Only then does the impartiality required by the moral rules demand that one be willing to make the same judgment in all situations that have the same morally relevant features. When the moral judgment containing "ought" only concerns following a moral ideal, all that is necessary is that any impartial rational person could make the same judgment.

When no violations of moral rules are involved, there is nothing wrong with telling two people to whom all the same morally relevant considerations apply that they ought to do different things, such as telling one that she ought to help those in her home town and telling the other that she ought to join the Peace Corps and help those in the poorer countries. When the judgment concerns the violation of a moral rule, even though one must always make the same judgment, one does not have to maintain that anyone who makes an incompatible judgment is mistaken. The objectivity of a moral judgment does not require all impartial rational persons to make the same judgment, only that they all could make the same judgment. Morality is an informal public system, so two impartial rational persons can correctly base their judgment on the moral system and still disagree.

I pointed out previously that fully informed, impartial rational persons sometimes will make incompatible moral judgments about what ought to be done. In these situations, an impartial rational person who makes a moral judgment saying what ought to be done is expressing her personal attitude. Of course, she is not doing just this. For even if there are several different courses of action that could be advocated by impartial rational persons, there are far more that no impartial rational person would advocate. Even when impartial rational persons disagree about what action ought to be done, if they are making moral judgments, there is a clear limit to what they can say. When making a moral judgment a rational person must believe that at least some fully informed, impartial rational person would make the same judgment.

Two people who make different moral judgments about what ought to be done can sometimes be led to agree, not by producing new information, but by one person coming to see that no one who was impartial and rational, not even she, would make this same judgment if, for example, it were not her child that was involved. But even in those cases where impartial rational persons cannot agree about what morally ought to be done, there is agreement about what the morally relevant considerations are, and about what considerations are not morally relevant. Although people disagree about many cases, they can usually agree that if the facts were changed in some specified way, they would agree. And in most cases, there is usually considerable agreement on what ought not be done, even when people do not agree on the action that should be done. But in many actual cases all impartial rational persons do agree on what morally ought to be done, for in many cases there is only one morally right course of action.

All impartial rational persons agree that one ought to do what is morally right, and that one ought not to do what is morally wrong. These are mere tautologies. But, given the analysis of morally right and morally wrong, it shows that moral judgments about what one ought to do are capable of being mistaken. Someone making the moral judgment that X ought to be done can be shown that she is mistaken by showing that doing X is morally wrong. Also, moral judgments about what one ought to do, even if they cannot be lies, can be deceitful. For one can know that an action is morally wrong and claim to be making the moral judgment that one ought to do it. Acceptable moral judgments containing "ought" or "should" cannot be made simply according to the whim, or even the sincere reflective attitude, of the person making them. In some cases, only one "ought" judgment is correct; in others, although there may be several acceptable "ought" judgments, this number will generally be quite small in proportion to the "ought" judgments that are not morally acceptable.

"Ought" occurs in moral judgments in which one advocates obeying a moral rule, justifiably violating it, or when one advocates following a moral ideal. In any of these cases, there may be complete agreement, or partial disagreement. I have already pointed out that there are occasions in which all impartial rational persons agree that one ought not obey a moral rule and others in which impartial rational persons disagree about whether one ought to obey the rule. It is even clearer that impartial rational persons can sometimes disagree about whether one ought to follow a moral ideal. The latter case allows room for much more disagreement, since although all impartial rational persons favor following the moral ideals, they do not, as with the moral rules, favor everyone's following them all of the time, unless they are at least weakly justified in violating them.

When "ought" is used in those moral judgments advocating obeying a moral rule and no impartial rational person would advocate violating the rule, then "ought" has a greater force than when advocating a weakly justified violation or following the moral ideals. For in the first case all impartial rational persons not only agree in advocating obeying the rule, they also advocate liability to punishment for not obeying it. This sense of "ought" can be described by saying that it is used when all impartial rational persons *require* that a certain course of action be followed.[7] Some philosophers now recognize that "must" rather than "ought" is generally used in situations where there is a clear moral requirement.[8]

Although a judgment that Jane ought to do X is not correct unless a rational person concerned with her could make that judgment, one need not be concerned for a person in order to make a moral judgment that she ought to do X. However, when actually making a moral judgment to some person about what she ought to do, one is generally expected to have some concern for her. If I tell a person for whom I obviously have no concern "You ought to do X," even if I intend this to be a moral judgment, she may legitimately reply, "You can't tell me what I ought to do; you don't care about me." The legitimacy of this reply stems in part from the fact that moral and nonmoral judgments are not totally distinct. Making the judgment to someone that she ought to do something, even when it is a moral judgment, suggests that one is concerned with her. Most moral judgments telling people what they ought to do, thus, must have a characteristic of similarly worded nonmoral practical judgments, namely that one be concerned with the person to whom one is making the judgment. It is with this understanding of "should" that the question "Why should one be moral?" will be discussed in the next chapter.

Notes

1. Using the terminology of J. L. Austin, the linguistic accounts are about the illocutionary force of the judgment.

2. Paul McNamara has forcefully argued that moral judgments telling someone that he is morally required to do something are usually expressed using the term "must" rather than "ought" or "should." See his articles, "Must I Do What I Ought? (Or Will the Least I Can Do Do?)," in *Deontic Logic, Agency and Normative Systems,* edited by José Carmo and Mark Brown (Berlin: Springer Verlag, 1996), 154–173, and "Making Room for Going Beyond the Call," *Mind* 105 (July 1996): 415–450.

3. These are sometimes call "thick concepts" because they have specific moral content independent of context, as opposed to "thin concepts" like "good," which have no specific moral content independent of context. But this just shows that it is the content of a judgment that determines if it is a moral judgment.

4. This view is one that has been put forward most forcefully in several books by R. M. Hare. See especially *The Language of Morals* (Oxford: Oxford University Press, 1952) and *Freedom and Reason* (Oxford: Oxford University Press, 1963). It is one factor responsible for the failure to realize that moral judgments can be hypocritical.

5. Having taught a course in Argentina using an earlier version of this book, I am not certain that moral judgments in Spanish can be summarized by these same words. The differences are likely to be even greater in languages that differ more than Spanish and English. However, I do not think these differences will have any significant effect on the philosophical points that I am making.

6. The neglect of this point has had disastrous consequences for the account of morality offered by many consequentialists. See especially R. M. Hare, *Moral Thinking: Its Levels, Method and Point* (Oxford: Oxford University Press, 1981).

7. Some philosophers claim that when we are morally required to do something "ought" should be replaced by the words "oblige" or "obligation." I prefer not to use these words, for it seems to me that they have their normal use primarily in connection with the three positively stated moral rules: "Keep your promise," "Obey the law," and "Do your duty." To stretch the use is to invite misunderstanding. I have not been concerned with obligations because it is not philosophically important to distinguish the positively stated rules from the negatively stated ones. It is not that there is nothing philosophically interesting to say about obligations, it is, rather, that the concept of obligation does not play any significant role in moral philosophy.

8. See note 2, above.

Chapter 13

"Why Should I Be Moral?"

When people ask, "Why should I be moral?" they may be asking why they should act morally on a particular occasion but usually they are asking why they should obey the moral rules in general. They want to know why they should not cause harm to others, why they should not deceive or cheat, and why they should keep their promises, obey the law, and perform their duties. The question "Why should I be moral?" would make no sense if one did not have a fairly clear idea of what morality prohibits, requires, encourages, and allows. The account of morality as an informal public system that every rational person wants others to follow, and knows that others want him to follow, both explains why the question "Why should I be moral?" has a clear sense and provides the foundation for a sensible answer.

"Why should I be moral?" need not be taken as a request for an account of morality such that, by itself, it provides adequate reasons for following it. However, I shall try to show that the most satisfactory answers to this question do arise from the very nature of morality. Since it is not irrational to be immoral, it will be impossible to provide an account of morality such that it is irrational not to use morality as one's supreme guide to conduct. On the other hand, since it is always rational to be moral, it should be possible to show that morality, by itself, always provides an adequate reason for following it. It may even be possible to show that when morality conflicts with self-interest or even the interests of friends or country, there are often stronger or better reasons for acting morally than for acting immorally.

I am concerned with the question "Why be moral?" only when it is posed with regard to a justified moral system, that is, one that all rational persons would put forward as a public system that applies to all of them. Philosophers who hold that the question "Why should I be moral?" is a senseless or pointless question often conceive of morality primarily as a guide to conduct that each person adopts for himself. But it is only on an account of morality as a guide to conduct that each person wants everyone else to obey that the question "Why should I be moral?" has a point. I want everyone else to be moral, and I know everyone wants me to be moral, but why should I be moral? Why is it rational for me to be moral? What are the rea-

338

sons for me to be moral? These are the questions that will be discussed and answered in this chapter.

Using the analysis of "should" provided in the previous chapter, it is most fruitful to interpret these questions as asking why a rational person, not necessarily impartial, but concerned for me, would advocate that I be moral. Understood in this way the question becomes "Why would a rational person (possibly myself) concerned for me advocate that I be moral?" This is not a senseless question. It may very well be that some rational persons concerned for me will advocate that I not be moral. However, some rational persons concerned for me will advocate that I be moral. Why they would advocate this provides the answers to the question "Why should I be moral?" It is pointless to interpret the question "Why should I be moral?" as "Why would an impartial rational person advocate that I be moral?" Interpreted in this way, the answer to the question is too obvious; all impartial rational persons advocate that everyone act morally. But some rational persons who are concerned with me may also be impartial and so what impartial rational persons would favor is relevant.

For the most part, morality does not require a person to act differently than he would act without these moral constraints. Most of the time a person has no inclination or interest in doing what morality prohibits his doing. The occasions on which one wants to kill, deceive, or cheat do not occupy a high percentage of most persons' waking hours. However, morality sometimes does constrain one's behavior, prohibiting one from doing what one wants to do, or what is in one's interest to do, or what is in the interests of one's friends to do. It makes sense to ask why I should constrain my behavior by the moral rules at all, not doing what I want to do, simply because no rational person (including myself) would favor everyone knowing that they can violate these rules in the same circumstances. The moral rules impose constraints, so it is quite plausible for a person to ask why he should follow them if he does not feel like it or if it is not in his interest or that of his friends for him to obey the rules.

The moral ideals do not raise the same question, for the moral ideals impose no constraints. No one is required to follow the moral ideals at any time, let alone at all times. To follow the moral ideals is to be morally good, and asking why one should be morally good is a different question than asking why one should be moral. However, it will turn out that most of the reasons for being moral, which involves not unjustifiably violating the moral rules, are very similar to the reasons for being morally good, which involves justifiably following the moral ideals. Although this chapter is concerned primarily with the question "Why should I be moral?" the answers provided will be closely related to the answers to the question "Why should I be morally good?"

Talking to Children

Taken literally, the question "Why should I be moral?" does not seem to be about why one should act morally either in general or in a particular case. Rather, it seems to be about why one should be a certain kind of person, namely, a moral person. Thus the question seems more closely related to the moral virtues than to the moral system. Indeed, it is easier to answer why one should have the moral virtues rather than why one should act morally in a particular situation when it is in one's interest to act immorally. This may be part of the explanation why morality was traditionally thought of in terms of the virtues rather than in terms of a moral system that determines what acts are morally acceptable in particular occasions. I shall try to provide adequate reasons for acting morally in all particular situations, but I know that sometimes these reasons will involve the reasons for having the moral virtues. Indeed, the answers that I give for being moral will, for the most part, be answers both to why one should act morally on particular occasions and why one should be a moral person. Training children to be moral persons or to have the moral virtues is the same as training them to act morally, so that when the questions concern children, the same answers should be given no matter which way the question is interpreted.

Given the analysis of "should" given in the previous chapter, this question is best thought of as being asked by someone who believes that you are concerned for him. To appreciate its force, consider that you have been asked it by one of your children or by a younger sister or brother. How would you answer? There are many things you could say. You could point out that it is generally in one's self-interest to be moral, that people who are moral are generally happier than those who are not. When talking to a child, whose character is not yet formed, this point takes on even more significance. You could point out that recognition of one's own vulnerability and fallibility makes acting morally one's best option. This appeal to humility is appropriate whether or not one is religious. If you were religious, you could add that God wants one to be moral and will reward those who are. You could point out that since the child wants others to be behave morally with regard to her and will most likely be making moral judgments on the behavior of others, it would be hypocritical not to act morally herself. You could also point out the advantages of avoiding guilt, shame, and remorse.

Finally, you could point out to her that though you were concerned for her, you were also concerned for others, and that in large measure, you advocate her being moral, not so much out of your concern for her as out of your concern for everyone. There is nothing wrong, morally or otherwise, with advocating a course of action to someone for whom you are concerned, which is not advocated out of concern for her. As long as you would advocate this course of action to anyone for whom you are concerned, you need not advocate it out of your concern for her. The appropriateness of this kind of answer shows that the question "Why should I be moral?" need not be taken as asking for reasons of self-interest. However, since the answers to this question are supposed to provide not only reasons but also motives, it is not surprising that most reasons that are offered are related to self-interest. However, if a child has been brought up to have a concern for others, then pointing out that being moral lessens the chances of harming others may have more force than any other answer. If she has not, then there is a good chance that none of your answers will seem persuasive, for lacking concern for others makes it very unlikely that one will be always be motivated to act morally.

The Point of Being Moral

Many attempts to answer the question "Why should I be moral?" take it as asking for reasons of self-interest for being moral. But although it is usually in one's self-interest to be moral, it will sometimes not be so. Sometimes, it is not even in one's self-interest to seem moral, though in any morally acceptable society it almost always will be. Thus, no answer in terms of self-interest is completely satisfactory because self-interest does not always provide reasons for acting morally. The only completely satisfactory answers to the question "Why should I be moral?" are answers that always provide reasons. Unless morality itself provides such reasons, there is no answer that always provides reasons for acting morally. This was realized by Plato, who tried to offer reasons of self-interest for being moral, but at the same time to make these reasons an essential part of the nature of morality. The result of this was to make morality essentially self-interested, though with a strange kind of self-interest, to wit, harmony of the soul. Unfortunately, acting morally is not always or necessarily in one's self-interest. Self-interest and morality are related, but to claim that morality and self-interest never provide motives for conflicting actions results in a distortion of the concept of morality or of the concept of self-interest, or both.

Fortunately, not all reasons are reasons of self-interest. Rationality is a wider concept than self-interest, and beliefs that one's action will prevent harm to others are reasons for acting.[1] In asking "Why should I be moral?" one need not be asking and, I think, one generally is not asking "What's in it for me?" but rather "What is the point of my being moral?" Since being moral is often regarded as simply obeying a certain set of rules, it is not self-evident that anyone would gain anything by a person acting morally. This is especially true if there is no distinction made between those moral rules that can be justified, either with or without reference to the customs or institutions of one's society, and those that do not have a justification at all. In many societies the genuine or justifiable moral rules are not distinguished from those rules or traditions that a society, by some accident or design, has grouped together with them.[2]

Many take the question "Why should I refrain from having sexual intercourse before marriage?" simply to be a particular instance of the question "Why shouldn't I do it if I want to?" Saying it is immoral to have sexual relations before marriage is not a sufficient answer. If no one is hurt, what is wrong with breaking what many in one's society consider a moral rule? There may not be an adequate reason to obey these rules, for many of them may not be justified. I do not attempt to provide an answer to the question "Why should I obey the rules that many in my society regard as moral rules?" I am concerned with the question "Why should I be moral?" only when it is restricted to justified moral rules. Without a distinction between justified moral rules and unjustified ones, there is no satisfactory answer to the question "Why should I obey the moral rules?" But that there is often not an adequate reason to obey unjustified moral rules does not mean that there is ever not an adequate reason to obey justified moral rules.

It could, of course, be claimed that there is often an adequate reason to obey even unjustified moral rules, namely, you will be punished if you are caught violating these rules. Though this answer is correct, its very correctness shows that it is not the kind of answer most people are looking for, for this answer provides no better reason for obeying justified moral rules than for obeying unjustified ones. Even though the account of morality provided in the previous chapters makes clear why punishment is not just accidentally related to unjustified violations of the moral rules, punishment does not provide the kind of answer that is wanted. For "You will be punished if you are not" does not really answer the question "Why should I be moral?" but only the question "Why should I seem moral?" One might, of course, claim that it is impossible to seem moral without being moral. But this claim, though it may hold generally, certainly does not hold universally. In particular it does not hold in just those cases where one believes that one can be immoral without anyone else finding out about it, and these are precisely the kinds of cases for which philosophers and others want to provide adequate reasons for being moral.

Religious Answers

One way of making the answer "You will be punished if you are not" hold universally is to bring in God. God always knows if you are really moral or only seem to be, and you will be punished if you are not really moral. This is why some claim that belief in God is a necessary support of morality. In this context, this claim seems to be based on the view that only self-interest, in this case avoidance of the wrath of God, can provide an adequate reason for acting morally. The answer in terms of religious self-interest avoids one of the difficulties that all answers in terms of natural self-interest have. It is simply false that it is always in a person's natural self-interest to act morally. However, the religious self-interest answer is not primarily an answer to the question "Why should I be moral?" but rather to the question "Why should I do as God commands?" Of course, if God commands everyone to be moral, then this provides an answer to the original question also.

The religious self-interest answer to the question "Why should I be moral?" is not the only religious answer. There is also what I prefer to call the genuine religious answer, namely, the love of God. The genuine religious answer to the question "Why should I be moral?" is that it will please God if you are. Since God knows when one only seems to be moral, it provides a reason for actually being moral. But this reason, like that of religious self-interest, does not distinguish moral from nonmoral rules. In both cases people have an adequate reason to obey the moral rules only if they justifiably believe that God commands them to. However, God does not always command people to act morally; some of his commands seem to concern only matters of religious ritual. In fact, he sometimes issues commands to break one of the moral rules unjustifiably, as when he commanded Abraham to sacrifice his son Isaac.

On a practical level, there are serious defects with both religious answers. First, they do not distinguish between genuine moral rules and those religious rules that apply only to those who accept a particular religion. The Ten Commandments are an example of this failure, so that killing and failing to keep the Sabbath are both regarded as violations of moral rules. Second, both religious answers depend upon belief in a God, and a God of a very special sort, one who commands that one always act morally. A rational person need not believe in such a God, so these answers provide no reason at all for him to be moral. A completely satisfactory answer must be one that all rational persons acknowledge as providing adequate reasons for acting morally, so that it would never be irrational for any person to act contrary to their own self-interest in order to act morally. Although a satisfactory answer must be acknowledged as an adequate reason by any rational person, it must also be rational not to act on that adequate reason; otherwise all immoral action would be irrational.

Immoral Action and Irrational Action

I am not claiming to be able to provide an answer to the question "Why should I be moral?" such that every rational person, if aware of this answer, would act morally. I am not even claiming to provide an answer that would at least slightly incline every rational person to always act morally. An adequate reason for being moral need not provide any motive at all for some rational persons such as rational egoists. I am claiming that an adequate answer to the question "Why should I be moral?" must provide an answer such that it would always be rational to act on the reasons provided by that answer. It cannot be irrational to act morally, but it cannot be irrational to act immorally either, otherwise those who were most immoral would be too irrational to be held responsible for their actions. That it is only rationally allowed to act morally may not be strong enough for some philosophers, but that it is always rationally allowed to act morally is the most that can be shown.

Some philosophers, however, would maintain that all immoral action either is based on a mistaken belief or is irrational. Plato tried to show, at least on some interpretations, that no one ever knowingly acts immorally. However, Plato did not clearly distinguish between immoral action and irrational action. It is true that unless one has an adequate reason, acting so as to cause harm to oneself or to those one cares about is acting either unknowingly or irrationally. It is not true that all immoral action is either unknowing or irrational. Immoral action usually involves causing or risking harm to those one does not care about (or care about enough) in order to please or benefit oneself or those one does care about. There is nothing irrational about this, unless one accepts the very dubious Platonic account of the harmony of the soul. There is a great temptation to accept such an account. Freud has sometimes been twisted in such a way as to yield the conclusion that an immoral person is always suffering from a mental disorder. Although many murders may be due to mental illness, it is implausible to account for all murder, let alone all immoral action in this way.

It is equally implausible to hold that all immoral action is followed by painful feelings of guilt, shame, or remorse. The wicked suffer torments of the soul only if they have been brought up in a certain way, which not all of them have. Even if all of the wicked do suffer some guilt, shame, or remorse (a very doubtful view), it is quite likely that their ill-gotten gains often more than compensate for such feelings. To hold that the wicked never profit from their wickedness is a view that I, as much as anyone, would prefer to be true. Unfortunately, all of the evidence appears to show that it is false. But there is another view, which the present account of morality supports, namely, that a moral person stands a better chance of being happy than an immoral one. The evidence appears to show that those having the moral virtues are more likely to live successful lives than those who have the moral vices. But as I noted in an earlier section, 'Talking to Children,' there are stronger reasons for having the moral virtues than for acting morally on each particular occasion. There is no plausible account of human nature such that it is never in one's self-interest, even one's long-term self-interest, to unjustifiably violate a moral rule. Morality requires resisting the temptation to make false statements in order to persuade people to be moral.

The Moral Answer

The question "Why should I be moral?" is most likely to be asked by those who take morality seriously, such as Glaucon and Adimantus. Thus the question should not be dismissed as a request for proving the self-interest of morality. Trying to provide an answer to this question is a good way of distinguishing bogus from genuine or justifiable morality. If an adequate answer cannot be given to the question, then one should begin to question the justification of that morality. Since a justification of the common moral system has been provided, an adequate answer should be able to be given, though, of course, not one of self-interest.

The moral rules prohibit acting in those ways that cause or increase the likelihood of someone suffering an evil. This provides a ready-made answer to the question why one should be moral, namely that one will cause or increase the likelihood of someone suffering some harm or evil if one is not. Note that this is a moral answer to the question "Why should I be moral?" As such, it should apply in all cases rather than merely generally. Being moral can now be distinguished from the reasons for being moral. Included among these reasons is what I call *the moral reason*, to avoid causing or increasing the likelihood of someone suffering an evil. Note that this is a perfectly acceptable answer to the question. It is one that might serve to convince someone who had actually asked the question. Pointing out to him that others may suffer because of his immoral action may be sufficient to make him give up that course of action, for he may not have thought of this, or have given it sufficient weight.

It is because one usually knows the moral rules before one knows their justification that it is possible to fail to distinguish justifiable moral rules from unjustifiable ones. And it may be the presence of unjustifiable moral rules that leads some to ask "Why should I be moral?" It is important and interesting that "Because you will cause or increase the likelihood of someone suffering an evil if you are not" is an appropriate answer only when asked about the justifiable moral rules. It also is a reason for actually being moral rather than only seeming to be so. It thereby differs from all answers in terms of self-interest, including religious self-interest. Unlike all of the religious answers, it is also an answer that derives from the point of morality itself, not one that presupposes the existence of a God who is appropriately related to morality.

This answer, indeed an even stronger one, "You will cause someone to suffer an evil if you are not" can always be appropriately given to anyone contemplating a violation of the first five rules. However, it is not always an appropriate reply to someone contemplating a violation of one of the second five rules. And it is with regard to the second five rules that the question is more likely to be asked. Although violation of any of the second five rules generally results in at least an increase in the probability of someone suffering some harm, some unjustifiable violations of each of the second five rules do not seem to increase this probability. When no one will suffer harm because of a particular violation, one may wonder why one should not deceive or cheat when doing so would be in one's best interest. Why should one be moral in this case? The straightforward answer, "Because you will cause or increase the likelihood of someone suffering an evil," is not adequate here. Although this is an appropriate answer for not lying most of the time, it does not seem appropriate in the kind of case under consideration.

I am not concerned now with the question "Why in general shouldn't one deceive, break one's promise, cheat, disobey the law, or neglect one's duty?" The answer to this question is the same as for the first five rules: "You will cause or increase the likelihood of someone suffering an evil." Thus it might seem as if the answer to the question "Why in this particular case shouldn't one deceive, cheat, and so on?" is the same answer, "You will cause or increase the likelihood of someone suffering evil consequences." But in some cases this is not true, a particular act will not cause or increase the likelihood of someone suffering evil consequences. From the fact that disobeying these rules generally results in someone suffering evil consequences, it follows that many individual acts of this sort are likely to have these consequences. But it does not follow that some particular act is likely to have them. It is the offering of this reason in the cases where it does not fit that renders it suspect. It is a good reason not to violate a moral rule on a particular occasion when it causes or increases the likelihood of someone suffering evil consequences. But it is not a good reason when this is not the case, although given the fallibility of persons, one may never be sure that a particular violation will cause no harm.

Given this fallibility, it may always be appropriate to claim that one might cause harm by violating a moral rule, but in some particular cases this risk will be so small that it does not provide a reason that is adequate for acting contrary to one's self-interest. Of course, in some of these cases, it may be at least weakly justifiable to violate a moral rule, but I am not concerned with these cases. I am concerned with answering "Why should I be moral?" when this question is asked about an unjustifiable violation of a justifiable moral rule, and cannot be adequately answered by "Your act will cause or increase the likelihood of someone suffering evil consequences." If this question cannot be adequately answered, then there is an unbridgeable gap between the justification of morality and the possibility of always adequately answering the question "Why should I be moral?" Of course, in all of the important and clear-cut cases, there is no gap. The justification of morality provides an adequate answer to the question "Why should I be moral?" namely, "You will cause or increase the likelihood of someone suffering evil consequences." This answer is not based on self-interest or on religion, but rather is based on the nature of morality itself. It is therefore appropriately called the moral answer. Nonetheless, it is troubling that there is any gap at all. If an adequate reason cannot always be given for going against one's self-interest whenever this is morally required, then it will not always be rational to be moral, and this is an unacceptable conclusion.

The Role of the Virtues

This discussion concerns a very limited class of actions, those actions that are an unjustifiable violation of a moral rule, and yet one cannot seriously claim that someone will suffer or is more likely to suffer evil consequences because of that particular act. These violations are violations of the second five rules, particularly the last three, where a single violation causes no harm, but an impartial rational person cannot publicly allow such a violation because publicly allowing such a violation would have serious harmful consequences. These are the cases where the moral virtues are needed to fill the gap between the justification of morality and providing an adequate reason for being moral. There are no moral virtues specifically related to each of the first five moral rules. They are not needed, for when the first five rules are involved the moral reason is sufficient to offer an answer to the question "Why should I be moral?" But each of the second five moral rules is closely related to a moral virtue: to the rule concerning deceit, truthfulness; to promises, trustworthiness; to cheating, fairness; to obeying the law, honesty; and to duty, dependability. (Relating the virtues to the second five rules somewhat differently will make no difference to anything that follows.)

The answer to the question "Why should I be moral?" when it is not likely that the particular violation will have harmful consequences for anyone, is related to the moral answer by means of the virtues. As noted in chapter 11, virtues and vices are based on one's intentional, free, voluntary actions. Justifiably following the moral rule builds the virtue and unjustifiably violating the rule builds the vice. The reason for following the moral rule in the peculiar situation when no one would be harmed by an unjustified violation sounds like a prudential one, namely, it builds your character. Although this may sound more like a Platonic reason of self-interest than a moral reason, it is not, for a virtuous person is much less likely to cause harm to others. A virtuous person is less likely to unjustifiably break moral rules when this will increase the likelihood of someone suffering evil consequences.

It should not be surprising that the moral answer to the question "Why should I be moral?" is directly related to the first five moral rules and only indirectly related to the second five. The first five rules are directly related to the evils that all rational persons desire to avoid, but the second five are only indirectly related to these evils. Every violation of the first five rules causes or increases the likelihood of someone suffering evil consequences. But even though general violation of the second five rules causes or increases the likelihood of someone suffering evil consequences, not every particular violation does so. Hence it is not surprising that the moral answer to the question "Why should I be moral?" is sometimes indirect when applied to these second five rules. Nor is it surprising that this indirect answer involves the moral virtues, for each of the second five rules is closely tied to a moral virtue. These moral virtues, when properly understood, necessarily lead to less evil being suffered than the associated vices, and hence are quite closely related to the moral reason.

As pointed out in chapter 11 on the virtues, underlying all of the moral virtues is the spiritual virtue of humility. Humility could also be called an intellectual virtue, for it involves having correct beliefs about one's own vulnerability, limited knowledge, and fallibility. Humility involves the recognition that one cannot know how unjustifiably violating a moral rule will affect one's character. It involves realizing that it may affect it in a way that increases the likelihood that one will violate a rule in the future when doing so will cause harm. To think that one can know that an immoral act will have no bad effects on one's future behavior is a clear example of arrogance and explains why arrogance normally leads to immoral behavior.[3]

Fallibility is far more significant when talking about the effect on one's character from unjustifiably violating a moral rule than it is when talking about the consequences of a particular unjustified violation. It is extremely plausible that one might know that a particular unjustified violation will cause no harm; it is much less plausible that one knows how one's character will be affected by unjustifiably violating a moral rule. To know that one is unjustifiably violating a moral rule is to know that one is acting in a way that one cannot publicly allow. The resulting hypocrisy may also have bad effects. Recognition by a person of his limited knowledge and fallibility not only is likely to help him avoid causing harm to others, it also decreases the chances of his suffering harm himself.

The Virtuous Answer

Although the virtues are used to support the moral answer to the question "Why should I be moral?" they also provide an independent answer to this question. The virtuous answer to the question "Why should I be moral?" is that acting morally is necessary in order to have the moral virtues. The motivating power of this answer makes use of the fact that some persons aspire to have all of the virtues, both moral and personal. Aspiring to a character of this sort requires acting morally. For clearly a person cannot have the moral virtues unless she acts morally. One who acts morally because she aspires to a good character need not even be concerned with others. Rather she need only be concerned with attaining a goal that she has set herself. It is certainly a worthy goal, one that all impartial rational persons would favor all persons seeking. If one has been brought up in a certain way, this answer will have considerable force. However, I cannot see why anyone would be brought up so that the virtuous answer will have much appeal without being brought up to regard the moral answer as having great force. Although one needs no reason for aspiring to a character that includes the moral virtues, it is very unlikely that one will aspire to it unless she does have an additional reason. The strongest additional reason for wanting such a character is provided by the moral answer.

Like the moral answer, the virtuous answer is not merely contingently related to the nature of morality; rather, it is essentially related to it. But perhaps surprisingly, unlike the moral answer, the virtuous answer always provides by itself a direct answer to the question "Why be moral?" Indeed, it always provides an adequate reason for being moral. Of course, it will not serve as a motive for someone who has no desire to have the moral virtues, but it has already been shown that not all reasons serve as motives for all rational persons. Although the virtuous answer does not need to be supplemented by any other answer, it is far more likely to serve as a motive to a person who accepts the moral answer. However, any adequate account of morality must be such that there is always an adequate reason for acting morally, and it is only by bringing in the virtues that one can always provide an adequate reason for acting morally. This, together with the fact that attaining the virtues always provides an adequate reason for being moral, may provide one explanation of why morality has traditionally been regarded as being concerned primarily with the virtues.

The Impartial Rationality Answer

The third answer that has an essential relation to morality is what I call the impartial rationality answer to the question "Why should I be moral?" This answer makes use of the fact that all rational persons, insofar as they are advocating an attitude toward the moral rules that could be accepted by all other rational persons, must advocate the attitude of a person who is impartial with regard to all moral agents. Since impartial rationality requires acting morally, a person may be motivated to act morally because impartial rationality requires acting in this way. The impartial rationality answer is similar to the virtuous one in that neither one requires concern for anyone else, yet both can always provide a direct answer to the question "Why be moral?" Also, as with wanting to have the moral virtues, one needs no reason for wanting to act as impartial rationality requires. However, I do not think that many who are not motivated by the moral answer will be motivated by the impartial rationality answer.

The impartial rationality answer may have significant motivating force because of a confusion concerning rationality. This is a confusion about the relationship between what impartial rationality requires and what rationality requires. It is irrational not to act as rationality requires; it is not irrational not to act as impartial rationality requires. That impartial rationality requires acting morally does not mean that rationality requires acting morally. As I have continually pointed out, and shall discuss again later in this chapter, rationality does not require acting morally, although it always allows acting in this way. Rationality does not require acting in the way impartial rationality requires; it is not irrational not to be impartial in the way morality requires. The failure to clearly distinguish between what rationality requires and what impartial rationality requires may lead one to the false conclusion that it is irrational to act immorally. Since no one wants to act irrationally, this false conclusion may provide motivation for one to act morally. Many followers of Kant seem to be involved in this kind of confusion.[4]

Feminist moral theory is correct in citing care for others rather than impartial rationality, or the attaining of the virtues, as the fundamental reason for acting morally.[5] However, it is not the only motivation for doing so. Although the moral answer is more fundamental than either the impartial rationality answer or the virtuous answer, the latter two answers are also important. Some persons may have been brought up having virtuous persons as role models and so desire to have a character including all the moral virtues. Other persons may have been brought up to provide reasons to defend their actions and so desire to act in the way that impartial rationality requires. Still others may have been brought up to despise hypocrisy. Even if they have been brought up to have concern for all and so find the moral answer most persuasive, the virtuous and impartial rationality answers may provide additional motivation for acting morally. It may be that the moral answer, making no reference to oneself, is, by itself, not a sufficient motive to lead some people to act morally. The virtuous and impartial rationality answers, though normally grounded in the moral answer, go beyond it and carry some significant force of their own. Evidence for this is the fact that some common emotions, with obvious power to move people, are related to both of these answers as well as to the moral one.

Moral Emotions: Compassion, Remorse, Pride, Shame, and Guilt

Compassion and remorse are intimately related to the moral answer. Combined with a proper understanding of morality, compassion provides additional motivational force to the moral answer, although without such an understanding, compassion may lead to immoral actions. Those who sincerely ask "Why should I be moral?" need not lack the necessary compassion. They can have compassion for others, but not see how morality, which they regard as simply a traditional set of rules, has any relationship to it. The moral answer may provide adequate motivation, if it is clearly explained and presented. Even some who do not generally feel compassion often suffer remorse when they see someone suffering because of something they have done, even if unintentionally. To feel remorse is to suffer because of some harm you have caused. Unlike compassion, remorse is felt only in circumstances in which you consider yourself responsible for someone suffering some evil. A compassionate person will often feel remorse when someone suffers because of his immoral actions, especially violations of the first five rules. But even violations of the second five rules that result in someone suffering harm are likely to cause remorse. Compassion is more closely related to the moral ideals than to the moral rules, but remorse is related primarily to the moral rules.

The emotions most closely related to the virtuous answer are pride and shame. Of course, pride is appropriate to more than one's moral virtues. One can take pride in one's abilities, work, family, or country. To feel pleasure in anything because one believes that it is related to oneself and lives up to a standard that one accepts or that makes one believe oneself better than average is to feel pride in that thing. Since most rational persons consider a character containing the moral virtues to live up to an accepted standard and to make one better than average, it is obviously appropriate to take pride in one's moral virtues. Someone who does take pride in her moral character will suffer shame when she acts immorally. To feel shame is to feel sad due to loss of pride or because of something related to one that fails to live up to an accepted standard or that one believes makes one worse than average. Since the groups with regard to which one determines what counts as average may differ quite considerably, one can feel pride when comparing oneself to a larger group, but shame when comparing oneself to a smaller one. And it may not be under one's control which group one uses. The desire to maintain one's pride and to avoid feeling shame provide strong motives to some for being moral. Pride and shame are more closely related to the moral ideals than to the moral rules. One often feels pride when acting on the moral ideals, and shame is commonly caused by failure to act on them.

Guilt feelings seem most closely related to the impartial rationality answer. Although guilt is often closely associated with legal rules or laws, guilt feelings were originally related to violating those rules that were established by one's parents. These rules were usually regarded as moral rules, and so it is not surprising that people often feel guilty if they have unjustifiably broken some moral rule. If one unjustifiably violates a rule that one knows that all impartial rational persons favor everyone's following, it is appropriate to feel anxiety. Even though this anxiety may originally be due to one's belief that if found out, one will be punished, one may feel guilt later simply because one believes that one is guilty. Children often feel guilt when they violate the rules laid down by their parents or teachers; adults may not feel guilt unless the rules they violate are ones that they consider justified. The impartial rationality answer emphasizes that the moral rules are rules toward which all impartial rational persons, including oneself, favor obedience, including liability to punishment for unjustified violations. Accepting the impartial rationality answer should lead one to feel guilt even for unjustified violations of the second five moral rules when no one is hurt. The desire to avoid feeling guilt may provide a strong motive for acting morally.

Conscience, Authenticity, Integrity, and Dignity

The impartial rationality answer can also be used to explain and justify some of the talk about conscience. This should not be surprising, as pangs of conscience are often considered identical to guilt feelings. Conscience is best regarded as one's public attitude, that is, the attitude one takes when considering something as part of a public system that applies to all rational persons. This account of conscience allows people to have some differences in what their consciences tell them to do, but assures that conscience always tells one to avoid morally unacceptable actions. Letting one's conscience be one's guide becomes equivalent to guiding one's actions by morality. Going against one's conscience is acting as one knows that one's public attitude not only would not favor but would even favor liability to punishment for such action. Regarding a person's conscience as his public attitude rather than as his superego takes conscience out of psychology and brings it back to morality where it belongs. However, it is easy to understand how conscience came to be identified with the superego. Most of one's public attitude was learned from one's parents. Concerned primarily with the explanation of behavior and not its justification, Freud and his followers made no attempt to distinguish between that internalized parental teaching which was justifiable and that which was not. Thus conscience was swallowed up by the superego and lost its moral significance. By identifying conscience with one's public attitude, conscience regains its traditional moral authority.

The impartial rationality answer is also related to the concept of authenticity. Authenticity excludes hypocrisy. Hypocrisy is not exactly deceit, but is closely related to it. It consists in making moral judgments about other persons' behavior, thereby suggesting that one acts in accordance with those judgments, when, in fact, one does not. Some people have maintained that authenticity is all that is required for acting morally. That is correct only if one makes moral judgments. However, since most people do make moral judgments it is plausible to maintain that an authentic person must be a moral person. If one makes judgments according to one's conscience and acts accordingly, one would be acting authentically. In somewhat older terminology, which I prefer, such a person would be called a person of integrity.

Taking cheating as the model of immoral action may lead one to look upon the moral rules as the rules that govern the game of life. Looking at them in this way, a person may regard it as beneath her dignity to be immoral. She may think that if she cannot win the game of life without violating the moral rules, she does not deserve to win. Viewing morality in this way may lead one to find the impartial rationality answer persuasive. The difference between dignity and integrity is very small; however, dignity has a closer relationship to pride. To act beneath one's dignity is to suffer shame; to violate one's integrity is to suffer guilt. A person of dignity is one who sincerely believes "It matters not whether you win or lose, but how you play the game." Although there are many explanations why a person may accept the moral rules as the rules for the game of life, the moral answer provides the best reason for doing so. Thus dignity, which is a completely self-regarding reason for acting morally, is supported by concern for others.[6]

Although desires for authenticity, integrity, or dignity may lead people to act morally, compassion makes it more likely that they will do so. However, if one has dignity and integrity, in addition to compassion, then one has additional reasons for being moral. Being moral is required to avoid not only remorse, but also shame and guilt. But all of these reasons have an air of self-interest about them. Self-interest, no matter how far it is extended, does not provide the fundamental reason for being moral. The fundamental reason for being moral is to avoid causing harm to others. The fundamental reason for being morally good is to prevent or relieve the suffering of others. None of these other reasons seems very strong unless supported by the moral reason. The motivating force of all of the reasons is primarily determined by the way one has been brought up, but it is clear that the motivating force of the moral reason can be increased significantly by the addition of these other reasons.

Summary of Answers to the Question "Why Should I Be Moral?"

I have considered a number of answers to the question "Why should I be moral?" Some, like the answers in terms of self-interest and those that involve religious belief, I have found wanting. Self-interest does not always provide a reason for acting morally, and religious answers do not provide reasons at all for those who do not have the appropriate religious beliefs. I agree that acting morally is generally in one's self-interest and have tried to show why this is so, but unfortunately morality and self-interest do not always coincide. Fortunately, those who ask "Why should one be moral?" are normally not looking for an answer in terms of self-interest but for one that explains the point of morality. The religious answers may satisfy some, but a rational person need not believe in any God, let alone one that commands people to always act morally.

The fundamental answer is the moral answer. This answer stems from the very nature of morality and provides an adequate reason for being moral in all of the most important moral situations. Although, without bringing in the virtues, it does not provide an adequate reason for being moral in every case, when the virtues are brought in, it does do so. The virtuous answer and the impartial rationality answer are compatible with the moral answer, and the three together are stronger than anyone of them all by itself. Although the virtuous answer and the impartial rationality answer can each stand alone, the moral answer provides the reason that these other reasons have significant force. The moral reason can be supported by many other reasons, including those involving the emotions of compassion, remorse, pride, shame, and guilt, but the fundamental reason for being moral is to avoid causing harm to others.

The moral answer, supported by the virtuous answer and the impartial rationality answer, provides the best reasons for acting morally. Even though acceptance of some religious reasons might make it irrational to be immoral, that does not mean that religious reasons are better reasons than the moral reason and its supporting reasons. Indeed, even were one to make the highly dubious hypotheses about human nature or the nature of the world that some philosophers make, it is unlikely that one could provide better reasons than these reasons. Although the reasons provided by the moral, virtuous, and impartial rationality answers are good enough to make it completely rational for any person to act morally at any time, they do not make it irrational for one ever to act immorally. That some religious reasons can make it irrational to be immoral may be taken as an argument for accepting these religious reasons. However, once one realizes that punishment is more appropriate for immoral actions than for irrational ones, it becomes apparent that regarding all immoral actions as irrational creates serious problems. Although the moral reason, even with its supporting reasons, will not motivate all rational persons to act morally, it will motivate some. Further, even those who are not motivated by these reasons for acting morally would be acting rationally if they were so motivated.

Impossibility of Giving Conclusive Reasons for Acting Morally

Some might take the previous paragraph to be an admission of ultimate failure to answer the question "Why should I be moral?" I have admitted that it is perfectly rational to act immorally even when one knows that acting immorally will cause harm to others. This correctly suggests that it is sensible to ask "Why should I avoid causing harm to others?" But if one can ask for reasons to avoid causing harm to others, then it might seem that giving the answer "You will avoid causing harm to others" does not provide an adequate reason for acting morally. However, simply because it is sensible to ask "Why should I avoid causing harm to others?" it does not follow that avoiding causing harm to others does not provide an adequate reason for being moral. The claim that if I can sensibly ask "Why should I do X?" when X is the reason for doing Y, then X cannot be an adequate reason for doing Y, is based on a mistaken view of reasons. The mistake involved is due to a concept of a reason that has been shown to be false, that an adequate reason for doing a particular action is one that provides a motive for all rational persons.

As the popularity of answers in terms of self-interest shows, some people want an answer to the question "Why should I be moral?" that shows that it is always rationally required to act morally. They are not satisfied with answers that merely show that it is always rationally allowed to act morally. I have already shown that rationality does not require acting morally. The reluctance to accept this answer may be due to the belief that rationality does always require one kind of action, namely action in one's own self-interest. Rational egoism, which was discussed in chapter 3, is the view that it is irrational to act contrary to one's self-interest. Those who accept this view think that if they can show that acting morally is acting in one's self-interest, they will have shown that rationality requires acting morally. The equation of rational action with action in one's self-interest is so strong that the question "Why should I do X?" is often taken to mean no more than "How will doing X benefit me?"

The answer "Because you will avoid causing harm to others" is not considered satisfactory, because although it gives an adequate reason for being moral, it is not a conclusive reason. It does not provide a motive for all rational persons, and so not all rational persons will act in accord with it. Supposedly, the only answer that provides a motive for all rational persons is a reason of self-interest, so the only answer that all rational persons will act on is "Because it is in your self-interest." However, this answer cannot always be truthfully given, so that self-interest cannot always provide conclusive reasons for acting morally. But even if one could show that it is always in one's self-interest to act morally, this would still not show that there are conclusive reasons for acting morally, that is, reasons that would make it irrational not to act morally.

Self-Interest Does Not Always Provide Conclusive Reasons

I agree that only reasons of self-interest provide motives to all rational persons and that when no one else is involved, it provides conclusive reasons. However, I should now like to show that when other people are involved, the answer "Because it is in your self-interest" does not provide conclusive reasons, that is, reasons that all rational persons must act on. First I shall discuss a slightly different question so as to provide as close a parallel to the moral case as possible. Consider the question "Why should I be prudent?" This is a question that is asked, though perhaps not in exactly these terms, by many people, especially by teenagers. Just as "Why shouldn't I do it if I want to?" is sometimes equivalent to "Why should I be moral?" so it is also sometimes equivalent to "Why should I be prudent?" In the former case, the answer is "You will harm others"; in the latter, "You will harm yourself." It is plausible to think it perfectly rational to go on and ask "Why shouldn't I harm others ?" but to be irrational to reply "Why shouldn't I harm myself?" This plausibility is not merely due to a prejudice in favor of oneself over others. The two questions are not usually asked in the same circumstances. With the question, "Why shouldn't I harm others?" a further clause is generally understood, namely, "if it benefits me." The question is really "Why should I refrain from harming others if it benefits me?" I have already stated that rationality does not require refraining from harming others, especially when one would benefit from causing them harm.

The question "Why shouldn't I harm myself?" cannot be understood in the same way, that is, with the unstated clause "if it benefits me." With the question "Why shouldn't I harm myself?" the unstated clause is generally something like "if I want to." When asking why one should not harm others, the interests of others is implicitly opposed to self-interest. When asking why one should not harm oneself, self-interest is opposed to irrational desires. Someone who smokes, drinks, or takes other drugs, when told that his excessive use will harm him, may reply, "So what, I want to." Here, if the harm is regarded as significant, the person is considered to be acting irrationally. Thus, when the harm is serious, "Why shouldn't I harm myself?" is a question that no rational person would ask. Hence it seems that the answer "You will harm yourself if you do that" is one that all rational persons would accept as conclusive for not doing something, whereas "You will harm someone else if you do that" is not a conclusive reason to all rational persons.

However, the question "Why shouldn't I harm others?" was asked when the alternative was benefiting myself. But the question "Why shouldn't I harm myself?" was opposed not to the prevention of harm to others but to an irrational desire. It is not that, considered by themselves, "Why shouldn't I harm others?" is a perfectly sensible question and "Why shouldn't I harm myself?" is a senseless one. The sense of the question depends upon the unstated clause that goes with the question. It is not senseless to ask "Why shouldn't I harm myself?" if the unstated clause is "if I can thereby prevent greater harm to others." This question with this unstated clause is one that is asked, though perhaps not in these words, by many people, particularly idealistic young men and women. It is not unusual to hear parents try to persuade their daughter not to join the Peace Corps or not to join the fight for civil rights, by pointing out that she may suffer harm. And it is not unusual to hear the daughter reply that this is not a good enough reason, that avoidance of harm to herself does not take precedence over trying to help others. Thus it can be seen that "Why shouldn't I harm myself?" is not always a senseless question. Avoidance of harm to oneself does not always provide a conclusive reason for all rational persons, one that they will always act on in preference to preventing harm for others.

Only an inadequate account of the concept of rationality like rational egoism leads to the view that it is irrational to sacrifice one's own interests for the interests of others. Rational egoism has already been shown to be an oversimplification of the concept of rationality. It is irrational to harm oneself for no reason, but it is not irrational to sacrifice your own interests for the interests of others. When the interests of others are involved, the reply "You will harm yourself if you do that" is not a conclusive reason for all rational persons. It does provide a good reason for not doing something, but in doing this it does no more than the reply "You will harm others if you do that." Although avoidance of harm to oneself provides a motive for all rational persons, whereas avoidance of harm to others does not, this does not mean that when they conflict the former motive is always stronger than the latter. Indeed, one reason counts as a better or stronger reason than another if the former can make rational every otherwise irrational action that the latter can make rational and more besides. Beliefs about avoiding harm to oneself and beliefs about avoiding harm to others are such that it is usually rationally allowed to guide one's action by either one. Of course, one who usually acts so as to avoid greater harm to others is very likely to act morally, while one who always acts in his own self-interest will probably not, but neither person will be acting irrationally.

Rationality, Self-Interest, and Morality

It may now seem as if rationality is of no use as a guide to action. This, of course, is not so; rationality is incompatible with many kinds of action, as pointed out in chapters 2 and 3. It is true that in the important decisions about whether or not to act morally, rationality does not provide a guide. When morality and self-interest conflict, even when morality and the interests of friends or family conflict, rationality takes no sides. Disappointing as this conclusion seems at first, any other conclusion would be worse. Were rationality ever to prohibit acting morally, one would be forced, in the case of conflict, to advocate either irrational or immoral behavior. If rationality were always to require acting morally, one would be forced to regard all immoral action as irrational, including that which was clearly in the self-interest of the agent. Contrasted with either of these alternatives, the conclusion seems far less disappointing than before.

I have shown that in a conflict between morality and self-interest, rationality allows one to act either morally or in one's self-interest. This may lead one to think that rationality prohibits acting in any way that is both immoral and contrary to one's self-interest. This has not been shown. Indeed, it is false. Rationality allows action that is both immoral and contrary to one's self-interest, such as self-sacrificing action done to support the immoral behavior of one's friends or colleagues. Indeed, the most serious immoral actions are those done for some cause or group, not from simple self-interest. Those philosophers who talk as if all rational actions are either moral actions or those of self-interest seem to overlook this obvious fact. Further, some seem to hold not only that moral actions and self-interested actions exhaust the category of rational actions, but that they are mutually exclusive. This has the odd consequence that self-interest never provides an additional reason and motive for acting morally, and that knowing that one's action is morally right never provides an additional reason and motive for acting in one's self-interest.

It is hard to believe that anyone who has thought about the matter thinks that self-interest and morality are always in conflict. So many actions that are in one's self-interest fall outside the sphere of morality that this view is not even plausible. Further, even when one's actions are covered by a moral rule or ideal, self-interest may provide additional reasons for acting morally. It is in one's self-interest to avoid shame, guilt, and remorse, and one must act morally if one wishes to avoid them. Further, the risk of punishment and the enmity of those affected by immoral action may also lead one to act morally. Good governments pass laws in order to make self-interest and morality provide reasons for doing the same action. It should now be clear that self-interest and morality are not only not mutually exclusive, but that they often reinforce each other.

Reasons for Acting Immorally

Although self-interest and morality often provide reasons for doing the same action, they also often conflict. But it has already been shown that even if self-interest and morality always did support doing the same action, this would not make it irrational to act immorally. There are other reasons for acting immorally besides reasons of self-interest, such as beliefs that one's action will benefit a friend or those who share one's religious beliefs. Since one is concerned for these people, these beliefs will also be motives for benefiting them. Such beliefs may lead people not only to act in ways that they know are both immoral and contrary to their own self-interest, they may also make acting in that way rational. Parents often act both immorally and contrary to their own self-interest for the sake of their children. Their interest in their children is greater than their concern for themselves or for morality. Lovers not only sacrifice themselves, but others, for the sake of their loved ones. Parents and lovers who act in these ways are not acting irrationally. Neither are those who sacrifice their lives for their country, even when their country is fighting an immoral war.

However, some actions, such as those motivated by revenge, which lead to actions that are both contrary to one's self-interest and immoral, are irrational. It may be that concentrating on these kinds of actions is what leads some to think that all actions that are contrary to both self-interest and morality are irrational. But revenge that is contrary to both self-interest and morality is irrational because it does not benefit anyone. When one's action benefits someone, such as a friend, relative, racial or religious group, or country, it can be both contrary to one's self-interest and to morality and still be rational. Benefiting anyone provides a reason. Physicians and scientists sometimes act both immorally and contrary to their own self-interest in order to protect their colleagues. Indeed, misguided loyalty is not only one of the leading causes of immoral actions, it is one of the leading causes of confusion about morality. Many well-intentioned people cannot understand how it can be immoral to risk their own careers in order to cover up the mistakes of their colleagues. They confuse morality with altruism or unselfishness. They forget that morality does not allow violating a moral rule unless an impartial rational person can publicly allow such a violation.

Failure to realize that a rational action can be both immoral and contrary to one's self-interest, together with the view that all rational actions must be either self-interested or moral, reinforces the view that whenever a rational person sacrifices himself for others he is acting morally. Unjustified violations of the moral rules that are contrary to one's self-interest, perhaps even requiring risking one's life, are ubiquitous. Even granting the enormous amount of evil caused by immoral actions done from motives of self-interest, considerably more evil has been caused by immoral actions that were contrary to the self-interest of the agent. Religions have provided both reasons and motives for people to act in ways that were both immoral and contrary to their self-interest. Many of these actions were rational because God was believed to be pleased by them. The amount of evil caused by self-sacrificing immoral actions for religious reasons is incredible. So many persons have not only slaughtered others but risked their own lives in advancing the interests of their religion that it is impossible to hold that self-interest is the sole or even primary cause of immoral action.

Religion is only one of many sources of reasons for acting immorally. People often act immorally in order to advance the interests of their social or economic class. And sometimes these immoral actions require some sacrifice of self-interest. Persons often act both immorally and contrary to their self-interest, in order to advance the interests of their race or ethnic group. But today probably the greatest and most serious source of reasons for acting immorally comes from one's country. Many persons are not only willing, but anxious, to sacrifice their lives for their country even when their country is engaged in an immoral war. The evil caused by immoral actions due to nationalism probably outweighs the evil caused by the immoral actions due to all other reasons put together. Taking an interest in one's country need not lead to immoral actions. To be willing to do whatever is in the best interests of one's country, except act immorally, is the mark of a patriot. A nationalist is one who is willing to advance the interests of his country even when this requires him to act immorally. To keep patriotism from degenerating into nationalism is impossible without a clear understanding of morality.

There are many sources of reasons for acting immorally: self, children, friends, lovers, colleagues, race, religion, and country. If immoral actions are done for any of these reasons besides self-interest, an action can be rational even though it is both immoral and contrary to self-interest. Moral impartiality requires not merely that one make no exceptions for oneself, but also that one make no exceptions for one's children, friends, lovers, colleagues, race, religion, or country. That is why concern for others, unless it is an impartial concern for all those protected by morality, does not guarantee that one will act morally. Although it is true that concern for others often leads one not only to avoid doing immoral actions, but also to do morally good ones, if that concern is not governed by an adequate understanding of morality, it can lead to morally bad actions. In the conflict between feminist moral theory, which champions care as the fundamental reason for moral action, and Kant, who champions an impartial respect for the moral law, the feminists are correct. However, in order for care not to result in any morally unacceptable actions, an adequate understanding of morality, including the requirements of moral impartiality, is required.

Reasons for Acting Morally

As pointed out above, self-interest often is not an opponent of morality at all but often sides with morality against the demands of friends, colleagues, country, race, or religion. To avoid misunderstanding it should also be pointed out that friends, colleagues, religion, country, and race sometimes provide reasons for acting morally when self-interest would lead to immoral action. In other words, self-interest, friends, colleagues, religion, race, and country, all provide reasons that sometimes support morality and sometimes support immoral action. Why then has self-interest received so much attention as the opponent of morality? Perhaps because of a misunderstanding of morality, and probably also because of an over simple account of rational action, but there is another explanation that deserves some consideration.

Concern for others is often the primary motivating force for acting in accordance with the moral rules and for following moral ideals. Concern for others also motivates acting to advance the interests of one's religion, race, or country. However, when considering violations of the moral rules, morality, unlike religion, race, and country, requires impartial concern for all. On the other hand, if one is not violating any moral rule, the moral ideals encourage one to minimize the evil suffered by any person or group of persons. If self-interest provides the only motive for one's actions, then one will not be a morally good person, whereas acting for patriotic, racial, or religious motives may lead one to justifiably follow the moral ideals. However, although race, religion, and country, unlike self-interest, may provide motives for morally good actions, they also provide more powerful motives for immoral action. Indeed, except for those motives provided by the moral answer and related virtuous and impartial rationality answers, the motives that have the most power for morally good actions also have the most power for morally bad ones. But when religious conviction, racial pride, and patriotism come together in a person who has great compassion for all humankind, as they did in Dr. Martin Luther King Jr., moral goodness achieves such power that even death seems to be overcome.

Are Reasons for Acting Morally Stronger or Better Than Reasons of Self-Interest?

The account of the stronger or better reasons given in chapter 3 may make it seem that in any conflict between morality and self-interest, the stronger reasons would always support acting morally. As was pointed out in that chapter, one reason counts as stronger than another if it makes rational every otherwise irrational action that the other reason makes rational, plus others besides. On this account, when morality and self-interest conflict, it will often be the case that the reasons for acting morally are better than the reasons for acting in one's own self interest, for one will often be causing greater harm for others than one is avoiding for oneself. Indeed, often one will be causing great harm to others simply to gain lesser goods for oneself. People do not usually ask why they should be moral when there are clearly better reasons for being moral than for acting immorally. The situation in which this question is most often asked is when acting morally requires acting in a way that will result in great harm to oneself, whereas acting immorally does not seem to have a serious bad effect on anyone.

　　It is when the reasons for acting morally are not clearly better than the reasons for acting immorally, for example, when one can avoid harm to one's friends by deceiving others, that people are more likely to ask why they should be moral. Taking self-interest to be the primary opponent of morality obscures those particular cases where acting immorally can benefit one's friends or colleagues at the expense of others, but the overall harm and benefits involved either do not change or one's friends gain more than the others lose. But I deny that there are ever cases where there are clearly better reasons for acting immorally than for acting morally. If the better reasons were reasons of self-interest, that would make it irrational to act morally, and this is clearly an unacceptable conclusion. If the better reasons for acting immorally involved the interests of those for whom one was concerned rather than oneself, it might not be irrational to act morally, but it would be unreasonable. But no adequate account of morality can allow that it is ever unreasonable to act morally; that there are ever situations where there are better reasons for acting immorally than for acting morally. The reasons for acting morally must always be at least as good as those for acting immorally, but they do not always have to be clearly better reasons.

Some people might claim that in every situation the reasons for acting morally are better than the reasons for acting immorally once the possible effect of one's immoral action on one's character is taken into account. I do not deny that taking the possible effect of one's immoral action on one's character is an important reason for acting morally. Indeed, that reason is sometimes needed in order to make it rational to act morally. However, there is no point in claiming that in every situation the reasons for acting morally are better than those for acting immorally. Even if that were true, it would still not be irrational to act immorally, for it is not always irrational not to act on the better reasons. If it were, everyone would be acting irrationally when they spend money on luxuries for themselves rather than contributing the money to buy necessities for many others. There are many philosophers who claim that everyone who spends money on luxuries for himself rather than giving that money to worthy charities is acting immorally, but I do not know of any who claim that all of these people are acting irrationally.

Conclusion

I realize that the question "Why should I be moral?" will be answered differently by different rational persons. I would expect most readers of this book to advocate that everyone be moral and to give some or all of the answers to the question that I have provided in this chapter. However, I am fully aware that rational persons, who lack that concern for all humankind that is essential for dependable moral action, may not advocate to those for whom they are concerned that they always act morally. A rational mother, perhaps with bitter experience with persons outside of her family, may advocate to her daughter not to be moral, but only to seem to be. Such a person might provide her daughter with reasons why she should not be moral. She may argue that she will generally get the best of others if she is immoral and that she will be able to satisfy her own desires and the desires of those whom she loves much more completely and easily. In some situations this may be persuasive, but in others it will not.

Equally common will be the father who advocates to his son to put his country above all else. He can also provide some powerful reasons for his son to adopt this course of action. His life will have a largeness of purpose and ideals that are lacking to the person who is concerned only with himself and some few loved ones. Indeed, such a person may have all the rewards that are normally associated with a moral life, including great respect and esteem. Putting one's race or religion above all else may be supported by similar reasons. It is not a service to morality to minimize the persuasiveness of these answers; they do not lose their persuasiveness if they are ignored. However, I think that stage in human history may now have arrived where the moral answer may prove to be more persuasive to many to whom it is clearly presented. Many persons now do have a concern for all humankind, and many religions now support this concern. Many nations have come to realize how small the Earth is. And the harms that result from dividing the races have become apparent to all.

The difficulties of providing persuasive answers to the question "Why should I be moral?" are no greater than the difficulties of providing persuasive answers to the question "Why should I be immoral?" Unfortunately, in some societies, and in some parts of all societies, the answers to "Why should I be immoral?" may be more persuasive than the answers to "Why should I be moral?" It is, perhaps, the most important measure of a society which answers are most persuasive to most of its citizens.

Notes

1. Robert Hannaford in *Moral Anatomy and Moral Reasoning* (Lawrence: University Press of Kansas 1993) incorrectly lumps me together with David Gauthier and claims that I hold that reason is essentially egoistic. I do hold the similar-sounding, but very different, view that it is always irrational to go against one's self-interest for no reason, but I explicitly state that reasons involving the interests of others are sometimes stronger than reasons of self-interest. My claim is that insofar as one is rational, whether egoistic, completely impartial, or somewhere in the middle, one will still put forward what I list as the moral rules and moral ideals as essential parts of the public system that will govern all rational persons. Indeed, that all rational persons put forward common morality as the public system governing their behavior is what justifies common morality. Hannaford seems to think that it is somehow inconsistent to have different motives for being moral than for wanting others to be moral. I do not say that everyone does have different motives for wanting to be moral and wanting others to be so, but I see no inconsistency in the primary motive for wanting to be moral being impartial concern for others and the primary motive for wanting others to be moral being self-interest and the interests of friends.

Since Hannaford correctly states that my views are closely related to Hobbes, it may be significant that he also has a mistaken interpretation of Hobbes's views. Hobbes does not hold that all people act only on motives of self-interest. He explicitly points out that all the moral "virtues are contained in justice and charity." Hobbes does claim that an absolutely impartial concern for all humankind, or even for all citizens of one's country, is so rare that it cannot serve as the foundation of civil society. On both of these points Hobbes is correct. See my introduction to *Man and Citizen* by Thomas Hobbes (Indianapolis: Hackett, 1991), and my article "Hobbes's Psychology," in *The Cambridge Companion to Hobbes*, edited by Tom Sorell (Cambridge: Cambridge University Press, 1996), 157–174.

2. The Ten Commandments are an excellent example of this kind of grouping.

3. There are exceptional cases where one might know that a harmless unjustified violation will not affect one's character, such as when one knows that one will die almost immediately. In such cases, there is a strong temptation to claim that since there is not an adequate reason to sacrifice one's self-interest in order to obey the moral rule against cheating, the violation is in fact a justified one. It is not implausible to claim that at least some rational persons would publicly allow a harmless violation of a rule by someone who is going to die very shortly. However, whether or not one accepts this claim is not important, for if one does accept it, the violation is at least weakly justifiable, and if one does not, there must be some reason why no impartial rational person would publicly allow such a violation, and this reason will be an adequate reason for obeying the rule.

4. This confusion is primarily a confusion about the concept of rationality. See Alan Gewirth, "Can Any Final End Be Rational?" *Ethics* 102 (October 1991), where Gewirth wants to hold both that rationality requires impartiality and that everyone always wants to be ratio-

nal. "For if a final end can be shown to be rational, then it is truly worth maintaining or pursuing, and we can know this to be so" (p. 68). On the previous page he claims, "I shall here use 'reason' in its most traditional and general sense to mean the power of ascertaining and preserving truth." But, as in his book *Reason and Morality* (Chicago: University of Chicago Press, 1978), Gewirth does not try to show that ascertaining and preserving truth is always "truly worth maintaining or pursuing," but, like almost all other philosophers putting forward an account of rationality, he assumes that his philosophical definition of "rational" accords with the standard meaning of "rational" described in previous chapters.

5. Unfortunately, feminist moral theory often starts by attacking Kohlberg's claims about the stages of moral development, without recognizing a serious flaw in his description of each of those stages. Kohlberg links together questions about how what counts as a morally acceptable, encouraged, or required action is determined, with questions about the reasons and motives for acting morally. His confusion was probably due to his acceptance of a Kantian view, where these two kinds of questions are presented as linked together. Even though care for others provides the fundamental reason and best motive for moral action, it does not determine what actions are moral.

6. This sense of dignity is distinct from its sense when it is used in expressions such as "You should treat people with dignity" or "Do not take away anyone's dignity." When used in this way, to treat a person with dignity is to treat her with respect, that is, as a moral agent and as someone fully protected by morality. It is to regard the person as competent to engage in moral reasoning. Humility requires that one regard all moral agents as protected by morality and as competent to engage in moral reasoning. It is what Kant meant, or should have meant, by saying that persons should be treated as ends and never merely as means. I have been helped to understand this sense of dignity by conversations with Maria Julia Bertomeu and George Ulrich.

Chapter 14

Morality and Society

In chapter 8 I showed that all societies, no matter how small, have a legal system, that is, a system of rules that applies to all persons in the society and that most of them use to guide their behavior and to make judgments about the behavior of others. I suspect that many people would call these simple legal systems moral systems and that is why they claim that different societies have completely different moralities. But this claim ignores the fact that morality is a public system; a moral judgment cannot be made on the action of someone who is justifiably ignorant of what he should have done. But a legal system is not a public system; ignorance, even completely justified ignorance, of the law sometimes does not exempt one from legal judgments. Further, a legal system can be based on authority; for example, a rule can be a law because the ruler, or God, is thought to have authorized it. A legal rule need not have the kind of content that would allow a rational person to favor it being part of a public system that governs the behavior of all those to whom it applies. A moral system must be a public system; that is, it must be understood by all those to whom it applies, and it cannot be irrational for any of them to use the system as a guide for their actions.

Everyone agrees that morality, at least in the sense that is of philosophical interest, is a public system, so that it is confusing and misleading to call a legal system, even of the kind I have been describing, a moral system. Even those who do not agree that morality applies to all rational persons recognize that all moralities are public systems. I do not claim that all people in all societies actually use a public system that even applies to all persons in their society in making their decisions or judgments about moral matters. In many small societies most people make their decisions and judgments about moral matters based upon their societies' legal system. These legal systems do not have the bureaucratic characteristics of legal systems in large industrialized societies, but in fundamental ways they resemble these legal systems more than they resemble morality. To emphasize the similarity of these judgments about what is right and wrong and about what ought to be done to judgments about an action being legally required or prohibited, I shall call them "personal legal judgments." They are not moral judgments. Thus I am not making the false empirical claim that all persons in all societies base their decisions and judgments about moral matters on the kind of moral system that I have been describing in this book. I do claim that all readers of this book make at least some judgments about moral matters based on the kind of moral system that I describe.

The failure of many people or societies to make genuine moral decisions and judgments is not due to lack of knowledge but rather to a lack of sufficient interest in a public system that applies to all people in their society, let alone all rational persons. Many simple legal systems, and even some complex ones, do not distinguish between religious matters and moral matters. Many people, even in large modern societies, make personal legal decisions and judgments about moral matters, especially when the legal systems on which they are based incorporate religious beliefs. Many people are more concerned with a system of conduct derived from their religious or metaphysical beliefs about the nature of the world and their place in it than with a public system that applies to all rational persons. Many people care seriously only about a limited group of people and are no more concerned with those not in this group, even members of their own society, than most rational persons are concerned with sheep. Rational persons need not make any decisions or judgments based on morality as I have described it. However, once people recognize that morality is the only system for governing behavior between people that is understood and can be followed by all rational persons, it is quite likely that they will, at least publicly, take the moral attitude toward the moral rules and sometimes even make decisions and judgments based on the moral system. All readers of this book make moral judgments, not only on individuals and their actions but also on governments and their actions.

These readers are not "like mushrooms, come to full maturity, without all kind of engagement with each other."[1] They are actual persons raised by families in societies. Their views about morality, like their views about everything else, are profoundly shaped by the family and society in which they are educated and trained. In chapter 8, I pointed out that different societies may interpret the moral rules differently, and in the previous chapter I noted that one's attitude toward morality is strongly affected by the way one has been brought up. Even though I believe that all readers of this book accept common morality, I am aware that there are many important differences concerning interpretation and scope. Rationally allowed beliefs, including both religious and scientific beliefs, differ both within societies and between societies. Rankings of the goods and evils and views about human nature and society also differ. All of these differences may affect one's moral decisions and judgments. However, since morality is an informal system, these differences should not lead one to accept the view that different persons or even different societies use different moral systems. They are simply using different variations of the same universal moral system.

Morality Applies to Governments

In this chapter I shall try to show that the moral system that applies to individuals is the same moral system that explains our moral judgments about governments. Indeed, there can only be one moral system, for if there were different moral systems for governments and for individuals and they sometimes required incompatible actions, any individual who was acting for a government could not avoid acting immorally. However, that a government has a duty to violate some moral rules with regard to its citizens independent of their consent (see chapter 9, the section on morally relevant features, question 4) results in some morally significant differences between governmental actions and actions by individuals. One consequence of a positive answer to question 4 and a government's being in a unique or almost unique position in this regard results in a government's sometimes being morally justified in violating a moral rule when individuals would not be.

For example, a government may be justified in depriving its citizens of some freedom when it is not morally justified for one citizen to deprive others of the same amount of freedom, even when all of the other morally relevant features are the same, including the same amount of evil caused, avoided, and prevented and the same rational desires of the persons being deprived of the freedom. That is why governments are justified in setting speed limits and imposing other safety regulations but individuals are not. That the actions of a government and of an individual, even if similar in all other respects, are not the same kind of act explains why impartial rational persons may publicly allow a violation of a moral rule by a government and not allow what seems like the same violation by an individual. But in both cases an action is morally justifiable only if an impartial rational person can publicly allow that kind of violation of a moral rule.

Persons in Government Not Morally Required to Be Morally Good

The persons who compose the government and who make the laws are subject to the moral rules in exactly the same way that all other persons are. This means that they are required to obey the moral rules except when an impartial rational person can publicly allow violating them, and that they are encouraged to follow the moral ideals. It may seem that unlike others they are required to follow some of the moral ideals, for it is acknowledged by all that governments have a duty to protect their citizens from the harms resulting from unjustified violations of the moral rules. Some people in government are not merely encouraged to follow those moral ideals that encourage persons to prevent unjustified violations of moral rules; they have a duty to follow these ideals. I agree that some persons in their roles as members of the government, such as members of the police force, do have such a duty, but since it is their duty, this does not change their relationship to the moral rules and ideals. People outside of government, such as nurses, often have duties that require them to act toward their patients in ways that would otherwise only be encouraged by the moral ideals. If one is required by one's duty, or by any of the moral rules, to prevent others from suffering some harm, acting in this way does not count as following a moral ideal, but as obeying a moral rule.

Awareness of the vast number of deprived persons in almost every country, may make it seem that more is required of persons, especially persons in government, than simply to obey the moral rules. To say that following the moral ideals is only encouraged, not required, may seem to provide an easy way out for those who self-ishly seek to preserve the status quo. Much as I would like to encourage people to act so as to lessen the evils suffered by deprived persons, it is worse than pointless to claim that morality requires helping the deprived. Of course, people who do noth-ing to help are not morally good, but no one should be forced to be morally good. Indeed, distinguishing between moral rules and moral ideals is intended to explain why there are limits to the behavior that people can be forced to do. But in the pre-vious chapter, I had shown that those who are motivated to act morally because they accept the moral answer will not care whether they are obeying moral rules or fol-lowing moral ideals, for their goal is to lessen the amount of evil suffered. No practi-cal purpose is served by distorting the concept of morality to make it require every-one to be morally good. If persons do not wish to be morally good, even a correct account of morality will not persuade them to be.

Even though it will probably have no practical effect, I should like to point out that, contrary to appearances, the present account of morality will not result in gov-ernments doing nothing to aid their deprived citizens. It might do so if no person in government were morally good, but one need not be naively optimistic to believe that in every country and in every government there are some morally good persons. If these persons introduce good laws to aid deprived citizens, laws that are strongly justi-fied, then morality requires that one not oppose such legislation unless an impartial rational person can advocate such opposition. To do so is to unjustifiably deprive peo-ple of freedom or pleasure. So although the moral rules do not require legislators to introduce good laws, they do prohibit them from preventing such legislation from being enacted. Holding that morality only encourages, but does not require, following the moral ideals will not lead to societies failing to address any of their social evils. If a morally good person tries to get the government to lessen the evils suffered by deprived persons, then morality requires that no one stand in her way as she seeks to get the gov-ernment to help them. If there is not even one morally good person who tries to help, it is absurd to think that distorting the understanding of morality will be of any use.

Clearly much more needs to be said to clarify the relationship between moral-ity and government. To be completely clear about this relationship one would need a complete political theory, which includes accounts of rational persons' public and personal attitudes toward government. I hope to provide such accounts some day, but in this chapter I am concerned only with showing that what I have said about morality applies to governments as well as to individuals. Governments are like indi-viduals in that they are not justified in violating a moral rule unless a fully in-formed, impartial rational person can publicly allow such a violation. It is only be-cause governments have a duty to violate moral rules with regard to their citizens without their consent that they are sometimes morally justified in violating moral rules when individuals would not be justified. I believe that this morally relevant feature is sufficient to account for the differences between governments and individ-uals and thus to show that the moral system I have described applies not only to the actions, intentions, and so on, of individuals, but also to those of governments.

Minimal Duties of Government

The primary function of governments is to keep the peace, to protect their citizens from one another and from those outside the state.[2] In order to avoid conflict over what counts as a violation of a rule, governments must deprive their citizens of freedom to interpret the moral rules. Governments must not only interpret these rules, they must also determine which weakly justified violations of the rules they will legally prohibit. In order to enforce obedience to the moral system as interpreted by them, governments must sometimes set up an enforcement system, with judges, police, and prisons. This requires money and so citizens have to pay taxes, or provide resources in some other way, in order to provide the government with the money to protect them from the morally unacceptable behavior of each other. Even those who support a minimal state admit that governments have a duty to protect their citizens from the harms caused by immoral behavior. This duty requires governments to violate the moral rules with regard to their citizens even without the latter's consent. Further, only governments have this duty with regard to all citizens, so that they are in a unique or close to unique position in this regard.

Keeping the peace also allows governments to restrict freedom in order to prevent serious internal disorder. Perhaps surprisingly, this means that the less stable and secure the government, the more justified it is in limiting freedom to prevent internal disorder. The more stable and secure the government, the more freedom it should allow its citizens, for their freedom does not threaten the state and increase the chances of a civil war.[3] Civil war usually brings with it even more harm to the citizens of a state than individual acts of immoral behavior. Riots and general lawlessness threaten many with serious harm. Governments are allowed to limit the freedom of people in order to prevent civil disorder. As long as governments have an adequate justification for limiting freedom, they are not acting immorally in doing so. But impartial rational people will sometimes disagree whether the risk of evil that the limitation of freedom is intended to prevent is sufficient to justify that limitation. Most of these disagreements are about the answers to the following questions: How serious is the risk of evil? And how much freedom needs to be deprived in order to prevent it? If there is disagreement on the answers to these questions, even complete agreement on the nature of morality will not resolve disputes. As pointed out in chapter 9, disagreement on the facts is one of the primary causes of moral disagreement.

Although impartial rational persons do not always agree in their rankings of the different goods and evils, everyone agrees that governments are morally allowed to deprive their citizens of some freedom and pleasure in order to prevent both civil war and war with other countries, for all war results not only in loss of freedom and pleasure, it also results in death, pain, and disability. Although "Give me liberty or give me death" has powerful rhetorical force, taken literally it would not be used by any rational person as a guide to behavior. The death penalty is a greater punishment than life imprisonment, and no one outside of prison is deprived of freedom more completely than a person in life imprisonment. Thus it is generally agreed that governments are allowed to deprive their citizens of a substantial amount of freedom in order to prevent the greater evils that generally accompany war, either civil war or war with other countries.

Governments May Violate Moral Rules for Moral Ideals

If necessary to prevent significant evils, governments are often not only morally allowed to deprive people of their money by taxes, but also allowed to deprive people of their freedom and pleasure in other ways, such as by health and safety regulations. However, individuals also are sometimes morally allowed to violate moral rules to follow moral ideals, so being allowed to do so does not distinguish governments from individuals. The difference is that governments may be allowed to violate moral rules in situations that would be unjustifiable for individuals, such as supporting medical research. Governments may tax in order to support medical research, for medical research is a significant help in following the three positive moral ideals of preserving life, relieving pain, and lessening disability. The same considerations allow a government to provide support for the training of doctors and nurses, the building of hospitals and, more generally, doing those things that it justifiably believes will help lessen the amount of suffering of the evils such as death, pain, and disability. That a government is allowed to violate a moral rule in order to follow a moral ideal should not be surprising in the least, for even individuals are also sometimes allowed to violate a moral rule in order to follow a moral ideal. The serious problem arises in explaining why, without consent, a government is sometimes allowed to violate a moral rule in order to follow some utilitarian ideals.[4]

Governments May Violate Moral
Rules for Utilitarian Ideals

If governments were never justified in violating moral rules for utilitarian ideals, it would seem to follow that most of them act immorally when they tax in order to promote the arts, parks, or better schools for all. For in these cases taxation deprives people of freedom or pleasure, not in order to prevent death, pain, or disability, or even the deprivation of freedom or pleasure, but in order to increase knowledge and pleasure. Libertarians, as well as some philosophers who support a minimal state, accept the conclusion that it is immoral to tax in order to provide schooling for all children, for they mistakenly hold that whatever it is immoral for an individual to do, is also immoral for a government to do. However, most rational persons agree that governments are often justified in violating some of the moral rules in order to promote pleasure and increase knowledge, both of which are utilitarian ideals.

As a practical matter, it may turn out that governments do not accomplish utilitarian goals as well as private individuals. That is an empirical matter, but theoretically, it is clear that it is sometimes justified for governments to violate moral rules for utilitarian ideals. Although it is clear that it is not immoral to tax in order to provide better schools, it is not clear that it is morally unacceptable for a government not to do so. Showing that an impartial rational person can support taxation to provide better education for all children, even though it involves some deprivation of freedom, is not the same as showing that all impartial rational persons would favor such taxation. I am only attempting to show why it can be morally acceptable for a government to violate a moral rule for utilitarian ideals when it would not be morally acceptable for an individual to perform what would otherwise be the same kind of act.

Social Contract Theory

One answer to the question why it is justifiable for a government to violate moral rules for utilitarian ideals is offered by social contract theory. According to one version of social contract theory, citizens agree to obey the laws if the government agrees not only to prevent evil, but also to promote the general welfare. Since, on this account, the government has promised to promote the general welfare, in doing so, it is not merely following an utilitarian ideal, it is also obeying the moral rule "Keep your promises." It is generally acknowledged that providing schooling for all children promotes the general welfare, therefore the government would be violating a moral rule if it did not provide schooling for all children. In carrying out its promise, it is permitted to deprive people of some freedom or pleasure by taxation, for were it not permitted to do this, it would be unable to fulfill its promise. Although this argument can also be applied to supporting arts and parks, it is not quite as persuasive, for supporting arts and parks is not as closely related to the general welfare as is providing schooling.

However this argument, even when applied to schools, is extremely implausible. It depends upon there being some contract, probably implicit, between the citizens and the government concerning promotion of the general welfare. Although some politicians make promises to do various things if elected, governments, in general, do not make even implicit promises to their citizens. It is extremely implausible to claim that there is an implicit promise by the government when there is often no one who even claims that a promise was made to him. Some modern versions of social contract theory claim the government is unfair if it does not promote the general welfare, but this claim is equally implausible. Governments do not usually enter into voluntary activities with their citizens such that failure to abide by the rules of that activity counts as cheating. ("Unfair" is often taken simply as a synonym for "immoral," but taken in this way it clearly does not explain why it is immoral not to provide schooling.) The most plausible version of a social contract theory is that put forward by Hobbes, where he claims that the government would show ingratitude if it did not promote the general welfare. However, even this version has difficulties, for among other problems, no one is allowed to violate moral rules simply in order to show gratitude.

Another kind of answer rests upon the fact that individuals are allowed to violate the moral rules with regard to someone else if they have good specific reasons for thinking that the person has a rational desire to have the rule disobeyed with regard to himself, such as deceiving someone in order to throw a surprise party for him. Similarly, governments are allowed to violate a moral rule with regard to their citizens if they have good specific reasons for thinking that the citizens have a rational desire to have the rule disobeyed with regard to themselves. One problem with this answer is that it justifies only violations of a moral rule by the government toward citizens who it has good reason to believe want the rule violated with regard to themselves. This answer would not justify universal taxation in order to provide schooling for all children, for not everyone wants to be taxed for this reason.

Using the Moral System to Justify Government Promoting the General Welfare

Since the same moral system applies to both individuals and governments, it should be possible to show how the moral system explains why governments may often be justified in depriving its citizens of some freedom and pleasure to promote the general welfare but not justified in violating the other moral rules. When no evil is being prevented, and not even deprived persons are benefited but only additional ability, freedom, or pleasure are being promoted, no impartial rational person would publicly allow government violations of any of the second five moral rules. No impartial rational person would publicly allow governments to deceive, break promises, cheat, disobey the law, or fail to perform its duties simply in order to promote more ability (knowledge), or freedom (opportunities), or pleasure. One consequence of violations of these rules being publicly allowed would be significant loss of trust in a government. The benefits gained by publicly allowing these violations (there are no harms prevented) does not compensate for the anxiety and other harms caused by this lost of trust. Further, in the real world, the benefits cannot be distributed impartially to all citizens. Thus bias and suspicions of bias with all of the attendant risks are inevitable. Appropriate humility makes clear that the consequences of violations of any of the second five moral rules being publicly allowed for purely utilitarian ideals cannot be plausibly claimed to be better than their not being publicly allowed.

Similarly, without consent, no impartial rational person would publicly allow any significant violation of the first three rules in order to follow some utilitarian ideal, either by individuals or governments. There may be particular situations in which a rational person would be willing to suffer death, pain, or disability simply in order to achieve some good. However, no rational person would be willing to let someone he did not know decide when he should suffer these evils and for what goods. No impartial rational person would favor governments having the authority to kill, or cause significant pain or disability in order to follow any utilitarian ideal. Recognizing that all justified violations of a moral rule must be those that an impartial rational person could publicly allow, makes it clear that throwing the Christians to the lions is not justifiable, no matter how many people enjoy it and no matter how much they enjoy it; nor does gaining added knowledge about lions or Christians or their interaction justify it.

The fourth and fifth rules, "Do not deprive of freedom" and "Do not deprive of pleasure," are the two rules that can be plausibly described as more concerned with goods than with evils. Impartial rational persons can publicly allow governments to violate these rules in order to follow utilitarian ideals, for allowing governments to do this is simply allowing governments to take away some goods in order to promote others. Of course, impartiality toward all citizens must be maintained, and the goods that are promoted must be significantly greater than the goods that are taken away. If these limitations are heeded, then there are some situations in which all impartial rational persons would publicly allow the government to violate the fourth and fifth moral rules in order to follow utilitarian ideals. Governments have, in fact, generally been thought justified in depriving people of freedom by taxation in order to promote utilitarian ideals, such as increased knowledge, more opportunities, and greater pleasure.

The question that now naturally arises is "If some government violations of the fourth and fifth moral rules for utilitarian ideals are morally justified, why are similar violations by individuals not also justified?" If all impartial rational persons would sometimes publicly allow the deprivation of freedom and pleasure for utilitarian ideals by a government, why would they not also publicly allow what would otherwise be the same kind of violation by individuals? The answer is that governments have a duty to violate some moral rules with regard to their citizens, and individuals do not. Further, governments are in a unique or close to unique position with respect to their duties to violate moral rules with regard to their citizens. This morally relevant feature also explains why parents are sometimes morally allowed to violate these two rules with regard to their children in order to increase their ability, freedom, or pleasure. If all individuals were publicly allowed to violate these moral rules in order to promote utilitarian ideals, the additional goods would not compensate for the resulting disorder with all of its attendant significant evils. Allowing the government to violate these moral rules in order to follow utilitarian ideals does not normally lead to disorder.

Individuals may never need to violate a moral rule without consent, but governments must always do so. Simply enforcing those laws that are necessary in order to prevent unjustified and some weakly justified violations of the moral rules, requires depriving people of freedom and pleasure. Since governments must violate the moral rules, they are faced with a decision about the way in which they will do so. When governments need money they must get it from their citizens, but the manner in which they get it, such as by an income tax or sales tax, is a matter for decision. Whatever decision they make will result in different people being deprived of different amounts of money. Since governments violate, though justifiably, the moral rules with regard to all of its citizens, they have a different relationship to them than any individual has with regard to his fellow citizens. Governments are morally allowed to violate a rule when individuals would not be justified in doing so because of a positive answer to question 4.

This special relationship also blurs the distinction between utilitarian ideals and some moral ideals where governments are concerned. Promoting the utilitarian ideals (increasing freedom and pleasure) can often be plausibly described as following the moral ideals (preventing the depriving of freedom and pleasure), for a government may claim that it is simply trying to lessen the amount of freedom and pleasure that it takes away from its citizens. This is why classical utilitarianism is more plausible when applied to governments. That a government has a duty to violate the moral rules with regard to its citizens, even without their consent, makes an action by a government with regard to its citizens a different kind of act than an action by an individual that is identical in all of its other morally relevant features. However, this does not put governments outside of the moral sphere, for governments cannot justifiably violate any moral rule unless an impartial rational person can publicly allow that violation.

Political Judgments

In some situations, all impartial rational persons would publicly allow a government to violate a moral rule; in others, no impartial rational person would publicly allow a violation. However, most cases, at least those that are seriously discussed, are those in which impartial rational persons disagree about whether the government should violate a moral rule. Of course, not all disagreements will concern whether the government should violate a moral rule; many will concern how they should do it. Political judgments involve more than is usually relevant in moral judgments about individuals, namely, a consideration of the goods that will result. Political judgments differ from other moral judgments in that promoting goods as well as causing, avoiding, and preventing evils is normally a relevant consideration. Although one can make political judgments about family matters, most political judgments are moral judgments of governments. This makes the distinction between the moral and utilitarian ideals less significant for governments. It was undoubtedly the classical utilitarians' preoccupation with governmental action that led them to neglect the importance of the distinction between promoting goods and preventing evils.

Who Counts as a Deprived Person?

The blurring of the distinction between some moral and utilitarian ideals may also occur because rational persons disagree about when the government is lessening the deprivation of freedom and pleasure of those who are deprived, and when it is simply increasing freedom and pleasure. This disagreement stems in part from disagreement about the minimal amount of freedom and pleasure that members of this society should have. In this context "should have" means "an impartial rational person knowing the resources and problems of this society would favor every member of this society having." I think that there is also something of "a rational person knowing the resources and problems of this society would expect every member of this society to have." In every society there is some minimal amount of freedom and pleasure, such that all rational persons, knowing the resources and problems of that society would regard anyone having less than that amount as deprived. When members of this society have slightly above this amount, rational persons may disagree, some claiming that those who do not have this higher amount are deprived, others claiming that they are not. Whether a person counts as deprived depends upon the resources and problems of his society. Since deprivation is society-relative, persons who would not count as deprived in a poor society will count as deprived in a wealthier one.

Conservative versus Liberal (American Usage)

Nowadays those who favor more governmental action to aid the less fortunate members of the society are called, in America, liberals; their opponents, conservatives. (In European and other countries, the terminology is different, and those who favor more such governmental action are called socialists or social democrats and those who are opposed sometimes are called liberals. In this discussion I shall follow American usage.) Generally speaking, liberals claim that they are following moral ideals rather than utilitarian ones. They claim that in a society with these resources and problems, no person should have less freedom and pleasure than will be provided by the governmental action they favor. Indeed, they generally claim that even this governmental action will leave too many people with less freedom and pleasure than the minimum they should have. Conservatives claim that no one or almost no one is below the minimum amount of freedom and pleasure that all members of the society should have. They regard most welfare programs not as lessening the deprivation of freedom and pleasure but simply as increasing these goods. They oppose such welfare programs because they hold that they unjustifiably deprive other people of freedom and pleasure. Conservatives believe that it is not justifiable for governments to violate a moral rule for purely utilitarian ideals.

Perhaps even more important than this difference about what counts as the minimum that every member of the society should have are ideological differences. Conservatives generally believe that governments do not operate as efficiently as private enterprises and that welfare programs have bad effects on the recipients. Liberals generally believe that private enterprises do not help those who are deprived and that welfare programs do help deprived persons become more productive. There are, of course, other ideological differences about the practical effects of governmental action, but generally, even when the effects are agreed upon, there is often disagreement between conservatives and liberals. Liberals tend to emphasize the moral ideals; Conservatives generally place more emphasis on the moral rules. They also differ in the degree to which they think the distinction between utilitarian and moral ideals breaks down when dealing with governments.

Extreme liberals hold that the distinction breaks down completely; extreme conservatives, that it does not break down at all. Extreme conservatives hold that the only duty of governments is to prevent unjustified violations of the moral rules. They are against most governmental actions to relieve or prevent evils not due to violations of moral rules, and they regard as immoral any governmental action that seeks to increase goods, for they consider this an unjustified violation of a moral rule for utilitarian rather than moral ideals. Extreme liberals hold that with regard to government the status quo is of no importance. They hold that with regard to governments, there is no morally relevant difference between lessening the deprivation of freedom and pleasure and promoting more freedom and pleasure. I do not accept either of these extreme views.

Extreme liberals do not recognize the importance of the status quo in moral matters. For them, the appropriate governmental action is one that more evenly distributes the freedom and pleasure enjoyed by members of the society. They see nothing wrong in depriving people who have more pleasure in order to give the same amount of pleasure to others who now have less. Of course, taking a thousand dollars from a rich person and giving it to a poor one usually gives significantly more pleasure to the poor person than it takes away from the rich person. I do not regard the negative income tax as an extreme liberal measure. Further, attempts to help those people who are deprived, even though this involves depriving others of some goods, are usually justifiable. However, if the people to be aided are not deprived, morality will require a much greater difference between what is given and what is taken away. Morality does not allow a government to deprive some people of goods unless a significantly greater amount of good will result. But impartial rational persons can disagree about how much greater the resulting goods must be.

I regard the dispute between liberals and conservatives as limited to violations of the fourth and fifth moral rules. So I do not regard the extreme liberal as a classical utilitarian, simply advocating achieving the greatest happiness. I think utilitarianism not only an incorrect position but an extremely dangerous one. Significant violations of the first three moral rules are never justifiable in order to promote goods, only to prevent or relieve significant evils. Someone who holds that it is justifiable to violate the first three moral rules in order to promote goods, as a classical utilitarian might, opens the door to the most extreme forms of totalitarianism. Classical utilitarianism in action is devoted to the greatest overall happiness regardless of the consequences for some. Strange as it may seem, the path from John Stuart Mill, who defended liberty on utilitarian grounds, to Communism, which denies it on the same grounds, is both short and easy to travel. Although the originators of the greatest happiness principle certainly did not intend it, their principle can be used to justify governmental actions that all rational persons would agree are immoral.

I have already shown that extreme conservatism is inadequate because there is a morally relevant difference between governments and individuals. Even extreme conservatives admit that governments have a duty to violate some moral rules toward its citizens without their consent, for they must enforce the moral rules and punish those who unjustifiably violate them. Thus a positive answer to question 4 distinguishes governmental actions from actions by individuals that have all of the same other morally relevant features. Further, governmental action to enforce morality must be paid for, and how the government chooses to raise that money has the effect of increasing freedom and pleasure for some and decreasing it for others. In the real world, the distinction between some moral and utilitarian ideals does indeed become extremely blurred when applied to governments, especially governments of any size. Insofar as both liberals and conservatives accept the account of the moral system and its application to governments, they will not be extreme. Both will acknowledge that a government is justified in breaking a moral rule only if a fully informed, impartial rational person can publicly allow that the rule be broken in this case. If they both agree on this, then both of their positions on whether the government should undertake a certain course of action will count as morally acceptable. Even though some political disagreements cannot be settled by the moral system, employing the concept of what an impartial rational person would publicly allow may be more helpful in deciding political issues than is initially apparent.

Just Governments and Laws versus Good Governments and Laws

Although distinguishing between moral and utilitarian ideals is less important when talking about governments than when talking about individuals, this does not make political judgments about governments significantly different from moral judgments about individuals. A perfectly just government is one that never does what is morally wrong. It never unjustifiably violates any of the moral rules with regard to any of its citizens, nor does it do so with regard to other governments or individuals. All violations of a moral rule by such a government are those that at least some impartial rational persons would publicly allow. There are probably no perfectly just governments, so a government can be called just if it does what is morally wrong far less than most governments. This is similar to the use of moral standards in making moral judgments about individuals. As with judgments about individuals, one government will be better than another if all fully informed, impartial rational persons prefer it to the other. Of course, since fully informed, impartial rational persons sometimes disagree, there may be disagreement about which government is better, and so neither is.

As with other moral disagreements, if agreement is reached on all the facts (a particularly difficult task when considering governmental action), there will be a large measure of agreement. Disagreements should continue only in a very limited sphere. Like individuals, governments are judged not only by their actions, but also by their intentions and motives. If a government does what, to the best of its knowledge, will result in the least amount of evil being suffered, then it does not become unjust simply because its policies actually result in more evil being suffered. Well-intentioned programs can go wrong. But good intentions are not sufficient to make a government just. A just government must avoid bad results. A government that means well may not be an unjust one, but unless it actually carries out its intentions, it will not be a just one either.

The necessity of governments to constantly violate the moral rules by restricting freedom makes the distinction between a just government and a good one more difficult to make than the parallel distinction between a just person and a morally good one. Nonetheless, there is some point in the distinction. A just government is one that by positive action, as distinguished from not acting, neither intends to nor does unjustifiably violate any of the moral rules. A just government does not unjustifiably increase the evil suffered by anyone, but a just government may not be a good government. A morally good government, or simply a good government, is not only just, but intends to and does follow the moral and appropriate utilitarian ideals. A good government both decreases the amount of evil suffered and increases the amount of good enjoyed. A government that does not follow the moral or utilitarian ideals, but simply refrains from unjustifiably violating the moral rules, can be just without being good. A good government must also be a just government. A government that is unjust cannot be a good one no matter how much it decreases evil and increases good. For if it is unjust, this means that it unjustifiably violates the moral rules, and no impartial rational person would favor a government that acts in this way.

It is also possible to judge individual laws. A just law never intentionally unjustifiably violates a moral rule; if a law intentionally violates a moral rule unjustifiably, it is an unjust law. If a law simply results in greater harms than benefits, it is a bad law. If it does so intentionally, it is also an unjust law. A just law is more than a law that is not unjust; it is also a law that is not bad. All just laws are good, for all laws restrict freedom, and such laws are justified only if they prevent sufficient evils or promote sufficient goods to justify that restriction. An unnecessary law, that is, one not needed either to lessen evils or to promote goods, is a bad one. Some just laws can be better than others, if they have better results. But, of course, fully informed rational persons can disagree about which law is better, or even whether a law is good or bad, for they can disagree in their rankings of the goods and evils. Whether or not a law is unjust is an objective matter, for it requires that the government intentionally violate a moral rule when no impartial rational person would publicly allow such a violation. No law about which fully informed, impartial rational persons disagree is an unjust law. But fully informed rational persons can disagree about whether a law is just, for they can disagree about whether a law is bad, and a bad law cannot be a just law.

This discussion about governments and laws may leave the impression that I am overlooking that governments are composed of persons and that laws are made by these persons. Although I am aware of these obvious facts, I do not think there is any simple way, if there is any way at all, to replace talk about governments and laws with talk about the persons who compose the former and make the latter. Although it is extremely unlikely, a good government may be composed primarily of bad persons, and a good law may be passed by persons whose motives were not morally good. It is more likely that a bad government be composed primarily of good persons, and that a bad law be passed by persons whose motives were morally good. Of course, most often, good governments will be composed of good persons, and bad governments of bad persons; good laws will be passed with good motives, and bad laws with bad motives. The goodness and badness of laws and governments are not, however, to be judged by the goodness or badness of the motives of those who make the former or the moral character of the persons who compose the latter.

Theories of Justice

This account of just governments and just laws is in conflict with the most influential current theory of justice, that put forward by John Rawls in his book, *A Theory of Justice.* In that book Rawls put forward two principles: first, that all citizens of a country should have the greatest amount of liberty compatible with an equal amount of liberty for all, and second, that any deviation from an equality of goods can be justified only by that deviation benefiting those who are worst off.[5] This powerful theory is superior to its two major rival theories, the marxist or egalitarian theory, and the utilitarian or capitalist theory.[6] The utilitarian or capitalist theories also give special status to freedom, but it seems to be secondary. John Stuart Mill, one of the leading proponents of the utilitarian theory, clearly regards liberty as essential for achieving the greatest happiness, and in the capitalist version economic liberty is essential for maximum productivity.

As a practical matter, liberty or freedom is an extremely important political good, and strong justification is required for governments to justify depriving their citizens of any freedom. Of course, it is justified for governments to deprive their citizens of the freedom to act immorally, for all impartial rational citizens want the government to enforce the moral rules. But, as shown in the discussion of punishment, impartial rational citizens do not want enforcement of morality to be so harsh that more harm is caused than is prevented by that enforcement. Governments are also justified in depriving of freedom in order to prevent other harms as well. They can prohibit polluting behavior and can require preventive health measures, such as vaccinations. The justifiability of these deprivations of freedom is determined in the same way as all violations of the moral rules are determined, by going through the two-step procedure described in chapter 9.

According to the egalitarian view, a government should seek to have goods distributed to its citizens in such a way as to make them as equal as possible. The egalitarian view holds that it is always appropriate for governments to redistribute goods, taking away goods from those who have more in order to give them to those who have less. Much less emphasis seems to be put on the requirement that the government should also seek to distribute the evils in order to achieve equality. An extreme form of egalitarianism, in which it does not matter if this distribution will result in fewer overall goods and more overall evils as long as the result is greater equality among the citizens, is not held by anyone. This is because egalitarianism presupposes some basic rationality in which it is irrational to have goods taken away from those who have more goods, or evils inflicted on those who have less evils, simply to make the citizens more equal. However, if redistribution is impossible, it could be rational to simply destroy the goods of those who have more if this lessens the envy felt by those who have fewer. This may be why egalitarianism is sometimes called the politics of envy.

According to the capitalist view, a government should always seek to improve the general welfare, which is taken to mean that it should seek to increase the overall balance of goods over evils. It should seek this goal regardless of how these goods are distributed. On the capitalist account, except for considerations of marginal utility, it makes no difference who gets more goods, those who already have a great many or those who have very few. This capitalist view suffers, as do all utilitarian views, from the problem of determining how one balances one good against another. For example, how much pleasure is equivalent to a given increase in freedom? Balancing goods against evils is even more difficult. For example, how much pleasure is needed to compensate for a specified amount of pain, for a specified disability, or for a specified increased risk of death?[7] Even though these problems remain unsolved, the capitalist theory holds that increasing the overall balance of goods over evils is the primary goal of government and that distribution considerations are largely irrelevant. On this theory, a government should favor a policy that decreases the incomes of the poor and increases the incomes of the rich if it will result in the overall balance of benefits over harms being significantly greater.

These accounts of the egalitarian and capitalist theories of how governments should act (theories of justice) caricature the theories being put forward, but they show what would happen if one took either equality or increase in overall goods as the primary goal of government. Rawls's theory starts with the egalitarian premise that equality is a legitimate goal of government, but he explicitly rules out envy as irrational, and so he also accepts as a legitimate goal of government increasing the overall good.[8] He combines these two goals by taking the point of view of those who are worst off. This results in inequalities being justified if they benefit the worst off. While the egalitarian is concerned solely with distribution and the capitalist, solely with overall benefits, Rawls claims that government should be concerned with both increasing overall welfare and with assuring equality of distribution. Rawls's theory is clearly superior to the other two in accounting for judgments of how governments should act.

Unlike the other two theories, Rawls explicitly gives liberty pride of place, holding that assuring the greatest liberty compatible with a like liberty for all is more important than increasing the goods of those who are worst off or even distributing them more equally. Perhaps, surprisingly, this is because Rawls's theory, like the other two, concentrates on distributing goods rather than preventing evils. If Rawls were to have concentrated on preventing harms rather than distributing benefits, he may have come to realize that preventing loss of freedom is not more important than preventing all of the other evils. All three theories are mistaken in concentrating on promoting and distributing benefits rather than on avoiding and preventing harms. All three theories are also mistaken in holding that in every situation there is, at least theoretically, a unique right answer to what a just government should do.

Common Morality Applied to Government Policy: Health Care

In this section I am only concerned with the actions of government. A government that acts in a morally acceptable way acts justly. But what is required for a government to act in a morally acceptable way? A full answer to this question would require a whole book in political theory; I shall not try to provide even an outline of a full answer. However, knowing that common morality applies to the actions of governments as well as to the actions of individuals is sufficient to clarify some points. The recognition that morality is an informal public system suggests the most important point: it is extremely unlikely that there is a unique right answer to how the government should act with regard to almost any controversial political matter, for example, the allocation of health care. Even if, contrary to fact, there were substantial agreement on factual matters like the result of a given law or policy, there would still be no unique right answer. There are too many ideological disagreements about human nature and the nature of human society as well as disagreement about the rankings of the harms and benefits involved.

One of the primary responsibilities, if not the primary responsibility, of government is to lessen the amount of harm suffered by its citizens. There are several sources of these harms. The first is immoral behavior by other members of the society; the second is immoral behavior by people outside of the society, including other governments. Everyone agrees that governments have duties to enforce the moral rules with regard to their own citizens and to provide security against attacks by those outside of the society. A third source of harms is the environment, both natural and artificial, for example, floods and toxic wastes. Governments should seek to prevent and relieve the harms caused by these conditions. A fourth source of harms is diseases and injuries, and so on, all of which can be classified as maladies.[9] One of the duties of government is to prevent and relieve the harms involved in maladies, especially if they can be most effectively prevented by governmental action, such as ensuring safe drinking water and universal vaccinations. No one disagrees that these are justifiable governmental expenses. However, after a certain amount of money is spent on health care, including public health, it is appropriate to question whether more ought to be spent. It is doubtful that these questions have uniquely correct moral answers. The same is true of questions about how much ought to be spent on the criminal justice system, education, public defense, and so on.

Assuming that agreement has been reached on the amount of government spending on health care, there is still the question of what would count as a morally acceptable way of spending that money or what would count as a just health care system. A formal, but not very useful answer to that question is whatever system a fully informed, impartial rational person could favor adopting. What kind of system could such a person favor adopting? The answer to this is slightly more informative: any system that such a person could regard as resulting in the least amount of harm being suffered due to maladies. If no fully informed person could regard a particular health care system as resulting in the least amount of harm being suffered, then such a system cannot be regarded as just. The present health care system in the United States is not regarded by anyone as resulting in the least amount of harm being suffered, which explains why no one regards the present health care system as just. But this does not mean that there is agreement on what would be a just health care system or how the government should act with regard to health care.

All that is required of a just health care system is that a fully informed, impartial rational person can regard that system as resulting in the least amount of harm being suffered. It requires nothing about equality, nor about providing the most aid to those who are worst off. This is not because equality and aiding the worst off are irrelevant; rather, it is because, insofar as they are relevant, they are encompassed by the goal of lessening the amount of harm suffered. Unlike the capitalist account of justice, which has a goal of increasing the amount of net benefits and so would allow massive inequality, the moral goal of lessening the amount of harm suffered sets strict limits on inequality. It also necessarily results in great concern for those who are worst off, for they are suffering greater harm than others, and so relieving their suffering will normally be included in the goal of lessening harm.

Justice does not, however, require that the government spend a given amount of money in order to aid one thousand who are worst off if that same amount of money will prevent more harm for a hundred thousand who are not as badly off. For example, it is not required that the government spend a given amount of money on treating one thousand children with a serious genetic malady rather than spending that same amount on preventing a hundred thousand children from getting some lesser malady. It is also not required that they do not spend the money on the one thousand who are worst off, for impartial rational persons can disagree on which alternative most lessens the amount of harm suffered. But keeping the cost the same, if the number of the worst off gets smaller and the number who can be prevented from suffering some lesser disease gets greater, it is quite likely that a point will be reached where it will be unjust to spend that amount of money on the worst off.

Since a government that acts in a morally acceptable way acts justly and there is usually more than one morally acceptable way for a government to act, it is very likely that there will not be a unique right answer to the question of how health care should be allocated. Agreement that the goal of a health care allocation is to lessen the amount of harm suffered due to maladies still leaves unresolvable any disagreement about what counts as the lesser amount of harm suffered. Some may claim that what is most important is minimizing the suffering of the worst off, those suffering the greatest harm, whereas others may maintain that it is irrelevant whose suffering is minimized, as long as the total amount of harm suffered is minimized. Since there is no agreed-upon way to weigh and balance different evils, there is no way to resolve any plausible disagreement. But, even with all of this disagreement, there is universal agreement that the present health care system in the United States is not just. Often this is expressed by claiming that the health care system is unfair, but this is simply to use the term "unfair" to mean morally unacceptable.

Reflective Equilibrium

It is, of course, a test of the adequacy of any account of morality that it not be inconsistent with one's considered moral judgments. However, given that morality is an informal public system, it is extremely unlikely that any considered moral judgment will be incompatible with common morality. Trying to arrive at a correct moral judgment by going back and forth between one's considered moral judgments and an account of morality, presupposes the mistaken view that there is a unique correct answer to every genuine moral controversy. Common morality allows wide variation in moral judgments, even among those who agree on all of the facts of a particular case. Not only can there be some differences in the interpretation of the moral rules, there is also considerable latitude in the rankings of the different goods and evils, and there are different ideological beliefs concerning human nature and the nature of human societies. A moral theory cannot and should not be used to settle controversial moral questions.

It has, unfortunately, become common for philosophers to talk about "reflective equilibrium" as a method for testing the correctness of one's moral theory as well as being a test of one's moral judgments. The phrase "reflective equilibrium" was introduced into moral theory by John Rawls as such a method. It presupposes that a moral theory provides a decision procedure for making moral judgments. When the moral theory yields a moral judgment that is in conflict with a person's considered moral judgments, he must decide whether or not to change the theory or his considered moral judgments. He must bring the theory and his considered moral judgments into reflective equilibrium. This strongly suggests that if a person changes his moral judgment on some controversial moral question, for example, abortion or the death penalty, he must change his moral theory. This may be true if one conceives of a moral theory, as Kant and the utilitarians did, as generating moral judgments, that is, as generating a moral system. Rawls seems to share this misleading way of characterizing a moral theory.

However, as pointed out in chapter 1, a moral theory is best regarded as providing an explicit description of common morality and then attempting to justify that system. It is only the descriptive part of a moral theory that it even makes sense to bring into reflective equilibrium with one's considered moral judgments. And even this is misleading, for the descriptive part of a moral theory is simply an attempt to provide an explicit, precise, and coherent description of the considered moral decisions and judgments of all moral agents. That part of a moral theory which is an attempt to justify common morality cannot be inconsistent with the descriptive part, for it is an attempt to justify the moral system that has been described. Reflective equilibrium not only mistakenly seems to presuppose that there is a unique right answer to all moral questions, it also mistakenly seems to regard a moral theory as generating that answer.

Democratic Implications of Morality as an Informal System

Rawls, together with most other moral and political philosophers, seem to hold that a moral system that provides unique answers to every moral and political question is preferable to one that allows for some questions to have more than one morally acceptable answer. For them a moral system is supposed to provide a way of settling disputes, so that a moral system that settles all disputes is clearly preferable to one that does not. However, as a practical matter, it would not make much difference if the moral system did provide unique answers, for there would still be disagreements about the facts, including the nature and probability of the consequences of alternative policies. And as I have pointed out before, most moral and political disagreements are disagreements about the facts. Nonetheless, it is still a mistake to think that a moral system provides unique answers to every moral and political question, for fully informed, impartial rational persons do not always agree on all moral matters.

The view that morality always provides unique answers is not only mistaken, it is also dangerous. It may lead one to hold that someone who takes a different view in a moral dispute must be either uninformed, partial, or irrational. Regarding one's opponents in this way is not conducive to fruitful negotiation and compromise. Accepting a theory that claims to provide unique answers also has a tendency to lead one to accept as the ideal form of government, a kind of Platonic Republic, where philosopher-kings, who are supposed to most closely approximate impartial rational persons, make all of the decisions. Regarding morality as providing unique answers leads to a tendency to regard democracies, where significant decisions are made by the votes of the mass of the population, as employing a defective decision procedure. If there is only one right answer, then why not have those who are most qualified determine what it is? There is no need to involve all the people in these decisions, any more than the captain of a ship needs to consult his passengers about how to run his ship.

A captain need not consult his passengers concerning the technical details of running the ship, but if there has not been some prior agreement that he should make the decision about where the ship is to go, then he must consult them concerning its destination. He should tell them the capabilities of the ship, the risks they would encounter, and also the benefits, if they choose one destination rather than another, but if he is running the ship on their behalf, then he should consult them on the destination. Even if they are equally informed, it is doubtful that all of them prefer one destination over all of the others. The captain's rational desires and preferences, assuming that he is simply hired by the passengers to run the ship, have no special status. It is the morally acceptable rational desires and preferences of the passengers that should determine where they go. Even the voting procedure should be determined by them.

Not all members of a society rank the goods and evils in the same way. Some rank a higher material standard of living ahead of more personal freedom, at least until the standard of living has become as high as Scandinavia or Switzerland. Others prefer more personal and political freedom to greater material prosperity, even though the standard of living is lower than that of Bolivia or Brazil. Impartial rational persons need not always agree which to choose if there is a conflict between raising the material standard of living and having more personal and political freedom. Of course, if more personal freedom always increases the material standard of living, there is no conflict. However, there is another matter on which there is clearly a conflict, concern about some environmental health issues. Impartial rational persons may disagree on how much freedom and material prosperity they are willing to give up in order to alleviate air and water pollution, thereby improving the health of the population.

All of the fundamental issues on which there is political debate between moderate liberals and moderate conservatives involve issues on which impartial rational persons can decide either way. Since both ways are morally acceptable, there is no morally right way, and it is quite appropriate to vote on which policy to adopt. This is not a second best way of arriving at the correct answer to the moral question; it is not a way of arriving at the correct answer to the moral question at all. It is the best practical way of deciding what to do, for voting allows not only for all persons to express their own preference, it also allows for intensity of preference. Those who care more can work harder to win more votes. Of course, if one prefers democracy to oligarchy, care will have to be taken to avoid undue influence by those with extreme wealth or power. Force and fraud are already ruled out by the moral system. That there is no single morally right action does not mean that there are not many ways of acting that are ruled out as morally wrong, so that lack of a unique answer to every moral question does not mean that anything goes. Morality is conceptually prior to politics, for one task of politics is to avoid morally unacceptable policies and to decide between morally acceptable policies when more than one of the competing policies is morally acceptable.

Many Moral Issues Are Not Resolvable

Not only does morality not resolve the issues between conservatives and liberals, as long as they are not extreme, it does not resolve any of the moral issues on which fully informed, impartial rational persons would favor different positions. Morality sometimes leaves an individual with that dreadful freedom of choice about which some existentialist thinkers have written so fully and brilliantly. Because there is sometimes no morally right course of action, even a morally good person may be forced to choose between alternative courses of action in a situation where it is impossible not to break one or more moral rules and all choices are only weakly justified. This kind of situation is likely to be distressing to any morally sensitive person and may explain why many morally sensitive people have claimed that objective morality is a fraud or useless or both. This reaction, though understandable, is not correct. Just because morality does not always provide a unique answer, it does not follow that it never or even generally does not. Of course, those cases where morality provides a unique answer are usually not morally perplexing, so they have not attracted the attention of those fascinated by moral perplexity. To desire morality always to provide a single clear answer may be a rational desire, but it is irrational to reject morality simply because it does not satisfy this desire.

Morality and Religion

One of the proper functions of religion is to offer guidance in those cases in which there is no morally right course of action. Since these cases are truly about moral matters, it is very easy for a person to conclude that the answer given by her religion is *the* morally right answer. But it is not. This is not to say that it is a morally wrong answer, but simply to repeat that in this kind of situation there is no morally right answer. The occurrence of this kind of situation makes it possible to talk of Buddhist ethics, Christian ethics, Hindu ethics, Jewish ethics, Moslem ethics, Shinto ethics, and so on. When there is no morally right course of action, Buddhist ethics can differ from Christian ethics. An impartial rational Buddhist will choose one course of action, while an impartial rational Christian will choose another. However, a misunderstanding of morality may lead a Buddhist to claim falsely that the Christian is immoral, and vice versa. In truth, neither will be, but both must be extremely clear about the nature of morality and distinguish it clearly from what their religion tells them to do. Otherwise it may be impossible for them to avoid unjustified moral intolerance.

The previous paragraph assumes that all religions are morally acceptable, that they never advocate doing morally unacceptable actions. Unfortunately, that is not always true. Although there are interpretations of all of the major religions such that they never advocate acting immorally, there are also interpretations such that some immoral actions seem supported by a religion. Since religion provides the motive to so many people for being moral, they may fail to realize that it is not religion that determines what is morally acceptable. People may not only fail to distinguish between a morally required action and their particular religion's requirement of a morally allowed action, they may also fail to distinguish between morality and their religion's support for its own nonmoral religious requirements. This may lead some people to unjustifiably punish others for actions that are not even violations of any moral rule but simply fail to conform to the rules or ideals of their religion. Some religions have interpretations that actually require this kind of immoral action.

Even the Ten Commandments combine moral and purely religious rules without distinguishing between them. The commandment to keep the Sabbath day to sanctify it is not distinguished from the commandment not to kill. Even worse, some of the commandments seem to condone the clearly immoral practice of slavery. The commandment to keep the Sabbath includes the following passage: "But the seventh day is the Sabbath of the Lord thy God: in it thou shalt not do any work, thou, nor thy son, nor thy daughter, nor thy manservant, nor thy maidservant, nor thine ox, nor thine ass, nor any of thy cattle, nor the stranger that is within thy gates; that thy manservant and thy maidservant may rest as well as thou" (Deuteronomy 5:14). "Manservant" and "maidservant" refer to male and females slaves. This commandment does recommend more humane treatment of slaves than was customary at the time, so that in historical context, it constitutes a moral improvement. However, it is clear that not all of the Ten Commandments can be included as rules in a justified moral system.

The Value of Recognizing That Common Morality Is Universal

Although one might think that the extraordinary growth in applied and professional ethics, such as business ethics, engineering ethics, and medical ethics, would prompt increased interest in an account of a universal moral system, the reverse seems to be true. Many philosophers seem to hold that each particular field or profession has its own moral system. Those who attempt to justify punishment usually do not even consider whether that same moral system is appropriate for them to use when doing medical ethics.[10] However, one of the most important features of good work in applied ethics is that it shows how what may look like an acceptable solution to a moral problem in one field is not adequate, because applying that same solution to another field comes up with a clearly unacceptable solution. It was only when physicians saw that there was no special moral system just for them that any progress was made in medical ethics.

Another virtue of having an account of a universal moral system is that it enables one to organize a vast array of particular moral intuitions and thus to discover if they are all consistent. When moral decisions are made in individual cases without checking them against a universal system, sometimes different decisions are made in cases where all the morally relevant facts are the same. This may happen because people are swayed by morally irrelevant features, such as their friend being the one who is punished, or simply because they do not see that the cases were morally similar. If an explicit description of a universal moral system does, in fact, yield the answers that would be given in all of the clear cases, then that moral system can be used to help deal with problems in which it is difficult to discover what decisions are morally acceptable.

The primary practical function of a moral theory is to provide an explicit description of the moral system that determines the status of violations of the moral rules: unjustified, weakly justified, or strongly justified. Making explicit the morally relevant features and explaining the two-step procedure helps one to determine how to decide whether a violation counts as unjustified, weakly justified, or strongly justified. Since morality is a public system that applies to all rational persons, any moral problem in business, medicine, government, as well as in any other activity of rational persons, can be adequately described in terms that all rational persons will understand. That the same moral system applies to all of these problems allows one to take advantage of solutions arrived at in one field and apply them to another. It also shows the inadequacies of some solutions.

Summarizing the Moral Guide

To act morally is to act in a way that an impartial rational person can publicly allow when the action is covered by either a moral rule or a moral ideal. It is very easy to forget this final qualification and to equate acting morally with acting in any way that an impartial rational person can publicly allow. There is no great harm in this; acting as an impartial rational person can publicly allow does rule out immoral action. However, ignoring the qualification counts doing morally indifferent actions as acting morally and blurs the distinction between acting morally and acting according to personal or utilitarian ideals. This tends to obscure the important fact that morality is primarily concerned with protecting and preventing people from suffering harm, not with self-realization or promoting benefits. It is only for those who have duties in a political situation that achieving greater goods sometimes justifies violations of the moral rules.

The Golden Rule, "Do unto others as you would have them do unto you," though it provides a guide that closely resembles the moral guide, is not identical with it. In fact, as Kant pointed out, taken literally, it provides incorrect moral advice. It advises police and judges, at least those who have normal human desires, not to arrest or sentence criminals. Nor is there any simple way in which to modify it so that it does always provide the right moral advice in a complex situation. Even incorporating into the Golden Rule, the concept of what an impartial rational person would advocate does not provide a completely adequate moral guide. "Do unto others as an impartial rational person would advocate that they do unto you," though it eliminates many objections to the Golden Rule, still encourages one to do more than the moral guide. Changing it to the negative, "Do not do unto others what an impartial rational person would advocate that they not do unto you," may be equivalent to the guide provided by the moral rules, but it leaves out those actions encouraged by the moral ideals. If one thinks of politics as involving more than morality, as involving not only the moral ideals, but also acting on the utilitarian ideals, then the Golden Rule, in its positive modification, might be regarded as a political guide to life.

The moral guide can perhaps be best summarized in that ancient command "Eschew evil; do good," where this is understood as meaning "Obey the moral rules; follow the moral ideals." It is unfortunate that the most familiar moral injunctions have to be modified or interpreted before they provide an adequate summary of the moral guide to life. I should have liked to be able to present an account of morality simple enough to be compressed into a saying as forceful as the more familiar moral injunctions. The best I can think of is "Always be just; be kind when you can." To which religion would add "And let the kindness be loving-kindness." More forceful is the patently derivative "What doth morality require of thee but to do justly and love mercy?" It is not mere coincidence that the familiar moral injunctions come so close to expressing the view of morality described in this book. For I do not consider myself as having presented a new morality, but simply as describing with more precision the nature of the morality that has been preached by all of the great moral and religious teachers of humankind.

The importance of presenting a clear, precise, and coherent account of morality lies primarily in the effect it may have on people's behavior. Although I do not hold that if people know what is morally right they will always do it, I do think that many persons of good will do what is morally wrong because they are unclear about the nature of morality. I fully agree with Hobbes's remark quoted at the beginning of this book, that "the utility of moral and civil philosophy is to be estimated, not so much by the commodities we have by knowing these sciences, as by the calamities we receive from not knowing them."

Philosophical understanding, such as that provided by this book, is not enough. People must come to care for all other persons. Yet it is extremely hard to come to care for all other persons if it is clear that they do not care for you. To the deprived citizens of a country it seems clear that other persons do not care for them. To show them that other persons do care, individuals and governments must actively seek to eliminate deprivation. It is also necessary for the natural compassion of humankind to be broadened and deepened. People must learn to care for those who are suffering regardless of their country, race, or religious beliefs. This is a task for art, literature, and religion. They, and not philosophy, have the power to increase a person's compassion and to widen its scope. More important, this compassion must yield a concern for humankind that is active even apart from the compassion that generates it. Parents and teachers, indeed all those who are responsible for the teaching of children, have a crucial role. For if children do not learn to care for others while they are young, it may be impossible to teach them when they are older. I have shown what morality is. Others are needed to teach people to follow it.

Notes

1. Thomas Hobbes, *De Cive*, chap. 8, sec. 1.
2. This is the foundation of Hobbes's political theory.
3. Hobbes recognizes this point, and it is one of the reasons he argues for the sovereign having absolute authority, for the closer the sovereign is to having no challenge to its authority, the more freedom it can and should allow its citizens. This leads to a virtuous circle, for the more freedom the citizens have, the less likely they are to challenge the sovereign, and so the sovereign's authority becomes even less challenged. This is why sovereignty in the wealthiest and freest countries is the least challenged and the closest to having absolute authority. This interpretation of Hobbes was made clear to me by Leiser Madanes in a meeting of the Asociación de Estudios Hobbesianos at the Universidad de Buenos Aires in November of 1995.
4. Except for parents or parent surrogates, an individual is almost never justified in violating a moral rule in order to follow a utilitarian ideal without consent. A positive answer to question 4 explains why parents' relationship to their children is similar to governments' relationship to their citizens, without suggesting that citizens should be treated like children.
5. Rawls's own final statements in A *Theory of Justice* of these principles are as follows: "Each person is to have an equal right to the most extensive total system of equal basic liberties compatible with a similar system of liberty for all" (250) and "Social and economic inequalities are to be arranged so that they are both (a) to the greatest benefit to the least advantaged and (b) attached to offices and positions open to all under conditions of fair equality of opportunity" (83).

6. As mentioned earlier in this chapter, utilitarianism can also lead to a totalitarian communist state, for marxists can claim that Mill was mistaken in thinking that liberty was essential for achieving the greatest happiness. In this context, I group marxists with egalitarians in order to emphasize that both are primarily concerned with distribution, and group utilitarians with capitalists to emphasize that both are primarily concerned with the total amount of goods.

7. These difficulties may explain why it is so enticing to reduce all goods to a single one, pleasure, and all evils to a single one, pain. They also explain why there is so little talk of pain, for it is at least initially plausible that all people who compare one set of pleasures with another will reach the same decision on which is greater. It is completely implausible that there will be complete agreement on the rankings of the goods and evils or on how much good is needed to compensate for a given evil. The attempt to use money to compare goods and evils is a feature of the capitalist version of utilitarianism. Of course, using money makes clear that different people rank different goods and evils differently, so it naturally leads to a "maximizing the satisfaction of desires" view, with intensity of desire measured by the amount of money a person would be willing to pay to satisfy the desire. I shall not discuss the many problems with this view.

8. For a fuller account of Rawls, including his account of rationality and envy, see chapter 13 of *Morality: A New Justification of the Moral Rules* (New York: Oxford University Press, 1988), the predecessor of this book.

9. For the relationship of maladies to the suffering of harm see chapter 4. See Bernard Gert, Charles M. Culver, and K. Danner Clouser, *Bioethics: A Return to Fundamentals* (New York: Oxford University Press, 1997), chap. 5, for a fuller analysis of the concept of malady.

10. Indeed, ethical relativism — or what we call the "anthology approach" to ethics — is common within the field. Many medical ethics anthologies have an introductory chapter containing brief excerpts from various kinds of moral theories, such as consequentialism, deontology, and virtue theory, and the reader is told to use whatever theory she thinks best for thinking about each of the problems that are presented in the remainder of the anthology. See Gert, Culver, and Clouser, *Bioethics*, chap. 1, for detailed discussion of this issue.

Index

Goods (benefits) (*continued*)
  and evils, 89–108
  inherent, 93
  instrumental, 95
  intrinsic, 93
  list of, 92, 94, 107
  as morally relevant features, 231
  personal, 93–94
  positive, 91
  promoting, 90, 124–125
  no rational person avoids, 94
  and rewards, 103–105
  several different kinds of, 98
  social, 95–97
Goods and evils, 89–108
  choice between, 97–98
  no unique ranking, 58, 97–99
  objective, 97, 101
  personal, 93–94
  social, 95–96
Gossip, 193
Governments, 96, 125, 224, 231, 364–367
  and general welfare, 369–370
  good, 355, 374
  just, 374–375
  and health care, 377–379
  versus individuals, 231, 364, 367, 370
  minimal duties of, 366, 377
  persons in, 364–365
  and violations of moral rules, 231, 367
Grammar, 4–5
Gratitude, 62, 74–75
  and loyalty, 256–257
Groundwork of the Metaphysics of Morals (Kant), 129n 6
Gregarious, 279
"Greet people with a smile," 124
Group,
  and impartiality, 130–132
  minimal, 141
  protected by morality, 137–146
  significant, 32, 57–58
Guariglia, Oswaldo, xii
Guides,
  to conduct, 6, 8, 10, 13–15, 17–18
  to life, 258, 271, 384
Guilt, 350
Gunnarsson, Logi, 54n 12

Habermas, Jürgen, 218n 3
Habits, 280
Haksar, Vinit, xiii
Hannaford, Robert, 360n 1
Happiness, 261
  Aristotle's view, 259, 261

  and pleasure, 261
  and utilitarian paradox, 261
Hardin, Russell, 219nn 14, 22
Hare, R. M., 154n 12, 205, 219n 15, 237, 246n 17, 335, 337nn 4, 6
Harman, Gilbert, 174
Harms. *See* evils (harms)
Hate, 269
Hate speech, 272n 9
Health, 39, 92, 93, 106
Health care, 377–379
Hedonism, 18
Heroism, 104
Hindu ethics, 382
Hitler, 9
Hobbes, Thomas, xi, xiv, 2, 6, 9, 12, 15, 27n 13, 32, 74, 90, 129n 5, 185n 18, 203, 205, 246n 10, 272n 1, 306, 307n 1, 308n 9, 360n 1, 368, 385nn 1–3
"Hobbes, Mechanism, and Egoism" (Gert), 87n 15
"Hobbes's Psychology" (Gert), 28n 14, 360n 1
Hollywood, Amy, xii
Homosexual behavior, 264, 315
Homosexuals, 5
Honesty, 94, 260, 283–284
Hospitals, 247, 366
Human nature, 6–7, 32, 47, 140, 238
Human Genome Project, xi
Hume, David, 40–41
Humility, 262, 306–307, 340. *See also* arrogance
Hurricanes, 96
Hursthouse, Rosalind, 308nn 5, 7
Hypocrisy, 9, 169, 178, 262, 284, 314, 350

Ice, 193
Ideal observer, 239
The Ideal of Rationality: A Defense within Reason (Nathanson), 87nn 10, 20, 88n 30
Ideals,
  ethnic, 258
  moral (*see* moral ideals)
  national, 257–258
  particularistic, 258
  personal (*see* personal ideals)
  racist, 258
  religious (*see* religious ideals)
  utilitarian (*see* utilitarian ideals)
Ideology, 237–239, 244, 372, 377
Ignoring the modifier, 87n 16, 215, 290
Immoral person, 300
Immoralist, The (Gide), 262
Impartial rational persons,
  agree usually, 148–149, 239